CRIMINAL DEFENCES AND PLEAS IN BAR OF TRIAL

by

James Chalmers,
Senior Lecturer in Law, University of Aberdeen

and

Dr Fiona Leverick,
Senior Lecturer in Law, University of Aberdeen

Published under the auspices of
SCOTTISH UNIVERSITIES LAW INSTITUTE LTD

Published in 2006 by
W. Green & Son Ltd
21 Alva Street
Edinburgh EH2 4PS

www.wgreen.thomson.com

Typeset by YHT Ltd, London
Printed and bound in Great Britain by Athenaeum Press Ltd, Gateshead, Tyne and Wear

No natural forests were destroyed to make this product; only farmed timber was used and replanted

A CIP catalogue record for this book is available from the British Library.

ISBN-10 0 414 01521 5
ISBN-13 9780 414 01521 0

CRIMINAL DEFENCES AND PLEAS IN BAR OF TRIAL

AUSTRALIA
Law Book Co.
Sydney

CANADA and USA
Carswell
Toronto

HONG KONG
Sweet & Maxwell Asia

NEW ZEALAND
Brookers
Wellington

SINGAPORE and MALAYSIA
Sweet & Maxwell Asia
Singapore and Kuala Lumpur

PREFACE

The idea for a jointly authored book about defences was born several years ago in the St Machar Bar in Old Aberdeen. Unknown to each other, we had both independently been thinking about writing a book covering the range of Scottish criminal defences. As a result of a chance conversation in the bar, we discovered each other's intentions and, after a series of misunderstandings worthy of a particularly bad British situation comedy from the 1970s, we eventually decided to pool our resources.

A scholarly text devoted solely to criminal defences in Scotland fills a clear gap in the market. Most of the defences we deal with are covered in Gordon's *Criminal Law* but because our focus is solely on defences, we have the luxury of being able to give them more detailed treatment. This has allowed us to take full account of the case law and academic literature on defences, which has grown exponentially since the first edition of "Gordon" was published in 1967, and has even developed somewhat since the third edition of Gordon, published in two volumes in 2000 and 2001. Our text also deals with pleas in bar of trial, which are not covered by Gordon (rightly so in a text which is concerned with the substantive criminal law). It might be debated whether pleas in bar of trial are rightly classified as criminal defences proper, but we have taken a wide interpretation of defences and included them in our analysis. This book, therefore, includes chapters not only on the substantive defences, but also on time bar and delay, *res judicata*, renunciation of the right to prosecute, insanity in bar of trial, entrapment and oppression (based both on prejudicial publicity and more generally).

Some aspects of our approach require a little further explanation. We have tried to write a book that is of interest both to practitioners and to the academic community. Thus, for each defence that we cover, we address both its theoretical basis and the legal requirements of the defence. The balance between these two elements varies from chapter to chapter. For most of the pleas in bar of trial, very little theoretical debate arises. A plea in bar based on prejudicial publicity, for example, is justified for the very simple reason that the accused has a right to a fair trial, and so it is possible to set out the theoretical basis of this defence in short compass. This is, however, not always the case. There is, for example, considerable debate about the basis of the plea in bar based on entrapment, and so we set this out at much greater length.

As well as dealing with the theoretical issues surrounding each defence and providing an up-to-date account of the law in Scotland, we have also taken a historical and comparative approach. The former is especially important where no detailed historical account of a particular defence's development already exists in the case law or the academic literature, as might be said for the defence of insanity. The latter is particularly important where there is a lack of Scottish authority, as there is in relation to the availability of necessity or coercion as a defence to murder, for example. Where this is the case, we have attempted to provide as much useful guidance to practitioners as possible, drawing on comparative material from the major common law jurisdictions and on discussions in the academic literature to assist us.

Some of our editorial decisions relating to individual defences also require some explanation. One aspect of our approach that might initially seem surprising is the combination of the defences of insanity and automatism in a single chapter. Our original plan was, in fact, to have two separate chapters, but it soon became clear that this would lead to a great deal of repetition and cross-referencing. The two defences are—in many ways—very similar and, in Scots law at least, rely on the same concepts, probably more so even than the other closely related defences of necessity and coercion. The only real difference between insanity and automatism in Scots law is in the source of the "alienation of reason" that is required to ground the defence and thus it makes little sense to treat them separately.

Another aspect of our approach that requires some explanation is our treatment of alibi, incrimination and consent in sexual offences. These defences are examples of what might be termed "failure of proof defences": defences that operate because the prosecution is unable to prove a required element of the offence. As such, they might not, strictly speaking, be regarded as defences at all, but we have taken a broad approach to the definition of a defence and thus they are included here. We have taken the decision, however, not to devote any substantial attention (or indeed a separate chapter) to any of them. Instead, each is briefly considered in Chapter 2, which deals with the procedural requirements relating to defences. There are two main reasons for this.

First, alibi, incrimination and consent differ from the other defences we cover in that they are entirely uncontroversial: there is absolutely no debate about whether they should be accepted as defences. Secondly, the defences of incrimination and alibi, at least, have no substantive content and the only issues of any significance which arise are procedural notice requirements. This is clearly not the case for consent in sexual offences—on the contrary, there is considerable debate about the meaning of consent—but the defence itself simply involves denying that the *actus reus* of a particular sexual offence has been made out. If we were to enter the debate about the nature of consent in sexual offences, we would by logical implication have to consider the definition of every criminal offence (and there is a question anyway of how much we could add to a debate that has already received extensive coverage in the academic literature). Our concern here is purely with the statutory provisions which place consent in sexual offences on the same footing as special defences for the purposes of notice.

Although this book is jointly authored, there was a clear division of labour in terms of which of us took primary responsibility for writing particular chapters. In all cases, one of us wrote a first draft of a particular chapter, which was then passed to the other for comment. (This was also the point at which one author attempted to persuade the other to cut down on the number of time he used the word "however", while that author objected to the use of 10,000 words when 5,000 would do and what he saw as the lack of sufficient references to obscure cases.) The process of dividing up the chapters between us worked remarkably smoothly. Our interests turned out to be almost entirely mutually exclusive and not once did one of us 'claim' a chapter the other wanted to write (although admittedly there were a couple of chapters that neither of us particularly wanted to write).

The result of this process is that lead authorship of the 20 chapters is split equally between us. Chapters 1–6 (classification of defences, procedural issues, self-defence, necessity, coercion, superior orders); chapter 9 (nonage); chapter 12 (error of fact); chapter 13 (error of law); and chapter 20 (entrapment) were written by Fiona Leverick. Chapter 7 (insanity and automatism); chapter 8 (intoxication); chapter 10 (provocation); chapter 11 (diminished responsibility); and chapters 14–19 (insanity in bar of trial, *res judicata*, time bar and delay, renunciation of the right to prosecute, prejudicial publicity, oppression and abuse of process) were written by James Chalmers.

Finally, a big thank you is due to all the people who helped us to write this book.

Shona Wilson worked as a research assistant for us during most of the time we were writing the book. We quite simply could not have managed without her. She sought out materials (and always presented them to us beautifully organised and labelled), researched points of law, and proof read most of the chapters. Her amazing talent for spotting bold full stops and double spaces between sentences has become legendary.

Michael Plaxton read a significant proportion of the chapters in first draft form in a very short space of time over the summer of 2005. Without his help in brutally pruning unnecessary words, some chapters would have been twice as long (and this book would have been even heavier). Pete Duff, Victor Tadros and Sharon Cowan were also kind enough to read and comment on various draft chapters and discuss various issues with us. We are extremely grateful (and apologies if we have left anyone else who commented on draft chapters off this list).

Over the course of writing the book, we both also had invaluable discussions about defences with various people, including Chris Gane and David Irvine. A special thank you is also due to David who—while himself working on the second edition of *Corporeal Moveables in Scots Law*—supported us (both morally and with jaffa cakes) over the summer of 2004 when the whole project still seemed very daunting and a long way off being completed.

A big thank you is due to all the staff at W. Green and Son who have been involved in various ways and at various stages. Particular thanks are due to Neil McKinlay for his enthusiasm for the initial book proposal some years ago; Philippa Blackham for her excellent editorial work; Jill Hyslop for overseeing the whole process and always being efficient and supportive in doing so; and Rebecca Johnston for organising the publicity material.

The original intention was for this book to be published as a Greens Practice Library text. Thanks are due to Joe Thomson and Jill Hyslop (again) for, after the manuscript had been submitted, raising the possibility of publication in the Scottish Universities Law Institute (SULI) series. The book was accepted as a SULI book after being reviewed by three anonymous referees and we are very grateful for their comments.

A final thank you is due to the staff of the Taylor Library at Aberdeen University. We were very lucky to be able to draw on the assistance of such helpful and professional librarians. Writing the book would have been a far more difficult process without them.

The law is stated on the basis of the materials available to us at the end of July 2006.

James Chalmers and Fiona Leverick
Aberdeen
August 2006

CONTENTS

Page

Para.

CHAPTER 1

THE CLASSIFICATION OF DEFENCES

CHAPTER 2

PROCEDURAL ISSUES RELATING TO DEFENCES

CHAPTER 3

SELF-DEFENCE

CHAPTER 4

NECESSITY

CHAPTER 5

COERCION

CHAPTER 6

SUPERIOR ORDERS

CHAPTER 7

INSANITY AND AUTOMATISM

Chapter 8

INTOXICATION

Chapter 9

NONAGE

Chapter 10

PROVOCATION

Chapter 11

DIMINISHED RESPONSIBILITY

Chapter 12

ERROR OF FACT

Chapter 13

ERROR OF LAW

Chapter 14

INSANITY IN BAR OF TRIAL

Chapter 15

RES JUDICATA

Chapter 16

TIME BAR AND DELAY

Chapter 17

RENUNCIATION OF THE RIGHT TO PROSECUTE

Chapter 18

OPPRESSION: PREJUDICIAL PUBLICITY

CHAPTER 19

OPPRESSION AND ABUSE OF PROCESS

CHAPTER 20

ENTRAPMENT

TABLE OF CASES

TABLE OF EUROPEAN AND INTERNATIONAL CASES

TABLE OF STATUTES

TABLE OF STATUTORY INSTRUMENTS

TABLE OF EUROPEAN TREATIES AND CONVENTIONS

LIST OF ABBREVIATIONS

(excluding standard law reports and journals)

Alison, *Principles*	A. Alison, *Principles of the Criminal Law of Scotland* (1832).
Alison, *Practice*	A. Alison, *Practice of the Criminal Law of Scotland* (1833).
Anderson	A.M. Anderson, *The Criminal Law of Scotland* (2nd edn, 1904).
Ashworth, *Principles of Criminal Law*	A. Ashworth, *Principles of Criminal Law* (5th edn, 2006).
Bayne	A. Bayne, *Institutions of the Criminal Law of Scotland* (1730).
Burnett	J. Burnett, *A Treatise on Various Branches of the Criminal Law of Scotland* (1811).
Casebook	C.H.W. Gane, C.N. Stoddart and J. Chalmers, *A Casebook on Scottish Criminal Law* (3rd edn, 2001).
CPSA 1995	Criminal Procedure (Scotland) Act 1995.
Draft Criminal Code	Scottish Law Commission, *A Draft Criminal Code for Scotland with Commentary* (2003).
Draft English Code	Law Commission, *A Criminal Code for England and Wales* (Law Com. No. 177, 1989).
ECHR	European Convention on Human Rights
Fletcher, *Rethinking Criminal Law*	G.P. Fletcher, *Rethinking Criminal Law* (1978).
Forbes	W. Forbes, *The Institutes of the Law of Scotland* (1730).
Gordon	G.H. Gordon, *The Criminal Law of Scotland* (3rd edn, in two volumes, by M.G.A. Christie): Vol.1 (2000), Vol.2 (2001).
Hume	D. Hume, *Commentaries on the Law of Scotland Respecting Crimes* (4th edn, 1844).
Jones and Christie	T.H. Jones and M.G.A Christie, *Criminal Law* (3rd edn, 2003).
Macdonald	J.H.A. Macdonald, *A Practical Treatise on the Criminal Law of Scotland* (3rd edn, 1894; 4th edn 1929; 5th edn, 1948). References are to the 5th edition unless otherwise stated.
Mackenzie	G. Mackenzie, *The Laws and Customes of Scotland in Matters Criminal* (2nd edn, 1699).

Renton and Brown	Renton and Brown's Criminal Procedure According to the Law of Scotland (6th edn, 1996 by G.H. Gordon, assisted by C.H.W. Gane).
Robinson, *Criminal Law Defenses*	P.H. Robinson, *Criminal Law Defenses* (1984).
Walkers on Evidence	A.G. Walker and N.M.L. Walker, *The Law of Evidence in Scotland* (2nd edn, 2000 by M.L. Ross with J. Chalmers).

CHAPTER 1

THE CLASSIFICATION OF DEFENCES

INTRODUCTION

This chapter sets out to explore the various ways in which criminal defences might be classified and examines some of the implications of classification. Before doing so, it is necessary to set out what we mean by a criminal defence.[1a] In Robinson, *Criminal Law Defenses*, Paul Robinson defines a criminal defence as "any set of identifiable conditions or circumstances which *may* prevent conviction for an offence".[1] But, as Husak has quite correctly pointed out, this definition is too wide, lacking as it does a normative element, and thus potentially including such circumstances as avoiding being caught, murdering a witness or bribing a judge.[2] It also fits uneasily with defences that operate as pleas in bar of trial, such as entrapment or time-bar and delay. The basis of pleas in bar of trial is not that they prevent conviction as such, but that they provide a reason why the accused ought not to stand trial in the first place.[3] **1.01**

An improvement on Robinson's definition might then be as follows. A criminal defence is 'any identifiable set of conditions or circumstances that provides sufficient reason why the accused *ought* not to be convicted of a particular offence or *ought* not to stand trial for a particular offence'. This is a relatively wide definition, including as it does not only defences that relate to the conduct and blameworthiness of the accused, such as self-defence, insanity and coercion, but also defences that relate to the conduct of the state (or indeed other bodies), such as entrapment, time-bar and delay, and other pleas in bar of trial, such as prejudicial pretrial publicity.

Although it overcomes Husak's objections, the definition is still not a perfect one, including as it does the simple claim by an accused "I didn't do it". It is actually extremely difficult to define a criminal defence in such a way as to exclude a claim of this nature and the definition above may well be the best that can be achieved in the circumstances.

Defences can be distinguished on at least four grounds: whether they are complete or partial defences; whether they are general or specific defences; whether they are common law or statutory defences; and according to the rationale for admitting the defence.[4] Each of these

---

[1a] Although this book is titled "Criminal Defences and Pleas in Bar of Trial", this is not to suggest that the two are mutually exclusive. In our view, pleas in bar of trial may be regarded as a category of criminal defence. Because pleas in bar of trial are sometimes regarded as separate from defences "proper", however, the title has been chosen to make the scope of the book clear.

[1] Robinson, *Criminal Law Defenses*, §21 (emphasis added).

[2] D. Husak, "The serial view of criminal law defenses" (1992) 3 *Criminal Law Forum* 369–400 at p.370.

[3] It might be said in response to this that pleas in bar of trial are not "proper" defences at all, but a wide definition of defences is taken here and they are included in our discussion.

[4] A fifth distinction is whether or not the defence is classed as a "special defence". This is covered in Ch.2 where the procedural issues relating to defences are discussed.

dimensions of classification is explored here, and, in doing so, this chapter sets out some limits to the scope of remainder of the book.

Complete and Partial Defences

1.02 The first way in which defences might be classified is according to whether they are complete or partial defences. Complete defences are defences that, if successfully pled, enable the accused to escape conviction entirely.[5] Partial defences, if successfully pled, operate merely to reduce the seriousness of the crime with which the accused was charged. This can happen in one of two ways. Either the accused is convicted of a lesser offence than the one with which he was charged or the partial defence operates as a mitigating factor, resulting in a reduction in sentence.

Only two partial defences are recognised by Scots law: provocation and diminished responsibility. The effect of a successful plea of either of these partial defences on a murder charge is to reduce it to culpable homicide.[6] Where the original charge was one of assault, the result will be that sentence is mitigated accordingly.[7] Both of these partial defences are covered in detail in subsequent chapters.[8] Scots law does not formally recognise other potential partial defences, such as infanticide, mercy killings, suicide pacts or excessive force in self-defence.[9]

The terminology of "partial" defence is problematic, and has, in the context of diminished responsibility, led to occasional judicial objections that a person cannot be "partially" responsible: they are either responsible or not.[10] It is, in fact, possible to avoid the terminology altogether, by regarding provocation and diminished responsibility as *complete* defences to murder, but inapplicable to other crimes (thus not precluding convictions for culpable homicide).[11] That, however, does not answer such objections, which are probably best met by regarding partial

[5] Although the point should be made here that this does not necessarily mean that the accused entirely escapes any consequences stemming from his or her act. The defence of insanity is a complete defence to a criminal charge, but might still result in any of the disposals listed in s.57(2) of the CPSA 1995 (e.g. a hospital order, a guardianship order or a supervision and treatment order).

[6] The appeal court disapproved of this terminology in *Drury v HM Advocate*, 2001 S.L.T. 1013, but it has continued to be used in subsequent cases: see Ch.10. For the effect of a successful plea of provocation or diminished responsibility on a charge of attempted murder, see para.10.24 (provocation) and para.11.18 (diminished responsibility).

[7] See para.10.25 (provocation) and para.11.20 (diminished responsibility).

[8] See Chs 10 (provocation) and 11 (diminished responsibility). For a detailed examination of partial defences to murder undertaken by the Law Commission for England and Wales, see *Partial Defences to Murder* (Consultation Paper No. 173, 2003). The study was undertaken in the context of the partial defences available in England/Wales to women who have killed their partners after suffering domestic violence, but the study is a comparative one, including detailed examination of the law on partial defences in Scotland, Australia, Canada, South Africa and New Zealand, among other jurisdictions.

[9] Although at one point it seemed that Scots law might recognise excessive force in self-defence as a partial defence to murder, this was ruled out in *Crawford v HM Advocate*, 1950 J.C. 67 (see paras 3.17–3.18).

[10] *Kirkwood v HM Advocate*, 1939 J.C. 36 at 41, *per* the Lord Justice-General (Normand); *HM Advocate v Higgins* (1913) 7 Adam 229 at 233, *per* Lord Johnston. See below, para.11.01.

[11] See Robinson, *Criminal Law Defenses*, §64(a).

defences as pleas in mitigation,[12] but pleas in mitigation which have the formal effect of reducing murder to culpable homicide in order to allow the accused to avoid both the mandatory penalty of life imprisonment and the label "murderer".[12a]

General and Specific Defences

A second way in which defences might be categorised is according to whether they are general defences that can be pled in relation to all offences, or whether they can be pled in relation to certain specific offences only. Provocation and diminished responsibility, for example, operate solely as partial defences to murder. Defences such as insanity and nonage, on the other hand, operate across the whole range of offences. Then there are defences such as necessity and coercion which are not linked by definition to specific offences, but where restrictions have been placed on their availability to a charge of murder.[13] **1.03**

In this book, we cover both the general defences and the specific (partial) defences of provocation and diminished responsibility. It should be noted that provocation and diminished responsibility are not the only specific defences that exist at common law and thus the coverage of this book might be seen as incomplete. The most obvious omission is the defence of reasonable chastisement that operates as a complete defence to a charge of assault.[14] There are two reasons for covering provocation and diminished responsibility in this book while not providing coverage of other specific defences. First, the status of these defences as "specific" defences in Scots law is contested, and it has occasionally been suggested that they might operate as defences to crimes other than murder.[15] Secondly, unlike the "reasonable chastisement" defence, both provocation and diminished responsibility represent extensive and complex bodies of

[12] The appeal court accepted this characterisation of diminished responsibility in *Lindsay v HM Advocate*, 1997 J.C. 19, but more recently has stated that provocation operates by negating the *mens rea* of murder (in *Drury v HM Advocate*, 2001 S.L.T. 1013), a position which has been heavily criticised: see para.10.05.

[12a] However, the labelling consideration has carried limited weight with the Law Commission in its recent review of English homicide law. The Commission has provisionally proposed that the partial defences of provocation and diminished responsibility should only reduce "first degree murder" to "second degree murder" (rather than manslaughter, which is to be retained as a separate offence). See *A New Homicide Act for England and Wales* (Consultation Paper No. 177, 2005), criticised by O. Quick and C. Wells, "Getting tough with defences" [2006] Crim. L.R. 514–525 at pp.515–518.

[13] It is generally thought that neither coercion nor necessity can be pled as a defence to murder in Scots law, although there is an almost complete lack of authority and some doubt might now be cast on this in relation to necessity. This is because of the English Court of Appeal case of *Re: A (Children)* [2001] 2 W.L.R. 480, the case involving the separation of two conjoined babies, in which one of the three Court of Appeal judges held that necessity would provide a defence to murder for any doctor carrying out a separation. See paras 4.23 *et seq.* (necessity) and paras 5.27 *et seq.* (coercion).

[14] *Stewart v Thain*, 1981 J.C. 13; *Guest v Annan*, 1988 S.C.C.R. 275; *Peebles v MacPhail*, 1990 S.L.T. 245. The case law must now be read in conjunction with s.51 of the Criminal Justice (Scotland) Act 2003, which provides guidance as to how the defence should be applied.

[15] See below, paras 10.24–10.25 (provocation); 11.18–11.20 (diminished responsibility). In English law, by contrast, both defences are found in the Homicide Act 1957 (ss.2–3), are clearly restricted to murder as a result, and it is, therefore, conventional to treat them as part of the law of homicide: see, e.g. D.C. Ormerod, *Smith and Hogan: Criminal Law* (11th edn, 2005), pp.442–471. The Draft Criminal Code includes diminished responsibility and provocation within the section (38) which defines culpable homicide.

law and theory which are worthy of detailed treatment in their own right. Accordingly, although the view is taken here that provocation and diminished responsibility are in fact restricted to murder, they have nevertheless been considered as part of the general law of 'defences', as has been done elsewhere.[16] Admittedly, such a distinction between partial defences to homicide and other specific defences is not particularly convincing, as there is little conceptually to separate reasonable chastisement from other specific defences such as provocation and diminished responsibility: both are common law defences operating as defences to one particular common law offence. Nonetheless, it is a distinction followed here.

Common Law and Statutory Defences

1.04 A third way in which defences might be categorised is according to whether they are common law or statutory defences. In Scots law, the vast majority of defences are common law defences: self-defence, necessity, coercion, insanity, provocation and diminished responsibility are all to be found in case law rather than statute,[17] although this may change if the Draft Criminal Code for Scotland ever becomes law.[18] At the time of writing, there were also proposals in existence from the Scottish Law Commission to place the defences of insanity and diminished responsibility on a statutory basis, but no suggestion as to whether or when these might become accepted.[19]

Some defences are provided for in Scotland by statute, but these are almost exclusively defences that operate in relation to specific statutory charges rather than having more general application. Examples are the defence of "lawful authority or reasonable excuse" in relation to a charge of carrying offensive weapons[20]; the defence of "good reason or lawful authority" in relation to a charge of having in a public place an article with a blade or a point[21]; the defence of "reasonable excuse" in relation to

[16] E.g. both provocation and diminished responsibility are addressed in D. O'Connor and P.A. Fairall, *Criminal Defences* (3rd edn, 1996), a discussion of the law in the various Australian jurisdictions. In the third edition of Gordon's *Criminal Law*, diminished responsibility is included in Vol.1 ("General Theory"), although provocation is included in Vol.2 ("Specific Crimes"), where it is discussed in the context of culpable homicide.

[17] *cf.* Canada and England/Wales, where many defences are codified. In relation to England and Wales, see, e.g. s.3 of the Homicide Act 1957 (defence of provocation); s.3 of the Criminal Law Act 1967 (defence of force used in the prevention of crime). In Canada, see the Criminal Code, ss.16 (defence of mental disorder); 17 (defence of compulsion by threats); 33 (defence of self-induced intoxication); 34 (self-defence). Both jurisdictions also recognise a number of common law defences.

[18] The Code has been in the process of preparation by Scottish criminal law academics for a number of years and at the time of writing had reached the stage of being issued as a Scottish Law Commission consultation paper. See *A Draft Criminal Code for Scotland* (2003). For discussion of the Draft Code, see T.H. Jones, "Towards a good and complete Criminal Code for Scotland" (2005) 68 M.L.R. 448–463; P.R. Ferguson, "Codifying criminal law: the Scots and English Draft Codes compared" [2004] Crim. L.R. 105–119; E.M. Clive, "Submission of a Draft Criminal Code for Scotland to the Minister of Justice" (2003) 7 Edin. L.R. 395–398; L. Farmer, "Enigma: decoding the Draft Criminal Code" (2002) 7 S.L.P.Q. 68–80; E. Clive and P.R. Ferguson, "Unravelling the enigma: a reply to Professor Farmer" (2002) 7 S.L.P.Q. 81–86.

[19] See the draft legislation in their *Report on Insanity and Diminished Responsibility* (Scot. Law Com. No.195, 2004).

[20] Criminal Law (Consolidation) (Scotland) Act 1995, s.47(1).

[21] *ibid.*, s.49(4).

a charge of vandalism[22]; the defence of "lawful authority or excuse" in relation to the charge of counterfeiting or falsifying a monetary instrument[23]; the defence of taking possession "for the purpose of preventing another from committing an offence" in relation to a charge of the possession of controlled drugs[24]; and the defence of belief in the owner's consent in relation to a charge of taking a motor vehicle without the consent of the owner.[25]

Our focus in this book is primarily on common law defences, rather than on provisions that have a narrow application to a single statutory charge. There are some minor exceptions to this, such as the discussion of time-bar and delay,[26] but this is because these statutory provisions relate not to a single statutory offence, but have general application across a range of offences.[27]

THE RATIONALE FOR ADMITTING THE DEFENCE

Fourth, and finally, defences can be categorised according to the basis upon which they prevent conviction for a particular offence. In this context, much attention has focused on the distinction between so called "justification" and "excuse" defences, but these two categories do not account for the full range of defences that would fall into the definition above. It is proposed here that criminal defences can be divided into five broad categories as follows: **1.05**

1. Failure of proof defences
2. Justifications
3. Excuses
4. Lack of capacity defences
5. Non-exculpatory defences

At this point, it should be acknowledged that our classification is based in part on that of Paul Robinson,[28] although it differs from his in two important respects. First, we make a distinction between excuse defences and lack of capacity defences, which he does not.[29] Secondly, Robinson includes in his classification a category of defences which he terms "offence modifications",[30] which operate on the basis that "while the actor has apparently satisfied all elements of the offence charged, he has not in fact caused the harm or evil sought to be prevented by the statute

[22] Criminal Law (Consolidation) (Scotland) Act 1995, s.52(1).

[23] *ibid.*, s.46A(2).

[24] Misuse of Drugs Act 1971, s.5(4).

[25] Specifically where "the accused acted in the reasonable belief that he had lawful authority, or in the reasonable belief that the owner would, in the circumstances of the case, have given consent if he had been asked for it, the accused shall not be liable to be convicted of the offence" (Road Traffic Act 1988, s.178).

[26] See Ch.16.

[27] See also the discussion of the Statutory Instruments Act 1946 in the chapter on error of law (para.13.22), and the various statutory defences of reasonable mistake in relation to sexual offences with under-age persons contained in the Criminal Law (Consolidation) (Scotland) Act 1995, discussed in relation to error of fact in para.12.17.

[28] See Robinson, *Criminal Law Defenses*, at §21. Robinson identifies five general categories of defence: failure of proof defences; offence modification defences; justifications; excuses; and non-exculpatory public policy defences.

[29] This is defended later.

[30] Robinson, *Criminal Law Defenses*, §23.

defining the offence".[31] These are not, however, considered here to be a distinctive category of defence in their own right; rather they are a collection of 'defences' that are better regarded either as failure of proof defences or as falling into one of the other categories above.[32]

Failure of proof 'defences'

1.06 The first category—failure of proof defences[33]—refer to those instances where the prosecution, because of the 'defence', are unable to prove all of the required elements of the offence. Into this category would be placed 'defences' including mistakes of law or fact[34] and non-insane automatism that negate an element of the offence.[35]

If one accepts that there is a valid distinction to be made between offences and substantive defences, failure of proof defences are not, strictly speaking, defences at all, referring as they do to a failure on the part of the prosecution to prove an element of the *offence*. That offences and defences are distinct in this way is not a view that is universally held. Williams[36] has suggested that the distinction is an artificial one and that it is merely by chance and historical accident that various elements in the criminal law have been attributed to either the offence or defence side of the equation.[37] Equally, the conceptual distinction was not recognised in *Drury v HM Advocate*,[38] where the Court of Appeal revised the definition of murder in order to exclude cases of killing under provocation from its scope.[39]

The view taken here is that offences and substantive defences are distinguishable, although, admittedly, the distinction between offence elements and defence elements is sometimes difficult to place. Offences are prima facie wrongs; acts (or omissions) that there is reason not to do and

[31] Robinson, *Criminal Law Defenses*, §23(a). Robinson provides examples including the impossibility defence in attempts (in legal systems where this is recognised); the principle that a victim of crime cannot be an accomplice; or the "de minimus" defence (in legal systems where this is recognised), where all conditions of the offence are satisfied but the harm caused is so minimal as not to be worth convicting. They can also be offence specific, for example the possession of a valid prescription for otherwise prohibited drugs.

[32] For a more detailed discussion of Robinson's classification scheme, see Ch.2 of F. Leverick, *Killing in Self-Defence* (2006). For an alternative classification that takes into account partial defences, see J. Horder, *Excusing Crime* (2004), p.103. In most respects, Horder's classification does not differ significantly from ours (with the exception that he deals with partial defences separately and leaves out non-exculpatory defences from his scheme).

[33] The terminology is borrowed from Robinson, although he alternatively refers to them as "absence of an element defences" (see Robinson, "Criminal law defenses: a systematic analysis" (1982) 82 *Columbia Law Review* 199–291 at p.204). Victor Tadros, in *Criminal Responsibility* (2005), terms them "evidential defences" (at p.103).

[34] See Chs 13 and 12 respectively.

[35] See Ch.7.

[36] G. Williams, "Offences and defences" (1982) 2 L.S. 233–256.

[37] But see K. Campbell, "Offence and defence" in *Criminal Law and Justice: Essays from the W.G. Hart Workshop 1986* (I.H. Dennis (ed), 1987), pp.73–86.

[38] 2001 S.L.T. 1013. But *cf.* the case law of the Canadian Supreme Court, especially *R. v Parent*, 2001 S.C.C. 30 at [6] and *R. v Kerr*, 2004 S.C.C. 44 at [28], *per* Bastarache J.; at [93] *per* LeBel J.

[39] Although as para.3.11 discusses, this aspect of *Drury* is not one that has been followed in later appeal court decisions on defences.

which require explanation if criminal liability is not to be imposed. Defences are conditions or circumstances which provide a reason why this prima facie assumption of criminal liability should be displaced.[40]

1.07 While they are not considered to be defences strictly speaking in this narrow sense of the term, failure of proof 'defences' are considered here, as the intention of this book is to offer coverage of defences in the fullest sense: the conditions that do—or ought to—operate to prevent conviction for an offence or to prevent a trial taking place.

The primary focus in this book is on failure of proof defences that negate the *mens rea* element of an offence. Thus the main failure of proof defences discussed here are error of fact,[41] error of law[42] and non-insane automatism,[43] where these conditions or circumstances operate to negate *mens rea*.

That is not to recognise that failure of proof defences cannot equally affect the *actus reus* element of an offence. The most obvious defences that operate in this way are alibi, incrimination and consent in sexual offences. All three of these defences are special defences and, as such, are discussed in this context in Ch.2, which deals with the procedural issues relating to defences. The decision has been taken not to give more detailed consideration to failure of proof defences that negate *actus reus*, primarily because there simply is not a body of case law surrounding the conditions of these defences in the same way as there is in relation to failure of proof defences that affect *mens rea*. In short, the issues involved in negating *actus reus* are far less complex than those involved in negating *mens rea*, where there exist greater difficulties of proof and various policy debates over questions such as whether any mistakes in relation to perception must be reasonable.

Justifications and excuses

1.08 The next two categories of defence respectively are justifications and excuses. Unlike failure of proof defences, both operate as substantive defences arising once the *actus reus* and *mens rea*[44] of the completed crime have been made out. Thus before it is appropriate for a claim of justification or excuse to be made, there needs to be *something to justify or excuse*. The two concepts are, however, distinct. As a working definition, it might be said that an individual claiming a justification defence asserts that what he did was, all things considered, an acceptable thing to do, even though it satisfied the definition of an offence. An individual claiming an excuse defence claims that, although what he did was wrong, *there is a reason why he should not be blamed for it*.

The distinction between justifications and excuses is a topic that has attracted an enormous amount of literature. The starting point for

---

[40] On this, see Campbell, above, fn.37; J. Gardner, "In defence of defences" in *Flores Juris et Legum: Festskrift till Nils Jareborg* (P. Asp, C.E. Herlitz and L. Holmqvist (eds), 1992); J. Horder, *Excusing Crime* (2004); S. Shute "Second Law Commission Consultation Paper on Consent: (1) Something old, something new, something borrowed: three aspects of the project" [1996] Crim. L.R. 684–693 at p.690.

[41] Discussed in Ch.12.

[42] Discussed in Ch.13.

[43] Discussed in Ch.7.

[44] Assuming the offence is not one of absolute liability.

discussion is often taken to be the work of George Fletcher, writing in the 1970s,[45] although interest in the distinction can be traced back further than that, at least to the philosophers J.L. Austin[46] and H.L.A. Hart.[47]

According to Austin, when we are claiming a justification, "we accept responsibility but deny that it was bad".[48] When we are claiming an excuse, "we admit that it was bad but don't accept full or even any responsibility".[49]

Immediately, some concerns arise over Austin's use of the term "responsibility". His claim *could* be taken to mean that, when we claim an excuse, what we are doing is denying responsibility in the sense that we did not cause the "bad thing" to happen *at all*. If this is what Austin meant, he would, in Hart's terms, be referring to causal responsibility. Hart distinguishes between four types of responsibility: role responsibility (the specific duties attached to a particular role such as a parent or doctor); causal responsibility (responsibility in the sense that the individual caused or made a contribution to an outcome); legal liability responsibility (the connection between the individual and the act is sufficient that he is legally liable for it—act responsibility might be another term); and capacity responsibility (the ability to understand, reason and control conduct).[50] Subsequent parts of Austin's article suggest that what he meant by responsibility was not causal responsibility, but was closest to liability responsibility (although he may have been alluding to capacity responsibility too).

1.09 Hart himself referred to justification as "something the law does not condemn or even welcomes".[51] According to Hart, an excuse is claimed when:

> "... what has been done is something which is deplored, but the psychological state of the agent when he did it exemplified one or more of a variety of conditions which are held to rule out public condemnation and punishment of individuals".[52]

Hence, the basic distinction between justifications and excuses for both Austin and Hart is similar. A claim of justification involves a claim primarily about the act itself. An individual claims responsibility for that act but denies that, all things considered, it was an unacceptable thing to do. A claim of excuse is a claim primarily about the individual. He accepts

45 G.P. Fletcher, "The individualisation of excusing conditions" (1974) 47 *Southern California Law Review* 1269–1309; G.P. Fletcher, "The right deed for the wrong reason: a reply to Mr Robinson" (1975) 23 *UCLA Law Review* 293–321; Fletcher, *Rethinking Criminal Law* (1978).

46 In 1956, Austin gave a paper at the Aristotelian Society entitled "A plea for excuses". This has since been reproduced in various edited collections, such as J.L. Austin, "A plea for excuses" in *The Philosophy of Action* (A.R. White (ed), 1968), pp.19–42.

47 In 1957, Hart addressed the New York Institute of Philosophy on the subject "legal responsibility and excuses", a paper that was later published in Hart's own book: H.L.A. Hart, *Punishment and Responsibility: Essays in the Philosophy of Law* (1968).

48 Austin, above, fn.46, at p.20.

49 Austin, above, fn.46, at p.20.

50 H.L.A. Hart, *Punishment and Responsibility: Essays in the Philosophy of Law* (1968), pp.212–222.

51 Hart, above, fn.50, at p.13.

52 Hart, above, fn.50, at p.14.

that what he did was wrong but claims that, for some reason pertinent to him as an individual, we should not blame him for his conduct.[53]

The same themes are reflected in Fletcher's work. Fletcher locates the difference between justifications and excuses in a distinction between wrongdoing and culpability:

> "Claims of justification concede that the definition of the offense is satisfied, but challenge whether the act is wrongful; claims of excuse concede that the act is wrongful, but seek to avoid the attribution of the act to the actor. A justification speaks to the rightness of an act; an excuse, to whether the actor is accountable for a concededly wrongful act."[54]

Indeed, it is likely that few of those who have written about justifications and excuses in the criminal law would argue about this basic distinction.[55] Rather, debate has tended to focus on issues such as which particular defences fall into each category (and, especially, on how mistake is to be treated)[56] and on attempting to provide an overarching rationale for why certain types of conduct should be justified or excused. **1.10**

It should be pointed out that, to some extent, the category that a particular defence falls into can depend on the way in which the defence is formulated in the particular jurisdiction in question. There is no absolute rule, for example, that necessity must *always* be characterised as a justification defence or that coercion must *always* be characterised as an excuse.[57] That said, based on the definitions above, the category of justification defences would include most claims of self-defence,[58] and some claims of necessity and coercion.[59]

Excuse defences would include the vast majority of claims of coercion and necessity and claims of superior orders. The excuse category would also include some claims of error of law, if reasonable error of law is accepted as a defence.[60] It would not, however, include a claim of nonage, as this more properly falls into the fourth category, lack of capacity defences.[61] The defence of insanity is more difficult to classify: it has

---

[53] Although, as will be noted in due course, some would argue that it is simplistic to conclude that justifications are solely concerned with acts and excuses with actors.

[54] Fletcher, *Rethinking Criminal Law*, p.759.

[55] See, e.g. J. Dressler, "Reflecting on excusing wrongdoers: moral theory, new excuses and the moral penal code" (1988) 19 *Rutgers Law Journal* 671–716 at pp.675–676; K. Greenawalt, "Distinguishing justifications from excuses" (1986) 49 *Law and Contemporary Problems* 89–108 at p.91; P.H. Robinson, "Criminal law defenses: a systematic analysis" (1982) 82 *Columbia Law Review* 199–291 at p.203; D.N. Husak, "Justifications and the criminal liability of accessories" (1989) 80 *Journal of Criminal Law and Criminology* 491–520 at p.496; M. Moore, *Placing Blame: A General Theory of the Criminal Law* (1987), p.483.

[56] A theme to which we return later: see paras 1.19 *et seq.*

[57] On this, see M.N. Berman, "Justification and excuse, law and morality" (2003) 53 *Duke Law Journal* 1–77 at p.68.

[58] At least those where the accused was not mistaken about his belief in the need to use self-defensive force, although not all theorists would agree with our conception of mistaken belief in self-defence as an excuse: see the discussion of the reasons theory of justification in para.1.21 and the discussion in relation to self-defence in para.3.04.

[59] Where the harm prevented far outweighed the harm threatened. See paras 4.03 and 5.04 for a defence of this categorisation in relation to necessity and coercion respectively.

[60] In Scots law it is not at present. See Ch.13.

[61] See para.1.12 below.

variously been regarded either as an excuse or a lack of capacity defence.[62] The partial defence of provocation is also difficult to classify, but it is most commonly categorised as a partial excuse (with a justificatory component).[63] There is some suggestion that claims of diminished responsibility might also fall into this category, although they might equally fall into the next category, lack of capacity defences.

Lack of capacity defences

1.11 Until relatively recently, debate about the categorisation of *substantive* defences[64] had focused almost exclusively on the distinction between justifications and excuses. It has been suggested, however, that a further distinction can be made between so called "true" excuses, such as coercion, and defences such as nonage that operate not as excuses, but as *lack of capacity defences*.[65]

Lack of capacity defences differ from excuses in that true excuse defences relate only to those who are regarded as capable of complying with the law. The actor claiming an excuse defence asserts responsibility for his acts *in general*, but realises that he should have acted differently on this particular occasion and puts forward for assessment a reason why he should not be blamed. As Wallace puts it, excuses "give us a reason to withdraw the attitudes we would ordinarily take in response to a particular *action*, but they do not give us a reason to view the *agent* as anything other than an ordinary, accountable person in general".[66]

Conversely, the actor who claims a lack of capacity defence does not need to bother making excuses as, due to an incapacity stemming from, for example, mental illness, he is regarded as incapable of making his conduct conform to the criminal law.

1.12 The distinction between excuses and lack of capacity defences might, then, be drawn as follows. An excuse defence is granted to those who are capable of conforming to the demands of the criminal law, but offer an excuse for one act (or omission). A lack of capacity defence is granted to those who are not capable of conforming to the demands of the criminal

---

[62] See paras 1.12–1.13 below.

[63] See paras 10.03–10.04 for discussion.

[64] Setting aside for the moment absent element defences and non-exculpatory defences.

[65] See R.J. Wallace, *Responsibility and the Moral Sentiments* (1994); A. Duff, "Law, language and community: some preconditions of criminal liability" (1998) 18 O.J.L.S. 189–206; J. Gardner, "Justifications and reasons" in *Harm and Culpability* (A.P. Simester and A.T.H. Smith (eds), 1996); J. Gardner, "In defence of defences" in *Flores Juris et Legum: Festskrift till Nils Jareborg* (P. Asp, C.E. Herlitz and L. Holmqvist (eds), 1992); J. Horder, *Excusing Crime* (2004), pp.9–10; V. Tadros, *Criminal Responsibility* (2005), pp.124–129; M. Baron, "Justifications and excuses" (2005) 2 *Ohio State Journal of Criminal Law* 387–406. The term "exemptions" is sometimes used (e.g. by Wallace and Tadros) instead of "lack of capacity defences". Lack of capacity defences is, however, a more appropriate term for the type of defence being described here. Exemptions could be viewed as including some non-exculpatory defences, such as diplomatic immunity. Horder terms lack of capacity defences as "out and out denials of responsibility" (above, fn.65, at p.8).

[66] Wallace, above, fn.65, at p.155 (emphasis in original).

law and are, therefore, exempt from its scope on the basis of a more pervasive mental disorder or condition.[67]

The two defences most commonly described as lack of capacity defences are insanity[68] and nonage.[69] Describing nonage as a lack of capacity defence is relatively uncontroversial, although in Scots law it is based on the legal fiction that children do not have the capacity to form *mens rea,* rather than evidence about the capacity of the particular child accused of an offence.[70]

Describing insanity as a lack of capacity defence, as some criminal law theorists have done,[71] is more controversial. The leading US criminal law theorists, Dressler,[72] Fletcher,[73] Robinson,[74] Greenawalt[75] and Kadish,[76] all classify insanity as an excuse and do not, normally, even consider the possibility that it might better be thought of as a different type of defence altogether.[77]

Although the courts have not discussed the issue, the way the sub- **1.13**
stantive defence of insanity[78] is formulated in Scots law is indicative of an excuse, not a lack of capacity defence. The insanity defence, as currently understood, rests entirely on the condition of the accused *at the time when the offence was alleged to have been committed*, and an acquittal on the ground of insanity may say nothing about whether the accused is now a proper subject for the sanction of the criminal law.[79]

However, the criminal law has run into difficulties in the past by treating insanity as if it were *both* an excuse and a lack of capacity defence. While it has been treated, in its substance, as an excuse (by

---

[67] Colvin makes a similar distinction, using the phrase "defences of mental impairment" to cover defences where the individual concerned is not a proper subject for handling within the standard structure of criminal liability. However, unlike others who have argued for the recognition of lack of capacity defences, he does not proceed to make a further distinction between justifications and excuses. Instead he places all other defences into a single category called "defences of contextual permission", which comprises all defences in which it was judged reasonable for the accused to act as he did. See E. Colvin, "Exculpatory defences in criminal law" (1990) 10 O.J.L.S. 381–407 at p.383.

[68] Discussed in Ch.7.

[69] Discussed in Ch.9.

[70] See Ch.9.

[71] See, e.g. V. Tadros, "Insanity and the capacity for criminal responsibility" (2001) 5 Edin. L.R. 325–354 at p.341; N. Lacey, *State Punishment* (1988), p.74.

[72] J. Dressler, "Reflecting on excusing wrongdoers: moral theory, new excuses and the moral penal code" (1988) 19 *Rutgers Law Journal* 671–716 at p.682.

[73] G.P. Fletcher, "The individualisation of excusing conditions" (1974) 47 *Southern California Law Review* 1269–1309 at p.1293; G.P. Fletcher, "Rights and excuses" (1984) 3 *Criminal Justice Ethics* 17–27 at p.17.

[74] Robinson, *Criminal Law Defenses*, §28.

[75] K. Greenawalt, "The perplexing borders of justification and excuse" (1984) 84 *Columbia Law Review* 1897–1927 at p.1915.

[76] S.H. Kadish, "Excusing crime" (1987) 75 *California Law Review* 257–289 at p.262.

[77] Fletcher does consider the possibility in *Rethinking Criminal Law* (1978), at pp.836–839. Trying to squeeze insanity into the category of excuses perhaps accounts for some of the difficulties commentators have in coming up with a single "theoretical basis" for excuse defences. It is not easy to make a convincing argument of why we excuse people that has to account for both insanity and coercion on the same basis. See, e.g. Joshua Dressler's attempt at explaining why insanity is an excuse: "An insane person is not a whole human being. We sense this inadequacy in a mentally ill person. We feel sorry for him. We try to reduce his suffering by freeing him from the blame, stigma and pain that results from a criminal conviction" (Dressler, above, fn.72, at p.682).

[78] As opposed to the plea in bar of trial (see Ch.14).

[79] See below, paras 7.03–7.04.

examining the accused's condition at the time of the alleged offence), its consequences have been defined as if it were a lack of capacity defence. This is because the law has assumed that a finding that an accused was insane at some point in the past means that he should be detained in a mental hospital, a question which should logically be decided on the basis of his present and not his past condition. It is only very recently that the last vestiges of mandatory detention for those acquitted on the ground of insanity have been removed from Scots law, largely because detaining persons who were not presently of "unsound mind" on the basis that they had been "insane" at some point in time in the past would have been contrary to the ECHR.[80]

Non-exculpatory defences

1.14 The fifth and final category of defences in our classification scheme is non-exculpatory defences. These operate where, despite the fact that the accused *might* have satisfied all of the requirements of the offence,[81] there is a reason why the state should be prevented from bringing the accused to trial.[82] Procedurally, non-exculpatory defences operate in a different way to all of the other defences considered thus far in that they are (or ought to be)[83] considered pre-trial and, if successful, prevent a trial from taking place at all.[84]

Defences falling into this category would include renunciation of the right to prosecute; entrapment; other pleas in bar of trial, such as those based on pretrial publicity or insanity; time bar and delay; and *res judicata.*[85] It would also include claims of diplomatic immunity, although this defence is not discussed here.[86] Depending on the view taken of the underlying rationale of the defence, it might also include some claims of

---

[80] Detention is now possible, but not mandatory. See CPSA 1995, s.57(2), and below, para.7.02.

[81] As non-exculpatory defences are considered pre-verdict, this is not an issue that is enquired into.

[82] Or, if facts giving rise to a non-exculpatory defence only come to light or occur during the trial, a reason why the state should not have embarked upon the trial in the first place, or why the trial should now be abandoned. On the procedural issues involved, see below, para.2.17.

[83] It is possible to raise a non-exculpatory defence once a trial has commenced, in which case the same principles as govern the plea in bar of trial should be applied (see para.2.17).

[84] On this, see R.A. Duff, "I might be guilty, but you can't try me: estoppel and other bars to trial" (2003) 1 *Ohio State Journal of Criminal Law* 245–259 at p.252. Although *cf.* the contrary approach taken to the plea of entrapment by the Canadian Supreme Court in *R. v Mack* [1988] 2 S.C.R. 903 (see para.2.17).

[85] Discussed in Chs 20 (entrapment); 14 (insanity as a plea in bar of trial); 15 (*res judicata*); 16 (time bar and delay); 17 (renunciation of the right to prosecute); and 18 (pretrial publicity as a plea in bar of trial).

[86] There is no body of specifically Scottish case law in relation to diplomatic immunity, which is governed by international law, principally the 1961 Vienna Convention on Diplomatic Relations, given effect to in domestic law by the Diplomatic Privileges Act 1964 (see also the International Organisations (Immunities and Privileges) Act 1950; the Diplomatic Immunities (Commonwealth Countries and Republic of Ireland) Act 1952; the Diplomatic Immunities (Conferences with Commonwealth Countries and Republic of Ireland) Act 1961; and the Diplomatic and Other Privileges Act 1971). The immunity of heads of state or government is not discussed here either, for the same reason (on this, see the State Immunity Act 1978). There is extensive discussion of both diplomatic and head of state immunity in *R. v Bow Street Metropolitan Stipendiary Magistrate, ex parte Pinochet Ugarte (No. 3)* [2000] 1 A.C. 147.

error of law, specifically those where the error was induced by reliance on official advice.[87]

Non-exculpatory defences may be justified by reference to two aims of the criminal justice system: "protecting the innocent from wrongful conviction and protecting the moral integrity of the criminal process".[88] The first of these aims is uncontroversial in Scots law, and has been dealt with principally under the heading of oppression, a plea in bar based on prejudice to the accused's right to a fair trial.[89] A body of case law exists only in respect of oppression due to delay and prejudicial publicity, although in principle it should be possible for an accused person to plead that he cannot receive a fair trial for other reasons (for example, that crucial evidence has been lost or destroyed).[90] In practice, the issue appears to have arisen—at least in the reported cases—outside of the context of delay or prejudicial publicity only once, in *Stewart v HM Advocate*,[91] where a juror claimed to have been approached by a man who wished to bribe her to persuade the jury to acquit one of the accused. It was recognised that events of this nature might require the trial diet to be deserted unless the trial judge was satisfied (as he was in this case) that the risk of prejudice could be corrected by appropriate directions to the jury.[92] The avoidance of wrongful conviction is also one reason (although not the only reason) for recognising insanity as a plea in bar of trial.[93]

Protecting the "moral integrity" of the criminal process, by contrast, is **1.15** a less clearly acknowledged aim of the criminal justice process in Scots law. In part, this may reflect the fact that criminal prosecutions in Scotland are almost exclusively in the hands of the public prosecutor and that the courts have not felt it necessary to rein in the prosecutor's discretion. However, it has recently been explicitly acknowledged in *Brown v HM Advocate*,[94] where the appeal court recognised entrapment as a plea in bar of trial.[95] In that case, Lord Clarke remarked that were the courts to countenance proceeding with a criminal prosecution where entrapment has occurred, this "may be to countenance the pollution of the moral integrity of the machinery of justice".[96]

These twin justifications are not mutually exclusive, and a non-exculpatory defence may rest on a combination of the two. The proper justification for each plea in bar of trial recognised by Scots law is considered in each chapter, as appropriate.

[87] See Ch.13 for discussion.

[88] A. L.-T. Choo, *Abuse of Process and Judicial Stays of Criminal Proceedings* (1993), p.13.

[89] As to whether a plea of oppression can succeed without such prejudice being established, see Ch.19.

[90] *cf. R. (Ebrahim) v Feltham Magistrates' Court* [2001] EWHC Admin 130, discussed by S. Martin, "Lost and destroyed evidence: the search for a principled approach to abuse of process" (2005) 9 *International Journal of Evidence and Proof* 158–182; D. Corker and D. Young, *Abuse of Process in Criminal Proceedings* (2nd edn, 2003), Ch.3.

[91] 1980 J.C. 103.

[92] This case, in fact, has formed the basis for subsequent decisions on the scope of pleas in bar of trial based on prejudicial publicity: see below, para.18.02.

[93] See below, para.14.01.

[94] 2002 S.L.T. 809.

[95] On which, see Ch.20.

[96] At [2].

The classification scheme summarised

1.16 *1. Failure of proof defences.* A failure of proof defence operates where the prosecution, because of the 'defence', are unable to prove all of the required elements of the offence. Into this category would be placed 'defences' that negate *mens rea* (including mistake of law or fact and non-insane automatism) and 'defences' that negate *actus reus* (such as consent in sexual offences, alibi and incrimination).

2. Justification defences. A justification defence is claimed where the accused has engaged in the wrongdoing prohibited by the offence but, all things considered, his conduct is judged to be acceptable. This category includes most claims of self-defence, some claims of necessity and a small minority of claims of coercion.

3. Excuse defences. An excuse defence is claimed where the accused has acted unacceptably, but, for some reason, we do not blame him for what he did. We hold an excused individual morally accountable for his acts in general but do not blame him for the particular act in question. This category includes some claims of self-defence,[97] claims of superior orders; those claims of necessity and coercion that do not fall into the justification category; and, if indeed such claims are recognised as defences at all, claims of intoxication that do not go as far as affecting the individual's ability to form *mens rea* and claims of reasonable error of law. This category might include claims of insanity, although insanity might equally be regarded as a lack of capacity defence.[98] The partial defence of provocation is most commonly regarded as a partial excuse (although with an element of justification) and there is some suggestion that the partial defence of diminished responsibility might be similarly regarded.[99]

1.17 *4. Lack of capacity defences.* A lack of capacity defence is claimed where the accused is not regarded as sufficiently capable to be held accountable for his behaviour at the time of the alleged offence. This category comprises primarily nonage but might also be argued to include insanity, as discussed earlier.[1]

5. Non-exculpatory defences. This category covers cases where, for reasons *other than* blamelessness or a lack of capacity, a trial should not occur. It includes renunciation of the right to prosecute; entrapment; other pleas in bar of trial, such as those based on pretrial publicity or insanity; time bar and delay; and *res judicata*. It might also include some claims of diplomatic immunity and of error of law, specifically those where the error was induced by reliance on official advice.

---

[97] Specifically those where the accused is mistaken in his belief that he is under attack, although as has already been noted, this depends on how one regards mistake in relation to a justification. This issue will be discussed in detail in paras 1.19 *et seq.*

[98] See paras 1.12–1.13 above.

[99] See para.11.01.

[1] See paras 1.12–1.13 above.

A hierarchy of defences?

It has been suggested by John Gardner,[2] among others,[3] that the classification above has a normative structure in terms of the defence that reflects most favourably on the accused. For Gardner, justifications are the most preferable type of defence to claim, followed by excuses and then lack of capacity defences. This is because it is morally preferable to have acted acceptably (a justification) than to be excused for acting unacceptably.[4] It is also morally preferable to be excused for acting unacceptably than not to have the capacity where one's behaviour can be judged acceptable or unacceptable at all.[5] Gardner does not mention absent element defences and does not make anything other than passing reference to non-exculpatory defences in this context. It might be assumed, though, that on a moral basis the former 'rank' above justifications and excuses in the sense that the accused has not even caused the harm prohibited by the offence definition, thus has done nothing which requires justification or excuse. It might equally be assumed that non-exculpatory defences, like lack of capacity defences, rank below absent element defences, justifications and excuses in terms of the manner in which they reflect on the accused, given that the defence is granted for reasons other than blamelessness.[6] **1.18**

What cannot be said is that the hierarchy operates in terms of the order in which the defences would be considered in practice. For one thing, although morally they may be considered inferior to claims of justification, most of the non-exculpatory defences are matters which would be considered pre-trial and which operate to prevent a trial actually taking place. Likewise, if an accused had potentially a defence of lack of capacity (such as nonage) and a justification defence (such as self-defence), it would make little sense, given the ease of proving nonage,[7] to plead the justification first and only move on to the nonage defence if the justification was unsuccessful.

[2] J. Gardner, "The mark of responsibility" (2003) 23 O.J.L.S. 157–171; J. Gardner, "The gist of excuses" (1998) 1 *Buffalo Criminal Law Review* 575–598 at p.590; J. Gardner, "In defence of defences" in *Flores Juris et Legum: Festskrift till Nils Jareborg* (P. Asp, C.E. Herlitz and L. Holmqvist (eds), 1992), p.262.

[3] See also M. Baron, "Justifications and excuses" (2005) 2 *Ohio State Journal of Criminal Law* 387–406 at p.389; J. Horder, *Excusing Crime* (2004), p.99; V. Tadros, "The structure of defences in Scots criminal law" (2003) 7 Edin. L.R. 60–79 at pp.60–61.

[4] Although not everyone would agree. For a contrary view, see D. Husak, "The serial view of criminal law defenses" (1992) 3 *Criminal Law Forum* 369–400; D. Husak, "On the supposed priority of justification to excuse" (2005) 24 *Law and Philosophy* 557–594; D. Klimchuk, "Necessity, deterrence and standing" (2002) 8 *Legal Theory* 339–358 at p.355.

[5] It might be questioned whether or not this is indeed true of the plea of nonage. It might be thought, though, that the self-respecting child would prefer to have his conduct deemed justified and therefore acceptable than he would to be told that he was not to be held accountable by virtue of his age. Although *cf.* Tadros, above, fn.3, at p.61 (fn.5).

[6] Support for this is provided by the Canadian Supreme Court case of *R. v Mack* [1988] 2 S.C.R. 903, which held that entrapment (which in Canada is regarded as a non-exculpatory defence) should only be considered after the trial has been completed and the accused found guilty in order to preserve the right of the accused to the more favourable verdict of an acquittal on the basis of justification or excuse.

[7] At least in the Scottish context. Circumstances can be envisaged whereby proof of age would be more difficult to come by.

Mistakes relating to justifications

1.19 An issue that has received a great deal of discussion—in fact it is probably the most hotly debated issue in relation to the classification of defences—is the way in which mistake about a justification is treated. There are two factual situations in which this issue arises.

The first is the actor who mistakenly believes that his act is justified. An example might be the accused who acts in 'self-defence' under the mistaken belief that he is about to be attacked. The debate here centres around whether such a person is best described as justified or excused.

The second is the so-called "unknowingly justified" actor. In this situation, the accused fulfils the requirements of the offence but, unknown to him, circumstances exist in which his act would have been justified. The debate here centres around whether or not such an actor should receive the benefit of a defence *at all*.[8] Claims of unknowing justification have only arisen very rarely. The most well known example is probably *R. v Dadson*,[9] in which a police constable shot and wounded a man who was running away from a forest carrying stolen goods. Unknown to the officer concerned, the victim had previously been convicted twice for theft and, under the law of England at the time, a police officer would potentially have been justified in using such force against him. More recent cases that could possibly be put in this category are the Scottish case of *Dawson v Dickson*[10] and the Northern Irish case of *R. v Thain*.[11]

The debate over the treatment of both the mistaken justification case and the unknowingly justified actor is a longstanding and extensive one in criminal law theory. Until relatively recently, it could be characterised as a debate between those who would support what has been termed a

---

[8] For an extensive discussion of this question, see A.M. Dillof, "Unravelling unknowing justification" (2002) 77 *Notre Dame Law Review* 1547–1600. See also Ch.2 of F. Leverick, *Killing in Self-Defence* (2006).

[9] (1850) 4 Cox C.C. 358. For comment see B. Hogan, "The *Dadson* principle" [1989] Crim. L.R. 679–686.

[10] 1999 J.C. 315. In the S.L.T. report of the case (1999 S.L.T. 1328), it is reported under the alternative name of *Dawson v McKay*. This appears to have stemmed from a mistake in recording the name of the procurator fiscal involved. The facts of *Dawson v Dickson* are described in para.1.23 below.

[11] [1985] N.I. 457. Here the defendant shot and killed a man who was running away from an army patrol. The defendant was unaware that he may potentially have been justified on the basis of effecting an arrest (instead he claimed that he had acted in self-defence, a defence that unsurprisingly failed because the deceased was running away at the time). For a case in which the issue would have arisen had it been prosecuted (in the event no prosecution actually took place), see P. Robinson, "The bomb thief and the theory of justification defenses" (1997) 8 *Criminal Law Forum* 387–409. Here a thief stole an innocent looking backpack that had been left in a public place. Unknown to him at the time, it contained a terrorist bomb that was shortly to explode. When he discovered the bomb, he handed it in to the police, thus potentially saving numerous lives.

"deeds theory" of justification and those who would support a "reasons theory" of justification,[12] but to these two possibilities must now be added the "dual requirement" theory of justification.

The deeds theory of justification

Those who support a deeds theory of justification would essentially grant a justification defence to the accused wherever potentially justifying circumstances were present, regardless of whether or not the accused was aware of them. For a deeds theorist, the unknowingly justified actor would be justified, despite the fact that he was not aware of the potentially justificatory circumstances. The primary proponent of the deeds theory of justification is Paul Robinson,[13] although others have supported his position.[14] **1.20**

Robinson initially supported the deeds theory of justification on the basis that no harm has occurred as a result of the 'justified' act and therefore no liability should be incurred. This position has been extensively criticised on the basis that it is simply not accurate to say that no harm has occurred where the offence definition has been fulfilled.[15] Robinson has since modified his position and now argues that although some harm has been caused by the justified behaviour, this is outweighed by the beneficial consequences.[16] He accepts though that the unknowingly justified actor should incur some level of criminal liability and suggests that this should be in line with that incurred for an impossible attempt.[17] He still agrees with the fundamental premise of the deeds theory: that where an actor commits an offence in potentially justifying circumstances, he should be described as justified even when he is entirely unaware of these circumstances.[18] And although he no longer attempts to argue that no harm has occurred, his view that attempt liability should result is based on the assumption that a lesser harm has occurred in a case of

---

[12] The terminology is that of Paul Robinson: see P.H. Robinson, "Competing theories of justification: deeds v reasons" in *Harm and Culpability* (A.P. Simester and A.T.H. Smith (eds), 1996), pp.45–70. Others have framed the debate as one between "subjective" and "objective" theories of justification (see J. Dressler, "New thoughts about the concept of justification in the criminal law: a critique of Fletcher's thinking and re-thinking" (1984) 32 *UCLA Law Review* 61–99). A more accurate description than either of these might be "factual circumstances alone" (deeds theory) and "actor's reasons alone" (reasons theory).

[13] P.H. Robinson, "A theory of justification: social harm as a prerequisite for criminal liability" (1975) 23 *UCLA Law Review* 266–292; P.H. Robinson, "Criminal law defenses: a systematic analysis" (1982) 82 *Columbia Law Review* 199–291; Robinson, "Competing theories of justification: deeds v reasons", above, fn.12.

[14] S.B. Byrd, "Wrongdoing and attribution: implications beyond the justification-excuse distinction" (1987) 33 *Wayne Law Review* 1289–1342; H. Hurd, "Justification and excuse, wrongdoing and culpability" (1999) 74 *Notre Dame Law Review* 1551–1573.

[15] G.P. Fletcher, "The right deed for the wrong reason: a reply to Mr Robinson" (1975) 23 *UCLA Law Review* 293–321. See also Leverick, above, fn.8, at Ch.2; T.M. Funk, "Justifying justifications" (1999) 19 O.J.L.S. 631–647; C.K.Y. Lee, "The act-belief distinction in self-defence doctrine: a new dual requirement theory of justification" (1998) 2 *Buffalo Criminal Law Review* 191–247.

[16] Robinson, "Competing theories of justification", above, fn.12, at p.45.

[17] Robinson, "Competing theories of justification", above, fn.12, at p.47. The unknowingly justified individual attempts to engage in an unjustified action in circumstances where this was impossible (due to the existence of justifying circumstances). For Robinson this is sufficiently conceptually similar to the impossible attempt that he feels a similar level of liability should attach.

[18] Robinson, "Competing theories of justification", above, fn.12, at p.48.

unknowing justification and thus a lesser punishment should result.[19] This is an assumption that has been questioned.[20]

The main objection that has been made to the deeds theory of justification, however, is that the actor who acts entirely unaware of potentially justificatory circumstances simply does not deserve the benefit of a justification defence. On this view, the accused has caused the harm that the offence was designed to prevent and has done so with a blameworthy mental state. That, entirely by chance, some good came out of his conduct is irrelevant to his liability.[21]

The reasons theory of justification

1.21 Those who support a "reasons theory" of justification would grant a justification defence to the accused on the basis of his belief in justificatory circumstances, regardless of whether or not the justificatory circumstances existed in reality. The reasons theorist would consider the unknowingly justified actor unjustified but, more importantly, would consider the mistaken actor justified, merely on the basis of his mistaken belief in the circumstances of justification. Thus the actor who comes to the assistance of a teenage boy who appears to be under attack from two men would be justified in assaulting the men (and breaking the legs of one of them), even though his belief is mistaken and the men were, in fact, plain clothes police officers legitimately attempting to arrest the boy.[22] The primary supporter of the reasons theory of justification is Joshua Dressler,[23] although many other theorists have since echoed his views.[24]

The main argument that Dressler puts forward for his position is that it is difficult to make a moral distinction between the individual who

---

[19] Robinson, "Competing theories of justification", above, fn.12, at p.58.

[20] Take the example of the accused who kills a five-year-old child for sexual pleasure. Unknown to him, the child has a gun and is about to shoot him. The deeds theory would describe the accused's conduct as justified on the basis of self-defence, but it is difficult to see how the harm involved is less than where no potentially justificatory circumstances exist. See Ch.2 of F. Leverick, *Killing in Self-Defence* (2006); A.P. Simester, "Mistakes in defence" (1992) 12 O.J.L.S. 295–310 at p.304. In this respect, George Fletcher has criticised Robinson for failing to distinguish between justified *acts* and just *events*: "It might be helpful to distinguish between *justified* acts and *just* events. It might be just for a would-be murderer to be killed by his intended victim ... but it does not follow that the act of killing is *justified*" ("The right deed for the wrong reason", above, fn.15, at p.293, emphasis in original).

[21] G.P. Fletcher, "The nature of justification" in *Action and Value in Criminal Law* (S. Shute, J. Gardner and J. Horder (eds), 1993), pp.175–186; Leverick, above, fn.20, at Ch.2.

[22] The facts of *People v Young*, 183 N.E. 2d 319 (1962).

[23] J. Dressler, "New thoughts about the concept of justification in the criminal law: a critique of Fletcher's thinking and re-thinking" (1984) 32 *UCLA Law Review* 61–99; J. Dressler, "Reflecting on excusing wrongdoers: moral theory, new excuses and the Model Penal Code" (1988) 19 *Rutgers Law Journal* 671–716.

[24] K. Greenawalt, "The perplexing borders of justification and excuse" (1984) 84 *Columbia Law Review* 1897–1927; K. Greenawalt, "Distinguishing justifications from excuses" (1986) 49 *Law and Contemporary Problems* 89–108; R.L. Christopher, "Mistake of fact in the objective theory of justification: do two rights make two wrongs make two rights ...?" (1994) 85 *Journal of Criminal Law and Criminology* 295–332; F. McAuley, "The theory of justification and excuse: some Italian lessons" (1987) 35 *American Journal of Comparative Law* 359–380; T. Morawetz, "Reconstructing the criminal defences: the significance of justification" (1986) 77 *Journal of Criminal Law and Criminology* 277–307; M. Baron, "Justifications and excuses" (2005) 2 *Ohio State Journal of Criminal Law* 387–406; H. Stewart, "The role of reasonableness in self-defence" (2003) 16 *Canadian Journal of Law and Jurisprudence* 317–336; V. Tadros, *Criminal Responsibility* (2005), pp.280–290.

proceeds in line with a reasonably mistaken belief[25] and the individual who has correctly perceived the circumstances: both, for Dressler, are morally faultless. This argument has been criticised on the basis that it fails to distinguish between justified *beliefs* and justified *acts*.[26] The mistaken actor may not be at fault in forming the *belief* that he did, but this is not the same as saying that his *act* was justified. In reality, he was mistaken and, in the example used above, has seriously injured an entirely innocent person. It is this fact that provides the moral distinction that Dressler is looking for. Conceptually, this has the gist of an excuse: the accused has done something unacceptable, but we do not *blame* him for it, on the basis that he had good reason for his mistaken belief.

The dual requirement theory of justification

More recently, John Gardner has suggested that in order to benefit from a justification defence, the key features of the deeds theory and the reasons theory should *both* be present; that is, the justificatory circumstances must exist in fact *and* the accused must have acted for the justificatory reason.[27] This has been termed the dual requirement theory of justification by Paul Robinson.[28] Under the dual requirement theory, the mistaken actor would have an excuse defence, if his mistaken belief was reasonable. The unknowingly justified actor would not be granted a defence at all, and nor would an actor who was aware of potentially justificatory circumstances but who did not act for this reason. A slight variation on this argument has been put forward by Dillof,[29] whereby "regard" for the justificatory circumstances is sufficient to ground a justification defence.[30] **1.22**

The dual requirement theory has found little support among mainstream US theorists. Robinson, for example, devotes only a single page to dual requirement theories of justification in a 25-page article on competing theories of justification and concludes that he finds them "puzzling".[31] Yet if one accepts the limitations of the deeds theory and the reasons theory set out above, then it is difficult not to reach the conclusion that the dual requirement theory is preferable. By requiring both that the justificatory circumstances actually exist (and thus that the accused has not caused harm to an innocent victim) and that the accused acted for the justificatory reason (and thus deserves the benefit of a defence), the dual requirement theory overcomes these objections.

---

[25] Dressler does not indicate how he would deal with an accused person who holds an *unreasonably* mistaken belief.

[26] Leverick, above, fn.20, at Ch.2; G.P. Fletcher, "Domination in the theory of justification and excuse" (1996) 57 *University of Pittsburgh Law Review* 553–578 at p.563; R.F. Schopp, *Justification Defences and Just Convictions* (1998), p.38.

[27] J. Gardner, "Justifications and reasons" in *Harm and Culpability* (A.P. Simester and A.T.H. Smith (eds), 1996), pp.103–129. Gardner's argument is paraphrased here as he actually formulates the two requirements in terms of reasons for acting.

[28] P.H. Robinson, "Competing theories of justification: deeds v reasons" in *Harm and Culpability* (A.P. Simester and A.T.H. Smith (eds), 1996), pp.45–70, at p.68. Baron has termed it the "material rightness thesis" (above, fn.24, at p.397).

[29] A.M. Dillof, "Unravelling unknowing justification" (2002) 77 *Notre Dame Law Review* 1547–1600 at p.1597.

[30] By which he means "shorthand for the more bulky phrase 'takes into account in his reasoning process when deciding what to do' or 'functions as a reason (even if not the sole reason) relevant to the actor's choice'" (at pp.1597–1598).

[31] Robinson, "Competing theories", above, fn.28, at p.68.

The practical consequences of the competing theories

1.23 Does the choice between the deeds theory, reasons theory and dual requirement theory matter in practice? One answer to this is that it can certainly make a difference in relation to the unknowingly justified actor, as under the deeds theory of justification he will be granted a defence, whereas under the reasons or dual requirement theory he will not. In Scots law, it seems that the unknowingly justified actor would not receive the benefit of a justification defence.

The issue was dealt with, up to a point, in *Dawson v Dickson*.[32] Here, the appellant had been convicted of driving with excess alcohol and careless driving after his defence of necessity had been rejected by the presiding sheriff. He claimed the defence after driving a fire engine that was blocking the path of an ambulance waiting to take a seriously injured casualty to hospital, but admitted in evidence that he would have driven the fire engine regardless of the emergency circumstances. An issue immediately arises of quite how best to describe Dawson. He was not, after all, *unknowingly* justified in the sense that he was unaware of the potentially justifying circumstances. On the contrary, he was fully *aware* of the nature of the emergency situation and the need to move the fire engine in order to clear the way for the ambulance. It was simply that he admitted that he would have responded to a request to move the fire engine *regardless* of the existence of these circumstances. In that sense, he might best be described as failing to act *for* the justificatory reason.

In any event, the appeal court declined to quash his conviction, and held that the justification defence of necessity can only be successful where the justifying circumstances "dominated the mind" of the accused.[33] Here, the defence of necessity had not been made out on the facts as:

> "... the defence of necessity only arises when there is a *conscious dilemma* faced by a person who has to decide between saving life or avoiding serious bodily harm on the one hand and breaking the law on the other hand".[34]

1.24 Quite what the appeal court meant by this is difficult to gauge.[35] What can be said with a reasonable degree of confidence is that (assuming this passage has a wider application to justification defences other than necessity) the unknowingly justified accused will not receive the benefit of a defence in Scots law as his mind could not possibly have been "dominated" by something of which he was unaware.[36]

If this is the correct interpretation of *Dawson v Dickson*, this places Scots law in line with English law, where, in *Dadson*,[37] the unknowingly justified defendant was similarly unsuccessful in his defence. A similar line

[32] 1999 J.C. 315.

[33] Although the judgement was not an entirely clear one. See paras 4.17–4.18, where *Dawson v Dickson* is discussed in more detail.

[34] *Dawson v Dickson*, 1999 J.C. 315 at 319, emphasis added.

[35] The judgement is discussed in detail in relation to the defence of necessity in paras 4.17–4.18.

[36] And, given the outcome of the case, it would seem that the accused who does not act for the justificatory reason will also be denied a justification defence.

[37] *R. v Dadson* (1850) 4 Cox C.C. 358.

was taken by the Northern Ireland Court of Appeal in the case of *R. v Thain*.[38]

Whether or not the choice between the three approaches has any implications in the mistaken belief scenario is less clear. Here, the choice of one theory over another only makes the difference between whether or not the accused has a justification or an excuse defence; in both instances, he would be acquitted (assuming the conditions of the defence were made out). One response might be that, as John Gardner suggests, the accused would *prefer* to be justified rather than excused, because of the more favourable way in which this reflects on a person. Indeed, Gardner professes "astonishment" that anyone would doubt this:

> "Criminal lawyers, in particular ... tend to take it for granted that any doctrine that serves to acquit the accused, and therefore to avert the adverse normative consequences of her action, is as good as any other so far as the accused is concerned. I have always found this an astonishing assumption, which implies that nobody who is tried in the criminal courts has, or even deserves to have, any self-respect ... The self-respecting person aspires to live up to the proper standards for success in and fitness for the life she leads, and holds herself out to be judged by those standards ... She wants it to be the case that her actions were not truly wrongful, or if they were wrongful, that they were at any rate justified, or if they were not justified, that they were at any rate excused."[39]

Given that, at present, the criminal justice system makes no pronouncement on declaring an acquittal as to whether any successful defence was a justification or an excuse, the accused is, however, likely to be entirely unaware of this fact.

Another way in which it has been suggested that the distinction matters **1.25**
is in relation to rights of resistance and assistance. It has been suggested that whereas an excused act can justifiably be resisted, an individual has no right to resist a justified act. In other words, no two parties can be justified in the same conflict.[40] Thus, the third party who has her mobile phone forcibly taken from her in order that an individual can phone an ambulance for the dying victim of a road traffic accident cannot permissibly resist what is, prima facie, a robbery, if the justification defence of necessity is recognised.[41] In contrast, the victim of an excused attack or robbery (where, for example, the attacker is acting under the excuse of coercion) is permitted to resist that attack.

Likewise, it has been suggested that, whereas it is permissible for a third party to assist someone in performing a justified act, this permission does not extend to assistance in performing an excused act.[42] Hence, it is permissible for a third party to come to the aid of someone attempting to

---

[38] [1985] N.I. 457. See also *North Dakota v Leidholm*, 334 N.W. 2d 811 (N.D. 1983) at 815, *per* Walle J.

[39] J. Gardner, "The gist of excuses" (1998) 1 *Buffalo Criminal Law Review* 575–598 at p.590.

[40] S.B. Byrd, "Wrongdoing and attribution: implications beyond the justification-excuse distinction" (1987) 33 *Wayne Law Review* 1289–1342 at p.1332; Fletcher, *Rethinking Criminal Law*, p.760; Robinson, *Criminal Law Defenses*, §36(a).

[41] It *might* be the case that someone resisting justified action could be granted an *excuse* defence but the suggestion here is that they would not be *justified* in resisting.

[42] Byrd, above, fn.40, at p.1332; Fletcher, *Rethinking Criminal Law*, p.760; Robinson, *Criminal Law Defenses*, §36(a).

repel an attacker in legitimate self-defence, but it would not be permissible for a third party to assist someone who is undertaking a bank robbery under coercion.

Whether or not these consequences follow, however, depends in turn on the particular theory of justification and excuse that is preferred, at least in relation to rights of assistance.[43] If all that is required for a claim of justification is the existence of justificatory circumstances (the deeds theory of justification), then it is true that anyone who assists a justified individual in those circumstances will be similarly justified, regardless of his own knowledge or motivation. Under the dual requirement theory this would not necessarily be the case, as the individual who assists would not be justified unless he acts for the justificatory reason.[44]

---

[43] Whether or not it is permissible to resist justified conduct depends on whether or not it is accepted that two parties can both be justified in the same conflict. On this, compare R.L. Christopher, "Mistake of fact in the objective theory of justification: do two rights make two wrongs make two rights ...?" (1994) 85 *Journal of Criminal Law and Criminology* 295–332 with A.M. Dillof, "Unravelling unknowing justification" (2002) 77 *Notre Dame Law Review* 1547–1600 at pp.1558–1565.

[44] Or, under Dillof's version of the theory, "has regard" to the justificatory circumstances before acting.

Chapter 2

PROCEDURAL ISSUES RELATING TO DEFENCES

Disclosure of Defences to the Prosecution

Special defences

Certain defences—termed special defences—require the defence to give advance notice to the prosecution if they are to be pled at trial under solemn procedure.[1] As such, s.78(1) of the Criminal Procedure (Scotland) Act 1995 provides that: **2.01**

> "It shall not be competent for an accused to state a special defence or to lead evidence calculated to exculpate the accused by incriminating a co-accused unless—
>
> (a) a plea of special defence or, as the case may be, notice of intention to lead such evidence has been lodged and intimated in writing ...
> (b) the court, on cause shown, otherwise directs."

Where the case is to be tried in the High Court, the plea of special defence must be lodged with the Clerk of Justiciary and intimated to the Crown Agent and to any co-accused not later than seven days before the preliminary hearing.[2] Where the case is to be tried in the sheriff court, the plea must be lodged with the sheriff clerk and intimated to the procurator fiscal and to any co-accused at or before the first diet.[3] Any reference to a court diet in the 1995 Act includes any continuation of that diet.[4] Thus, in *O'Connell v HM Advocate*,[5] the appeal court held that the presiding sheriff was wrong to refuse to accept the accused's notice of special defence when it was lodged at a continued first diet.[6]

Where a special defence is lodged under solemn procedure, it should

[1] The provisions governing summary procedure are different and are dealt with later in this chapter (see para.2.12).

[2] CPSA 1995, s.78(3)(a). Preliminary hearings were introduced into High Court procedure in April 2005 by the Criminal Procedure (Amendment) (Scotland) Act 2004 as a result of Lord Bonomy's report *Improving Practice: 2002 Review of the Practices and Procedure of the High Court of Justiciary* (2002) and the proposals contained in the White Paper resulting from that report, *Modernising Justice in Scotland* (2003). Preliminary hearings typically take place around a month before the trial diet. Their purpose is to improve efficiency in the High Court by, among other things, identifying prior to trial whether or not the parties are ready to proceed. Prior to their introduction, special defences merely had to be notified 10 days before the trial diet.

[3] CPSA 1995, s.78(3)(b).

[4] CPSA 1995, s.307.

[5] 1997 S.L.T. 564.

[6] In *O'Connell*, the accused had actually attempted to lodge the notice of special defence at the previous first diet but the sheriff had refused to accept it because it was insufficiently specific. The diet was continued and at the continued first diet the special defence, now in the correct form, was rejected by the presiding sheriff on the basis that it was late.

always be read to the jury at the commencement of the trial after the indictment or the summary of the indictment has been read, although if this is not done, it does not necessarily amount to a miscarriage of justice.[7]

Notification of special defences is said to be necessary in order to prevent so-called ambush defences taking the prosecution by surprise.[8] If defences such as alibi could be pled without notice, then the task of the prosecution in negativing fabricated defences would be that much more difficult, as they would not have been able to undertake their own investigations into the background and credibility of the witnesses in question. As Hume puts it:

> "... although a pannel is thus allowed to prove, without a previous and minute detail of all the particulars which are to establish his defence, it is not and ought not to be the law, that he is entitled to make a mystery of his case, and withhold from the prosecution and the Court, all knowledge of what his line of defence and grounds of exculpation are to be. To let him maintain silence in that respect, till the proof in support of the libel has been closed, would be downright injustice to the prosecutor, who might thus lose the fair means of meeting the defences, and strengthening his own case with evidence, in the relative and proper parts."[9]

Which defences are special defences?

2.02 Exactly which defences are special defences that require advance notification has at times been the subject of some confusion. The issue is not helped by the fact that nowhere in the 1995 Act does it define what is meant by a special defence or list the defences that fall into this category. Hume notes a requirement of intimation only in relation to "insanity for instance, or justifiable act of duty, or the like".[10] Bell's Notes expands on this, listing in addition self-defence and alibi,[11] but also the intention "to discredit the principal witness for the Crown, by proving him to be of weak intellect and incapable of giving rational evidence"[12] and the intention in a trial for rape "to impugn the character of the woman alleged to have been ravished, by the testimony of other witnesses".[13]

---

[7] *Moar v HM Advocate*, 1949 J.C. 31 at 35, *per* the Lord Justice-Clerk (Thomson). The requirement to read the notice to the jury does not apply where the accused lodges a notice of intention to incriminate a co-accused (see para.2.04).

[8] N. Gow, "Scotland's right of silence" (1988) 138 N.L.J. 781. Although *cf.* R. Leng, "Losing sight of the defendant: the Government's proposals on pre-trial disclosure" [1995] Crim. L.R. 704–711, who presents evidence from England, at a time when the notice requirements governing defences were far less stringent than in Scotland, suggesting that the prevalence of ambush defences is over-estimated. See also R.W. Stayton and T.N. Watkins, "Is specific notice of the defense of alibi desirable?" (1939–1940) 18 *Texas Law Review* 151–158 at pp.153–154.

[9] Hume, ii, 301.

[10] *ibid.*

[11] Although leaving out incrimination.

[12] Bell's Notes, ii, 236. See *David Adams and Lachlan Macintosh* (1829) Bell's Notes, ii, 236.

[13] Bell's Notes, ii, 236. See *Thomas Wight* (1836) Bell's Notes, ii, 236. It is now the case that if the defence wishes to lead evidence of the complainer's character or past sexual history in a case involving a sexual offence, he must seek permission to do so: ss.274–275 of the CPSA 1995, as amended by ss.7–8 of the Sexual Offences (Procedure and Evidence) (Scotland) Act 2002.

Alison clearly thought that provocation was a special defence, stating that:

> "There is indeed a regulation, that where any special defence, such as alibi or provocation, is to be set up, it must be stated in written defences lodged before the trial begins."[14]

More recently, in *Adam v MacNeill*,[15] Lord Walker defined a special defence as:

> "... one which puts in issue a fact (1) which is not referred to in the libel, and (2) which, if established, necessarily results in acquittal of the accused".[16]

This is too wide a definition,[17] however, including as it does defences such as necessity and superior orders, which are clearly not special defences.[18]

It is now reasonably well settled that there are only four special **2.03** defences: insanity, alibi, incrimination and self-defence.[19] In addition to these, the 1995 Act lists three defences that are to be treated *as if* they are special defences: automatism, coercion and consent as a 'defence' to a sexual offence.[20] The view taken in Renton and Brown is that the wording of this section means that the list of special defences cannot be extended by the High Court.[21] Support for this view can be found in *Thomson v HM Advocate*[22] and *Ross v HM Advocate*[23] where the appeal court declined to recognise coercion and automatism respectively as special

[14] Alison, *Practice*, xxi. See also *HM Advocate v William Crumley* (1871) 2 Coup. 27 where the accused gave notice that he planned to plead the somewhat unusual special defence that "he was married according to the law of Scotland to the mother of the children prior to the date of birth of either of the children, and that the entries were correct" (at 27). The charge was one of causing the birth of two illegitimate children to be registered as legitimate.

[15] 1972 J.C. 1.

[16] *ibid.* at 5.

[17] Casebook, para.7.02.

[18] In relation to necessity, see *Dawson v Dickson*, 1999 J.C. 315 and the *Lord Advocate's Reference (No. 1 of 2000)*, 2001 J.C. 143, in which necessity was pled without notice being given. Likewise, in *HM Advocate v Sheppard*, 1941 J.C. 67 a defence of superior orders appears to have been pled without notice. Lord Walker might be forgiven in the context of necessity, as the appeal court only confirmed the existence of the defence in 1997, in *Moss v Howdle*, 1997 J.C. 123.

[19] Renton and Brown, para.14–26; *Stair Memorial Encyclopaedia Reissue*, Criminal Procedure, para.183; G. Gordon, "The burden of proof on the accused", 1968 S.L.T. (News) 29–34 at p.30. See also Macdonald, although in addition to alibi, insanity, incrimination and self-defence, he lists "[a]llegations that the accused was asleep, or was suffering from temporary mental dissociation, or from hysterical amnesia at the time of the alleged crime" (at p.265). Sleepwalking, if it is a defence at all, is normally considered under the auspices of non-insane automatism (see below, para.7.31) and thus is not a special defence, although under s.72(2) of the CPSA 1995 it would be treated as such.

[20] CPSA 1995, s.78(2): "Subsection (1) above shall apply to a defence of automatism, coercion or, in prosecution for an offence to which section 288C of this Act applies, consent as if it were a special defence." The sexual offences covered by s.288C are listed in para.2.08.

[21] Para.14–26.

[22] 1983 J.C. 69.

[23] 1991 J.C. 210.

defences, despite accepting in both cases that there was a good argument to be made that they were defences requiring advance notification.[24]

Aside from these seven defences, evidence may be led in the course of a trial of any defence or mitigating factor without prior notice.[25] Thus, none of necessity, superior orders, diminished responsibility[26] or provocation presently requires notification,[27] although the Scottish Law Commission has proposed that diminished responsibility should be added to the list.[28] There is little by way of logic supporting the distinction between defences requiring notice and those that do not. The list seems to have come about by way of historical accident rather than any over-arching guiding principles.[29] The treatment of coercion as if it was a special defence, but not necessity, is particularly baffling, given that the appeal court has held that the same principles should govern the two defences.[30]

The substantive requirements of the pleas of self-defence, coercion, automatism and insanity are discussed in detail in the relevant chapters of this book.[31] Incrimination, alibi and consent in sexual offences are not given detailed treatment in the book[32] and therefore some brief discussion of each is necessary here.

Incrimination

2.04 Incrimination (sometimes termed impeachment[33]) is a plea that "the crime was not committed by the person accused but by another person, named and designated".[34] As late as 1858, there was some doubt over

---

[24] In *Thomson*, see Lord Hunter, at 70–71. In *Ross*, see the Lord Justice-General (Hope), at 222 and 223; Lord Allanbridge, at 224; Lord McCluskey, at 228; Lord Weir, at 223. Although *cf.* Lord Brand in *Ross*, at 233, who did not think that notification of automatism was necessary. As noted earlier in the text (see para.2.03), both defences *are* now treated as if they are special defences by the CPSA 1995. For further discussion of coercion, see Ch.5. For further discussion of automatism, see Ch.7.

[25] *cf. HM Advocate v Cunningham*, 1963 J.C. 80, where a potential defence of automatism was rejected because it did not fall into the category of recognised special defences (at 84 *per* the Lord Justice-General (Clyde)). This seemed to suggest that if a defence was not "special" it did not exist at all and could not be pled. This (and other) aspects of *Cunningham* were over-ruled in *Ross v HM Advocate*, 1991 J.C. 210 and it can now be said that the accused may rely by way of defence on any plea that would have the effect of excluding guilt or raising a reasonable doubt as to guilt, regardless of whether or not it is a special defence (for discussion, see the Casebook, para.7.02).

[26] *cf.* F. Raitt, *Evidence* (3rd edn, 2001): "Insanity and *diminished responsibility* are known in criminal law as special defences" (para.2.13, emphasis added).

[27] Although, as Gordon has pointed out, there is nothing to prevent the generous accused from giving notice of them if he so chooses (G. Gordon, "The burden of proof on the accused", 1968 S.L.T. (News) 29–34).

[28] *Report on Insanity and Diminished Responsibility* (Scot. Law Com. No. 195, 2004), at para.5.39.

[29] Gordon, "The burden of proof on the accused", above, fn.27 at p.30.

[30] *Moss v Howdle*, 1997 J.C. 123 at 127–128. This might be said to be excusable on the basis that the appeal court only confirmed that the defence of necessity existed in Scots law after the CPSA 1995 was passed (in 1998, in *Moss v Howdle*). This would not, however, have prevented it from being added to the list subsequently, as was consent in sexual offences by the Sexual Offences (Procedure and Evidence) (Scotland) Act 2002 (discussed in para.2.08).

[31] See Ch.3 (self-defence); Ch.5 (coercion); and Ch.7 (insanity and automatism).

[32] All three of these defences are defences that, if successfully pled, negate *actus reus*. They are not discussed in detail here primarily because there is not a body of case law on the requirements of these defences in the same way as there is in relation to failure of proof defences that affect *mens rea* (such as error of fact, error of law and non-insane automatism).

[33] G. Gordon, "The burden of proof on the accused", above, fn.27, at p.30.

[34] Renton and Brown, para.14–26.

whether or not incrimination was a special defence requiring notice,[35] but it is now clear that it is one of the four special defences.[36]

Where the person blamed is a co-accused, incrimination is not a special defence, but notice must still be lodged in the same way.[37] The only difference is that, unlike the special defence of incrimination,[38] a notice of intention to incriminate a co-accused need not be read to the jury nor referred to by the judge in his charge.[39]

Discussion of incrimination is extremely limited in both case law and criminal law texts.[40] The only reported case in which there is any discussion of the substantive requirements of the defence is *McQuade v HM Advocate*.[41]

In *McQuade*, the two appellants were charged with murder, alongside a third co-accused, Smith. The Crown case was that Smith shot and killed the deceased in the course of all three accused trying to leave the scene of a bank robbery. Smith gave evidence at trial that implicated the two appellants, but had not lodged a notice of intention to incriminate. They appealed against their conviction on the basis that the evidence should not have been admitted in the absence of notice.

The appeal court held that the special defence of incrimination only applies where the evidence led by the accused has the effect of *transferring* blame from the accused to another person or persons. In other words, where the evidence led would have the effect, if accepted, of exculpating the accused entirely:

> "The concept is a simple one, namely that if an accused is to seek to remove the blame from himself entirely and to place that blame on to his co-accused he must give notice of his intention to do this both to the Crown and to the co-accused ... The essential point is that the evidence seeks to achieve an acquittal by stating that it was the co-accused who committed the crime ... It is to be noted that it is not enough to bring this requirement into effect that the intention is to lead evidence which is calculated to incriminate the co-accused. It must have the dual character and effect which was referred to by the trial judge in his reasons for deciding to repel the objection [namely that the evidence was calculated to *exculpate* the accused and was also of a character that would *inculpate* the co-accused]."[42]

---

[35] See *HM Advocate v Robertson* (1858) 3 Irv. 328 and the discussion of the case in G. Gordon, "The burden of proof on the accused", above, fn.27, at p.30.

[36] *McQuade v HM Advocate*, 1996 S.L.T. 1129.

[37] CPSA 1995, s.78(1). See also *Pike v HM Advocate*, 1987 S.C.C.R. 163.

[38] See para.2.01.

[39] *McShane v HM Advocate*, 1989 S.C.C.R. 687 at 688, *per* the Lord Justice-Clerk (Ross); *Collins v HM Advocate*, 1991 J.C. 204 at 210, *per* the Lord Justice-Clerk (Ross).

[40] It is covered in a single paragraph by Jones and Christie, who state simply that "[t]he defence of incrimination (otherwise known as impeachment) is that the crime was not committed by the accused, but by another person, named if known. It is not a special defence where the accused utilises a 'cut-throat' defence and incriminates his co-accused, but the same statutory requirement that notice of intention to lead such evidence be lodged is applicable" (para.8–10). Gordon makes no mention of it at all. The Casebook mentions it only to note that it is a special defence (para.7.02).

[41] 1996 S.L.T. 1129.

[42] *ibid.* at 1132–1133, emphasis added.

Alibi

2.05 The special defence of alibi is a plea that "at the time libelled the person accused was not at the place libelled, but at some other specified place".[43] While alibi is one of the most frequently tendered special defences,[44] like incrimination, there is little by way of case law or academic discussion of the plea.[45] Hume expressed some scepticism about the defence, stressing that the plea "requires to be carefully scrutinised"[46] on the basis that:

> "... it is a plea of that short and simple nature, with respect to which the pannel's witnesses can easily contrive an uniform, though a false story, such as the prosecutor cannot well disprove, more easily as he can cite no new witnesses in reply".[47]

The notice of alibi must state where the accused actually was at the relevant time and cannot simply state that at the relevant time he was not at the locus of the alleged offence.[48]

2.06 A plea that the accused was at the locus for an innocent purpose does not constitute the special defence of alibi and advance notice need not be provided. This is clear from *Balsillie v HM Advocate*,[49] one of the few cases that deals with the substantive requirements of the defence. In *Balsillie*, the appellant had been convicted of theft by housebreaking. No special defence of alibi had been lodged, but in the course of the trial he gave evidence that, although he had been near the houses that were broken into, he had an innocent explanation for this. In this context, a question was put to a defence witness as to where they last saw the accused on the day of the offences. The Crown objected to this and the presiding sheriff sustained the objection on the basis that, in his view, this was an attempt to establish that the appellant was elsewhere at the time of the offence and this was a defence of alibi requiring special notice.

The appeal court disagreed and quashed the conviction. The Lord Justice-Clerk (Ross) stated that:

> "A special defence of alibi means that an accused is claiming that at the time libelled he was not at the place libelled but was at some other specified place. What the appellant here was trying to do was

---

43 Renton and Brown, para.14–26.

44 *Criminal Procedure in Scotland (Second Report)* (Cm. 6218, 1975), para.37.02.

45 Like incrimination, it merits only a single paragraph in Jones and Christie (para.8–09). Gordon makes no mention of it at all. The Casebook mentions it only to note that it is a special defence (para.7.02). For a rare exception, see the book devoted to the defence: R. Gooderson, *Alibi* (1977), including a section on Scotland (at pp.41–43). (The majority of the book is concerned with US law and, primarily, with the implications of the requirement of notice.)

46 Hume, ii, 410.

47 Hume, ii, 410–411. Hume's concerns about the ease with which witnesses can contrive a false alibi is repeated by Alison (Alison, *Practice*, 624–625). Burnett objects to the plea on the basis that "it is a circumstance of that kind, which corrupt witnesses may swear to, and which at the moment cannot be disproved, it ought in many cases to be entertained with caution" (at p.596).

48 On this, see *HM Advocate v Gairdner, Robertson and Jamieson* (1838) 2 Swin. 180; *HM Advocate v Laing* (1871) 2 Coup. 23, where the Crown successfully objected to a notice of alibi that contained "no averment as to where the panel alleges that he was, and at what time" (at 24); and, more recently, *Lennie v HM Advocate*, 1946 J.C. 79, where the appeal court stated that "the defence of alibi means, not that the panel was not at the *locus delicti* at the material time, but that he was at another definite place" (at 82).

49 1993 J.C. 233.

> to say that he was at or near the place libelled in the charges and then to offer an explanation for his being present at or near the locus. We are not persuaded that a notice of a special defence of alibi requires to be given in such circumstances."[50]

The accused who wishes to plead the defence of alibi is entitled to obtain from the prosecutor sufficient information about the time and locus of the alleged offence in order to permit him to do so.[51] In *Winter v HM Advocate*,[52] it was made clear by the appeal court that where the Crown is not specific about the time of the alleged offence in the indictment, the accused is entitled to wait until he has heard the Crown's evidence before deciding whether or not to lodge an alibi. In *Winter*, the accused was charged with breach of the peace, but the indictment stated only that the alleged offence had been committed between October 1 and November 30, 1996. It emerged when the complainer was precognosed that he was to give evidence that it had happened on one of three occasions on which Heart of Midlothian football club had been playing at home during this period, but that he could not remember which of these three dates it was. No special defence of alibi was lodged, even though the accused claimed to have an alibi for two of the three dates in question.

The central issue in the appeal was one of defective representation, but in the course of his judgment, the Lord Justice-Clerk (Gill) stated that: **2.07**

> "Where the Crown take latitude in date such as they took ... they are formally giving notice that they do not intend to confine themselves to any particular date within that latitude ... If the Crown take advantage of latitude in such circumstances, they must accept that the accused is put at a disadvantage. If the accused says that he was not involved in any such incident and was never at the locus during that period, he cannot know from the indictment for what date he should consider and prepare an alibi. It may be that he can provide an alibi for the entire latitude; for example if he was abroad during that period. But if he cannot do that, it is clearly unreasonable to require him to provide an alibi specifying his movements throughout the entire period of the latitude."[53]

Where the accused does learn of the time of the alleged offence only during the prosecution evidence, and pleads the defence of alibi as a result, it is suggested in Renton and Brown that the prosecution can put forward evidence to contradict the alibi under the provisions of s.269 of

---

[50] 1993 J.C. 233 at 238. The court did accept that this would depend on the facts and that there may be cases where the accused is admitting to being near the place libelled in the charge and this does amount to trying to establish alibi, but in the present case this was not so.

[51] Renton and Brown states that the hours within which the offence was committed are not normally specified in an indictment or complaint, unless they are of the essence of the charge, but they should be disclosed to the accused on request (para.21–07).

[52] 2002 S.C.C.R. 720.

[53] At [38].

the 1995 Act.[54] It is also likely that an adjournment will be granted to the prosecution in order to give them time to investigate the alibi.[55]

Consent in sexual offences

2.08 The requirement to give advance notification of a 'defence' of consent in sexual offences stemmed from the review of evidence and procedure in sexual offence trials undertaken by the Scottish Executive in 2000. In the consultation paper, *Redressing the Balance*,[56] it was proposed that where the defence plans to claim that the complainer consented to the sexual behaviour contained in the charge, this should be made clear at the outset.[57] The main reason advanced for this was that, if the complainer knew in advance that the basic issue at trial was likely to be whether or not she consented, she would be "better prepared psychologically for the cross-examination" and would not be "taken by surprise when questions seeking to show that she did in fact consent, or had led the accused to believe she had, were put to her".[58] Even the Scottish Executive seemed to accept that this was not a particularly convincing argument, however, admitting that, in non-stranger rape cases at least, a defence of consent was "unlikely to come as much of a surprise to the complainer".[59]

Nonetheless, s.6 of the Sexual Offences (Procedure and Evidence) (Scotland) Act 2002 inserted into s.78(2) of the 1995 Act a provision that, like coercion and automatism, consent in sexual offences was to be treated in solemn procedure as if it was a special defence. It also inserted into s.149 of the 1995 Act a provision that notice should be given of the defence of consent in summary prosecutions for sexual offences.[60]

The sexual offences to which this requirement applies are listed in a new s.288C of the 1995 Act, inserted by s.1 of the Sexual Offences (Procedure and Evidence) (Scotland) Act 2002. Specifically they are:

- rape;
- sodomy;
- clandestine injury to women[61];
- abduction of a woman or girl with intent to rape;
- assault with intent to rape;
- indecent assault;
- indecent behaviour (including any lewd, indecent or libidinous practice or behaviour);

---

[54] On "evidence in replication". Section 269(1)(a) of the CPSA 1995 allows the prosecution to lead additional evidence for, among other things, contradicting a defence witness, where the evidence could not reasonably have been anticipated by the prosecutor.

[55] *Murray v HM Advocate*, 1987 S.C.C.R. 249 at 251.

[56] *Redressing the Balance: Cross Examination in Rape and Sexual Offence Trials* (2000).

[57] *ibid.*, para.131.

[58] *ibid.*, para.132.

[59] *ibid.*, para.132.

[60] Discussed in para.12.12.

[61] This offence is effectively abolished as a result of the *Lord Advocate's Reference (No. 1 of 2001)*, 2002 S.L.T. 466. See *HM Advocate v Shearer*, 2003 S.L.T. 1354.

- an offence under s.106(1)(a) or s.107 of the Mental Health (Scotland) Act 1984 (unlawful sexual intercourse with a mentally handicapped female or with a patient)[62];
- an offence under any of the following provisions of the Criminal Law (Consolidation) (Scotland) Act 1995: ss.1–3 (incest and related offences); s.5 (unlawful sexual intercourse with a girl under 13 or 16); s.6 (indecent behaviour towards a girl between 12 and 16); s.7(2) and (3) (procuring a woman to engage in sexual services); s.8 (abduction and unlawful detention); s.10 (seduction, prostitution, etc. of a girl under 16); and s.13(5) (homosexual offences);
- any attempt to commit any of the offences listed above.[63]

Non-compliance with the notice requirements

Where an accused attempts to lead evidence of a special defence but has **2.09** not complied with the notice requirements contained in s.78 of the 1995 Act, it is open to the prosecution to object to the line of evidence. The court will then decide whether or not, "on cause shown"[64] the evidence should be admitted. In deciding whether or not the evidence should be admitted, the court will have regard to the position not only of the prosecution but also of the prejudice that might be suffered by any co-accused, since they too are entitled to advance notification.[65]

Reported cases where evidence has actually been disallowed or where a defence has actually been withdrawn from the jury's consideration on the basis that the notice requirements have not been complied with are few and far between. In *Trotter v HM Advocate*,[66] the presiding sheriff decided to withdraw the defence of coercion from the jury on the basis that no notice of the defence had been lodged, as required by s.72(2) of the 1995 Act.[67] The accused appealed against his conviction on this basis (among others), but the appeal court declined to comment on whether or not the sheriff had erred in doing so since the defence of coercion was, in their view, unarguable on the facts of the case.[68]

In *Benson v Tudhope*,[69] the defence were prevented from leading evidence of alibi because, although notice had been given of intention to plead the defence, the Crown had not been given a list of witnesses who were going to speak to the alibi, as was then required in summary procedure under s.339 of the Criminal Procedure (Scotland) Act 1975.[70] The Crown had objected to the defence leading evidence of an alibi provided

---

[62] The requirement to give notice does not appear, however, to apply to an offence under s.311 of the Mental Health (Care and Treatment) (Scotland) Act 2003 (non-consensual sexual acts with a mentally disordered person). This is presumably an oversight.

[63] CPSA 1995, s.288C. For a more detailed discussion of the issue, see R.S. Shiels, "The special defence of consent", 2002 S.L.T. (Notes) 276–277.

[64] CPSA 1995, s.78(1)(b).

[65] R. Shiels, I. Bradley and P.W. Ferguson, *Criminal Procedure (Scotland) Act 1995* (5th edn, 2006), p.263 (see General Note on s.78).

[66] 2001 S.L.T. 296.

[67] There was some debate over whether the sheriff decided *ex proprio motu* to withdraw the defence or whether the Crown had objected to the defence being led. The grounds of appeal suggested the former; the sheriff in his report to the court, the latter (*Trotter*, at [4]).

[68] At [4]. For discussion of *Trotter* in the context of the substantive requirements of the defence of coercion, see Ch.5.

[69] 1986 J.C. 107.

[70] This requirement is now contained in s.149 of the CPSA 1995. The notice requirements relating to defences under summary procedure are discussed in para.2.12.

by the accused's wife and the justice upheld the Crown objection, intimating that no further evidence relating to the alibi was to be led. In what was the central issue in the case, however, the justice's decision caused the accused's solicitor to walk out of the court, leaving the accused to conduct the rest of the trial without representation and, once the trial continued, the prosecutor withdrew his objection to the alibi evidence. In the course of the resulting bill of suspension, no comment was made by the High Court on the justice's initial decision to prevent the accused from leading evidence of alibi.[71]

In *Lowson v HM Advocate*,[72] the presiding sheriff prevented the appellant from leading evidence of witnesses whose names had not been lodged in accordance with the rules then governing advance notice.[73] As a result, the appellant was deprived of the evidence of eight witnesses and was convicted of lewd, indecent and libidinous behaviour. The appeal court was highly critical of the sheriff's decision[74] and ordered that the witnesses be called to give evidence in front of the appeal court itself.[75] The case is complicated, though, by the fact that the failure to lodge the notice was not entirely the fault of the appellant, whose agent had left two copies of the notice at the sheriff court on the understanding it would be passed on to the procurator fiscal.[76]

2.10 In an earlier edition of Renton and Brown,[77] the authors stated that, since the introduction of criminal legal aid, the statutory notice requirements[78] were being rigidly enforced, with defences being disallowed where no satisfactory explanation has been given for delayed notification.[79] They refer only to one case in this respect, however, namely the unreported case of *HM Advocate v Young and Cater*.[80]

On the basis of these limited authorities it is difficult to reach a firm conclusion on whether in modern practice an accused would actually be prevented from leading evidence of a special defence if he had not given notice of his intention to do so. It is submitted that this is unlikely, even in the face of Crown objection. To exclude such evidence would be to run the risk of being seen to be unfair and oppressive and could lead to a successful appeal. The most likely outcome of a failure to lodge notice of a special defence is that late lodging would be permitted and the Crown (and any co-accused) would be granted an adjournment in order to

---

[71] The accused argued that he ought to have been given an adjournment when his solicitor walked out and the appeal court agreed.

[72] 1943 J.C. 141.

[73] As then required by s.36 of the Criminal Procedure (Scotland) Act 1887.

[74] *Lowson v HM Advocate*, 1943 J.C. 141 at 147, *per* the Lord Justice-General (Normand); at 148 *per* Lord Fleming; at 150 *per* Lord Moncrieff.

[75] In the event, once the appeal court had heard from the eight witnesses, they upheld the conviction.

[76] *Lowson v HM Advocate*, 1943 J.C. 141 at 144.

[77] Renton and Brown (4th edn, 1972).

[78] Then contained in s.36 of the Criminal Procedure (Scotland) Act 1887.

[79] Para.7–14.

[80] Glasgow High Court, August 1966 (para.7–14, fn.31). The same observation is made in G. Gordon, "Criminal Justice Bill 1966", 1967 S.L.T. (News) 21–27 at p.23. See also Alison: "In several late cases the Court have ... refused to allow an alibi to be proved, unless notice was given of it in the defences, so as to put [the prosecutor] on his guard in the examination of his own witnesses." (Alison, *Practice*, 370). See also the *Stair Memorial Encyclopaedia Reissue*, Criminal Procedure, which states that "failure to give proper notice or obtain the consent of the court where the notice was late could result in the line of defence no longer being available and no evidence being led in support of it" (para.182), although no cases are cited by way of example of this.

investigate the defence. Some support for this is found in *Murray v HM Advocate*.[81] In *Murray*, the Crown had been unspecific about the date of the alleged offence in the indictment which, it was claimed on appeal, had made it difficult for the appellant to put forward an alibi. The appeal court commented that if putting forward an alibi is only possible at a late stage or if evidence emerges during the trial that means the accused wishes to put forward an alibi "the remedy of adjournment is well recognised as one which is available in circumstances of this kind".[82]

Where the prosecution does *not* object to the leading of evidence of a special defence without advance notification, it seems that the court will simply allow the evidence to be led. There are several examples of reported cases where evidence has been led of a special defence in the absence of prior notification and where this does not appear to have resulted in an objection or caused any other difficulties.[83]

Implications of special defences other than the requirement to give notice

It is now well settled that the only implication of a defence being categorised as a special defence is the requirement of notice. At one time, it had been thought that special defences might also have implications for the burden of proof, with a number of cases suggesting that the burden of proof for a special defence lay with the accused on the balance of probabilities. In *Lennie v HM Advocate*,[84] for example, a case concerning alibi, it was stated that: **2.11**

> "... it is also true that the onus of proving the alibi was on the appellant. That that has been from the earliest times our law is made clear by [Hume]".[85]

It was made clear in *Lambie v HM Advocate*,[86] however, that, even if this ever was a correct statement of the law, it is certainly no longer the case.

---

[81] 1987 S.C.C.R. 249.

[82] At 251. Admittedly, the appeal court is referring here to late notification that is not the fault of the accused.

[83] In none of these cases was the late lodging of the special defence the central issue. In *Walker v HM Advocate*, 1999 S.L.T. 1388, the accused tendered a special defence of alibi at the trial diet and the court allowed it to be received. The Crown made no objection to this late lodging and did not seek any adjournment to investigate the facts. In *Ross v HM Advocate*, 1998 S.C.C.R. 445, the case report states that: "[i]t appears that in the course of the trial the appellant gave evidence to the effect that at the relevant time he was not at the locus but was elsewhere in Inverness. That evidence was therefore, in substance, evidence of an alibi, although no special defence had been lodged" (at 446). No further comment was made on this by the appeal court. In *Venters v HM Advocate*, 1999 S.L.T. 1345, the accused initially lodged notice to plead alibi and incrimination but, once the trial had commenced, changed his mind and decided that he wished to plead self-defence instead (a decision that caused the withdrawal of his counsel). He was allowed to do so without an adjournment being granted (and, in fact, the decision of the court not to grant an adjournment so that he could seek alternative representation was the basis of a successful appeal against conviction).

[84] 1946 J.C. 79.

[85] At 81. See also: *Owens v HM Advocate*, 1946 J.C. 119 at 125, *per* the Lord Justice-General (Normand); *HM Advocate v Cunningham*, 1963 J.C. 80 at 84, *per* the Lord Justice-General (Clyde).

[86] 1973 J.C. 53.

The persuasive burden of proving a special defence does not lie with the accused.[87] In *Lambie*, the trial judge withdrew the special defence of incrimination from the jury on the basis that it was not supported by corroborated evidence. In the event, the appeal was successful on another ground but, in the course of his judgment, the Lord Justice-General (Emslie) stated that:

> "In light of this review of the law and practice before 1946 we have come to be of the opinion that the references in *Lennie* and *Owens* to there being an onus upon the defence were unsound ... The only purpose of the special defence is to give fair notice to the Crown and once such notice has been given the only issue for a jury is to decide upon the whole evidence before them, whether the Crown has established the accused's guilt beyond reasonable doubt."[88]

An exception to this rule is the defence of insanity, which must be proved by the accused on the balance of probabilities.[89]

At one time, it seemed that special defences might also have implications for the issue of disclosure. In *Smith v HM Advocate*,[90] it was held that there was no obligation on the Crown to disclose information that was potentially exculpatory (on the basis of self-defence) in the absence of notice being given that a special defence of self-defence was being pled.[91] Like the issue of the burden of proof, however, this is now of only historical interest, as the requirements of Crown disclosure have changed beyond recognition since *Smith* was decided.[92]

[87] The accused must, however, be able to point to some evidence supporting the claim (the evidential burden). See *Walkers on Evidence*, para.2.12. The confusion over the burden of proof would seem to stem from the historical rule that the accused was not allowed to raise any defence at trial that was contrary to the averments in the libel. The only way in which a defence *could* be considered was to hold a separate hearing on relevancy before the trial itself (Mackenzie, 60). This practice seems to have died out around the 1730s. For discussion, see Hume, ii, 297–300; G. Gordon, "The burden of proof on the accused", 1968 S.L.T. (News) 29–34 at p.29; F. Leverick, *A Critical Analysis of the Law of Self-defence in Scotland and England*, unpublished Ph.D. thesis, at pp.114–115. See also the account in *Moar v HM Advocate*, 1949 J.C. 31.

[88] *Lambie v HM Advocate*, 1973 J.C. 53 at 58–59. See also *Dunn v HM Advocate*, 1986 J.C. 124 at 130. This did not prevent the presiding sheriff in *Gilmour v HM Advocate*, 1989 S.L.T. 881 from telling the jury that: "[t]here is no special burden on the accused to prove his special defence—corroboration is not necessary—if you are satisfied from the evidence that you have heard that it has been substantiated" (at 882), a direction that was described by the appeal court as "quite unsatisfactory" (at 882, *per* the Lord Justice-Clerk (Ross)). A recent re-statement of the principle that it is for the prosecution to disprove beyond reasonable doubt that the accused acted in self-defence can be found in *Irvine v Orr*, 2003 S.L.T. 1193.

[89] *HM Advocate v Mitchell*, 1951 J.C. 53 at 54–55. See para.2.16. The same applies to the partial defence of diminished responsibility, although it is not a special defence: see *HM Advocate v Savage*, 1923 J.C. 49; *HM Advocate v Braithwaite*, 1945 J.C. 55; *Lindsay v HM Advocate*, 1997 S.L.T. 67.

[90] 1952 J.C. 66 at 75.

[91] The accused was convicted of assault after stabbing the complainer in a Glasgow club. In a search of the premises, the police had found a second knife (other than the one used by the accused) but this was not disclosed to the defence.

[92] See the Privy Council cases of *Holland v HM Advocate* [2005] UKPC D1; *Sinclair v HM Advocate* [2005] UKPC D2 and the subsequent discussion in para.2.14.

Disclosure of defences under summary procedure

Advance notification is required under summary procedure only in relation to the defences of alibi and consent in sexual offences. The provision relating to alibi is to be found in s.149 of the 1995 Act, which provides that: **2.12**

> "It shall not be competent for the accused in a summary prosecution to found on a plea of alibi unless he gives, at any time before the first witness is sworn, notice to the prosecutor of the plea with particulars as to time and place and of the witnesses by whom it is proposed to prove it; and, on such notice being given, the prosecutor shall be entitled, if he so desires, to an adjournment of the case."[93]

Unlike the provisions relating to solemn proceedings, whereby written notice of a special defence must be provided,[94] s.149 does not specify that notification must be made in writing and it is suggested in Renton and Brown that oral notification would be sufficient.[95]

The requirement of notice of the defence of consent in sexual offences is found in s.149A of the 1995 Act, added by s.6 of the Sexual Offences (Procedure and Evidence) (Scotland) Act 2002. The list of sexual offences to which this provision applies is the same as that under solemn procedure.[96] The notice requirements are more stringent than those relating to alibi, s.149A(1) providing that:

> "It shall not be competent for the accused in a summary prosecution for an offence to which section 288C of this Act applies to found on a defence of consent unless, not less than *10 clear days* before the trial diet, he gives notice to the prosecutor of the defence and the witnesses by whom he proposes to maintain it."[97]

Section 149A(2) does allow the accused, on cause shown, to be permitted to plead the defence if less than 10 days notice is given.

Aside from alibi and consent in sexual offences, notification is not required of any other defence under summary procedure.

Withdrawal of a special defence from the jury

Where the accused has given notice of a special defence, the trial judge should not withdraw consideration of the defence from the jury unless there is no evidence at all to support the defence. This was made clear in *Crawford v HM Advocate*,[98] where the Lord Justice-General (Cooper) set out the way in which trial judges should approach the issue of special defences as follows: **2.13**

93 CPSA 1995, s.149.

94 CPSA 1995, s.78(1).

95 Renton and Brown, para.21–07.1.

96 Namely, those offences listed in s.288C of the CPSA 1995 (see para.2.08).

97 CPSA 1995, s.149A, emphasis added. The reason for the more stringent requirement is almost certainly the desire to give advance warning of a defence of consent to the complainer in cases involving sexual offences: this was the justification for introducing a notice requirement of this nature in relation to sexual offences prosecuted under solemn procedure (see para.2.08 above).

98 1950 J.C. 67.

"The withdrawal of a special defence is always a strong step, but there are circumstances in which it is the duty of the presiding Judge to take that step ... I am prepared to affirm that it is the duty of the presiding Judge to consider the whole evidence bearing on self-defence and to make up his own mind whether any of it is relevant to infer self-defence as known to the law of Scotland. If he considers that there is no evidence from which the requisite conclusion could reasonably be drawn, it is the duty of the presiding Judge to direct the jury that it is not open to them to consider the special defence. If, on the other hand, there is some evidence, although it may be slight, or even evidence about which two reasonable views might be held, then he must leave the special defence to the jury subject to such directions as he may think proper."[99]

Crawford was applied in *Whyte v HM Advocate*,[1] where the appellant's conviction *was* quashed on the basis the trial judge was wrong to withdraw the special defence of self-defence. The Lord Justice-General (Hope) stated that:

"It is clear from what was said in [*Crawford*] that a special defence of self-defence should be left with the jury to consider if there is some evidence, however slight, on which a jury might properly come to the view that the defence was made out."[2]

The Crown's Duty to Disclose

2.14 Thus far, it has been established that the defence have a duty to disclose to the prosecution any special defences they intend to plead in a solemn case (including any defences that are treated as if they are special defences) and, in a summary case, their intention to plead alibi or consent in sexual offences. It should also be noted that the Crown has a duty of disclosure to the defence that is far wider than the defence's duty to disclose to the Crown.

It is not within the scope of this book to embark on a detailed discussion of the rules relating to prosecution disclosure. Suffice to say, the Crown duty of disclosure has undergone a complete transformation recently, in the Privy Council cases of *Holland v HM Advocate*[3] and *Sinclair v HM Advocate*,[4] which develop the duty of disclosure far beyond that previously held to be the case, in *McLeod v HM Advocate*.[5] Prior to *McLeod*, there was no formal duty on the prosecution to disclose to the defence the information it had collected during the course of its investigations,[6] although it had generally acted in "a generous fashion" and would reveal information when the "interests of justice" required it.[7] In

[99] At 70.
[1] 1996 J.C. 187.
[2] At 190.
[3] [2005] UKPC D1.
[4] [2005] UKPC D2. For a detailed discussion, see P. Duff, "*Sinclair* and *Holland*: a revolution in disclosure", 2005 S.L.T. (News) 105–111. Because of the significant changes introduced by these cases, any discussion of disclosure published prior to 2005 should be read with caution.
[5] 1998 J.C. 67.
[6] *Higgins v HM Advocate*, 1990 S.C.C.R. 268.
[7] *McLeod v HM Advocate*, 1998 J.C. 67 at 72; Duff, above, fn.4, at p.105.

McLeod, it was established that there *was* a duty on the prosecution to "disclose to the defence information ... which would tend to exculpate the accused"[8] and to respond positively to any request for information "where the defence can explain why [it] would be material to the defence".[9]

In *Sinclair*, it was held by the Privy Council that the Crown is under a duty to disclose to the defence in advance of trial all statements given to the police by witnesses likely to be called at trial. In *Holland*, it was held that the prosecution should also disclose to the defence the details of all prosecution witnesses' previous convictions and any outstanding charges against such witnesses. Duff has suggested that the combined effect of these two cases is to create a rule that "the prosecution must disclose prior to trial all the evidence which it has against the accused as well as any other information which might possibly have a bearing on the case."[10] The only exception to this rule is where there is a public interest in non-disclosure, such as witness safety or national security. It was made clear that decisions about whether disclosure is in the public interest are not the Crown's to make but must be subject to independent scrutiny.[11]

Sinclair and *Holland* were High Court cases conducted under solemn procedure, but the new duty of prosecution disclosure is likely to apply to all cases, whether solemn or summary and regardless of venue.[12]

Pleading Mutually Inconsistent Defences

Where the accused attempts to plead mutually inconsistent defences, it is unlikely that both will be left to the jury. This would seem to be indicated by *Surman v HM Advocate*,[13] where the trial judge withdrew the defence of self-defence from the jury, despite a notice of special defence having been lodged, on the basis that it was inconsistent with the defence of accident that was put forward at trial. The appeal court held that the trial judge was wrong to do so in this case, but that there could well be other cases where the special defence of self-defence would not be consistent with a defence of accident and, where this did occur, the correct course of action would be to withdraw the defence. **2.15**

A similar issue arose in *MacKenzie v HM Advocate*,[14] where the trial judge withdrew the defence of accident from the jury on the basis that it was entirely inconsistent with a special defence of self-defence that had been lodged. While the appeal court once again held that the trial judge had been wrong to do so, as the appellant had given evidence during the course of the trial that *was* consistent with a defence of accident, it was commented that it was actually the defence of self-defence that should have been withdrawn.[15]

Aside from these cases involving self-defence and accident, there does not appear to be any reported case law providing guidance on how to

[8] *McLeod v HM Advocate*, 1998 J.C. 67 at 80.

[9] *ibid.*

[10] Duff, above, fn.4, at p.110.

[11] *Sinclair v HM Advocate* [2005] UKPC D2 at [33], *per* Lord Hope; *Holland v HM Advocate* [2005] UKPC D1 at [71], *per* Lord Rodger.

[12] Duff, above, fn.4, at p.108.

[13] 1988 S.L.T. 371.

[14] 1983 S.L.T. 220.

[15] At 224 *per* Lord Robertson. *Cf. HM Advocate v Woods*, 1972 S.L.T. (Notes) 77.

treat an attempt to plead mutually inconsistent defences.[16] The issue has arisen in the English context where, in *R. v Bonnick*,[17] the trial judge refused to leave the defence of self-defence to the jury on the basis that it was not consistent with the defence of alibi, notice of which had been given. Evidence of alibi had been led, but in response to a remark from the trial judge that the only issue in the case was identification, defence counsel submitted that self-defence was also an issue. The Court of Appeal agreed with the trial judge that, in this case, the two defences were completely contradictory and the trial judge had been right to exclude self-defence from the jury's consideration.[18] The Court commented that:

> "Common sense indeed rebels against allowing a defendant to say on his oath 'I was not there and did not do it' and through his counsel 'I did it but I was acting in self-defence'. It might indeed be thought to confuse judgment and hinder justice if counsel were to be encouraged, in the proper discharge of their duty to do their best to ensure that their clients are not improperly convicted, to raise defences so completely contrary to their instructions."[19]

The appeal court did not entirely rule out the possibility that the defences of self-defence and alibi might sometimes both be allowed to be pled, but were of the opinion that this would be in only an exceptional case:

> "... there may be evidence of self-defence even though a defendant asserts that he was not present ... but in the nature of things it would require to be fairly cogent evidence, when the best available witness disables himself by his alibi from supporting it".[20]

The Burden of Proving Defences

2.16 The burden of proof of any criminal charge rests with the Crown throughout the trial. It is for the Crown to prove the accused's guilt beyond reasonable doubt.[21] The accused, with some minor exceptions,[22] does not have a persuasive burden of proof in relation to any defence, regardless of whether or not it is a special defence.[23]

---

[16] Although see *Venters v HM Advocate*, 1999 S.L.T. 1345, where the accused's counsel withdrew from acting after the accused, having given notice that he intended to plead alibi and incrimination, changed his mind on the second day of the trial and indicated that he wished to plead self-defence instead. In the event, he was permitted to do this and proceeded with his defence of self-defence without representation. See also *Gemmill v HM Advocate*, 1980 J.C. 16, where the accused appears to have been permitted to plead both alibi and diminished responsibility (at 18), a fact that was not commented upon by the appeal court when his appeal was decided on unrelated grounds, and *Adam v HM Advocate*, 2006 S.L.T. 621, where the accused lodged special defences of alibi, incrimination and insanity (at [1]), none of which were withdrawn from the jury. Once again, the appeal court did not comment.

[17] (1978) 66 Cr.App.R. 266.

[18] At 270.

[19] At 269.

[20] At 269.

[21] *Lambie v HM Advocate*, 1973 J.C. 53.

[22] See below.

[23] *Lambie v HM Advocate*, 1973 J.C. 53 at 59–60; *King v Lees*, 1993 J.C. 19. Thus, cases such as *Lennie v HM Advocate*, 1946 J.C. 79 and *Owens v HM Advocate*, 1946 J.C. 119, in which it was suggested that the burden of proving a special defence lay with the accused, were wrongly decided (*Lambie v HM Advocate*, 1973 J.C. 53 at 59–60). See para.2.11.

The exceptions are the defences of insanity and diminished responsibility, which must be proved by the accused, although only on the balance of probabilities[24] and there is no requirement for corroboration.[25]

Procedural Issues Relating to Pleas in Bar of Trial

2.17 Pleas in bar of trial are described in Renton and Brown as being "normally taken prior to the commencement of a trial",[26] but there is no further general discussion of the procedure involved. An earlier edition states that "with regard to pleas of this sort ... if proof is required in their support, the court can hear it without empannelling a jury".[27] The appeal court has suggested that leading evidence might be competent (and even required) in order to reach a decision on at least certain pleas in bar of trial,[28] although in practice the relevant facts may not be in dispute and the point appears to have arisen only rarely. The decision on the plea in bar is one for the judge and not the jury.[29] It is for the accused to "establish" the plea in bar,[30] and the standard of proof required appears to be on the balance of probabilities.[31]

---

[24] In relation to insanity, see *HM Advocate v Mitchell*, 1951 J.C. 53. In relation to diminished responsibility, see *HM Advocate v Savage*, 1923 J.C. 49; *HM Advocate v Braithwaite*, 1945 J.C. 55; *Lindsay v HM Advocate*, 1997 S.L.T. 67. In *Lindsay*, the High Court declined to submit the question of the burden of proof of diminished responsibility for reconsideration by a full bench on the basis that the law on this issue had been settled for a very long time.

[25] *King v Lees*, 1993 S.L.T. 1184. There are also some statutory defences where the burden of proof rests with the accused, e.g. the defences of reasonable belief in age contained in Part 1 of the Criminal Law Consolidation (Scotland) Act 1995. For further discussion of the burden of proof in relation to criminal defences, see *Walkers on Evidence*, paras 2.12.1 to 2.12.6.

[26] Renton and Brown, para.9–01. It might be thought that there is no other logical time for such a plea to be determined—subject to the caveat that the facts giving rise to the plea in bar might only arise or become clear at a later stage—but in *R. v Mack* [1988] 2 S.C.R. 903 the Canadian Supreme Court held that entrapment should be considered *after* the trial process has been completed and guilt has been established by a jury. The rationale for this is that it "protects the right of an accused to an acquittal where the circumstances so warrant" (at [160]). See also *R. v Pearson* [1998] 3 S.C.R. 620 at [10].

[27] Renton and Brown (4th edn), para.9–18. No authority is cited for this statement, which does not appear in subsequent editions.

[28] See *McCartney v Tudhope*, 1986 J.C. 7. This case concerned a plea to the competency on the basis that the six-month time limit for commencing a summary prosecution (on which see para.16.25) had been breached because a warrant granted within the six-month period had not been executed without undue delay. The court observed (at 13) that "[w]hen a plea to competency [on this basis] is taken, unless the relevant facts can be agreed between the parties ... the preferable course would be for the judge to hear evidence on the preliminary plea". See also *McGlennan v Johnston*, 1991 S.C.C.R. 895. Although the case is concerned with one particular plea in bar of trial, there would seem no reason why this same procedure might not be followed elsewhere.

[29] Historically, juries were sometimes asked to consider pleas of insanity in bar of trial (after, rather than before, the substantive evidence for the prosecution had been led), but in modern practice the decision is one for the judge alone. See paras 14.10–14.12 and *Stewart v HM Advocate (No.1)*, 1997 J.C. 183 at 190, *per* the Lord Justice-Clerk (Cullen). *Cf.* R.A. Duff, "'I might be guilty, but you can't try me': estoppel and other bars to trial" (2003) 1 *Ohio State Journal of Criminal Law* 245–259 at p.249, who suggests that it should not be assumed as a matter of principle that pleas in bar are matters appropriately decided by a judge rather than a jury.

[30] See *HM Advocate v McGill*, 1997 S.L.T. 1156 at 1158, *per* the Lord Justice-General (Rodger); *Brown v HM Advocate*, 2002 S.L.T. 809 at [12], *per* Lord Marnoch.

[31] *Jessop v Stevenson*, 1989 S.C.C.R. 600; *Report on Insanity and Diminished Responsibility* (Scot. Law Com. No. 195, 2004), para.5.58.

It is possible that the basis for a plea in bar of trial might only become clear during the trial, and form the basis for a motion to desert the diet.[32] That might be appropriate, for example, where media publicity prejudicing the right to an accused's fair trial appears during the course of proceedings.[33] On principle, it would seem that any necessary evidence might be led in the absence of any jury—a process which would be essentially identical to a trial within a trial.[34]

The procedure required where an issue otherwise giving rise to a plea in bar has arisen only mid-trial has been discussed on two occasions, and neither case is conclusive. In *Brown v HM Advocate*,[35] Lord Marnoch noted that the issue of entrapment might only arise during the course of the trial, and suggested that "then clearly the proper course will be to intimate an objection at the earliest opportunity".[36] It is not clear whether this is intended to refer to an objection to the admissibility of evidence, or an "objection" in some broader sense. It would be odd if the former were intended, as this would weaken the protection afforded to the accused, as the evidence in question might not be crucial to the prosecution case.

In *HM Advocate v Walsh*,[37] where the accused became insane during the course of the trial, the prosecutor moved the court to desert the diet against him *simpliciter* and the jury returned a verdict of "not guilty" on the direction of the trial judge. It may be, however, that the prosecutor's actions were more favourable to the accused than was strictly required, and the modern statutory provisions on insanity in bar of trial make it clear that the same procedure is to be followed whether or not the trial has already commenced.[38] Insanity remains an unusual plea in bar of trial, in that it may in fact be raised by the Crown, or by the court itself. In such a case, it appears that the burden of proof will rest with the Crown, but the standard of proof will remain the balance of probabilities.[39]

---

[32] On the extent of the court's power to desert the diet, see Renton and Brown, paras 18–21 to 18–24.

[33] See para.18.02..

[34] On which, see *Thompson v Crowe*, 2002 J.C. 173.

[35] 2002 S.L.T. 809.

[36] At [14].

[37] 1922 J.C. 82.

[38] CPSA 1995, s.54.

[39] *Jessop v Stevenson*, 1989 S.C.C.R. 600; *Report on Insanity and Diminished Responsibility* (Scot. Law Com. No. 195, 2004), para.5.58.

CHAPTER 3

SELF-DEFENCE

INTRODUCTION

Self-defence[1] is a complete defence that, if successful, results in an acquittal. Self-defence is most commonly pled as a defence to murder,[2] attempted murder[3] or assault,[4] but it is also competent to plead self-defence as a defence to a charge of breach of the peace.[5] **3.01**

Compared to the conceptually similar defences of necessity and coercion, self-defence is relatively well-established. The availability of the plea, even in cases of homicide, can be traced back at least to the thirteenth century.[6] It receives detailed treatment in both Mackenzie, first published in 1678, and the first edition of Hume, published in 1797.

Perhaps because of its long history, the requirements of the defence are well-settled. They are also relatively strict in comparison to other jurisdictions. The retreat rule comprises an independent requirement of the defence[7] and only reasonable mistakes about the need to use self-defensive force can provide the basis for the plea.[8]

This chapter concerns the common law defence of self-defence. Thus it excludes discussion of the various statutory provisions covering acts preparatory to the use of self-defensive force. For example, ss.47 and 49 of the Criminal Law (Consolidation) (Scotland) Act 1995 make it an offence to carry an offensive weapon in public without reasonable excuse and it may be a reasonable excuse if the accused picked up the weapon with the intention of using it in defence against an imminent attack.[9]

---

[1] Although the term self-defence is used throughout this chapter, this is not to suggest that Scots law does not recognise a defence where the accused has acted in defence of others (see para.3.27). The term private defence has been proposed as an umbrella term to cover self-defence and the defence of others (see the Casebook, para.7.04), but although it is occasionally used in criminal texts (see, e.g. J. Burchell, *Principles of Criminal Law* (3rd edn, 2005)), it has not been widely adopted.

[2] See, e.g. *Jones v HM Advocate*, 1990 J.C. 160; *Burns v HM Advocate*, 1995 J.C. 154; *Pollock v HM Advocate*, 1998 S.L.T. 880; *McBrearty v HM Advocate*, 1999 S.L.T. 1333.

[3] See, e.g. *Hendry v HM Advocate*, 1985 J.C. 105; *Brady v HM Advocate*, 1986 J.C. 68.

[4] See, e.g. *Moffat v McNaughton*, 1987 S.C.C.R. 497; *Moore v MacDougall*, 1989 S.C.C.R. 659; *Fitzpatrick v HM Advocate*, 1992 S.L.T. 796; *Whyte v HM Advocate*, 1996 J.C. 187; *Friel v HM Advocate*, 1998 S.L.T. 1327.

[5] See *Derrett v Lockhart*, 1991 S.C.C.R. 109, where the Lord Justice-Clerk (Ross) confirmed that self-defence is available as a defence to breach of the peace, if the charge is expressed in language that alleges an assault type incident has taken place.

[6] See the case of *one Richard, accused of the murder of Adam the Miller*, reported in T. MacKay Cooper, *Select Scottish Cases of the Thirteenth Century* (1944), p.58.

[7] See paras 3.12–3.13.

[8] See paras 3.10–3.11.

[9] *Miller v Douglas*, 1988 S.C.C.R. 565. These provisions are not discussed further here, but see the Casebook, paras 8.65–8.68.

THEORETICAL BASIS

Distinguishing self-defence from other conceptually similar defences

3.02 Self-defence is part of a family of defences (which would also include necessity and coercion) that all involve the commission of a crime in order to avert a threatened harm. Self-defence has much in common conceptually with necessity and coercion, but can be distinguished from both.

Self-defence involves an act directed towards someone who poses a direct threat to the life or physical integrity of the accused,[10] whether as an aggressor or as a passive threat.[11] The defining feature of a claim of self-defence is that it involves defensive force being directed towards the *source* of the threat posed.[12]

This factor distinguishes self-defence from necessity. Like self-defence, the defence of necessity can also involve the infliction of harm on a person.[13] Unlike self-defence, the defence of necessity would involve harming a bystander, who was not posing a direct threat to the accused. That is not to say that the distinction between cases of self-defence and necessity is always a clear one, especially where passive threats are concerned.[14]

Distinguishing cases of self-defence from cases of coercion is comparatively straightforward. Here, the distinction lies in the nature of the act undertaken by the accused. In a case of self-defence, the accused avoids harm by *warding off* or *blocking* a threat. In a case of coercion, the accused avoids harm by *complying with the demands* of the threatener. For example, the accused, A, is threatened with death, by B, unless he commits theft. If A complies with the threat (and commits the theft), his

---

[10] Or a third party.

[11] An aggressor is someone who attacks the accused, or threatens to do so, either using physical force or a weapon. A passive threat is someone who directly threatens the life or physical integrity of the accused by means *other* than an attack (for an example, see fn.14 below). What both aggressors and passive threats have in common is that they pose a direct threat to the life or physical integrity of the accused. The important point is that both aggressors and passive threats can be distinguished from bystanders, who pose *no direct threat* to the life or physical integrity of the accused.

[12] T. Kasachkoff, "Killing in self-defence: an unquestionable or problematic defence?" (1998) 17 *Law and Philosophy* 509–531 at p.513.

[13] Although this is not always the case and the vast majority of reported cases of necessity have involved charges of reckless/careless driving or driving with excess alcohol (see Ch.4).

[14] The case of the roped mountaineer (A) who falls from a cliff edge while attached to a companion (B) is often used as an example (for a real life case of this nature, see J. Simpson, *Touching the Void* (1988) and the 2004 film of the same title). If B cuts the rope, causing A to fall to his death, this is surely a case of self-defence. A is a passive threat and poses a direct threat to the life of B (although *cf.* Brooke L.J. in *Re: A (Children)* [2001] 2 W.L.R. 480 at 585, and the Commentary to the Draft Criminal Code, at 62). One of the most difficult cases to classify is that of the conjoined twins in *Re: A (Children)*, where the judges themselves were unable to agree on whether the most appropriate defence for the doctors who undertook the separation of the twins was one of self-defence (or more accurately the defence of others) or necessity: compare the opinions of Ward L.J. and Brooke L.J. For discussion, see S. Uniacke, "Was Mary's death murder?" (2001) 9 *Medical Law Review* 208–220 at p.213.

act is one committed under coercion. If A wards off the threat of death (for example by disabling or killing B), his act is one of self-defence.[15]

3.03 These conceptual distinctions have not prevented Clarkson[16] from arguing that the defences of self-defence, necessity and coercion should be brought together under a unified defence governed by the same rules. While it is true that the defences have much in common, there is nonetheless something to be said for treating necessity, coercion and self-defence as distinct defences. Self-defence differs from necessity and coercion in that it involves action against one or more persons who pose a *direct threat* to life or bodily integrity. This fact alone is sufficient reason for having a set of distinct rules; distinct, that is, from those governing necessity and coercion, where the victim, if indeed there was one, would not have posed such a threat. The most obvious example relates to whether or not the defence can be pled to a charge of murder. This is generally accepted in relation to self-defence *because* the murder victim was himself a direct threat to the life of the accused, but it is extremely controversial in relation to necessity and coercion, where any victim was likely to have been an innocent bystander.

Likewise, the public policy issues relating to each of the three defences are not identical. For example, there is an argument for placing more stringent restrictions on coercion than on the other two defences because of the risk that the defence is abused by terrorist groups or other criminal organisations.[17]

Aside from anything else, there is a compelling argument to be made for conceptual separation of the three defences on the grounds of fair labelling.[18] The accused is surely entitled to the nature of his defensive act being labelled as accurately as possible by the courts, rather than subsumed under a general heading of "necessary defence", simply because he may be morally judged by society on the basis of this label. "I did this in self-defence" (a justification defence and thus a claim that his behaviour was acceptable) arguably reflects more favourably on the accused than "I did this under coercion" (most commonly an excuse defence and thus a claim that his behaviour was unacceptable but not blameworthy).[19]

The theoretical basis of the defence

3.04 Self-defence can operate both as a justification and as an excuse.[20] The justification form of the defence applies when the accused correctly perceives that he is facing, or is about to face, an attack and uses force to

[15] The distinction and the example are drawn from J. Horder, "Killing the passive abuser: a theoretical defence" in *Criminal Law Theory: Doctrines of the General Part* (S. Shute and A.P. Simester (eds), 2002), pp.283–297, at p.296. This relatively clear-cut distinction has not stopped Dressler from confusing acts of self-defence with acts of coercion. See J. Dressler, "Battered women who kill their sleeping tormenters: reflections on maintaining respect for human life while killing moral monsters" in Shute and Simester, above, at pp.275–281. For criticism, see Horder, above, at p.296.

[16] C.M.V. Clarkson, "Necessary action: a new defence" [2004] Crim. L.R. 81–95.

[17] On this, see the Commentary to the Draft Criminal Code, at 63 and para.5.03. Indeed, this was precisely the reason given by the House of Lords in *R. v Hasan* [2005] UKHL 22 for imposing stricter conditions on the defence of duress (where the defendant is judged according to an objective test) than on the defence of self-defence (where the defendant is judged according to a subjective test). See Lord Bingham at [22] and [38].

[18] See Ashworth, *Principles of Criminal Law*, pp.88–90.

[19] On this, see J. Gardner, "The mark of responsibility" (2003) 23 O.J.L.S. 157–171. *Cf.* Clarkson, above, fn.16, at p.94, who assumes that fair labelling is important only in terms of sending a message to the public about rules of conduct.

[20] For the distinction, see above, paras 1.08–1.10.

defend himself. The excuse form of the defence applies when the accused believes that he is acting in self-defence, but is actually mistaken in his belief that he is facing, or is about to face, an attack.[21]

The argument most commonly advanced for treating self-defence as a justification is one based on the right to life, with an accompanying theory of forfeiture.[22] In brief,[23] all human beings have a right to life and therefore a right to protect themselves from an aggressor[24] who threatens to deprive them of life.[25] It is acceptable for the accused to kill an aggressor because the aggressor, in becoming an unjust immediate threat to the life of another, temporarily forfeits his right to life, at least as long as he remains a direct threat. Once the immediate threat he poses ceases, his right to life is regained.[26]

The excuse form of self-defence applies where the accused is *mistaken* in his perception that he is being attacked. The right to life and forfeiture arguments, that justify self-defence in cases of genuine attack, do not apply here. The perceived 'attacker' has done nothing to suggest that the accused is permitted to kill him. He, like all human beings, possesses a right to life in so far as he does not become a threat to the life of another, which he has not done. Instead of killing someone who was threatening to violate his right to life, the accused has killed an entirely 'innocent' person who was unfortunate enough to do something that suggested he was about to commence an attack. The accused cannot therefore be justified if he kills in self-defence. A justification defence implies that the conduct of the accused is acceptable or even welcomed by the criminal law. This is surely not the case where an innocent victim has been killed because of a

---

21 *cf.* V. Tadros, *Criminal Responsibility* (2005), pp.280–290.

22 S. Uniacke, *Permissible Killing: The Self-defence Justification of Homicide* (1994); J.J. Thomson, "Self-defence" (1991) 20 *Philosophy and Public Affairs* 283–310; F. Leverick, *Killing in Self-Defence* (2006).

23 In the philosophical literature, the basis of the defence has received intense discussion, much of which lies beyond the scope of this book. For some of the most influential contributions, see Uniacke, above, fn.22; Thomson, above, fn.22; T. Kasachkoff, "Killing in self-defence: an unquestionable or problematic defence?" (1998) 17 *Law and Philosophy* 509–531; M. Gorr, "Private defence" (1990) 9 *Law and Philosophy* 241–268; S. Levine "The moral permissibility of killing a material aggressor in self-defence" (1984) 45 *Philosophical Studies* 69–78; P. Montague, "Self-defence and choosing between lives" (1981) 40 *Philosophical Studies* 207–219; B.J. Smart, "Understanding and justifying self-defence" (1989) 4 *International Journal of Moral and Social Studies* 231–244.

24 Or a passive threat: see fn.11 above.

25 The discussion proceeds here on the basis that the accused has killed in self-defence. The explanation holds equally well where the accused has used non-lethal force. Here it would be based on the right to bodily integrity.

26 The rights based account of self-defence has been subject to some criticism, the detail of which is beyond the scope of this book. See T. Kasachkoff, above, fn.23; C. Ryan, "Self-defence, pacifism and the possibility of killing" (1983) 93 *Ethics* 508–524. For a detailed discussion of the rights/forfeiture account and its critics, see Ch.3 of F. Leverick, *Killing in Self-Defence* (2006). It is certainly not the only way in which the use of force in self-defence can be justified. In some cases, it can be justified on the basis that it is the lesser evil, such is the disparity between the two harms in question. An example might be the use of physical force in order to overcome an aggressor who threatened to kill several people. This fails to account for the more difficult cases, however, in which the harms are similar in nature, such as the use of lethal force to prevent a life threatening attack. Here, rights based accounts are the most convincing, or at least if they are not accepted, then it is difficult to explain why self-defence is a justification defence, and it might have to be conceded that it is merely an excuse.

mistake on the accused's part, however reasonable that mistake might have been.[27]

Historical Development

Hume's two categories of self-defence

Although no previous Scottish writer had done so,[28] Hume distinguishes between two categories of homicide in self-defence. The first is "that slaughter which is committed in the necessary defence of one's life against an attempt feloniously to take it away".[29] This covers all situations where the self-defender was attacked suddenly, without warning and without any suggestion of blame on his part. 3.05

The second is self-defence that becomes necessary "in the course of an affray, or occasional quarrel, between persons who have fallen out upon the spot and have probably, at the outset, been both of them less or more in fault".[30] It is not entirely clear what Hume would include in this category. One interpretation is that it only includes situations where the self-defender was the initiator of the physical violence, although this seems unlikely, given later comments by Hume that self-defence is never available to the originator of a fight.[31] Another interpretation is that quarrel self-defence covers situations where the self-defender is in some other way to blame for the incident, for example by using provocative words or actions.

Hume suggests that entirely different rules govern the two categories; the main difference being that, in situations of blameless self-defence, there is no retreat rule.[32]

Hume's distinction between blameless and quarrel self-defence is puzzling for at least two reasons. First, it is entirely unsupported by Scots law prior to 1797.[33] Secondly, it seems to contradict other parts of Hume's own text. Hume draws the distinction at the start of his account of homicide in self-defence, before proceeding to discuss homicide to prevent rape and homicide in defence of property. By the time he embarks on a more detailed discussion of the rules governing self-defence, four pages later, the distinction appears to have been abandoned, with Hume advocating a retreat rule in relation to all cases of self-defence.[34]

Gordon[35] has suggested that Hume's approach can be explained by the fact that he briefly allowed himself to get carried away by his sympathy for the plight of the person suddenly and randomly attacked in the street

---

[27] This conclusion does depend on accepting John Gardner's dual requirement theory of justification defences: J. Gardner, "Justifications and reasons" in *Harm and Culpability* (A.P. Simester and A.T.H. Smith (eds), 1996), pp.103–129. *Cf.* Tadros, above fn.21, at pp.280–290. For further discussion of the dual requirement theory, see Ch.1.

[28] For the treatment of self-defence prior to Hume, see Mackenzie, 58; Bayne, 84–85; Forbes, 110.

[29] Hume, i, 217. Subsequently referred to as "blameless" self-defence

[30] Hume, i, 217. Subsequently referred to as "quarrel" self-defence.

[31] Hume, i, 230.

[32] Hume, i, 217–218. For discussion of the retreat rule, see paras 3.12–3.13.

[33] There is no suggestion of it in the work of Mackenzie and it finds no real support in the case law of the time (although *cf. John Symons* (1810) Hume, i, 228).

[34] Hume, i, 226. For a more detailed discussion, see Ch.4 (and section 4.3.3 in particular) of F. Leverick, *A Critical Analysis of the Law of Self-Defence in Scotland and England* (2003), unpublished Ph.D. thesis.

[35] Gordon, para.24.06.

and never intended to suggest that such an individual should be allowed to kill where this was not necessary to save his life.

An alternative explanation is that Hume was unduly influenced by English texts of the time. Hume cites no direct authority for the distinction between blameless and quarrel self-defence but it reflects a longstanding distinction in English law between justifiable and excusable homicide, with no duty to retreat in relation to the former and a retreat rule in relation to the latter.[36]

The requirements of the defence under Hume

3.06 Hume sets out four requirements of the defence.[37] First, "the pannel must have killed *to save his life*",[38] lethal self-defensive force being permissible only in response to a life threatening attack.[39]

Secondly, the act must be one of "just and *necessary* self-defence; the only refuge which the killer has in this high peril of his person. Thus the plea is not good in those, not unfrequent situations, where the party has other ways of escape from the assault".[40]

Thirdly:

> "... the manslayer must have observed the due temperance and reserve (*moderamen inculpatae tutelae* as it is termed by lawyers) in conducting his defence. The meaning of which is, that with respect to the weapons employed, the season and way of using them, and all other particulars, he must have confined himself to the just degree and measure of resistance."[41]

This appears on the face of it simply to be a statement of the rule of proportionality between attack and defence. This is a little misleading because Hume goes on not to discuss proportionality, but to set out a requirement for imminence of danger, stating that:

> "... any excess in the article of time scarcely seems to be reconcilable to the notion of self-defence. This is, where the homicide is not immediate on the attack or danger, but at some interval of time. For in these circumstances, at least unless the interval is very short, the deed can only be attributed to the principle of revenge; which always makes a case of murder."[42]

---

[36] M. Hale, *The History of the Pleas of the Crown* (1736), p.478. If Hume did borrow material from English law, it would not be the first time he had done so. It is well documented that Hume draws without direct acknowledgement on English material when discussing the issue of marital rape (see the Casebook, para.9.15 and *Stallard v HM Advocate*, 1989 S.L.T. 469 at 472). Indeed, Hume himself admits in the introduction to *Commentaries* that he has "made liberal use of the sentiments, and sometimes even of the words of the English writers on law" (Hume, i, 13).

[37] Despite his brief preoccupation with blameless self-defence (discussed in para.3.05 above), it is probably safe to assume that Hume intended these conditions to govern all cases of self-defence.

[38] Hume, i, 223, emphasis in original.

[39] Hume, i, 223.

[40] Hume, i, 226, emphasis in original. Hume's fleeting abandonment of the retreat rule in relation to blameless self-defence is discussed in para.3.05 above.

[41] Hume, i, 227.

[42] Hume, i, 228. Hume's view that, where danger is not imminent, the accused's only possible motive is revenge can be questioned. An individual can surely act for motives of self-preservation or fear even if the danger he perceives is not an imminent one.

At one point, Hume takes an extremely restrictive approach to the issue of imminence, using the example of John drawing his sword on James and James killing him before it is fully drawn. This, he states, represents "a precipitancy and an excess, for which the killer shall be answerable".[43] **3.07**

These first three of Hume's requirements, with some minor relaxations,[44] still govern the defence today. This is not true of Hume's fourth requirement: that the plea of self-defence is unavailable to the accused who "has himself in any degree been the cause of the fatal strife".[45] If this is interpreted to mean that someone who is the first to use physical violence will always be denied the plea of self-defence, then it is no longer a correct statement of the law.[46]

Requirements of the Defence

A successful plea of self-defence has three substantive requirements: imminence of danger; the absence of a reasonable opportunity to escape; and for any force used to have been proportional to the threat faced. The first two relate to the *necessity* of having to use defensive force; the third to *proportionality*.[47] **3.08**

Imminence of danger

The requirement for imminent danger[48] can be found in Hume and has been repeated in modern case law. Thus in *Owens v HM Advocate*,[49] the court held that: **3.09**

> "... self-defence is made out when it is established to the satisfaction of the jury that the panel believed that he was in imminent danger and that he held that belief on reasonable grounds".[50]

This is not to say that any attack must actually be underway before the accused is permitted to use defensive force. Even Hume, who took a relatively strict view of the imminence requirement,[51] conceded that:

[43] Hume, i, 228. Although *cf.* Hume, i, 229.

[44] For example in relation to retreat (see below, paras 3.12–3.13).

[45] Hume, i, 230.

[46] See below, paras 3.23–3.26.

[47] Force used in self-defence can be necessary without being proportionate and vice versa. Necessity refers to the need to use defensive force *at all*. In other words, if an attack could have been avoided without resorting to force (by, for example, taking an opportunity to escape the aggressor), then any force used in self-defence was not necessary. Proportionality refers to the degree of force that is permitted, once it has been established that it is necessary to use *at least some force* to avoid an attack. If an individual uses lethal force to avoid being slapped in the face, the force might have been necessary to avoid the slap (perhaps it was the only way of doing so) but it was not proportional.

[48] If the accused killed his attacker, then the accused must have faced an imminent danger specifically of death or great bodily injury. If less than lethal force was used, then an imminent attack of a lesser nature will suffice. See paras 3.16 *et seq.*

[49] 1946 J.C. 119.

[50] At 125. The requirement for the belief to be held on reasonable grounds is discussed below in paras 3.10–3.11. The imminence requirement has been re-iterated in *HM Advocate v Doherty*, 1954 J.C. 1 at 5; *McCluskey v HM Advocate*, 1959 J.C. 39 at 43; *Fenning v HM Advocate*, 1985 J.C. 75 at 78; *Hendry v HM Advocate*, 1985 J.C. 105 at 111, *per* the Lord Justice-Clerk (Wheatley); and *Friel v HM Advocate*, 1998 S.L.T. 1327 at 1328, *per* the Lord Justice-Clerk (Cullen).

[51] See para.3.06 above.

> "... it cannot be exacted of any one, to wait till the pistol is in the very act of being fired at him; or if the enemy have drawn, and be rushing towards him, he may meet him with his fire, before the point be at his breast".[52]

The purpose of the imminence rule, it has been suggested,[53] is to deny the defence of self-defence where there were alternative courses of action open to the accused other than killing or injuring the aggressor. If a threatened harm is not imminent, it is assumed that the accused could have summoned help or protection or could otherwise have avoided the threat.

Critics have argued that this assumption is unwarranted; that it may not always be possible to avoid a non-imminent threat. This criticism is sometimes made in "battered women" cases.[54] A violent partner might not threaten imminent harm but, because the authorities are unable to offer protection, there may be no way to avoid a threat that seems inevitable.[55]

An alternative approach would be to follow English[56] and Canadian law,[57] which treats imminence of danger as merely one factor in determining whether the use of defensive force is reasonable.

Mistake as to imminence of danger

3.10 Scots law has long required mistake in relation to self-defence to be based on reasonable grounds. Thus Hume stated:

> "It is not sufficient that the pannel have killed out of an apprehension, though ever so serious on his part, of danger to his life, if it was not also a reasonable apprehension, and well grounded in the circumstances of the situation ... In a matter of this kind, the law cannot entirely pardon any vain terror or sudden panic; for against

---

[52] Hume, i, 229.

[53] R. Rosen, "On self-defence, imminence and woman who kill their batterers" (1993) 71 *North Carolina Law Review* 371–411 at p.379.

[54] S. Estrich, "Defending women" (1990) 88 *Michigan Law Review* 1430–1439; J. Dressler, "Battered women who kill their sleeping tormenters: reflections on maintaining respect for human life while killing moral monsters" in *Criminal Law Theory: Doctrines of the General Part* (S. Shute and A.P. Simester (eds), 2002), pp.259–282; J. Horder, "Killing the passive abuser: a theoretical defence" in Shute and Simester, above. For a rare example of someone who supports the imminence requirement, see K.F. Ferzan, "Defending imminence: from battered women to Iraq" (2004) 46 *Arizona Law Review* 213–262. Debate has tended to centre on the paradigm case of a woman who has killed her violent male partner. This is not to suggest that this is the only situation in relation to which the criticism can be made. See, e.g. *Whipple v Indiana*, 523 N.E. 2d 1363 (Ind. 1988) (male defendant killed his two abusive parents while they slept); *State v Schroeder*, 261 N.W. 2d 759 (1978) (defendant was a male prisoner who killed his abusive cellmate while he slept).

[55] The argument that the imminence rule is unfair to women who have killed their abusive partners is perhaps a little overstated. Cases in which there are genuinely no reasonable alternatives to killing in self-defence are likely to be very rare. For detailed discussion, see F. Leverick, *Killing in Self-Defence* (2006), at Ch.5.

[56] *Shaw v R.* [2001] UKPC 26. See also *Re: A (Children)* [2001] 2 W.L.R. 480 for a case that at least one of the judges classified as self-defence and in which there was no question of the imminence requirement being met.

[57] *Lavallee v R.* [1990] 1 S.C.R. 852, approved in *R. v Pétel* [1994] 1 S.C.R. 3 and *R. v Cinous* [2002] S.C.R. 3. *Cf. R. v Charlebois* [2000] 2 S.C.R. 674.

this, so far at least as concerns his conduct towards others, it is the duty of every man to be on his guard."[58]

The reasonableness requirement was reiterated in the leading case of *Owens v HM Advocate*,[59] where it was held that:

> "... self-defence is made out when it is established to the satisfaction of the jury that the panel believed that he was in imminent danger and that he held that belief on reasonable grounds. Grounds for such belief may exist though they are founded on a genuine mistake of fact."[60]

Owens has been followed in a line of cases including *Crawford v HM Advocate*[61]; *McCluskey v HM Advocate*[62]; *McLean v Jessop*[63]; *Jones v HM Advocate*[64]; and *Burns v HM Advocate*.[65] The reasonableness requirement remained intact despite *Jamieson v HM Advocate*,[66] where Scots law followed English law in accepting that an honest but unreasonable belief in consent can ground an acquittal on a charge of rape.[67]

There is some suggestion that the comments made by the appeal court **3.11** on the definition of murder in *Drury v HM Advocate*[68] have the potential to change Scots law in relation to reasonable mistake in self-defence. In *Drury*, a provocation case,[69] the *mens rea* of murder was defined not simply as an intention to kill but a *wicked* intention to do so,[70] where the term wickedness referred to the absence of any applicable justification or excuse defence, such as self-defence.[71] If murder requires a wicked intention (that is, one which excludes action taken in self-defence), then it is arguable that the accused who honestly believes he is acting in self-defence, whether or not his mistake is reasonable, may not act with wicked intent and will therefore not have the requisite *mens rea* for murder.[72] At worst, this would leave him facing a conviction for culpable homicide.

Until a case involving mistaken belief in self-defence arises for decision, this interpretation of *Drury* cannot be ruled out conclusively. This does, however, appear unlikely. *Drury* has not proved influential outside the narrow confines of the provocation defence. It was not mentioned at all in two subsequent appeal court judgments on defences: the *Lord Advocate's*

---

58 Hume, i, 244.
59 1946 J.C. 119.
60 At 125, *per* the Lord Justice-General (Normand).
61 1950 J.C. 67 at 72.
62 1959 J.C. 39 at 43.
63 1989 S.C.C.R. 13 at 17.
64 1990 J.C. 160 at 172.
65 1995 J.C. 154 at 159.
66 1994 J.C. 88.
67 In *Jamieson*, the appeal court ruled out the extension of this principle to other defences (at 93). See Ch.12 for further discussion.
68 2001 S.L.T. 1013.
69 See Ch.10 for detailed discussion of the case.
70 Or alternatively as wicked recklessness.
71 At [11], *per* the Lord Justice-General (Rodger). See also Lord MacKay at [9]; Lord Johnston at [18] and Lord Nimmo-Smith at [3]. *Cf.* the Canadian Supreme Court in *R. v Kerr* [2004] 2 S.C.R. 371 at [28], *per* Bastarache J., and at [93], *per* LeBel J.; *R. v Parent* [2001] 1 S.C.R. 761 at [6]. For criticism, see F. Leverick, "Mistake in self-defence after *Drury*", 2002 Jur. Rev. 35–48 at pp.41–43.
72 See Leverick, above, fn.71, at pp.40–42 and J. Chalmers, "Collapsing the structure of criminal law", 2001 S.L.T. (News) 241–245.

Reference (No.1 of 2000)[73] or *Galbraith v HM Advocate (No.2)*.[74] Likewise, it was referenced only in passing by the appeal court in *Cochrane v HM Advocate*.[75] For the time being, it is probably safe to assume that the reasonable mistake requirement still forms part of the law of self-defence in Scotland.[76]

In requiring mistake to be reasonable, Scots law is in line with Canadian law, where the Canadian Supreme Court has consistently required mistaken belief in self-defence to be reasonable.[77] This was also the approach taken by the Australian High Court in *Zecevic v DPP*.[78] By contrast, English law does not require mistake in relation to the existence of an attack to be reasonable; an honest but unreasonable belief will suffice.[79]

The absence of a reasonable opportunity to retreat

3.12 The accused must have had no reasonable opportunity to escape the threat other than by using defensive force. If the threat could have been avoided by taking an opportunity to escape, and the accused did not take that opportunity, then he cannot plead self-defence.[80]

Thus in *HM Advocate v Doherty*,[81] the trial judge, in his charge to the jury, was impliedly critical of the accused for not taking a means of escape rather than resorting to the use of force. The incident alleged took place in a building in a Glasgow park. (The accused and his attacker had both broken into the building.) Reference is made in the case report to a possible escape route: an open door to a set of stairs which led down to a

---

[73] 2001 J.C. 143. The *Lord Advocate's Reference* concerned necessity and is discussed in Ch.4. In fact, in the *Reference*, it was made clear that necessity does not negate *mens rea* but is a separate defence in its own right (at [31]).

[74] 2002 J.C. 1. *Galbraith* concerned diminished responsibility and is discussed in Ch.11.

[75] 2001 S.C.C.R. 655. *Cochrane* dealt with coercion and is discussed in Ch.5.

[76] For an account of why requiring reasonable belief is the morally preferable option, see Leverick, above, fn.71, at pp.43–47; O.E. Woodruff Jnr, "Mistake of fact as a defense" (1958–1959) 63 *Dickinson Law Review* 319–333 at pp.325–326. *Cf.* R. Singer, "The resurgence of *mens rea*: II—honest but unreasonable mistake of fact in self defense" (1986–1987) 28 *Boston College Law Review* 459–519.

[77] *R. v Pétel* [1994] 1 S.C.R. 3 at [12]; *R. v Cinous* [2002] S.C.R. 3 at [41].

[78] (1987) 162 C.L.R. 645.

[79] *R. v Williams* [1987] 3 All E.R. 411; *R. v Beckford* [1988] A.C. 130; *R. v Martin* [2001] EWCA Crim 2245. See also the Privy Council case of *Shaw v R.* [2001] UKPC 26. It has been suggested that in allowing an unreasonable mistake to ground the defence of self-defence, English law violates Art.2 of the ECHR. For discussion, see F. Leverick, "Is English self-defence law incompatible with Article 2 of the ECHR?" [2002] Crim. L.R. 347–362; J.C. Smith, "The use of force in public or private defence and Article 2" [2002] Crim. L.R. 958–962; F. Leverick, "The use of force in public or private defence and Article 2: A reply to Professor Sir John Smith" [2002] Crim. L.R. 961–965; Ch.10 of F. Leverick, *Killing in Self-Defence* (2006).

[80] *McCluskey v HM Advocate*, 1959 J.C. 39 at 44, *per* Lord Russell; *Fenning v HM Advocate*, 1985 J.C. 76 at 78; *Burns v HM Advocate*, 1995 J.C. 154 at 157; *Pollock v HM Advocate*, 1998 S.L.T. 880 at 882. *Cf.* Hume, i, 217, who advocates a retreat rule only in cases of quarrel self-defence and not for cases of blameless self-defence (see earlier para.3.05). The retreat requirement only applies to the accused who is defending *himself*. A retreat rule would make little sense in relation to the defence of others (see para.3.27).

[81] 1954 J.C. 1.

yard. Lord Keith, in his charge to the jury, noted that "certainly there does not seem to have been any attempt to make an escape by the door".[82]

The accused is not, however, required to take any opportunity to escape, regardless of whether this would expose him to greater danger than using force to defend himself. Only the failure to take advantage of a *reasonable* opportunity to retreat will bar a plea of self-defence. This was emphasised in the leading case of *McBrearty v HM Advocate*.[83] Here, the accused appealed against his murder conviction on the basis (among others) that the trial judge did not emphasise that any opportunity to escape must be reasonable before it barred a plea of self-defence.[84]

The Lord Justice-General (Rodger) commented that it would have been more precise if the trial judge had mentioned that a means of escape must be reasonable, rather than just any opportunity, however risky.[85] Lord Coulsfield agreed:

> "... it is no doubt true that a person who is under threat cannot be expected to use a means of escape which exposes him to equal or greater danger rather than use force to defend himself. In that sense, it is no doubt correct that, in appropriate circumstances, a jury may have to consider whether any means of escape open to the person under threat were reasonable."[86]

In making a retreat rule an independent requirement of the defence of self-defence, Scots law is out of line with a number of other common law jurisdictions. The Canadian Criminal Code contains a retreat rule in relation to provoked attacks but not unprovoked attacks.[87] In English law, the failure to take an opportunity to retreat is merely one of a number of factors to be taken into account in deciding whether or not any force used in self-defence was reasonable.[88] In a number of US states[89] and in German law,[90] there is no duty whatsoever on the accused to retreat, even if a safe opportunity exists to do so. **3.13**

[82] At 6. On the facts as reported, this seems rather harsh. The accused was faced with immediate danger to his life from a man armed with a hammer. Requiring him to escape via a door, a staircase and a yard could be seen as requiring an unnecessary level of risk. In the event, Doherty's defence of self-defence was rejected by the jury, although whether they were influenced by Lord Keith's comments on retreat is impossible to tell. The case was reported in 1954 and Lord Keith did not refer to the requirement that any means of escape be reasonable before the accused is bound to utilise it, a qualification that clearly does now form part of Scots law (see below).

[83] 1999 S.L.T. 1333.

[84] At 1334.

[85] At 1336.

[86] At 1337.

[87] Canadian Criminal Code, s.34(2) (self-defence against unprovoked assault); s.35(c) (self-defence in case of aggression). Although see *R. v McIntosh* [1995] 1 S.C.R. 686, which left the distinction between these provisions in a state of some confusion. For reform proposals, see Canadian Department of Justice, *Provocation, Self-Defence and Defence of Property: A Consultation Paper* (1998).

[88] *R. v Bird* [1985] 1 W.L.R. 816.

[89] See, e.g. the Texas Penal Code (s.9.3.2). R.M. Brown, *No Duty to Retreat: Violence and Values in American History and Society* (1994) has further examples.

[90] German Penal Code, s.32; see also the discussion in K. Bernsmann, "Private self-defence and necessity in German penal law and in the penal law proposal: some remarks" (1996) 30 *Israel Law Review* 171–187.

Some argue that Scots law takes the morally superior position.[91] To permit the accused to stand his ground and injure or kill an aggressor when a safe opportunity to escape from the attack exists is to suggest that, in some circumstances, there are values that outweigh the value of saving the life of the aggressor. It is difficult to see what these values might be, other than honour or self-respect[92]—values which clearly do not outweigh the value of human life unless one takes the extreme view that the aggressor, by virtue of his attack, renders his own life worthless.

Retreat from the home

3.14 In some jurisdictions where the law of self-defence requires the accused to take any safe opportunity to retreat, an exception to that rule is made when an attack takes place in the accused's own home. This is, for example, the case in a number of US states.[93]

There is no direct authority on this point in Scots law, but given the relatively strict approach taken to the law of self-defence in Scotland it is assumed here that the same rule would apply regardless of whether an attack took place in the home or elsewhere: the accused could not claim the defence of self-defence if he failed to take any reasonable means of escape.

Proportionality

3.15 The response of the accused must have been proportionate to the danger he faced. The defence will be ruled out if the accused has used excessive force.

This requirement has been expressed in various ways. In *McCluskey v HM Advocate*,[94] the Lord Justice-General (Clyde) held that the accused must observe "due restraint" in defending himself and that he must not use force that was "cruelly excessive".[95] In *Fenning v HM Advocate*,[96] Lord Cameron referred to a requirement that the accused should not have used "force grossly in excess of that necessary to defend himself"[97] and stated that the benefit of the defence would be lost "where the force used to repel the attack is excessive". The degree of excess required to rule out the defence is "cruel" excess.[98]

It has been stressed by the courts that, in determining whether or not cruelly excessive force has been used, the accused will not be judged on too fine a scale. Account is taken of the circumstances in which the accused finds himself and especially of the fear that he is likely to experience if threatened with an unexpected attack. As such, in *HM*

---

[91] F. Leverick, *Killing in Self-Defence* (2006), at Ch.4. See also (although they do not refer directly to Scots law) A. Ashworth, "Self-defence and the right to life" [1975] C.L.J. 282–307 at p.290; J.H. Beale, "Retreat from a murderous assault" (1903) 16 *Harvard Law Review* 567–582 at p.581.

[92] On this, see the US case of *Runyan v State*, 57 Ind. 80 (1877), where the court thought that enforcing a duty to retreat would legitimise cowardice, which would be un-American (at 82).

[93] See, e.g. Pennsylvania Criminal Code, Part 1, s.505(b)(2)(ii); Connecticut Criminal Code, s.53a–19(a) and (b). Article 20(4)(a) of the Louisiana Criminal Code applies the same principle to an attack taking place in a motor vehicle.

[94] 1959 J.C. 39.

[95] At 43.

[96] 1985 J.C. 76.

[97] At 81.

[98] At 81.

Advocate v Doherty,[99] the trial judge, Lord Keith, charged the jury as follows:

> "You do not need an exact proportion of injury and retaliation; it is not a matter that you weigh in too fine scales (*sic*), as has been said. Some allowance must be made for the excitement or the state of fear or the heat of blood at the moment of the man who is attacked ... For instance, if a man was struck a blow by another man with the fist, that could not justify retaliation by the use of a knife, because there is no real proportion at all between a blow with a fist and retaliation with a knife."[1]

In *Fraser v Skinner*,[2] the accused's conviction for assault was overturned by the appeal court on the basis that the presiding sheriff *had* weighed the degree of force used too finely.[3] In *Whyte v HM Advocate*,[4] the accused's plea of self-defence was not defeated despite his admission in a police interview that he felt that he had used excessive force.

Equally, there are examples of reported cases in which the defence has been ruled out on the basis that excessive force *was* used, most commonly when a weapon has been used to repel an attack from an unarmed aggressor. For example, in *Moore v MacDougall*,[5] the defence was ruled out where the appellant had used a pair of scissors to stab in the buttocks an unarmed man who was assaulting her friend. Her conviction for assault was upheld, on the basis that she had used a weapon whereas the complainer was unarmed.[6]

Killing to prevent a non-fatal attack

Lethal self-defensive force is permissible only when the accused faced a **3.16** threat to life or a threat of serious bodily injury. Thus, in *Owens v HM Advocate*,[7] the court held that only "danger of his life (or ... reasonable apprehension of danger to his life)" would justify the accused in killing his attacker in self-defence.[8] Likewise, in *Burns v HM Advocate*,[9] the Lord Justice-General (Hope) refers to killing that was "necessary to preserve [the accused's] own life or protect himself from serious injury".[10]

---

[99] 1954 J.C. 1.

[1] At 4–5.

[2] 1975 S.L.T. (Notes) 84.

[3] The defence does not appear to be defeated if the trial judge does not mention the need to make allowance for the heat of the moment or does not warn the jury not to judge the accused's use of force on too fine a scale; a direction that the force used must not constitute a cruel excess is sufficient. See *Friel v HM Advocate*, 1998 S.L.T. 1327 at 1328, *per* the Lord Justice-Clerk (Cullen); *Maher v HM Advocate*, 1999 G.W.D. 31–1471.

[4] 1996 J.C. 187.

[5] 1989 S.C.C.R. 659.

[6] At 663 *per* the Lord Justice-Clerk (Ross). See also *Moffat v McNaughton*, 1987 S.C.C.R. 497; *Surman v HM Advocate*, 1988 S.L.T. 371.

[7] 1946 J.C. 119.

[8] At 124.

[9] 1995 J.C. 154.

[10] At 159.

Excessive force in self-defence

3.17 In Scots law, excessive force in self-defence cannot operate as a partial defence to murder, where the accused has acted in self-defence but has used cruelly excessive force in doing so.[11]

There is some suggestion in Hume that excessive force in self-defence might once have operated as a partial defence or as a factor in mitigation of punishment.[12] Both Alison[13] and Macdonald[14] advance the proposition that excessive force in self-defence can reduce what would otherwise have been murder to culpable homicide. The issue was addressed directly in *Hillan v HM Advocate*,[15] an appeal against conviction for assault on the ground, among others, that the trial judge misdirected the jury on the issue of excessive force in self-defence. In the course of his judgment, the Lord Justice-Clerk (Aitchison) stated of self-defence that the plea:

> "... is subject to the same qualifications as the plea of provocation, with which it often coincides. Thus the attack may afford a complete justification for what the panel has done, or it may reduce the quality of the crime, as, for example, from murder to culpable homicide, where the panel has struck in his own defence but with a measure of violence that cannot be justified."[16]

If excessive force in self-defence ever was a partial defence in Scots law, however, it was conclusively ruled out in *Crawford v HM Advocate*.[17] Here, the Lord Justice-General (Cooper) attributed the idea that self-defence can operate as a partial defence to confusion between the pleas of self-defence and provocation and stated that:

> "Exculpation is always the sole function of the special defence of self-defence. Provocation and self-defence are often coupled in a special defence, and often I fear confused; but provocation is not a special defence and is always available to an accused person without a special plea. The facts relied upon to support a plea of self-defence usually contain a strong element of provocation and the lesser plea may succeed where the greater fails; but when in such a case murder is reduced to culpable homicide, or a person accused of assault is found guilty subject to provocation, it is not the special defence of self-defence which is sustained but the plea of provocation."[18]

---

[11] This is contrary to the view expressed in the House of Lords Select Committee *Report on Murder, Manslaughter and Life Imprisonment* (HL Paper No. 78–I, 1988–1989). The Committee recommended the establishment of a partial defence of excessive force in self-defence and claimed that this would bring the law of England and Wales into line with that of Scotland (at para.89). The issue is one that has attracted the attention of the English Law Commission, in its review of the law on partial defences. See *Report on Partial Defences to Murder* (Law Com. No. 290, 2004), at paras 4.1–4.31. The discussion that follows is based heavily on J. Chalmers, C.H.W. Gane and F. Leverick, "Partial defences to homicide in the law of Scotland: a report to the Law Commission for England and Wales" in *Partial Defences to Murder* (Consultation Paper No. 173 (Appendices), 2003), pp.151–183.

[12] See, e.g. Hume, i, 223, 227. See also the cases of *John Govan* (1710) Hume, i, 227; *John Macmillan* (1690) Hume, i, 227; *Urquhart and Webster* (1685) Hume, i, 228.

[13] Alison, *Principles*, 102.

[14] Macdonald, 131.

[15] 1937 J.C. 53.

[16] At 58. *Hillan* was followed in *HM Advocate v Kizileviczius*, 1938 J.C. 60 at 63.

[17] 1950 J.C. 67.

[18] At 69.

Further confirmation came in *Fenning v HM Advocate*[19] where, despite *Crawford*, the accused appealed against his conviction for murder on the ground, among others, that the trial judge misdirected the jury by failing to mention the possibility of a verdict of culpable homicide if excessive force was used in self-defence. Lord Cameron once again conclusively rejected that argument, stating that: **3.18**

> "... a direction in law that a plea of self-defence 'might result in a verdict of culpable homicide' ... was a wrong direction in law and confused two entirely separate matters ... If a special defence of self-defence fails, the only proper and competent verdict is one of murder, unless [provocation is established]".[20]

In ruling out excessive force in self-defence as a partial defence to murder, Scots law is in line with the majority of common law jurisdictions.[21] In Canada, the Supreme Court ruled out its availability in *R. v Faid*,[22] a decision confirmed in *Reilly v The Queen*.[23] In England, it has been clear since *R. v Palmer*[24] that excessive force in self-defence is not a partial defence, this being re-affirmed by the House of Lords in *R. v Clegg*[25] and the Court of Appeal in *R. v Martin*.[26] The English Law Commission's 2004 review of partial defences to murder recommended that this remain the case.[27] In Australia, despite the concept gaining some currency in *R. v Viro*,[28] the partial defence was ruled out by the High Court in *Zecevic v DPP*,[29] at least in part because it was thought to be too complex for juries to understand.[30] The partial defence is also ruled out by statute in New Zealand.[31]

---

19 1985 J.C. 76.

20 At 80. See also *Low v HM Advocate*, 1994 S.L.T. 277 at 286. Some doubt might be cast on this conclusion by the appeal court's definition of murder in *Drury v HM Advocate*, 2001 S.L.T. 1013. If, as it was held in *Drury*, murder requires a wicked intention (that is, one which excludes action taken in self-defence), then it is possible that the accused who honestly believes that he is acting in self-defence, albeit using excessive force, is not acting with wicked intent and will therefore not have the requisite *mens rea* for murder. See para.3.11 above for discussion. *Cf. Bennett v Criminal Injuries Compensation Appeal Panel*, December 9, 2003, Court of Session, unreported, at [18] where it is suggested that wicked intent might be inferred in such circumstances.

21 An exception is India. See s.300 of the Indian Penal Code.

22 [1983] 1 S.C.R. 265 at [9]–[19], *per* Dickson J.

23 [1984] 2 S.C.R. 396 at [5]–[10], *per* Ritchie J.

24 [1971] A.C. 814.

25 1995 A.C. 482.

26 [2001] EWCA Crim 2245. *Cf. R. v Scarlett* [1993] 4 All E.R. 629 at 636, *per* Beldam L.J.

27 *Report on Partial Defences to Murder* (Law Com. No. 290, 2004), at para.4.31.

28 (1978) 141 C.L.R. 88.

29 (1987) 162 C.L.R. 645.

30 At 660 *per* Wilson, Dawson and Toohey JJ. Some Australian states have since re-introduced the partial defence of excessive force through legislation. In South Australia, see s.15(2) of the Criminal Law Consolidation Act 1935 (SA), as amended by the Criminal Law Consolidation (Self Defence) Amendment Act 1997 (SA). In New South Wales, see s.421 of the Crimes Act 1900 (NSW), as amended by the Crimes Amendment (Self-defence) Act 2001 (NSW).

31 The Crimes Act 1961, ss.48 and 62, as amended by the Crimes Amendment Act 1980.

Killing to prevent rape

3.19 The proportionality requirement is satisfied where a female person uses lethal force to prevent a threat of rape.[32] This is clear from Hume, who states that:

> "In like manner as a man may kill in resistance of an attempt on his life, so may a woman in resistance of an attempt to commit a rape on her person, an attempt at which she is entitled to feel the highest indignation and resentment."[33]

Hume's account is gender specific: the person threatened with rape must be female, although the prevention of the attack can be undertaken by either the victim or by another person.[34] As Hume refers specifically to rape, which is a gender specific crime,[35] this is not surprising. But it seems that it would not be permissible to kill in order to prevent an equivalent sexual assault on a male person under Hume's account. This is because of the very serious injury rape is assumed to cause to the honour of (specifically) a woman. Hume describes rape as "cruel and irreparable injury"[36] and "a robbery of that in which a woman's honour, her place in society, and her estimation in her own eyes depend".[37] Presumably he does not consider non-consensual sexual intercourse to carry the same degree of harm to a male person.[38]

The leading (relatively) modern authority is *McCluskey v HM Advocate*.[39] *McCluskey* concerned a claim by the (male) accused that he killed in order to prevent a sexual assault by another man. He was convicted of

---

[32] Even where she faces no accompanying threat of death or serious bodily injury. In practice, it may be difficult to separate the two, although in a survey of 464 female rape victims undertaken in the US, only 54% reported that they thought that they might be killed or seriously injured during the incident. See R. Acierno, M. Gray, C. Best, H. Resnick, D. Kilpatrick, B. Saunders and K. Brady, "Rape and physical violence: comparison of assault characteristics in older and younger adults in the National Women's Study" (2001) 14 *Journal of Traumatic Stress* 685–695 at p.690.

[33] Hume, i, 218.

[34] In the first edition of Hume, published in 1797, only the victim herself or the husband, father and brother of the victim were permitted to kill to prevent a rape. By the time of the fourth edition in 1844, this permission had been widened to include "anyone who is with her".

[35] At the time of writing, rape can be committed only by a male perpetrator on a female victim. The definition of rape was considered in the *Lord Advocate's Reference (No. 1 of 2001)*, 2002 S.L.T. 466. While the case was noteworthy in that it re-defined rape as sexual intercourse with a female person without her consent (a change from the previously accepted definition of sexual intercourse with a female person by overcoming her will), the gender specific nature of the crime was not addressed, leaving Scots law out of line with almost every other common law jurisdiction. The Scottish Law Commission's *Discussion Paper on Rape and Other Sexual Offences* (D.P. 131, 2006) recommends the adoption of a gender neutral definition (at para.4.18).

[36] Hume, i, 218.

[37] Hume, i, 301.

[38] On this, see also Burnett: "[A] woman may kill with impunity in hindrance of a rape; but the same will not hold in other injuries, though of the grossest kind; a man will not be *justified* in killing another to prevent an indignity to his person, as if one should wantonly invade him, to horsewhip, or to pull his nose; though his killing the invader in such circumstances would not infer the guilt of murder. To extenuate, however, in any great degree, the injury must be *real*, and of the higher class" (at 53, emphasis in original).

[39] 1959 J.C. 39. Although see also *HM Advocate v Forrest* (1837) 1 Swin. 404 and *Crawford v HM Advocate*, 1950 J.C. 67.

culpable homicide after the trial judge directed the jury that homicide was justified by self-defence only "if the homicidal acts are done to save the man's own life".[40] This was confirmed on appeal.[41] In the course of his judgment, the Lord Justice-General (Clyde) contrasted this with the situation of a woman faced with a threat of rape, who would be permitted to kill in her defence.[42]

Since *McCluskey*, the only two reported Scottish cases to touch on the issue are *Elliott v HM Advocate*[43] and *Pollock v HM Advocate*.[44] In *Elliott*, it was confirmed that a man who kills in order to avoid a sexual assault cannot plead self-defence, although no mention was made of whether or not a woman would be permitted to kill in similar circumstances. In *Pollock*, the accused claimed to have killed to prevent the deceased from raping his girlfriend, but was convicted of culpable homicide after the trial judge withdrew the defence of self-defence from the jury. On appeal, the High Court did not address the issue of defence against rape directly,[45] but it did seem to accept that killing to prevent a rape was permissible: **3.20**

> "... the crucial point is not whether the appellant had or had not a genuine belief that the deceased might still rape [his girlfriend] but rather whether a reasonable jury could consider that the steps he took were taken to defend her".[46]

It seems, then, from a line of authorities stretching from Hume through *McCluskey* to *Pollock*, that Scots law does permit a woman (or a third party acting on behalf of a woman) to kill in order to prevent a threat of rape.[47] What is less clear is why this is so. Hume grounded his argument in the particularly serious injury that rape caused to a woman's personal honour. But modern Scots law surely cannot sanction killing in defence against a threat to personal honour or dignity? Indeed, in *McCluskey* it was made very clear that this would not be permitted. The trial judge withdrew the plea of self-defence in the first place because it could not be extended to cover killing "to avoid some great indignity, some attack upon virtue or even some bodily harm".[48] The Lord Justice-General agreed. In his view, only a threat to life justified killing in self-defence. Threats to honour, personal dignity, or even of bodily harm, were not seen as sufficiently serious to justify killing:

> "Dishonour, it is suggested, may be worse than death. But there are many ways of avoiding dishonour without having to resort to the taking of a human life, and, so far as I am concerned, I do not see how the taking of a human life can ever be justified by the mere fact

---

40 At 41.

41 It will be interesting to see whether or not this remains the case if, as expected, the Scottish Law Commission's recommendation in its *Discussion Paper on Rape and Other Sexual Offences* that the definition of rape is widened to include male victims (see para.4.18) becomes law. On this, see below, para.12.18.

42 The Lord Justice-General quoted with approval the following passage from Alison: "A private individual will be justified in killing in defence of his life against imminent danger, of the lives of others connected with him from similar peril, or a woman or her friends in resisting an attempt at rape" (at 43).

43 1987 J.C. 47.

44 1998 S.L.T. 880.

45 The appeal was rejected on unrelated grounds.

46 *Pollock v HM Advocate*, 1998 S.L.T. 880 at 883.

47 *cf.* Draft Criminal Code, s.23(3).

48 *McCluskey v HM Advocate*, 1959 J.C. 39 at 41.

that there have been threats of dishonour or indignities or even of some bodily harm, which falls short of creating reasonable apprehension of danger to life".[49]

3.21 But if the threat to honour and dignity, or the threat of bodily harm, does not explain why a woman is permitted to kill in defence against rape, what alternative rationale is advanced in *McCluskey*? The answer is not at all clear. The only explanation given by the Lord Justice-General is the following passage, in which he attempts to explain why killing in defence against rape is permissible but killing in defence against "sodomy" is not:

> "It seems to me impossible to assimilate the present case to a woman threatened with rape. For rape involves complete absence of consent on the part of the woman. This is not the situation in sodomy."[50]

With respect, this is not a particularly convincing explanation. It is possible to imagine many different types of act to which the reasonable person would not consent, but this alone does not permit him or her to kill in order to prevent them. Presumably what the Lord Justice-General meant was that there is something about non-consensual *sexual intercourse* that is especially harmful to a woman. But elsewhere in his judgment, he rules out the possibility of killing to protect honour or dignity, or to prevent a threat of bodily injury "which falls short of creating reasonable apprehension of danger to life".[51] The most likely explanation is that the Lord Justice-General never gave the issue of why it is permissible to kill to prevent rape any great thought and that he, like so many others,[52] simply assumed that it should be permissible.[53]

Killing in defence of property

3.22 Somewhat surprisingly, Hume seems to regard the proportionality requirement as being met where the accused has killed in defence of property. For example, at one point, he sanctions the killing of a thief where a robbery takes place "on the highway, in the night and in a solitary place".[54] This is *not* primarily because of the accompanying danger to the person (although this is a consideration) but because it is unlikely that the property will be recovered unless the thief is killed:

---

[49] *McCluskey v HM Advocate*, 1959 J.C. 39 at 43.

[50] *McCluskey v HM Advocate*, 1959 J.C. 39 at 43–44. What the Lord Justice-General was presumably implying was that at the time when the case was decided (1959), a lack of consent (or at least the fact that sexual intercourse was against the will of the victim) was part of the definition of rape, whereas this was not the case in relation to the specific offence of sodomy, a wider offence criminalizing even consensual homosexual acts between males. Homosexual acts between males were not decriminalised in Scotland until s.80 of the Criminal Justice (Scotland) Act 1980.

[51] *McCluskey v HM Advocate*, 1959 J.C. 39 at 43.

[52] This can be said of Gordon who simply states that rape is a "unique exception" (at para.24.18) to the rule that lethal force can only be used where there is a danger to life, without considering why this might be so.

[53] For detailed discussion of whether or not killing in defence against rape *should* be permissible, see Ch.8 of F. Leverick, *Killing in Self-Defence* (2006); D.B. Kates Jr and N.J. Engberg, "Deadly force self-defence against rape" (1982) 15 *University of California Davis Law Review* 873–906. For a discussion of why rape is so wrongful that it might constitute an injury of equal gravity to serious bodily harm, see J. Gardner and S. Shute, "The wrongness of rape" in *Oxford Essays in Jurisprudence, Fourth Series* (J. Horder (ed.), 2000), pp.193–217.

[54] Hume, i, 220.

> "... once surrendered, my property is gone, *and with but little hope of recovery*. Meeting in this way, the assailant and I are here in a state of open warfare: I have no terms to keep with him, and am under no obligation in law, whatever generosity may suggest, to consult his safety, but may prevent and chastise his felony on the spot."[55]

Hume's account is surprising not least because it is not supported by the case law of the time. *Ewart*,[56] *Kennedy*,[57] *HM Advocate v McBryde*[58] and *HM Advocate v Wright*[59] all ruled out the possibility of an acquittal for the accused who had killed to defend property. In *Earl of Eglinton v Campbell*,[60] the issue was considered in detail, with the court holding that the only occasion justifying the use of lethal force in the defence of property was where an intruder had broken into the accused's home at night and then *only* because of the presumed element of personal danger involved, not because of the threat to property. The same conclusion was reached in *James Craw*,[61] a five judge decision on the relevancy of a charge of murder where the accused had set an automatic gun trap to catch poachers. Here, Lord Mackenzie summed up the rationale for restricting the justification of homicide in defence of property to those cases where there is an actual (or assumed) element of danger to life:

> "The law of Scotland is peculiarly tender of human life; and, except in some very particular cases, does not allow it to be taken, unless in defence of life."[62]

The only two cases that provide support for Hume's view are *Edward Lane*[63] and *William Williamson*.[64] In *Lane*, Lord Moncreiff charged the jury that a servant might be justified in killing an intruder found in his master's house "if he could not otherwise protect his master's property".[65] In *Williamson*, the accused was acquitted of murder after shooting a thief who was stealing cloth from an outhouse. Hume is critical of the decision in *Williamson*, but his criticism focuses on the absence of necessity in the case, not on the absence of proportionality.[66]

No modern reported case has directly addressed the issue of homicide in defence of property.[67] The leading authorities on self-defence suggest, however, that it would not be sanctioned. Admittedly, in *Crawford v HM Advocate*,[68] Lord Keith did include resistance to a housebreaker or to a robber as two of his classic examples of self-defence but he did not suggest

---

55 Hume, i, 220, emphasis added. See also Hume, i, 221.
56 (1828) Hume, i, 219.
57 (1829) Alison, i, 23.
58 (1843) 1 Broun 558.
59 (1835) 1 Swin. 6.
60 (1769) MacLaurin 505.
61 (1826) Syme 188 at 219, *per* the Lord Justice-Clerk (Boyle).
62 At 214.
63 (1830) Bell's Notes 77.
64 (1801) Hume, i, 220–221.
65 *Edward Lane* (1830) Bell's Notes 77 at 77.
66 Hume, i, 220–221.
67 Although see *Gillingham v HM Advocate*, January 1999, unreported. See the *Scotsman*, April 24, 2001. Here, a man who set an automated trap in a toolshed on his land in order to try and catch vandals who had been causing damage to the property was convicted of attempted murder when the trap injured an intruder.
68 1950 J.C. 67.

that lethal force would be permissible in this context. In *McCluskey v HM Advocate*,[69] the Lord Justice-General (Clyde) refused to extend the plea of self-defence to cover defence against an attempted sexual assault by one man on another because of the "principle of the sanctity of human life".[70] When the same issue was considered in *Elliott v HM Advocate*,[71] the Lord Justice-General (Emslie) approved the trial judge's charge to the jury that "homicide will not be justified by self-defence unless it is committed of necessity in the just apprehension on the part of the killer that he cannot otherwise save his own life".[72] Given these comments, and the strict rules relating to other aspects of self-defence, it can probably be concluded that the acquittal of an accused who had killed in defence of property could not be legally justified.[73]

Can an initial aggressor plead self-defence?

3.23 Hume seems to rule out the availability of self-defence to an initial aggressor, although his account is a confused one. Hume recognises two forms of the defence: blameless self-defence and quarrel self-defence.[74] The latter is self-defence that becomes necessary:

> "... in the course of an affray, or occasional quarrel, between persons who have fallen out upon the spot and have probably, at the outset, been both of them less or more in fault".[75]

This would seem to suggest that Hume would allow an initial aggressor to plead self-defence. The basis of Hume's quarrel self-defence is that it is a defence available to someone who was at least partially to blame for the conflict. Nonetheless, Hume proceeds to *deny* the availability of self-defence to someone who is responsible for starting the trouble,[76] even where the initial provoking incident did not constitute a physical assault.[77]

---

[69] 1959 J.C. 39.

[70] At 43.

[71] 1987 J.C. 47.

[72] At 50.

[73] *cf.* the South African case of *Ex parte die Minister van Justisie: In re S. Van Wyk*, 1967 (1) SA 488 (AD), translated in J. Burchell and J. Milton, *Cases and Materials on Criminal Law* (2nd edn, 1997), p.151 and D.R. Stuart, "Killing in defence of property" (1967) 84 S.A.L.J. 123–131. It may be, however, that if a case of this nature were now to arise for decision in South Africa, the outcome would be different (see *Ex parte The Minister for Safety and Security and the National Commissioner of the South African Police Service: In re The State v Walters and Walters* (2002) 7 B.C.L.R. 663 (CC) at [53]). For a discussion of whether lethal force should ever be permitted in defence of property, see A.P. Simester and G.R. Sullivan, *Criminal Law: Theory and Doctrine* (2nd edn, 2004), at p.626; R.J. Muth and A.L. Blumstein, "The use of deadly force in the protection of property under the Model Penal Code" (1959) 59 *Columbia Law Review* 1212–1232 at p.1225; S.P. Green, "Castles and carjackers: proportionality and the use of deadly force in defence of dwellings and vehicles" (1999) *University of Illinois Law Review* 1–41.

[74] See para.3.05.

[75] Hume, i, 217.

[76] The "full plea of self-defence is ... out of the question" (Hume, i, 230) and there "seems scarcely to be room for a difference of opinion" (Hume, i, 233).

[77] "There does not even seem to be any good reason why [the accused] should not be liable to the moderate pains of fine and imprisonment ... who brings the assault on himself, by the provocation of contumelious words, or derisive signs and gestures" (Hume, i, 233). See also his criticism of the decision in *HM Advocate v Lieutenant Robertson* (1758) Hume, i, 233.

Thankfully, modern case law has clarified the matter. Hume's notion that an initial aggressor cannot plead self-defence does not appear to have been followed in *HM Advocate v Kizileviczius*.[78] In this case, the accused was the first to use physical violence and there was no suggestion that this should have prevented him from pleading self-defence.

Kizileviczius was followed by *Robertson and Donoghue v HM Advocate*.[79] This case concerned a plea of self-defence by the accused, who had robbed and killed a café proprietor. In the course of the robbery, the accused had not used a weapon, but the café proprietor responded violently, which prompted the accused to produce a knife and kill him. The accused was convicted of culpable homicide and appealed. The appeal failed, but in the course of his judgment, the Lord Justice-General (Normand) made the following comment: 3.24

> "It is necessary to observe that although an accused person may commit the first assault and may be, in general, the assailant, he is not thereby necessarily excluded from a plea of self-defence. If the victim, in protecting himself or his property, uses violence altogether disproportionate to the need, and employs savage excess, then the assailant is in his turn entitled to defend himself against the assault by his victim ... Accordingly, in a case in which there is a struggle, the right of self-defence may be invoked by the original assailant as well as by a man who was at the outset his victim."[80]

Further clarification came in *Boyle v HM Advocate*.[81] The accused had willingly entered into a fight and, in the course of the trouble, he stabbed and killed a man who was about to attack his friend. The trial judge withdrew the defence of self-defence (or perhaps more accurately, defence of others) and the accused was convicted of murder. On appeal, it was held that the trial judge was in error. The appeal court drew on *Kizileviczius* and *Robertson and Donoghue*, concluding that:

> "... it was a misdirection for the trial judge to tell the jury that the appellant could not plead self-defence if he was a willing participant in the sense that he joined in the fight willingly. Even if he was a participant in the sense that he stepped forward into the fight, it would all depend upon the circumstances whether self-defence could be pleaded. If the jury accepted that part of his evidence in which he described how he came to step forward to go to the assistance of [his friend] then, in our opinion, it would be open to the jury to accept that he was acting in self-defence."[82]

Boyle was swiftly followed by *Burns v HM Advocate*.[83] Burns had started the trouble by assaulting the complainer's cousin. The complainer then entered the fight, only for Burns to strike him on the head with a metal bar. The trial judge charged the jury that it was a condition of the plea of 3.25

---

78 1938 J.C. 60.

79 High Court at Edinburgh, October 1945, unreported. See Gordon, at para.24.10.

80 At para.24.10 of Gordon. This passage is also quoted in *Boyle v HM Advocate*, 1993 S.L.T. 577 at 587.

81 1993 S.L.T. 577.

82 At 588.

83 1995 J.C. 154.

self-defence that "the accused must not have started the trouble".[84] On appeal, the Lord Justice-General (Hope) stated that, in the light of *Kizileviczius*, *Robertson and Donoghue* and *Boyle*:

> "It is not accurate to say that a person who kills someone in a quarrel which he himself started, by provoking it or entering into it willingly, cannot plead self-defence if his victim then retaliates. The question whether the plea of self-defence is available depends, in a case of that kind, on whether retaliation is such that the accused is entitled then to defend himself. That depends on whether the violence offered by the victim was so out of proportion to the accused's own actings as to give rise to the reasonable apprehension that he was in immediate danger from which he had no other means of escape, and whether the violence which he then used was no more than was necessary to preserve his own life or protect himself from serious injury."[85]

Thus, even where the accused was the first to use physical violence, he will be able to plead self-defence if the victim responded disproportionately and the accused had no other means available to save his own life.[86]

In permitting an initial aggressor to plead self-defence, Scots law is in line with other jurisdictions. For example, the Canadian Criminal Code specifically provides for this possibility, with a separate provision relating to the accused who was the first to use aggression or who otherwise provoked the attack upon himself.[87] In Australia, the Supreme Court of Victoria has held that an initial aggressor is entitled to claim self-defence if "he reasonably believes that the victim is not defending himself against the initial threat or attack but has become the aggressor and he the defender".[88] In England, it was held in *R. v Rashford*[89] that: "the mere fact that a defendant goes somewhere in order to exact revenge from the victim does not of itself rule out the possibility that in any violence that ensues self-defence is necessarily not available as a defence".[89a] The Court of Appeal relied heavily on *Burns*, which was described as an "important decision [that] should be more widely known than it appears to be".[89b]

3.26 It might be said that this is inconsistent not with the law in other jurisdictions, but with the law in Scotland *relating to other defences*, where prior fault on the part of the accused *does* operate to rule out the defence. This is certainly the case in relation to intoxication[90] and automatism[91] and is probably also the case in relation to coercion[92] and necessity.[93]

---

[84] At 156.

[85] At 159.

[86] This still leaves open the question of the case where the victim responds *proportionately*, but the initial aggressor ceases his attack and communicates this to the victim, who continues to use physical force regardless. For a discussion of the principled arguments involved in denying the defence to an initial aggressor, see Ch.6 of F. Leverick, *Killing in Self-Defence* (2006).

[87] Canadian Criminal Code, s.35.

[88] *R. v Lawson and Forsythe* [1985] 18 A.Crim.R. 360 at 375, *per* McGarvie J.

[89] [2005] EWCA Crim 3377.

[89a] At [19]. Although *cf.* the Northern Ireland case of *R. v Browne* [1973] N.I. 96, where the defence of self-defence was denied to the appellant on the basis that "[t]he need to act must not have been created by conduct of the accused in the immediate context of the incident which was likely or was intended to give rise to that need" (at 106–107 *per* Lowry L.C.J.).

[89b] At [19].

[90] *Brennan v HM Advocate*, 1977 J.C. 38. See the discussion in Ch.8.

[91] *Finegan v Heywood*, 2000 J.C. 444. See the discussion in Ch.7.

[92] *Thomson v HM Advocate*, 1983 J.C. 69. See the discussion in Ch.5.

[93] *McNab v Guild*, 1989 J.C. 72. See the discussion in Ch.4.

There are two possible explanations for this apparent inconsistency. First, self-defence, unlike any other complete defence, involves causing harm to someone who was a direct threat to the accused. The availability of the defence derives from the conduct of the victim.[94] Unlike self-defence, the availability of defences such as automatism, coercion and intoxication does *not* depend on the conduct of the victim. If a victim is harmed under coercion or under the influence of intoxication, he is likely to be an innocent bystander, who posed no threat to the accused and made no contribution to the situation in which the accused finds himself. Under these circumstances, it would seem reasonable to require that the accused, in order to benefit from a complete defence, is himself free from fault in creating the situation.[95]

The second is that, unlike the justification defence of self-defence, and except in some limited circumstances,[96] defences such as coercion and intoxication operate as excuse defences. The basis of an excuse defence is that we accept that the accused has done something wrong but we do not blame him for doing so. There is a far more compelling argument for withholding the defence from someone who is partially blameworthy. The accused who voluntarily associates with a criminal gang or voluntarily becomes extremely intoxicated is not free from fault and it may be quite consistent that he is denied the benefit of an excuse defence.[97]

The defence of others

Scots law permits force to be used not only in self-defence, but also in the defence of others. This was made clear in *HM Advocate v Carson*,[98] where Lord Wheatley, in his charge to the jury, stated that where the accused had seen an attack on another person or had reasonable grounds for believing such an attack was occurring: **3.27**

> "... then according to the law of Scotland he was entitled to interfere and intervene in order to prevent such attack because, he would then be justified in killing in defence of his own life against imminent danger or of the lives of those connected with him. If a man sees another man being unlawfully attacked he is entitled to try and stop that unlawful attack, and if within reason he uses methods that otherwise would constitute an assault he will be excused because his intention is not to commit a criminal assault on the victim but to prevent the victim from carrying out an assault, an illegitimate assault, on another person."[99]

---

[94] The only other defence where this can be said to be the case is the partial defence of provocation. Although there is no Scottish authority on the issue, the Privy Council has held that the fact that provocation was self-induced does not necessarily rule out the defence. See *R. v Edwards* [1973] A.C. 648; *R. v Johnson* [1989] Crim. L.R. 738 and the discussion in Ch.10.

[95] Lowry L.C.J. makes something akin to this point in the Northern Irish case of *R. v Fitzpatrick* [1977] N.I. 20 at 30, which concerned the availability of duress.

[96] On coercion, see para.5.04.

[97] This is perhaps a less convincing argument. Even if it is accepted, it does not apply to the excuse form of self-defence (where the accused is mistaken about the need to use self-defensive force).

[98] 1964 S.L.T. 21.

[99] At 21. Despite Lord Wheatley's use of the phrase "the lives of those connected with him", it can probably be assumed that the defence of self-defence would be available if the accused defended a complete stranger. This is certainly the case in relation to the closely related defence of necessity: see *Lord Advocate's Reference (No. 1 of 2000)*, 2001 J.C. 143 at [44]. See also *Bennett, Petitioner*, Court of Session, January 11, 2005, unreported, at [2].

Where the accused acts in the defence of others, the rules governing the defence are the same as those governing self-defence. The one exception is that the accused is not required to take any reasonable opportunity to escape. This would make little sense where he acted to defend someone other than himself, as it would mean he would no longer be able to prevent the attack.[1]

[1] See *Fitzpatrick v HM Advocate*, 1992 S.L.T. 796, where the accused's conviction for assault was quashed on the basis that the presiding sheriff had directed the jury that, in order to benefit from the defence of self-defence, the accused was required to have no means of running away or otherwise avoiding the threat. As the accused was acting in defence of both himself *and his brother*, this direction was incorrect, as it failed to distinguish between someone defending himself and someone defending a third party.

CHAPTER 4

NECESSITY

INTRODUCTION

4.01 The defence of necessity is a plea by the accused that he broke the law on the basis that it was the least harmful of two (or more) alternative courses of action.[1] It is a defence that has tended to be accepted with a great deal of caution on the part of the criminal courts and Scots law is no exception.[2]

Until 1997 there was no clear statement from the appeal court confirming the existence of the necessity defence.[3] This is perhaps not surprising, given that Hume was openly hostile towards the defence and argued strongly against its recognition.[4] Successful pleas of necessity are rare[5] and the parameters of the defence have been kept within tight bounds in Scotland, more so than in other jurisdictions.[6]

---

[1] Or, if the excuse form of the defence is recognised, that the choice he made was a reasonable one in the circumstances that he faced (see para.4.03). The concern of this chapter is with the common law defence of necessity. It excludes the various statutory provisions that are similar in nature to the common law defence (see Gordon, para.13.09, fn.20).

[2] For discussion of the issues raised by the defence, see E.B. Arnolds and N.F. Garland, "The defence of necessity in criminal law: the right to choose the lesser evil" (1974) 65 *Journal of Criminal Law and Criminology* 289–301; M.D. Bayles, "Reconceptualising necessity and duress" (1987) 33 *Wayne Law Review* 1191–1220; S. Gardner, "Instrumentalism and necessity" (1986) 6 O.J.L.S. 431–438; D. Klimchuk, "Necessity, deterrence and standing" (2002) 8 *Legal Theory* 339–358; J.M. Paley, "Compulsion, fear and the doctrine of necessity" (1971) *Acta Juridica* 205–247; G. Williams, "The defence of necessity" (1953) 6 *Current Legal Problems* 216–235.

[3] It was finally recognised in *Moss v Howdle*, 1997 J.C. 123.

[4] See para.4.04.

[5] To date, the only *reported* Scottish case in which it has been successful remains *Tudhope v Grubb*, 1983 S.C.C.R. 350, a case where the accused was acquitted in the sheriff court. To this one might add *HM Advocate v Zelter*, the case that led to the *Lord Advocate's Reference (No. 1 of 2000)*, 2001 J.C. 143. The three accused were acquitted in the sheriff court of charges of malicious mischief, after claiming the necessity defence, but the Lord Advocate referred the point of law to the High Court for consideration. *Zelter* is unreported, but see the *Lord Advocate's Reference (No. 1 of 2000)*, 2001 J.C. 143. Another example of an unreported case in which the defence appears to have been successful is *Procurator Fiscal v Hughes*, Perth Sheriff Court, June 4, 1998. See the *Scotsman*, "Detective forced to take wheel in fog is cleared of drink driving", June 5, 1998. Here, the accused's girlfriend was driving a car on a motorway in which the accused was a passenger. Thick fog began to descend, which caused her to panic and stop the car on the hard shoulder. The accused took over driving, despite having been drinking, and drove for a short time before pulling over at the first service station. The presiding sheriff appears to have accepted his defence of necessity in acquitting him of a charge of driving with excess alcohol.

[6] See paras 4.12 *et seq.* on the immediacy of danger and paras 4.08 *et seq.* on the requirement for a threat of death or great bodily harm.

Concerns have been raised that the defence is open to abuse and could permit individuals to break the law on the basis that it conflicted with what they perceived as a higher social value, regardless of whether or not their perceptions were shared by the legal system or society as a whole.[7] It would be a harsh system of criminal law, however, that did not provide for some sort of necessity defence[8] and abuse can largely be prevented by placing tight restrictions on the conditions in which it can be pled.

Theoretical Basis

Distinguishing necessity from other conceptually similar defences

4.02 The gist of a plea of necessity is that the accused avoids harm by engaging in criminal wrongdoing. The harm avoided may be man-made or may be one arising from natural causes. While necessity has much in common conceptually with self-defence and coercion, it can be distinguished from both.[9]

The distinction between necessity and self-defence has already been discussed in detail in Ch.3.[10] Necessity can be distinguished from coercion on the basis that, whereas coercion involves avoiding harm by *complying with the demands* of a threatener, the nature of the wrong undertaken in necessity is not specified by a threatener, but is determined (albeit reluctantly) by the accused himself.[11]

Despite the conceptual distinctions that can be made between the three defences, the rules governing their operation in practice have much in common. This is especially so in relation to necessity and coercion, with

---

[7] See A. Norrie, *Crime, Reason and History: A Critical Introduction to Criminal Law* (2nd edn, 2001), p.160; F.A. Allen, *The Habits of Legality: Criminal Justice and the Rule of Law* (1996), p.22; *London Borough of Southwark v Williams* [1971] Ch. 734 at 744, *per* Lord Denning, and at 746, *per* Lord Edmund Davis; *Perka v The Queen* [1984] 2 S.C.R. 232 at [32], *per* Dickson J.

[8] See *R. v Kitson* (1955) 39 Cr.App.R. 66 for a case that illustrates the unfairness of denying the defence. Here, the defendant had been drinking and had fallen asleep in a car being driven (or so he thought) by his brother-in-law. When he awoke, it was to discover that there was no longer anyone else in the car which, by this time, was rolling down a hill in the rain. Having decided that the handbrake would prove ineffective in the slippery conditions, he attempted to control the car by steering it onto a grass verge, where it came to a halt. He was convicted of driving under the influence of excess alcohol and was sentenced to six months' imprisonment.

[9] For an argument that coercion, necessity and self-defence should be brought together under a single unified defence, see C.M.V. Clarkson, "Necessary action: a new defence" [2004] Crim. L.R. 81–95. For detailed discussion and criticism, see para.3.03.

[10] See para.3.02.

[11] P. Westen and J. Mangiafico, "The criminal defense of duress: a justification not an excuse and why it matters" (2003) 6 *Buffalo Criminal Law Review* 833–950 at p.846. It has sometimes been suggested that the distinction between necessity and coercion is that coercion involves avoiding harm from a human source (the threatener) and necessity involves avoiding harm from a non-human source. See, e.g. Forensis, "The excuse of necessity in Scots law" (1985) 30 J.L.S.S. 151–154 at p.152; P.R. Glazebrook, "The necessity plea in English law" [1972] C.L.J. 87–119 at p.88; the Law Reform Commission for Ireland, *Consultation Paper on Duress and Necessity* (LRC CP 39-2006, 2006) at para.1.06. This was also the approach taken by the House of Lords in *R. v Hasan* [2005] UKHL 22 (at [18] *per* Lord Bingham). While this may sometimes be true, it is not a defining feature of necessity that it involves avoiding harm from a non-human source. A plea of necessity might involve the accused driving under the influence of excess alcohol in order to avoid an immediate threat of violence from another individual (as was the case in *Tudhope v Grubb*, 1983 S.C.C.R. 350 and *Ruxton v Lang*, 1998 S.C.C.R. 1).

the appeal court stating that the rules governing the two defences should be the same:

> "... we consider that, where an accused commits a crime in an endeavour to escape an immediate danger of death or great bodily harm, it makes no difference to the possible availability of any defence that the danger arises from some contingency such as a natural disaster or illness rather than from the deliberate threats of another".[12]

The theoretical basis of the defence

It has sometimes been argued that necessity can operate only as a justification defence, on the basis that the accused has acted acceptably by choosing the lesser of two evils.[13] Others have argued that it can only operate as an excuse, on the basis that the accused engaged in a wrongful act while under extreme pressure.[14] **4.03**

The view is taken here that necessity can potentially operate either as a justification or as an excuse depending on the circumstances in which it is pled.[15] The justification form of the defence operates where there is a disparity between the two harms in question. The accused who breaks into the house of a neighbour in order to obtain a fire extinguisher and prevent the spread of a house fire is surely justified in doing so, rather than excused for undertaking a wrongful act.[16] In the cases where necessity operates as a justification, the basis of the defence is that the accused was justified in acting because, in choosing the lesser of two possible harms, the choice he made was an acceptable one.[17]

The excuse form of the defence operates where the harms involved are similar in nature. The accused who injures a pedestrian in an attempt to drive away from a threat of violence does not do so on the basis that his conduct was acceptable. Rather he claims an excuse on the basis that, although what he did was wrong, there is a reason why he should not be blamed for his act.[18]

The basis upon which necessity should excuse is essentially the same as that for coercion: in a situation of extreme pressure caused by fear for his

---

[12] *Moss v Howdle*, 1997 J.C. 123 at 128. English law goes further and views what Scots law would term necessity and coercion as simply two species of duress governed by the same rules: duress of circumstances (necessity) and duress by threats (coercion) (see para.4.07).

[13] E.B. Arnolds and N.F. Garland, "The defence of necessity in criminal law: the right to choose the lesser evil" (1974) 65 *Journal of Criminal Law and Criminology* 289–301 at p.290; A. Brudner, "A theory of necessity" (1987) 7 O.J.L.S. 339–368 at p.352; Robinson, *Criminal Law Defenses*, §124.

[14] See the Canadian Supreme Court case of *Perka v The Queen* [1984] 2 S.C.R. 232 at [31]–[34]. For comment, see C. Wells, "Necessity and the common law" (1985) 5 O.J.L.S. 471–475.

[15] On this, see P.A. Alldridge, "The coherence of defences" [1983] Crim. L.R. 665–672 at p.667; M.D. Bayles, "Reconceptualising necessity and duress" (1987) 33 *Wayne Law Review* 1191–1220 at p.1192; Fletcher, *Rethinking Criminal Law*, at p.774 and p.818. *Cf.* Norrie, above, fn.7, at p.154.

[16] The example is taken from the Casebook, para.7.71, where it is used to argue that restricting the defence to cases where death or serious bodily harm is threatened (as Scots law does: see below, para.4.08) is contrary to principle.

[17] For an alternative argument for recognising necessity as a justification, see S.M. Bauer and P.J. Eckerstrom, "The state made me do it: the applicability of the necessity defence to civil disobedience" (1987) 39 *Stanford Law Review* 1173–1200 at p.1174.

[18] Whether or not this would be accepted as an excuse depends on the legal system in question.

life or bodily integrity (or that of another person),[19] the accused's choice was a reasonable one in the circumstances.[20]

Whether in practice necessity operates as a justification, an excuse, or both, depends on the circumstances in which any particular legal system allows the defence.[21] It might be concluded from the language used by the appeal court[22] and from the conditions attached to the defence[23] that necessity operates as an excuse in Scots law, but it is difficult to draw any firm conclusions on this.[24] Unlike the Canadian Supreme Court, which has considered the theoretical basis for the necessity defence in some detail,[25] the Scottish courts have shown no inclination to engage in such discussions.

Historical Development

Necessity under Hume

4.04 Whereas the defence of coercion is recognised by Hume,[26] albeit with strict conditions attached, the defence of necessity finds no such acceptance, with Hume expressing his strong disapproval of the plea. He begins his account of the defence by noting a form of the plea of necessity that appears in *Regiam Majestatem* termed "burthynsack". Under the law of burthynsack, a man goes unpunished for the theft of a sheep or calf or, alternatively, as much meat as he can carry on his back, if he is compelled to do so by hunger.[27]

Hume is dismissive of the plea, viewing it not as a complete defence but as a mitigating factor whereby the thief is spared from what would otherwise be capital punishment.[28] Hume's views on burthynsack set the tone for his views on the defence of necessity in general. He disapproves of any defence based on "the pressure of extreme want",[29] primarily on the basis that it would be difficult to distinguish between genuine cases of necessity and cases where the accused was undeserving of the defence.[30]

---

[19] Only threats to life or of serious bodily harm can ground the defence in Scots law. See para.4.08.

[20] See paras 5.05–5.06.

[21] The German Penal Code, for example, clearly recognises both forms of the defence (see para.4.20), whereas the Canadian Supreme Court has made it clear that only the excuse form is recognised (see *Perka v The Queen* [1984] 2 S.C.R. 232).

[22] The only reported cases where any reference has been made to the theoretical basis for the defence are *Tudhope v Grubb*, 1983 S.C.C.R. 350, where the sheriff referred to the accused's will being "overborne by threats" (at 352), and *Moss v Howdle*, 1997 J.C. 123, where the appeal court quoted a passage from *Perka v The Queen* [1984] 2 S.C.R. 232, where it was stated that the defence applies when the accused "has control over his actions to the extent of being physically capable of abstaining from the act. Realistically, however, this act is not a 'voluntary' one. His 'choice' to break the law is not true choice at all; it is remorsefully compelled by normal human instincts" (at 129).

[23] Especially the requirement for a qualifying level of danger: that of death or great bodily harm (see para.4.08).

[24] And, indeed, the importance of doing so is arguably overstated.

[25] In *Perka v The Queen* [1984] 2 S.C.R. 232.

[26] Under the name "compulsion". See paras 5.07 *et seq.*

[27] Hume, i, 55. See also Mackenzie, 98; Bayne, 122–123; Forbes, 148.

[28] Hume, i, 55.

[29] *ibid.*

[30] *ibid.*

Hume wrote specifically in the context of theft or other offences against property. Thus it might be argued that he left open the possibility of necessity being a valid defence to other types of offence.[31]

The pre-*Moss v Howdle* case law

It was only relatively recently, in *Moss v Howdle*,[32] that the appeal court confirmed the existence of the necessity defence.[33] The defence was not, however, entirely dormant prior to 1997. Necessity was actually pled successfully in the sheriff court in *Tudhope v Grubb*.[34] Here, the accused had left his car with a mechanic whom he had paid in advance to undertake repairs. After six months, the repairs had not been carried out and the accused, after consuming six pints of beer, went to see the mechanic in an attempt to retrieve it. On doing so, he was attacked by the mechanic and his friends. The accused, in a bid to escape, got into his car and attempted to start it.[35] He was charged with attempting to drive with excess alcohol in his blood, but was acquitted by the presiding sheriff on the basis of necessity. **4.05**

In arguing for an acquittal, the defence relied on statements made by Anderson and Hume on the defence of coercion, rather than necessity, which Hume rejected. The presiding sheriff relied on these authorities as well as *Docherty v HM Advocate*,[36] another coercion case. The sheriff described the accused as "the innocent victim of an unprovoked and violent assault" who "attempted to drive away ... in an attempt to save himself from further injury". He concluded that "[i]n these circumstances, I found the defence of necessity established."[37]

---

[31] In modern day case law, necessity has most commonly been pled not in relation to theft, but in relation to road traffic offences. See *Tudhope v Grubb*, 1983 S.C.CR. 350 (attempting to drive with excess alcohol); *McNab v Guild*, 1989 J.C. 72 (reckless driving); *McLeod v MacDougal*, 1989 S.L.T. 151 (driving with excess alcohol); *Morrison v Valentine*, 1991 S.L.T. 413 (reckless driving); *Moss v Howdle*, 1997 J.C. 123 (speeding); *Ruxton v Lang*, 1998 S.C.C.R. 1 (driving with excess alcohol); *Dolan v McLeod*, 1999 J.C. 32 (driving with excess alcohol); *Dawson v Dickson*, 1999 J.C. 315 (driving with excess alcohol and careless driving). One exception to this is the case from which the *Lord Advocate's Reference (No. 1 of 2000)*, 2001 J.C. 143 stemmed, which involved malicious mischief.

[32] 1997 J.C. 123.

[33] Gordon (at para.13.21) suggests that the lack of recognition given to the defence prior to 1997 sometimes led to a harsh outcome. For a particularly compelling example, see *Watson v Hamilton*, 1988 S.L.T. 316. Here, the accused pled guilty to driving with excess alcohol in his blood and was sentenced to a period of disqualification. He had been a guest at a party and was staying overnight when one of the other guests, a pregnant woman, started bleeding and became anxious that she was about to have a miscarriage. The accused and another guest (who did not have a car) attempted to phone an ambulance, but there was no telephone in the flat and the nearest and next nearest public telephone boxes were out of order. An attempt to stop a passing taxi to ask the driver to telephone for assistance also failed. Only then did the accused decide to drive the increasingly distressed woman to hospital, knowing that he was likely to be driving under the influence of excess alcohol, but deciding he was justified because of medical emergency.

[34] 1983 S.C.C.R. 350. For comment, see T. Jones, "The defence of necessity in Scots law", 1989 S.L.T. (News) 253–256; M. Wasik, "A case of necessity" [1984] Crim. L.R. 544–548.

[35] In the event, he was unable to do so because the battery was flat.

[36] (1976) S.C.C.R. Supp. 146.

[37] *Tudhope v Grubb*, 1983 S.C.C.R. 350 at 352.

Tudhope v Grubb led at least one commentator[38] to state that Scots law recognised a defence of necessity at a time when English law did not.[39] This was perhaps a little premature, given that, following *Tudhope v Grubb*, there were a number of occasions on which the appeal court had the opportunity to confirm the existence of the defence, but chose not to do so. In *McNab v Guild*,[40] for example, the accused appealed against his conviction for reckless driving on the basis that the presiding sheriff had wrongly rejected his defence of necessity. On appeal, the appeal court chose not to remark upon the availability of the defence, concluding that it was not made out on the facts. Similar opportunities for the appeal court to recognise the defence occurred in *McLeod v MacDougall*,[41] *Morrison v Valentine*,[42] *Hamilton v Neizer*[43] and *Downie v HM Advocate*.[44] In all of these cases, as in *McNab v Guild*, the defence was rejected on the facts.

Moss v Howdle and beyond

4.06 In *Moss v Howdle*[45] the appeal court finally ruled that the defence of necessity existed in Scots law. By this time, Scotland was lagging behind other common law jurisdictions. In English law, a form of the defence was recognised by the Court of Appeal in *R. v Willer* in 1986,[46] albeit under the guise of duress of circumstances. In Canada, the defence was recognised by the Supreme Court in *Perka v The Queen*[47] in 1984.

In *Moss v Howdle*, the appellant had been convicted of speeding, after driving at over 100 mph on the motorway with a passenger he believed to be dangerously ill. This belief was formed on the basis of his passenger's shouts of pain and, instead of pulling over onto the hard shoulder in an attempt to establish what was wrong, the appellant drove at speed to the nearest motorway service station. On arrival, his passenger was able to tell him he was suffering only from cramp. An attempt to plead the defence of necessity at his trial was rejected by the presiding sheriff.

The appeal court drew heavily on *Thomson v HM Advocate*,[48] a case dealing with the related defence of coercion.[49] The court recognised the defence of necessity, stating that they could see no reason to exclude it when the defence of coercion was accepted.[50]

---

[38] Wasik, above, fn.34, at p.544.

[39] It was not until *R. v Willer* (1986) 83 Cr.App.R. 225 that the equivalent defence of duress of circumstances was recognised by the Court of Appeal.

[40] 1989 J.C. 72.

[41] 1989 S.L.T. 151.

[42] 1991 S.L.T. 413.

[43] 1993 J.C. 63.

[44] 1984 S.C.C.R. 365.

[45] 1997 J.C. 123. For comment, see M. Christie, "The mother of invention? *Moss v Howdle*" (1998) 1 Edin. L.R. 479–488; P.W. Ferguson, "Necessity and coercion in criminal law", 1997 S.L.T. (News) 127–130.

[46] (1986) 83 Cr.App.R. 225.

[47] [1984] 2 S.C.R. 232.

[48] 1983 J.C. 69.

[49] Perhaps unsurprisingly, no mention was made of Hume's rejection of the defence of necessity.

[50] *Moss v Howdle*, 1997 J.C. 123 at 128. In the event, the appeal was rejected on the basis that the appellant had a reasonable alternative course of action available to him. On this, see para.4.15.

Since *Moss v Howdle*, the defence of necessity has been given detailed consideration in *Dawson v Dickson*[51] and *Lord Advocate's Reference (No. 1 of 2000)*[52] and has received superficial treatment in *Dolan v McLeod*.[53] Reference can be also made to the parallel body of law on coercion given that, in *Moss v Howdle*, the appeal court stated that the same considerations should govern the two defences.[54]

English law and duress of circumstances

The paucity of Scottish authority on necessity, coupled with the appeal court's tendency to draw upon the parallel body of English case law on duress of circumstances,[55] means it is worth considering the development of English law. **4.07**

The duress of circumstances terminology first entered English law in *R. v Willer*.[56] At the time, it was unclear whether or not English law recognised a general necessity defence,[57] but it had for some time recognised a defence of duress.[58] In *Willer*, the defendant had driven on the pavement to escape from a gang of young men who were threatening him with violence. He attempted to plead necessity to a charge of reckless driving but the presiding judge refused to leave the defence to the jury. The Court of Appeal quashed the conviction, but found no reason to speculate on the existence of the defence of necessity, given that they considered the appropriate defence in this case to be one of duress.[59] They concluded that it should have been left to the jury to say whether the appellant "was wholly driven by the force of circumstance into doing what he did and did not drive the car otherwise than under that form of compulsion i.e. under duress".[60]

At no point in *Willer* did the Court use the phrase "duress of circumstances" (although they did use the terms "duress" and

[51] 1999 J.C. 315. In the Scots Law Times report of the case (1999 S.L.T. 1328), it is reported under the alternative name of *Dawson v McKay*. This appears to have stemmed from a mistake in recording the name of the procurator fiscal involved.

[52] 2001 J.C. 143. For comment, see S.C. Neff, "Idealism on appeal: the *Lord Advocate's Reference* on British nuclear policy" (2001) 5 Edin. L.R. 355–360; R.S. Shiels, "The defence of necessity and citizen interveners", 2002 S.L.T. (News) 47–49; C.J. Moxley, "The usefulness of the United Kingdom's policy of nuclear deterrence—the invalidity of the Scots High Court's decision in *Zelter*", 2001 Jur. Rev. 317–343.

[53] 1999 J.C. 32. One further sheriff court case involving necessity has been reported since *Moss v Howdle* but the defence was rejected and the case raises no significant issues (*Ruxton v Lang*, 1998 S.C.C.R. 1).

[54] *Moss v Howdle*, 1997 J.C. 123 at 127–128. For a detailed account of the coercion defence, see Ch.5.

[55] See *Moss v Howdle*, 1997 J.C. 123 at 125, 127; *Lord Advocate's Reference (No. 1 of 2000)*, 2001 J.C. 143 at [42].

[56] (1986) 83 Cr.App.R. 225. See T. Rees and J.C. Smith, "Official secrets: defence of duress of necessity" [2001] Crim. L.R. 986–990 at p.988.

[57] Compare P.R. Glazebrook, "The necessity plea in English law" [1972] C.L.J. 87–119 at p.88 with G. Williams, "The defence of necessity" (1953) 6 *Current Legal Problems* 216–235 at p.224.

[58] *R. v Hudson and Taylor* [1971] 2 Q.B. 202.

[59] At 227. This is a puzzling conclusion. Conceptually this does not have the gist of a duress defence (see para. 5.02).

[60] *R. v Willer* (1986) 83 Cr.App.R. 225 at 227.

"circumstance" separately) and it was only in the subsequent case of *R. v Conway*[61] that this terminology was first used.[62]

In *R. v Martin*[63] the principles governing duress of circumstances were summarised. The defence is only available "if, from an objective standpoint, the accused can be said to be acting reasonably and proportionately in order to avoid a threat of death or serious injury".[64] If that preliminary test is satisfied, the jury or judge should determine two further questions:

> "... first, was the accused, or may he have been, impelled to act as he did because as a result of what he reasonably believed to be the situation he had good cause to fear that otherwise death or serious physical injury would result; second, if so, would a sober person of reasonable firmness, sharing the characteristics of the accused, have responded to that situation by acting as the accused acted?"[65]

It is difficult to say whether or not English law recognises a separate defence of necessity in addition to the defence of duress of circumstances. In *Re: A (Children)*,[66] a case involving the separation of conjoined twins which was certain to lead to the death of one of the babies, at least one of the Court of Appeal judges, Brooke L.J., analysed the case in terms of necessity. He regarded this as a separate defence to that of duress of circumstances; in his view, necessity is a justification defence involving the choice of a lesser harm to prevent a greater harm whereas duress of circumstances is an excuse defence that applies where the defendant makes a reasonable choice under extreme pressure.[67] Other English cases have made no such distinction, either using the terms duress of circumstances and necessity interchangeably[68] or holding that necessity is an overarching concept of which duress of circumstances and duress by threats are two possible variants.[69]

---

[61] (1989) 88 Cr.App.R. 159.

[62] At 163.

[63] (1989) 88 Cr.App.R. 343. For comment on *Willer*, *Conway* and *Martin*, see D.W. Elliott, "Necessity, duress and self-defence" [1989] Crim. L.R. 611–621.

[64] At 346.

[65] At 346. See also *R. v Pommell* [1995] 2 Cr.App.R. 607; *R. v Baker* [1997] Crim. L.R. 497; *R. v Backshall* [1999] 1 Cr.App.R. 35; *R. v Abdul-Hussain* [1999] Crim. L.R. 570; *DPP v Tomkinson* [2001] EWHC Admin 182; *DPP v Lloyd* [2001] EWHC Admin 465; *R. v Shayler* [2001] EWCA Crim 1977; *R. v Safi* [2003] EWCA Crim 1809; *R. v Quayle* [2005] EWCA Crim 1415.

[66] [2001] 2 W.L.R. 480. The case is discussed in paras 4.23 *et seq.*

[67] At 569 *per* Brooke L.J. If he is correct in his analysis, this has important implications for English law, because the rules governing the two defences are not the same. Duress of circumstances requires a qualifying level of threat of death or serious injury (*R. v Martin* (1989) 88 Cr.App.R. 343 at 346). Necessity requires only that "the evil inflicted must not be disproportionate to the evil avoided" (*Re: A*, at 573 *per* Brooke L.J.).

[68] *R. v Rodger and Rose* [1998] 1 Cr.App.R. 143 at 145; *R. v Backshall* [1999] 1 Cr.App.R. 35 at 42; *Jones and Milling, Olditch and Pritchard, and Richards v Gloucestershire Crown Prosecution Service* [2004] EWCA Crim 1981 at [48]–[55]; *R. v Hasan* [2005] UKHL 22 at [22], *per* Lord Bingham.

[69] *R. v Cairns* [2000] R.T.R. 15 at 20; *R. v Safi* [2003] EWCA Crim 1809, at [24]. For a case that illustrates the confusion that can be caused by the terminology, see *R. v Bronson* [2001] EWCA Crim 1322.

Requirements of the Plea

Threat of death or serious bodily harm

4.08 The first requirement of the plea of necessity is that the accused must have "acted in the face of an immediate danger of death or great bodily harm".[70] The court in *Moss v Howdle* considered whether a lesser threat could ever suffice to ground the plea and concluded it could not.[71]

Critics have suggested that the defence should not be limited to cases where the accused faced a threat as extreme as serious bodily injury or death.[72] The restriction may make sense so long as necessity is understood as an excuse.[73] It is less obvious that the defence in its justification form should be limited to threats of death or serious bodily harm.[74] We would surely want someone to benefit from the defence if that person broke into a neighbour's house to obtain a fire extinguisher and put out a fire raging in an empty but valuable building.[75] If one believes in the conduct-guiding function of the law,[76] it seems foolish to rule out the defence in these circumstances.[77]

The high threshold level of threat effectively stemmed from the fact that, in *Moss v Howdle*, the appeal court linked the development of the necessity defence with coercion, where the rule was already well-established.[78]

The obvious alternative to having a minimum level of threat of death or serious bodily injury is to have some sort of balance of harms or proportionality test.[79] This is the approach taken in the Draft Criminal

70 *Moss v Howdle*, 1997 J.C. 123 at 126. See also *Lord Advocate's Reference (No. 1 of 2000)*, 2001 J.C. 143 at [42] and the *obiter* comments in *McNab v Guild*, 1989 J.C. 72 at 76; *Morrison v Valentine*, 1991 S.L.T. 413 at 414; and *Ruxton v Lang*, 1998 S.C.C.R. 1 at 5.

71 *Moss v Howdle*, 1997 J.C. 123 at 126.

72 M. Christie, "The mother of invention? *Moss v Howdle*" (1998) 1 Edin. L.R. 479–488 at p.487; P.R. Ferguson, "Codifying criminal law (1): a critique of Scots common law" [2004] Crim. L.R. 49–59 at p.56. See also criticism of the same condition as it applies to the defence of coercion (at para.5.12).

73 Indeed, it may be that the requirement for a certain level of threat before the defence can be considered, as opposed to a simple balance of harms test, is a clear distinguishing feature between the justification and excuse forms of the defence. There is some support for this view in English law: see *Cichon v DPP* [1994] Crim. L.R. 918.

74 E.B. Arnolds and N.F. Garland, "The defence of necessity in criminal law: the right to choose the lesser evil" (1974) 65 *Journal of Criminal Law and Criminology* 289–301 at p.290; D.W. Elliott, "Necessity, duress and self-defence" [1989] Crim. L.R. 611–621 at p.616.

75 Casebook, para.7.71. Gordon (para.13.19) points out that whereas English law also restricts the defence to threats of death or serious bodily injury, the practical consequences of the restriction are less severe than they are in Scotland, because action taken in necessity to prevent damage to property would generally be covered by English statutory provisions.

76 *cf.* P.H. Robinson and J.H. Darley, "Does criminal law deter? A behavioural science investigation" (2004) 24 O.J.L.S. 173–205.

77 H. Packer, *The Limits of the Criminal Sanction* (1968), p.114.

78 Hume, i, 53 and *Thomson v HM Advocate*, 1983 J.C. 69. See paras 5.11 *et seq.* for discussion. A similar result occurred in English law where the linking of duress of circumstances with duress by threats has meant that the minimum requirement for a threat of death or serious bodily harm applies to both. See *R. v Conway* (1989) 88 Cr.App.R. 159 at 164; *R. v Martin* (1989) 88 Cr.App.R. 343 at 346; *R. v Abdul-Hussain* [1999] Crim. L.R. 570 at 570. *Cf.* the *obiter* comment of Brooke L.J. in *DPP v Rogers* [1998] Crim. L.R. 202.

79 These are not *necessarily* alternatives. The *Lord Advocate's Reference* seems to suggest that there is a proportionality test in Scots law *as well as* a minimum threat level of death or serious bodily harm (see para.4.09).

Code, which requires only that conduct must be "immediately necessary and reasonable in order to prevent a greater harm".[80] Although the Commentary to the Code does not specifically state as much, this would allow action taken to prevent serious damage to property.[81] This is also the approach taken in Canadian law,[82] although it requires a threat of death or serious bodily injury in relation to the defence of compulsion (coercion).[83]

A proportionality test is not itself without difficulties. While some comparisons of harms will be relatively straightforward,[84] others will be less so, especially where they involve conflicts between different types of value, such as liberty, bodily integrity or property.[85]

Does Scots law contain a proportionality requirement?

4.09 The *Lord Advocate's Reference* raises the question of whether, in addition to a requirement that the harm to be avoided is death or serious bodily injury, Scots law also contains a proportionality test. In the *Reference*, the appeal court held that:

> "As a matter of general principle it appears clear that the conduct carried out must be broadly proportional to the risk. That will always be a question of fact to be determined in the circumstances of the particular case."[86]

It might be argued that, in the light of the requirement for a threat of death or serious bodily injury (and assuming that necessity is not available as a defence to murder or culpable homicide),[87] the proportionality test is redundant. It is possible, however, to think of some situations in which the proportionality test would not be satisfied, even if a threat of death or serious injury had been made.[88]

---

[80] s.24(2)(a).

[81] See P.R. Ferguson, "Codifying criminal law (2): the Scots and English draft codes compared" [2004] Crim. L.R. 105–119 at p.113.

[82] *Perka v The Queen* [1984] 2 S.C.R. 232 at [43]; *R. v Latimer*, 2001 S.C.C. 1 at [31]; *R. v Kerr*, 2004 S.C.C. 44 at [94], *per* LeBel J.

[83] See para.5.12.

[84] It might be said, for example, that the value of life (and possibly that of bodily integrity) will always outweigh the value of property, although not everyone would agree. See A.P. Simester and G.R. Sullivan, *Criminal Law: Theory and Doctrine* (2nd edn, 2004), at p.626; R.J. Muth and A.L. Blumstein, "The use of deadly force in the protection of property under the Model Penal Code" (1959) 59 *Columbia Law Review* 1212–1232 at p.1225.

[85] J.T. Parry, "The virtue of necessity: reshaping culpability and the rule of law" (1999) 36 *Houston Law Review* 397–469 at pp.415–417; G. Williams, "The defence of necessity" (1953) 6 *Current Legal Problems* 216–235 at p.234. There is also the difficulty of identifying the specific test to be applied. The law could require variously that the harm caused does not outweigh the harm avoided; that the harm avoided outweighs that caused; or that the harm avoided *clearly* outweighs that caused.

[86] *Lord Advocate's Reference (No. 1 of 2000)*, 2001 J.C. 143 at [47].

[87] The point is undecided in Scots law. See para.4.23.

[88] Depending on how the proportionality test is phrased, the scenario where the accused inflicts serious bodily injury on one or more victims in order to prevent serious bodily injury to himself could be one example.

Must the threat be directed specifically towards the accused?

4.10 If necessity is understood as a justification, there seems no reason in principle why action taken to prevent harm befalling even complete strangers should not be permitted, provided a general balance of harms test is satisfied.[89] As the appeal court stated in the *Lord Advocate's Reference*:

> "In our opinion there is no acceptable basis for restricting rescue to the protection of persons already known to and having a relationship with the rescuer at the moment of response to the other's danger. No doubt a close relationship may enter into the issue of necessity in some respects. Proportionality of response may be a function of relationship, for example. A parent's reaction to apprehended danger to a child might reasonably be more extreme than that of an unrelated bystander. But the existence of a prior relationship as a precondition of necessity has nothing to commend it, in our view."[90]

This view may be contrasted with the position in English law, where the defence of duress of circumstances has been restricted to the defendant who acts to prevent harm to those for whom he "has responsibility"[91] or "reasonably regarded himself as being responsible".[92]

Must the threat of harm come from a source extraneous to the accused?

4.11 Another issue relating to the nature of the threat is whether or not the harm threatened must stem from a source extraneous to the accused. The point has never arisen for decision in a Scottish case, but is illustrated by the English case of *R. v Rodger and Rose*.[93] Here, both appellants were serving a sentence of life imprisonment and were informed that their tariffs were to be substantially increased. Upon hearing the news, they escaped from prison, claiming the defence of duress of circumstances on the ground that they would have committed suicide if they had not escaped (a fact that was conceded for the purposes of the appeal). The defence was withdrawn from the jury on the basis that any threat posed did not stem from an extraneous source.

On the face of it, this seems a case satisfying all the conditions of a successful defence of duress of circumstances: the defendants acted as they did because they reasonably believed that otherwise death would

---

[89] M.D. Bayles, "Reconceptualising necessity and duress" (1987) 33 *Wayne Law Review* 1191–1220 at p.1201. Where the balance of harms test is not satisfied (because the harms are approximately equivalent in nature) and the accused is relying on the excuse form of the defence, the position is less clear. There seems little doubt that the imminent prospect of harm to close family members or loved ones could place the accused in a state of fear sufficient that it would not be reasonable to expect him to refrain from acting. Whether someone could be equally terrorised by the prospect of harm befalling a complete stranger is less immediately obvious, but is surely possible, especially if the harm was particularly serious.

[90] *Lord Advocate's Reference (No. 1 of 2000)*, 2001 J.C. 143 at [44]. See also *Moss v Howdle*, 1997 J.C. 123 at 129.

[91] *R. v Abdul-Hussain* [1999] Crim. L.R. 570, at 7 of the Lexis transcript of the case (this aspect of the case is not reported in the *Criminal Law Review*).

[92] *R. v Shayler* [2001] EWCA Crim 1977 at [63]. *Cf. Re: A (Children)* [2001] 2 W.L.R. 480.

[93] [1998] 1 Cr.App.R. 143.

result, and a sober person of reasonable firmness sharing their characteristics may well have responded to the situation in the same way.[94] The English Court of Appeal agreed with the trial judge, however, and ruled out the availability of the defence, stating that:

> "If allowed it could amount to a licence to commit crime dependent on the personal characteristics and vulnerability of the offender. As a matter of policy that is undesirable and in our view it is not the law and should not be the law."[95]

Thus, in English law, duress of circumstances is available only where the threat of harm stems from a source extraneous to the defendant.[96] The issue does not appear to have arisen in any other common law jurisdiction and it is assumed that if it did ever arise in Scotland, the appeal court would take the same approach as the English Court of Appeal.[97]

Immediacy of danger

4.12 The second requirement of the necessity defence is that the danger of death or great bodily harm must be an immediate one. This was made clear both in *Moss v Howdle*[98] and the *Lord Advocate's Reference*.[99]

The most common argument for requiring an immediate danger standard is to rule out the defence in circumstances where the accused had the opportunity to avoid the danger by taking some other, lawful, course of action. This is precisely the argument utilised by the appeal court in the *Lord Advocate's Reference*, who explain their insistence on the immediacy requirement as follows:

> "Unless the danger is immediate, in the ordinary sense of that word, there will at least be time to take a non-criminal course, as an alternative to destructive action. A danger which is threatened at a future time, as opposed to immediately impending, might be avoided by informing the owner of the property and so allowing that person to take action to avert the danger, or informing some responsible authority of the perceived need for intervention. That authority could then consider whether intervention was in its view necessary, and whether and how it could be carried out legally. If there is scope for legitimate intervention in the timescale set by the circumstances,

---

94 The conditions governing the defence of duress of circumstances, as set out in *R. v Martin* (1989) 88 Cr.App.R. 343.

95 *R. v Rodger and Rose* [1998] 1 Cr.App.R 143 at 147, *per* Sir Patrick Russell.

96 See *R. v Brown* [2003] EWCA Crim 2637, where the Court of Appeal relied on this limitation to rule out the availability of the defence to a defendant who cultivated cannabis for use in alleviating the symptoms of multiple sclerosis. See also *R. v Quayle* [2005] EWCA Crim 1415 at [73]–[75], a case involving similar facts where the same approach was taken (although here the defence was ruled out primarily on the basis that the legislature had already made a determination of values: see para.4.22 below).

97 The appeal court has been influenced by the English Court of Appeal in relation to other aspects of the necessity defence (see, e.g. para.4.19) and permitting such a defence would seem to be contrary to the generally objective approach taken to defences in Scots law (see, e.g. *Owens v HM Advocate*, 1946 J.C. 119).

98 1997 J.C. 123 at 126. See also *Ruxton v Lang*, 1998 S.C.C.R. 1 at 5.

99 *Lord Advocate's Reference (No. 1 of 2000)*, 2001 J.C. 143 at [37].

> it is difficult to see why the law should allow a third party to intervene by actions that would ordinarily be characterised as involving criminal conduct."[1]

The difficulty with this is that it cannot be assumed that because a danger is not immediate, it *can* necessarily be avoided in some other, lawful way. To illustrate this point, Paul Robinson uses the example of the ship's crew who discover a slow leak after leaving port. The captain of the ship unreasonably refuses to return to shore. The leak would not pose any danger to the integrity of the ship for at least two days but, Robinson argues, the crew are surely justified in mutiny because once the leak does start to threaten the seaworthiness of the ship, the crew will be too far from the shore to be able to do anything about it.[2] It might also be said that, if the purpose of the immediacy requirement is to prevent the accused from claiming the defence of necessity when he ignored a reasonable alternative (and lawful) course of action, then this is redundant in Scots law, as the absence of any reasonable alternative course of action is a separate requirement of the defence.[3]

It *might* be argued that an immediate danger standard is appropriate in relation to the excuse form of the defence of necessity. Here, the accused is arguing that under the extreme pressure of circumstances that he faced (and, perhaps, the fact that he had to make a split second decision in the face of immediate danger) his choice was a reasonable one.[4] In relation to the justification form of the defence, where the balance of harms is such that the harm avoided clearly outweighs the harm caused, for the reasons stated above, the requirement is surely redundant and has the potential to lead to unjust convictions. **4.13**

In requiring an immediate danger standard, Scotland is out of line with at least some other common law jurisdictions. English law does not contain an immediacy of harm requirement in relation to duress of circumstances, although it does require that the threat of harm be "imminent".[5] It seems, however, that the Court of Appeal does not regard this term as having the same meaning as the term "immediate".[6]

Conversely, Canadian law has retained an immediate danger standard (or at least something close to it), as illustrated by *R. v Latimer*,[7] where the Canadian Supreme Court held that, for the necessity defence to be

---

1 *Lord Advocate's Reference (No. 1 of 2000)*, 2001 J.C. 143 at [37].

2 Robinson, *Criminal Law Defenses*, §124(f).

3 See para.4.15. See also the argument made in favour of the immediacy standard by Fletcher (*Rethinking Criminal Law*, p.795) and the criticism made of Fletcher's argument by Robinson (*Criminal Law Defenses*, §124(f)).

4 Even here, however, the fact that the accused was under extreme pressure due to fear is not necessarily related to the fact that the danger he faced was immediate.

5 *R. v Abdul-Hussain* [1999] Crim. L.R. 570 at 570.

6 In *R. v Abdul-Hussain*, it was held that "the execution of the threat need not be immediately in prospect" and that the period of time which elapsed between the inception of the peril and the defendant's act "was a relevant but not determinative factor" (at 570). Interestingly enough, in the *Lord Advocate's Reference (No. 1 of 2000)*, 2001 J.C. 143, the appeal court use the terms imminent and immediate interchangeably (see, e.g. the court's reference to danger the accused "reasonably believed to be imminent" at [45]), but there is nothing in the *Reference* to suggest that the court is taking the same approach to imminence as the English Court of Appeal. There is some indication from very recent cases that the English courts are becoming more reluctant to recognise the defence in circumstances where the danger is not immediate: see *R. v Quayle* [2005] EWCA Crim 1415 at [79]; *R. v Hasan* [2005] UKHL 22 at [28], *per* Lord Bingham (on the related defence of duress by threats).

7 2001 S.C.C. 1.

made out, "disaster must be imminent, or harm unavoidable and near. It is not enough that the peril is foreseeable or likely; it must be on the verge of transpiring and virtually certain to occur".[8]

In relation to coercion, the appeal court has hinted that, were a case to arise in which the accused could not avoid a non-immediate harm, the immediacy requirement might be relaxed.[9] It is likely that the court would be equally flexible in relation to necessity, given that the requirement for immediacy was predicated on the assumption that a lack of immediacy would mean that alternative means of avoiding the danger could be undertaken.[10] It is also worth noting that the Draft Criminal Code has abandoned the immediate danger requirement, stating instead that acts are justified by necessity if "they are immediately necessary and reasonable in order to prevent a greater harm".[11]

Does the accused have to be present at the place of the danger?

4.14 While Scots law has taken a strict stance on the immediacy requirement, it does recognise that "the defence of necessity could be available where the place and person or persons under threat from the apprehended danger were remote from the locus of the [offence]."[12]

Existence of reasonable alternative courses of action

4.15 A further condition of the defence of necessity is that there must be no reasonable alternative (and lawful) course of action open to the accused. In the *Lord Advocate's Reference*, the appeal court concluded that:

> "... the defence is available only where there is so pressing a need for action that the actor has no alternative but to do what would otherwise be a criminal act under the compulsion of the circumstances in which he finds himself".[13]

This passage suggests that the defence is defeated if the accused fails to take any alternative legal course of action available, regardless of the possible dangers associated with this. *Moss v Howdle*, however, makes it clear that the question is only whether the accused had a "reasonable" alternative.[14]

---

[8] At [29]. Although *cf. R. v Kerr*, 2004 S.C.C. 44. The immediate danger requirement in relation to necessity is surprising given that, in *R. v Ruzic* [2001] 1 S.C.R. 687, the Canadian Supreme Court ruled that the same requirement is unconstitutional in relation to compulsion (coercion). See para.5.15.

[9] *Thomson v HM Advocate*, 1983 J.C. 69 at 78. For further discussion, see para.5.15.

[10] And bearing in mind that the appeal court stated in *Moss v Howdle* that the same considerations should govern coercion and necessity.

[11] Section 24(2). No reference is made in the Commentary to this departure from precedent.

[12] *Lord Advocate's Reference (No. 1 of 2000)*, 2001 J.C. 143 at [45].

[13] *Lord Advocate's Reference (No. 1 of 2000)*, 2001 J.C. 143 at [39].

[14] *Moss v Howdle*, 1997 J.C. 123 at 129–130. In this, Scots law is in line with the case law of the Canadian Supreme Court. See *R. v Latimer*, 2001 S.C.C. 1 at [3]; *R. v Kerr*, 2004 S.C.C. 44 at [94], *per* LeBel J. It is also consistent with the corresponding requirement in self-defence: see *McBrearty v HM Advocate*, 1999 S.L.T. 1333 at 1336, *per* the Lord Justice-General (Rodger); at 1337 *per* Lord Coulsfield. For discussion, see paras 3.12 *et seq.*

Act must have reasonable prospect of removing danger

In order for the defence of necessity to succeed, the act undertaken by the accused must have a reasonable prospect of removing the danger.[15] This point arose for the first time in the *Lord Advocate's Reference*, where it was argued for the Crown that the defence should be ruled out unless the accused had "reason to think that the acts carried out had some prospect of removing the perceived danger".[16] The appeal court agreed, stating that: **4.16**

> "What the defence is concerned with is conduct directly related to the avoidance of a particular danger which would cause harm if the acts of intervention were not carried out. If there were no prospect that the conduct complained of would affect the danger anticipated, the relationship between the danger and the conduct would not be established."[17]

In the majority of cases in which necessity potentially arises as a defence, meeting this requirement is unlikely to present a problem. In the *Reference*, the appeal court gives an example of a case where this condition would be unproblematic as the accused who damages a runaway vehicle in order to prevent it from injuring a group of pedestrians. Likewise, the accused who attempts to escape from a threat of violence by driving under the influence of excess alcohol, the factual scenario that has featured in many of the reported cases,[18] would have no difficulty in meeting this requirement.

This condition is potentially problematic in the type of case that led to the *Lord Advocate's Reference*. Here, in the original trial, the accused were acquitted of malicious mischief on the basis of necessity after damaging a ship that played a role in the Trident nuclear missile programme. Even if all of the other conditions of the defence were satisfied, damaging a single vessel involved in the UK's nuclear weapons programme was unlikely to change government policy in this area.

No authority was cited by the appeal court for the direct causal relationship requirement but the issue has arisen in a number of US cases involving necessity as a defence to civil disobedience charges and this body of case law may have influenced the Crown to propose such a requirement and the court to accept it.[19]

The subjective condition: the requirement that the threat dominates the mind

Thus far, the focus has been on the "objective" requirements of the necessity defence. There is, in addition, a subjective requirement: the threat must have dominated the mind of the accused at the time he engaged in the conduct in question. **4.17**

---

[15] What in the United States has been termed a direct causal relationship requirement: *United States v Seward*, 687 F 2d 1271 (10th Cir. 1982).

[16] *Lord Advocate's Reference (No. 1 of 2000)*, 2001 J.C. 143 at [46].

[17] *ibid.*

[18] *Tudhope v Grubb*, 1983 S.C.C.R. 350; *Ruxton v Lang*, 1998 S.C.C.R. 1; *Dolan v McLeod*, 1999 J.C. 32.

[19] See, e.g. *United States v Seward*, 687 F 2d 1271 (10th Cir. 1982). For comment, see S.M. Bauer and P.J. Eckerstrom, "The state made me do it: the applicability of the necessity defence to civil disobedience" (1987) 39 *Stanford Law Review* 1173–1200 at pp.1178–1183 and W.P. Quigley, "The necessity defence in civil disobedience cases: bring in the jury" (2003) 38 *New England Law Review* 3–72 at pp.50–51.

The point arose for direct consideration in *Dawson v Dickson*.[20] Here, the appellant had been convicted of driving with excess alcohol and careless driving after his defence of necessity had been rejected by the presiding sheriff. The appellant was a fire fighter who attended the scene of an accident despite being off-duty at the time and having been drinking. At the scene of the accident, the path of an ambulance waiting to take a seriously injured casualty to hospital was blocked by a fire engine and the paramedics asked for it to be removed. The appellant drove the fire engine away from the path of the ambulance but, in doing so, collided with a police patrol car. He was found to have excess alcohol in his blood. The crucial fact of the case was that the appellant admitted in evidence that he would have driven the fire engine regardless of the emergency circumstances. In other words, he never even considered the possibility that he was unfit to drive, and that by doing so he would be breaking the law.

The appeal court held that the defence of necessity had not been made out on the facts as:

> "... the defence of necessity only arises when there is a *conscious dilemma* faced by a person who has to decide between saving life or avoiding serious bodily harm on the one hand and breaking the law on the other hand".[21]

They continued:

> "Applying that principle to the circumstances of the present case, it can be seen that there was no question of the appellant making any choice at all. It never occurred to him that he should not be driving and the reason why he drove at the locus was simply because he was the driver of that pump ... The reason he did [drive] was because it never crossed his mind that he was unfit to drive and he would have driven anyway. In these circumstances it cannot be said that his mind was dominated at the time of the act by the extreme urgency of the situation which overrode the normal requirements that a driver should not drive with excess alcohol in his blood."[22]

It is not entirely clear from these two passages how this requirement should be interpreted.

One interpretation is simply that the defence of necessity is ruled out in cases where the accused is unknowingly justified; that is when potentially justificatory circumstances exist, but the accused is unaware of them. Another is that the defence is ruled out when the accused is *aware* of the potentially justificatory circumstances, but does not act for this reason.[23]

4.18 A third possible interpretation is that the accused must engage in some sort of *conscious* deliberation between the alternative courses of action available to him in order to benefit from the defence of necessity. If this was the case, it would rule out the defence of necessity to anyone who acted on the spur of the moment in an emergency situation, not having

---

[20] 1999 J.C. 315.

[21] At 318, emphasis added.

[22] At 318.

[23] The latter perhaps best describes Dawson's position. Both of these possible interpretations of *Dawson v Dickson* (and the issue of unknowing justification more generally) are discussed in detail in paras 1.23 *et seq*.

first consciously weighed up the alternatives. It seems unlikely that this is what the appeal court intended, given the authorities upon which they rely.

The Court in *Dawson v Dickson* based their conclusion on a passage contained in *Moss v Howdle*, a passage that was, in turn, taken from *Thomson v HM Advocate*,[24] an authority on coercion. In *Thomson*, the appeal court surveyed a number of English and Northern Irish authorities before concluding that these authorities were unanimous in requiring that "coercion or duress must have dominated the mind at the time of the act and that it was by reason of that domination that the act was committed".[25] In *Moss v Howdle*, the appeal court quoted this passage with approval[26] and went on to adopt a further passage of the Canadian Supreme Court's decision in *Perka v The Queen*,[27] where it was stated that where the defence applies, an accused:

> "... has control over his actions to the extent of being physically incapable of abstaining from the act. Realistically, however, this act is not a voluntary one. His choice to break the law is no true choice at all; it is remorselessly compelled by normal human instincts."[28]

This passage in *Perka* has generally been interpreted to refer to the theoretical basis of the necessity defence: that it is an excuse defence based on the principle of moral involuntariness. In *Dawson v Dickson*, however, the appeal court concluded from the dicta in *Perka* and "the way they were applied in *Moss*"[29] that a "conscious dilemma" was a requirement of the necessity defence. Yet there is nothing in *Moss v Howdle* (or in *Perka*) to suggest that the accused must face a "conscious dilemma" between two alternative courses of action. In *Moss v Howdle*, the appeal court made no further comment on the passage in *Perka*, other than to state that it follows that the defence of necessity cannot apply in circumstances where the accused was not, in fact, constrained by circumstances to break the law; in other words where there was a reasonable legal alternative course of action open to him.[30]

The requirement that the defence of necessity can succeed only where "there is a *conscious dilemma* faced by a person who has to decide between saving life or avoiding serious bodily harm on the one hand and breaking the law on the other hand" does seem to have injected some confusion into the law. No mention of it is made in the *Lord Advocate's Reference*, a case that sets out in some detail all of the other requirements of the defence. It is most likely that the effect of *Dawson v Dickson* is merely to rule out the defence to the accused who does not act for the potentially justificatory reason.[31]

---

[24] 1983 J.C. 69.

[25] At 80.

[26] *Moss v Howdle*, 1997 J.C. 123 at 129.

[27] [1984] 2 S.C.R. 232.

[28] [34] of *Perka*; quoted with approval in *Moss v Howdle*, 1997 J.C. 123 at 129.

[29] *Dawson v Dickson*, 1999 J.C. 315 at 318.

[30] *Moss v Howdle*, 1997 J.C. 123 at 129. The rule that the accused cannot claim the defence of necessity where a reasonable lawful alternative course of action was available to him is discussed in para.4.15.

[31] For further explanation and discussion of this, see paras 1.23 *et seq*

Relevance of personal characteristics

4.19 The three main requirements of the defence of necessity are an immediate danger of death or great bodily injury; an absence of reasonable lawful alternatives; and a reasonable prospect that the conduct concerned will remove the danger. A further issue arises as to whether the accused should be judged according to an objective or subjective standard in relation to these requirements and, if an objective approach is taken, which, if any, of the accused's personal characteristics are to be taken into account in deciding whether or not the objective test has been met.

It was not until the *Lord Advocate's Reference* that this issue was addressed at all. Here, the appeal court stated:

> "The actor must have good cause to fear that death or serious injury would result unless he acted; that cause for fear must have resulted from a reasonable belief as to the circumstances; the actor must have been impelled to act as he did by those considerations; and the defence will only be available if a sober person of reasonable firmness, sharing the characteristics of the actor, would have responded as he did."[32]

The test relies heavily on that set out by the English Court of Appeal in *R. v Martin*[33] and is clearly an objective one, but the issue of which particular personal characteristics are relevant is left open. Some guidance might be taken from the parallel body of case law on coercion where, in *Cochrane v HM Advocate*,[33a] the appeal court held that age, sex and physical ability are relevant characteristics for the purposes of assessing whether or not the accused should have responded as he did, whereas low intelligence and (relevant to the coercion defence) unusual levels of compliance are not. This leaves open the question of whether, for example, a recognised psychiatric condition, such as post-traumatic stress disorder, would be a relevant characteristic for the purposes of the defence. Some assistance might be provided by the case of *Bone v HM Advocate*.[33b] Here, the appeal court considered the relevance of personal characteristics in determining whether the accused should have been found guilty of culpable homicide by failing to protect her daughter from the acts of a violent partner. It was held that the relevant test of what is reasonable in this context is "whether the particular parent, with all her personal characteristics and in the situation in which she found herself, could reasonably have intervened to prevent the assault" and that personal characteristics meant "the appellant's physical, social and psychological circumstances".[33c] This included her size and strength, her advanced stage of pregnancy, her social and geographical isolation and, most significantly, her level of intellectual functioning and certain personality disorders from which she suffered, namely, avoidant personality disorder, dependent personality disorder and borderline personality disorder.[33d] *Bone*, however, was considering the relevance of personal characteristics in the context of a criminal *offence*, and whether the same approach would be taken in the context of the necessity defence (or indeed other defences, such as coercion or provocation) is not clear.

---

[32] *Lord Advocate's Reference (No. 1 of 2000)*, 2001 J.C. 143 at [42].
[33] (1989) 88 Cr.App.R. 343. For discussion see para.4.07.
[33a] 2001 S.C.C.R. 655. For discussion of this aspect of *Cochrane*, see paras 5.20 *et seq.*
[33b] 2006 S.L.T. 164.
[33c] At [9].
[33d] At [8].

Canadian law also takes an objective approach, but the Supreme Court of Canada has been equally vague as to exactly which personal circumstances can be taken into account in applying the objective test.[34] Some guidance might be taken from English law, where a court is entitled to take account of age, sex, pregnancy, serious physical disability or a recognised psychiatric condition.[35]

Fault in creating the circumstances of necessity

A further issue is whether or not the defence should be denied to the accused who is at fault in creating the circumstances of necessity. One reason why the courts might wish to rule out the defence in these circumstances is that its recognition sits uncomfortably with the notion of necessity as an excuse. The basis of excuse defences is that we accept that the accused has done something wrong but we do not blame him for doing so. The accused who voluntarily engages in blameworthy behaviour is not completely free from fault and it may be consistent with the theoretical basis of excuses that he is denied the benefit of an excuse defence.[36] If we accept this argument, however, it clearly does not apply to the situation where the balance of harms is such that necessity is operating as a justification.[37] Here, Dressler has suggested that, from a consequentialist perspective, it would be unwise to rule out the availability of the defence because the criminal law should provide an incentive to act in the way that prevents the greater harm.[38] **4.20**

In Scots law, the point has arisen only once, in *McNab v Guild*.[39] Here, the appellant had been convicted of reckless driving after reversing his car out of a car park and colliding with another vehicle. He claimed he had been trying to escape a threat of violence from two men who were also in the car park. His account was complicated by his admission that, when the threats were initially made, he had left the car park, only to return to it shortly afterwards. His defence of necessity was rejected by the presiding sheriff on the basis that he had voluntarily returned to the car park knowing that his assailants were likely to be there.

The appeal court were of the opinion that this in itself should not have ruled out the defence, but hinted that the issue might have been different had there been a finding in fact that the appellant returned to the car park specifically in order to confront his assailants.[40] Given that this was an

---

[34] *R. v Latimer*, 2001 S.C.C. 1 at [32]–[33].

[35] *R. v Graham* [1982] 1 W.L.R. 294; *R. v Bowen* [1997] 1 W.L.R. 372. *Graham* and *Bowen* are duress by threats cases, but the same rules govern the two defences (*R. v Safi* [2003] EWCA Crim 1809 at [13]). See para.4.07 where the approach of English law is discussed in more detail.

[36] Although whether the accused needs to be completely free from fault in claiming an excuse defence is open to question.

[37] On this, see Fletcher, *Rethinking Criminal Law*, pp.797–798; Gur-Arye, "Should the criminal law distinguish between necessity as a justification and necessity as an excuse?" (1986) 102 L.Q.R. 71–89 at p.77. This is precisely the approach taken by German law, which recognises a justification and an excuse version of the defence but, in relation to the excuse form, denies the defence to an accused who caused the danger in question. See German Penal Code, s.35(1) and the discussion in J. Herrmann, "Causing the conditions of one's own defence: the multifaceted approach of German law" (1986) 3 *Brigham Young University Law Review* 747–767.

[38] J. Dressler, *Understanding Criminal Law* (3rd edn, 2001), p.289. This assumes that the criminal law influences behaviour in this way. *Cf.* Robinson and J.H. Darley, "Does criminal law deter? A behavioural science investigation" (2004) 24 O.J.L.S. 173–205.

[39] 1989 J.C. 72.

[40] At 76–77.

obiter comment, though, it cannot be regarded as conclusive on the matter.

4.21 Little guidance can be taken from case law relating to other defences. The issue of prior fault is undecided in relation to coercion, although the trial judge's charge to the jury in *Thomson v HM Advocate*[41] suggests that voluntary association with a group where threats from one's associates might reasonably be expected would rule out the defence. There may, however, be public policy reasons for taking this approach to coercion that do not apply to necessity; namely, the danger that allowing the accused who voluntarily joins a criminal organisation to plead the defence opens up the possibility that members of that organisation can confer immunity on fellow members simply by issuing threats of death.[42]

In relation to self-defence, prior fault on the part of the accused does *not* necessarily rule out the defence.[43] Self-defence is a justification defence and thus it might be concluded that, at least in relation to the justification form of the necessity defence, the same rules should apply. There is, however, another possible reason why the defence might be withheld in relation to necessity and not self-defence, at least in circumstances that involve causing harm to another person. In self-defence situations, harm is caused to someone who poses a direct threat to the accused. In necessity situations, the accused is likely to harm an innocent bystander who posed no such threat and made no contribution to the situation in which the accused finds himself. Under these circumstances, it might be argued that in order to benefit from a complete defence, the accused should be free from fault in creating the situation.

A rare example from a common law jurisdiction in which the issue of prior fault and necessity has actually arisen is the Canadian Supreme Court case of *Perka v The Queen*.[44] Here, the Supreme Court took the view that the commission of an illegal act at the time the threat of harm arose was not in itself sufficient to defeat the availability of the necessity defence.[45] Nevertheless, the Court went on to suggest that prior fault in the sense of it being reasonably foreseeable that the initial conduct of the accused would lead to the circumstances of danger *is* a relevant consideration in deciding on the availability of the defence. While the Court did not state categorically that the defence would be ruled out in these circumstances,[46] they did comment:

> "... the better approach to the relationship of fault to the availability of necessity as a defence is based once again on the question of whether the actions sought to be excused were truly 'involuntary'. If the necessitous situation was clearly foreseeable to a reasonable observer, if the actor contemplated or ought to have contemplated that his actions would likely give rise to an emergency requiring the breaking of the law, then I doubt whether what confronted the accused was in the relevant sense an emergency. His response was in

---

[41] 1983 J.C. 69.

[42] Although whether or not this is a convincing reason for denying the coercion defence is open to question: see para.5.23.

[43] *Boyle v HM Advocate*, 1993 S.L.T. 577; *Burns v HM Advocate*, 1995 J.C. 154.

[44] [1984] 2 S.C.R. 232.

[45] At [49] *per* Dickson J.

[46] This was not the issue to be decided in *Perka*.

> that sense not 'involuntary'. 'Contributory fault' of this nature, but only of this nature, is a relevant consideration to the availability of the defence."[47]

These comments need to be viewed in light of the fact that the Canadian Supreme Court regards the necessity defence as an excuse and not a justification.[48] As discussed above, the prior fault doctrine is more consistent with the excuse form of the defence than the justification form. The same point might be made about English law, where the prior fault doctrine has been accepted in relation to duress by threats,[49] a defence that also seems to be regarded as an excuse rather than a justification.

The legislature must not already have determined the balance to be struck between the values in question

Some jurisdictions have placed an additional requirement on the defence that the legislature must not have anticipated the choice of evils and determined the balance to be struck between the competing values in a manner that conflicts with the defendant's choice. For example, in *United States v Oakland Cannabis Buyers Co-operative*,[50] the United States Supreme Court ruled out necessity as a defence to charges of the manufacture or distribution of marijuana for medical purposes on the basis that "the defence cannot succeed when the legislature has made a 'determination of values'".[51] The legislation in question, the Controlled Substances Act, provided only one exception to the offence of manufacturing and distributing marijuana; that being for the purpose of Government approved research projects. As such, the statute was deemed to reflect a determination on the part of the legislature that marijuana has no medical benefits worthy of an exception outside the confines of such a Government-approved research project and thus the defence of necessity could not succeed.[52] **4.22**

The rationale for restricting the defence in this way is to prevent individuals from being able to break the law on the basis that it conflicted with what they perceived as a higher social value, regardless of whether or not their perceptions were shared by the legislature.

No mention has been made of this possible requirement in Scots law and the type of case in which it would be likely to apply has not arisen.

---

[47] *Perka v The Queen* [1984] 2 S.C.R. 232 at [53], *per* Dickson J.

[48] *Perka v The Queen* [1984] 2 S.C.R. 232 at [31]–[33], *per* Dickson J. (Wilson J. dissenting on this point).

[49] The issue of prior fault has not arisen in relation to duress of circumstances but as the English courts have stressed on numerous occasions that the rules governing the two defences are the same, it must be assumed that it does apply. This is certainly the assumption made by Ashworth in *Principles of Criminal Law*, at p.223.

[50] 532 US 483 (2001).

[51] At 491 *per* Thomas J. For comment, see M. Pongratz, "Medical marijuana and the medical necessity defence in the aftermath of *United States v Oakland Cannabis Buyers Co-operative*" (2003) 25 *Western New England Law Review* 147–192.

[52] See also *State v Tate*, 505 A 2d 941 (N.J. 1986), at 946; *Commonwealth v Leno*, 616 N.E. 2d 453 (Mass 1993), at 455. The defence has been ruled out by the English Court of Appeal for the same reason: see *R. v Quayle* [2005] EWCA Crim 1415. *Quayle* also involved a number of defendants who had grown cannabis for purposes of pain relief. The Court of Appeal held that the defence of duress of circumstances was not available because its recognition would be "in conflict with the purpose and effect of the legislative scheme" contained in the Misuse of Drugs Act 1971 (at [56]).

Is Necessity a Defence to Murder?

4.23 No reported Scottish case has decided whether necessity could ever operate as a defence to murder.[53] If a case arose, guidance would most likely be taken from other common law jurisdictions, although even here the authorities are limited.

In England it had been assumed that *R. v Dudley and Stephens*[54] ruled out the availability of necessity as a defence to murder.[55] The case involved the killing of a cabin boy by two shipwrecked sailors in order to prevent death by starvation.[56] The defendants were found guilty of murder, the necessity defence being ruled out on the basis of moral and religious arguments about the sanctity of human life[57] and discomfort with the notion that it was the weakest member of the party that was chosen for sacrifice.[58]

In *Re: A (Children)*,[59] however, Brooke L.J. clearly allowed necessity to operate as a defence to murder.[60] Here, two babies, named Mary and Jodie for the purposes of reporting the case, were born with a shared heart. In any operation to separate them, only Jodie, the stronger of the two, would survive. If separation did not take place, both twins would eventually die. The Court of Appeal in England was asked to rule on whether or not the separation of the twins would be lawful. At least two members of the court accepted that performing the operation would involve the intentional killing of Mary[61] and thus if the doctors were not to be guilty of murder, an appropriate defence would have to be found.

4.24 Brooke L.J. reached the conclusion that the most appropriate defence was one of necessity[62] and held that the decision in *Dudley and Stephens* did not prevent him from finding necessity established. The two policy reasons for the decision in *Dudley*, he stated—that there was no reasonable basis for the cabin boy to be selected for sacrifice and that permitting the defence would mark a divorce of law from morality—did not apply in *Re: A*.[63]

Brooke L.J.'s analysis has been criticised on the basis that by classifying the case as one of necessity, he effectively implied that Mary's life was worth less than Jodie's, given that Mary could well have lived for up

[53] The Draft Criminal Code does allow for the possibility that necessity could be a defence to murder. See s.24(3) read in conjunction with s.24(2).

[54] (1884) 14 Q.B.D. 273.

[55] If indeed the defence of necessity (as opposed to that of duress of circumstances) is even recognised by English law (see para.4.07). In *R. v Abdul-Hussain* [1999] Crim. L.R. 570, the Court of Appeal ruled out the availability of the defence of duress of circumstances to murder (*per* Rose L.J. at 7 of the Lexis transcript of the case—this aspect of the case is not reported in the *Criminal Law Review*).

[56] The facts of the case are considered in more detail in para.4.28.

[57] *R. v Dudley and Stephens* (1884) 14 Q.B.D. 273 at 287.

[58] *ibid.* at 287–288.

[59] [2001] 2 W.L.R. 480. For comment, see the special issue of the *Medical Law Review* devoted to the case in 2001. See also J. Rogers, "Necessity, private defence and the killing of Mary" [2001] Crim. L.R. 515–526; S. Michalowski, "Sanctity of life: are some lives more sacred than others?" (2002) 22 L.S. 377–397.

[60] The other two members of the court did not think that the appropriate defence in the case was one of necessity: see below.

[61] *Re: A (Children)* [2001] 2 W.L.R. 480 at 531 (*per* Ward L.J.) and 549 (*per* Brooke L.J.).

[62] *Re: A (Children)* [2001] 2 W.L.R. 480 at 573.

[63] Where the victim was self-selected—"Mary is, sadly, designated for a very early death" (at 572)—and there is no obviously morally correct course of action—"All that a court can say is that it is not at all obvious that this is the sort of clear-cut case, marking an absolute divorce from law and morality" (at 572).

to six months if the separation had not taken place.[64] By concluding that this additional lifespan could be denied to Mary in order to save the life of Jodie, Brooke L.J. signalled that it was not a life from which she could benefit significantly, thus making an evaluation of the comparative worth of the respective lives of the twins that has proved troubling to some.[65]

The difficulties inherent in Brooke L.J.'s judgment would have been avoided if he had categorised the case as one of self-defence on the basis that Mary posed a direct threat to the life of Jodie. This was the route taken by one of his fellow judges, Ward L.J.,[66] and, arguably, it is the more convincing one.[67] In any case, it certainly cannot be concluded from *Re: A* that necessity is a defence to murder in England in anything other than the specific circumstances of the case and even that conclusion is doubtful, given that only one of the three Court of Appeal judges analysed the case in terms of necessity.[68]

In Canada, there is no direct authority on whether necessity can be a defence to murder. The issue arose in *R. v Latimer*,[69] but was left undecided, as the defence was not made out on the facts.[70] The Supreme Court did, however, express doubts that any factual scenario involving murder could arise in which the proportionality requirement of the defence would be met.[71] Likewise, in Australia, there is no direct authority on the point, although in *R. v Japaljarri*,[72] the Court of Appeal of the Supreme Court of Victoria stated that "it is unlikely that the defence of necessity is available for the crime of murder".[73]

The principled argument

The question of whether or not necessity should ever be a defence to murder has been debated at length by both lawyers and philosophers.[74] Debate has tended to centre around either the very few reported cases on **4.25**

[64] *Re: A (Children)* [2001] 2 W.L.R. 480 at 488.

[65] B. Hewson, "Killing off Mary: was the Court of Appeal right?" (2001) 9 *Medical Law Review* 281–298 at p.298.

[66] Ward L.J. described the case as a "plea of quasi self-defence, modified to meet the quite exceptional circumstances nature has inflicted on the twins" (*Re: A (Children)* [2001] 2 W.L.R. 480 at 536). The term "defence of others" is perhaps more appropriate than self-defence, given that the doctors were not acting in defence of their own lives, but in order to save Jodie.

[67] See Ch.1 of F. Leverick, *Killing in Self-Defence* (2006). *Cf.* S. Uniacke, "Was Mary's death murder?" (2001) 9 *Medical Law Review* 208–220 at p.213.

[68] The basis upon which the third member of the court, Walker L.J., decided the case is not clear, but he did not regard it as either a case of self-defence or necessity.

[69] 2001 S.C.C. 1.

[70] The defendant had killed his severely disabled 12-year-old daughter when, after many years of painful operations, it transpired that she would need a further operation in order to allow her to be fed through a tube. The Supreme Court held that none of the proportionality, imminent peril or lack of reasonable alternatives requirements of the defence were met.

[71] *R. v Latimer*, 2001 S.C.C. 1 at [40]. No reference was made in *Latimer* to *Re: A (Children)* [2001] 2 W.L.R. 480, which was decided four months earlier.

[72] (2002) 134 A. Crim.R. 261.

[73] At 270.

[74] See, e.g. L. Fuller, "The case of the Speluncean Explorers" (1949) 62 *Harvard Law Review* 616–645; J.J. Thomson, "The trolley problem" (1985) 94 *Yale Law Journal* 1395–1415; P. Foot, "The problem of abortion and the doctrine of double effect" (1967) *Oxford Review* 5–15; L. Katz, *Bad Acts and Guilty Minds: Conundrums of the Criminal Law* (1987).

the subject[75] or, perhaps because of the lack of case law, around numerous hypothetical examples drawn up by philosophers.[76]

One reason why debate has tended to focus on specific factual scenarios rather than the issue in the abstract is that there exists a wide range of circumstances in which necessity might potentially be pled as a defence to murder, varying from the accused who kills a number of innocent bystanders to save his own life, to the accused whose own life is under no threat, but who kills one person in order to save the lives of a larger group of people. As such, generalisations are difficult to draw. At one extreme, it has been argued that necessity should not be a defence to murder in any circumstances, on the basis that killing innocent bystanders who pose no direct threat to the lives of others is always morally wrong.[77] At the other extreme, some have argued that there is no reason why necessity should not be a defence to murder, even in cases where the accused acts to save himself and there is no net saving of lives.[78]

Cases of "self-interest" where there was no net saving of lives

4.26 The scenario that will be considered first is where the accused acts to save his own life and his conduct does not result in a net saving of lives. An example might be the accused who deflects his car into the path of one (or more) pedestrians rather than face death by crashing into a fallen tree that is blocking the road.

At the outset, it can be said that few, if any, would argue that this conduct is *justified* on the basis of necessity. The accused has taken an innocent life (or lives) in order to save his own and this can hardly be said to be justified on either the consequentialist basis that it was the lesser harm or under the rights based argument that the pedestrian posed a direct threat to the accused's life.[79] The innocent bystander in this situation possesses a right to life and has done nothing to suggest that this right be forfeited or over-ridden.[80]

A potentially more fruitful argument is that this conduct might be excusable. Those who argue that an excuse form of the defence of necessity should be available in this situation, do so on the basis that to rule it out as a defence would demand from individuals a standard of behaviour with which the vast majority of people would be unable to comply, such is the instinct for self-preservation. Demanding this standard might be appropriate if necessity operates only as a justification defence, but, if it is accepted that it can also be an excuse, then a lower standard of conduct should serve to ground the defence.[81]

---

[75] The case that has attracted the most extensive discussion to date is undoubtedly *Dudley and Stephens*. See A.W.B. Simpson, *Cannibalism and the Common Law* (1984); E. Rakowski, "Taking and saving lives" (1993) 93 *Columbia Law Review* 1063–1156; T. Stacy, "Acts, omissions and the necessity of killing innocents" (2002) 29 *American Journal of Criminal Law* 481–520; S. Gardner, "Instrumentalism and necessity" (1986) 6 O.J.L.S. 431–438.

[76] The most common of these are the trolley problem and the organ transplant problem. See para.4.29 below.

[77] L. Alexander, "A unified excuse of pre-emptive self-protection" (1999) 74 *Notre Dame Law Review* 1475–1505.

[78] P. Montague, "Self-defence and choosing between lives" (1981) 40 *Philosophical Studies* 207–219 at p.209; J.M. Taurek, "Should the numbers count?" (1976/1977) 6 *Philosophy and Public Affairs* 293–316 at p.307.

[79] As would be the case in relation to a self-defensive killing (see para.3.04).

[80] J.J. Thomson, "Self-defence" (1991) 20 *Philosophy and Public Affairs* 283–310 at p.290; S. Uniacke, *Permissible Killing: The Self-Defence Justification of Homicide* (1994), p.166.

[81] H. Packer, *The Limits of the Criminal Sanction* (1968), p.118.

As a counter-argument, it might be said that simply because the accused behaved in a way in which the majority of others would have behaved does not necessarily mean that his conduct is blameless and therefore excusable. Reference might be made here to the Milgram experiments, in which it was found that the vast majority of individuals would inflict extreme pain on another person simply because they were commanded to do so by an authority figure.[82] This fact alone does not mean that they should not be blamed for doing so. 4.27

Another argument for allowing necessity in the choice between lives situation is that there is no point in punishing those who kill in these circumstances as the instinct for self-preservation is so strong that a conviction is unlikely to act as a deterrent.[83] Once again, there are counter arguments that can be made. First, not everyone agrees that the drive for self-preservation is irresistible and thus that this type of conduct is undeterrable.[84] Secondly, the assumption is made that deterrence is the only basis for punishment. Even if it is accepted that killings under necessity are undeterrable, it may be that it is still appropriate to punish the accused on the ground of his moral blameworthiness for taking an innocent life in order to save his own.[85]

Consequently, the main argument against allowing even an excuse form of the necessity defence in the "no net saving of lives" example is that the sanctity of human life is such that taking the life of an innocent bystander in order to save one's own life is not only unjustifiable but is also *inexcusable*.[86]

Net saving of lives cases

The issue becomes more complex where the killing would result in a net saving of lives. At this point it is useful to consider in more detail the facts of *R. v Dudley and Stephens*.[87] The case involved three men and a cabin boy who were shipwrecked in an open boat at sea, with little food and water. After 18 days, seven of these without food, Dudley and Stephens decided that there was little chance of saving any of the lives of the four people involved other than by killing one of the others to eat. On the 20th day, Dudley and Stephens killed the cabin boy, on the basis that, of the four of them, he was in the weakest condition. All three of the men[88] fed 4.28

---

[82] S. Milgram, *Obedience to Authority: An Experimental View* (1974), pp.34–40.

[83] P.H.J. Huxley, "Proposals and counter-proposals on the defence of necessity" [1978] Crim. L.R. 141–149 at p.144; T. Stacy, "Acts, omissions and the necessity of killing innocents" (2002) 29 *American Journal of Criminal Law* 481–520 at p.504. A slightly different version of this argument is made by D. Klimchuk, "Necessity, deterrence and standing" (2002) 8 *Legal Theory* 339–358, who argues that the State simply does not have the standing to punish conduct that was not deterrable (at p.339).

[84] J. Hall, *General Principles of Criminal Law* (2nd edn, 1960), pp.445–446.

[85] It may be the case that the accused who acted under necessity is less morally blameworthy than, say, the accused who killed in a pre-meditated fashion, but this is something that can be taken into account at the sentencing stage.

[86] There is also the problem of what Simon Gardner has termed "quasi-justificatory drift". Gardner argues that as the legal system does not distinguish between verdicts of acquittal due to justification and due to excuse, allowing even an excuse form of the defence will lead the public to assume from the fact of the acquittal that the killing was condoned by the legal establishment. See S. Gardner, "Instrumentalism and necessity" (1986) 6 O.J.L.S. 431–438.

[87] (1884) 14 Q.B.D. 273.

[88] The third man involved did not agree to what was done by Dudley and Stephens, but he did eat the flesh of the cabin boy.

on his body and were rescued four days later.[89] Dudley and Stephens were convicted of murder.[90]

In a sense, the position adopted on whether or not necessity should be a defence to murder in these circumstances depends on one's moral viewpoint. On a purely consequentialist analysis, it is arguable that the defence should be permitted in these circumstances. It could be said that it is generally better for more to live than fewer and therefore the criminal law should encourage conduct that promotes this state of affairs by providing a defence.[91] By killing and eating the cabin boy, three lives were saved, whereas if Dudley and Stephens had done nothing, it was likely that all four would have died.[92]

Taking a deontological perspective,[93] however, it might be said that necessity should be ruled out as a defence, even in cases that do result in a net saving of lives, on the basis that killing violates the Kantian principle that innocent human life should never be used as a means to an end.[94]

4.29 As well as this, a second argument against recognising necessity as a defence in cases such as *Dudley and Stephens* is that the defence might then come to succeed simply on the basis that there *is* a net saving of lives, an outcome that most would find unpalatable. The classic example used by legal philosophers is the organ transplant hypothetical whereby a doctor who kills one healthy person in order to save the lives of five people who are in need of organ transplants can claim the defence of necessity.[95] To most, it is likely that this would be entirely unacceptable.

This "slippery slope" argument is perhaps overstated. For one thing, the conditions that have been placed on the defence, particularly the absence of reasonable alternative courses of action, mean that necessity is extremely unlikely to be successful in the organ transplant scenario where there are reasonable alternative courses of action available such as using donated organs or animal organs or keeping patients alive through other means.[96]

Furthermore, there is a key distinction that can be made between *Dudley and Stephens* and the organ transplant scenario. In *Dudley*, all of the actors involved in the situation faced the threat of death whereas in

---

[89] A fact that makes the issue slightly more complicated as it is not clear whether or not the killing was actually necessary, given that the cabin boy might have survived the additional four days until the rescue. It can probably be concluded, however, that it was reasonable for Dudley and Stephens to believe at the time that death would result if they did not act.

[90] In the event, the mandatory death sentence for murder was commuted to six months' imprisonment (A.W.B. Simpson, *Cannibalism and the Common Law* (1984), p.247).

[91] Stacy, above, fn.83, at p.502.

[92] It has been argued that Dudley and Stephens should have been found guilty of murder *if they had done nothing* and allowed the cabin boy to die. This is via omissions liability in that they had a duty to act, either on the basis of creation of danger (Dudley had apparently refused to replace rotting beams on the ship before setting sail) or on the basis of the special relationship between crew members. See Stacy, above, fn.83, at p.489; J.M. Paley, "Compulsion, fear and the doctrine of necessity" (1971) *Acta Juridica* 205–247 at p.236.

[93] Deontological theory holds that certain conduct is morally obligatory whether or not it results in a beneficial consequence.

[94] E. Kant, *Metaphysical Elements of Justice* (translated by John Ladd) (1965), p.41. The same argument is utilised by L. Alexander, "A unified excuse of pre-emptive self-protection" (1999) 74 *Notre Dame Law Review* 1475–1505.

[95] Stacy, above, fn.83, p.504; J. Horder, "Self-defence, necessity and duress: understanding the relationship" (1998) 11 *Canadian Journal of Law and Jurisprudence* 143–165 at p.157.

[96] Stacy, above, fn.83, p.506, also points out that the condition that the action taken has a reasonable prospect of removing the danger may not be met. There are significant risks of organ rejection and infection and the recipient of the organ is unlikely to gain as many years of life as the innocent bystander has lost. *Cf.* Horder, above, fn.95, who argues that unless necessity is confined to "emergency" situations, it *would* justify killing in the organ transplant scenario (at p.161).

the organ transplant situation the life of an innocent bystander who was not previously in any danger and who might have been expected to lead a long and healthy life is taken. It is certainly harder to argue on a moral basis that necessity should operate as a complete defence in the innocent bystander situation, given that an individual whose right to life was not previously threatened is appropriated to save the lives of others.[97]

Even in the situation where all of the parties involved face death, the position is not straightforward. It has been argued that, in *Dudley and Stephens*, one of the reasons why the defendants should not have been permitted to claim necessity is because, although all four passengers in the boat were in danger of starvation, they specifically selected the cabin boy as a victim.[98] Thus, there is another distinction that can be made: between cases where a victim has to be chosen and cases where the victim (or victims) are self-selected.[99] **4.30**

An example of the latter category is an incident that arose out of the *Herald of Free Enterprise* ferry disaster. At the inquest,[1] evidence was led that a man stood on a ladder blocking the path to safety of a number of other individuals, who were in freezing water and in danger of drowning.[2] One of those in the water shouted at him, for 10 minutes, asking him to move, but, when he did not, he instructed one of the other passengers to push him off into the water where, it was presumed, he drowned. No criminal proceedings were ever brought.[3]

If necessity is ever to be permitted as a defence to murder, it is this type of case, where the victim was self-selected and his death resulted in a net saving of lives, that the argument for its recognition is strongest.[4]

The question remains of whether necessity should ever be recognised as a defence to murder when the victim is *not* obviously self-selected and, if **4.31**

---

[97] This scenario is effectively the factual basis for what has been termed the "trolley problem". This hypothetical scenario, much loved by philosophers, involves a trolley with failed brakes that is running uncontrollably down a track towards five people at the bottom of the line. It is impossible to warn them or to stop the trolley. The only alternative course of action is for the driver of the trolley to switch the track and divert the trolley onto an alternative path towards a single individual who was not previously threatened. The problem was originally devised by Philippa Foot (in "The problem of abortion and the doctrine of double effect" (1967) 5 *Oxford Review* 5–15). Debate has raged between philosophers who consider it permissible to switch the path of the trolley (Foot herself, but also M.D. Bayles, "Reconceptualising necessity and duress" (1987) 33 *Wayne Law Review* 1191–1220 at 1205; J.J. Thomson, "The trolley problem" (1985) 94 *Yale Law Journal* 1395–1415 at 1414) and those who do not (G.C. Christie, "The defence of necessity considered from the legal and moral points of view" (1999) 48 *Duke Law Journal* 975–1042 at p.1041).

[98] A concern raised by Lord Coleridge in *R. v Dudley and Stephens* (1884) 14 Q.B.D. 273 (at 287–288). See also Ashworth, *Principles of Criminal Law*, p.152.

[99] Brooke L.J. used this factor to distinguish between *Dudley and Stephens* and *Re: A*, stating that, unlike the cabin boy in *Dudley*, "Mary is, sadly, self-designated for a very early death" (*Re: A (Children)* [2001] 2 W.L.R. 480 at 572).

[1] *R. v HM Coroner for East Kent ex. parte Spooner and others* (1987) 88 Cr.App.R. 10; *R. v P&O European Ferries (Dover) Ltd* (1990) 93 Cr.App.R. 72.

[2] Neither *R. v HM Coroner for East Kent* nor *R. v P&O European Ferries (Dover) Ltd* describes this incident in detail, but see J.C. Smith, *Justification and Excuse in the Criminal Law* (1989), pp.73–74.

[3] It *might* be argued that this was actually a case of self-defence, on the basis that the man on the ladder was a direct threat to those below. However, the majority of commentators have concluded that it is best regarded as a case of necessity, as the man was not a direct threat, but a bystander (the direct threat being the rising water). See Ch.1 of F. Leverick, *Killing in Self-Defence* (2006); S. Uniacke, *Permissible Killing: The Self-Defence Justification of Homicide* (1994), p.166; Horder, above, fn.95, at p.153.

[4] See Ashworth, *Principles of Criminal Law*, p.152; P.H.J. Huxley, "Proposals and counter-proposals on the defence of necessity" [1978] Crim. L.R. 141–149 at p.145.

so, what an acceptable method of selection might be. It has been argued that it should, provided that some sort of fair selection procedure is undertaken, such as drawing lots.[5] This point arose in *United States v Holmes*.[6] In *Holmes*, the crew and passengers of a ship were shipwrecked and the only means of survival was two lifeboats. The lifeboats could not hold everybody and Holmes—one of the crew members—was convicted of manslaughter after pushing 16 male passengers overboard from a lifeboat that was overcrowded and sinking. The trial judge, Baldwin J., charged the jury on the basis that the correct course of action in such circumstances would have been to select the victims by drawing lots:

> "When the ship is in no danger of sinking, but all sustenance is exhausted, and a sacrifice of one person is necessary to appease the hunger of others, the selection is by lot. This mode is resorted to as the fairest mode, and, in some sort, as an appeal to God, for selection of the victim."[7]

While there is something to be said for attempting to lay down rules, in that it provides an equitable basis for the participants to proceed and may help to enforce order,[8] the drawing of lots is not unproblematic. This is particularly so where not all parties agree to take part in the procedure, raising questions of whether a lot is then drawn on their behalf and, if the unwilling individual is selected as the victim, whether it is permissible to kill him.[9]

What is clear is that the question of whether or not necessity should ever be a defence to murder is a complex one and the answer rests, to a certain extent, on one's moral views about the sanctity of human life and whether or not it is ever acceptable to take the life of an innocent human being who was not posing any threat. A factor that makes the issue all the more difficult is the existence of the mandatory life sentence for murder,[10] which makes it difficult to distinguish between a pre-meditated, cold blooded killing and one where the accused killed only as a last resort to save his own life. It may be that some of the more borderline cases are best dealt with either by allowing necessity to operate as a partial defence,[11] reducing murder to culpable homicide, or by removing the mandatory life sentence for murder.[12] The latter option would be less palatable to those who believe that the accused who kills out of necessity is not sufficiently blameworthy to be labelled a murderer.

---

[5] Ashworth, *Principles of Criminal Law*, p.152; Robinson, *Criminal Law Defenses*, §124(g). In fact, Dudley and Stephens originally considered the idea of drawing lots but rejected it in favour of killing the weakest member of the party.

[6] (1842) 26 Fed. Cas. 360.

[7] At 367. This solution was considered but rejected by Lord Coleridge in *R. v Dudley and Stephens* (1884) 14 Q.B.D. 273 (at 285). This is surprising, given that one of his main concerns elsewhere in his judgment was that the weakest member of the party had been sacrificed to save the strongest.

[8] Gordon, at para.13.15.

[9] Or, as the Casebook notes (para.7.74), whether the husband or wife of the victim would be guilty of assault (or even murder) if he or she attempted to prevent the killing and injured (or killed) one of those involved.

[10] CPSA 1995, s.205(1).

[11] On this, see the English Law Commission's Consultation Paper, *A New Homicide Act for England and Wales?* (Consultation Paper No.177, 2005), where it is recommended that duress of circumstances should operate as a partial defence, reducing first degree murder to second degree murder, and thus avoiding the mandatory life sentence (para.7.31).

[12] There is also the argument that difficult borderline cases can be dealt with by the exercise of prosecutorial discretion. However, this leaves open the possibility of unfairness due to variable treatment and is not therefore a satisfactory solution. See E. Rakowski, "Taking and saving lives" (1993) 93 *Columbia Law Review* 1063–1156 at p.1152.

Chapter 5

COERCION

Introduction

5.01 The defence of coercion is a plea by the accused that he broke the law only because he was complying with the demands of a third party, who threatened him with harm unless he did so. Although Hume addressed it, the defence of coercion lay virtually dormant in Scottish criminal law for many years, experiencing a revival of interest only in the early 1980s, when the appeal court considered it in *Thomson v HM Advocate*.[1]

The defence raises a number of difficult public policy issues. Unless its availability is restricted, the defence might allow criminal organisations and terrorists to confer immunity on their colleagues and subordinates simply by issuing threats of death.[2] Furthermore, the defence might also permit the complete acquittal of someone who has harmed or killed an innocent third party in order to save his or her own life.

These concerns have led some commentators to argue that coercion should *never* operate as a complete defence.[3] More commonly, the defence is one that is accepted with reluctance and with the safeguard of tightly defined rules. This was the view of Hume, who expressed some scepticism about the plea, especially in the ordinary conditions of a well-regulated society, and envisaged it operating as a complete defence only if strict conditions were met.[4] There has been little Scottish case law on coercion. That which exists suggests that its availability as a defence continues to be tightly controlled. Indeed, in some respects, the conditions governing the defence in Scotland are stricter than in other common law jurisdictions.[5]

Before proceeding, a brief note about terminology is necessary. The term coercion is used in Scotland to describe what, in other jurisdictions, is referred to as duress[6] or compulsion.[7] It might be argued that duress and compulsion are actually more appropriate terms for the defence as "coercion" invites confusion with the English defence of *marital* coercion. This defence is still available to married women under English law and does not require a threat of death or bodily harm.[8] Indeed, the defence was originally called compulsion in Scots law[9] and it is not clear precisely

[1] 1983 J.C. 69.
[2] Although on this point, see para.5.03 below.
[3] See para.5.03 and the references contained therein.
[4] See para.5.09.
[5] See in particular paras 5.14 *et seq.* on immediacy of harm.
[6] The term used in English criminal law and the US Model Penal Code (s.2.09).
[7] The term used in the Canadian Criminal Code (s.17) and in the Criminal Codes of some Australian States.
[8] Criminal Justice Act 1925, s.47. See fn.56 below.
[9] The term compulsion was used by Hume and Alison, as it was in the fifth edition of Macdonald, published in 1948. The first reported case in which it was termed coercion appears to be *HM Advocate v Peters* (1969) 33 J.C.L. 209, in which Lord Thomson referred to "the defence of coercion, or compulsion or constraint" (at 210).

why or when the change in terminology arose. Modern Scottish case law is relatively consistent[10] in its reference to coercion, however, and thus this term will be used here.[11]

Theoretical Basis

Distinguishing coercion from other conceptually similar defences

5.02 The conceptual basis of a plea of coercion is that the accused avoids harm by *complying with the demands* of a threatener. Thus it can be distinguished from self-defence, where the accused avoids harm by *warding off or blocking a threat*.[12]

Coercion can also be distinguished from the closely related defence of necessity, on the basis that the nature of the wrong undertaken in necessity is not specified by a threatener, but is decided on by the accused himself.[13] Despite this conceptual distinction, it has been held that the rules governing coercion and necessity should be the same.[14]

Should coercion *ever* operate as a complete defence?

5.03 It has sometimes been suggested that coercion should *never* operate as a complete defence,[15] on the basis of concerns over the defence operating as a "terrorists' charter"[16] or a feeling that it is inappropriate to permit the complete acquittal of someone who has inflicted harm, or even death, on an innocent third party in order to save his own life.[17]

This seems unnecessarily harsh on the accused who, through no fault of his own, faces a choice between committing a criminal offence or the infliction of death or serious bodily harm on himself or members of his family. Many of the specific public policy concerns about the defence can be addressed by limiting the conditions in which it is available. For example, the concern that it acts as a terrorists' charter can be addressed by ruling out its availability to the accused who has voluntarily joined such an organisation or who has placed himself in a position where it was reasonably foreseeable that he would be subjected to coercion.[18]

---

[10] Although see *Sayers, Pears and Turner v HM Advocate*, 1981 S.C.C.R. 312, where the trial judge variously referred to "duress or coercion" (at 318, 319 and 320), "duress" (at 319 and 320) and "being forced or coerced" (at 319).

[11] It is also the term used in s.78(2) of the Criminal Procedure (Scotland) Act 1995, which provides for the treatment of coercion as if it is a special defence. On this, see Ch.2.

[12] See para.3.02.

[13] See para.4.02. For an argument that coercion, necessity and self-defence should be brought together under a single unified defence, see C.M.V. Clarkson, "Necessary action: a new defence" [2004] Crim. L.R. 81–95. For detailed discussion and criticism, see para.3.03.

[14] *Moss v Howdle*, 1997 J.C. 123 at 128. For further discussion, see para.4.06.

[15] Lord Kilbrandon, "Duress per minas as a defence to crime: I" in *Law Morality and Rights* (M.A. Stewart (ed.), 1983), pp.333–343, at p.341; R.F. Schopp, *Justification Defences and Just Convictions* (1998), p.141.

[16] On this, see *DPP for Northern Ireland v Lynch* [1975] A.C. 653 at 688, *per* Lord Simon.

[17] A. Kenny, "Duress per minas as a defence to crime: II" in *Law Morality and Rights* (M.A. Stewart (ed.), 1983), pp.345–354.

[18] On this, see paras 5.23 *et seq*.

The theoretical basis of the defence

5.04 It has sometimes been suggested that coercion operates to negate the *mens rea* element of criminal liability. This was the view of the defence taken by the High Court in *HM Advocate v Raiker*[19] where Lord McCluskey's charge to the jury included the following passage:

> "... the law is that where a person has a real, a genuine, a justifiable fear that if he does not act in accordance with the orders of another person, that other person will use life threatening violence against him or cause it to be used, and if as a result of that fear and for no other reason he carries out acts which have all the typical external characteristics of criminal acts like assault or theft, then in that situation he cannot be said to have the evil intention which the law says is a necessary ingredient in the carrying out of a crime. In other words, he lacks the criminal state of mind that is a necessary ingredient of any crime."[20]

If *mens rea* is defined as simple intent, knowledge or recklessness, it is difficult to see how coercion could possibly negate *mens rea*.[21] It seems wrong to say that the accused who robs a bank under coercion did not intend to do so or that the accused who assaults a victim under coercion did not intend to injure. This view is in line with that taken by the appeal court in the *Lord Advocate's Reference (No. 1 of 2000)*,[22] where it was stated quite clearly that the closely related defence of necessity does not negate *mens rea* but is a separate defence in its own right.[23] On the other hand, if *mens rea* is defined as, for example, evil or wicked intention, then the logical conclusion to draw is that coercion does operate to negate *mens rea*, as the accused acting under coercion would lack the requisite element of 'wickedness'.[24] This was precisely the view taken by the appeal court in *Drury v HM Advocate*,[25] albeit in a case concerning provocation.[26]

Assuming that coercion does not negate *mens rea*, we must situate the defence within the classification of defences set out in Ch.1. Some argue that coercion can operate only as a justification defence, on the basis that,

---

19 1989 S.C.C.R. 149.

20 At 154.

21 Ashworth, *Principles of Criminal Law*, p.224; L.K. Dore, "Downward adjustment and the slippery slope: the use of duress in defence of battered offenders" (1995) 56 *Ohio State Law Journal* 665–766 at p.740.

22 2001 J.C. 143.

23 At [31].

24 The issue is of more than purely academic interest. If coercion does operate in this way, then an honest but unreasonable belief in relation to any of the elements of the defence may serve to generate an acquittal on the basis that the accused would lack the necessary element of wickedness. See F. Leverick, "Mistake in self-defence after *Drury*", 2002 Jur. Rev. 35–48; J. Chalmers, "Collapsing the structure of criminal law", 2001 S.L.T. (News) 241–245.

25 2001 S.L.T. 1013. See paras 3.11 and 10.05 for discussion.

26 See also *Bennett v Criminal Injuries Compensation Appeal Panel*, December 9, 2003, Court of Session, unreported, at [18]. Although *cf. Lord Advocate's Reference (No. 2 of 1992)*, 1993 J.C. 43, where it was held that the *mens rea* of assault, evil intention, simply referred to an intention to injure or to make the victim fear injury. The English courts have recently made it clear that they regard duress not as a denial of *mens rea* but as a separate defence operating where *actus reus* and *mens rea* have been satisfied. See *R. v Fisher* [2004] EWCA Crim 1190; *R. v Hasan* [2005] UKHL 22 at [18], *per* Lord Bingham.

in complying with the demands of the coercer, the accused has chosen the lesser of two evils.[27] Others argue that it must be an excuse, on the basis that an accused who breaks the law to avoid harm to himself cannot be said to have chosen the 'lesser evil'.[28]

The view is taken here that coercion can operate either as a justification or as an excuse depending on the factual circumstances in which it is pled.[29] The justification form of the defence operates where there is a disparity between the two harms in question.[30] For example, in a situation where the accused commits a parking offence when faced with a threat of death, the conclusion must surely be that the accused has made a justifiable choice, given the balance of harms involved.[31]

5.05 The excuse form of the defence operates where the harms involved are similar in nature. The accused who takes part in a violent robbery under the threat of death does not do so on the basis that his conduct was acceptable. Rather, he claims an excuse on the basis that, although what he did was wrong, there is a reason why he should not be blamed for his act. Indeed, there is an argument for saying that coercion operates as an excuse whenever the accused physically harms an innocent third party. It would seem unjust to the victim if the law were to deem it acceptable for one person to choose to preserve his own life or bodily integrity over that of another.[32]

In cases where coercion operates as a justification, the accused was ostensibly justified because, in choosing the lesser of two possible harms, the choice he made was acceptable. The question of why coercion should excuse is less clear.

One possible line of argument is that we should not blame the accused because the degree of pressure he faced was such that he was unable to control his conduct.[33] The act may be *physically* voluntary, but is some-

---

[27] G. Williams, *Criminal Law: The General Part* (2nd edn, 1961), p.755; P. Westen and J. Mangiafico, "The criminal defense of duress: a justification not an excuse and why it matters" (2003) 6 *Buffalo Criminal Law Review* 833–950 at p.895.

[28] L. Alexander, "The philosophy of criminal law" in *The Oxford Handbook of Jurisprudence and Philosophy of Law* (J.L. Coleman and S. Shapiro (eds), 2002), pp.815–867 at p.849; T. Honoré, "A theory of coercion" (1990) 10 O.J.L.S. 94–105 at p.100. See also the House of Lords in *R. v Hasan* [2005] UKHL 22 at [18], *per* Lord Bingham.

[29] See also Ashworth, *Principles of Criminal Law*, p.219; M.N. Berman, "Justification and excuse, law and morality" (2003) 53 *Duke Law Journal* 1–77 at p.65; J. Dressler, "Exegis of the law of duress: justifying the excuse and searching for its proper limits" (1989) 62 *Southern California Law Review* 1331–1386 at p.1353; V. Tadros, "The structure of defences in Scots criminal law" (2003) 7 Edin. L.R. 60–79 at p.70.

[30] M.D. Bayles, "Reconceptualising necessity and duress" (1987) 33 *Wayne Law Review* 1191–1220 at p.1197.

[31] This is not to say that coercion might not also be an excuse in this scenario. It is just that, in addition to being an excuse, it is also a justification.

[32] The possible exception to this is in relation to the defence of self-defence where, arguably, the victim has forfeited his right to protection by virtue of becoming a direct threat to the life of the accused (see para.3.04).

[33] This comes close to suggesting that coercion negates *actus reus* on the basis that an act undertaken under coercion cannot be said to be voluntary. This conception of the defence must surely be rejected. The coerced individual retains free will in the sense that he chooses how to conduct himself, even though his choice is made under constrained circumstances. See M. Bayles, "A concept of coercion" in *Coercion* (R.J. Pennock and J.W. Chapman (eds), 1972), pp.16–29, at p.17.

how *morally* involuntary, since the accused's will has been overborne by threats.[34]

The "overborne will" terminology has found its way into Scottish case law. In *Thomson v HM Advocate*,[35] Lord Hunter charged the jury on the basis that:

> "... the will and resolution of the accused must in fact have been overborne and overcome by the threats and the danger. He must have found himself entangled in a share of the criminal enterprise ... 'entirely against his will'. There must have been an inability to resist the violence."[36]

The question arises of exactly what is meant by these terms. Robinson envisions "moral involuntariness" as "the impairment of the actor's ability to control his conduct"[37] or, alternatively, a "relative impairment of the psychological control mechanisms".[38] Fletcher states only that it "depends in a curious way on the competing interests as in cases of justification".[39]

Such explanations are unconvincing. Whereas some accused persons **5.06** acting under coercion might be so overcome by fear that they are temporarily prevented from controlling their conduct, others might make the choice coolly after a period of rational deliberation.[40] The legal system may choose to deny the defence to those who undertake such rational deliberation, and recognise it only in circumstances where the reasoning of the accused was disturbed. If this conceptualisation were to be accepted, however, an entirely different version of the defence would operate: one that is entirely subjective, where the main issue is the degree of pressure experienced by the accused.[41]

An alternative, and more convincing, conception of coercion is offered by Ashworth: we excuse the actor on the basis that his choice was a reasonable response to extreme danger.[42] In other words, the defence is based not on a disability that prevents rational thought, but on a moral evaluation of the accused's conduct. In Ashworth's words, the excuse form of the defence operates by recognising:

---

[34] This is the conception of the defence that has dominated the English Court of Appeal. It seems to have stemmed from *R. v Hudson and Taylor* [1971] 2 Q.B. 202, where Lord Parker asserted the need for threats "sufficient to destroy [the defendant's] will" (at 207). It was followed in *R. v Emery* (1993) 14 Cr.App.R. (S) 394 (at 398 *per* Lord Taylor) and *R. v Baker and Wilkins* [1997] Crim. L.R. 497 at 498. See also the Canadian Supreme Court in *Hibbert v The Queen* [1995] 2 S.C.R. 973 at [64]. *Cf.* the House of Lords in *DPP for Northern Ireland v Lynch* [1975] A.C. 653 and *R. v Howe, Bannister, Burke and Clarkson* [1987] A.C. 417.

[35] 1983 J.C. 69.

[36] At 73. See also *Docherty v HM Advocate*, 1976 S.C.C.R. Supp. 146 at 146; *Sayers v HM Advocate*, 1981 S.C.C.R. 312 at 319.

[37] Robinson, *Criminal Law Defenses*, §177(b).

[38] *ibid.*

[39] Fletcher, *Rethinking Criminal Law*, p.803.

[40] Ashworth, *Principles of Criminal Law*, p.225; J.L. Hill, "A utilitarian theory of duress" (1999) 84 *Iowa Law Review* 275–338 at p.300.

[41] Ashworth, *Principles of Criminal Law*, p.224. As such it would seem to have more in common with automatism. As paras 5.20–5.22 demonstrate, this is not how the defence operates in Scots law, which retains a strong objective requirement.

[42] Ashworth, *Principles of Criminal Law*, p.224.

> "... the dire situation with which D was faced and limiting the defence to cases where D responded in a way that did not fall below the standard to be expected of the reasonable citizen in such circumstances".[43]

Weston and Mangiafico[44] have argued that this sounds like a justification defence rather than an excuse. It is not being argued, however, that the choice made by the accused (for example, to inflict injury on an innocent bystander in order to escape a threat to himself) was acceptable. The criminal law hopes that citizens do not sacrifice the well-being of an innocent bystander or otherwise invade their rights in order to save themselves from injury.[45] What is being argued is that we do not blame the accused for acting in this self-preferential way as in doing so he behaved only as any reasonable person would have done in the circumstances. To term this a justification defence is to ignore the fact that an innocent bystander has been injured, something that is understandable but not acceptable.[46]

Whether coercion operates as a justification and/or an excuse in practice depends on the conditions attached to the defence within the legal system in question. Scots law allows coercion to operate as a complete defence to offences such as assault and armed robbery,[47] as well as to more minor offences, such as the possession of controlled substances.[48] We might infer from this that it recognises both the justification and excuse form of the defence. Some of the language used by the appeal court and the conditions attached to the defence,[49] however, suggest an excuse. It is therefore difficult to draw any firm conclusions,[50] especially as the Scottish courts have shown no great inclination to engage in theoretical discussion of this nature.[51]

Historical Development

Coercion under Hume

5.07 Hume distinguishes between subjection and compulsion. The plea of subjection covers commands made within the context of certain types of relationship: the command of a husband to a wife,[52] a parent to a child[53]

---

[43] Ashworth, *Principles of Criminal Law*, p.225.

[44] P. Westen and J. Mangiafico, "The criminal defense of duress: a justification not an excuse and why it matters" (2003) 6 *Buffalo Criminal Law Review* 833–950 at p.914.

[45] J. Horder, *Excusing Crime* (2004), p.59.

[46] For further criticism of Westen and Mangiafico's conceptualisation of coercion exclusively as a justification, see M.N. Berman, "Justification and excuse, law and morality" (2003) 53 *Duke Law Journal* 1–77 at pp.71–73.

[47] *Thomson v HM Advocate*, 1983 J.C. 69; *Cochrane v HM Advocate*, 2001 S.C.C.R. 655; *HM Advocate v Raiker*, 1989 S.C.C.R. 149; *HM Advocate v McCallum* (1977) S.C.C.R. Supp. 169.

[48] *Trotter v HM Advocate*, 2001 S.L.T. 296.

[49] Especially the requirement for a qualifying level of danger: that of death or great bodily harm (see para.5.11).

[50] And, indeed, the importance of doing so is perhaps overstated.

[51] In *Moss v Howdle*, 1997 J.C. 123 the appeal court stated that: "[t]here is much discussion in the cases and in the books about the juridical basis of a defence of coercion or duress. Happily there is no reason even to try to add to it in this case" (at 129). *Cf.* the Canadian Supreme Court in *Hibbert v The Queen* [1995] 2 S.C.R. 973 at [26]–[54].

[52] Hume, i, 47–48.

[53] Hume, i, 50.

and a master to a servant.[54] Subjection, it seems, need not involve a threat of violence and in this sense has more in common with superior orders[55] than it does with coercion. Hume makes it quite clear that subjection alone, without an accompanying threat of violence, does not exculpate the accused.[56]

Compulsion differs from subjection in that the demand made of the accused is backed by a threat of violence if the accused does not comply. Hume distinguishes between compulsion that occurs in "situations of great commotion, or extensive danger" and compulsion that occurs in "the ordinary condition of a quiet and well-regulated society".[57]

Compulsion in situations of great commotion

This type of compulsion occurs in times of war or rebellion when the protection of the Government, which would normally be available, is suspended. In these circumstances, states Hume, allowance must be made for individuals if "they suffer the great law of self-preservation to govern ... their conduct for the time".[58] For example, the accused who, at a time when the country is commanded by rebels, supplies them with arms or money, would not be guilty of treason if he reasonably feared execution for refusing.[59] Compulsion could also serve to exculpate if the accused "be with [the rebels] for a time in arms" provided he "quit their service on the first opportunity, and do no act of hostility while he remains with them, that is not fairly imputable to the constraint of his condition".[60] No reference is made by Hume to any requirement for an explicit threat of violence unless the accused complies with the demands of the rebels. It seems that, in this context, an implicit threat is sufficient.[61] **5.08**

Still writing in the context of situations of great commotion, Hume states that compulsion can also exculpate in cases where there is "a less extensive commotion, if the individual is truly in a state of helplessness and danger for the time".[62] He gives the example of a mob taking possession of people and compelling them to take part in what would

[54] Hume, i, 50–51. This type of subjection is discussed in more detail in para.6.06 in relation to superior orders.

[55] On which see Ch.6.

[56] *cf.* Mackenzie, 170. In relation to husband and wife, *cf.* also the statutory defence of marital coercion in English law provided for by s.25 of the Criminal Justice Act 1925. This is still in force, despite the recommendation of the English Law Commission that it should be repealed (*Report on Defences of General Application* (Law Com. No. 83, 1977), at para.3.9). For a modern attempt to plead the defence, see *R. v Shortland* [1996] 1 Cr.App.R. 116.

[57] Hume, i, 51. Gordon (at para.13.27) refers to this as a distinction between public and private compulsion. These terms are not used by Hume. Hume does describe compulsion occurring in the ordinary condition of a quiet and well regulated society as "a more special and private sort of violence" (Hume, i, 52) but does not use the term public compulsion to describe situations of great commotion.

[58] Hume, i, 51.

[59] *ibid.*

[60] Hume, i, 51. See *William and John Riddell* (1681) Hume, i, 51.

[61] On whether an implicit threat can ground the defence of coercion other than in situations of great commotion, see para.5.16.

[62] Hume, i, 51.

otherwise be unlawful acts.[63] Compulsion in this sense is used to describe a situation where the accused is almost physically forced to take part in a criminal act.[64]

Compulsion in a well-regulated society

5.09 Outside of situations of great commotion, Hume accepts that there "may even be situations, though not as common now as formerly, of a more special and private sort of violence, which shall be judged by the same rule".[65] The example he proceeds to give is that of some parts of Scotland that were "infested by gangs of ruffians, who levied contributions, and committed all sorts of mischief without fear or restraint", where "through fear of their enmity, a person nowise disposed to such a course of life might, for the time, find himself entangled in some share of a criminal enterprise, entirely against his will".[66] This example seems to have more in common with a situation of great commotion than with compulsion in a well-regulated society.[67]

Hume does concede that compulsion can be a valid plea in "the ordinary condition of a well-regulated society, where every man is under the shield of the law".[68] Because the accused "has the means of resorting to that protection",[69] however, compulsion "is at least somewhat a difficult plea".[70] It is in this context that Hume sets out four requirements that have, to a greater or lesser extent, formed the basis of the defence of coercion in the modern context. The first is that the accused must have faced "an immediate danger of death or great bodily harm".[71] The second is that the accused must have had "an inability to resist the violence".[72] The third is that the accused must have played "a backward and inferior part in the perpetration"[73] and the fourth is a requirement for "disclosure of the fact, as well as restitution of the spoil, on the first safe and convenient occasion".[74] In relation to the third and fourth, Hume elaborates by stating that "if the pannel take a very active part in the enterprise, or conceal the fact, and detain his share of the profit, when restored to a state of freedom, either of these replies will serve in a great measure to elide his defence".[75]

In *Thomson v HM Advocate*,[76] it was said that Hume restricted the availability of coercion to "atrocious crimes".[77] A more careful reading of his text, however, suggests that this was not Hume's intention. Rather, he

---

[63] For examples of cases in which the defence of compulsion served to exculpate the accused in these circumstances, see *Andrew Fairney* (1720) Hume, i, 52; *William Gilchrist* (1741) Hume, i, 52; *Robert Main* (1725) Hume, i, 52.

[64] Gordon (at para.13.27) refers to it arising when the accused's acts are "almost involuntary".

[65] Hume, i, 52.

[66] *ibid.*

[67] As does the case he refers to: *James Graham* (1717) Hume, i, 52–53.

[68] Hume, i, 53.

[69] *ibid.*

[70] *ibid.*

[71] *ibid.*

[72] *ibid.*

[73] *ibid.*

[74] *ibid.*

[75] *ibid.*

[76] 1983 J.C. 69 at 78, *per* the Lord Justice-Clerk (Wheatley).

[77] Hume gives the examples of treason, fire-raising and murder as crimes that would fall under this heading (Hume, i, 47). Atrocious crimes are contrasted with "less heinous offences" including theft, reset of theft and forgery (Hume, i, 48).

states that the plea of compulsion "can hardly be serviceable in the case of a trial for any atrocious crime, *unless it have the support of these qualifications*",[78] a reference to the four requirements outlined above.

Indeed, the appeal court itself subsequently rejected the *Thomson* interpretation in *Moss v Howdle*,[79] pointing out that it "would be an odd legal system indeed which, as a matter of principle, allowed coercion to elide guilt of the crime of armed robbery, but not guilt of the offence of exceeding the speed limit".[80]

This means, though, that Hume left open the requirements governing the plea in relation to non-atrocious crimes,[81] a point not addressed in subsequent case law.

Coercion in modern case law

The appeal court has given the defence of coercion detailed consideration on only two occasions: *Thomson v HM Advocate*[82] and *Cochrane v HM Advocate*.[83] In *Thomson*,[84] the appeal court held that the four requirements of the defence set out by Hume still represent the law of Scotland.[85] However, the court went on to conclude that only the first two (an immediate danger of death or great bodily harm and an inability to resist the violence) remain preconditions for the operation of the defence, with the last two (a backward and inferior part in the perpetration and a disclosure of the fact) relating to the credibility of the accused's plea.[86] **5.10**

Cochrane was primarily concerned with the relevance of personal characteristics to whether the accused's response to threats was reasonable, a point not addressed by Hume.[87] Here too, the appeal court commences its discussion by setting out Hume's four requirements, which were still regarded as authoritative.[88]

In addition to the authorities on coercion, reference can be made to the parallel body of case law on necessity given that, in *Moss v Howdle*,[89] the appeal court suggested that the same considerations should govern the two defences[90] and, indeed, made a number of comments on the defence of coercion itself.

---

[78] Hume, i, 53, emphasis added.

[79] 1997 J.C. 123. *Moss v Howdle* concerned the related defence of necessity and is discussed in detail in Ch.4.

[80] *Moss v Howdle*, 1997 J.C. 123 at 126.

[81] A point made by Gordon (at para.13.29).

[82] 1983 J.C. 69.

[83] 2001 S.C.C.R. 655. In *Cochrane*, the court refers to the defence lying "virtually dormant until about thirty years ago [when it re-surfaced in *Thomson*]" (at [1]).

[84] By which time the defence is referred to as coercion, rather than compulsion, the term used by Hume.

[85] *Thomson v HM Advocate*, 1983 J.C. 69 at 78.

[86] *ibid.*

[87] Although note Alison, *Principles*, 673.

[88] The only other reported decisions of the appeal court on coercion are *Sayers v HM Advocate*, 1981 S.C.C.R. 312; *Collins v HM Advocate*, 1991 S.C.C.R. 898; and *Trotter v HM Advocate*, 2001 S.L.T. 296. *Sayers* and *Collins* were both cases in which the trial judge gave a direction on coercion, but which were not appealed on this basis. In *Trotter*, the defence of coercion was excluded from the jury by the presiding sheriff, on the basis that no notice of the defence had been given (on this see Ch.2). The appeal court upheld the decision, not on the procedural point, but because the accused ignored a reasonable opportunity to seek the protection of the authorities. See para.5.14 for discussion.

[89] 1997 J.C. 123

[90] At 128.

Requirements of the Plea

Hume's first requirement: an immediate danger of death or great bodily harm

5.11 Hume limited the availability of the defence to threats of "death or great bodily harm".[91] This requirement was approved by the appeal court in both *Thomson*[92] and *Moss v Howdle*.[93] It has been subject to some minor variation by trial judges in their jury charges,[94] but there has been no explicit suggestion in the case law that lesser threats, for example threats to property, could ground the defence. The exception to this is Alison, who appears to take the view that threats to property might suffice.[95] Nevertheless, he provides no authority for this view and the relevant passage of his text has not found its way into subsequent case law.

It has been suggested[96] that *Cochrane* might recognise coercion stemming from lesser threats. In *Cochrane*, the presiding sheriff allowed the defence of coercion to charges of assault and robbery to go to the jury on the basis of a threat to blow up the accused's house and to "kick" him or "hammer" him.[97] Little significance can be attached to this, however, because the appeal court expressed some doubt about the sheriff's decision[98] and went on to refer on several occasions to the requirement for "immediate danger of death or serious bodily injury".[99]

Before conclusively ruling out the availability of coercion as a defence where the threats were not of death or serious bodily harm, it should be noted that the case law to date has centred around relatively serious offences.[1] Thus, until a case comes up for decision where the offence is a relatively minor one, one could take the view that the issue of lesser threats remains open.

5.12 If coercion can operate both as a justification and an excuse, there seems no reason why the defence, at least in its justification form, should be limited to threats of death or serious bodily harm.[2] It is surely the case that an accused would be justified in committing a minor offence, such as possession of controlled drugs, on the basis of a threat to damage valuable or irreplaceable property or even a threat to cause serious economic loss. In such circumstances, the harm caused by the offence appears outweighed by the harm threatened by the coercer.

---

[91] Hume, i, 53. See also Forbes, who limited the defence to "mortal threats" (at 10).

[92] *Thomson v HM Advocate*, 1983 J.C. 69 at 78.

[93] *Moss v Howdle*, 1997 J.C. 123 at 128.

[94] For example, in *Sayers, Pears and Turner v HM Advocate*, 1981 S.C.C.R. 312, Lord Ross charged the jury in terms of "threats of death or injury to an individual if a certain act isn't done" (at 319). In *HM Advocate v Raiker*, 1989 S.C.C.R. 149, Lord McCluskey referred to "life threatening violence" (at 154).

[95] Alison, *Principles*, 672. It is unusual (although not unknown) for Alison to depart from the views of Hume in this way.

[96] V. Tadros, "The structure of defences in Scots criminal law" (2003) 7 Edin. L.R. 60–79 at pp.67–68.

[97] *Cochrane v HM Advocate*, 2001 S.C.C.R. 65 at [6].

[98] *ibid.* at [11].

[99] *ibid.* at [10] and [11].

[1] *Thomson v HM Advocate*, 1983 J.C. 69, the leading case, was a case involving armed robbery and has to be read in this context.

[2] See P.R. Glazebrook, "Structuring the criminal code: functional approaches to complicity, incomplete offences, and general defences" in *Harm and Culpability* (A.P. Simester and A.T.H. Smith (eds), 1996), pp.195–214, at pp.209–210; Tadros, above, fn.96, at p.67.

In relation to the excuse form of the defence, restricting the qualifying level of threat to one of death or serious bodily harm is more understandable on the basis that an individual might reasonably be expected to resist threats of a less serious nature than those of death or serious bodily harm, especially if a wide definition of serious bodily harm is taken such that it includes, for example, a threat to cause serious psychiatric injury.[3]

The approach taken to the qualifying level of threat in other jurisdictions varies. For the most part, English law appears to have taken the view that the availability of duress is restricted to cases where the threats were of death or serious bodily harm.[4] A similar limitation is placed on the defence in Canada,[5] Australia[6] and New Zealand.[7]

Is the defence limited to threats directed at the accused?

A second issue in relation to the nature of the threats is whether they must be directed towards the accused or whether threats to harm others will suffice. For the justification version of the defence, there seems no reason why threats to harm members of the accused's family or even complete strangers should not be treated as "coercive" if, on the balance of harms, the harm threatened outweighs the harm that would result from compliance. Where the balance of harms test is not satisfied (because the harms are approximately equivalent in nature) and the accused relies on the excuse form of the defence, the position is less clear. There is little doubt that threats to harm close family members or loved ones could place someone in such a state of fear that it would not be reasonable to expect him to resist a coercer's demands. Whether someone could be equally terrorised by threats made to a complete stranger is less immediately obvious, but is surely possible, especially if the threats were of a particularly gruesome nature. **5.13**

Neither *Thomson* nor *Cochrane* address the issue of whether threats must be directed at the accused himself. *Docherty v HM Advocate*[8] and

---

3 This would be consistent with English law, where the House of Lords has held in the context of assault occasioning actual bodily harm that bodily harm encompasses psychiatric injury (see *R. v Ireland* [1998] A.C. 147). As to what might constitute a threat to cause serious psychiatric injury, the English Law Commission gives the example of threats to destroy the sanity of a defendant through exposure to drugs. See *Report on Defences of General Application* (Law Com. No. 83, 1977), at para.2.25. In *R. v Baker and Wilkins* [1997] Crim. L.R. 497, it was held that a threat to cause serious psychological injury would *not* be sufficient to ground the defence of duress (although *cf. R. v Steane* [1947] K.B. 997), but this must surely be questioned in the light of *Ireland*.

4 *R. v Bowen* [1996] 2 Cr.App.R. 157; *R. v Shayler* [2001] EWCA Crim 1977; *R. v Hasan* [2005] UKHL 22. See also *R. v Valderrama-Vega* [1985] Crim. L.R. 220, where it was held that a threat to disclose the fact that the defendant was homosexual was not sufficient in itself to ground a defence of duress, although if the defendant was influenced to act by this threat in combination with threats of death or serious bodily harm, the position would be different. English law has taken a strict approach to what constitutes serious bodily harm. In *R. v Aikens* [2003] EWCA Crim 1573 it was doubted that a threat to punch the defendant in the face would suffice.

5 Section 17 of the Canadian Criminal Code restricts the availability of the defence to threats of death or bodily harm. See also *R. v Hibbert* [1995] 2 S.C.R. 973 which states the common law position in similar terms.

6 *Williamson* [1972] 2 N.S.W.L.R. 281.

7 Crimes Act 1961, s.24(1). *Cf.* the South African case of *S v Mtewtwa* 1977 (3) S.A. 628 (E), where a threat of solitary confinement proved sufficient where the accused broke into premises.

8 (1976) S.C.C.R. Supp. 146.

HM Advocate v McCallum[9] seem to suggest that coercion can be grounded in threats to members of the accused's family. This is consistent with English law.[10]

It is probably equally safe to conclude that coercion is available when the threats of harm are made to persons who are *not* members of the accused's family, whether such persons be friends, acquaintances or complete strangers. While there is no direct authority in relation to coercion,[11] it was held in the *Lord Advocate's Reference (No. 1 of 2000)*[12] that the closely related defence of necessity is available when a threat is directed to an unrelated bystander.[13]

Immediacy of danger

5.14 The danger of death or great bodily harm must be "immediate".[14] The immediacy requirement rules out the defence in cases where the accused had a reasonable opportunity to avoid the threatened harm by taking some action other than compliance; for example, by seeking the protection of the authorities.

Critics argue that it is unfair to the accused to rule out the defence where seeking the protection of the authorities would be *possible*, in terms of the time period in question, but would most likely be ineffective.[15]

Nonetheless, the courts show little sign of departing from Hume's immediacy condition. In *Thomson*, the appeal court approved the requirement, stating that:

> "What [Hume] was saying was that it is only where, following threats, there is an immediate danger of violence, in whatever form it takes, that the defence of coercion can be entertained ... If there is time and opportunity to seek and obtain the shield of the law in a well-regulated society, then recourse should be made to it, and if it is not then the defence of coercion is not open. It is the danger which has to be 'immediate', not just the threat."[16]

---

[9] (1977) S.C.C.R. Supp. 169.

[10] *R. v Ortiz* (1986) 83 Cr.App.R. 173. See also the Supreme Court of Victoria case of *R. v Hurley and Murray* [1967] V.R. 526 and the Canadian Supreme Court in *R. v Ruzic* [2001] 1 S.C.R. 687.

[11] Although see the Draft Criminal Code, s.29(2)(a) where no limitation is placed on the class of person to whom the threat must be directed.

[12] 2001 J.C. 143.

[13] At [44]. See para.4.10. *Cf.* the English cases of *R. v Abdul-Hussain* [1999] Crim. L.R. 570 and *R. v Shayler* [2001] EWCA Crim 1977 which have restricted the availability of duress to cases where the threats were made to someone for whom the defendant reasonably feels responsible, an approach approved by the House of Lords in *R. v Hasan* [2005] UKHL 22 (at [21] *per* Lord Bingham).

[14] Hume, i, 53.

[15] V. Tadros, "The structure of defences in Scots criminal law" (2003) 7 Edin. L.R. 60–79 at p.68; Robinson, *Criminal Law Defenses*, §177(e). This criticism is made frequently in relation to battered women who might be denied the defence on the basis that a violent partner's threat might not be one of immediate harm, but, because the authorities are unable to protect them from their partner's future violence, seeking official protection would most likely be futile. See H.R. Skinazi, "Not just a conjured afterthought: using duress as a defence for battered women who fail to protect" (1997) 85 *California Law Review* 993–1042 at p.1003; S. Appel, "Beyond self-defence: the use of battered woman syndrome in duress defences" (1994) *University of Illinois Law Review* 955–980 at p.975.

[16] *Thomson v HM Advocate*, 1983 J.C. 69 at 77. The point was re-iterated in *Cochrane v HM Advocate*, 2001 S.C.C.R. 655 at [10]. The immediacy requirement is also retained in the Draft Criminal Code, s.29(20)(a).

The issue of immediacy arose directly in *Trotter v HM Advocate*.[17] Here, the accused attempted to plead coercion to a charge of possession of drugs with intent to supply. He had been discovered with the drugs when visiting his father in prison. He claimed that he was told by a third party to take the drugs to his father and that, if he refused, his father would "get done".[18] He had the opportunity to inform the authorities of this before visiting the prison but did not do so, he claimed, because he was "scared".[19] The presiding sheriff excluded the defence of coercion from the jury on the basis that no notice of the defence had been given.[20] The appeal court held that they were not required to address the procedural question because the defence was not arguable on the facts. The defence of coercion, they stated, is available only in the restricted circumstances outlined in *Thomson*, meaning that there must be immediate danger. In this case, however:

> "... the appellant had the opportunity to inform the authorities of the situation, but chose not to do so, because he was afraid. Such circumstances cannot amount to a complete defence to a criminal charge, although they may, if accepted, be taken into account in mitigation of sentence".[21]

In requiring a threatened harm to be immediate, Scots law is out of line with other jurisdictions. In England, it was conceded as long ago as 1971 that the defence of duress would not be disallowed merely because a threat of harm could not be carried out immediately[22] and a similar stance has been taken by the United States Court of Appeals for the Sixth Circuit.[23]

5.15 In Canada, the Supreme Court has gone as far as declaring the immediacy requirement to be unconstitutional, in *R. v Ruzic*.[24] Prior to *Ruzic*, the Canadian Criminal Code contained the requirement that threats must be of immediate death or bodily harm and they must be made by a person who is present at the commission of the offence.[25] Ruzic was charged with illegally importing drugs into Canada and claimed she had done so because of threats to kill her family living in Serbia. The threatener lived in Serbia and did not accompany her to Canada and, as

---

[17] 2001 S.L.T. 296.

[18] By which he understood that his father would be stabbed (at [2]).

[19] At [2].

[20] On this, see Ch.2.

[21] At [4]. See also *HM Advocate v McCallum* (1977) S.C.C.R. Supp. 169 at 169.

[22] *R. v Hudson and Taylor* [1971] 2 Q.B. 202 at 207, *per* Lord Widgery. *Hudson and Taylor* has since been applied in a line of cases including *R. v Lewis* (1993) 96 Cr.App.R. 412; *R. v Abdul-Hussain* [1999] Crim. L.R. 570; *R. v Baker and Ward* [1999] 2 Cr.App.R. 335; *R. v Lyness* [2002] EWCA 1759; and *R. v True* [2003] EWCA Crim 2255. See also the Privy Council case of *Subramaniam v Public Prosecutor* [1956] 1 W.L.R. 965, where the Privy Council held that the failure to satisfy the immediacy requirement should not have prevented the defence of duress from being left to the jury (at 972). *Cf. R. v Hasan* [2005] UKHL 22 at [28], *per* Lord Bingham.

[23] *United States v Riffe*, 28 F. 3d 565 (1994). For comment, see D.S. Rutkowski, "A coercion defence for the street gang criminal: plugging the moral gap in existing law" (1996) 10 *Notre Dame Journal of Law, Ethics and Public Policy* 137–226 at pp.195–196.

[24] [2001] 1 S.C.R. 687.

[25] Section 17.

such, the immediacy and presence requirements were not satisfied.[26] The Canadian Supreme Court declared these requirements to be unconstitutional on the basis that they infringe the principles of fundamental justice by permitting the conviction of persons whose conduct is morally involuntary.[27]

There is some indication in *Thomson* that, if a suitable case were to arise for decision, Scots law might be prepared to relax the immediacy requirement. In *Thomson*, the appeal court considered whether Scots law would allow the defence of coercion if facts corresponding to those of the English case of *Hudson and Taylor* arose.[28] They concluded that it would not "*unless* of course there was evidence to the effect that the processes of law and order could not afford a reasonable protection against the threats being carried out at some future date".[29]

The appeal court also made it clear that, in requiring immediacy, they assumed a well-regulated society in which the protection of the authorities would be available. In the rare cases in which this assumption cannot be made, it was accepted that "different considerations might have to apply".[30]

Will an implied threat suffice?

5.16 The issue of whether the threat of harm must be explicit or whether an implied threat will suffice has not arisen in Scots law. The issue has arisen in other jurisdictions. In Canada, the Ontario Court of Appeal has held that the defence of duress is not limited to explicit threats.[31] This was applied in *R. v McRae*,[32] where the appellant helped his cousin, who had killed three hitchhikers and their dog, to destroy the evidence of his act. No explicit threat was made, but the events took place in a remote location, the cousin had a gun, and one of the hitchhikers was executed and her body thrown on the fire in the appellant's presence. These circumstances were held to constitute an implied threat sufficient to ground the defence of compulsion.

---

[26] The issue is slightly complicated by the fact that Canadian criminal law recognises two forms of the defence. The version relied upon by Ruzic was that in s.17 of the Criminal Code, which applies to defendants who commit offences as principals. Where a defendant is liable as a party to the offence, however, the common law version can be evoked (*Paquette v The Queen* [1977] 2 S.C.R. 189). Only the Criminal Code version of the defence contained the immediacy and presence requirements. Ruzic was forced to rely on the Criminal Code because she was the principal actor in relation to the offence with which she was charged.

[27] *R. v Ruzic* [2001] 1 S.C.R. 687 at [55]. See also the Law Reform Commission for Ireland's *Consultation Paper on Duress and Necessity* (L.R.C. C.P. 39, 2006) which recommends that there be no immediacy requirement in relation to duress (at para.2.135).

[28] In *Hudson and Taylor*, two women called as witnesses gave false evidence in a case involving a criminal gang because they had been threatened with serious bodily injury if they told the truth. As they entered the court to give evidence, they saw one of the gang members sitting in the public gallery.

[29] *Thomson v HM Advocate*, 1983 J.C. 69 at 80, emphasis added. The appeal court appears to have concluded (erroneously) that the Court of Appeal in *Hudson and Taylor* did not take into account the availability and practicality of alternative methods of preventing the threat.

[30] *Thomson v HM Advocate*, 1983 J.C. 69 at 78. For a case in which it was conceded that the authorities (here the Serbian police) could not be relied upon to provide protection, see *R. v Ruzic* [2001] 1 S.C.R. 687.

[31] *R. v Mena* (1987) 34 C.C.C. (3d) 304 at 320.

[32] (2005) 199 C.C.C. (3d) 536. See also the Irish case of *Attorney General v Whelan* [1934] I.R. 518, where it was accepted that an implied threat could serve to ground the defence of duress.

Hume's second requirement: an inability to resist the violence

5.17 The accused must be unable "to resist the violence".[33] Hume does not explain this requirement and it has been all but ignored in subsequent case law. The only reference to it (other than simply repeating it verbatim) is found in *Cochrane*, where the Lord Justice-General (Rodger) explained:

> "... if when threatened with death or great bodily harm the accused is in a position to resist any attack—perhaps because he is stronger or more skilful in combat than the third party—then the defence of coercion cannot apply, since the accused should resist rather than commit the crime".[34]

The "inability to resist the violence" requirement appears to play a role similar to the retreat rule in self-defence[35] and means that the defence of coercion will be denied to the accused who fails to pursue a course of action other than compliance. Presumably the defence will only be denied where the opportunity to resist the demands of the coercer was a reasonable one that did not expose the accused to equal or greater danger.[36]

Hume's third requirement: a backward and inferior part in the perpetration

5.18 For Hume, the accused must play "a backward and inferior part in the perpetration".[37] The appeal court in *Thomson* relegated this requirement to something of a secondary role, stating that the defence should not be ruled out on this basis alone:

> "... we consider that the part which is taken in the perpetration, which can take place in a whole variety of ways and degrees, is simply one factor in the amalgam of factors which may point to the accused's voluntary or coerced conduct".[38]

This approach seems to be sensible and fair to the accused. As the appeal court stated:

> "If a man opens a safe, which is the major feature of the crime, but only does so because he has a revolver pointed at his head and he is told that his head will be blown off if he does not open it, it is difficult to see why the defence is not open to him because he played a major and not a backward or inferior part in the perpetration of the crime."[39]

Hume's fourth requirement: disclosure of the fact

5.19 According to Hume, the accused must make "a disclosure of the fact, as well as restitution of the spoil, on the first safe and convenient occasion".[40] This relates to the behaviour of the accused after he has complied

---

[33] Hume, i, 53.
[34] *Cochrane v HM Advocate*, 2001 S.C.C.R. 65 at [10].
[35] On which, see para.3.12.
[36] This would be consistent with the approach taken to self-defence (see *McBrearty v HM Advocate*, 1999 S.L.T. 1333 and para.3.12).
[37] Hume, i, 53.
[38] *Thomson v HM Advocate*, 1983 J.C. 69 at 77.
[39] *ibid.*
[40] Hume, i, 53.

with the demands of the threatener and, if strictly applied, would deny the defence to anyone who did not surrender himself to the authorities on the first safe occasion.[41] Like the requirement of a backward and inferior part in the perpetration, however, this requirement was held in *Thomson* not to be absolute:

> "... that is not something which could positively affirm or disprove that the accused was acting under coercion. Rather it is a test of whether such actings are or are not consistent with his proponed defence of coercion."[42]

The relevance of personal characteristics

5.20 One issue not addressed by Hume is the extent to which the personal characteristics of the accused are to be taken into account when determining whether or not he should have been expected to resist the threat made against him. Given that Hume (and indeed subsequent case law[43]) recognised only threats of death or great bodily harm as coercive, the point may be redundant. After all, it is difficult to imagine circumstances in which it would be reasonable to expect an accused to resist a threat of this nature, regardless of their personal characteristics.[44]

Nonetheless, this point has now been directly addressed in *Cochrane v HM Advocate*.[45] The appellant in *Cochrane* had been convicted of assault and robbery after his defence of coercion was rejected. He appealed on the basis that the presiding sheriff had misdirected the jury in stating that they had to consider whether the threats made against him were such as would have overcome the resolution of an ordinarily constituted person of the same age and sex. It was accepted that Cochrane had an extremely low IQ (in the bottom four per cent of the population) and was unusually susceptible as far as compliance was concerned. It was argued on appeal that these traits should have been taken into account in deciding whether or not he should have been expected to resist the threats.

The appeal court rejected his argument. They commenced their judgment by noting that an objective condition is relatively well established in relation to coercion in Scots law. Although Hume is silent on this matter,[46] Alison stated that:

> "... if an ordinary mob, or any unlawful assembly of persons, compel any individual by threats and violence to accompany them on any unlawful expedition, provided he did not yield too easily to intimidation, but held out as long as in such circumstances can be expected *from a man of ordinary resolution*".[47]

[41] Hume did include the condition that the occasion must be a safe one. He did not intend to require the accused to disclose the fact if the authorities would not be able to protect him from the coercer.

[42] *Thomson v HM Advocate*, 1983 J.C. 69 at 77.

[43] See para.5.11 above.

[44] Assuming all the other relevant conditions of the defence of coercion are met, such as the non-availability of avenues of escape, and setting aside for the time being issues such as whether the defence should be excluded in murder cases. On whether coercion should be a defence to murder, see paras 5.27 *et seq*.

[45] 2001 S.C.C.R. 655.

[46] *cf*. Gordon, who states incorrectly (at para.13.27, fn.9) that Alison follows Hume.

[47] Alison, *Principles*, 673; *Cochrane v HM Advocate*, 2001 S.C.C.R. 65 at [13] (emphasis added).

The first full formulation of the objective condition was set out, without authority, in Anderson's *The Criminal Law of Scotland*, where he wrote: **5.21**

> "The defence of compulsion ... is a valid plea, if threats have been used of such a nature as to overcome the resolution of an ordinarily constituted person of the same age and sex as the accused".[48]

The Anderson formulation was repeated by the trial judges in *McCallum*[49] and *Thomson*.[50] On this basis, the appeal court in *Cochrane* took the view that an objective test was part of Scots law and neither the appellant's low intelligence nor his unusually compliant nature could be taken into account in assessing whether he could have reasonably been expected to resist a particular threat.[51]

Aside from the weight of authority, the appeal court set out two policy reasons for their decision. First, the objective condition was necessary to keep relatively strict limits on what is a controversial defence that would otherwise be open to abuse.[52] Secondly, the adoption of an objective test is consistent with the stance taken by Scots law in relation to other defences, such as self-defence.[53]

Consequently, in deciding whether or not the accused should have been expected to resist the threats made to him, a jury should: **5.22**

> "... consider whether an ordinary sober person of reasonable firmness, *sharing the characteristics of the accused*, would have responded as the accused did. Therefore, in a case where the accused lacks reasonable firmness, the jury must disregard that particular characteristic *but have regard to his other characteristics*."[54]

The question then arises of which characteristics *are* relevant. According to the appeal court in *Cochrane*:

> "The test does not ... apply a single standard to all cases. It recognises that what may reasonably be required of ordinary people will depend on their age: a child cannot be expected to react like an adult. Similarly, when faced with a threat from a more powerful man, a woman cannot be expected to react in the same way as a man who is as powerful as the third party. A person who is physically handicapped cannot be expected to react to certain threats in the same way as someone who is physically fit."[55]

Thus, age, sex and physical ability are relevant when deciding whether the accused could reasonably have been expected to resist the threat. Low intelligence and unusual levels of compliance are clearly not.[56] Other than

---

48 Anderson, 16; *Cochrane v HM Advocate*, 2001 S.C.C.R. 65 at [13].

49 *HM Advocate v McCallum* (1977) S.C.C.R. Supp. 169 at 170.

50 *Thomson v HM Advocate*. 1983 J.C. 69 at 75. The charge was approved by the appeal court (at 80).

51 *Cochrane v HM Advocate*. 2001 S.C.C.R. 65 at [29]. *Cf. Bone v HM Advocate*, 2006 S.L.T. 164.

52 *Cochrane v HM Advocate*, 2001 S.C.C.R. 65 at [20].

53 *ibid.* at [20]. On the objective condition in self-defence, see para.3.15.

54 *Cochrane v HM Advocate*, 2001 S.C.C.R. 65 at [29], emphasis added.

55 *ibid.* at [21].

56 Although *cf. R. v Antar* [2004] EWCA Crim 2708 at [41]. In a different context, *cf. Bone v HM Advocate*, 2006 S.L.T. 164.

this, no further guidance is provided. This leaves open the question of whether, for example, a recognised psychiatric condition, such as post-traumatic stress disorder, would be a relevant characteristic.[56a]

This issue has been addressed in English law. Somewhat surprisingly, given the subjectivisation of both the self-defence and provocation defences,[57] English law retains an objective test in relation to duress. Indeed, it was from the leading English case, *R. v Graham*,[58] that the "sober person of reasonable firmness sharing the same characteristics of the accused" test adopted in *Cochrane* was taken. In applying this test, English law does not admit evidence that the defendant was more pliable, vulnerable, timid or susceptible to threats than an ordinary person and characteristics resulting from self-abuse (such as alcohol or drug abuse) are also excluded. The court is, however, entitled to take account of age, sex, pregnancy, serious physical disability or a recognised psychiatric condition.[59]

Voluntary exposure to the risk of coercion

5.23 A further issue that is not addressed by Hume is whether the accused who voluntarily exposes himself to the risk of coercion by, for example, joining a criminal organisation that has used violence against its members in the past, should be permitted to plead the defence. Two main arguments have been put forward for denying the defence in these circumstances.

The first is that it sits somewhat uncomfortably with the notion of coercion as an excuse. This has already been discussed in relation to necessity.[60]

The second, which would apply both to the justification and the excuse versions of the defence, is one of public policy. Allowing the accused who voluntarily joins a criminal organisation to plead the defence opens up the possibility that members of that organisation could confer immunity on their fellow members who commit crimes simply by issuing threats of death.[61] This does, however, seem a rather weak argument as it might be questioned that a threat issued in these circumstances is actually a true threat that would lead the recipient to fear death or serious bodily injury.

If a requirement of this nature is imposed, the question arises of how to formulate it. At one end of the spectrum—the end most favourable to the accused—the defence is denied only when it was reasonably foreseeable that pressure would be put on the accused to commit specifically the type of crime he was asked to commit in practice. Hence, if it was reasonably foreseeable that the accused might have been coerced into committing

---

[56a] On this, albeit in a different context, see *Bone v HM Advocate*, 2006 S.L.T. 164. *Bone* is discussed in more detail in para.4.19, in relation to necessity.

[57] *R. v Smith (Morgan James)* [2001] 1 A.C. 146 (provocation); *R. v Williams (Gladstone)* (1984) 78 Cr.App.R. 276 (self-defence); *R. v Beckford* [1988] A.C. 130 (self-defence). Although in relation to provocation, see now the decision of the Privy Council in *Attorney-General for Jersey v Holley* [2005] UKPC 23 (discussed in para.10.19).

[58] [1982] 1 W.L.R. 294. *Graham* was approved by the House of Lords in *R. v Howe* [1987] A.C. 417 at 459, *per* Lord Mackay of Clashfern.

[59] *R. v Bowen* [1996] 2 Cr.App.R. 157, approved in *R. v Lyness* [2002] EWCA Crim 1759, a case decided after the controversial decision on provocation in *R. v Smith (Morgan James)* [2001] 1 A.C. 146. See also *R. v Hurst* [1995] 1 Cr.App.R. 82. *Cf. R. v Martin (David Paul)* [2000] 2 Cr.App.R. 42.

[60] See para.4.20.

[61] Casebook, para.7.67; P.R. Glazebrook, "Structuring the criminal code: functional approaches to complicity, incomplete offences, and general defences" in *Harm and Culpability* (A.P. Simester and A.T.H. Smith (eds), 1996), pp.195–214, at p.209.

minor drugs offences (perhaps because the criminal gang involved had a history of suchlike) but, in the event, he was coerced into committing an armed robbery, the defence would not be denied.

Slightly less favourably to the accused, the defence could be ruled out whenever it was reasonably foreseeable that he might have been pressurised to commit not only the specific offence in question, but an offence of *any* nature. The defence would then be ruled out in the armed robbery example above.

Finally, at the other end of the spectrum—and least favourably to the accused—the defence could be denied whenever there was a reasonably foreseeable risk that the group or individual with which the accused voluntarily associated might engage in unlawful violence towards him. In this scenario, the defence would be denied when, for example, the accused associated with drug dealers who were known to use violence to collect their debts but had no history of subjecting their members to coercion in order to persuade them to commit crimes. **5.24**

The approach taken by Scots law to this question is unclear. The issue of voluntary exposure to the risk of coercion has never directly arisen. The only reference to the issue in reported case law is in *Thomson v HM Advocate*,[62] where the trial judge charged the jury in the following terms:

> "I am further of opinion, having regard to the principle lying behind the foregoing qualifications, that if the accused has joined an association where such threats from associates and the dangers arising from them are reasonably to be expected, a defence of coercion by such associates will not avail him."[63]

The issue has been controversial in English law where, after a series of conflicting authorities, it was recently settled by the House of Lords.[64] In *R. v Baker and Ward*,[65] the Court of Appeal had taken the position most favourable to a defendant, denying the defence only where the defendant was aware of the risk that he might be coerced into committing criminal offences of the type for which he is being tried.[66] In *R. v Heath*,[67] a differently constituted Court of Appeal ruled out the defence whenever the defendant was aware of the risk of duress, even if he did not foresee the particular type of offence he was, in fact, asked to commit.[68] In *R. v Harmer*,[69] yet another bench of the Court of Appeal took the position least favourable to a defendant and ruled out the defence in all cases where the defendant was aware that he was exposing himself to the risk of

---

[62] 1983 J.C. 69.

[63] At 73. The appeal court in *Thomson* made no specific reference to this part of the charge but stated that the trial judge "gave the proper directions in the circumstances of the case in a careful and meticulous manner" (at 80). *Cf. Sayers, Pears and Turner v HM Advocate*, 1981 S.C.C.R. 312, where coercion was allowed to go to the jury even though the accused was a member of a terrorist organisation, the Ulster Volunteer Force (UVF). The case was appealed but the appeal court made no mention of this point.

[64] *R. v Hasan* [2005] UKHL 22.

[65] [1999] 2 Cr.App.R. 335.

[66] At 344. See also *R. v Z* [2003] EWCA Crim 191 (the Court of Appeal's decision that preceded *R. v Hasan* [2005] UKHL 22), where the Court chose to follow the *Baker and Ward* formulation (at [72]). For comment, see A. Reed, "Duress and specificity of the threat: commentary on *R. v Z*" (2003) 67 J.C.L. 281–286.

[67] [2000] Crim. L.R. 109.

[68] See also *R. v Lewis* (1993) 96 Cr.App.R. 412; *R. v Ali* [1995] Crim. L.R. 303.

[69] [2001] EWCA Crim 2930.

violence, even where he did not foresee that he might be asked to commit a crime.[70]

5.25 Faced with these three conflicting authorities, the House of Lords chose to follow *Heath*,[71] Lord Bingham explaining that:

> "The defendant is, *ex hypothesi*, a person who has voluntarily surrendered his will to the domination of another. Nothing should turn on the foresight of the manner in which, in the event, the dominant party chooses to exploit the defendant's subservience."[72]

The English cases raise three further points. First, the defence will be denied in English law only if the accused voluntarily associated with the coercive organisation or individual.[73] If the defendant was coerced into association in the first place, the defence would not be withheld.[74] Although there is no authority on the point, the Scottish courts would presumably follow this approach.

The second is that English law applies an objective test to the question of whether or not the defendant voluntarily exposed himself to the risk of duress.[75] The defence will be ruled out whenever a person:

> "... voluntarily becomes or remains associated with others engaged in criminal activity in a situation where he knows or ought reasonably to know that he may be the subject of compulsion by them or their associates".[76]

It might be thought from the trial judge's charge in *Thomson*,[77] where he referred to dangers "reasonably to be expected",[78] that Scots law would likewise take this approach, but the issue is still open in the absence of any direct authority.

The third is that, under English law, the defence can be pled once the defendant has ceased to be a member of the criminal association in question or otherwise disassociated himself from the circumstances in which there was a risk of duress.[79] Once again, in the absence of any direct authority in Scots law, this question is still open.

---

[70] At [16]. In *Harmer* the defence was denied to an appellant who was a drug user and, after incurring debts with his supplier, was coerced by him into importing cocaine into the UK. The appellant admitted that he was aware that his supplier might resort to violence in order to enforce his debts but not that he might ask him to resort to crime.

[71] *R. v Hasan* [2005] UKHL 22 at [37], *per* Lord Bingham; at [77] *per* Baroness Hale.

[72] *R. v Hasan* [2005] UKHL 22 at [37], *per* Lord Bingham.

[73] See *R. v Sharp* [1987] 1 Q.B. 853 at 861, *per* Lord Lane C.J.; *R. v Harmer* [2001] EWCA Crim 2930 at [16].

[74] On this, see D.S. Rutkowski, "A coercion defence for the street gang criminal: plugging the moral gap in existing law" (1996) 10 *Notre Dame Journal of Law, Ethics and Public Policy* 137–226. *Cf.* C. Gearty, "Duress: members of criminal organisations and gangs" [1987] C.L.J. 379–381 at p.380.

[75] *R. v Hasan* [2005] UKHL 22 at [37], *per* Lord Bingham.

[76] *R. v Hasan* [2005] UKHL 22 at [38], *per* Lord Bingham. He explains: "The policy of the law must be to discourage association with known criminals, and it should be slow to excuse the criminal conduct of those who do so" (at [38]).

[77] *Thomson v HM Advocate*, 1983 J.C. 69.

[78] See para.5.24 above.

[79] *R. v Baker and Ward* [1999] 2 Cr.App.R. 335 at 346; *R. v Lewis* (1993) 96 Cr.App.R. 412 at 417.

The nature of the demand

Another possibility not addressed by Hume is that the nature of the demand made by the coercer might place some limits on the availability of the defence. In particular, the issue arises of how specific the demands of the threatener must be before coercion is available. 5.26

The issue has not been considered in Scotland but it did arise in the English case of *R. v Cole*.[80] Here, the defendant was threatened with serious bodily harm to himself and his family if he did not pay a debt he owed. He then attempted to plead duress in answer to a charge of the robbery of two building societies, claiming that he did so in response to the demands of the moneylenders. The moneylenders had demanded only that he repay the money that he owed and at no time specifically suggested that he should commit robbery. The Court of Appeal held that duress was not available on this basis but is limited to situations where the threatener has nominated the specific crime(s) to be committed.[81]

Is Coercion a Defence to Murder?

The authorities

The appeal court has never addressed the issue of whether coercion operates as a defence to murder. Hume places no such limitation on the availability of the defence and, although he otherwise draws to a great degree from Hale[82] in his views on the defence of coercion,[83] he does not repeat Hale's exclusion of the defence to charges of murder.[84] 5.27

In *HM Advocate v Peters*,[85] a case where the issue might have arisen,[86] the trial judge stated only that "[i]t has never been decided in Scotland whether coercion can ever be a defence to murder" and excluded the defence from the jury on unrelated grounds. In *Thomson*, the appeal court reserved their opinion on the point, which was not directly at issue.[87] In *Collins v HM Advocate*,[88] the issue was addressed by the trial judge, who directed the jury that coercion was not available to a charge of murder as follows:

> "I direct you [that] as a matter of law coercion is not a defence in Scotland to the crime of murder and the reason is quite simple. It is because of the supreme importance that the law affords to the protection of human life. It is repugnant that the law should recognise in any individual in any circumstances however extreme the right to choose that one innocent person should be killed rather than any other person including himself."[89]

---

80 [1994] Crim. L.R. 582.

81 At 583. On this, see A. Reed, "Duress and specificity of the threat: commentary on *R. v Z*" (2003) 67 J.C.L. 281–286 at p.283. It might have been arguable that the accused actually had a defence of necessity (or in English law duress of circumstances).

82 M. Hale, *The History of the Pleas of the Crown* (1736).

83 See especially the distinction made by Hale (above at p.49) but adopted by Hume, i, 51–52 (without direct acknowledgment) between the availability of the defence in times of war, or public insurrection, or rebellion and times of peace.

84 Hale, above, fn.82, p.51.

85 (1969) 33 J.C.L. 209.

86 The accused was charged with murder and lodged a special defence of coercion.

87 *Thomson v HM Advocate*, 1983 J.C. 69 at 78.

88 1991 S.C.C.R. 898.

89 At 902.

These comments on coercion must be treated as *obiter* because neither accused actually relied on the defence. In the subsequent appeal, lodged on the basis of evidential matters, the appeal court mentioned coercion only in passing and did not comment on this passage.

It would be surprising, should the issue directly arise, if the appeal court allowed coercion to operate as a defence to murder.[90] This would place Scotland out of line with the vast majority of common law and civil law jurisdictions and with international criminal law.

5.28 In England, the House of Lords ruled that duress is available neither as a defence to murder[91] nor to attempted murder.[92] Similar restrictions are placed on the availability of the defence in Ireland,[92a] some Australian states[93] and New Zealand.[94] In Canada, the restrictions placed on the availability of the defence are even more stringent; it is ruled out in cases of murder, attempted murder, sexual assault, abduction, hostage taking, robbery, assault with a weapon or assault causing bodily harm and arson, among other offences.[95]

In international criminal law, the issue has received detailed consideration in *Prosecutor v Erdemovic*,[96] a case decided by the Appeals Chamber of the International Tribunal for the Former Yugoslavia. In a majority decision, the Appeals Chamber held that duress did not afford a complete defence to a soldier charged with a crime against humanity and/or a war crime involving the killing of innocent human beings.[97]

A contrasting approach can be found in South Africa, where the Appellate Division accepted, in *S v Goliath*,[98] that compulsion could

[90] *cf.* the Draft Criminal Code, s.29(3).

[91] *R. v Howe* [1987] A.C. 417, recently confirmed in *R. v Hasan* [2005] UKHL 22 at [21], *per* Lord Bingham. Lord Bingham did, however, state that he found the argument for abandoning this restriction "irresistible" (*Hasan*, at [21]).

[92] *R. v Gotts* [1992] 2 A.C. 412 (Lord Lowry dissenting), recently confirmed in *R. v Hasan* [2005] UKHL 22 at [21], *per* Lord Bingham. It is available as a defence to all other crimes (with the exception of some forms of treason), including hijacking an aircraft (*R. v Abdul-Hussain* [1999] Crim. L.R. 570).

[92a] *Attorney-General v Whelan* [1934] I.R. 518 at 524.

[93] *McConnell* [1977] 1 N.S.W.L.R. (CCA) 714 (New South Wales); *Brown and Morley* [1968] S.A.S.R. 467 (South Australia).

[94] Crimes Act 1961, s.24(2). It is also ruled out in relation to robbery, kidnapping, wounding with intent and arson.

[95] Canadian Criminal Code, s.17. The Criminal Code governs cases of compulsion where the accused was the principal offender (in the case of murder this would be where the accused was the actual killer). Where the accused is liable as an accessory to the offence, the common law defence of duress applies. In *R. v Paquette* [1977] 2 S.C.R. 189, the Supreme Court held that duress *was* available as a defence to murder under the common law, where the accused was not the actual killer. However, the Supreme Court relied heavily on the House of Lords decision in the Northern Irish case of *DPP for Northern Ireland v Lynch* [1975] A.C. 653, which allowed duress as a defence to murder where the accused merely aided and abetted the principal offender. As *Lynch* has since been overruled by the House of Lords in *R. v Howe* [1987] A.C. 417, the decision in *Paquette* must be subject to some doubt. There have been several cases decided under the common law by the Supreme Court since *Paquette*, but none deals with this question.

[96] Case no. IT-96-22-A, October 7, 1997, Appeals Chamber of the International Tribunal for the Former Yugoslavia, unreported. See *www.un.org/icty*. For comment, see R.E. Brooks, "Law in the heart of darkness: atrocity and duress" (2003) 43 *Virginia Journal of International Law* 861–888.

[97] In fact, the issue being decided was slightly narrower even than this: whether or not duress afforded a defence to the killing of innocent human beings *who would have died regardless of the conduct of the accused.* If duress was ruled out in this context, however, then it can be assumed that it would also have been ruled out where the victims would have lived but for the actions of the accused.

[98] 1972 (3) S.A. 1 (AD).

operate as a defence to murder. This was applied in *S v Peterson*,[99] where the accused was acquitted of the murder of a fellow prisoner on the ground of compulsion. Likewise, in the Australian state of Victoria, duress is now a complete defence to murder. See s.6 of the Crimes (Homicide) Act 2005, which amends the Crimes Act 1958.[99a]

The principled argument

The main principled arguments against recognising duress as a defence to murder were set out in the English case of *R. v Howe*,[1] a decision much discussed and criticised in the academic literature.[2] In rejecting the availability of duress as a defence to murder, the House of Lords in *Howe* relied on three main arguments of principle. **5.29**

The first was that the law should not be seen to countenance the act of killing an innocent person in order to save one's own life. Lord Griffiths, for example, referred to the:

> "... special sanctity that the law attaches to human life and which denies to a man the right to take an innocent life at the price of his own or another's life".[3]

This line of argument has been criticised on two inter-related grounds. First, it assumes that duress operates only as a justification. If the view is taken that duress can operate as an excuse, the objection that the law is condoning the killing of an innocent human being is less convincing. This is because the recognition of an excuse defence does not, as a justification does, imply that the law approves or somehow condones the conduct in question. Rather it sends the message that, although the law disapproves of the conduct in question, the accused should not be blamed for it.[4] This argument might itself be subject to the counter-argument that, as the legal system does not distinguish between verdicts of acquittal due to justification and acquittal due to excuse, the public will assume from the fact of the acquittal that the conduct *is*, in fact, condoned.[5]

The second ground of criticism is that it is wrong for the law to demand that an individual sacrifice his own life in order to save the life of another, as this is a standard of behaviour that borders on saintliness and one with which the vast majority of people would be unable to comply.[6] This might be appropriate if duress operates only as a justification defence, but if it is **5.30**

---

[99] 1980 (1) S.A. 938 (A).

[99a] This was a change in the law recommended by the Victorian Law Reform Commission, in its report *Defences to Homicide* (No. 94, 2004).

[1] [1987] A.C. 417.

[2] H.P. Milgate, "Duress and the criminal law: another about turn by the House of Lords" [1988] C.L.J. 61–76; A. Reed, "The need for a new Anglo-American approach to duress" (1997) J.C.L. 209–224; K.J.M. Smith, "Must heroes behave heroically?" [1989] Crim. L.R. 622–628; L. Walters, "Murder under duress and judicial decision-making in the House of Lords" (1988) 8 L.S. 61–73.

[3] *R. v Howe* [1987] A.C. 417 at 439. See also Lord Griffiths, at 444; Lord Hailsham, at 432–434; Lord Mackay, at 456.

[4] P.A. Alldridge, "The coherence of defences" [1983] Crim. L.R. 665–672 at p.668; I. Dennis, "Duress, murder and criminal responsibility" (1980) 96 L.Q.R. 208–238 at p.238.

[5] Simon Gardner terms this problem quasi-justificatory drift. See S. Gardner, "Instrumentalism and necessity" (1986) 6 O.J.L.S. 431–438.

[6] A.L. Dienstag, "*Fedorenko v United States*: War crimes, the defence of duress and American nationality law" (1982) 82 *Columbia Law Review* 120–183 at p.144; J. Dressler, "Exegis of the law of duress: justifying the excuse and searching for its proper limits" (1989) 62 *Southern California Law Review* 1331–1386 at p.1373.

accepted that it can also be an excuse, a lower standard of conduct should serve to ground the defence. In response to this argument, it could be said that some forms of conduct are simply inexcusable and that the killing of an innocent human being in order to save one's own life falls into this category.[7]

Even if one cannot excuse the taking of an innocent human life to save one's own, it may be possible to excuse it when the life saved belongs to someone other than the accused. Consider a scenario where the accused is told that his child will be killed if he does not himself kill another innocent human being. Here the choice he faces is between two lives, neither of which is his own. It might be argued that it is still inexcusable for him to kill the innocent human being, but this is a weaker argument.[8] The difficulties become even more pronounced in circumstances where killing the innocent human being leads to a net saving of lives, or where the innocent victim would have died anyway, regardless of the actions of the accused.

An example of this latter scenario arose in *Prosecutor v Erdemovic*,[9] where the accused, who was attached to a military unit in the former Yugoslavia, killed approximately 70 unarmed Muslim citizens. He claimed that he had been threatened with death if he did not participate in the killing and, most pertinently, that the killing would have taken place anyway (by one of the other soldiers present) had he refused. The Appeals Chamber, in a majority decision, still chose to rule out the availability of the defence on the basis that it was wrong to take innocent human life even where the victims would most likely have been killed anyway. Judge Stephen, in a dissenting opinion, argued that the defence should have been available on the basis that nothing the accused could have done would have saved the lives of the victims and thus expecting him to sacrifice his own life would have been futile.[10] The disagreement on this point shows that ruling out coercion as a defence to murder on the basis of the sanctity of human life is more complex than might be assumed from a reading of *Howe*. Ultimately, the position one takes on the subject depends on the view one has of the value of human life and whether or not it is acceptable to balance one human life against one's own or another (or others).

5.31 The second of the arguments used in *Howe* to rule out the availability of the defence was that it is necessary to do so in order for the law to stand firm in the face of potential abuse of the defence by terrorists.[11] This is a rather weak argument, given that this can be avoided simply by ruling

[7] See J. Horder "Occupying the moral high ground: the Law Commission on duress" [1994] Crim. L.R. 334–342 at p.335. For an argument that suggests an individual should have the benefit of the defence of duress when, faced with a threat of death, she kills two innocent bystanders, see P. Westen and J. Mangiafico, "The criminal defense of duress: a justification not an excuse and why it matters" (2003) 6 *Buffalo Criminal Law Review* 833–950. (In fact Westen and Mangiafico argue that such an individual is not merely excused, but *justified*.) For criticism, see M.N. Berman, "Justification and excuse, law and morality" (2003) 53 *Duke Law Journal* 1–77 at pp.71–72.

[8] See Dennis, above, fn.4, at p.471; A. Norrie, *Crime, Reason and History: A Critical Introduction to Criminal Law* (2nd edn, 2001), p.168. It might be said that there is still an element of self-interest where the child is the accused's, but the factual scenario can easily be altered so that this is not the case.

[9] Case no. IT-96-22-A, October 7, 1997, Appeals Chamber of the International Tribunal for the Former Yugoslavia, unreported. See *www.un.org/icty*.

[10] Judge Cassese also issued a dissenting opinion in the case, along similar lines to that of Judge Stephen.

[11] *R. v Howe* [1987] A.C. 417 at 443–444, *per* Lord Griffiths; at 434 *per* Lord Hailsham.

out the availability of the defence whenever the accused has voluntarily joined such an organisation or has placed himself in a position where it was reasonably foreseeable that he would be subjected to coercion.[12]

The third of the arguments used in *Howe* was that there is no need formally to allow for duress as a defence to murder because executive discretion can deal with those cases in which it would be unfair to convict and/or punish the accused.[13] It might be argued, though, that this is an unsatisfactory solution. Allowing decision making to be made at this level means that the evidence against the accused is never properly tested and leaves open the possibility of inequality of treatment between cases.[14]

One argument for allowing duress as a defence for murder that is not dealt with in *Howe* is that there is simply no point in punishing those who kill under duress as this is unlikely to act as a deterrent.[15] This is because the rationally thinking person will choose life imprisonment over virtually certain death.[16] Assuming that one accepts the premise that the content of the criminal law does indeed deter,[17] this argument makes the additional assumption that deterrence is the only basis for punishment. It may be that killings under duress are indeed undeterrable but that it is still appropriate to punish the accused on the ground of his moral blameworthiness for taking an innocent life in order to save his own.

The difficulty with this is that the mandatory life sentence attached to murder[18] means that there is only limited opportunity when sentencing to take account of the relative moral blameworthiness of the accused who acted under coercion. One way to resolve this issue might be to take a compromise position whereby the accused is convicted of murder, but the mandatory life sentence is removed,[19] although this might be criticised on the grounds of fair labelling.[20] So another possible compromise position is for coercion to act as a partial defence which, in Scotland, could reduce a murder charge to culpable homicide. Such a move would allow the law on one hand to recognise and respect the sanctity of human life while, on the

---

[12] See paras 5.23–5.25.

[13] *R. v Howe* [1987] A.C. 417 at 432, *per* Lord Hailsham.

[14] Ashworth, *Principles of Criminal Law*, p.227; A. Reed, "The need for a new Anglo-American approach to duress" (1997) J.C.L. 209–224 at p.214.

[15] *Report on Defences of General Application* (Law Com. No. 83, 1977), at para.2.42; S. Shavell, "Criminal law and the optimum use of non-monetary sanctions as a deterrent" (1985) 85 *Columbia Law Review* 1232–1262 at p.1257.

[16] The 'irrationally' thinking person is unlikely to think of the consequences of his act anyway and so would also not be deterred.

[17] *cf.* P.H. Robinson and J.H. Darley, "Does criminal law deter? A behavioural science investigation" (2004) 24 O.J.L.S. 173–205.

[18] CPSA 1995, s.205(1).

[19] The solution advocated by Lord Kilbrandon, "Duress per minas as a defence to crime: I" in *Law Morality and Rights* (M.A. Stewart (ed.), 1983), pp.333–343, at p.342.

[20] Ashworth, *Principles of Criminal Law*, pp.88–90. See also M. Wasik, "Excuses at the sentencing stage" [1983] Crim. L.R. 450–465.

other hand, demonstrate compassion for the accused who was placed in the situation of having to choose between sacrificing his own life or killing an innocent human being.[21]

[21] This was the view taken by Lord Lane C.J. when *Howe* was decided by the English Court of Appeal (*R. v Howe* [1986] Q.B. 626). The idea was initially rejected by the English Law Commission (in *Defences of General Application*, above fn.15, at paras 30.17–31.8), but, in a more recent report, the Law Commission recommends that duress by threats *should* operate as a partial defence, reducing first degree murder to second degree murder, thus avoiding the mandatory life sentence but retaining the label of "murderer" for the defendant who kills under duress. See *A New Homicide Act for England and Wales* (Consultation Paper No. 177, 2005) at para.7.31. See also the Irish Law Reform Commission's *Consultation Paper on Duress and Necessity* (L.R.C. C.P. 39, 2006), which recommends that duress operate as both a complete defence to murder (where the accused has chosen the lesser of two evils) and a partial defence to murder, reducing murder to manslaughter, in other circumstances (at paras 3.100–3.101).

CHAPTER 6

SUPERIOR ORDERS

INTRODUCTION

The defence of superior orders is a plea that the accused engaged in prohibited conduct on the instructions of a superior whose orders he was bound to obey. Potentially, it arises in any context where there is a relationship of superior and subordinate and where the subordinate is duty bound to obey instructions. Its relevance is greatest, however, in the military context,[1] where the duty of soldiers to obey orders is more compelling than that of any subordinate in the civilian context.[2] **6.01**

Superior orders is a plea that is most likely to stem from events occurring in wartime. It has arisen only rarely in the Scottish context. Unlike a number of other common law jurisdictions,[3] Scots law does not conclusively rule out the defence.[4]

THEORETICAL BASIS

Distinguishing superior orders from coercion and error of law

There is some potential for overlap between the defence of superior orders and the related defences of coercion and error of law.[5] **6.02**

The gist of the superior orders defence is that the accused followed the instructions of a superior officer whose orders he was bound to obey. The coercion defence applies where the accused followed the instructions of a coercer on the understanding that the coercer would harm the accused if

[1] A wide definition of the military context might be taken here to include any of the armed forces. The plea may also be relevant in quasi-military contexts, such as the police force or the prison service, where employees are trained to obey the commands of superior officers.

[2] Although that is not to say that it has never arisen in the civilian context: see later paras 6.16 *et seq.*

[3] The plea has been ruled out in England and Wales and in Australia (see para.6.13). It has been allowed in Canada and South Africa, subject to what has been termed the "manifest illegality" test (see paras 6.12–6.13).

[4] For a more detailed discussion of the defence than that provided here, see: J.L. Baker, "The defense of obedience to superior orders: the *mens rea* requirement" (1989–1990) 17 *American Journal of Criminal Law* 55–80; M.C. Bassiouni, *Crimes against Humanity in International Criminal Law* (1992), pp.399–437; I.D. Brownlee, "Superior orders: time for a new realism" [1989] Crim. L.R. 396–411; Y. Dinstein, *The Defence of Obedience to Superior Orders in International Law* (1965); P. Eden, "Criminal liability and the defence of superior orders" (1991) 108 S.A.L.J. 640–655; L.C. Green, *Essays on the Modern Law of War* (1985), pp.43–72; M.J. Osiel, "Obeying orders: atrocity, military discipline and the law of war" (1998) 86 *California Law Review* 939–1129. See also the detailed discussions of the history of the defence in international law and in various common law jurisdictions in the Canadian Supreme Court case of *R. v Finta* [1994] 1 S.C.R. 701 (at [122]–[147] *per* Cory J.) and the South African case of *S v Banda*, 1990 (3) S.A. 466 (at 479–496).

[5] See Dinstein, above, fn.4, at p.56.

he did not carry out these instructions.[6] There is some common ground between the two defences if an order given by a superior officer is accompanied by a threat of violence. It has been suggested that orders accompanied by a threat of violence are properly dealt with under the defence of coercion and not superior orders,[7] but it will not always be easy to distinguish the two, especially if implied (as opposed to express) threats are permitted to ground the defence of coercion.[8]

There is also a potential overlap with the defence of error of law, if indeed such a defence is recognised. The accused ordered to undertake an unlawful act by his superior, who does so without realising that his conduct constitutes a criminal offence,[9] operates under an error of law, albeit one induced by the superior officer. In Scots law, the defence of error of law is not a valid plea,[10] so the accused, who operates under both an error of law and superior orders, has little choice but to plead superior orders. This would not be the case in a jurisdiction where both defences are recognised.[11]

Possible approaches to the defence

6.03 There are three possible approaches that can be taken to the defence of superior orders[12]:

1. It can provide a complete defence whenever a subordinate obeys the orders of a superior officer[13];
2. It can provide no defence at all[14]; or
3. An intermediate position can be taken, whereby the defence is permitted in certain circumstances. This may be whenever the order in question was not obviously unlawful[15] (an objective test) and/or where the accused did not realise it was unlawful (a subjective test).

The main argument for allowing superior orders to act as a complete defence in the military context[16] is that obedience to the orders of a superior officer is a fundamental aspect of military discipline, without

6 In Scots law, a threat of death or serious bodily harm is required: see *Thomson v HM Advocate*, 1983 J.C. 69 and the discussion in paras 5.11–5.12.

7 See the separate and dissenting opinion of Judge Cassese in *Prosecutor v Erdemovic*, Case no. IT-96-22-A, October 7, 1997, Appeals Chamber of the International Tribunal for the Former Yugoslavia, unreported, at [15]. See *www.un.org/icty*.

8 There is no Scottish authority on this, but implied threats have been accepted as a valid basis for the defence of coercion in Canadian law: see *R. v Mena* (1987) 34 C.C.C. (3d) 304 and the discussion in para.5.16.

9 This will not necessarily be the case. An accused *might* try and claim the defence of superior orders even when he realised that the order was an unlawful one. It is likely, however, that if the accused was aware that an order was unlawful, this would rule out the defence in Scots law (see para.6.11 below). Conversely, a soldier might make an error of law and act in the mistaken belief that his conduct was lawful without having received any orders from a superior officer.

10 Except in some very limited circumstances: see Ch.13.

11 Such as South Africa. On this, see Eden, above, fn.4, at p.653.

12 Dinstein, above, fn.4, at p.8; Brownlee, above, fn.4, at pp.397–398.

13 Termed the doctrine of *respondeat superior* by Dinstein, above, fn.4, at p.8. Dinstein discusses this approach at pp.38–67.

14 Termed the doctrine of absolute liability by Dinstein, above, fn.4, at p.8. Dinstein discusses this approach at pp.68–87.

15 A test most commonly formulated as the "manifest illegality" principle: see para.6.05 below.

16 The civilian context is discussed in paras 6.16–6.17 below.

which the functioning of military operations would be impaired.[17] Members of the armed forces are trained to obey orders; indeed, failing to do so (at least in relation to lawful orders) is a criminal offence.[18] As Gordon puts it:

> "... it is unfair to train a man in automatic obedience, and then to penalise him for acting in the way the state itself has trained him to act".[19]

The proposition that superior orders should *always* act as a complete defence finds little support.[20] It is not the case that soldiers are trained to follow orders unquestioningly, regardless of their legality. As the United States Military Tribunal at Nuremberg put it in *Einsatzgruppen*[21]:

> "The obedience of a soldier is not the obedience of an automaton. A soldier is a reasoning agent. He does not respond, and is not expected to respond, like a piece of machinery. It is a fallacy of widespread consumption that a soldier is required to do everything his superior officer orders him to do."[22]

Indeed, to allow the defence to be successfully pled even when the order in question is obviously illegal would, as Baker puts it, make "military obedience superior to the rule of law".[23] It may also mean that responsibility is simply passed up a chain of command with the eventual result that *no one* is held responsible for an unlawful act.[24] In this context, McCoubrey has noted the difficulties that have been encountered by the International Tribunal for the Former Yugoslavia in bringing superior officers to trial,[25] even in the absence of a superior orders defence.[26] **6.04**

These criticisms could be met by adopting the approach of absolute liability, whereby superior orders *never* provides a defence.[27] This position has been criticised on two fronts.

First, some argue that it is unfair to impose liability on a soldier for

---

[17] H. McCoubrey, "From Nuremberg to Rome: restoring the defence of superior orders" (2001) 50 I.C.L.Q. 386–394 at p.391.

[18] Disobedience to a *lawful* command constitutes a criminal offence: Army Act 1955, s.34; Air Force Act 1955, s.34; Naval Discipline Act 1957, s.12 (all as substituted by the Armed Forces Act 1971, s.8(2) and (3)).

[19] Gordon, para.13.31.

[20] For a rare exception, see L. Oppenheim, *International Law*, Vol.2 (1st edn, 1906), pp.264–265 (and the four subsequent editions of the book). The position changed from the sixth edition onwards, which was published in 1940, most likely because Oppenheim's view was not shared by the new editor of the treatise.

[21] *USA v Ohlendorf* (Einsatzgruppen case) (1948) 15 A.D.I.L. 656 (United States Military Tribunal at Nuremberg).

[22] At 665.

[23] J.L. Baker, "The defense of obedience to superior orders: the *mens rea* requirement" (1989–1990) 17 *American Journal of Criminal Law* 55–80 at p.60.

[24] I.D. Brownlee, "Superior orders: time for a new realism" [1989] Crim. L.R. 396–411 at p.408; Y. Dinstein, *The Defence of Obedience to Superior Orders in International Law* (1965), pp.70–71.

[25] McCoubrey, above, fn.17, at p.393. *Cf.* Brownlee, above, fn.24, who takes the view that passing responsibility up a hierarchy of command does not present a problem "unless the hierarchy of command is headed by a sovereign beyond redress" (at p.409).

[26] The defence is ruled out by the Statute of the International Tribunal for the Former Yugoslavia (see para.6.15).

[27] This is, in fact, the modern position taken in English and Australian law—see para.6.13.

following an order, when he would face severe punishment—perhaps even death—if he disobeyed.[28] Dicey has famously described this dilemma thus:

> "Hence the position of a soldier is in theory and may be in practice a difficult one. He may, as it has been well said, be liable to be shot by a court-martial if he disobeys an order, and be hanged by a judge and jury if he obeys it."[29]

It might be said, however, that there is no need for a defence of superior orders in this situation, as coercion would provide a defence.[30]

6.05 Secondly, it has been argued that it is too harsh to impose liability upon a subordinate when the order given by his superior was not either known to be unlawful or was not obviously unlawful, as the accused who follows such an order is simply not morally blameworthy.[31] The argument here mirrors that made in favour of recognising a reasonable error of law defence.[32]

The majority of academic commentators favour an intermediate position, whereby superior orders can provide a defence in certain limited circumstances. One formulation of the test might be that the defence is allowed where the order concerned was not "manifestly unlawful".[33] This is an objective test that requires the trier of fact to determine whether or not a reasonable person in the position of the accused would have realised that the order in question was unlawful. To this might be added an additional requirement: that the accused did not *know* that the order was unlawful.[34] Alternatively, one might propose a purely subjective approach, whereby superior orders is a defence only when the accused honestly believed that the order was lawful, regardless of whether or not his belief was reasonable.[35]

If superior orders is recognised as a defence at all, it is an excuse defence. In pleading superior orders, the accused puts forward a claim that, although what he did was wrong, he should not be blamed for it as he merely obeyed the orders of a superior officer.

---

28 Baker, above, fn.23, at p.65.

29 A.V. Dicey, *Introduction to the Study of the Law of the Constitution* (10th edn, 1961), p.303.

30 Unless the defence of coercion was ruled out on the basis that, by joining the armed services, the accused voluntarily exposed himself to the risk of coercion (see paras 5.23–5.25). On the overlap between the two defences, see para.6.02 above. There might be an additional difficulty here if the accused was ordered to kill, as coercion does not generally provide a defence to murder (see the discussion in paras 5.27 *et seq.*). Conceptually, the most appropriate defence is still one of coercion as the accused faces a threat of death or serious injury himself if he does not do as his commanding officer requires.

31 Baker, above, fn.23, at p.64.

32 See Ch.13.

33 Brownlee, above, fn.24, at p.410. This test has been adopted in Canada, South Africa and in international criminal law (see paras 6.12–6.13 and 6.15 respectively).

34 It is possible to envisage a situation where an order was not obviously unlawful but, nonetheless, the accused knew that the order was, in fact, unlawful, perhaps because of his knowledge of the criminal law.

35 This is the approach taken by the US Model Penal Code (see s.2.10). The subjective approach is also favoured in G. Creighton, "Superior orders and command responsibility in Canadian criminal law" (1980) 38 *University of Toronto Faculty Law Review* 1–32 at pp.16–17 and P. Eden, "Criminal liability and the defence of superior orders" (1991) 108 S.A.L.J. 640–655 at p.646.

Superior Orders in Scots Law

Superior orders under Hume

Hume considers superior orders under the auspices of "subjection", a plea involving commands made within the context of certain types of relationship. Of most relevance here is "subjection, which arises out of the relations of a public nature, as between the judge and the Legislature, the inferior ministers of the law and the magistrate, or soldier and commanding officer".[36] **6.06**

"Subjection of officer to the magistrate" covers those officials who act under the authority of an order given to them by a magistrate or other judge. Hume takes the view that, if the official knew or ought to have known that what he was ordered to do is illegal ("if he was in the knowledge of the nullity, or had reasonable ground of belief on the subject"), he should be held criminally responsible.[37] The examples used by Hume all relate to the pronouncement of unlawful sentences of execution.[38] One may doubt that this category of subjection has any relevance today.[39]

Of more obvious relevance is what Hume terms the "subjection of soldiers to officers".[40] In this context, Hume is relatively receptive to a plea of superior orders, on the basis that soldiers are specifically trained to obey orders and may face disciplinary measures if they do not do so:

> "It only remains to take notice of the case of soldiers, who are trained to a still stricter discipline, and are bound to obedience of orders by far higher penalties. It is obvious, nevertheless, that any plea which may be grounded upon these favourable conditions, must at least be received under certain provisions, without which it would be both dangerous and unjust."[41]

In order for the plea to succeed, certain conditions must be satisfied. First, the order must be one that "falls within the officer's commission, and known line of duty".[42] Hume does not explain what he means by this. It is most likely a requirement that (a) the subordinate falls under the command of the superior officer and is duty bound to obey him[43]; and (b) the order is one that falls within the scope of the subordinate's responsibilities.[44] Given Hume's use of the phrase "known line of duty", it is likely that this is to be judged on the basis of the subordinate's

---

[36] Hume, i, 53. Hume also discusses subjection in the context of the command of a husband to a wife and a parent to a child (both of which are discussed in para.5.07) and a master to a servant (discussed in para.6.16 below). Hume also touches on the issue of superior orders in the context of justifiable homicide by an officer in the execution of his duty (Hume, i, 195–217) but does not add anything of note to his earlier discussion of the topic.

[37] Hume, i, 54.

[38] A sentence of execution being pronounced in the sheriff court (which cannot pass such a sentence) (Hume, i, 53) and an order to poison a convict or privately to strangle him in his cell (Hume, i, 54).

[39] Gordon, para.13.30.

[40] Hume, i, 54.

[41] *ibid.*

[42] *ibid.*

[43] Thus ruling out, e.g. an order given by one soldier to another of identical rank.

[44] Consequently, ruling out, e.g. an order given to undertake a personal task for the superior officer.

knowledge, or at least on the basis of what it was reasonable for him to have known. If, unknown to the subordinate, the superior officer had been demoted, and no longer had the authority to issue orders, then it would seem unjust for the defence to be ruled out.

6.07 Secondly, the order:

> "... must be at least an excusable order, or such as may be the subject of different opinions; not a manifest injury or aggression on his part".[45]

Hume goes on to provide some examples of what he means by "manifest injury or aggression":

> "If an officer order out a party to rescue him from a messenger, who has him in custody for debt, any homicide or other injury which ensues on so irregular an enterprise, would be at the hazard even of all the private men concerned in the execution of it. Or put the case, that being on guard with his party, an officer orders them to fire on an inoffensive meeting of the people—a command which he is punishable for giving, and which they may lawfully disobey: Certainly they, as well as he, are answerable for the consequences."[46]

Thus Hume would allow a defence of superior orders (or, as he terms it, "subjection of soldiers to officers"[47]) where the order concerned was "not a manifest injury or aggression". It is not entirely clear whether Hume would rule out the defence where the order did not fall into this category but, nonetheless, the accused knew that it was an illegal order. It seems relatively safe to conclude, however, that he would, on the basis that he does apply this requirement to his earlier example of subjection of an officer to a magistrate.[48]

Alison, who also allows the defence in the military context, formulates the requirements of the defence slightly differently. For Alison, "[t]he express command of a magistrate or officer will exonerate an inferior officer or soldier, unless the command be to do something plainly illegal, or beyond his known duty".[49] Alison does not address the issue of whether the defence would be ruled out if the order was not "plainly illegal" but, nevertheless, the accused was aware of its illegality.

Superior orders in Scottish case law

6.08 Reported Scottish cases on superior orders are few and far between.[50] A rare example is the case of *Ensign Maxwell*.[51] Here, the accused was an officer working in a prison where French prisoners of war were detained.

---

[45] Hume, i, 54. Hume's test is not dissimilar to the "manifestly unlawful" test discussed earlier (see para.6.05) and which forms part of Canadian, South African and international criminal law (see paras 6.12–6.13 and 6.15 respectively).

[46] Hume, i, 54. See also the case cited by Hume of *William Ferguson* (1674) Hume, i, 54; Burnett, at 72. The clearest account of the facts of the case is in Burnett.

[47] Hume, i, 54.

[48] See para.6.06 above.

[49] Alison, *Principles*, 673.

[50] The defence is not mentioned at all in the Draft Criminal Code.

[51] (1807) Buch Part II 3; Burnett, 77 (although Burnett does not quote the charge to the jury). The case is not mentioned in Hume. It is noted in Gordon (at para.13.34, fn.42) but only in the context of an order that comes close to constituting coercion.

The commander of the prison had issued a verbal order that, when prisoners created a disturbance or refused to put their lights out, a guard (after giving due warning) could open fire. The accused ordered a private to fire his musket into a prisoner's room, following this practice. The private refused at first but eventually obeyed and a prisoner was killed. The private was not prosecuted, but the officer was, pleading in his defence that he was justified to open fire in the course of his duty.

Lord Hope charged the jury that the shooting would be justifiable if the accused acted "under specific orders, which he was bound to obey without discretion"[52] or if "in the general discharge of his duty, he was placed in circumstances which gave him discretion, and called upon him to do what he did".[53] On the subject of superior orders, Lord Hope stated:

> "... if he did [act under superior orders], be these orders right or wrong, he was bound to obey, and the crime will rest upon those who issued them, not upon him who obeyed them. There is some restriction, however, even upon this; because, if an officer were to command a soldier to go out into the street, and kill you or me, he would not be bound to obey. It must be a legal order given with reference to the circumstances in which he was placed; and thus every officer has a discretion to disobey orders against the known laws of the land."[54]

A similar stance was adopted in the case of *William Inglis*.[55] Here, the **6.09** accused had not acted in obedience to a specific order; in fact, if anything, he had acted contrary to orders. The case involved a soldier on duty guarding prisoners of war. He had been given general orders not to fire unless prisoners were escaping or attempting to escape. The accused fired towards the prison window and killed a prisoner who had been throwing stones at him. There was no evidence to suggest that the prisoner was trying to escape. Nonetheless, the court left the jury to consider whether the accused might have mistaken the nature of the orders he had been given which, it was stated, would make this a case not of murder but of culpable homicide. On the general issue of superior orders, the court took the opportunity to observe that:

> "... no orders can *justify* a manifestly illegal act. A soldier is inexcusable, might even be guilty of Murder, if, by *order*, he fired on persons lawfully and peaceably employed, there being no disturbance, or appearance of disturbance at the time, and nothing to create any such apprehension."[56]

The only other reported case in which anything is said specifically about the defence of superior orders is *HM Advocate v Hawton and Parker*.[57] Here, a Royal Navy marine was charged with murder and an alternative

---

[52] *Ensign Maxwell*, at 58.

[53] *ibid.*

[54] *ibid.* Lord Hope went on to express to the jury his opinion that this particular act was not justifiable. In the event, the accused was convicted of culpable homicide and sentenced to nine months' imprisonment.

[55] (1810) Burnett 79.

[56] At 80, emphasis in original.

[57] (1861) 4 Irv. 58.

charge of culpable homicide after he shot and killed a fisherman.[58] It had been the task of the marine and his superior to prevent illegal trawling in Loch Fyne. The superior officer ordered the marine to fire on trawlers in an attempt to prevent them from fishing and make them come to the shore. Blank shots were used at first, but eventually the marine fired live shots, although his intention was to fire wide and make the ships come in. One shot hit and killed a fisherman. At trial, the marine argued that he had acted under his superior's orders and that he was bound to obey unless ordered to do "what was obviously a grossly criminal and illegal act".[59] This, it was argued, did not come into that category since it was in accordance with usual navy practice.

6.10 The Lord Justice-General (McNeill) instructed the jury as follows:

> "One of the prisoners in this case had a certain command, the other was in the position of a subordinate; and it was the duty of the subordinate to obey his superior officer, unless the order given by his superior was so flagrantly and violently wrong that no citizen could be expected to obey it."[60]

Two other cases that are sometimes cited as authorities on superior orders[61] are *HM Advocate v Macpherson*[62] and *HM Advocate v Sheppard*.[63] Neither deals directly with the defence. The cases are perhaps better categorised as authorities on the extent of conduct justifiable in the course of public duty.[64]

In *Macpherson*, the accused was a soldier on leave in Edinburgh during the course of the Second World War and had shot at a car being driven at what he considered to be excessive speed and with undimmed lights during an air raid. In the event, the car turned out to contain the Assistant Chief Constable of Edinburgh, who was killed. The accused was charged with culpable homicide and claimed that he had acted in the course of what he thought was his duty.

The Lord Justice-Clerk (Aitchison) directed the jury that if the accused *reasonably* believed that he was acting in the course of his duty, he was entitled to an acquittal:

> "Even in a case where the soldier was on leave and had no specific duty to perform, if you are able to say that the accused acted under a mistaken sense of duty and that he had some reasonable cause for what he did, you would be entitled to acquit him."[65]

6.11 In *Sheppard*, another case stemming from the Second World War, the accused was a private in the Pioneer Corps in charge of a deserter at Dundee train station. While the lance corporal in charge of the escort party was buying a ticket, the accused shot and killed the prisoner, who was trying to escape. No direct order to shoot the prisoner had been

[58] The murder charge was subsequently dropped by the Crown.

[59] *HM Advocate v Hawton and Parker* (1861) 4 Irv. 58 at 70.

[60] *ibid.* at 71–72.

[61] For example by Gordon (paras 13.33 and 13.34) and in the Casebook (para.7.77).

[62] September 1940, Edinburgh High Court, unreported. See *HM Advocate v Sheppard*, 1941 J.C. 67 at 69.

[63] 1941 J.C 67.

[64] On this, see Hume, i, 205–217.

[65] Quoted at 69 of *HM Advocate v Sheppard*, 1941 J.C. 67.

given, but the lance corporal had told the accused not to stand any nonsense and to shoot if necessary to prevent the prisoner from escaping.[66] He was originally charged with murder, but at the end of the Crown case the advocate-depute amended the indictment by reducing the charge of murder to one of culpable homicide.[67]

Lord Robertson charged the jury as follows:

> "The accused was on duty, and his immediate duty was to keep in custody, and to deliver up, the man whom he was escorting. In such a case it is obviously not impossible by any means for a jury to take the view that, if the circumstances were such as to require the accused, for the due execution of his duty, to shoot in order to keep this man in custody, then the homicide was justifiable, and so to acquit the accused entirely of the crime charged against him. The question is—and it is a question for you the jury—whether on the facts the conclusion that there was no crime in this matter, but only the execution, painful as it might be, of a duty imposed upon the accused—whether that conclusion is a proper one."[68]

In the event, the accused was acquitted. Nothing was said by Lord Robertson specifically about the defence of superior orders. Indeed, the charge to the jury seems to indicate that it was open to the jury to find that the order given to the accused was actually lawful (on the basis that it was justifiable for the accused to shoot in the execution of his duty), in which case there would be no need for a superior orders defence at all.

In summary, superior orders is recognised in Scots law as a valid defence[69] provided that the order is not obviously unlawful[70] or (although this can be concluded with less certainty) nonetheless is known to be unlawful.[71] The absence of any recent authority in Scots law means, however, that if the issue arose, the courts would probably take account of case law in other jurisdictions and in the international context. Some brief discussion of both is therefore worthwhile.

Superior Orders in Other Jurisdictions

In other common law jurisdictions, two approaches to the defence are apparent: either the courts have ruled it out entirely or something akin to the manifest illegality test has been adopted. **6.12**

The latter approach was taken by the Canadian Supreme Court in *R. v*

[66] *HM Advocate v Sheppard*, 1941 J.C. 67 at 69.

[67] *ibid.* at 68.

[68] *ibid.* at 72.

[69] At least in the military or quasi-military context. Orders given in a civilian context are considered in paras 6.16–6.17 below.

[70] The language used in the various authorities differs slightly but effectively amounts to a similar test. See Hume, i, 54 (order must not be a "manifest injury or aggression"); *William Inglis* (1810) Burnett 79 at 80 ("no orders can justify a manifestly illegal act"); *HM Advocate v Hawton and Parker* (1861) 4 Irv. 58 at 72 (an order "so flagrantly and violently wrong that no citizen could be expected to obey it").

[71] Hume, i, 54 (in the context of orders issued by magistrates to officers of the law—see para.6.06 above). No mention of this requirement is made in the case law, unless one interprets the dicta in *Ensign Maxwell* (1807) Buch Part II 3 that "every officer has a discretion to disobey orders against the *known* laws of the land" (at 58, emphasis added) as such.

Finta,[72] a rare example of a case in modern times in which a defendant has relied upon the defence. The Supreme Court held that the defence of superior orders was available as a defence to charges of war crimes and crimes against humanity, subject to the proviso that the order concerned must not have been manifestly unlawful.

The defendant was a captain in the Hungarian Gendarmerie who had been involved in sending thousands of Jewish people to concentration camps during the Second World War. He claimed to have done this under the authority of the so called Baky Order, a decree of the Hungarian government directed to officials including commanding officers of gendarmerie sub-divisions. At trial, he was acquitted by the jury of all charges and the Crown appealed on the ground, inter alia, that the defence of superior orders should not have been left to the jury. The appeal was refused by the Supreme Court[73] and the majority concluded that:

> "The defence of obedience to superior orders [is] available to members of the military or police forces in prosecutions for war crimes and crimes against humanity. Those defences are subject to the manifest illegality test. That is to say, the defences will not be available where the orders in question were manifestly unlawful."[74]

The Court also provides some guidance on what is meant by a manifestly unlawful order, stating that it:

> "... must be one that offends the conscience of every reasonable, right-thinking person; it must be an order which is obviously and flagrantly wrong".[75]

The Supreme Court continues by citing with approval a passage in the Israeli District Court case of *Chief Military Prosecutor v Melinki*[76]:

> "The identifying mark of a 'manifestly unlawful' order must wave like a black flag above the order given, as a warning saying 'forbidden'. It is not formal unlawfulness, hidden or half hidden, not unlawfulness that is detectable only by legal experts, that is the important issue here, but an overt and salient violation of the law, a certain and obvious unlawfulness that stems from the order itself, the criminal character of the order itself or of the acts it demands to be committed, an unlawfulness that pierces and agitates the heart, if the eye be not blind nor the heart closed and corrupt. That is the degree of 'manifest' quality required in order to annul the soldier's duty to obey and render him criminally responsible for his actions."[77]

6.13 The same approach was taken in South African law in *S v Banda*,[78] a case involving an attack on the President of the State of Bophuthatswana. The

---

[72] [1994] 1 S.C.R. 701.

[73] On a 4/3 majority decision, although the dissent was unrelated to the issue of superior orders.

[74] *R. v Finta* [1994] 1 S.C.R. 701 at [166].

[75] *ibid.* at [134].

[76] Appeal 279–283/58 44 Psakim (Judgments of the District Courts of Israel) 362.

[77] Cited at [134] of *R. v Finta* [1994] 1 S.C.R. 701.

[78] 1990 (3) S.A. 466.

accused were charged with treason and attempted to plead the defence of superior orders. Friedman J. undertook a detailed analysis of the authorities in various common law jurisdictions and in international law[79] before formulating the defence as follows:

> "A soldier must obey orders issued by a lawful authority, and is under a duty to obey all lawful orders, and, in doing so, must do no more harm than is necessary to execute the order. Where, however, orders are manifestly beyond the scope of the authority of the officer issuing them, and are so manifestly and palpably illegal that a reasonable man in the circumstances of the soldier would know them to be manifestly and palpably ... illegal, he is justified in refusing to obey such orders. The defence of obedience to orders of a superior officer will not protect a soldier for acts committed pursuant to such manifestly and palpably illegal orders."[80]

There is some suggestion that, historically, English law did recognise a defence of superior orders.[81] More recently, however, the defence does seem to have been completely ruled out by the House of Lords[82] and the Privy Council,[83] albeit by *obiter* comments. Likewise, the defence has been ruled out by the Australian High Court,[84] although once again it was not the central issue in the case.

---

[79] At 479–496.

[80] At 496. See also *United States v Calley*, 48 C.M.R. 19 (1973), a case decided by the United States Court of Military Appeals, where something akin to the manifest illegality test was adopted (at 26–27).

[81] See *Keighley v Bell* (1866) 4 F&F 763; 176 E.R. 781; *R. v Trainer* (1864) 4 F&F 105; 175 E.R. 488.

[82] *R. v Clegg* [1995] 1 A.C. 482 at 498, *per* Lord Lloyd of Berwick. The central issue in *Clegg* was whether or not excessive force in self-defence can operate as a partial defence to a charge of murder and as such it is discussed in more detail in Ch.3. For discussion of the case in the context of superior orders, see S. Skinner, "Citizens in uniform: public defence, reasonableness and human rights" [2000] P.L. 266–281. See also *R. v Howe* [1987] A.C. 417, where the House of Lords approved a statement in the Nuremberg Charter ruling out the defence (at 427 *per* Lord Hailsham). The Nuremberg Charter's position is discussed in para.6.14. *Howe* was a case concerned primarily with whether or not duress can operate as a defence to murder and as such it is discussed in more detail in Ch.5.

[83] *Yip Chiu-Cheung v The Queen* [1995] A.C. 111 at 118, *per* Lord Griffiths (in an *obiter* comment). See also the *obiter* remark of Lord Hailsham in the Privy Council case of *Maharaj v Attorney General of Trinidad and Tobago (No. 2)* [1979] A.C. 385 at 404.

[84] *A v Hayden (No. 2)* (1984) 156 C.L.R. 532 at 540, *per* Gibbs C.J.; Mason J. at 550; Murphy J. at 562; Brennan J. at 582; Deane J. at 593. It should be noted though that the Criminal Codes of both Western Australia (s.31(2)) and Queensland (s.57(2)) provide for a defence of superior orders, subject to the manifestly unlawful test.

Superior Orders in International Law

6.14 Perhaps unsurprisingly, given the context in which the defence is likely to arise,[85] the defence of superior orders has received most attention in international law.[86] Until relatively recently the commonly accepted position was that, while superior orders did not constitute a defence in international criminal law, a court may consider it in mitigation of sentence.

Consequently, Art.8 of the Nuremberg Charter[87] provides that:

> "The fact that the Defendant acted pursuant to order of his Government or of a superior shall not free him from responsibility, but may be considered in mitigation of punishment if the Tribunal determines that justice so requires."[88]

The plea was raised in a number of trials of war criminals in relation to the events of the Second World War but was consistently ruled out as a defence.[89] It has been argued that this did not necessarily signal a complete rejection of the defence in international law but simply reflected the fact that the vast majority of those tried under the Nuremberg and Tokyo Charters were senior officers who actually participated in formulating and issuing orders:

> "Where politicians of cabinet rank and officers at the most senior levels of command are on trial it is difficult to see how, upon the face of this doctrine, a 'defence' of superior orders could have been available to them ... Viewed in this light it may be questioned whether the Nuremberg and Tokyo Charters necessarily altered the legal status of a plea of superior orders at all. It may rather be argued to be the case that they simply stated the natural application of the established 'ought to know' doctrine in the very particular context of the cases with which they were called upon to deal."[90]

---

[85] Analysis of the proceedings which took place against war criminals at the end of the Second World War shows that the plea of superior orders was raised as a defence to war crimes more frequently than any other defence. See Digest of Laws and Cases, United Nations War Crimes Commission, Law Reports of Trials, Vol.XV (1949).

[86] For a detailed account of the defence specifically in the international context, see: M.C. Bassiouni, *Crimes against Humanity in International Criminal Law* (1992), pp.399–437; I. Bantekas and S. Nash, *International Criminal Law* (2nd edn, 2003), pp.131–135; A. Eser, "Defences in war crimes trials" in *War Crimes in International Law* (Y. Dinstein and M. Tabory (eds), 1996), pp.251–273; Y. Dinstein, *The Defence of Obedience to Superior Orders in International Law* (1965); P. Gaeta, "The defence of superior orders: the Statue of the International Criminal Court versus customary international law" (1999) 10 *European Journal of International Law* 172–191; H. McCoubrey, "From Nuremberg to Rome: restoring the defence of superior orders" (2001) 50 I.C.LQ. 386–394. See also the account in the Canadian Supreme Court case of *R. v Finta* [1994] 1 S.C.R. 701 at [122]–[147], *per* Cory J.

[87] Nuremberg Charter (Charter of the International Military Tribunal) (1945).

[88] See also the Tokyo Charter (Charter of the International Military Tribunal for the Far East) (1945), Art.6. For discussion, see Bassiouni, above, fn.86, at p.427.

[89] See, e.g. *USA v Ohlendorf* (Einsatzgruppen case) (1948) 15 A.D.I.L. 656; *Re: Eck* (The Peleus) (1945) 12 A.D. 248.

[90] McCoubrey, above, fn.86, at pp.389–390. *Cf.* Gaeta, above, fn.86, at p.172.

More recently, the defence has been excluded under the statutes of the international tribunals set up to prosecute alleged offences in, respectively, the former Yugoslavia[91] and Rwanda.[92] 6.15

This approach was not followed in the Rome Statute of the International Criminal Court,[93] which allows the defence subject to the manifest illegality test. Article 33(1) of the Rome Statute provides that:

> "(1) The fact that a crime within the jurisdiction of the Court has been committed by a person pursuant to an order of a Government or of a superior, whether military or civilian, shall not relieve that person of criminal responsibility unless:
>
> (a) The person was under a legal obligation to obey orders of the Government or the superior in question;
> (b) The person did not know the order was unlawful; and
> (c) The order was not manifestly unlawful".

Article 33(2) provides that "for the purposes of [the Statute], orders to commit genocide or crimes against humanity are [always] manifestly unlawful".

While the position in international law is in no way conclusive as to domestic law, it is likely that a Scottish court would follow the Rome Statute, especially given that the position it sets out is so close to that of the existing (albeit limited) Scottish authorities.

Superior Orders in the Civilian Context

Thus far, the discussion of superior orders has focused on the plea in the military (or quasi-military) context. The plea may or may not be valid outside of this context, for instance in the context of a civilian employment relationship. The issue has arisen in case law, although not in any recent authorities. When it has arisen, it has tended to be in the historical context of the master-servant relationship. 6.16

---

[91] Statute of the International Tribunal for the Former Yugoslavia, Art.7(4). The International Tribunal for the Former Yugoslavia was established in order to bring to justice those suspected of committing war crimes and other offences against international humanitarian law during the former Yugoslavian armed conflict. See also the *obiter* comments of the Tribunal in *Prosecutor v Drazen Erdemovic*, Case no. IT-96-22-A, October 7, 1997, Appeals Chamber of the International Tribunal for the Former Yugoslavia, unreported. See *www.un.org/icty*.

[92] Statute of the International Tribunal for Rwanda, Art.6. The International Tribunal for Rwanda was established to prosecute persons suspected of committing genocide and other serious violations of international humanitarian law during the internal armed conflict in Rwanda.

[93] The jurisdiction of the International Criminal Court commenced with the entry into force of the Rome Statute on July 1, 2002, with 139 signatories and 76 state parties. The Court has jurisdiction over genocide (Art.6), crimes against humanity (Art.7) and war crimes (Art.8). For further discussion of the defence of superior orders under the Rome Statute, see Gaeta, above, fn.86; M. Scaliotti, "Defences before the International Criminal Court: substantive grounds for excluding criminal responsibility" (2001) 1 *International Criminal Law Review* 111–172; McCoubrey, above, fn.86.

Hume deals with the issue under the heading of subjection[94] between master and servant. He conclusively rules out any possibility that the orders of a master to undertake an unlawful act might provide a defence to his servant.[95] This might have been regarded as conclusive, but for the subsequent cases of *Calder v Robertson*[96] and *Jack v Nairne*.[97] In *Calder v Robertson*, a servant charged with poaching was acquitted by the presiding sheriff on the basis that he was "acting under the orders of his master . . . the tenant therein".[98] In *Jack v Nairne*, a case with similar facts, the appellant's conviction was quashed for the same reason, the court relying on *Calder v Robertson*.[99]

In *Richardson v Maitland*,[1] however, the defence was ruled out. The case was distinguished from *Calder* on the basis that the accused was not employed as a servant, but merely had a casual arrangement with the farmer that he would be employed to shoot rabbits once a year.[2]

6.17 A more relevant authority is perhaps that of *Gordon v Shaw*,[3] where the defence was also ruled out in a civilian context. Here, a member of the crew of a steam trawler was charged with a statutory offence of fishing in prohibited waters. The presiding sheriff found the charge not proven on the basis that the accused occupied a subordinate position and was "acting under orders of his superior officers".[4] The appeal court disagreed[5] and allowed the Crown's appeal, although in doing so said nothing specifically about the defence. Another case worthy of note is *HM Advocate v Boyd*,[6] where an employee of the Dundee and Arbroath Railway Company was charged with culpable homicide after he drove a train at speed through a village. In his charge to the jury, Lord Moncrieff stated that:

> "The conductor of an engine was not protected, any more than the driver of a stage coach, by reference to the authority of his masters, if the undertaking was either dangerous and illegal in itself, or conducted so as to be dangerous and illegal."[7]

---

[94] See para.5.07 for an account of the plea of subjection.

[95] The doctrine "is not grounded in the practice of the Court; nor indeed does it seem to be safe and reasonable in itself" (Hume, i, 50). Hume refers to a number of cases as authority for his view: *Dougal Macfarlane* (1737) Hume, i, 50; *James Hamilton* (1726) Hume, i, 51; *James Graham* (1717) Hume, i, 51. See also Alison, *Principles*, 672. *Cf.* Mackenzie, 170.

[96] (1878) 4 Coup. 131.

[97] (1887) 1 White 350.

[98] *Calder v Robertson* (1878) 4 Coup. 131 at 133. The High Court upheld the acquittal, Lord Young describing the sheriff's decision as "consistent with law and common sense" (at 134).

[99] *Jack v Nairne* (1887) 1 White 350 at 354.

[1] (1897) 2 Adam 243.

[2] At 248 *per* Lord Adam; at 251 *per* Lord Kinnear. Thus the case is not the conclusive authority on private orders between master and servant that Gordon claims it to be (at para.13.35).

[3] (1908) 5 Adam 469.

[4] At 472.

[5] At 478–479 *per* Lord McLaren; at 483 *per* Lord Kinnear.

[6] (1842) 1 Broun 7.

[7] At 20. See also *George Clarkson and Peter Macdonald* (1829) Bell's Notes 8 where, although the defence was ruled out, the court took account in sentencing of the fact that the offender had been ordered by his master to engage in a joint act of sheep stealing, sentencing the master to 14 years and the servant to 7 years of transportation.

Thus, the limited authorities suggest that a mere order to carry out an unlawful act, without any accompanying threat of death or bodily injury (which would take the plea into the realms of coercion),[8] does *not* constitute a defence in Scots law outside the military context.[9] The only suggestion to the contrary comes in the cases of *Calder v Robertson*[10] and *Jack v Nairne*,[11] both of which involved a relationship of master and servant that would be less likely to arise today.[12] While the authorities on the plea in a military context do not expressly limit the plea to this context, the underlying rationale of the defence suggests that this is the intention.[13]

---

[8] See Ch.5.

[9] This is certainly the conclusion of Gordon, at para.13.35. *Cf.* the English cases of *Lewis v Dickson* [1976] R.T.R. 431 and *R. v Salford Health Authority, ex parte Janaway* [1988] 2 W.L.R. 442 (the latter is discussed in detail in J.C. Smith, *Justification and Excuse in the Criminal Law* (1989), pp.70–72).

[10] (1878) 4 Coup. 131.

[11] (1887) 1 White 350.

[12] And both cases disregard the contrary view of Hume on the matter.

[13] See Hume's grounding of the plea in the position of soldiers "who are trained to a still stricter discipline, and are bound to obedience of orders by far higher penalties" (Hume, i, 54).

CHAPTER 7

INSANITY AND AUTOMATISM

INTRODUCTION

This chapter considers the defences of insanity and automatism together because, in Scots law, the defences have developed in a manner whereby they now operate as two sides of the same coin. Both defences are based on the accused having suffered from an "alienation of reason" at the relevant time, the distinction between the two being based on the cause of that alienation. Both defences are concerned with the mental state of the accused at the time of the alleged offence (unlike insanity as a plea in bar of trial, which is concerned with whether the accused is now fit to stand trial, regardless of his condition at any earlier stage).[1] **7.01**

The automatism defence, having been only formally recognised in 1991,[2] is of much more recent vintage than the insanity plea in Scots law. By contrast, the insanity plea has a long history which it is necessary to set out in some detail, particularly because of the frequent insistence that the (English) McNaghten Rules form no part of Scots law.[3] As is shown here, the McNaghten Rules have, in fact, been enormously influential in Scots law, and the history of the Scots defence of insanity is one of their rise, fall, and—most recently—rise again in Scots law. Intriguingly, their recent rise has come not in the context of insanity, but in the courts' development of "alienation of reason" within the context of the defence of automatism.

A second feature to the development of both pleas has been the distinction between cognitive and volitional tests of insanity, in other words, what is meant by an "alienation of reason"? A cognitive test considers whether the accused understood the nature and quality of his act, and whether it was wrong, while a volitional approach asks whether the accused was able to control his actions. Cognitive insanity has always been clearly accepted in Scots law, but volitional insanity—as an additional, rather than an alternative, basis on which the accused might escape criminal liability—has a more chequered history. Intermittently both rejected and accepted by judges, it now appears not to form a part of the modern law, but the situation remains uncertain. Automatism appears to be similarly restricted to impairments of the accused's cognitive faculties.

---

[1] On the plea in bar, see Ch.14.

[2] *Ross v HM Advocate*, 1991 J.C. 210.

[3] Most notably in *Brennan v HM Advocate*, 1977 J.C. 38 at 46, *per* the Lord Justice-General (Emslie).

The Insanity Defence

7.02 The defence of insanity is, in a number of ways, unique. Although, successfully pleaded, it results in an acquittal, it is far from an acquittal in the ordinary sense. As Walker has observed:

> "In a legal system in which the practical effect of an acquittal is normally the liberation of the accused, while a conviction renders him subject to a penal measure, how should we classify a verdict which is intended to subject him to indefinite detention in a mental hospital? It is a poor sort of acquittal. If it has anything in common with either of the ordinary verdicts, it is with the one which says 'guilty', since both at least render the accused liable to restraint."[4]

For that reason, a plea of insanity may well be unattractive from the accused's point of view, particularly where he faces trial for a relatively minor offence. Historically, the defence appears to have been of disproportionate significance in trials for murder, because it has enabled the accused to escape the mandatory penalty of death or (in modern practice) life imprisonment.[5] The plea's unattractiveness is reflected in the paradoxical murder case of *HM Advocate v Harrison*,[6] where the Crown found themselves contending for an acquittal (on the ground of insanity) against Harrison's claim that he was guilty of culpable homicide (on the ground of diminished responsibility).

Detention is no longer the inevitable result of an acquittal on the ground of insanity, although it remained so in murder cases up until 2003.[7] The plea remains unique, however, in that the accused, though acquitted, is still subject to the coercive power of the state where the court considers such a disposal to be appropriate.[8]

An acquittal on the ground of automatism, by contrast, carries with it no such power on the part of the courts to act to protect the public which, depending on the breadth with which the defence is made available, may be thought to be undesirable in certain cases.

---

[4] N. Walker, *Crime and Insanity in England, Volume 1: The Historical Perspective* (1968), p.192. See also *Criminal Procedure in Scotland (Second Report)* (Cmnd. 6218, 1975), para.53.07 ("...we find the present procedure somewhat illogical in that it provides for the acquittal of a person of a crime but at the same time requires the court to dispose of him in a manner probably more restrictive of liberty than a determinate prison sentence.")

[5] CPSA 1995, s.205. Almost all of the reported Scottish cases on insanity concern trials for murder (or other offences which were capital at the relevant time). Between 1900 and 1949, of 494 persons proceeded against for murder in Scotland, 105 were found insane and unfit to plead, while 23 were acquitted on the ground of insanity: see *Royal Commission on Capital Punishment 1949–1953: Report* (Cmd. 8932, 1953), 311 (table 9). The incidence of unsuccessful pleas is not recorded. Empirical evidence on the incidence of insanity pleas across different offences in Scotland is not readily available, although some information can be found in M. Burnam and C. Connelly, *Mentally Disordered Offenders and Criminal Proceedings* (1990). In England, see R.D. Mackay, *Mental Condition Defences in the Criminal Law* (1995), p.103 (noting that of 52 not guilty by reason of insanity disposals between 1975 and 1989, 15 (28.9%) were in cases where murder was charged).

[6] (1968) 32 J.C.L. 119.

[7] Criminal Justice (Scotland) Act 2003, s.2(b).

[8] For the disposals available to the court where an accused is acquitted on the ground of insanity, see CPSA 1995, s.57.

The nature of the insanity defence

Doubt has arisen in the past as to whether insanity is appropriately classified as an excuse, or as a lack of capacity defence. Is the insane actor excused because he committed a wrongful act, but one for which he cannot be blamed, or because his insanity means that is not "the appropriate kind of agent"[9] for the criminal law to concern itself with?[10] In other words, is the law concerned with "act-responsibility" or "capacity-responsibility"?[11] 7.03

The fact that, until relatively recently, detention was regarded as the inevitable consequence of an acquittal on the basis of insanity, might lead us to conclude that insanity was regarded as a lack of capacity defence.[12] Such a procedure suggests that a verdict of not guilty by reason of insanity is a statement of the accused's *current* condition: how else, after all, could automatic detention be justified? The law did not, however, clearly distinguish between act-responsibility and capacity-responsibility, as can be seen from Alison's description of the defence:

> "To amount to a complete bar to punishment, the insanity, *either at the time of committing the crime, or of the trial*, must have been of such a kind as entirely deprived him of the use of reason, *as applied to the act in question*, and the knowledge that he was doing wrong in committing it."[13]

The first of the italicised phrases is redolent of capacity-responsibility, in that it suggests the *timing* of the accused's insanity is of limited relevance, but the second makes it clear that Alison is formulating the plea in terms of act-responsibility.[14] Hume is even more clear on this point: "[t]he quality of the deed depends entirely on the man's state of mind at the time he does it".[15]

The fact that Scots law has not regarded insanity as founded on capacity-responsibility does not mean that such an approach would not be preferable, and it has sometimes been strongly argued that the law should move in this direction. Such arguments are often based on an analogy with nonage: just as we regard children under a certain age as improper subjects for the criminal law, so, it is argued, should we regard the insane.[16] The analogy is not an exact one, however, as reflected by the fact that, in Scots law, nonage operates as a plea in bar of trial,[17] while 7.04

---

[9] V. Tadros, "Insanity and the capacity for criminal responsibility" (2001) 5 Edin. L.R. 325–354 at p.341. Although the focus here is on the arguments made in this article, they have been developed further (and modified) in V. Tadros, *Criminal Responsibility* (2005), particularly Ch.4.

[10] See N. Lacey, *State Punishment* (1988), p.74: "Insane offenders must ... be removed from the ambit of normal criminal regulation not because they lack normal capacities of understanding and control, but because they do not and cannot participate in the normal discourse which underpins the enterprise of criminal justice."

[11] The terms are taken from Tadros, fn.9 above.

[12] Fletcher, *Rethinking Criminal Law*, p.839.

[13] Alison, *Principles*, 645 (emphases added). It is not clear how insanity "at the time ... of the trial" could be "applied to the act in question".

[14] This interpretation is strengthened by Alison's views that an "insane person having lucid intervals" would be criminally responsible for an offence committed in such an interval: *Principles*, 658–659. *Cf.*, however, Tadros, fn.9 above, at p.331.

[15] Hume, i, 39.

[16] Tadros, fn.9 above, at p.327. The analogy is noted (but not adopted) by Fletcher, fn.12 above, at p.836.

[17] Renton and Brown, para.9–06. On nonage generally, see Ch.9 below.

insanity operates as a substantive defence. Nonage rules are not based—or at least not *solely* based—on views as to the capacity of children for responsibility; otherwise it would be difficult to explain the enormous variation worldwide in the age of criminal responsibility.[18] Nonage rules reflect the fact that children, even where they have the capacity to be regarded as responsible for their actions, are not appropriate subjects for criminal prosecution.[19]

In the same way, an insane person may not be subjected to the process of a criminal trial where he lacks the capacity to effectively participate in that process, and thereby satisfies the requirements of a plea of insanity in bar of trial.[20] Although it has been argued that it would be open to the Scottish courts to develop a capacity-based account of insanity as a substantive defence, this might in practice add little to the plea in bar, even if the tests applied were different. Moreover, a capacity-based account should properly necessitate procedural changes: if insanity is to operate as a status excuse, it would be appropriately dealt with as a plea in bar rather than at trial,[21] and such a change would require statutory reform rather than judicial development of the law.

It is suggested, therefore, that arguments for a capacity-based account of insanity should properly be framed as arguments for a reform of the plea in bar of trial.[22] The plea of insanity in bar of trial does not, of course, render the substantive defence irrelevant: first, "insanity" has different meanings in each context, and an accused may be "insane" in one sense but not in another; secondly, an accused's condition may be different at the time of the alleged offence from the time of the trial. Even where an accused has capacity-responsibility, and is a fit subject to be tried, it may be shown that his state of mind at the time was such that his actions cannot properly be attributed to him *qua* agent.

Insanity and mens rea

7.05 The relationship between insanity and *mens rea* has not been fully explored by the Scottish courts. The weight of authority suggests that insanity may operate as a defence even where the accused does have *mens rea*, but the most recent formulation of the plea, in *Brennan v HM Advocate*,[23] frames it in terms of a "total alienation of reason"—a phrase which, in the context of automatism, has been regarded as referring to an

---

[18] See *Discussion Paper on Age of Criminal Responsibility* (Scot. Law Com. D.P. No. 115, 2001), Appendix D (noting ages ranging from 7 to 18 in different jurisdictions).

[19] See, on this point, the comments of the Kilbrandon Committee: "The legal presumption by which no child under the age of 8 can be subjected to criminal proceedings is not therefore a reflection of any observable fact, but simply an expression of public policy to the effect that in no circumstances should a child under the age of 8 be made the subject of criminal proceedings and thus liable to the pains of the law ... the 'age of criminal responsibility' is largely a meaningless term, and that in so far as the law refers to the age of 8 as being the minimum age for prosecution, this is essentially the expression of a practical working rule determining the cases in which a procedure which may result in punishment can be applied to juveniles." (*Report of the Committee on Children and Young Persons in Scotland* (Cmnd. 2306, 1964), para.65).

[20] See below, Ch.14.

[21] Fletcher, *Rethinking Criminal Law*, p.836. It would be inappropriate to deal with a capacity-responsibility form of the insanity defence at a full trial, because, reformulated in this way, "the insanity defence [would] no longer be connected importantly to the individual act that the agent has performed" (Tadros, fn.9 above, at p.353).

[22] On which, see Ch.14.

[23] 1977 J.C. 38.

absence of *mens rea*.[24] Given, however, that it was said in *HM Advocate v Kidd*[24a] that an insane offender "may know very well what he is doing, and may know that it is wrong, and he may none the less be insane",[24b] it seems to have been assumed that although an insane offender *may* lack *mens rea*, this is not the basis of the defence in Scots law.[24c] In England, the Divisional Court has held that the defence is based on the absence of *mens rea*, and is, therefore, not available where the offence is one of strict liability (in that case, driving with excess alcohol).[25] That decision, however, has been strongly criticised,[26] and the court did not refer to prior conflicting authority.[27] In Scotland, the point appears not to have arisen.[28]

Why is an accused whose insanity has negated *mens rea* not able simply to deny the offence charged and secure an unqualified acquittal which would not render him liable to coercive measures? In practice, it seems to have been assumed that such a course is not open, but it is not clear on what basis. It may be that there is a rule of evidence which prohibits an accused from relying on evidence probative of insanity where the special defence has not been lodged, but there does not appear to be any evidence for such a rule, and it is difficult to know how it would be applied if there were room for doubt as to whether the facts claimed by the defence amounted to insanity. The better view is probably that, as a matter of practice, it would always be open to the Crown to allege insanity where the accused denied *mens rea* based on such evidence.[29] For that reason, it is suggested that recent proposals to remove the Crown's right to allege that the accused was insane[30] should not be enacted, at least in an unqualified form.[31] If they were, then they would have the consequence that a potentially dangerous individual, who should be subject to the coercive measures available to the court where a plea of insanity is

---

[24] See *Ross v HM Advocate*, 1991 J.C. 210 at 218, *per* the Lord Justice-General (Hope). See also *Cardle v Mulrainey*, 1992 S.L.T. 1152. *Cf.*, however, *Finegan v Heywood*, 2000 J.C. 444, where it was assumed that the defence of automatism was available despite the accused having been charged with offences of strict liability.

[24a] 1960 J.C. 61.

[24b] At 71, *per* Lord Strachan. See below, para.7.19.

[24c] It would be peculiar if automatism involved a denial of *mens rea* and insanity did not, given that both defences rest on the common concept of "alienation of reason". See below, paras 7.37–7.43.

[25] *DPP v H* [1997] 1 W.L.R. 1406, and see the discussion of automatism and *mens rea* at para.7.06 below.

[26] See, e.g. T. Ward, "Magistrates, insanity and the common law" [1997] Crim. L.R. 796–804; Ashworth, *Principles of Criminal Law*, p.208.

[27] *R. v Hennessy* [1989] 1 W.L.R. 287, where it was assumed without discussion that the defence was available.

[28] It is noted by Gordon, para.8.28: "... insanity as a defence may depend on showing that the accused was incapable of *mens rea*, in which case it should strictly speaking be irrelevant in an offence of strict responsibility. But it is almost inconceivable that insanity would not be accepted as a defence in an offence of strict responsibility".

[29] *HM Advocate v Harrison* (1968) 32 J.C.L. 119.

[30] As the Scottish Law Commission has suggested: *Report on Insanity and Diminished Responsibility* (Scot. Law Com. No. 195), para.5.37.

[31] The difficulty inherent in such an approach was recognised by North J. in the case of *R. v Cottle* [1958] N.Z.L.R. 999 at 1027: "Now, however, it is asserted that it is competent for counsel for the prisoner to seek 'a complete and unqualified acquittal notwithstanding the fact that the prisoner relies on his mental incapacity to know the nature of his act', to quote the words of Sir Owen Dixon. This, it is said, can be achieved by the simple expedient of not pleading temporary insanity and relying on the statement of the law laid down in *Woolmington's* case [*Woolmington v DPP* [1935] A.C. 462], that it is the duty of the Crown to prove the existence of a criminal intent on the part of the accused. This is a rather startling proposition, and it seems to me to threaten the very foundation of the criminal law."

successful, could simply deny *mens rea* rather than plead insanity, and thereby receive an acquittal *simpliciter*. Such a result would be undesirable and contrary to public policy.

The Nature of the Automatism Defence

7.06 It is commonly assumed, both in the academic literature and in other jurisdictions, that automatism operates as a negation of *actus reus*: that is, where a person "acts" in an automatistic state, there is in fact no act at all, or at least no *voluntary* act. As expressed by Lord Denning in *Bratty v Attorney-General for Northern Ireland*,[32] "[n]o act is punishable if it is done involuntarily and an involuntary act in this context—some people nowadays prefer to speak of it as 'automatism'—means an act which is done by the muscles without any control by the mind ..."[33]

That is not, however, the approach which has been taken in Scots law, where the leading case on automatism, *Ross v HM Advocate*,[34] is predicated firmly on the absence of *mens rea* on the part of the person in an automatistic state. *Mens rea*, *Ross* suggests, is a necessary condition for an act (at least in most cases) to be attributed to a person for the purposes of criminal liability, and the automatistic "actor" must be acquitted because he will lack the *mens rea* required for the offence with which he is charged.

It is sometimes argued that this approach is inadequate, and that automatism must negate the *actus reus* of an offence, as otherwise it would not be a defence to strict liability crimes (most obviously, motoring offences).[35] That argument is, however, open to two objections. First, the fact that an offence is one of strict liability only means that no *mens rea* is required as to a particular element of the *actus reus*.[36] An offence such as driving with excess alcohol does not require *mens rea* as to the accused's intoxicated state,[37] but it might well require an intention to drive—although in practice such a question could hardly arise, as it is difficult to see how one could drive other than intentionally. It might be, however, that such an intention could be considered to be absent where a person "acts" in an automatistic state. Alternatively, automatism could simply be regarded as a freestanding excuse defence so far as offences of strict liability are concerned. The fact that the defence is available to offences of strict liability does not necessitate treating it as a negation of *actus reus*.

---

32 [1963] A.C. 386.

33 At 409.

34 1991 J.C. 210.

35 I. Patient, "Some remarks about the element of voluntariness in offences of absolute liability" [1968] Crim. L.R. 23–32; C. Finkelstein, "Involuntary crimes, voluntarily committed" in *Criminal Law Theory: Doctrines of the General Part* (S. Shute and A.P. Simester (eds), 2003), pp.143–169, at p.148.

36 *Whitehouse v Gay News Ltd* [1979] A.C. 617 at 617, *per* Lord Edmund-Davies.

37 See, e.g. *DPP v H* [1997] 1 W.L.R. 1406.

THE DEVELOPMENT OF THE DEFENCE OF INSANITY IN SCOTS LAW

The Scots law of insanity prior to McNaghten

Whatever significance a Scots lawyer may attach to the McNaghten Rules of 1843,[38] the date itself is of at least coincidental significance. Prior to the 1842 case of *Eugene Whelps*,[39] there appears to be no report of any charge delivered to a jury on the defence of insanity—and the charge in *Whelps* is itself rather brief. Any analysis of the Scots law prior to the mid-nineteenth century is, therefore, reliant on the institutional writers, and such short notes of cases as may be found in Hume and Alison.[40] **7.07**

The similarity between the McNaghten Rules and the earlier accounts offered by Hume and Alison is a striking one. Alison concisely formulates the plea as follows:

> "To amount to a complete bar to punishment, the insanity, either at the time of committing the crime, or of the trial, must have been of such a kind as entirely deprived him of the use of reason, as applied to the act in question, and the knowledge that he was doing wrong in committing it."[41]

Hume treats the defence at greater length, the essence of it being summarised in the following paragraph:

> "To serve the purpose of a defence in law, the disorder must therefore amount to an absolute alienation of reason, '*ut continua mentis alienatione, omni intellectu careat*,'—such a disease as deprives the patient of the knowledge of the true aspect and position of things about him,—hinders him from distinguishing friend or foe,—and gives him up to the impulse of his own distempered fancy."[42]

Hume goes on to discuss in some detail to what extent the accused's failure to appreciate the wrongfulness of his act may amount to insanity, noting that the relevant question is not whether the accused understood the crime to be wrong in the abstract, but one which must be answered "taking into account the whole circumstances of the situation"[43]: did the accused, given what he understood the situation to be, "as at that moment understand the evil of what he did? Was he impressed with the consciousness of guilt, and fear of punishment?"[44] **7.08**

These accounts, broadly stated, are concerned with cognitive insanity, focusing on the question of the accused's knowledge. They recognise insanity in two senses: first, where the accused fails to understand his actions, or secondly, where the accused fails to understand that his actions are wrong. Neither account, however, treats those two

[38] See below, para.7.09.

[39] (1842) 1 Broun 378.

[40] Two cases are noted in Maclaurin: *HM Advocate v Caldwall* (1737) Maclaurin 85 and *William Herries* (1770) Maclaurin 533, but neither of these brief notes shed much light on the plea. Two other cases discussed by Hume are also noted more briefly in Maclaurin: *Robert Thomson* (1739) Hume, i, 40; Maclaurin 85; *Robert Spence* (1747) Hume, i, 39; Maclaurin 98.

[41] Alison, *Principles*, 645.

[42] Hume, i, 37.

[43] *ibid.*

[44] *ibid.*

possibilities as alternatives: instead, they appear to be regarded as largely concurrent. But although the language is different, there is nothing radically at variance in Hume or Alison's account with that offered in the McNaghten Rules a few decades later, something which may explain the ready reception of the Rules by the Scottish courts.

The McNaghten Rules: their rise, fall and rise in Scots law

7.09 The basic history of the McNaghten Rules is well known. In 1843, Daniel McNaghten, in the paranoid belief that he was being persecuted by the Tories, attempted to kill the Prime Minister, Sir Robert Peel. Instead, he killed Peel's private secretary, Edward Drummond, whom he mistook for Peel. He was acquitted on the ground of his insanity.[45] As a result of the ensuing public controversy, the House of Lords elected to put a series of questions to the English judges to establish the scope of the defence. The core of the answers (or rules) is the following passage:

> "[T]o establish a defence on the ground of insanity it must be clearly proved that, at the time of the committing of the act, the party accused was labouring under such a defect of reason from disease of the mind, as not to know the nature and quality of the act he was doing; or if he did know it, that he did not know he was doing what was wrong."[46]

The judges also addressed the question of partial delusions, advising as follows:

> "[Where persons] labour under ... partial delusions only, and are not in other respects insane, we are of opinion that notwithstanding the party accused did the act complained of with a view, under the influence of insane delusion, of redressing or revenging some supposed grievance or injury, or of producing some public benefit, he is nevertheless punishable according to the nature of the crime committed, if he knew at the time of committing such crime that he was acting contrary to law; by which expression we understand your Lordships to mean the law of the land ... [A person who] labours under [a] partial delusion only and is not in other respects insane ... must be considered in the same situation as to responsibility as if the facts with respect to which the delusion exists were real. For example if under the influence of his delusion he supposes another man to be in the act of attempting to take away his life, and he kills that man, as he supposes, in self defence, he would be exempt from punishment. If the delusion was that the deceased had inflicted a serious injury to his character and fortune, and he killed him in revenge for such supposed injury, he would be liable to punishment."[47]

---

[45] See, generally, N. Walker, *Crime and Insanity in England, Volume 1: The Historical Perspective* (1968), Ch.5.

[46] *McNaghten's Case* (1843) 10 Cl & F 200 at 210; 8 E.R. 718 at 722. The Rules are also excerpted in an appendix to Broun's Justiciary Reports, which is demonstrative of their contemporary influence in Scotland: see the appendix to the second volume, and the editor's footnote to *James Gibson* (1844) 2 Broun 332 at 355 ("These opinions are of such general importance, that it has been judged proper to insert them at length in an Appendix to this volume.").

[47] *McNaghten's Case* (1843) 10 Cl & F 200 at 209–211; 8 E.R. 718 at 722–723.

The McNaghten Rules have been massively influential throughout the common law world, having formed the basis of the law of insanity for at least some period in almost every common-law jurisdiction.[48] It is, however, sometimes asserted that Scots law is distinct in this respect, and Lord Justice-General Emslie insisted in *Brennan v HM Advocate* that the McNaghten Rules are "no part of our law".[49]

Such statements, however, have a tendency to mislead. It is clear that the McNaghten Rules were quite explicitly considered to be part of Scots law for a time[50]—and so it would have been more (if perhaps not entirely) correct to state, as Lord Walker did in the civil case of *Mackenzie v Mackenzie*, that they are "no *longer* part of our law".[51] The history of the Scots law of insanity up until *Brennan* is, in fact, one of acceptance and then rejection of the McNaghten Rules. Furthermore, the more recent decision of the appeal court in the later case of *Cardle v Mulrainey*[52] seems to—at least in part—rephrase the Scots law of insanity in terminology close, if not identical, to that of the McNaghten Rules.

The reception of the McNaghten Rules into Scots law

The first major Scottish case dealing with insanity after *McNaghten* is 7.10
James Gibson.[53] Gibson set fire to a factory under the belief that "he was appointed by the landed gentry to punish all monopolists"[54] and "that there was no use in keeping back, for her majesty Queen Victoria was lying off in a ship of war ready to blow up the town if it was not done".[55]

In addressing the jury, Gibson's counsel appears to have placed heavy reliance on Issac Ray's *Treatise on the Medical Jurisprudence of Insanity*. In this text, Ray (a medical doctor) provided a highly critical review of the English cases on insanity (and also Hume and Alison's treatment of the subject), arguing that it was fallacious to regard the ability to distinguish right from wrong as determinative of any question of sanity or insanity.

---

48 For a survey of approaches in foreign jurisdictions, see Appendix 9 of the *Report of the Royal Commission on Capital Punishment* (Cmd. 8932, 1953).

49 1977 J.C. 38 at 46. See also *Breen v Breen*, 1961 S.C. 158 at 185, *per* Lord Patrick, and at 193, *per* Lord Mackintosh; *HM Advocate v Kidd*, 1960 J.C. 61 at 71, *per* Lord Strachan; *Mackenzie v Mackenzie*, 1960 S.C. 322 at 325, *per* Lord Walker. In giving evidence to the Royal Commission on Capital Punishment, Lord Cooper (then Lord Justice-General) stated that "I had some difficulty in finding in Scotland a copy of the M'Naghten Rules, and I had eventually to get them from a copy of an English textbook. So it is quite wrong to suppose that the M'Naghten Rules in their full vigour are current in Scotland. They were once reported in a foot-note to a Scottish decision about 100 years ago ..." *Minutes of Evidence Taken Before the Royal Commission on Capital Punishment* (1950), para.5465. This is strong rhetoric, but it is misleading: the Rules were reported in full as an appendix to Broun's Reports (see fn.46 above), while the two most significant textbook treatments of the defence published post-McNaghten in Scotland framed the insanity defence in terms of the Rules: see Macdonald, 9; Anderson, 5–6. Macdonald cites McNaghten's case as authority, while Anderson quotes from *James Gibson* (1844) 2 Broun 332, where the trial judge (Lord Justice-Clerk Hope) read the Rules to the jury.

50 See, most obviously, *James Gibson* (1844) 2 Broun 332, discussed below, para.7.10.

51 1960 S.C. 322 at 328 (emphasis added).

52 1992 S.L.T. 1152.

53 (1844) 2 Broun 332. *Adam Sliman* (1844) 2 Broun 138 is concerned with insanity as a plea in bar of trial.

54 At 337.

55 At 335. Both this and the preceding quote are taken from the evidence of witnesses in the case.

Instead, Ray argued, "delusion" was its "true character, of which the criminal act in question must be its immediate, unqualified offspring"[56]:

> "One man kills his neighbor, whom he fancies to have joined a conspiracy to defraud him of his property or his liberty; or for having insulted and exposed him to scorn and derision; or for standing in the way of his attaining certain honors or estates; yet the insanity is not to excuse him, unless it deprived him of the consciousness, that he was doing a wrong act. The existence of the illusion is obvious and cannot be mistaken; but what may be the views of the maniac, respecting the moral character of the criminal acts which he commits under its influence, can never be exactly known; and, therefore, they ought not to be made the criterion of responsibility. But it is known, that one of the most striking and characteristic effects of insanity in the mental operations is, to destroy the relationship between end and means—between the object in view and the course necessary to pursue in order to obtain it."[57]

7.11 Lord Hope, however, was scathing about this approach. After quoting the core of the McNaghten Rules (that, for a successful defence of insanity, it must be shown that "the party accused was labouring under such a defect of reason from disease of the mind, as not to know the nature and quality of the act he was doing; or if he did know it, that he did not know he was doing what was wrong"),[58] and directing the jury that this expressed the law of Scotland as well as England, he went on to direct the jury that:

> "You are not to consider insanity according to the definition of medical men, especially such fantastic and shadowy definitions as are to be found in Ray, whose work was quoted by the counsel for the pannel, and in many other medical works on the subject. We are not to make law but to administer it; and whether medical writers, differing as widely from each other, as they do from the law, approve of the law on the subject or not, the insanity to be proved must be that which the law holds to be the insanity which exempts men from punishment. The man must believe, not that the crime is wrong in the abstract (for most madmen do admit murder to be wrong, and punishable in the abstract), but that *the particular act* committed under the influence of the motive which seems to have prompted it, was not an offence against the law."[59]

Gordon observes that Lord Hope "seems to have taken a much narrower view of insanity than any other Scots judge, and the driving force behind his attitude seems not to have been any psychological or legal principle, but a religious view that freewill was absolute, and that people must not

---

[56] Isaac Ray, *A Treatise on the Medical Jurisprudence of Insanity* (1838), p.29. A second edition of this text was published in 1844 (and a third in 1860). It is likely, although not absolutely clear from the report, that counsel was relying on the first edition. While the report indicates that counsel read passages from Ray's text to the jury, there is no indication of which passages these were.

[57] Isaac Ray, *A Treatise on the Medical Jurisprudence of Insanity* (1838), p.41.

[58] See above, para.7.09.

[59] (1844) 2 Broun 332 at 356–357.

be allowed to escape punishment for their sinfulness on the excuse that they were not responsible for their acts."[60]

It is true that religious references loomed large in Lord Hope's jury charges on insanity,[61] but his approach does not go so far as rejecting the defence entirely. Lord Hope was quite prepared to accept *cognitive* insanity,[62] the question being "whether the party had any notion that the act was one of which the law would take cognisance"[63] (either because they did not understand the nature and quality of the act, or because they did not know it was wrong), but this was for him "the only test which a Jury is at liberty to take".[64] There could be no question of *volitional* insanity, and it was here that religious references came into his reasoning. Where a person's reasoning was disturbed, but not overthrown, that is, where he was aware that what he was doing was criminal, but was unable to resist the impulse to commit the act: **7.12**

> "The view of such cases taken by the law is the doctrine of the Bible—the man *chooses* to commit the act: he *gives way* to the suggestions and temptations which are strong, only because he has long indulged in such thoughts. Rely upon it, he was not tempted above what he was able to bear. If there was not an absolute alienation of reason, the law holds he can resist, and must resist, the suggestions to commit an act, which would be against the law."[65]

Such acts were, according to Lord Hope, "acts of a mind rebelling against the decrees of God, impatient of the condition in which the individual is placed, and desirous rather of rushing into the presence of God than submitting to His decrees".[66] Even if this view is narrower than later Scottish judges, however, it would be wrong to regard Lord Hope as having narrowed the then-understood concept of insanity. Neither Hume nor Alison appear to have accepted a volitional test of insanity,[67] and Lord Hope's approach is no narrower than that adumbrated in *McNaghten*'s case. Moreover, it is unsurprising that Lord Hope should have relied on *McNaghten*'s case, given the absence of any Scottish judicial authority, and the fact the McNaghten Rules were phrased in

---

[60] Gordon, para.10.25.

[61] See *James Gibson* (1844) 2 Broun 332 at 360–361; *Elizabeth Yates* (1847) Arkley 238 at 240–241; *George Lillie Smith* (1855) 2 Irv. 1 at 60 and 62. There are no such references in *Eugene Whelps* (1842) 1 Broun 378, but the charge here is much briefer. Lord Hope also presided in *Jane Smith* (1852) 1 Irv. 77, but the terms of his charge to the jury are not included in the report of that case.

[62] The distinction between cognitive and volitional insanity is noted briefly above, para.7.01. See also *Report on Insanity and Diminished Responsibility* (Scot. Law Com. No. 195), Ch.2.

[63] *Elizabeth Yates* (1847) Arkley 238 at 241.

[64] *ibid.*

[65] *James Gibson* (1844) 2 Broun 332 at 360–361.

[66] *Elizabeth Yates* (1847) Arkley 238 at 241. See also *George Lillie Smith* (1855) 2 Irv. 1 at 59 ("That perversion of moral feeling is not insanity, nor is its existence sufficient to make out such a plea...").

[67] See above paras 7.07–7.08. *Cf.* Gordon, para.10.22, who suggests that "it seems to be going too far to say, as did Lord Dunedin, [HL Debs, Vol.57, col.475 (May 15, 1924)] that nothing in Hume countenances a defence of irresistible impulse". It is correct that Hume refers to the accused being given up "to the impulse of his own distempered fancy" (i, 37), but Hume treats this as a consequence of the accused suffering from an "absolute alienation of reason". Hume's use of the term "impulse" is not addressed to the situation where the accused is aware of the nature, quality and wrongfulness of his actions but is unable to control them.

terms more suitable for directing a jury than the discussions to be found in Hume or Alison.

The rise of irresistible impulse

7.13 Unlike Lord Hope, subsequent judges were prepared to countenance a defence of irresistible impulse. This was not a rejection of the McNaghten Rules as such: the inability to understand the nature or quality of the act, or to appreciate its wrongfulness, remained a valid test of insanity. But an alternative volitional element was added to the law: if an accused failed to demonstrate that he was insane under the McNaghten Rules, he might succeed in the plea by demonstrating that he had acted under an irresistible impulse. This was recognised by Lord Cockburn in two cases,[68] and by Lord Cowan in a third, *John McFadyen*:

> "The defence is not utter deprivation of reason; but *weakness of intellect* to such an extent as to render him irresponsible for his conduct as a rational being. Did the panel possess intellect enough to know the distinction between right and wrong, and *that*, in the very commission of the crime charged, and at the time? Or, if he knew that distinction, was he under disability, from want of sufficient rational power, to govern his actions, and to control his emotions and desires?"[69]

This expansion of the defence to include irresistible impulse may have been a response to certain contemporary medical writings which regarded the McNaghten Rules as unduly narrow because of their failure to recognise a volitional test of insanity.[70] This expansion was not uniform, however, and as Gordon observes, "whether or not an insane person was convicted was likely to depend more on which judge happened to try him, than on any accepted legal principle".[71] Lord Hope, during this period, continued to adhere to the view that irresistible impulse was not a valid defence.[72] His successor as Lord Justice-Clerk, Lord Inglis, took the same view in *Alexander Milne*, although the harshness of this approach was

---

[68] *James Denny Scott* (1853) 1 Irv. 132 at 142 ("the case in which, though aware what he was doing, the prisoner was under *an impulse, so irresistible to him, that he was not a free agent*."). Lord Cockburn did not, however, encourage the jury to bring in a verdict of insanity on this basis, noting that "though it be occasionally a real condition, [it] is always to be regarded with great jealousy", as it was "pretended very often". See also his *Circuit Journeys* (2nd edn, 1889), p.388 ("I did not discourage the jury from convicting him, and thus avoiding the usual dangerous verdict, but recommending him to mercy on the ground of his intellect being *defective*.") In *Isabella Blyth* (1852) J. Shaw 567, Lord Cockburn effectively halted the accused's trial for murder midway through the evidence being led on the basis that the defence of insanity had already been made out. No reasons were given, but the accused's declaration (at 573) states that she knew what she was doing but did not know why she did it, which is clearly not insanity in terms of the McNaghten Rules and indicates that the case was at most one of irresistible impulse. See also *Circuit Journeys*, 381.

[69] (1860) 3 Irv. 650 at 665.

[70] See, e.g. G.F. Blandford, *Insanity and Its Treatment* (1884), p.360 ("Between the legal and the medical professions there has always been a conflict, and always will be, so long as this test remains. For what we say is, that an insane person may know right from wrong, may know that the act is unlawful and a wicked act, but may, through insanity, be totally unable to control himself, and may, either on account of a delusion or an insane impulse, commit a crime. Our test is not a knowledge of the nature or quality of an act, but the capability or incapability of abstaining from it.")

[71] Gordon, para.10.28.

[72] In *George Lillie Smith* (1855) 2 Irv. 1.

mitigated by Lord Inglis' view that once insane delusions were established, "the law at once presumes from that that he cannot appreciate what he is doing".[73] As a matter of substantive law, however, Lord Inglis' charge to the jury in *Milne* is pure McNaghten: "if he knows the act that he is committing, if he knows also the true nature and quality of the act, and apprehends and appreciates its consequences and effects—that man is responsible for what he does".[74]

Indeed, Lords Cockburn and Cowan appear to have been in a minority at this time. Subsequent charges to juries in *George Bryce*[75] (by Lord Justice-General McNeill), *Andrew Brown*[76] (again by Lord Inglis) and *Alexander Dingwall*[77] (by Lord Deas) were again framed in terms of McNaghten, with no hint of any defence of irresistible impulse.

Lord Moncrieff's approach to insanity

Every significant jury charge between 1871 and the turn of the century **7.14**
was delivered by the then Lord Justice-Clerk, Lord Moncrieff,[78] who took a rather different view of this area of law from his predecessors. In his first reported jury charge, in *Eliza Sinclair or Clafton*,[79] he doubted the validity of a test of knowledge of right from wrong, and directed the jury that they might find insanity proven on the basis of irresistible impulse: "[t]he question here is whether the unsoundness of the prisoner's mind prevented her from having the power to resist the impulse to kill her children when it occurred."[80]

Subsequently, he explicitly rejected knowledge of right from wrong as a test of sanity:

> "... it is entirely imperfect and inaccurate to say that if a man has a conception intellectually of moral or legal obligation, he is of sound mind. Better knowledge of the phenomena of lunacy has corrected some loose and inaccurate language which lawyers used to apply in such cases. A man may be entirely insane, and yet may know well enough that an act which he does is forbidden by law. Probably a large proportion of those who occupy our asylums are in that position. It is not a question of knowledge, but of soundness of mind. If the man have not a sane mind to apply his knowledge, the mere intellectual apprehension of an injunction or prohibition may stimulate his unsound mind to do an act simply because it is

[73] (1863) 4 Irv. 301 at 343.

[74] (1863) 4 Irv. 301 at 343. *Cf.* Gordon, paras 10.28–10.31, who treats *Milne* as one of a group of cases representing a movement away from the McNaghten Rules. At most, however, *Milne* was a relaxation of the evidential requirements for the plea: the McNaghten Rules continued to govern, and it is clear from the terms of Lord Inglis' charge to the jury in the later case of *Andrew Brown* (1866) 5 Irv. 215 that he continued to accept the validity of the Rules.

[75] (1864) 4 Irv. 506.

[76] (1866) 5 Irv. 215.

[77] (1867) 5 Irv. 466 at 475–476 ("if the jury believed that the prisoner, when he committed the act, had sufficient mental capacity to know, and did know, that the act was contrary to the law, and punishable by the law, it would be their duty to convict him."). This case is more significant for its recognition of a partial defence of diminished responsibility, on which see paras 11.05–11.06.

[78] See also *Thomas Ferguson* (1881) 4 Coup. 552. That case is primarily concerned with the plea of diminished responsibility, but Lord Deas' brief directions on insanity appear to be consistent with the McNaghten Rules.

[79] (1871) 2 Coup. 73.

[80] At 93.

forbidden, or not to do it because it is enjoined. If a man has a sane appreciation of right and wrong he is certainly responsible; but he may form and understand the idea of right and wrong and yet be hopelessly insane. You may discard these attempts at definition altogether. They only mislead."[81]

7.15 His approach came remarkably close to abrogating any attempt at legal definition: insanity was, he informed juries, "not a question of medical science, neither is it one of legal definition, although both may materially assist you. It is a question for your common and practical sense."[82] In his last reported charge to the jury on the subject, in *Thomas Barr*, he reiterated his view that knowledge of right from wrong was a "very inadequate" test, and continued:

> "The question is, was this man's mind diseased,—was he the victim of unsound thought,—thought which was the product of the working of an unsound mind. It is not whether the impulses or passions by which he was actuated were too strong for his power of moral restraint—which in a greater or lesser degree may be true of every man—but whether, in the ordinary relations of life, you think it proved that the prisoner was or was not responsible for his actions—was he a man whom you would have been prepared to treat, upon the evidence before you, in the ordinary dealings between man and man, as one who was not responsible for his actions in respect of his mind being diseased ..."[83]

It is not clear what sort of test this is, if indeed it is a test at all. The jury are being asked to decide whether the accused is responsible for his crime, but are told that they cannot decide this on the basis of whether the accused knew right from wrong, or on whether he was unable to control his actions.[84] Instead, they must decide whether he "was or was not responsible for his actions", which is no more than a tautology. Effectively, the result of Lord Moncrieff's approach seems to have been to hand over the question of insanity in its entirety to the jury—although that may well be consistent with the occasionally-expressed view that the jury will disregard directions from the trial judge on insanity anyway.[85]

Later judges, with the possible exception of Lord Strachan in *HM Advocate v Kidd*,[86] appear to have been able to draw little from Lord Moncrieff's views, although some dicta from his charges have occasionally been grafted on to passages taken from Hume or the earlier cases, particularly his preliminary observation in *Barr* that insanity is "a question of fact, to be judged by [the jury] on the ordinary rules on which men

---

[81] *Archibald Miller* (1874) 3 Coup. 16 at 18. See also *James Macklin* (1876) 3 Coup. 257, which is to similar effect.

[82] *Archibald Miller* (1874) 3 Coup. 16 at 17.

[83] (1876) 3 Coup. 261 at 264.

[84] *cf.* Gordon, para.10.35, where the view is expressed that Lord Moncrieff "more or less expressly stated the causal criterion adopted in New Hampshire" (on which see Gordon, paras 10.15–10.18). However, although Lord Moncrieff refers to the accused's *thought* being the "product" of the working of an unsound mind—which is redolent of the New Hampshire or *Durham* test, it is not clear that he requires that the conduct in question be itself the product of the accused's unsound mind.

[85] See Lord Cooper's evidence to the Royal Commission on Capital Punishment, quoted below, para.7.38.

[86] 1960 J.C. 61. See below, para.7.19.

act in daily life".[87] They appear, however, not to have been able to share Lord Moncrieff's enthusiasm for abandoning attempts at definition—and so, as Gordon observes, "Lord Moncrieff can be regarded as an eccentric in this branch of the law."[88]

The Scottish cases before *Kidd*

In the first reported twentieth-century case dealing with insanity, the Lord Justice-General (Kinross) appeared to revert to the McNaghten Rules, directing the jury that insanity required "such an alienation of reason that the accused did not know the nature or quality of the act which he was committing, or that if he did know its nature and quality, he was in such a state of mind that he was not aware that it was wrong."[89] However, at the conclusion of his charge he grafted on a volitional prong to this test, directing the jury that "if the malady from which the accused was suffering rendered him wholly incapable of controlling his actions, he would not, in the eye of the law, be a sane man."[90] In so directing the jury, he quoted a passage of Lord Moncrieff's in *Archibald Miller* to the effect that a man "may be entirely insane, and yet know well enough that an act which he does is forbidden by law".[91] Nonetheless, it seems clear that Lord Kinross did not intend to adopt wholesale Lord Moncrieff's approach to the plea of insanity, but simply sought to use one passage in *Miller* to support the recognition of irresistible impulse as a form of insanity.[92] **7.16**

Lord Constable, however, used the same passage from *Miller* to rather different effect in deciding *HM Advocate v Sharp*.[93] That case recognised that the failure of an accused to realise that his actions were morally wrong might amount to insanity—even if he realised that they amounted to a crime for which he was liable to be punished. The case is significant, particularly given the variant approaches to this problem which have been adopted in other jurisdictions, and is discussed more fully later in this chapter.[94]

The only other reported case of any significance in this period is *HM Advocate v Mitchell*,[95] where it was claimed that the accused had been suffering from "psychic epilepsy" at the time of the offence, with the

---

[87] (1876) 3 Coup. 261 at 263.

[88] Gordon, para.10.35. See also *Minutes of Evidence Taken Before the Royal Commission on Capital Punishment* (1950), para.5190 (evidence of Lord Keith).

[89] *HM Advocate v McClinton* (1902) 4 Adam 1 at 25.

[90] (1902) 4 Adam 1 at 28.

[91] (1874) 3 Coup. 16 at 18. The full passage is quoted above, para.7.14. Lord Kinross omitted the last two sentences of that passage ("You may discard these attempts at definition altogether. They only mislead.") in charging the *McClinton* jury.

[92] *cf.* Gordon, para.10.36, who argues that Lord Kinross "added to *James Denny Scott* a reference to *Miller* without apparently realising that *Miller* represented a wholly different approach to the question, and could not just be tacked on to the Rules as could irresistible impulse." Although *Miller* does as a whole represent a "wholly different approach", it seems clear from the terms of the charge in *McClinton* that Lord Kinross sought only to adopt an isolated passage from Lord Moncrieff's charge in order to justify "tacking on" irresistible impulse to the Rules.

[93] 1927 J.C. 66 at 69 ("where the mental condition of the accused has not changed, the test of whether he is able to give proper instructions is exactly the same as the test of whether he can be held responsible for the act he has committed") (citing *HM Advocate v Robertson* (1891) 3 White 6). See further para.14.02.

[94] See below, paras 7.40–7.41.

[95] 1951 J.C. 53. *HM Advocate v Brown* (1907) 5 Adam 312 is concerned with insanity as a plea in bar of trial.

consequence that he did not know what he was doing. Lord Justice-Clerk Thomson charged the jury that if they accepted this claim, they should acquit on the ground of the insanity. That is uncontroversial, at least if "psychic epilepsy" is accepted as a disease of the mind for the purposes of the plea of insanity,[96] as, although the Rules are not specifically mentioned in Lord Thomson's charge, the case clearly falls within them.

The Royal Commission and its immediate aftermath

7.17 As Gordon observes, the Scottish witnesses who gave evidence to the Royal Commission on Capital Punishment "had some difficulty in explaining to the Commission just what the Scots law on insanity was".[97] Neither Lord Cooper nor Lord Keith was prepared to accept the Rules as authoritative, but they seem to have been considered at least as the starting point. Lord Cooper stated that, if charging a jury:

> "I am not prepared to say that I would charge in the exact terms of the M'Naghten Rules ... I would take as the broad rule only the third one, that insanity arises when a person is labouring under such a defect from reason from disease of the mind that he does not know the nature and quality of the act he is doing, or if he does know it, he does not know he is doing wrong."[98]

That, however, is essentially to accept the Rules, as the "third" rule is, as discussed earlier, their core: the first and fourth rules (dealing with delusions)[99] are logical consequences of that rule, while the second rule is simply a statement of the burden of proof and is identical to the Scottish position.[1] This acceptance notwithstanding, Lord Cooper asserted that the Rules were "not part of our law. We talk about it, but we do not use it as an authoritative formula."[2] Lord Keith indicated that the McNaghten Rules "would be considered", but that the law was perhaps "rather more flexible" than it had previously been.[3]

As has been demonstrated, however, almost all the Scottish cases prior to the Royal Commission (with the exception of those in which Lord Moncrieff presided) had proceeded on the basis of *McNaghten*, albeit that a defence of irresistible impulse was occasionally, but not consistently, added to the Rules. Although no Scottish judge since Lord Hope, in the immediate aftermath of *McNaghten's* case, had explicitly adopted the Rules as part of his charge to the jury, jury directions were almost always framed in terms of knowledge of the "nature and quality" of the act, or knowledge that it was wrong. By the time of the Royal Commission, Scots and English law had diverged sharply on whether "wrong" in this context meant morally wrong, or legally wrong,[4] but otherwise there is little to support a claim of real divergence in approach. It is true that the Rules were not, in Scotland, given the quasi-statutory status accorded

[96] See below, paras 7.33–7.35.

[97] Gordon, para.10.39.

[98] *Minutes of Evidence Taken Before the Royal Commission on Capital Punishment* (1950), para.5465.

[99] See above, para.7.09.

[1] See above, para.2.16.

[2] *Minutes of Evidence Taken Before the Royal Commission on Capital Punishment* (1950), para.5506.

[3] *ibid.*, para.5189.

[4] See below, paras 7.40–7.41.

them by the English courts, but the core of the insanity defence remained the same.

7.18 The Scots law of insanity prior to the Royal Commission's report is perhaps best viewed as a liberalised version of *McNaghten*: relying on the same principle, but occasionally (not consistently) recognising a defence of irresistible impulse, and interpreting knowledge that the act in question was "wrong" as meaning morally, rather than legally, wrong—thus avoiding the criticism of undue severity that has been directed against *McNaghten* as applied in the English case of *R. v Windle*.[5]

There was, however, no decision of an appellate court firmly acknowledging the Rules as part of Scots law. Accordingly, when the Royal Commission concluded that "the test of responsibility contained in the M'Naghten Rules cannot be defended in the light of modern medical knowledge and modern penal views",[6] it was open to Lord Walker to denounce them as alien English rules which formed no part of Scots law:

> "In their origin they are English rules, without any basis either in statute or judicial decision. The extent to which they have been followed and departed from in the practice of the criminal Courts in England, and all that has been urged against them, and in their favour, is fully summarised in the Report of the Royal Commission on Capital Punishment, which came to the conclusion that the rules were so defective that English law on the subject ought to be changed ... In these circumstances, I should not be prepared to hold that the rules form any part of the law of Scotland, unless compelled by binding authority."[7]

The emergence of the modern law

7.19 The first reported charge to a jury on insanity subsequent to the Royal Commission's report is that given by Lord Strachan in *HM Advocate v Kidd*.[8] It is not easy to isolate any single "operative" part of the charge, and it is therefore necessary to quote it at some length. It is as follows:

> "The question really is this, whether at the time of the offences charged the accused was of unsound mind. I do not think you should resolve this matter by inquiring into all the technical terms and ideas that the medical witnesses have put before you. Treat it broadly, and treat the question as being whether the accused was of sound or unsound mind. That question is primarily one of fact to be decided by you, but I have to give you these directions. First, in order to excuse a person from responsibility for his acts on the ground of insanity, there must have been an alienation of reason in relation to the act committed. There must have been some mental defect, to use a broad neutral word, a mental defect, by which his reason was overpowered, and he was thereby rendered incapable of exerting his reason to control his conduct and reactions. If his reason was alienated in relation to the act committed, he was not responsible for

---

[5] [1952] 2 Q.B. 826, where it was held that wrong in the Rules meant "legally wrong" and so a belief on the part of the accused that his actions were morally right was not a basis for the defence. For criticisms, see below, paras 7.40–7.41.

[6] *Report of the Royal Commission on Capital Punishment* (Cmd. 8932, 1953), para.291.

[7] *Mackenzie v Mackenzie*, 1960 S.C. 322 at 326 (a civil case on insanity as a defence to an action of divorce for cruelty).

[8] 1960 J.C. 61.

that act, even although otherwise he may have been apparently quite rational. What is required is some alienation of the reason in relation to the act committed. Secondly, beyond that, the question in this case whether the accused's mind was sound or unsound is to be decided by you in the light of the evidence, in the exercise of your commonsense and knowledge of mankind, and it is to be judged on the ordinary rules on which men act in daily life. Thirdly, the question is to be decided in the light of the whole circumstances decided in the evidence. You must have regard to the evidence which has been given by the medical witnesses, but the medical evidence by itself is not conclusive. The question is to be decided by you, and not by the mental specialists. In coming to your decision you are entitled, and indeed bound, to regard the whole evidence. You are entitled in particular to consider the nature of the acts committed and the conduct of the accused at and about the relevant times, and his previous history. Those are the directions which I give you on this matter.

At one time, following English law, it was held in Scotland that if an accused did not know the nature and quality of the act committed, or if he did know it but did not know he was doing wrong, it was held that he was insane. That was the test, but that test has not been followed in Scotland in the most recent cases. Knowledge of the nature and quality of the act, and knowledge that he is doing wrong, may no doubt be an element, indeed are an element, in deciding whether a man is sane or insane, but they do not, in my view, afford a complete or perfect test of sanity. A man may know very well what he is doing, and may know that it is wrong, and he may none the less be insane. It may be that some lunatics do an act just because they know it is wrong. I direct you therefore that you should dispose of this question in accordance with the directions which I have given, which briefly are, that there must be alienation of reason in regard to the act committed, otherwise the question is one for you to decide whether the accused was at the time of sound or unsound mind."[9]

It is not clear to which cases Lord Strachan is referring when he says that the test at the core of the Rules "has not been followed in Scotland in the most recent cases". As demonstrated earlier, the reported cases closest to *Kidd*—although some years earlier—do indeed appear to follow the Rules. It may be that Lord Strachan's directions are in part a response to the Royal Commission's condemnation of the Rules. In the absence of any other test to fall back on (those offered by Hume and Alison being little different from McNaghten),[10] Lord Strachan appears to have come close to Lord Moncrieff's abrogation of a test, and much of the charge to the jury in *Kidd* is taken directly from Lord Moncrieff's earlier charges. The language of "alienation of reason" is taken from Hume, but it is significant that while Hume insisted on an "absolute alienation of reason",[11] Lord Strachan directs the jury that only "some alienation of reason" is required.

At the outset of his charge, Lord Strachan seems to go so far as

[9] At 70–71.

[10] See above, paras 7.07–7.08. In *Mackenzie v Mackenzie*, 1960 S.C. 322 at 328, Lord Walker appears to have considered Alison to have laid down an identical test of insanity to that applicable under the Rules. Hume is not referred to.

[11] Hume, i, 37.

advocating a test of irresistible impulse, directing the jury that "a mental defect, by which his reason was overpowered, and he was thereby rendered incapable of exerting his reason to control his conduct and reactions" will suffice for insanity. When, therefore, he observes that "knowledge of right from wrong" is not a "complete or perfect test of sanity", it might be thought that his position is little different from Lords Cockburn or Cowan in the mid-nineteenth century, who reacted to the perceived inadequacy of a cognitive test by grafting on a defence of irresistible impulse.[12] However, both of these judges accepted knowledge of right from wrong as a valid test—simply not a conclusive one—whereas Lord Strachan appears to deny its validity altogether. Insofar as a test is formulated in Lord Strachan's charge, it is a volitional one, concerned with the accused's ability to control his actions, but it is not clear that his intention was to adumbrate any particular test, as opposed to simply handing the matter over to the jury as had Lord Moncrieff in the earlier cases.

Handing over the matter to the jury in this way might well have been consistent with the views of the Royal Commission, which had concluded "that a preferable amendment of the law would be to abrogate the Rules and to leave the jury to determine whether at the time of the act the accused was suffering from disease of the mind (or mental deficiency) to such a degree that he ought not to be held responsible".[13] There are, however, serious objections to abdicating responsibility to the jury in such cases, not least that it is likely to lead to arbitrary and inconsistent verdicts.[14] **7.20**

Lord Strachan's charge was subsequently used as a basis for the Court of Session to assert in two cases that the McNaghten Rules formed no part of Scots law.[15] The plea later fell to be reconsidered by a court of seven judges in *Brennan v HM Advocate*.[16] Although the court was technically only concerned with the question of whether the plea could be founded on the temporary effects of self-induced intoxication,[17] the court took the opportunity to offer a general (and concise) statement of the law on insanity:

> "In short, insanity in our law requires proof of total alienation of reason in relation to the act charged as the result of mental illness, mental disease or defect or unsoundness of mind and does not comprehend the malfunctioning of the mind of transitory effect, as the result of deliberate and self-induced intoxication."[18]

This is not identical to *Kidd*, but there are close parallels. It makes it clear that there are two components to the defence of insanity in Scots law: first, an aetiological component[19] (in *Brennan*, "mental illness, mental

[12] See above, para.7.13.

[13] *Report of the Royal Commission on Capital Punishment* (Cmd. 8932, 1953), para.333.

[14] J. Chalmers, "Merging provocation and diminished responsibility: some reasons for scepticism" [2004] Crim. L.R. 198–212 at pp.204–207, and see below, para.7.38.

[15] *Mackenzie v Mackenzie*, 1960 J.C. 61; *Breen v Breen*, 1961 S.C. 158.

[16] 1977 J.C. 38.

[17] As had previously been suggested to be the case in *HM Advocate v Aitken*, 1975 S.L.T. (Notes) 86 and doubted in *McGowan v HM Advocate*, 1976 S.L.T. (Notes) 8. See below, para.8.07.

[18] *Brennan v HM Advocate*, 1977 J.C. 38 at 45, *per* the Lord Justice-General (Emslie).

[19] The term "aetiological component" is used here to refer to the cause of the "impairment" suffered by the accused.

disease or defect or unsoundness of mind"; in *Kidd*, simply "unsound mind"),[20] and secondly, the impairment suffered by the accused (in *Brennan*, "*total* alienation of reason in relation the act charged"[21]; in *Kidd*, "*some* alienation of reason in relation to the act committed").[22] As is clear from the juxtaposition of these phrases, the law is less than certain. Not only is the difference between "some" and "total" crucial[23]—although this disparity between *Kidd* and *Brennan* has largely been ignored in the reported cases[24]—the exact meaning and scope of the two components has received little attention. Although, therefore, *Kidd* and *Brennan* may provide the basis for a formulation to be offered to juries, they say relatively little about the exact boundaries of the insanity plea.

The Development of the Defence of Automatism in Scots Law

7.21 In contrast to the plea of insanity, the history of the defence of automatism in Scots law is remarkably short and can be outlined much more briefly. The defence did not properly crystallise in law until the 1991 decision of *Ross v HM Advocate*.[25] Prior to that date, the law progressed through two main stages: first, the tentative, but irregular recognition of the defence prior to *HM Advocate v Cunningham*[26] in 1963, which appeared to exclude the possibility of any such defence. Secondly, following *Cunningham*, the defence was intermittently recognised (probably in disregard of that decision), until the landmark case of *Ross*.

The law prior to *Cunningham*

7.22 Although it has been observed that "[b]y a chronological accident Scotland may claim to have led the English-speaking world in developing the defence of automatism",[27] the cases prior to *Cunningham* did not reflect any structured approach to the issue. Instead, automatism-type excuses were recognised on a rather *ad hoc* basis: in *Simon Fraser*,[28] based on somnambulism; in *HM Advocate v Ritchie*,[29] on "temporary mental dissociation due to toxic exhaustive factors"; and in *HM Advocate v Hayes*,[30] on "temporary dissociation due to masked epilepsy or other pathological condition". The term "automatism" was not used in these cases, and the court seems to have regarded itself as having, at least, limited powers to protect the public despite the nature of the defence, with Fraser and Hayes both agreeing to certain conditions in return for

---

[20] *Brennan*, at 46 *per* the Lord Justice-General (Emslie); *Kidd*, at 71 *per* Lord Strachan.

[21] The phrase is based on Hume's requirement of an "absolute alienation of reason" (Hume, i, 37). See also *Lindsay v HM Advocate*, 1997 S.L.T. 67 at 69, *per* Lord Hamilton.

[22] *Brennan*, at 45 *per* the Lord Justice-General (Emslie); *Kidd*, at 71 *per* Lord Strachan (emphases added).

[23] See below, para.7.37.

[24] In *Carmichael v Boyle*, 1985 S.L.T. 399 at 406, the Lord Justice-Clerk (Wheatley) refers to Lord Strachan's definition of insanity in *Kidd* as "definition which has been accepted ever since as a classical one, and which has been approved and used in many subsequent cases, as for instance in the seven-judge case of *Brennan v HM Advocate*".

[25] 1991 J.C. 210.

[26] 1963 J.C. 80.

[27] G.H. Gordon, "Automatism, insanity and intoxication" (1976) 21 J.L.S.S. 310–316 at p.310.

[28] (1878) 4 Coup. 70.

[29] 1926 J.C. 45.

[30] High Court, November 1949, unreported. See further below, para.7.33.

their liberty (which raises the question of whether they were in fact acquitted at all).[31] All of these cases, in fact, raise important questions about the boundary between automatism and intoxication, and are discussed in more detail in this context, later in this chapter.[32]

HM Advocate v Cunningham

In *Cunningham*, the accused was charged with three offences: taking and driving away a motor van without the owner's consent, causing death by reckless driving, and driving while unfit through drink or drugs.[33] He lodged a special defence to the effect that, during the relevant time, "he was not responsible for his actings on account of the incidence of temporary dissociation due to an epileptic fugue or other pathological condition".[34] The trial judge certified the matter to the High Court, where the case came before the Lord Justice-General (Clyde), the Lord Justice-Clerk (Grant) and Lord Carmont. **7.23**

In a brief opinion delivered by the Lord Justice-General, the court advised the trial judge that the defence was incompetent. The reasons for this conclusion are not clearly stated, with Lord Clyde simply asserting that proof of the alleged defence "would not, in my opinion, justify a verdict of not guilty. On the contrary, these factors only bear upon mitigation of sentence and not upon guilt".[35] Why this is the case is not explained, and it is significant that the court does not consider the manner in which the "defence" lodged by Cunningham might have operated. If it was a denial of *mens rea* (or even of the *actus reus* of the relevant offences), then it is difficult to see how its relevance could have been denied, but instead Lord Clyde took the view that the onus of proving any special defence was "of course, upon the accused".[36] It was later decided—in *Lambie v HM Advocate*[37]—that this was not the law, and that (apart from insanity and diminished responsibility) any common law defences must be disproved beyond reasonable doubt by the prosecution once the defence has discharged the evidential burden.[38]

Although *Cunningham* was referred to with approval in some subsequent appeal court decisions,[39] it had alarming consequences. As Gordon observed, it could be interpreted in one of two ways: either automatism was irrelevant where it did not amount to insanity, which led "to the startling proposition that a man may be convicted of a common-law offence when he not only lacked *mens rea* but acted involuntarily",[40]

[31] See further below, para.7.31 (*Fraser*), para.7.33 (*Hayes*).

[32] See below, paras 7.26–7.36.

[33] Then offences under ss.271(1), 1 and 6(1) respectively of the Road Traffic Act 1960.

[34] 1963 J.C. 80 at 81. The language of the special defence is noticeably similar to that lodged in *HM Advocate v Hayes* (para.7.33 below).

[35] At 84.

[36] At 84.

[37] 1973 J.C. 53.

[38] See above, para.2.16.

[39] *HM Advocate v Clark*, 1968 J.C. 53; *Carmichael v Boyle*, 1985 S.L.T. 399. See also *HM Advocate v Murray*, 1969 S.L.T. (Notes) 85.

[40] G.H. Gordon, "Automatism, insanity and intoxication" (1976) 21 J.L.S.S. 310–316 at p.312.

or alternatively, automatism, "however caused" should be treated as a defence of insanity, meaning—given the limited flexibility of disposal available at the time in such cases—that the accused should be acquitted but committed to a mental hospital, even where this was an entirely inappropriate outcome.[41]

Neither of these possibilities is satisfactory, and *Cunningham* was not always applied by trial judges.[42] It was, however, reaffirmed by the appeal court in *Carmichael v Boyle*,[43] where the court allowed an appeal against a sheriff's decision to acquit the accused, who appeared to have committed various offences whilst in a hypoglycaemic state. The sheriff's view that *mens rea* had not been proven was rejected by the appeal court, which considered that *mens rea* could be inferred from the accused's actions, and that the facts did not disclose any defence which might rebut that inference. Because Boyle's condition did not amount to a mental illness, there could be no question of insanity (suggesting that the first of Gordon's two possible interpretations of *Cunningham* was correct) and so Boyle should have been convicted. *Cunningham*, it was said, was completely general in its terms and it was not open to the sheriff to distinguish it.[44] Matters stood there until the landmark decision in *Ross v HM Advocate*.[45]

Ross v HM Advocate

7.24 The appellant in *Ross v HM Advocate*[46] went to trial on a charge of malicious damage, nine charges of assault (in all but two of which he was charged with attempted murder), one charge of breach of the peace and one of police assault. Most facts were agreed by joint minute except those relating to the police assault charge, of which he was found not guilty by the jury. The jury found him "guilty on all the other charges under deletion of the references to attempted murder, and subject to the rider that at the time of these offences he was acting under the influence of drugs administered to him without his knowledge".[47] There was evidence to the effect that these drugs (temazepam and LSD) had been introduced into a can of lager from which he was drinking, and that he had shortly afterwards violently attacked various complete strangers with a knife until he was restrained by police officers.

The jury's decision was based on directions by the trial judge—themselves based on *Cunningham*—that the evidence of Ross's drink having been spiked, and any consequent effects on his mental state, could not

---

[41] It appears that this is what happened in *HM Advocate v Aitken*, 1975 S.L.T. (Notes) 86 (a successful plea of insanity based upon ingestion of LSD), but the accused was, unsurprisingly, released shortly thereafter: see A.M. McLean, "Insanity—a very special defence" (1976) 21 J.L.S.S. 175 at p.175. In modern practice, Aitken's defence would be treated as one of automatism but would fail due to the fact that the ingestion of LSD was voluntary: see below, para.7.44.

[42] See *McGregor v HM Advocate* (1973) S.C.C.R. Supp. 54; *HM Advocate v Raiker*, 1989 S.C.C.R. 149. In *Farrell v Stirling*, 1975 S.L.T. (Sh. Ct) 71, Sheriff Stewart distinguished *Cunningham* by concluding that a person in a hypoglycaemic state could not be said to be "driving" for the purpose of certain road traffic offences. See also Gordon, fn.40 above, at p.312, noting that *Cunningham* had been ignored "in some unreported cases".

[43] 1985 S.L.T. 399.

[44] At 405 *per* the Lord Justice-Clerk (Wheatley).

[45] 1991 J.C. 210.

[46] *ibid.*

[47] At 212 *per* the Lord Justice-General (Hope).

form the basis for an acquittal. On appeal, it was held that *Cunningham* had been wrongly decided and should be overruled.

Although most theoretical discussions of the defence of automatism, and leading cases in other jurisdictions, have tended to characterise it as a denial of *actus reus*, that was not the approach taken by the majority of the court in *Ross*. Instead, the majority based its decision on considerations of *mens rea*. In describing the defence, the Lord Justice-General (Hope) drew a close parallel with the defence of insanity:

> "... if a person cannot form any intention at all because, for example, he is asleep or unconscious at the time, it would seem impossible to hold that he had *mens rea* and was guilty in the criminal sense of anything he did when he was in that state. The same result would seem to follow if, for example, he was able to form intention to the extent that he was controlling what he did in the physical sense, but had no conception whatever at the time that what he was doing was wrong. His intention, such as it was, would lack the necessary evil ingredient to convict him of a crime. Insanity provides the clearest example of this situation, but I do not see why there should be no room for the view that the lack of evil intention in cases other than insanity, to which special considerations apply, should not also result in an acquittal. Indeed, since it is for the Crown to prove *mens rea* as well as the *actus reus* of the offence, it would seem logical to say that in all cases where there is an absence of *mens rea* an acquittal must result."[48]

There are hints of a *McNaghten* approach to insanity in this passage, **7.25** which were to become even more explicit in the subsequent automatism case of *Cardle v Mulrainey*.[49] More importantly, it presents automatism and insanity as two sides of the same coin: this approach suggests that they are both based on denials of *mens rea*. Automatism is, however, a sub-set of denials of *mens rea*, and Lord Hope specifies three requirements for the defence to operate: first, there must be an external factor; secondly, it must be one which was not self-induced or which the accused was bound to foresee,[50] and, thirdly, it must result in a total alienation of reason.[51] The phrase "total alienation of reason" is, it should be noted, identical to that used in the formulation of the insanity plea offered in *Brennan v HM Advocate*.[52]

It is suggested here that the pleas of insanity and automatism each comprise what may be termed an aetiological and an impairment component. The impairment component—the "total alienation of reason"—is common to both defences. The difference between the two rests with the aetiological component: that is, the cause of the alienation of reason. The question of which causes are properly regarded as a basis for each defence is discussed in detail below.[53]

[48] At 213–214 *per* the Lord Justice-General (Hope).

[49] 1992 S.L.T. 1152, discussed below, para.7.37.

[50] On this requirement, see below, para.7.44.

[51] See *Ross v HM Advocate*, 1991 J.C. 210 at 222, *per* the Lord Justice-General (Hope). At this particular point, the terminology of "total loss of control" is used, but the phrase "alienation of reason" is used elsewhere in the opinions delivered in *Ross* and has prevailed in later cases.

[52] 1977 J.C. 38, discussed above, para.7.20.

[53] See below, paras 7.26–7.36.

Beyond that, a further restriction is placed on the availability of the automatism plea. The external factor must not be one which was self-induced or which the accused was bound to foresee. This preserves the decision in *Brennan v HM Advocate*[54] that voluntary intoxication is no defence, but it is, as the court implicitly acknowledges, contrary to the principle that an absence of *mens rea* should result in an acquittal. Here, the principle is evaded by employing a legal fiction: where the condition which has resulted in an absence of *mens rea* is self-induced, "the accused must be assumed to have intended the natural consequences of his act".[55] This does not wholly answer the question, as *mens rea* will frequently be required as to conduct or circumstances as well, but such cases will be dealt with in a similar basis. So, for example, in *Donaldson v Normand*,[56] the accused was convicted of culpable and reckless conduct in that he had falsely denied carrying any sharp instruments to a turnkey before a search. His claim that he had forgotten that there was a syringe inside his left sock because he had taken drugs shortly before the search was of no avail. Although the court's decision to refuse his appeal was reasoned on the basis that his having taken the drugs was in itself reckless (and therefore demonstrated *mens rea*), it could equally have been refused on the basis that, because the condition which had resulted in an absence of *mens rea* was self-induced, he must have been assumed to know the relevant surrounding circumstances. Such an approach would avoid an acquittal in cases where the relevant offence required *knowledge* of the circumstances, rather than simple recklessness, for a conviction.[57]

Automatism and Insanity: The Modern Law

The aetiological component

7.26 As has been explained, the defences of insanity and automatism in Scots law each comprise what might be termed an aetiological and an impairment component.[58] The impairment component has been expressed in similar "alienation of reason" terms in respect of both defences, and it appears to be identical across both, as is demonstrated by the fact that the courts have drawn on case law relating to insanity when considering the scope of automatism.[59]

The distinction between the two defences therefore lies in the aetiological component. In respect of insanity, the requirement has been formulated (in *Brennan*) as "mental illness, mental disease or defect or unsoundness of mind",[60] while, in respect of automatism, *Ross v HM Advocate* specifies that an "external factor" is required.[61] Given that, as is

---

54 1977 J.C. 38.

55 *Ross v HM Advocate*, 1991 J.C. 210 at 215, *per* the Lord Justice-General (Hope).

56 1997 J.C. 200.

57 See further below, paras 7.44–7.45 and 8.10–8.13.

58 See above, para.7.20.

59 See, in particular, *Cardle v Mulrainey*, 1992 S.L.T. 1152.

60 *Brennan v HM Advocate*, 1977 J.C. 38 at 46, *per* the Lord Justice-General (Emslie).

61 *Ross v HM Advocate*, 1991 J.C. 210 at 214, *per* the Lord Justice-General (Hope). In *HM Advocate v Aitken*, 1975 S.L.T. (Notes) 86, the trial judge allowed (voluntary) ingestion of LSD to be considered by the jury as a basis for a plea of insanity. The appeal court subsequently expressed "grave doubts" as to whether this charge was correct (*McGowan v HM Advocate*, 1976 S.L.T. (Notes) 8) and, following *Ross*, it is clear that the transient effects of ingesting such a substance should properly be considered under the heading of automatism rather than insanity.

recognised in *Ross*, an absence of *mens rea* should logically result in an acquittal,[62] any cause which has resulted in the requisite "alienation of reason" should—unless some hitherto unknown third defence is to be recognised—fall into one of these two categories.[63] (There would be limited value in recognising any "third defence": the crucial difference is between the unqualified acquittal which results from the automatism defence, and the qualified acquittal consequent upon a successful plea of insanity.)

The distinction is influenced by two factors: public protection and labelling, and both these factors push in opposite directions. On the one hand, public protection is likely to push in the direction of a broad construction of the insanity plea, because the court retains the power to make appropriate orders for the protection of the public (and, indeed, the accused) in such cases. On the other hand, considerations of labelling are likely to push the courts towards a broad construction of the automatism plea, in order to avoid such odd consequences as labelling sleepwalkers as "insane". Such difficulties would, of course, be considerably alleviated were the insanity plea to be renamed.[64]

In Scotland, considerations of labelling have thus far taken precedence, 7.27 and so the courts have been prepared to assume (without discussion) that conditions such as sleepwalking and hypoglycaemia are properly regarded as bases for a defence of automatism, without any real consideration being given to the alternative of an insanity plea.[65]

How is it to be determined whether the aetiological component falls within the ambit of insanity or automatism? There are at least three ways in which the distinction might be drawn. In each case, it is appropriate to consider the way in which the insanity defence should be circumscribed, as that is the defence which leaves the accused open to coercive measures even where the plea is successful. Once the scope of the insanity defence is established, any other causes which lead to an alienation of reason must lead to an unqualified acquittal—presumably via the automatism defence—on the basis that the accused lacked *mens rea* at the relevant time. The possibilities are as follows.

(1) Distinguishing between "external" and "internal" causes

First, given the language of "external cause" in *Ross*, it may be that the 7.28 distinction is properly drawn between external and internal causes, and any internal cause which results in an alienation of reason is to be treated as falling within the scope of the insanity plea. A strong argument for such an approach is that, where the accused is not responsible due to some internal cause, the accused should not receive an unqualified acquittal, but the court's powers to protect the public should be triggered.

---

62 *Ross v HM Advocate*, 1991 J.C. 210 at 215, *per* the Lord Justice-General (Hope).

63 The defence may still fail, however, if the aetiology is itself self-induced: see below, para.7.44.

64 The Scottish Law Commission has proposed that the defence should no longer be known as "insanity", but without an alternative term being specified in legislation: *Report on Insanity and Diminished Responsibility* (Scot. Law Com. No. 195), para.2.23. *Cf.* V. Tadros, "Insanity and the capacity for criminal responsibility" (2001) 5 Edin. L.R. 325–354 at pp.352–353 (proposing that the insanity defence should be supplemented with a defence of "temporary incapacity").

65 See below, para.7.31–7.32.

For this reason, Lord Denning suggested in *Bratty v Attorney-General for Northern Ireland*[66] that:

> "The major mental diseases, which the doctors call psychoses, such as schizophrenia, are clearly diseases of the mind. But in *Charlson's* case, Barry J. seems to have assumed that other diseases such as epilepsy or cerebral tumour are not diseases of the mind, even when they are such as to manifest themselves in violence. I do not agree with this. It seems to me that any mental disorder which has manifested itself in violence and is prone to recur is a disease of the mind. At any rate it is the sort of disease for which a person should be detained in hospital rather than be given an unqualified acquittal."[67]

(2) Restricting the insanity plea to mental illness and cognate conditions

7.29 Alternatively, it may be that the insanity plea is properly restricted to mental illness and cognate conditions, and that any other internal cause which leads to an alienation of reason must result in an unqualified acquittal. This is supported by the Scottish cases which have assumed that sleepwalking and hypoglycaemia are properly bases for a plea of automatism rather than insanity,[68] but similar approaches in other jurisdictions have been criticised as giving insufficient weight to considerations of public protection.[69] This approach does, however, avoid the "gross unfairness"[70] of labelling such people as insane.

(3) A policy-based distinction

7.30 A third possible approach is that suggested by the treatment of sleepwalking in the Canadian case of *R. v Parks*[71]: to regard the automatism-insanity boundary as a question of policy, to be decided upon the factual basis for the aetiology presented to the court in any particular case. On this approach, it would be wrong to regard some conditions, such as sleepwalking, as necessarily falling into the category of either insanity or automatism, although in most cases, established practice will be such that the aetiology will clearly fall within one defence rather than the other. It is not clear, however, what the relevant policy factors are, and the point is not fully developed in *Parks*. If this approach were adopted, it is suggested that the court might properly have regard to at least the following:

---

[66] [1963] A.C. 386.

[67] [1963] A.C. 386 at 412 (citing *R. v Charlson* [1955] 1 W.L.R. 317). *Cf. R. v Burgess* [1991] 2 Q.B. 92 at 99 (noting that while the danger of recurrence may be a reason for categorising a condition as amounting to insanity, the absence of such danger does not preclude such a categorisation).

[68] *Finegan v Heywood*, 2000 J.C. 444 (sleepwalking); *MacLeod v Mathieson*, 1993 S.C.C.R. 488 (Sh. Ct) (hypoglycaemia).

[69] See, e.g. *R. v Charlson* [1955] 1 W.L.R. 317, where the jury were allowed to consider a defence of automatism based on the defendant's cerebral tumour. As was observed by C. Howard, "Automatism and insanity" (1962–1964) 4 *Sydney Law Review* 36–48 at p.40, "it is difficult to accept with equanimity a state of the criminal law in which it is more than possible, it is proper, to set free someone who on his own showing is likely to be suffering from a condition which may make him repeat an irrational and savage attack on a child with whose welfare he is entrusted by law". See also A. Brudner, "Insane automatism: a proposal for reform" (2000) 45 *McGill Law Journal* 65–85 at p.67.

[70] Ashworth, *Principles of Criminal Law*, p.208.

[71] [1992] 2 S.C.R. 871. See below, para.7.31.

(a) whether the condition is likely to recur and in what circumstances;
(b) whether the condition is likely to manifest itself in violence or in other ways dangerous to the public[72];
(c) to what extent the condition will be manageable by the accused in the future[73];
(d) whether the condition is such that it is appropriate to label the accused as "insane"; and
(e) whether the condition is one which would provide a basis for detention under Art.5(1)(e) of the ECHR, which permits the lawful detention of persons of "unsound mind".[74]

Against that background, the following sections consider how the courts have approached particular aetiologies.

Sleepwalking[75]

Attention here tends to focus on the well-known case of *Simon Fraser*,[76] where the accused killed his young son whilst dreaming that he was being attacked by a "wild beast". The jury, on the invitation of the trial judge, returned a verdict that "the panel killed his child, but that he was in a state in which he was unconscious of the act which he was committing by reason of the condition of somnambulism, and that he was not responsible".[77] After an adjournment of two days the Crown deserted the diet *simpliciter,* Fraser and his father having signed an agreement to the effect that Fraser would always sleep alone in the future and that his father would undertake to see that his son kept his word in the matter.[78] There is some doubt as to whether this verdict was one of conviction or acquittal,[79] although it is significant that it is referred to in Macdonald's *Criminal Law* as an acquittal,[80] given that it was Macdonald himself, as Solicitor-General, who prosecuted Fraser at his trial.[81] The question is, however, hypothetical—the Crown's decision to desert the diet meant that the **7.31**

[72] On points (a) and (b), see *Bratty v Attorney-General for Northern Ireland* [1963] A.C. 386 at 412, *per* Lord Denning, quoted above, para.7.28.

[73] See the discussion of hypoglycaemia and hyperglycaemia below, para.7.32.

[74] See *Winterwerp v Netherlands* (1979) 2 E.H.R.R. 387. The point is of less importance now that detention is no longer the inevitable result of an acquittal on the ground of insanity (see above, para.7.02).

[75] See, generally, C. Shapiro and A. McCall Smith (eds), *Forensic Aspects of Sleep* (1997); I. Ebrahim *et al*, "Violence, sleepwalking and the criminal law: (1) the medical aspects" [2005] Crim. L.R. 601–613; W. Wilson *et al*, "Violence, sleepwalking and the criminal law: (2) the legal aspects" [2005] Crim. L.R. 614–623.

[76] (1878) 4 Coup. 70. See R.S. Shiels, "Simon Fraser's case" (1998) S.L.G. 15–17.

[77] (1878) 4 Coup. 70 at 75.

[78] The text of the agreement (held in the National Archives of Scotland as AD/14/78/166) can be found in Jones and Christie, para.4–38.

[79] See Jones and Christie, para.4–38, who consider that "the preponderance of the evidence points to conviction". See, to similar effect, *Ross v HM Advocate*, 1991 J.C. 210 at 217–218, *per* the Lord Justice-General (Hope).

[80] Macdonald, 347.

[81] *Simon Fraser* (1878) 4 Coup. 70 at 70.

court never had to properly consider the meaning or effect of the jury's verdict. For that reason, *Fraser* is authority for very little, if anything.[82]

In the more recent case of *Finegan v Heywood*,[83] where the accused had committed several motoring offences whilst in a parasomniac state, the court treated the accused's condition as giving rise to a plea of automatism rather than insanity, and one which was unsuccessful given the sheriff's finding that the parasomniac state was the self-induced result of alcohol consumption.[84] It does not appear that the court considered the case to be one of automatism merely because an external factor (the consumption of alcohol) was involved, and it is implicit in the court's decision that sleepwalking unaccompanied by alcohol consumption should have resulted in Finegan receiving an unqualified acquittal.[85]

It would be unsatisfactory to always regard sleepwalking as a form of automatism, because the unqualified acquittal would leave the court unable to act to protect the public even where it was shown that the accused might act dangerously in the future. *Simon Fraser* is itself demonstrative of the need for flexibility of disposal in certain cases, and the English Court of Appeal, in a case where the charge was one of wounding with intent to do grievous bodily harm, regarded sleepwalking as the basis for a plea of insanity,[86] seemingly on the basis of the need to protect the public.[87] In *R. v Parks*,[88] the Supreme Court of Canada offered a solution to this difficulty, holding that it was wrong to state that

---

[82] It has been said that the case "cannot be regarded as anything other than very special": *Finegan v Heywood*, 2000 J.C. 444 at [4], *per* the Lord Justice-General (Rodger), citing *Ross v HM Advocate*, 1991 J.C. 210 at 217, *per* the Lord Justice-General (Hope).

[83] 2000 J.C. 444. Successful claims of somnambulism are likely to be rare, but in *PF (Dunfermline) v Kellman (Allan)*, Dunfermline Sheriff Court, September 2000, unreported, the accused was acquitted of indecent assault on the basis that he was sleepwalking at the time.

[84] On the exclusion of the defence of automatism where the alienation of reason is self-induced, see below, para.7.44.

[85] In England, it has been accepted that "although sleepwalking can no doubt be triggered by external factors such as stress, such factors are merely to be regarded as external triggers of a condition the primary source of which is internal to the accused": R.D. Mackay, *Mental Condition Defences in the Criminal Law* (1995), p.46, citing *R. v Burgess* [1991] 2 Q.B. 92. Accordingly, in English law, the presence or absence of an "external trigger" seems not to be determinative, but in *Burgess* sleepwalking was treated as the basis for a plea of insanity rather than automatism.

[86] *R. v Burgess* [1991] 2 Q.B. 92. The court noted (at 101) expert evidence from Dr Peter Fenwick stating that "... should [such] a person be detained in hospital? The answer to that is: Yes, because sleep walking is treatable. Violent night terrors are treatable. There is a lot which can be done for the sleep walker, so sending them to hospital after a violent act to have their sleep walking sorted out, makes good sense." In *R. v Lowe (Jules)*, Manchester Crown Court, March 2005, unreported, the defendant, who had killed his father while sleepwalking, was acquitted of murder by reason of insanity.

[87] I. Mackay, "The sleepwalker is not insane" (1992) 55 M.L.R. 715–720. *Burgess* is at odds with a number of earlier English trial cases (and *obiter* comments in appellate decisions) where it was assumed that the sleepwalker was entitled to an unqualified acquittal: see F. Boland, *Anglo-American Insanity Defence Reform* (1999), pp.8–10. See also *R. v Cogdon*, Supreme Court of Victoria, December 1950, unreported, discussed by N. Morris, "Somnambulistic homicide: ghosts, spiders and North Koreans" (1951) 5 *Res Judicatae* 29–33.

[88] [1992] 2 S.C.R. 871.

sleepwalking could never be a disease of the mind. Instead, the court should consider both medical and "policy factors", including the likelihood of recurrence, in deciding whether the appropriate defence was insanity or automatism.[89]

Hypoglycaemia and hyperglycaemia[90]

In *MacLeod v Mathieson*,[91] the sheriff was "prepared to accept"[92] that hypoglycaemia amounted to an external factor for the purposes of the automatism defence, but convicted the accused of careless driving—he had suffered a hypoglycaemic attack at the wheel of his car, resulting in a crash—on the basis that he should have foreseen the possibility of such an attack.[93] **7.32**

In England, the courts have applied the internal/external cause distinction to conclude that hypoglycaemia is a basis for a plea of automatism,[94] while hyperglycaemia grounds a plea of insanity.[95] This position has been labelled an "absurdity"[96]: as one commentator has pointed out, "[t]he distinction between external and internal factors only makes sense if it differentiates between those who can be safely acquitted, and those in need of restraint".[97]

It is suggested here that the appropriate response will normally be to treat such conditions as a basis for the defence of automatism, rather than insanity. Consider the situation where the accused's condition is a manageable one,[98] of which he was aware, but has nevertheless has failed to manage, or where an alienation of reason has occurred despite him taking reasonable efforts to manage his condition.[99] In such a case, the automatism defence will be excluded on the basis that he was "bound to foresee" the potential alienation of reason,[1] and the public interest will be served by a conviction. If the alienation of reason was unforeseeable, then there would—in the normal case—be no reason to assume that the accused would not take proper care to avoid similar situations in the

[89] What these other policy factors are is not made clear in *Parks*, although there is some reference to the possibility of an automatism defence being feigned (which is presumably more difficult if the aetiology is treated as amounting to insanity, given the differing burdens of proof). See *R. v Parks* [1992] 2 S.C.R. 871 at [16], *per* La Forest J. See above, para.7.30.

[90] The term hypoglycaemia refers to an abnormally low concentration of sugar in the blood, while hyperglycaemia refers to an abnormally high concentration.

[91] 1993 S.C.C.R. 488 (Sh. Ct).

[92] 1993 S.C.C.R. 488 at 492.

[93] See, to similar effect, *Moses v Winder* [1981] R.T.R. 37. Hypoglycaemia was rejected as the basis for a defence in *Carmichael v Boyle*, 1985 S.L.T. 399, but that decision pre-dated the recognition of a defence of automatism in *Ross v HM Advocate*, 1991 J.C. 210.

[94] *R. v Quick* [1973] Q.B. 910 (eating insufficient food to neutralise insulin taken earlier that day). See also *R. v Bingham* [1991] Crim. L.R. 433.

[95] *R. v Hennessy* [1989] 1 W.L.R. 287 (failure to take insulin).

[96] Ashworth, *Principles of Criminal Law*, p.208. See also G.T. Laurie, "Automatism and insanity in the laws of England and Scotland", 1995 Jur. Rev. 253–265 at p.256.

[97] N.M. Padfield, "Exploring a quagmire: insanity and automatism" [1989] C.L.J. 354–357 at p.356.

[98] This assumes that hypoglycaemia and hyperglycaemia are readily manageable, and manageable by the particular accused. If the evidence in a particular case demonstrates otherwise, that may be a policy reason for treating the case as one of insanity rather than automatism: *cf.* the discussion of *R. v Parks* [1992] 2 S.C.R. 871 at para.7.30 above.

[99] *cf. Farrell v Stirling*, 1975 S.L.T. (Sh. Ct) 71.

[1] See below, para.7.44.

future, events having put him on notice that he should do so.[2] Accordingly, there would seem to be no need to trigger the court's power to make one of the various disposals available on a finding of insanity[3] (and it is questionable whether these would be suitable in any case).

Physical illnesses[4]

7.33 Although recent Scottish Law Commission proposals would largely restrict the ambit of the insanity plea to "mental disorders",[5] it has extended more broadly—that is, to cover "physical illnesses"—in the past. In *HM Advocate v Mitchell*,[6] the Lord Justice-Clerk (Thomson) directed the jury that if they accepted the accused's claim that he had been suffering from "psychic epilepsy" at the relevant time, which it was said resulted in a loss of consciousness, then they should acquit on the ground of insanity.[7]

It is less clear how the case of *HM Advocate v Hayes*[8] should be interpreted. There, the accused was charged with culpable homicide, in that he had driven a bus which collided with two vehicles and overturned, resulting in death and injury. The jury returned a verdict finding both (1) that a charge of culpable homicide had been proved against the accused, and (2) that a "special defence" that he was, at the time, suffering from "temporary dissociation due to masked epilepsy or other pathological condition", had been established, as a result of which he had not seen the other vehicles. The case was certified to a Full Bench of the High Court, where it was agreed that Hayes should be dismissed from the bar if he undertook to surrender his public service and driving licenses and not to drive again in future. That arrangement, however, leaves it unclear as to whether or not Hayes had been convicted, although it seems likely that he was.[9] He was certainly not acquitted on the ground of insanity, or the court could not have adopted the course it did. The court was, however, adamant that its decision was "by no means to be regarded as a necessary precedent in any other case".[10]

It may well be that *Hayes* cannot be regarded as anything other than "very special",[11] but a similar case cannot be discounted in this way.

---

[2] In *Farrell v Stirling*, 1975 S.L.T. (Sh. Ct) 71, the accused was found guilty of one motoring offence committed during the onset of a state of hypoglycaemia, something which the accused had not suffered previously and would not have recognised when it commenced. In the circumstances, the sheriff (A.L. Stewart) granted an absolute discharge and did not proceed to conviction.

[3] CPSA 1995, s.57(2).

[4] The distinction between mental and physical illness is contested. See, e.g. R.E. Kendell, "The distinction between mental and physical illness" (2001) 178 *British Journal of Psychiatry* 490–493; M. Baker and M. Menken, "Time to abandon the term mental illness" (2001) 322 *British Medical Journal* 937.

[5] *Report on Insanity and Diminished Responsibility* (Scot. Law Com. No. 195), para.2.30, proposing that the plea should require a "mental disorder", meaning (a) mental illness; (b) personality disorder; or (c) learning disability. The definition of "mental disorder" proposed by the Commission is taken from the Mental Health (Care and Treatment) (Scotland) Act 2003, s.328(1).

[6] 1951 J.C. 53.

[7] See also *HM Advocate v Brown* (1891) 3 White 6, although that case is concerned with insanity as a plea in bar of trial rather than as a substantive defence, and is discussed further below, para.14.03.

[8] High Court, November 1949, unreported. See C.H.W. Gane and C.N. Stoddart, *A Casebook on Scottish Criminal Law* (2nd edn, 1988), p.70.

[9] Jones and Christie, para.4–32.

[10] Gane and Stoddart, fn.8 above, at p.71.

[11] As with *Simon Fraser* (1878) 4 Coup. 70: see fn.82 above.

Unfortunately, it has invariably been misinterpreted. That case is *HM Advocate v Ritchie*.[12] Ritchie was charged with culpable homicide, by knocking down a pedestrian whilst driving a car. He lodged a special defence in the following terms:

> "The panel pleads not guilty in respect that by the incidence of temporary mental dissociation due to toxic exhaustive factors he was unaware of the presence of the deceased on the highway and of his injuries and death, and was incapable of appreciating his immediately previous and subsequent actions."[13]

In modern practice, the reference to "toxic exhaustive factors" has **7.34** invariably been taken to mean that Ritchie had been overcome by the exhaust fumes from his vehicle.[14] It appears, however, that this is not the case. It should be noted that Ritchie's defence was that his condition of dissociation had lasted from Stirling until Doune (a drive the best part of 10 miles)[15]: this was not simply a case of falling asleep at the wheel. Evidence was led that he had been seriously wounded in the war and had undergone "several operations for abscess in the lungs", the last just a few months before the incident in question.[16] It was noted that a condition of dissociation ("a well-known morbid condition ... in which the patient might continue to carry on the operations in which he was engaged without being conscious, or with only a partial consciousness, of what he was doing ...")[17] might be "induced by a variety of causes, one of them, undoubtedly, being the absorption of poison into the blood".[18]

In his charge to the jury, Lord Murray said that the "defence of irresponsibility" put forward by Ritchie rested on a "disordered condition of the mind", which might be "induced by various causes. It may be congenital; it may be induced by illness, fever, palsy, accident, injury or shock ..."[19] There is no mention of any cause analogous to exhaust fumes in the charge. It appears that Ritchie's defence was *not*, in fact, based on any such external factor: the "toxic exhaustive factors" referred to were poison entering the blood from the abscess in his lungs.[20] In other words, the cause of his "alienation of reason"[21] was not external, but internal.

Nevertheless, Ritchie received an unqualified acquittal. Why should

---

[12] 1926 J.C. 45.

[13] 1926 J.C. 45 at 46.

[14] See, e.g. *Ross v HM Advocate*, 1991 J.C. 210 at 215, *per* the Lord Justice-General (Hope); Gordon, para.3.20; "In the Scottish Courts: non-insane automatism" (1964) 28 J.C.L. 42–44 at p.42–43; R.A.A. McCall Smith and D. Sheldon, *Scots Criminal Law* (2nd edn, 1997), p.26; Casebook, paras 7.41 to 7.42. *Cf.* Jones and Christie, para.4–30, who proceed on the assumption that Ritchie's defence was based on exhaust fumes but note that "the reports of the case fail to make this clear".

[15] See *HM Advocate v Ritchie*, 1926 J.C. 45 at 48.

[16] At 46.

[17] 1926 J.C. 45 at 47–48.

[18] 1926 J.C. 45 at 48.

[19] 1926 J.C. 45 at 48–49.

[20] The authors are indebted to Jenifer Ross, who uncovered this information in the Scottish Record Office in the course of her own researches, for generously sharing this information.

[21] Lord Murray did not in fact use that term, but adopted the language of the McNaughten Rules. See *HM Advocate v Ritchie*, 1926 J.C. 45 at 48–49: "... it amounts to this, that, owing to some disordered condition of the mind which affects its working, the afflicted person does not know the nature of his act, or, if he does know what he is doing, he does not know that what he is doing is wrong". For the Rules, see above, para. 7.09.

this be? It may be, of course, that the medical evidence was to the effect that his condition was unlikely to recur, but even if that was not the case (and there is no indication that it was), it is submitted that it is correct to treat his defence as one of automatism, rather than insanity. Lord Murray directed the jury that Ritchie was only entitled to an acquittal if he had ceased to be the "master of his own action" "owing to a cause which he was not bound to foresee, and which was outwith his control",[22] language which was later to form the basis for the defence of automatism as formulated in *Ross v HM Advocate*.[23] Accordingly, Ritchie would not have been able to succeed in his defence had he known that he was liable to enter such a state whilst driving and had nevertheless driven (or, at least, driven alone).[24] If he did so in the future, the defence would not be available to him. The facts of the case do not suggest that Ritchie would be unable to manage the consequences of his condition in future, nor that detention or some other restriction of liberty would have been a useful disposal. Policy factors, therefore, would point towards treating Ritchie's case as one of automatism rather than insanity, notwithstanding that the cause of his irresponsibility was an internal one.[25]

7.35 In England, the view has been taken that physical disorders, as internal causes, can fall within the concept "disease of the mind" for the purposes of the McNaghten Rules.[26] In *R. v Kemp*,[27] Devlin J. explained why counsel's argument that arteriosclerosis, as a "purely physical" illness,[28] was outwith the scope of the Rules and should be rejected:

> "In my judgment, the words 'from disease of the mind' are not to be construed as if they were put in for the purpose of distinguishing between diseases which have a mental origin and diseases which have a physical origin ... Hardening of the arteries is a disease which is shown on the evidence to be capable of affecting the mind in such a way as to cause a defect, temporarily or permanently, of its reasoning, understanding and so on, and so is in my judgment a disease of the mind which comes within the meaning of the Rules."[29]

In proposing to restrict the scope of the Scottish insanity plea to "mental disorder", it is not clear that the Commission gave any consideration to *Mitchell*,[30] the analogous English cases, or to the general question of whether physical disorders should provide a basis for the plea. The proposal is presented simply as giving statutory form to the existing law,

---

[22] 1926 J.C. 45 at 49.

[23] 1991 J.C. 210. See above, para.7.24.

[24] *cf. MacLeod v Mathieson*, 1993 S.C.C.R. 488 (Sh. Ct), discussed above, para.7.32.

[25] See further above, para.7.30.

[26] *R. v Sullivan* [1984] A.C. 156. See also *Bratty v Attorney-General for Northern Ireland* [1963] A.C. 386. *Cf.*, however, *R. v Charlson* [1955] 1 W.L.R. 317. In *R. v Kemp* [1957] 1 Q.B. 399 at 403, Devlin J. distinguished *Charlson* on the basis that the doctors who gave evidence at Charlson's trial "were apparently agreed that the accused was not suffering from any disease of the mind which would render him insane at the time of the commission of the acts".

[27] [1957] 1 Q.B. 399.

[28] The language adopted by the defendant's counsel, at 401.

[29] At 408.

[30] *HM Advocate v Mitchell*, 1951 J.C. 53. See above, para.7.33.

rather than as a substantive change.[31] If physical disorders were excluded from the plea, it would seem to follow that an alienation of reason caused by a physical disorder should result in an unqualified acquittal (as the accused would lack *mens rea* and the criteria for the insanity defence would not be satisfied): whether that is in the public interest, where the disorder has manifested itself in violence and is liable to recur,[32] is doubtful.

Dissociative states[33]

Both the Australian and the Canadian courts have had occasion to consider the criminal responsibility of persons who commit violent acts in what have been termed transient "dissociative states" caused by a psychological blow. The two jurisdictions have diverged on their treatment of these cases: in *R. v Rabey*,[34] the Supreme Court of Canada treated a dissociative state as a disease of the mind within the meaning of the McNaughten Rules, while in the Australian case of *The Queen v Falconer*,[35] the High Court of Australia treated it as a basis for a plea of non-insane automatism. The issue has not arisen in Scotland and, if it does, it is suggested that the courts should consider whether it properly falls within insanity or automatism by reference to the policy considerations identified above[36] in conjunction with the expert evidence presented at trial. **7.36**

The impairment component

As noted earlier, *Brennan v HM Advocate*[37] describes the impairment component of the insanity defence as a "total alienation of reason", a phrase adopted for the purposes of the automatism defence in *Ross v HM Advocate*.[38] The language is taken from Hume, who states: **7.37**

> "To serve the purpose of a defence in law, the disorder must therefore amount to an absolute alienation of reason, '*ut continua mentis alienatione, omni intellectu careat*,'—such a disease as deprives the patient of the knowledge of the true aspect and position of things about him,—hinders him from distinguishing friend or foe,—and gives him up to the impulse of his own distempered fancy."[39]

---

[31] Indeed, the Commission appears to have, at least initially, considered "mental disorder" to be analogous with "disease of the mind" in terms of the McNaughten Rules: *Discussion Paper on Insanity and Diminished Responsibility* (Scot. Law Com. D.P. No. 122, 2003), para.2.22. See also *Report on Insanity and Diminished Responsibility* (Scot. Law Com. No. 195), para.2.39, where reference is made to arteriosclerosis as a form of "mental disorder", even though it appears to fall outwith the definition of "mental disorder" proposed by the Commission.

[32] *cf. Bratty v Attorney-General for Northern Ireland* [1963] A.C. 386 at 412, *per* Lord Denning, quoted above, para.7.28.

[33] See, generally, B. McSherry, "Getting away with murder? Dissociative states and criminal responsibility" (1998) 21 *International Journal of Law and Psychiatry* 163–176; S. Gault, "Dissociative state automatism and criminal responsibility" (2004) 28 *Criminal Law Journal* 329–350. On the medical aspects, see A. Moskowitz, "Dissociation and violence: a review of the literature" (2004) 5 *Trauma, Violence and Abuse* 21–46.

[34] [1980] 2 S.C.R. 513.

[35] (1990) 171 C.L.R. 30. See also *The Queen v Radford* (1985) 42 S.A.S.R. 266.

[36] Para.7.30.

[37] 1977 J.C. 38.

[38] 1991 J.C. 210.

[39] Hume, i, 37.

The use of the words "absolute" and "total" is apt to mislead. As Hume's discussion shows, the phrase does not mean that the accused should have had *no* awareness of the circumstances and nature of his actions; a disordered understanding may suffice. Some flesh was given to the phrase in the automatism case of *Cardle v Mulrainey*,[40] where the accused, after a can of lager from which he had been drinking was spiked with amphetamine, attempted to steal a number of motor cars (successfully driving away one). The sheriff found that, although he was aware of his actions and that they were wrong, he had been unable to properly reason or refrain from committing them because of the effects of the amphetamine. Accordingly, he acquitted the accused, a decision which resulted in a successful appeal by the Crown. In remitting the case back to the sheriff, the appeal court stated that:

> "Where, as in the present case, the accused knew what he was doing and was aware of the nature and quality of his acts and that what he was doing was wrong, he cannot be said to be suffering from some total alienation of reason in regard to the crime with which he is charged which the defence requires."[41]

The court's language is almost a verbatim quotation from the McNaghten Rules.[42] While that sits uneasily with the mid-twentieth century insistence that the Rules are no part of Scots law,[43] Scots law has still failed to develop an adequate alternative formulation of the impairment component. Hume's phrase "alienation of reason" is inadequate without further explanation, while Alison defines insanity as that which "takes away from the pannel the power of distinguishing right from wrong, or knowing what he is doing",[44] language which is hardly any different in principle from the Rules, if at all.[45]

7.38 The only alternative developed by Scots law is the approach taken by Lord Moncrieff in the late nineteenth century—that is, not to "formulate" the law in any way, but to simply hand over insanity to the jury, without definition, as a question of fact. That approach is sometimes referred to as the "New Hampshire Rule", on the basis of the approach adopted in that state.[46] That approach may be seen as attractive on the basis that formulating a test is close to pointless anyway: as Lord Cooper famously said to the Royal Commission on Capital Punishment, "[h]owever much you charge a jury as to the M'Naghten Rules or any

---

[40] 1992 S.L.T. 1152.

[41] At 1160 *per* the Lord Justice-General (Hope). The phrase "some total alienation" is peculiar, and appears to conflate phrases from *Brennan v HM Advocate*, 1977 J.C. 38 ("total alienation") and *HM Advocate v Kidd*, 1960 J.C. 61 ("some alienation"). See above, para.7.20. In the earlier case of *Ross v HM Advocate*, Lord Hope suggested that lack of knowledge of wrong negated *mens rea*: 1991 J.C. 210 at 213.

[42] "... as not to know the nature and quality of the act he was doing; or if he did know it, that he did not know he was doing what was wrong". See above, para.7.09.

[43] See above, paras 7.17–7.18.

[44] Alison, *Principles*, 644.

[45] The language of the Rules also appears in Macdonald, 9 and Anderson, 5–6 (via *James Gibson* (1844) 2 Broun 332, where they were quoted to the jury).

[46] Gordon, para.10.16. See also J. Reid, "The companion of the New Hampshire doctrine of criminal insanity" (1961–1962) 15 *Vanderbilt Law Review* 721–767, where the Scottish position (understood by that writer to be analogous to that in New Hampshire) is discussed in some detail.

other test, the question they would put to themselves when they retired is—'Is the man mad or is he not?'"[47] But research with shadow juries has demonstrated convincingly that the formulation of jury directions on insanity *does* affect the verdict returned,[48] and even without such evidence it would be an abdication of responsibility to abandon attempts to formulate a legal rule and leave the accused's fate to depend on the arbitrary matter of jury composition.[49] In any event, there is little, if any, support in modern day case law for such an abolitionist approach.

Even accepting the "reception" of *McNaghten* in *Cardle v Mulrainey*,[50] three important questions remain. First, what is meant by knowing the "nature and quality" of one's actions? Secondly, if not knowing that one's actions are wrong amounts to an "alienation of reason", what does "wrong" mean in this context? Thirdly, and notwithstanding *Cardle v Mulrainey*, is there any room for irresistible impulse to amount to an alienation of reason? There is, unfortunately, relatively little guidance to be found on these issues in the Scottish case law. Partly, this is because most of the law on insanity is found in the charges of trial judges to juries rather than in decisions of the appeal court.[51] Accordingly, although the McNaghten formula has been quoted to juries on a number of occasions, its nuances have received relatively little attention. Such guidance as can be drawn from these cases can, however, be supplemented by reference to Hume, Alison and comparative material.

Nature and quality

It seems logical to regard this limb as being restricted to the "physical character" of the accused's actions: questions of the accused's appreciation of their moral or legal character—to the extent these are relevant at all—are appropriately dealt with under the "wrongfulness" limb.[52] Nevertheless, ambiguity remains, and as with the concept of wrongfulness, it has been said that this element of the defences admits of either a narrower or wider interpretation.[53] Some cases will be uncontroversial: 7.39

[47] *Minutes of Evidence Taken Before the Royal Commission on Capital Punishment* (1950), para.5479.

[48] R.J. Simon, *The Jury and the Defense of Insanity* (1967), especially Ch.3. See also N. Walker, *Crime and Insanity in England, Volume 1: The Historical Perspective* (1968), pp.242–243.

[49] To adopt an argument made in a slightly different context, see P.H. Robinson, "The modern general part: three illusions" in *Criminal Law Theory: Doctrines of the General Part* (S. Shute and A.P. Simester (eds), 2002), pp.75–102, at p.90: "Ad hoc determination means that similar cases are likely to be treated differently, that the law will be unpredictable, and that there is created the possibility of abuse of discretion by decision-makers, judge or juror ... [such] decisions may seem principled but are in fact the product of unguided and undisclosed discretion."

[50] 1992 S.L.T. 1152.

[51] Most of the case law dates from the period before the Criminal Appeal (Scotland) Act 1926 established a court of criminal appeal, permitting the review of convictions on indictment.

[52] *R. v Codère* (1916) 12 Cr.App.R. 21.

[53] G.L. Williams, *Criminal Law: The General Part* (2nd edn, 1961), §159.

the man who kills another believing them to be the devil,[54] or a "wild beast"[55] is clearly unaware of the "nature or quality" of his actions. But what of the accused who understands the actions he is performing but cannot appreciate their consequences? McAuley explains the difficulty clearly:

> "... the concept of the 'physical character' of an action is ambiguous. It could be taken to refer to the behavioural component of the defendant's conduct, in which case it would be confined to the surface features of an action—i.e., to the bodily movements or physical activity involved in shooting, stabbing, choking etc. Or it could be taken to refer to the accused's conduct as a whole, in which case it would include the consequences of his actions as well as their surface features. Nor is this a distinction without a difference, since the first interpretation would remove the insanity defence from a defendant who knew he was engaged in the physical activity of squeezing his victim's throat even if he was too ill to appreciate that that activity was likely to cause her death."[56]

Similar difficulties might arise where the accused was aware of the "surface features" of his actions but was unable to appreciate the attendant circumstances on which their criminality depended. One way of addressing these difficulties is to observe that the significance of consequences and circumstances varies from offence to offence. Consider the accused who sets fire to another's property but, because of mental disorder, does not appreciate the risk to further property, or persons, inherent in this conduct.[57] On one view, a failure to appreciate consequences is irrelevant if he is charged with wilful fire-raising of the property to which he sets fire directly, but highly relevant if he is charged with reckless fire-raising of the other property, or with reckless endangerment.

At any rate, it seems unduly restrictive to adopt the narrow approach in its full extent. Indeed, if appreciation of certain circumstances or consequences is an element of the *mens rea* of a particular offence, then the narrow approach might conflict with the basic principle that an actor who lacks *mens rea* cannot be held criminally liable.[58] Indeed, it might—while apparently narrowing the scope for the mentally disordered offender to be acquitted on the ground of insanity—actually mean that an actor who lacked *mens rea* because of mental disorder was entitled to an unqualified acquittal rather than the qualified acquittal offered by the

---

[54] *Robert Thomson* (1739) Hume, i, 40. The point made in the text assumes that the accused perceives the victim as the devil and not a human being in any sense; if he perceives the victim as a person then he would know the "nature and quality" of his act but might escape conviction on the basis that he did not know it was morally wrong: see, e.g. *R. v Landry* [1991] 1 S.C.R. 99. This depends on whether not knowing that an act is morally wrong is a basis for the plea (a point discussed below, para.7.40), but the distinction between the two cases is thin and this may be taken as an argument in favour of recognising the plea in such circumstances.

[55] *Simon Fraser* (1878) 4 Coup. 70.

[56] F. McAuley, *Insanity, Psychiatry and Criminal Responsibility* (1993), p.27, who notes that the example given is taken from the facts of *R. v Cooper* [1980] 1 S.C.R. 1149. As to the actor who understands that death is likely to result but does not fully appreciate the nature or significance of death, see *R. v Porter* (1933) 55 C.L.R. 182 at 188, *per* Dixon J.; McAuley, at p.28 (discussing *O* (1959) 3 *Criminal Law Quarterly* 151).

[57] *cf. R. v Dickie* [1984] 1 W.L.R. 1031, as discussed by McAuley, fn.56 above, at p.27.

[58] *Ross v HM Advocate*, 1991 J.C. 210 at 215, *per* the Lord Justice-General (Hope).

insanity defence. These issues have yet, however, to be properly addressed by the Scottish courts.

Wrongfulness

In contrast to "nature and quality", this aspect of alienation of reason has been addressed by the Scottish courts—but primarily in a case that has generally been misinterpreted. That case is *HM Advocate v Sharp*[59] (technically a decision on the plea in bar of trial, but one taken on the basis that the relevant rules of law were the same in the circumstances).[60] Sharp was charged with the murder of two of his children. It appeared that he was suffering serious financial difficulties, and had a large family of "five or six"[61] with a new child due, and to have "formed the idea that he must get rid of the two youngest members of his family in order to ease the burden upon his wife when he left her."[62] As Lord Constable noted, while such an attitude was "on the face of it, irrational and insane", it was not strictly illogical, and it was clear that Sharp understood his actions. It was the fact that he felt such actions to be justifiable and even compelled by the circumstances that demonstrated that he had "lost the sense of distinguishing between right and wrong".[63] 7.40

One of the medical witnesses, in his report, expressed the view that Sharp was nevertheless fit to plead because he understood the nature and quality of his deed. Lord Constable rejected that conclusion, observing that:

> "I think that when Dr Skeen put that in his report he was seeking to express the view of a lawyer, and did not express it quite correctly, because the legal view, as developed in recent years, is that a man may be quite in a position to appreciate the nature and quality of his deed as an illegal act, which by the law of the country will be punished in a certain way, and may nevertheless be insane, his insanity consisting in a failure to recognise that the act is morally wrong ... while [the accused] regarded his act as a justifiable and even meritorious one, he fully realised the penalty that would follow, and regarded it as a solemn sacrifice which he was called upon to make. Legally, therefore, I see no difficulty in applying the same reasoning which the medical gentlemen applied when they arrived at the conclusion that the accused was insane."[64]

Sharp is treated by Gordon as a case in which the McNaghten Rules were "dispensed with",[65] but it is difficult to understand this conclusion. It will be remembered that the Rules require that the accused was "labouring 7.41

[59] 1927 J.C. 66.

[60] See 1927 J.C. 66 at 69, *per* Lord Constable ("where the mental condition of the accused has not changed, the test of whether he is able to give proper instructions is exactly the same as the test of whether he can be held responsible for the act he has committed") (citing *HM Advocate v Robertson* (1891) 3 White 6). On the plea in bar, see Ch.14.

[61] At 68 *per* Lord Constable.

[62] *ibid.*

[63] *ibid.*

[64] 1927 J.C. 66 at 68–69. As to the more difficult situation where the accused recognises that an act is understood as both legally and morally wrong but rejects both sets of societal values, see *R. v W (JM)* (1998) 123 C.C.C. (3d) 245, where a majority of the British Columbia Court of Appeal held that the insanity plea was not available in such a case.

[65] Gordon, para.10.37.

under such a defect of reason from disease of the mind, as not to know the nature and quality of the act he was doing; or if he did know it, that he did not know he was doing what was wrong".[66] Lord Constable's opinion is no more than a particular interpretation of the latter part of that test, concluding that "wrong" in the Rules means "morally wrong" as opposed to "legally wrong". Once that interpretation of the Rules is accepted, there is little difficulty in bringing Sharp's case within their terms.

In that respect, *Sharp* stands in stark contrast to the leading English decision in *R. v Windle*.[67] In that case, Windle was married to a woman who spoke constantly of suicide and whom it was later concluded had been certifiably insane. He gave her 100 aspirin tablets, causing her death. He told the police what he had done, adding "I suppose they will hang me for this?" The medical evidence was to the effect that he was suffering from a form of "communicated insanity" known as *folie à deux* as a result of his constant contact with his wife's illness. Devlin J. withdrew insanity from the jury, who found Windle guilty of murder. The Court of Appeal upheld his decision:

> "In the opinion of the court there is no doubt that in the McNaghten rules 'wrong' means contrary to law and not 'wrong' according to the opinion of one man or of a number of people on the question whether a particular Act might or might not be justified. In the present case, it could not be challenged that the appellant knew that what he was doing was contrary to law, and that he realized what punishment the law provided for murder."[68]

The decision in *Windle* has been criticised,[69] rejected in other jurisdictions,[70] and appears to have often been ignored in practice in England and Wales.[71] Its pre-emptive rejection in Scots law appears, however, not to have been properly recognised. Such a rejection is to a certain extent

---

[66] See above, para.7.09.

[67] [1952] 2 Q.B. 826.

[68] [1952] 2 Q.B. 826 at 834, *per* Lord Goddard C.J. The consequences of such an interpretation were more acute in English law at the time than would have been the case in Scots law, as the plea of diminished responsibility was not then available (only being introduced into English law by s.2 of the Homicide Act 1957), and the rejection of Windle's plea of insanity had the consequence that he was convicted of murder and sentenced to death. The sentence was, however, commuted to life imprisonment by means of the prerogative of mercy: N. Walker, *Aggravation, Mitigation and Mercy in English Criminal Justice* (1999), p.158.

[69] See, e.g. McAuley, fn.56 above, at pp.30–35. See also *Report of the Committee on Mentally Abnormal Offenders* (Cmnd. 6244, 1975), para.18.8 (criticising *Windle* but rejecting "knowledge of wrong" entirely as a satisfactory test).

[70] In Australia, see *Stapleton v R.* (1952) 86 C.L.R. 358. In Canada, see *R. v Chaulk* [1990] 3 S.C.R. 1303 (overruling *Schwartz v R.* [1977] 1 S.C.R. 673). See also *R. v Ratti* [1991] 1 S.C.R. 68; *R. v Landry* [1991] 1 S.C.R. 99. See also Robinson, *Criminal Law Defenses*, §173(d)(2).

[71] See R.D. Mackay, *Mental Condition Defences in the Criminal Law* (1995), p.104. R.D. Mackay and G. Kearns, "More fact(s) about the insanity defence" [1999] Crim. L.R. 714–725 at p.722.

supported by other *dicta* to the effect that a man may know that what he is doing is criminal and yet be insane,[72] although the meaning of such dicta is not always clear and they can, alternatively, be interpreted as supporting the recognition of irresistible impulse as a form of insanity.

Volitional insanity, or irresistible impulse[73]

The question of whether Scots law recognises a "volitional element" in the defence of insanity—and, perhaps by extension, in automatism—was a vexed one during the nineteenth century. As discussed earlier, such an element to the defence was trenchantly rejected by Lord Hope in *James Gibson*,[74] but accepted (with some reluctance) by Lord Cockburn in two subsequent cases,[75] and by Lord Cowan in a third.[76] Other judges, however, chose not to mention the possibility of an "irresistible impulse" in their charges to juries,[77] but it is impossible to be certain whether this represented a rejection of the concept or simply a belief that the question did not arise on the facts of the particular case.[78] The absence of a criminal appeal court meant that the variant practice could not be resolved. **7.42**

In the twentieth century, the possibility of an irresistible impulse has been left to juries in two reported cases, *HM Advocate v McClinton*[79] and *HM Advocate v Kidd*,[80] where Lord Strachan suggested that insanity could be established by proof of "a mental defect, by which [the accused's] reason was overpowered, and he was thereby rendered incapable of exerting his reason to control his conduct and reactions".[81]

It has been suggested, on the basis of these authorities, that Scots law does in fact recognise irresistible impulse as a form of insanity.[82] It is submitted that this conclusion is doubtful, for several reasons. First, the institutional writers do not acknowledge it: the treatment of the insanity plea offered by Hume and Alison is framed in purely cognitive terms.[83] Secondly, none of the authorities which may be taken to support such a

---

[72] See *Archibald Miller* (1874) 3 Coup. 16 at 18, *per* Lord Moncrieff (a man "may be entirely insane, and yet know well enough that an act which he does is forbidden by law"); *HM Advocate v McClinton* (1902) 4 Adam 1 at 25, *per* the Lord Justice-General (Kinross); *HM Advocate v Kidd*, 1960 J.C. 61 at 72, *per* Lord Strachan ("A man may know very well what he is doing, and may know that it is wrong, and he may none the less be insane. It may be that some lunatics do an act just because they know it is wrong.")

[73] The language of "irresistible impulse" has been described as melodramatic: J. Burchell, *Principles of Criminal Law* (3rd edn, 2005), p.382. Depending on how it is defined, a volitional form of the insanity defence may, while including an "irresistible impulse", operate in a rather wider fashion: see *S v Kavin*, 1978 (2) S.A. 731 at 737, *per* Irving Steyn J.

[74] (1844) 2 Broun 332. See above, para.7.10.

[75] *James Denny Scott* (1853) 1 Irv. 132; *Isabella Blyth* (1852) J. Shaw 567. See above, para.7.13.

[76] *John McFadyen* (1860) 3 Irv. 650. See above, para.7.13.

[77] See above, para.7.13.

[78] A similar tendency of some, but not all, trial judges to graft on a volitional prong to the McNaghten Rules appears to have been evident in English cases: see *R. v Davis* (1881) 14 Cox C.C. 563; *R. v Fryer* (1915) 24 Cox C.C. 405.

[79] (1902) 4 Adam 1.

[80] 1960 J.C. 61.

[81] 1960 J.C. 61 at 71.

[82] V. Tadros, *Criminal Responsibility* (2005), p.323 fn.3, who cites *Kidd* and observes: "Given the existence of a volitional limb in Scots law in the nineteenth century... it is fair to assume that such a limb still exists in Scotland."

[83] Hume, i, 37–38; Alison, *Principles*, 645.

plea are decisions of more than a single judge,[84] and there are as many authorities which ignore the possibility of irresistible impulse (although it is only explicitly rejected once, in *James Gibson*).[85] Thirdly, the two relevant appellate decisions—*Brennan v HM Advocate*[86] and *Cardle v Mulrainey*[87]—appear to leave no room for such a possibility. Although *Cardle v Mulrainey* is concerned with automatism rather than insanity, it turns on the meaning of "alienation of reason", which appears to be a common feature of both insanity and automatism in Scots law.[88] In holding that the accused was not entitled to be acquitted because he knew the nature and quality of his acts, and knew that they were wrong, the appeal court appears to have excluded the possibility of any consideration of irresistible impulse in future cases.

7.43 This would, of course, be regrettable if a defence of irresistible impulse were a desirable one, but it is far from clear that this is the case. This is not the place for a full treatment of the theoretical debate,[89] but it may be noted that one of the major difficulties for advocates of a volitional test of insanity is identifying a case which should properly be treated as one of insanity despite failing to amount to cognitive insanity: that is, a case where an actor knows the nature and quality of his act, and knows that it is wrong, but nevertheless should not be criminally liable.[90] Furthermore, it is difficult to understand how a finder of fact is to sensibly distinguish between an actor whose capacity for self-control is substantially impaired (and who may, therefore, in cases of homicide, be entitled to the partial defence of diminished responsibility) and the actor who has lost such capacity entirely.[91]

A volitional test of alienation of reason may, in some cases, ameliorate a narrow interpretation of the cognitive limb. So, for example, the

---

[84] At least so far as the criminal cases are concerned: in the civil context, see *Breen v Breen*, 1961 S.C. 158.

[85] See above, para.7.10.

[86] 1977 J.C. 38.

[87] 1992 S.L.T 1152.

[88] See above, para.7.26.

[89] See F. McAuley, *Insanity, Psychiatry and Criminal Responsibility* (1993), Ch.3; F. Boland, *Anglo-American Insanity Defence Reform* (1999), Ch.2.

[90] *Report on Insanity and Diminished Responsibility* (Scot. Law Com. No. 195), para.2.54 ("It was of some significance that none of the consultees could provide any example where a person might fail the test for the defence on the appreciation criterion but satisfy it on a purely volitional one. It is also worth nothing that the mental health experts whom we met were virtually unanimous in rejecting a category of mental disorder which was purely volitional in nature and which had no impact on cognitive functions.") The Atkin Committee appears to have recommended a defence of irresistible impulse purely on the basis of a reference to "mothers... seized with the impulse to cut the throats of or otherwise destroy their children to whom they are normally devoted": *Report of the Committee on Insanity and Crime* (Cmd. 2005, 1923), 8.

[91] This was one of the objections levelled against Lord Darling's Criminal Responsibility (Trials) Bill (which would have created a defence of uncontrollable impulse in English law) when it was unsuccessfully introduced into the House of Lords in April 1924: *Report of the Royal Commission on Capital Punishment* (Cmd. 8932, 1953), 405. See also M. Smith, "Irresistible impulse" in *Intention in Law and Philosophy* (N. Naffine, R. Owens and J. Williams (eds), 2001), pp.37–56, who argues that a plausible account of the concept is possible, but his suggested characterisation of an irresistible impulse (at p.50) illustrates the difficulties involved: "an irresistible impulse might be characterised as any impulse which causes an agent to act when that impulse is of a kind such that the agent lacks the capacity to have desires of that kind that accord with her beliefs about what she would want herself to do in her present circumstances if she had a maximally informed and coherent set of beliefs". How is a finder of fact supposed to assess such "capacity"?

accused in the South African case of *S v Kavin*[92] was held entitled to a defence of volitional insanity after he attempted to kill his family in order to be reunited with them in heaven after he had committed suicide. Such a case may be capable of being accommodated within a cognitive test of insanity provided that an inability to appreciate moral wrongness is accepted as sufficient.[93] If the accused, however, appreciates that his actions are morally wrong but nevertheless deliberately proceeds with them, it is difficult to see why an acquittal is appropriate. For reasons similar to this, the Scottish Law Commission has recently concluded that a statutory definition of insanity "should not contain any reference to volitional incapacities or disabilities of the accused",[94] taking the view that the case for a volitional limb no longer stands when the cognitive limb is properly defined.

The rejection of a volitional limb to the "alienation of reason" test may operate rather more harshly in respect of automatism than insanity. Where, for example, an actor's drink has been spiked and he has acted out of character, it may seem unsympathetic to refuse him a defence, but it is clear from *Cardle v Mulrainey* that he does not currently have a defence in law. There are ways in which such a defence might be tailored while reducing the possibility for abuse, such as resorting to a reverse burden of proof,[95] allowing the defence only where an ordinary person might have been liable to react to the external factor in the same way,[96] or allowing the defence on a "one-off" basis only,[97] but any such reforms would be likely to require legislative intervention.

Prior fault and the automatism defence

In recognising the defence of automatism, *Ross v HM Advocate*[98] makes it clear that the defence is unavailable where the alienation of reason results from a "self-induced" external factor, or is one which the accused was "bound to foresee". Forseeability is necessarily essential in either case: Ross's own alienation of reason was "self-induced" in the limited sense that he had voluntarily drunk the can of lager in which drugs had been placed, but since he did not know of their presence his alienation of reason was not foreseeable. Where prior fault is present, the accused will, by the application of a legal fiction, be presumed to have *mens rea* despite its absence in fact.[99] **7.44**

Where an individual takes drugs, knowing that they are likely to have an intoxicating effect, he will not be able to plead automatism if an alienation of reason results. This is most obviously applied in cases of

---

92 1978 (2) S.A. 731.

93 See above, para.7.40.

94 *Report on Insanity and Diminished Responsibility* (Scot. Law Com. No. 195), para.2.56. The Commission's thinking on this matter appears to have been strongly influenced by F. McAuley, *Insanity, Psychiatry and Criminal Responsibility* (1993), particularly Ch.3.

95 Which would address some of the concerns raised by J.R. Spencer, "Involuntary intoxication as a defence" [1994] C.L.J. 6–9.

96 In that way, a defence might be allowed to the accused in *Cardle v Mulrainey*, but denied to the accused in *R. v Kingston* [1995] 2 A.C. 335, on the basis that his paedophiliac tendencies, which he was caused to act on by involuntary intoxication, were not a characteristic that could be attributed to the "ordinary person".

97 See G.R. Sullivan, "Making excuses" in *Harm and Culpability* (A.P. Simester and A.T.H. Smith (eds), 1996), pp.131–152.

98 1991 J.C. 210.

99 See above, para.7.25.

intoxication through alcohol,[1] but is not restricted in that way. It is not essential that the accused should have taken the substances for their intoxicating effect. In *Ebsworth v HM Advocate*,[2] the accused had taken "grossly excessive" quantities of proprietary painkillers and illegally purchased diamorphine in order to deal with the pain caused by a broken leg. The court held that he was rightly denied the defence of automatism on the basis that he had acted recklessly:

> "The element of guilt or moral turpitude lies in the taking of drink or drugs voluntarily and reckless of their possible consequences. That recklessness may take various forms, of which the most familiar no doubt is consuming the intoxicating substance deliberately to excess without regard to the effect which the excessive consumption may produce. But it may also, especially when powerful drugs are taken for a legitimate purpose, such as to reduce stress or alleviate pain, involve doing so in defiance of, or without taking, medical advice. The same applies where ordinary proprietary drugs are taken in grossly excessive quantities or in combination with other more powerful drugs without seeking and complying with medical advice."[3]

It would seem to follow from this that where the accused has not acted "recklessly"—for example, where he has complied with medical advice in taking certain drugs and was unaware that he risked an alienation of reason by doing so—the defence should not be denied to him.[4] That approach was not, however, taken in the sleepwalking case of *Finegan v Heywood*,[5] where the accused's parasomniac state (during which he took the keys to a friend's car and drove it some distance) had been induced by his consumption of alcohol earlier that evening. The appeal court took the view that, as the appellant knew that he was liable to parasomniac episodes after drinking, the defence of automatism was not available to him. *Ebsworth* was not referred to by the court. Although Mr Finegan may have known that he was liable to sleepwalk after consuming alcohol, it seems harsh to deny him the defence given the apparent lack of any evidence that he was aware that he might behave dangerously or criminally in such a state.[6] It is doubtful that he can be said to have been "reckless" in the sense required by *Ebsworth*.

7.45 It is not clear from *Ebsworth* what sort of "recklessness" will serve to elide the defence. Is it recklessness as to the possibility of an alienation of reason, or recklessness as to the possibility of an alienation of reason during which the actor may behave in a dangerous and/or criminal fashion? It is submitted that the latter is the preferable approach, as otherwise (for example) the individual who takes sleeping tablets, following medical advice to the letter, would seem to be precluded from

---

[1] *Brennan v HM Advocate*, 1977 J.C. 38.

[2] 1992 S.L.T 1161.

[3] At 1166 *per* the Lord Justice-General (Hope).

[4] See the English case of *R. v Hardie* [1985] 1 W.L.R. 64. For discussion, see P.W. Ferguson, "Automatism, responsibility and recklessness", 1992 S.L.T. (News) 375–377.

[5] 2000 J.C. 444.

[6] Newspaper reports of the trial indicate that the appellant had previously, whilst in parasomniac states, woken his parents in the middle of the night to ask which colour shoe polish to use, climbed into bed with his in-laws, cleaned, and made sandwiches. See "Sleepwalker banned for drink-driving", *Press & Journal*, October 2, 1998; "The sleep driver", *Daily Record*, October 2, 1998.

raising the defence if they have unwarranted and unexpected effects given that his precise aim in taking the tablets was to induce sleep.

The defence has been similarly denied to persons who suffer a foreseeable alienation of reason whilst driving motor vehicles, such as the driver who suffers a hypoglycaemic attack at the wheel of a car.[7] Although it may be possible to say that an individual is guilty of "driving without due care and attention" simply by virtue of driving in knowledge of their condition and without taking safeguards,[8] that is not in itself necessarily sufficient to justify a conviction for further offences committed during the alienation of reason, and here the normal rule about presuming *mens rea* will apply.[9]

[7] *MacLeod v Mathieson*, 1993 S.C.C.R. 488 (Sh. Ct).
[8] See Gordon, para.3.28.
[9] See above, para.7.25 and below, paras 8.10–8.13.

Chapter 8

INTOXICATION

Introduction

Intoxication is a peculiar topic to include in a text on the Scottish law of criminal defences. This is because, in Scots law, intoxication is effectively treated as inculpatory rather than exculpatory. The institutional writers, followed by the courts, have been adamant that it should not be accepted as an excuse—or even, it seems, as a denial of *mens rea*. As a result, it seems that pleading intoxication as a "defence" in any form is of no avail to an accused in the Scottish courts, and may indeed assist the prosecution rather than the defence. **8.01**

Accordingly, this chapter seeks simply to outline the development of the current legal position, and to highlight some of the ambiguities and problems which remain. It has been said that the problems associated with the topic are such that "a satisfactory common-law solution seems impossible" and that "there is no alternative but to hope that Parliament (or whoever in future has the power) will provide an answer".[1] Statutory reform has not been forthcoming, however, although possible avenues for reform are noted briefly at the end of this chapter.

Hume and Alison on Intoxication

Both Hume and Alison state quite clearly that intoxication may not be regarded as a defence to a criminal charge. For Alison, the reasons for this are rooted firmly in public policy: **8.02**

> "Nothing is better established in our law than that intoxication, so far from being an alleviation, is an aggravation of a criminal charge; and indeed such is the tendency to this brutalizing vice, among the lower orders in this country, that if it were sustained as a defence, three-fourths of the whole crimes in the country would go unpunished; for the slightest experience must be sufficient to convince every one, that almost every crime that is committed, is directly or indirectly connected with whisky. For these reasons, our law utterly disowns any such defence..."[2]

Hume does not go so far as to describe intoxication as an aggravation, but—comparing it to insanity—notes that the law treats "wilful distemper" quite differently from something "which is the visitation of Providence", "and if it does not consider the man's intemperance as an

[1] G.H. Gordon, "Automatism, insanity and intoxication" (1976) 21 J.L.S.S. 310–316 at p.316.

[2] Alison, *Principles*, 661.

aggravation, at least sees very good reasons why it should not be allowed as an excuse".[3]

Both Hume and Alison, however, note that intoxication might be relevant as a plea in mitigation where the offence is one which is, in Alison's words, "not so much *mala in se* as proscribed for the good order of society".[4] The courts were prepared to go slightly further than this, it seems, in giving weight to intoxication as a mitigating factor and so, in *James Ainslie*,[5] the accused's intoxication enabled him to avoid transportation upon conviction for aggravated assault, malicious mischief and breach of the peace. Instead, a sentence of 18 months' imprisonment (followed by his being required to find security to keep the peace for three years thereafter) was imposed. The court's decision, however, was clearly influenced by the fact that Ainslie's plea in mitigation was not based on intoxication *simpliciter*, but rather on its tendency to make him "furious" due to wounds he had received during "frequent encounters with the bush rangers" while working as a farm-steward in Australia.[6]

It is clear from the—remarkably brief—treatment of intoxication in Hume and Alison that it was firmly excluded as a defence in Scots law. Neither writer (perhaps unsurprisingly, given the limited attention paid to culpable mental states at the time) discusses whether intoxication, even if it cannot be regarded as an "excuse", might be relevant as evidencing a lack of *mens rea*. When Hume writes that intoxication cannot be an excuse, he is clearly referring to "excuse" in the broadest sense, rather than the more technical meaning which a criminal lawyer might attribute to it today.[7]

The Development of Intoxication as a Defence in Scots Law: The Murder-Culpable Homicide Boundary

8.03 Despite the views of Hume and Alison, the Scottish courts in the late nineteenth and early twentieth century did gradually recognise intoxication as a factor which might lead to an acquittal—or at least a reduction of murder to culpable homicide. The development of intoxication as a defence in Scots law prior to the leading case of *Brennan v HM Advocate*[8] was concerned largely with the murder-culpable homicide boundary. A body of case law prior to *Brennan* (the best known case being *HM Advocate v Campbell*[9]) regarded intoxication as a factor which could negate the *mens rea* required for murder, rendering the accused guilty of culpable homicide only. This approach in itself was, at least in some of the cases, based on a particular interpretation of the *mens rea* of murder which would no longer be regarded as correct. The development is explained below.

---

[3] Hume, i, 45.

[4] Alison, *Principles,* 663.

[5] (1842) 1 Broun 25. See also *James Alves* (1830) 5 Deas and Anderson 147; Gordon, para.12.24.

[6] See Pyper's plea in mitigation, at 27.

[7] On which see above, paras 1.08–1.10.

[8] 1977 J.C. 38. See below, para.8.08.

[9] 1921 J.C. 1.

The law prior to *HM Advocate v Campbell*

8.04 For some time, Scots law permitted intoxication, in certain cases, to effectively act as a partial defence to murder, reducing that crime to culpable homicide. Although this is often treated as a reception of the English decision in *Beard*,[10] it dates from rather earlier than that. The first case is *Margaret Robertson or Brown*,[11] where the accused, who was looking after her two grandchildren, put them on the fire while under a drink-induced hallucination. There, Lord McLaren directed the jury that "[i]n violent crimes, and where the crime involves malice or criminal intention, intoxication might be a relevant matter to take into consideration, as showing that there could be no malicious intention. And in the present case it might be said that, although the panel was in such a stupid state from drink as to negative the malice essential to the constitution of the crime of murder, it would not absolve her from the charge of culpable homicide."[12] The jury were directed that they might bring in a verdict of culpable homicide if they were of the opinion that the accused had put the children on the fire "under the influence of some momentary hallucination induced by drunkenness",[13] and they did so unanimously.

This development occurred independently of the recognition of a partial defence of diminished responsibility.[14] Indeed, in *Alexander Dingwall*,[15] which is generally regarded as the foundation of that defence,[16] Lord Deas directed the jury that—although it appeared that Dingwall was not drunk when he killed his wife (he "had had a good deal of drink, no doubt, but he was habitually accustomed to it")[17]—if he had in fact been drunk, that "would have afforded neither excuse for nor palliation of the crime".[18] Juries were, however, permitted to consider applying the nascent doctrine of diminished responsibility in two later cases (both prior to *Margaret Robertson*) where the accused's weakness of mind had possibly been triggered (or at least exacerbated by) the transient effects of intoxication.[19]

8.05 It will be noted that the charge in *Margaret Robertson*[20] does not regard intoxication as an excuse in any form,[21] but rather a factor which may

---

[10] *DPP v Beard* [1920] A.C. 479. For the claim that the rule in *Beard* was improperly "received" into Scots law, see *Brennan v HM Advocate*, 1977 J.C. 38, discussed below, paras 8.08–8.09.

[11] (1886) 1 White 93.

[12] At 104.

[13] At 104–105.

[14] See Ch.11.

[15] (1867) 5 Irv. 466.

[16] See below, paras 11.05–11.06.

[17] *Alexander Dingwall* (1867) 5 Irv. 466 at 476.

[18] *John McLean* (1876) 3 Coup. 334 at 338, *per* Lord Deas (referring to his charge in *Dingwall*). The report of *Dingwall* at (1867) 5 Irv. 466 notes Lord Deas simply as saying (at 476) that "the plea of intoxication could not be regarded".

[19] *Andrew Granger* (1878) 4 Coup. 86; *Thomas Ferguson* (1881) 4 Coup. 552. Although the jury were permitted to consider diminished responsibility in *Ferguson*, they rejected it. It appears that Ferguson's weakness of mind was such that he was "very violent" when intoxicated, but there was evidence that he was sober at the relevant time and the report of Lord Deas' charge to the jury does not touch on the question of intoxication. See also the earlier case of *William Douglas* (1827) Shaw 192, Syme 184, where a successful plea of insanity appears to have been based upon the accused's disease having been "rekindled" by the consumption of alcohol.

[20] (1867) 5 Irv. 466.

[21] The notion of intoxication as an excuse is quite vehemently rejected by the Lord Justice-Clerk (Macdonald) in *HM Advocate v McDonald* (1890) 2 White 517 at 524, and *HM Advocate v Kane* (1892) 3 White 386 at 387.

evidence a lack of *mens rea* on the part of the accused. This approach was followed in the later case of *HM Advocate v McDonald,*[22] where the Lord Justice-Clerk (Macdonald) explained the position in this way:

> "If a man walks up to another with a revolver and fires at him and kills him, or if a person goes to the bedside of a sick father, mother, or other person, and puts poison in the cup from which that person drinks, there is no doubt about malignant intention to cause death. But where a person, drunk or sober, begins smashing about him, it does not necessarily follow that there was at the outset a murderous intent."[23]

While expressing some doubts about whether allowing drunkenness to be considered "in determining the question between murder and culpable homicide" was "consistent with principle", Lord Macdonald considered the point to have been established by prior cases, and accordingly left it open to the jury to take the accused's intoxication into account in reaching their verdict.

Although Lord Macdonald delivered a similar charge in another case two years later,[24] something of a rearguard action was mounted by Lord Young and Lord Stormonth Darling, charging juries in *HM Advocate v Paterson*[25] and *HM Advocate v Aitken*[26] respectively. In each case, the jury was directed that the effects of drink could not reduce murder to culpable homicide, although the jury in *Paterson* was allowed to consider culpable homicide on the basis that the accused might have suffered sunstroke many years ago "and was therefore more passionate and excitable when in drink than he might have been".[27]

HM Advocate v Campbell

8.06 In *HM Advocate v Campbell,*[28] the accused was charged with the murder of his wife. The evidence disclosed that he had returned home in a state of "acute intoxication" before the attack, and that "as a result of an injury to his head some ten years before, the accused was abnormally susceptible to alcohol, and abnormally violent when under its influence."[29] The Lord Justice-Clerk (Scott Dickson) charged the jury as follows:

> "... do you believe that injuries such as these were inflicted upon this woman when he had no intention, and was so drunk that he could not form the intention, to do serious injury? It is not necessary that he intended to kill; if he intended to do serious injury, and did do serious injury, and as a result of these injuries his wife died, then that

---

22 (1890) 2 White 517.

23 At 523.

24 *HM Advocate v Kane* (1892) 3 White 386.

25 (1897) 5 S.L.T. 13.

26 (1902) 4 Adam 88.

27 At 13 *per* Lord Young, inviting the jury to consider whether they could "take that as any reasonable alleviation of his conduct. If they could take that view, then they were at liberty in the exercise of their judgment to find accordingly."

28 1921 J.C. 1.

29 At 1.

is murder. Thus the question for you is whether he was so drunk that he had no intention, and could form no intention, of doing her serious injury . . ."[30]

A number of points fall to be noticed. First, on the state of the law at the time, it is arguable that it should have been open to Campbell to plead diminished responsibility on the basis of his abnormal susceptibility to alcohol, combined with its actual effects.[31] That plea was not, however, made, and it would not be open today.[32] Secondly, the charge proceeds on the basis that, while one form of the *mens rea* of murder is an intention to kill, the alternative is an intention to do serious injury,[33] and not wicked recklessness, as is the established alternative form in the modern law.[34] There was, therefore, no purpose in arguing that the accused had been "wickedly reckless" simply by virtue of becoming intoxicated, an argument which was to form the basis of the later decision in *Brennan v HM Advocate*.[35] Thirdly, although the Lord Justice-Clerk refers to the decision in *DPP v Beard*,[36] stating that on this matter "there is no difference between the law of England and the law of Scotland",[37] there is no reason to treat *Campbell* as a "reception" of *Beard*, given that there is ample authority in Scots law, pre-*Beard*, for allowing the effects of intoxication to reduce murder to culpable homicide. The importance of *Campbell* is that it resolved the inconsistency in the earlier case law in favour of the exculpatory position, putting to one side the doubts expressed by Lord Macdonald in *McDonald*[38] and *Kane*.[39]

In *Kennedy v HM Advocate*,[40] a Full Bench expressed the view that both *Campbell* and *Beard* correctly stated the law of Scotland. Strictly speaking, the point was probably *obiter*. Counsel on both sides (the Lord Advocate and the Dean of Faculty) were agreed that the charge in *Campbell* was correct, and the question for the *Kennedy* court was whether the trial judge had been permitted, on the facts of the case, to withdraw drunkenness from the consideration of the jury.

The position immediately prior to *Brennan v HM Advocate*

The tenability of the approach demonstrated in the cases up until *Kennedy v HM Advocate*[41]—or, at least, the extent to which it could be reconciled with the strict approach to intoxication found in Hume and **8.07**

---

[30] At 3.

[31] See below, para.11.05.

[32] See below, paras 11.11–11.12.

[33] This view of the law was common at the time: see, e.g. *HM Advocate v Marshall* (1896) 4 S.L.T. 217 at 217, *per* Lord Young; J.S. More, *Lectures on the Law of Scotland* (1864), Vol. ii, 364. See also Anderson, 148–149, who appears to recognise six different forms of the *mens rea* of murder, including both wicked recklessness and an intention to cause "grievous bodily injury".

[34] See Macdonald, 89; *Drury v HM Advocate*, 2001 S.L.T. 1013.

[35] 1977 J.C. 38. See below, para.8.08.

[36] [1920] A.C. 479.

[37] At 3.

[38] *HM Advocate v McDonald* (1890) 2 White 517. See above, para.8.05.

[39] *HM Advocate v Kane* (1892) 3 White 386.

[40] 1944 J.C. 171. The court's approach to intoxication in cases of murder was referred to with approval by the appeal court in the later case of *Carraher v HM Advocate*, 1946 J.C. 108. In *HM Advocate v McLeod*, 1956 J.C. 20, Lord Hill Watson referred (at 21) to the possibility of drink causing a "total incapacity to form an intention", but said that the issue did not arise on the facts of the case.

[41] 1944 J.C. 171.

Alison—was called into question by a number of cases in the mid 1970s. Because the case law was based on the premise that intoxication could negate an intention (either to kill or do serious bodily harm), it seemed to leave open the possibility of a complete acquittal where the accused was charged with an offence which could only be committed intentionally, and where there was no lesser included offence (in the way that culpable homicide relates to murder) of which he could be convicted if *mens rea* could not be proven.

Most obviously, the problem might arise with a charge of assault or of attempted murder (assuming that a verdict of "attempted culpable homicide" is not a competent one).[42] Those were the offences charged in the cases of *HM Advocate v Whitton*[43] (assault with intent to ravish) and *HM Advocate v Aitken*[44] (attempted murder), where in each case the accused was under the influence of LSD at the time of the relevant events. If intoxication was capable of negating *mens rea,* at least where the relevant *mens rea* was an intention to cause a certain consequence, then it should have followed that the jury were entitled to acquit the accused in both cases if they were not satisfied that *mens rea* had been made out. That was the result in both cases, but the verdicts returned were not ones of acquittal *simpliciter*.[45] In both cases, on the direction of the trial judge, the juries returned verdicts of not guilty by reason of insanity. Such verdicts are clearly unsatisfactory, as neither individual was in need of detention in a mental hospital (as was then compulsory where such a verdict was returned),[46] and both were released from hospital shortly after being detained.[47]

Around a year later, the appeal court expressed "grave doubt" as to the correctness of *Aitken* in *McGowan v HM Advocate*,[48] doubts which form the backdrop to the question being considered by a court of seven judges in *Brennan v HM Advocate*.[49]

---

[42] As seems to have been assumed in the context of provocation and diminished responsibility: see below, paras 10.24 and 11.18–11.20. In such cases, it has been assumed that a verdict of guilty of assault is appropriate, but that would not be a workable solution in the case of the intoxicated killer, as the intoxication might operate to negative both the *mens rea* of attempted murder and of assault.

[43] Dundee Sheriff Court, October 1973, unreported. See J.W.R. Gray, "A purely temporary disturbance", 1974 Jur. Rev. 227–248 at pp.246–247.

[44] 1975 S.L.T. (Notes) 86.

[45] It appears, however, that in the earlier case of *Alexander Winchester*, High Court at Glasgow, October 1955, unreported, the jury were directed "that if the accused had been too drunk to form the intention of assaulting the victim he must be acquitted of assault" (Gordon, para.12.23, fn.42). Gordon suggests that "this would be difficult to justify nowadays", but it seems to be the logical consequence of the pre-*Brennan* approach to intoxication.

[46] See above, para.7.02.

[47] See Gray, fn.43 above, at p.247; A.M. McLean, "Insanity—a very special defence" (1976) 21 J.L.S.S. 175 at p.175.

[48] 1976 S.L.T. (Notes) 8.

[49] 1977 J.C. 38. Shortly before the decision in *Brennan*, the jury in *Berry v HM Advocate* (1976) S.C.C.R. Supp. 156 were directed in accordance with *Campbell* and *Kennedy*, although Lord Keith said (at 156) that he did not think it was suggested that the accused's state of intoxication "went the length that he was incapable of forming the necessary intent".

Brennan v HM Advocate

In *Brennan v HM Advocate,*[50] the accused was indicted on a charge of murder and lodged a special defence of insanity. It appeared that he had stabbed his father in the chest with a knife after a quarrel "about the playing of a gramophone record". Earlier in the day, he had "voluntarily consumed between 20 and 25 pints of beer, and about half an hour before the killing had taken in addition a microdot of LSD, a hallucinogenic drug".[51] **8.08**

He was convicted of murder (the defence of insanity having been withdrawn from the jury), and unsuccessfully appealed. In a single opinion delivered by the Lord Justice-General (Emslie), the court noted that Brennan's plea of insanity "was no doubt encouraged" by the trial judge's charge in *HM Advocate v Aitken,*[52] but held that *Aitken* should be disapproved. This aspect of the decision was based on the conclusion that intoxication could not form the basis for a plea of insanity in Scots law[53] (or indeed a basis for diminished responsibility).[54] But, of course, this is not a full answer to the question: even without relying on these defences, a jury might still consider that Brennan lacked the *mens rea* of murder.

Here, the court excluded this possibility almost by sleight of hand. *Campbell* is treated as a case where the court wrongly adopted an English rule (that in *Beard*) as part of Scots law. The court notes that there is "in the report [of *Campbell*] no trace of any argument that *Beard* did not represent the law of Scotland", and that the Lord Justice-Clerk (Scott Dickson) had charged the jury as he did "without having had the advantage of a full debate or further examination of the relevant Scots authorities".[55] He had, indeed, failed to "appreciate that there was no trace in the law of Scotland before 1920 of self-induced intoxication being a recognised defence to a charge of murder".[56] *Kennedy* was of little importance, having proceeded on the assumption that the law as set out in *Campbell* was correct.

As noted earlier, however, there is indeed authority which holds that intoxication could have the effect of rendering the accused guilty of culpable homicide rather than murder.[57] The *Brennan* court simply failed to refer to two of these—*Margaret Robertson or Brown*[58] and *HM Advocate v Kane*[59]—and distinguished *HM Advocate v McDonald,*[60] arguing that the Lord Justice-Clerk (Macdonald)'s directions were based on a particular set of facts: "(1) absence of malicious or criminal intent to kill; and (2) use of modes of assault not of themselves likely to lead to bad results",[61] which might render a verdict of culpable homicide proper even without any evidence of drunkenness. **8.09**

Distinguishing *McDonald* in this way does not, of course, answer the

[50] 1977 J.C. 38.

[51] The text is taken from the reporter's summary at page 39 of the Justiciary Cases report. The Scots Law Times report (1977 S.L.T. 151) states that Brennan had also taken a glass of sherry in addition to the 20 to 25 pints of beer.

[52] At 41.

[53] At 45, and see above, para.7.20.

[54] At 46–47, and see below, paras 11.11–11.14.

[55] At 48–49.

[56] At 50.

[57] See above, paras 8.04–8.05.

[58] (1886) 1 White 93.

[59] (1892) 3 White 386.

[60] (1890) 2 White 517.

[61] At 48.

point of principle: what if, as a result of self-induced intoxication, the accused simply lacked the *mens rea* required for the offence? The court addressed the point in this way:

> "If according to our law the *mens rea* in murder may be deduced from the wicked recklessness of the actings of the accused, it is extremely difficult to understand how actings may lose the quality of recklessness because the actor was in an intoxicated state brought about by his own deliberate and conscious purpose... There is nothing unethical or unfair or contrary to the general principle of our law that self-induced intoxication is not by itself a defence to any criminal charge including in particular the charge of murder. Self-induced intoxication is itself a continuing element and therefore an integral part of any crime of violence, including murder, the other part being the evidence of the actings of the accused who uses force against his victim. Together they add up or may add up to that criminal recklessness which it is the purpose of the criminal law to restrain in the interests of all the citizens of this country."[62]

Accordingly, by denying that the *mens rea* of murder requires an intention either to kill or to do serious bodily harm, the court is able to treat the decision to become intoxicated as itself evidencing sufficient *mens rea*—in the form of "wicked recklessness"—to render the accused guilty of the crime.

The Modern Law: Intoxication as Inculpatory

8.10 *Brennan* was a step towards explaining why the intoxicated offender might be guilty despite seemingly lacking *mens rea*, but it was not a complete answer. To regard intoxication as evidencing recklessness does not prevent it operating to exculpate an accused charged with a crime requiring intention as the relevant *mens rea*. Here, a partial explanation is found in *Ross v HM Advocate*,[63] the leading case on the defence of automatism,[64] where the Lord Justice-General (Hope) referred to "the exception on grounds of public policy which applies where the condition which has resulted in an absence of *mens rea* is self-induced", saying that "[i]n all such cases the accused must be assumed to have intended the natural consequences of his act".[65]

In other words, evidence of intoxication is now regarded as inculpatory rather than exculpatory. Where the crime charged requires recklessness as the relevant *mens rea*, evidence of intoxication will serve to demonstrate recklessness. Where intention is required, evidence of intoxication may result in it being presumed—at least in regard to consequences.

This approach remains unsatisfactory for at least the following reasons:

8.11 (1) It assumes that "recklessness" is a single, interchangeable, concept. While the concept of recklessness is not well-developed in Scots law,[66] it is at least possible (and appropriate in principle) that it requires that the accused is reckless as to a particular circumstance or consequence. For

---

62 At 50–51.

63 1991 J.C. 210.

64 On which see Ch.7 above.

65 At 215.

66 See generally Gordon, paras 7.35–7.68.

example, the appeal court held in *Lord Advocate's Reference (No.1 of 2001)*[67] that the *mens rea* of rape was present where "the man... knows that the woman is not consenting [to sexual intercourse] or at any rate is reckless *as to* whether she is consenting".[68] An individual who becomes extremely intoxicated and has sexual intercourse with a non-consenting woman may fairly be described as "reckless" in the general sense of the word, but that is not the same thing as being reckless "as to" consent, and he may in fact be incapable of comprehending the issue.

(2) It is not clear what is meant by the concept of a condition **8.12** "resulting" in an absence of *mens rea*. Intoxication may result in a person ceasing to be aware of relevant circumstances—or failing to appreciate them when they arise, in which case such language may be intelligible.[69] In what sense, however, can intoxication be said to "result" in a lack of *mens rea* as to consequences? In *Ross*,[70] the accused had lunged out in all directions with a knife after drinking lager from a can spiked with temazepam and LSD. It seems to have been accepted that he did not have the *mens rea* required for attempted murder, but this is surely not a "result" of his intoxication.[71] The connection is not a causal one: it cannot be said that Ross would have had the *mens rea* for murder "but for" his intoxication, because he would not have acted in the way he did had he not been intoxicated. If Ross, in his intoxicated state, had fallen down the stairs, knocking another person over and fatally injuring them, he would not have the *mens rea* for murder either. Does this mean that, if his falling over were attributable to self-induced intoxication, he would be regarded as having the *mens rea* of murder and therefore guilty of that crime? Such a consequence would clearly be absurd, but the law as it currently stands provides no clear basis for distinguishing the two cases.

The matter is somewhat better dealt with in the Draft Criminal Code, which provides that:

> "For the purposes of criminal liability, a person cannot found on a temporary state of mind which is culpably self-induced, and accordingly ... where such a state of mind precludes the intention or other mental element required for an offence, the person is to be regarded as having that intention or mental element".[72]

Importantly, this recognises that intoxication will, strictly speaking, operate to *preclude* a mental state being formed, rather than to negative one which already exists. Difficulties remain, however. What is meant by "precludes"? Does it mean that the accused would have formed the mental state had he not been intoxicated? If so, then the provision is of

[67] 2002 S.L.T. 466.

[68] At 44 *per* the Lord Justice-General (Cullen) (emphasis added).

[69] Lord Hope's dictum is, however, concerned with *mens rea* as to consequences and not to circumstances, a point which is discussed further below at para.8.13.

[70] 1991 J.C. 210.

[71] Although *Ross* was a case of involuntary rather than voluntary intoxication, that goes only to the question of whether the intoxication was "self-induced". The issue discussed here would equally arise if Ross's intoxication had been voluntary.

[72] Draft Criminal Code, s.12(1), which also provides that "where such a state of mind gives rise to the availability of a defence or exception, that defence or exception is to be regarded as not being available". A "culpably self-induced" temporary state of mind includes both voluntary intoxication and a "voluntary failure to take any medication or precautionary measures" where the person knew or ought to have known that the taking of intoxicants or the failure was likely to lead to a loss of self-control: s.12(2).

limited inculpatory effect, since the intoxicated offender will frequently be able to argue the contrary—that he would not have behaved in the way he did had he been sober. But if it does not mean that, what does it mean? Does it mean any state of mind which he might possibly have formed? If so, then for the intoxicated offender, the entirety of the criminal law is transformed into offences of absolute liability, and he may be convicted of any offence on the proof of *actus reus* alone. Neither extreme is satisfactory.

8.13 (3) Lord Hope's dicta in *Ross* is concerned only with the *consequences* of the accused's actions. What of cases where criminality depends on *circumstances*? Here, there is in fact authority suggesting that intoxication might have exculpatory effect. In *James Kinnison*,[73] the accused was charged with knowingly and wilfully making false entries in the Registers of Births and Deaths. There was no dispute that the relevant entries were false and had been made by Kinnison, but no motive could be suggested. It was, however, established that "on at least two of the three occasions he was the worse of drink at the time".[74] The Lord Justice-Clerk (Moncreiff), noting that the word "wilfully" in the statute must be read "as meaning with the intention of doing the thing which is prohibited",[75] charged the jury that:

> "... the question you have to consider is, not whether the prisoner did wrong in being in the state in which he was when he was required to attend to that business; nor that he did wrong in the error which he made in filling up the register, but that when he made these errors he meant not to make a true entry, but meant to make a false entry. You must be satisfied that he knew it was false, and intended to put in the register an entry which he knew was false."[76]

It is not clear whether this decision can still be regarded as good law post-*Ross*. On the one hand, it seems to involve *mens rea* as to circumstances (whether the entry being made is a false one) rather than to consequences. But there seems no good reason why a legal fiction should be applied to deny a "defence" of intoxication in one type of case but not the other.

Any disparity between the two cases could be resolved by regarding *Kinnison* as a case concerned with *mens rea* as to consequences (the consequence of Kinnison's actions being a false entry in the register) rather than circumstances. That does not, however, resolve the underlying problem (it does not explain, for example, how intoxication would affect *mens rea* if the charge were one of rape, the relevant circumstance being the victim's lack of consent).

The point could have arisen, but was not discussed, in the case of *Donaldson v Normand*.[77] There, the accused was charged with culpable and reckless conduct. He had denied having any sharp instruments in his possession before being searched at a police station, but did in fact have an unguarded hypodermic syringe within his sock, and so exposed a civilian turnkey to the risk of injury and infection. His claim was that he had no memory of the needle being in his sock due to having taken heroin and temazepam. The appeal court applied *Brennan* to conclude that his

---

73 (1870) 1 Coup. 457.

74 At 459.

75 At 461.

76 At 461–462.

77 1997 J.C. 200.

intoxication was itself reckless, and that this recklessness was a "continuing element" continuing up until the time of the alleged offence. The case could have been analysed differently, however, by holding that Donaldson would have known of the relevant circumstance (the hypodermic's presence in his sock) had he not been intoxicated, and that he should therefore, in assessing whether *mens rea* was present, be presumed to be aware of circumstances which he would have known of but for his intoxication.

Comparative Perspectives and Options for Reform

The inculpatory Scottish approach is at one end of a spectrum of approaches to the question of intoxication in common law jurisdictions. At the other end of the spectrum, some jurisdictions have held that evidence of intoxication should always be admissible to show that the accused lacked *mens rea* (or, indeed, had acted involuntarily). Such alternative approaches as exist are very briefly sketched out here. **8.14**

In the middle of the spectrum lies the English approach, according to which voluntary intoxication may operate as a defence to crimes which require a *mens rea* of "specific intent", but not to those which require only a *mens rea* of "basic intent".[78] This classification of offences, which is not recognised in Scots law,[79] is complex,[80] and it has been remarked that it "is regrettable that the distinction is so obscure that the Law Commission felt unable confidently to state what the law was".[81] One attempt to state the distinction runs as follows:

> "The most popular view appears to be that offences of specific intent are those which have intention as their *mens rea*; whereas crimes of basic intent are those which require recklessness. Greater uncertainty surrounds crimes which contain elements of intent and elements of recklessness. For example rape, where the *mens rea* is an intent to engage in sexual intercourse with recklessness as to whether the victim consented. Commentators are divided on such crimes. Some suggest that the court will decide whether a crime is predominantly one of recklessness or intent and label it one of specific or basic intent accordingly. Others argue that it is simply a case of applying the specific intent rule to the intent part of the crime, but the basic intent rules to the basic intent part."[82]

---

78 *DPP v Majewski* [1977] A.C. 443.

79 *Brennan v HM Advocate*, 1977 J.C. 38 at 48, *per* the Lord Justice-General (Emslie).

80 For discussion, see A.R. Ward, "Making some sense of self-induced intoxication" [1986] C.L.J. 247–261.

81 D. Ormerod, *Smith and Hogan: Criminal Law* (11th edn, 2005), p.281 (referring to *Intoxication and Criminal Liability* (Law Com. No. 229, 1995), para.3.27). See also Ashworth, *Principles of Criminal Law*, at p.212.

82 J. Herring, *Criminal Law: Text, Cases and Materials* (2004), p.169, who acknowledges the argument of Ward (fn.80 above) that "no one explanation seems able to fit every case". Ormerod (fn.81 above) states (at p.279) that "[i]n order to know how a crime should be classified for this purpose we can look only to the decisions of the courts", citing a series of decisions which have held that certain crimes are ones of either specific or basic intent. See also Ashworth, *Principles of Criminal Law*, p.212 (noting that "[v]arious theories" have been advanced to explain the distinction, "but none is satisfactory ... However, this rather ramshackle law has proved workable.")

One important defence of the English position has been not that it is meritorious in itself, but simply that it is less bad than the available alternatives.[83] Proposals to replace the current English law with a special offence of "criminal intoxication", mooted by the Law Commission in a consultation paper,[84] did not find favour,[85] and the Commission's eventual report suggested restatement of the existing rule in a codified form rather than abolition.[86]

8.15 At the other end of the spectrum, some jurisdictions have adopted a fully "exculpatory" approach. Most notably, the Canadian Supreme Court held in *R. v Daviault*[87] that the rule which had existed up until that point, that intoxication could not be a defence to a crime of "basic intent",[88] violated ss.7 (fundamental justice) and 11(d) (the presumption of innocence) of the Canadian Charter of Rights and Freedoms. That decision was, however, met with legislative reform to restrict the scope of any defence of intoxication.[89] New Zealand and Australia (at least in some constituent jurisdictions) have also rejected the *Majewski* approach,[90] although it has been argued that this rejection, in Australia at any rate, has not been entirely successful.[91]

An alternative approach is that adopted in South Africa, where it was held in *S v Chretien*[92] that the distinction between crimes of basic and specific intent should be rejected and that evidence of intoxication could have full exculpatory effect. The legislature there chose not to amend the intoxication "defence", but instead to create a new criminal offence in the following terms:

> "Any person who consumes or uses any substance which impairs his faculties to appreciate the wrongfulness of his acts or to act in accordance with that appreciation, while knowing that such

[83] S. Gough, "Surviving without *Majewski*" [2000] Crim. L.R. 719–733.

[84] *Intoxication and Criminal Liability* (Law Com. C.P. No. 127, 1993).

[85] See J. Horder, "Sobering up? The Law Commission on criminal intoxication" (1995) 58 M.L.R. 534–546.

[86] *Intoxication and Criminal Liability* (Law Com. No. 229, 1995), and see now Home Office, *Violence: Reforming the Offences Against the Person Act 1861* (1998), para.3.23, making proposals which are similar in principle but are said to differ from the Law Commission's proposals in that they are "readily comprehensible": J.C. Smith, "Offences against the person: the Home Office Consultation Paper" [1998] Crim. L.R. 317–322 at p.321.

[87] [1994] 2 S.C.R. 63.

[88] *Leary v The Queen* [1978] 1 S.C.R. 29.

[89] See s.33.1 of the Canadian Criminal Code, which provides as follows:

"(1) It is not a defence to an offence referred to in subsection (3) that the accused, by reason of self-induced intoxication, lacked the general intent or the voluntariness required to commit the offence, where the accused departed markedly from the standard of care as described in subsection (2).

(2) For the purposes of this section, a person departs markedly from the standard of reasonable care generally recognized in Canadian society and is thereby criminally at fault where the person, while in a state of self-induced intoxication that renders the person unaware of, or incapable of consciously controlling, their behaviour, voluntarily or involuntarily interferes or threatens to interfere with the bodily integrity of another person.

(3) This section applies in respect of an offence under this Act or any other Act of Parliament that includes as an element an assault or any other interference or threat of interference by a person with the bodily integrity of another person."

For discussion, see K. Smith, "Section 33.1: denial of the *Daviault* defence should be held constitutional" (2000) 28 *Criminal Reports* (5th) 350–366.

[90] *R. v Kamipeli* [1975] 2 N.Z.L.R. 610; *R. v O'Connor* (1980) 146 C.L.R. 64.

[91] S. Gough, "Surviving without *Majewski*" [2000] Crim. L.R. 719–733.

[92] 1981 (1) S.A. 1097 (A).

substance has that effect, and who while such faculties are thus impaired commits any act prohibited by law under any penalty, but is not criminally liable because his faculties were impaired as aforesaid, shall be guilty of an offence and shall be liable on conviction to the penalty ... which may be imposed in respect of the commission of that act".[93]

This is not dissimilar to some proposals which have been made for the reform of English law in the past,[94] but, as noted earlier, such approaches have not found favour.[95]

[93] Criminal Law Amendment Act 1 of 1988, s.1(1). See, generally, J. Burchell, *Principles of Criminal Law* (3rd edn, 2005), pp.408–416.

[94] *Report of the Committee on Mentally Abnormal Offenders* (Cmnd. 6244, 1975), paras 18.51–18.59; *Intoxication and Criminal Liability* (Law Com. C.P. No. 127, 1993).

[95] See above, para.8.14, and see also E. Paton, "Reformulating the intoxication rules: the Law Commission's Report" [1995] Crim. L.R. 382–388.

[illegible] substances than [illegible] which [illegible] such, the offender [illegible] [illegible] consents [illegible] in [illegible] any part [illegible] [illegible] commonly liable [illegible] these [illegible] were imposed [illegible] [illegible] shall be [illegible] [illegible] liable [illegible] the penalty [illegible] which [illegible] in respect of the [illegible] of the [illegible]

[illegible] proposals which have been made for the [illegible] of English law [illegible] [illegible] [illegible] such appears [illegible] [illegible]

Chapter 9

NONAGE

The Relevance of Age to Criminal Responsibility

The present position

A child under the age of eight years old cannot be found guilty of a criminal offence. This rule is contained in s.41 of the Criminal Procedure (Scotland) Act 1995, which provides that: **9.01**

> "It shall be conclusively presumed that no child under the age of eight years can be guilty of any offence."[1]

The appeal court has held that the rule in s.41 deems a child under eight incapable of forming *mens rea*.[2] This might suggest that nonage is a substantive defence. In Scots law, however, nonage operates as a plea in bar of trial.[3] This suggests that the rule is not solely based on the capacity of children to commit criminal offences but that there is the additional concern that a child under the age of eight is not an appropriate subject for prosecution in the criminal courts.[4]

At eight years old, Scotland's age of criminal responsibility is lower

---

[1] CPSA 1995, s.41. For a detailed account of the history of the plea of nonage in Scots law, see *Discussion Paper on the Age of Criminal Responsibility* (Scot. Law Com. D.P. No. 115, 2001) (henceforth "Discussion Paper"), at paras 2.8–2.16. For a wider discussion, see A.W.G. Kean, "The history of the criminal liability of children" (1937) 53 L.Q.R. 364–370.

[2] *Merrin v S*, 1987 S.L.T. 193 at 196, *per* the Lord Justice-Clerk (Ross); at 199 *per* Lord Brand. For a discussion of the theoretical basis of the nonage defence, see S.J. Morse, "Immaturity and irresponsibility" (1997–1998) 88 *Journal of Criminal Law and Criminology* 15–67; G. Williams, "The criminal responsibility of children" [1954] Crim. L.R. 493–500; N. Richards, "Criminal children" (1997) 16 *Law and Philosophy* 63–89. For a discussion of the criminal liability of children from a developmental psychology perspective, see C.S. Fried and N.D. Reppucci, "Criminal decision making: the development of adolescent judgment, criminal responsibility, and culpability" (2001) 25 *Law and Human Behaviour* 45–61; T. Grisso, "What we know about youths' capacities as trial defendants" in *Youth on Trial: A Developmental Perspective on Juvenile Justice* (T. Grisso and R.G. Schwartz (eds), 2000), pp.139–171.

[3] Renton and Brown, para.9–06; Gordon, para.8.28. The other pleas in bar of trial are discussed in more detail in Chs 14–20.

[4] On this, see the *Report on Children and Young Persons, Scotland* (Cmnd. 2306, 1964): "The legal presumption by which no child under the age of 8 can be subjected to criminal proceedings is not therefore a reflection of any observable fact, but simply an expression of public policy to the effect that in no circumstances should a child under the age of 8 be made the subject of criminal proceedings and thus liable to the pains of the law ... the 'age of criminal responsibility' is largely a meaningless term, and that in so far as the law refers to the age of 8 as being the minimum age for prosecution, this is essentially the expression of a practical working rule determining the cases in which a procedure which may result in punishment can be applied to juveniles" (at para.65). Of course, the fact that nonage is considered as a plea in bar of trial could simply be because, procedurally, this ensures that it can be dealt with prior to any trial.

than that of most other European and Commonwealth jurisdictions.[5] While other jurisdictions may have a higher age of criminal responsibility in the sense of criminal capacity, however, comparisons of this nature can be misleading: once they reach the age of criminal responsibility, children in other jurisdictions may automatically be dealt with by the adult criminal courts, something which would rarely happen in Scotland.[6]

The children's hearings system

9.02 The provisions on the age of criminal responsibility in s.41 are not the only way in which age affects criminal responsibility.[7] In Scotland, the vast majority of children under the age of 16 who are alleged to have committed an offence are dealt with not by the adult courts but by the children's hearings system.[8] Children under the age of 16 can still be prosecuted in the adult courts, but only on the instructions of the Lord Advocate or at his instance, and then only in the High Court or the sheriff courts.[9] The numbers involved are tiny compared to those who are referred to a children's hearing on the ground that he has committed an offence.[10]

It was held in *Merrin v S*[11] that a child below the age of eight cannot be referred to a children's hearing on the ground that he has committed an offence. While this might seem to follow from the provisions of s.41 of the

[5] See Appendix D of the Discussion Paper, which notes ages ranging from seven to 18 in different jurisdictions.

[6] See para.9.02. In this context, the Scottish Law Commission singles out the example of Romania where the age of criminal responsibility is 14, but where children over 14 are prosecuted in the adult courts (Discussion Paper, para.2.36).

[7] As the Scottish Law Commission has pointed out, there are two senses in which age might potentially affect criminal responsibility. The first is that there may be a certain age below which a child is deemed to lack the capacity to commit a crime. The second is that age may affect the way in which an individual is treated within the criminal justice system; in particular, there may be an age at which the accused becomes subject to the full adult system of prosecution (Discussion Paper, at paras 1.2–1.3).

[8] Children up to the age of 17 years and 6 months may also be referred to a children's hearing in certain circumstances: CPSA 1995, s.49. A detailed discussion of the children's hearings system is beyond the scope of this book. It was established as a result of the Kilbrandon Committee's *Report on Children and Young Persons, Scotland* (Cmnd. 2306, 1964) which espoused the philosophy that a child who commits an offence is a child in need of care and protection and thus, in the vast majority of cases, should not be dealt with in the adult courts. The Committee's recommendation that a special system of children's hearings be set up was put into practice in the Social Work (Scotland) Act 1968, which came into force in 1971. The relevant law is now contained in the Children (Scotland) Act 1995, s.52(2)(i) of which (when read alongside s.65) provides that one ground of referral to a children's hearing is that the child has committed an offence. For detailed discussion of children's hearings, see: K. McK. Norrie, *Children's Hearings in Scotland* (2nd edn, 2005); B. Kearney, *Children's Hearings and the Sheriff Court* (2nd edn, 2000); A. Lockyer and F. Stone (eds), *Juvenile Justice in Scotland* (1998); S. Asquith and M. Docherty, "Preventing offending by children and young people in Scotland" in *Criminal Justice in Scotland* (P. Duff and N. Hutton (eds), 1999).

[9] CPSA 1995, s.42(1).

[10] The number of children under 16 prosecuted in the criminal courts was 189 in 1997; 179 in 1998; and 105 in 1999. This can be compared to the numbers dealt with by a children's hearing on the offence ground: 27,562 in 1997/1998; 28,213 in 1998/1999; and 30,633 in 1999/2000 (Discussion Paper, at para.3.11).

[11] 1987 S.L.T. 193. For comment, see J.M. Thomson, "Statutory interpretation of child care legislation" (1988) 104 L.Q.R. 21–24.

1995 Act,[12] the decision has been criticised on the basis that a small number of children under the age of eight might slip through the net and not receive the care and protection they require if they cannot be referred to a children's hearing on one of the other grounds contained in s.52(2) of the Children (Scotland) Act 1995.[13]

The treatment of mentally impaired children

It is clear from *HM Advocate v S*[14] that age refers to chronological age and not mental age. The accused was a 13-year-old child who was charged with culpable homicide in relation to an incident that had occurred when he was 12. He had set fire to some petrol, as a result of which his friend, who was standing nearby, suffered severe burns and later died. The accused suffered from a developmental delay as a result of which his ability in certain aspects of his functioning corresponded to that of the average eight or nine-year-old. A plea in bar of trial was successful, but on the basis of insanity and not nonage.[15] The court held that nonage would not have been an appropriate plea in these circumstances.[16] **9.03**

The compatibility of the Scottish approach with the ECHR

The age of criminal responsibility was considered by the European Court of Human Rights in *T and V v United Kingdom*,[17] a case in which the applicants challenged under Art.3[18] various aspects of their treatment by the UK authorities, including their public trial in an adult court and the power of the Home Secretary to set tariffs for juveniles sentenced to detention. At the time of the offence, both were 10 years old.[19] At the time of their trial, which took place in an adult court, they were 11. **9.04**

The European Court concluded that setting the age of criminal responsibility at 10, while on the low side, did not in itself breach Art.3.[20] What was more important, in terms of compatibility with Art.3, was that:

---

[12] The presumption that a child under the age of eight cannot commit a criminal offence. This was the view taken by the majority in *Merrin*. See the Lord Justice-Clerk (Ross) at 196; Lord Brand at 199. *Cf.* the dissenting opinion of Lord Dunpark, who took a more purposive approach to interpreting the legislation.

[13] J.P. Grant, "The under age offender", 1987 S.L.T. (News) 337–340. See also the Draft Criminal Code, Sch.2, para.3.

[14] High Court, October 15, 1999, unreported. See C. Connelly and C. McDiarmid, "Children, mental impairment and the plea in bar of trial" (2000) 5 S.L.P.Q. 157–168.

[15] On insanity as a plea in bar of trial, see Ch.14.

[16] Lord Caplan states quite clearly that: "I do not consider that the fact that S had certain limitations of capability more appropriate to a younger child did itself merit reducing his responsibility to that of a substantially younger child."

[17] (2000) 30 E.H.R.R. 121. For comment, see E. Henderson, "The European Convention and child defendants" [2000] C.L.J. 235–238; F.G. Davies, "Right to a fair trial for very young offenders" (2000) 64 J.C.L. 257–259; A. Ashworth, "Human rights: right to fair trial: very young defendants: imposition of 'sentence'" [2000] Crim. L.R. 187–189.

[18] The right not to be subjected to torture or to inhuman or degrading treatment or punishment.

[19] The age of criminal responsibility in England: Children and Young Persons Act 1933, s.50, as amended by Children and Young Persons Act 1963, s.16(1).

[20] At [74]. Five judges dissented on this issue but all seemed to be equating the age of criminal responsibility not with the capacity to commit a criminal offence, but with the entry of the accused into the adult criminal justice system.

> "... a child charged with an offence is dealt with in a manner which takes full account of his age, level of maturity and intellectual and emotional capacities, and that steps are taken to promote his ability to understand and participate in the proceedings".[21]

Thus setting the age of criminal responsibility at eight years old does not appear in itself incompatible with the ECHR. Compatibility difficulties, if they were to arise, are more likely to do so in the few cases where Scottish children are tried in the adult court system.[22]

S v Miller[23] makes clear that a child who is dealt with under the children's hearings system is not "charged with a criminal offence" in terms of Art.6 of the ECHR. This means that the various protections contained in Art.6(3) do not apply to children's hearings, although the more general guarantees contained in Art.6(1) would still be invoked.

The Possibility of Reform

9.05 The age of criminal responsibility has been considered by the Scottish Law Commission, which issued a discussion paper in 2001[24] and a report in 2002.[25] The Discussion Paper proposed that the rule on criminal capacity contained in s.41 of the 1995 Act be abolished,[26] but that the power to prosecute children under 16 be retained.[27] This provoked criticism on the basis that it left open the possibility that an extremely young child could be prosecuted in the adult courts.[28] The Discussion Paper anticipated this criticism[29] but suggested that this outcome would be

---

[21] At [86]. In the event, it was held that certain aspects of the applicants' trial in an adult court were a violation of Art.3 on this basis.

[22] For discussion of the compatibility of the Scottish approach with other international standards (such as the 1989 United Nations Convention on the Rights of the Child), see the Discussion Paper, paras 2.26–2.34; E.E. Sutherland, "The age of reason or the reasons for an age?", 2002 S.L.T. (News) 1–5 at p.3.

[23] 2001 S.C. 977. In *Miller*, a devolution issue was raised as to whether the children's hearings system was compliant with the ECHR. In particular, the court was asked to consider the nature of the proceedings (and whether or not a child appearing at a children's hearing on the offence ground was "charged with an offence" in which case the protections contained in Art.6(3) would be invoked); whether the hearing was an independent and impartial tribunal; whether it was unfair that a child had no access to legal aid at a hearing; and whether it was unfair that a child had no access to the various reports drawn up by social workers. For comment, see L. Edwards, "*S v Miller*: The end of the children's hearing system as we know it?", 2001 S.L.T. (News) 187–193; K. McK. Norrie, "*S v Miller (No 1)*: Case Comment", 2001 S.L.T. (News) 150; I. Jamieson, "*S v Miller*: should a declaration of incompatibility be made?", 2001 S.L.T. (News) 137–138; K. McK. Norrie, "Legal representation at children's hearings: the interim scheme" (2002) 7 S.L.P.Q. 131–133.

[24] See fn.1 above.

[25] *Report on the Age of Criminal Responsibility* (Scot. Law Com. No. 185, 2002) (henceforth "Report").

[26] Discussion Paper, para.3.5.

[27] Discussion Paper, para.3.12.

[28] C. McDiarmid, "Age of criminal responsibility: raise it or remove it?", 2001 Jur. Rev. 243–257 at p.250; Sutherland, above fn.22, at p.4.

[29] Discussion Paper, para.3.14.

prevented by "the duty on the Crown to prove criminal capacity, the requirement to adapt trial procedures to enable full and effective participation by the child, and guidelines limiting prosecution to only those cases in the public interest".[30]

Perhaps unsurprisingly, the Scottish Law Commission modified their proposals in their subsequent report. The recommendation is now that s.41 be abolished,[31] but replaced with a provision barring the prosecution of a child under 12.[32] It is also proposed that the existing provisions in s.42 should remain.[33] If the Commission's proposals were implemented, the vast majority of children between the ages of 12 and 16 would still be dealt with by way of a children's hearing.[34] The proposals have been impliedly criticised by the authors of the Draft Criminal Code, who point out that a child who committed an offence when aged under 12 could be prosecuted for it when he or she reached the age of 12 (assuming no statutory time limits applied).[35] As such, s.15 of the Draft Criminal Code proposes simply that the existing age of criminal responsibility be raised from 8 to 12.[36]

---

[30] Discussion Paper, para.3.14. *Cf.* McDiarmid, above fn.28, at p.257; Sutherland, above fn.22, at p.4 (citing cases from the US where very young children have been prosecuted in the wake of public outcry over their alleged offences). To be fair to the Scottish Law Commission, it was said in the Discussion Paper that the proposals as they stood did not form their concluded view and the issue was put out to consultation (paras 3.15–3.16).

[31] Report, para.3.5.

[32] Report, para.3.20.

[33] That a child can be prosecuted only on the instructions of the Lord Advocate or at his instance. See para.9.02 above.

[34] The Report also recommends the abolition of the rule in *Merrin v S*, 1987 S.L.T. 193 that the offence ground cannot be used to refer a child under the age of eight (or, if the other proposals in the Report are put into effect, a child under 12) to a children's hearing. See para.9.02 above.

[35] Commentary to s.15 of the Draft Criminal Code, at 42.

[36] The Draft Code also dispenses with the slightly confusing language contained in s.41 of the 1995 Act (which refers to a "conclusive presumption" that a child cannot be guilty of a criminal offence). The Draft Code provides instead that: "A person is not guilty of an offence by reason of anything done when the person is or was a child under 12 years of age." In the commentary to s.15 of the Code, it is stated that the figure of 12 is inserted provisionally and that the choice of age is a policy matter.

Chapter 10

PROVOCATION

Theoretical Basis

From the perspective of comparative law, the partial defence of provocation is one of the most controversial doctrines of the criminal law, at least within the common-law world. The literature is replete with calls for its abolition or restriction,[1] while law reform bodies worldwide have regularly grappled with its content.[2] Scotland, by contrast, represents something of an oasis of calm. The plea has been the subject of relatively little academic writing, and no decision on the law of provocation has provoked any significant controversy.[3] **10.01**

This may be a mere coincidence of the type which one would expect to find in any small jurisdiction, but it is significant that the Scottish variant of the plea is framed more narrowly than in almost any other jurisdiction. Scotland, therefore, has largely avoided the modern criticism that the plea allows those killers who should properly be convicted of murder to be convicted of a lesser offence.[4] This does, of course, leave Scots law open to the charge that the law of provocation is overly harsh and restrictive.

Why allow a partial defence of provocation?

It has been suggested that the "lifeline of provocation as a separate defence is the mandatory penalty for murder."[5] While it is all but inconceivable that the plea could be abolished for as long as the mandatory penalty is retained,[6] it does not follow that the *only* justification for the partial defence is the mandatory life sentence for murder. Even if the **10.02**

[1] See, e.g. C. Wells, "Provocation: the case for abolition" in *Rethinking English Homicide Law* (A. Ashworth and B. Mitchell (eds), 2000), pp.85–106; V. Nourse, "Passion's progress: modern law reform and the provocation defense" (1997) 106 *Yale Law Journal* 1331–1448; M. Goode, "The abolition of provocation" in *Partial Excuses to Murder* (S. Yeo (ed.), 1991), pp.37–60. It has been abolished in Victoria: Crimes Act 1958, s.3B, as inserted by the Crimes (Homicide) Act 2005, s.3. For the background to this reform, see Victorian Law Reform Commission, *Defences to Homicide: Final Report* (2004), Ch.2.

[2] See, e.g. *Partial Defences to Murder* (Law Com. No. 290, 2004); Law Reform Commission (Ireland), *Homicide: The Plea of Provocation* (LRC CP 27–2003); Department of Justice (Canada), *Reforming Criminal Code Defences: Provocation, Self-Defence and Defence of Property* (1998); New South Wales Law Reform Commission, *Partial Defences to Murder: Provocation and Infanticide* (1997).

[3] The one exception is *Drury v HM Advocate*, 2001 S.L.T. 1013. The academic criticism of that decision, however, relates largely to the possibility that the High Court's approach may have unforeseen consequences for defences other than provocation, rather than the court's treatment of provocation itself. See, in relation to self-defence, para.3.11.

[4] See, e.g. R.B. Mison, "Homophobia in manslaughter: the homosexual advance as insufficient provocation" (1992) 80 *California Law Review* 133–178.

[5] C. Wells, "The death penalty for provocation?" [1978] Crim. L.R. 662–672 at p.662.

[6] *cf. Partial Defences to Murder* (Law Com. C.P. No. 173, 2003), para.12.25 ("We know of no common law system where provocation has been abolished but a mandatory sentence of life imprisonment retained, nor of any law reform body which has made such a recommendation.").

legislature were to abolish the mandatory sentence, it is likely that a distinction would continue to be drawn between unlawful killings of greater and lesser seriousness.[7] Allowing provocation to reduce what would otherwise be murder to culpable homicide is an important tool in the assessment of culpability. In other words, this is an application of the principle of "fair labelling"[8]—a person who kills under provocation, while deserving of conviction and punishment, does not deserve to be stigmatised as a murderer.

Partial justification or partial excuse?

10.03 There is some doubt as to whether provocation is properly characterised as a partial justification or a partial excuse. In a 1956 paper, the question was formulated by J.L. Austin in the following way:

> "When we plead, say, provocation, there is genuine uncertainty or ambiguity as to what we mean—is *he* partly responsible, because he roused a violent impulse or passion in me, so that it wasn't truly or merely me acting 'of my own accord' (excuse)? Or is it rather that, he having done me such injury, I was entitled to retaliate (justification)?"[9]

Dressler, in particular, has argued that provocation should be regarded as a partial excuse. To support this, he gives the following example, presented on the basis that M and W have entered into a sexual relationship which is not one of fidelity, due to W's refusal to commit to a relationship:

> "One day, M comes to W's apartment and finds W in bed with X. Perhaps M is not justified in becoming angry—W has not wronged M, since she never promised sexual fidelity to him—but few people would disagree that M may be excused for being disturbed by the sighting. His emotions are excusable because an ordinary person, with an ordinary temper and ordinary feelings, would likely become emotionally overwrought in such circumstances. Therefore, if M kills W while he is overwrought (assuming, of course, that M did not have reasonable time to cool off), the homicide may be partially excusable."[10]

This example, however, assumes too much. There is no doubt that, *if* a provocation defence were to be recognised in such a case, it would have to be regarded as having no justificatory component whatsoever. But there is no necessary reason why the plea of provocation *should* be allowed in such a case, and Scots law certainly would not allow it,[11] although

---

[7] See, generally, W. Wilson, "Murder and the structure of homicide" in *Rethinking English Homicide Law* (A. Ashworth and B. Mitchell (eds), 2000), p.21. *Cf.* L. Blom-Cooper and T. Morris, *With Malice Aforethought: A Study of the Crime and Punishment for Homicide* (2004), arguing for a *single* offence of criminal homicide.

[8] See Ashworth, *Principles of Criminal Law*, pp.88–90.

[9] J.L. Austin, "A plea for excuses" in *The Philosophy of Action* (A.R. White (ed.), 1968), p.20.

[10] J. Dressler, "When 'heterosexual' men kill 'homosexual' men: reflections on provocation law, sexual advances and the 'reasonable man' standard" (1995) 85 *Journal of Criminal Law and Criminology* 726–763 at p.748.

[11] *McKay v HM Advocate*, 1991 J.C. 91. See below, para.10.11.

another legal system might choose to do so.[12] Whether provocation is a partial justification or partial excuse depends upon the circumstances in which any particular legal system is prepared to accept the validity of the plea.

One cannot, as Dressler does, argue that provocation must be regarded as a partial excuse because certain cases are decided in a particular way (as in the example given above), and then go on from this to argue that the status of provocation as a partial excuse defence means that certain results must be obtained in other cases.[13] This form of reasoning is entirely circular. This is not to say that the characterisation of the provocation defence as a partial justification or partial excuse is irrelevant, although its usefulness may easily be overstated.[14] It might, for example, be useful in determining whether the rules governing the plea are internally consistent.[15] **10.04**

It should be clear, however, that a legal system is entitled to formulate the plea as it sees fit. Ireland, for example, has at least flirted with a form of provocation which would allow the plea in all cases where the accused had lost his or her self-control, regardless of the nature of the provocation or the extent of the accused's reaction.[16] This type of plea is quite clearly a partial excuse, but proposals which would reintroduce an element of partial justification to the Irish law of provocation are currently under consideration.[17] Both formulations of the plea are logically coherent: the choice between the two is one of policy.

In Scots law, the plea is probably best regarded as containing elements of both justification and excuse.[18] Because the plea is restricted to cases where the accused has been provoked by violence or infidelity,[19] we may say that the accused's *anger* is justified.[20] If it is not, then he will not be entitled to plead provocation. For example, in *McKay v HM Advocate*,[21] the accused killed his wife after she alleged that he was not the father of their child. Because the accused already knew that the child had been conceived before their marriage at a time when the parties had not been living together and the deceased had been seeing other men, her statement could not be taken as disclosing infidelity. The accused, therefore, had no basis for a plea of provocation, because his anger could not be regarded as justified.

---

[12] Dressler formulates the example given under reference to the New York case of *People v Casassa*, 404 N.E. 2d 1310 (NY 1980). *Casassa*, however, is a peculiar case to refer to in this context, as it involves a plea of extreme emotional disturbance rather than provocation and Dressler has argued elsewhere that it should not be regarded as a provocation case: J. Dressler: "Why keep the provocation defense? Some reflections on a difficult subject" (2002) 86 *Minnesota Law Review* 959–1002 at pp.987–988.

[13] See J. Dressler, "Provocation: partial justification or partial excuse?" (1988) 51 M.L.R. 467–480 at p.468.

[14] *cf.* J. Dressler, "Provocation: partial justification or partial excuse?", at p.468 for an argument as to why the distinction is valuable.

[15] It would be odd, for example, if the plea were restricted to cases where the accused had lost control as a result of violence (which would seem characteristic of a partial justification), but was thereafter available regardless of the severity of the response offered by the accused (which would seem characteristic of a partial excuse).

[16] *People v MacEoin* [1978] I.R. 27.

[17] See Law Reform Commission (Ireland), *Homicide: The Plea of Provocation* (L.R.C. C.P. 27–2003).

[18] *cf.* A.J. Ashworth, "The doctrine of provocation" [1976] C.L.J. 292–320 at p.307.

[19] See below, paras 10.08–10.14.

[20] Or, in some cases, that the accused's *fear* is justified: see *van den Hoek* (1986) 161 C.L.R. 158.

[21] 1991 J.C. 91.

Although the accused's anger may be justified, this does not permit him to act violently in consequence of that anger. His *actions*, therefore, are merely excused (and even then, only partially). In other words, the plea is ultimately a partial excuse, but with a "justificatory" component.[22] The provoked killer is justified in being angry, but not in acting on that anger.

Provocation and the structure of homicide

10.05 In *Drury v HM Advocate*,[23] it was said that provocation operates by negating the *mens rea* for murder. Prior to that case, it was thought that the *mens rea* requirement for murder could be satisfied by proof of an intention to kill, or of wicked recklessness.[24] According to the *Drury* court, however, an intention to kill must also be "wicked" in order to satisfy the *mens rea* requirement, and provocation operates by negating "wickedness".[25]

This position has been heavily criticised.[26] The criticisms relate largely to the implications of such an approach for other defences (and, in particular, the consequences for the general rule that mistakes in defence must be reasonable).[27] Whether provocation is understood to operate as a plea in mitigation, or by negating *mens rea*, has little consequence for the plea itself.[28]

The *Drury* court did observe that, if provocation operated by negating *mens rea*, it was incorrect to refer to provocation as "reducing" murder to culpable homicide.[29] Nevertheless, the appeal court has since reverted to this terminology of "reduction" in the context of diminished responsibility,[30] and this language will be used throughout this chapter. The point is terminological rather than substantive.

Historical Development

10.06 Hume explains that the plea of provocation in Scots law has its origins in the ancient distinction between murder and "slaughter on suddenty, or *chaude melle*".[31] Under that distinction, the "manslayer on suddenty"[32] was entitled to sanctuary in a church or other holy place. While he could be taken for trial, he was to be returned if *chaude melle* were proved. Although the privilege of sanctuary was abolished at the Reformation,

[22] See J. Dressler, "Why keep the provocation defense? Some reflections on a difficult subject" (2002) 86 *Minnesota Law Review* 959–1002 at p.971.

[23] 2001 S.L.T. 1013.

[24] Macdonald, 89.

[25] At [20] *per* the Lord Justice-General (Rodger).

[26] See J. Chalmers, "Collapsing the structure of criminal law", 2001 S.L.T. (News) 241–245; M.G.A. Christie, "The coherence of Scots criminal law: some aspects of *Drury v HM Advocate*", 2002 Jur. Rev. 273–290; F. Leverick, "Mistake in self-defence after *Drury*", 2002 Jur. Rev. 35–48. There are, however, *dicta* in some of the earlier Scottish cases which suggest that provocation might operate by negating *mens rea*, although the point does not appear to have been argued prior to *Drury*. See *Hillan v HM Advocate*, 1937 J.C. 53; *Berry v HM Advocate* (1976) S.C.C.R. (Supp.) 156 at 157, *per* Lord Keith; *Gray v HM Advocate*, 1994 S.L.T 1237 at 1243, *per* the Lord Justice-Clerk (Ross).

[27] See above, paras 3.11 and 12.22–12.23.

[28] Except in the unusual case of provocation based on a mistake of fact (below, para.10.15), and possibly also provocation in assault (below, paras 10.25–10.26).

[29] *Drury v HM Advocate*, 2001 S.L.T. 1013 at [17], *per* the Lord Justice-General (Rodger).

[30] *Galbraith v HM Advocate (No. 2)*, 2002 J.C. 1.

[31] Hume, i, 241.

[32] *ibid.*

the distinction persisted,[33] and homicide on "gross and excessive provocation" was recognised as amounting to culpable homicide rather than murder.[34]

Historically—and this remains the case today—the scope of the plea was framed more narrowly than English law:

> "To have a good plea of extenuation, the pannel must have been, at the time of the killing, in the situation of an assaulted and a grossly injured person; one who was in a manner constrained to strike, by the violence he was suffering at the moment."[35]

Hume expressly rejected what he perceived to be the position in English law: that "*any* assault on the person of the killer materially extenuates his guilt, and brings his case within the privilege of manslaughter".[36] Instead, Hume appears to have viewed the plea as a doctrine addressing the use of excessive force on a justified occasion[37]: it was the "excess of the just measure of retaliation"[38] which left the killer open to criminal liability.

While a number of early nineteenth-century decisions, shortly after the first edition of Hume's *Commentaries*, appear to have adopted a more liberal approach to the scope of the plea,[39] subsequent decisions and writings suggest that this was, if anything, merely a temporary relaxation of attitudes. In particular, it became clear in later cases that the plea would not be open where the accused had responded to an unarmed assailant by using a weapon.[40]

It follows from this approach that there was no question of recognising provocation by words alone or by interference with property.[41] An exception was made for the "peculiar case of a husband killing the adulterer caught in the fact",[42] although there appears to be only one such

---

[33] Hume, i, 240–244; Alison, *Principles*, 16–18.

[34] Alison, *Principles*, 18.

[35] Hume, i, 247.

[36] *ibid.*

[37] Hume appears to have considered that provocation, as a separate plea from self-defence, could itself operate as a complete justification in cases of (non-fatal) assault. See Hume, i, 334–335. This is no longer the law. See further below, paras 10.25–10.26.

[38] Hume, i, 248. See also Alison, *Principles*, 93 ("it generally turns out, that both parties were at first to blame, although the sufferer has received more than his due chastisement from the intemperate revenge of the survivor").

[39] See *Andrew Burt* (1804) Hume, i, 258; *William Goldie* (1804) Hume, i, 249; *Walter Redpath* (1810) Hume, i, 252; *James Macara* (1811) Hume, i, 252. Each of these cases involved provocation by minor assaults. In noting these decisions by way of footnotes in later editions of his *Commentaries*, Hume took the opportunity to express doubts about the soundness of the verdicts.

[40] See Alison, *Principles*, 12; *Mrs Mackinnon* (1823) Alison, *Principles*, 14; *Peter Scott* (1823) Alison, *Principles*, 15; *Edward Armstrong* (1826) Alison, *Principles*, 15 (although the jury acquitted in the face of directions from the presiding judge in that case). See also *James Craw* (1826) Syme 188 at 211, *per* Lord Gillies. *Cf. William Wright* (1835) 1 Swin. 6, where the presiding judge charged the jury in such circumstances by (at 12) "expressing a clear opinion that a case of murder was established, but informing the jury that they might competently return a verdict of culpable homicide", which they did.

[41] Hume, i, 246–247. See also *William Aird* (1693) Hume, i, 248, where a defence of provocation based on the deceased's having tossed the contents of a chamber-pot in the accused's face was rejected; *HM Advocate v Robert Smith* (1893) 1 Adam 34 at 49, *per* Lord McLaren. *Cf.*, however, *Andrew Burt* (1804) Hume, i, 258.

[42] Hume, i, 248.

reported case prior to the twentieth century.[43] The exception clearly sat uneasily with the restrictive general approach to provocation, as Hume acknowledged,[44] but its validity does not appear to have been doubted.

The Requirements of the Plea

10.07 Following the decision in *Drury*,[45] the plea of provocation may be regarded as having a tripartite structure. There must have been (a) provocative conduct, which (b) caused the accused to lose self-control and (c) the accused's reaction to the provocation must have been such as might have been expected from an ordinary person. Where provocation is in issue, the prosecution must prove the absence of each and all of these elements beyond a reasonable doubt. If they fail to do so, the accused should be convicted of culpable homicide rather than murder.

Recognised provocations

10.08 Scots law only recognises two types of provocation as providing a basis for the plea: provocation by violence and provocation by infidelity, although it has at times flirted with the possibility of allowing other acts to ground the plea.

Provocation by violence

10.09 Violence on the part of the deceased is the usual basis for a plea of provocation. That is not to say that any killing following on from an assault will be culpable homicide rather than murder, and Hume was careful to reject what he perceived to be the position in English law: that "*any* assault on the person of the killer materially extenuates his guilt, and brings his case within the privilege of manslaughter".[46]

It used to be the case that the plea would not succeed unless the accused's reaction was in some way proportionate to the deceased's violence. Now, as a result of *Drury v HM Advocate*,[47] it may be that the crucial question is not whether the accused responded in a proportionate manner, but whether his reaction was such as might have been expected of the "ordinary person". The point is considered further below.[48]

Provocation by infidelity

10.10 Although Hume was prepared to accept that infidelity was properly recognised as a ground of provocation, he did not consider it as strong a ground as violence:

> "though the provocation is high, yet it is in some respects not so favourable as that of some other injuries; because the homicide is here done on the principle of rage and revenge, unaccompanied with

---

[43] *James Christie* (1731) Maclaurin 625. Hume notes an earlier (1510) case where the killer was given a free remission: Hume, i, 245.

[44] Hume, i, 246.

[45] *Drury v HM Advocate*, 2001 S.L.T. 1013.

[46] Hume, i, 247.

[47] 2001 S.L.T. 1013.

[48] See below, paras 10.18–10.19.

> that fear of further violence, or that trepidation and alarm, which in the ordinary case of an assault on the body of the killer, concur with his resentment, and materially strengthen his defence."[49]

Hume remarked that apart from "the peculiar case of a husband killing the adulterer caught in the fact"[50]—a reference to the 1731 case of *James Christie*[51]—there was no recorded case where a plea of provocation had been successful in the absence of violence.[52]

For some time, it was assumed that the plea was only available to a "husband instantly killing the seducer of his wife, when caught in the act of adultery".[53] However, a plea of provocation was successful in an unreported 1940 case where a husband killed his wife after finding letters from another man in his wife's handbag.[54] This was confirmed the following year in *HM Advocate v Hill*,[55] where Lord Patrick allowed the jury to consider a plea of provocation based on the fact that the accused's wife and her paramour had confessed to adultery in his presence prior to his fatally shooting both of them.[56]

It has now been confirmed that the plea is not restricted to marital **10.11**
relationships, but is also available where the relationship between the parties was "of such a character that fidelity, as in marriage, [was] expected on both sides."[57] It would seem to follow from this that there is no basis for restricting the plea to heterosexual relationships, a conclusion which was accepted by the trial judge in *HM Advocate v McKean*.[58]

---

[49] Hume, i, 246.

[50] Hume, i, 248.

[51] (1731) Maclaurin 625. After the court had ruled that the plea was open to the accused, the jury found the charge not proven. As Michael Christie has observed, this is "not an option that one would have thought was open to them in terms of the law laid down by the court. But, it is not unknown for juries to bring in verdicts which a lawyer would consider perverse." M.G.A. Christie, "The coherence of Scots criminal law: some aspects of *Drury v HM Advocate*", 2002 Jur. Rev. 273–290 at p.279. *Cf.* J.S. More, *Lectures on the Law of Scotland* (1864), pp.365–366, where the view is taken that a killing in such circumstances is a justified homicide, although no authority is cited in support of this proposition.

[52] There is an earlier case where the killer was given a free remission: *Robertus Shanke* (1510) Hume, i, 245.

[53] Macdonald (4th edn, 1929), 138–139. See also Anderson, 153. This formulation of the rule has two implications: (i) the parties must have been caught in the act, and (ii) the plea would only have applied where the paramour (rather than the spouse) is killed. It is implicitly assumed (although probably not considered to be any part of the rule) that factually such cases will involve the husband, rather than the wife, as the killer. There are now at least two recent Scottish cases involving female accused and male victims: *HM Advocate v McKean*, 1997 J.C. 32; *Houghton v HM Advocate*, 1999 G.W.D. 17–789.

[54] *HM Advocate v McWilliam*, High Court at Edinburgh, November 5, 1940, unreported. See *The Times*, November 6, 1940, 9. In a 1924 case, prior acts of adultery (an incestuous affair between the deceased (the accused's father) and the accused's wife) were left to the jury along with an allegation of assault immediately prior to the killing. *HM Advocate v Green*, High Court at Jedburgh, February 26–27, 1924, unreported. See the *Scotsman*, February 28, 1924, 5.

[55] 1941 J.C. 59.

[56] Hill was a corporal in the military police who was required to carry his revolver even when on leave.

[57] *McKay v HM Advocate*, 1991 J.C. 91 at 95, *per* the Lord Justice-General (Hope). See also *McDermott v HM Advocate*, 1973 J.C. 8.

[58] 1997 J.C. 32.

Although a confession of infidelity will now suffice, the appeal court has established two important caveats.[59] First, the confession must be "clear and unequivocal". Accordingly, the plea was unavailable in *McKay v HM Advocate*,[60] where the deceased had claimed that the accused was not in fact the father of their child, because the accused was already aware that the deceased had been seeing other men around the time when the child was conceived, and they had not been in a relationship of fidelity at that point.

10.12 Secondly, the accused must have accepted the confession of infidelity. In *McCormack v HM Advocate*,[61] the accused claimed that he had been provoked into killing his wife by her repeated statements that he was not the father of their child. He had, he said, not believed the claim, but had been provoked into strangling her because he "just wanted [her] to shut up". The appeal court held that because he had been provoked into the killing because he "did not wish to continue to hear these allegations, and not because he actually believed them,"[62] the plea was unavailable.[63]

The plea is not necessarily excluded by the fact that the accused was already aware of some infidelity on the part of his or her partner. In *Rutherford v HM Advocate*,[64] the accused had been aware of his partner's infidelity for two days prior to the killing, at which point he believed that the affair had involved intercourse on only two occasions and was now at an end. Immediately before the killing, she revealed that the affair had in fact been much more extensive and was continuing. The appeal court held that this was a "substantially different" and "fresh" account which could amount to provocation despite the earlier revelations by the deceased.

Other forms of provocation

10.13 Scots law does not allow words alone to amount to provocation sufficient to reduce murder to culpable homicide. English law has accepted the possibility of such provocation ever since the Homicide Act 1957, and it appears that consideration was given to applying the relevant section of the Act to Scotland when the Bill was passing through Parliament.[65] The Lord Advocate of the time rejected such an extension, on the remarkable basis that this was (he claimed) already the law of Scotland:

> "the common law of Scotland is extremely flexible. There is nothing that I have been able to find which would indicate that a judge in Scotland would be precluded from leaving provocation by words to a jury."[66]

---

[59] Although the reported cases are all concerned with confessions of infidelity (and this terminology is therefore adopted in the text), there is no reason, in principle, why a discovery of infidelity, such as the discovery of incriminating letters in *McWilliam* (above, para.10.10), would not suffice provided the other requirements of the plea are met.

[60] 1991 J.C. 91.

[61] 1993 S.L.T. 1158.

[62] At 1164 *per* the Lord Justice-General (Hope).

[63] McCormack's case was later referred back to the appeal court by the Scottish Criminal Cases Review Commission: *McCormack v HM Advocate*, 2003 J.C. 1. In those proceedings, it was argued that the earlier decision of the appeal court was overly restrictive. The court, in continuing the appeal to allow fresh evidence to be led, declined to express any opinion on the point. The appeal was eventually refused: *McCormack v HM Advocate*, 2005 HCJAC 38.

[64] 1998 J.C. 34.

[65] Section 3. See HC Deb, cols 769–788 (January 28, 1957).

[66] HC Deb, col.784 (January 28, 1957).

It is not easy to understand why the Lord Advocate took this view—which, as Gordon observes, is at odds with every textbook in use at that time.[67] Although there are three cases shortly prior to 1957 where provocation appears to have been left to the jury in the absence of any assault by the deceased (or revelation of infidelity),[68] none of these is conclusive, nor was there any support in the decisions of the appeal court for such a position.[69]

Two further cases subsequent to the 1957 Act did, however, suggest that Scots law might be prepared to adopt a more relaxed approach to the question of verbal provocation. In *Berry v HM Advocate*,[70] the accused's plea of provocation was based on a claim that, in the course of a sexual encounter, the deceased had "taunted [him] with his inadequate prowess, compared him unfavourably to his uncle in that regard and made some critical observations about whether or not he might be the father of his children".[71] The trial judge left the plea to the jury (who rejected it). The appeal court, however, expressed "great doubt" about whether the judge had been right to do so. In *Stobbs v HM Advocate*,[72] the accused claimed that he had been having a sexual relationship with the deceased, and that she had provoked him by threatening to tell his wife of the relationship unless he changed his mind about ending it. Again, the trial judge left the defence to the jury, who rejected it.

The appeal court did not endorse the trial judge's decision to leave provocation to the jury in either of these cases, and subsequent appellate decisions appear to have ruled out the possibility of verbal provocation. First, in *Thomson v HM Advocate*,[73] the appeal court expressed doubts about both of these cases, taking the view that they were difficult to reconcile with the established authorities. In the later case of *Cosgrove v HM Advocate*,[74] the appeal court quoted the following statement from Macdonald with approval: **10.14**

> "Words of insult, however strong, or any mere insulting or disgusting conduct, such as jostling, or tossing filth in the face, do not serve to reduce the crime from murder to culpable homicide."[75]

Taken together, *Thomson* and *Cosgrove* appear firmly to reject the possibility of verbal provocation in Scots law, and such cases should, therefore, not be left to the jury. It was also accepted in the later case of

---

[67] Gordon, para.25.26. It may be, however, that there was some confusion as to the distinction between (a) the test for provocation and (b) the circumstances in which the matter could be left to the jury. Although it is now accepted that a judge may withdraw provocation from the jury's consideration, this does not appear to have actually happened in any reported case prior to *Thomson v HM Advocate*, 1986 S.L.T. 281. It may have been that the Lord Advocate considered that the trial judge would have been unable to withdraw a plea of provocation by words from the jury's consideration, but even so, it must have been clear at the time that the authorities would require him to direct the jury that words alone would be insufficient for the plea to succeed.

[68] *HM Advocate v McGuinness*, 1937 J.C. 37; *Crawford v HM Advocate*, 1950 J.C. 67. The third is an unreported case referred to by T.B. Smith, "Capital punishment", 1953 S.L.T. (News) 197 at p.199.

[69] For an analysis of the cases, see Gordon, paras 25.27–25.28.

[70] (1976) S.C.C.R. (Supp.) 156.

[71] (1976) S.C.C.R. (Supp.) 156, 158.

[72] 1983 S.C.C.R. 190.

[73] 1986 S.L.T. 281.

[74] 1990 J.C. 333.

[75] At 340 *per* Lord Cowie (quoting Macdonald, 93).

Robertson v HM Advocate[76] that a homosexual advance, unaccompanied by violence, could not form a basis for the plea—which is of significance given the concern which has been expressed about this aspect of the plea in other jurisdictions.[77] The alleged advance in *Robertson* was in fact accompanied by the use of a knife, but it was held that the plea was nevertheless excluded because of the accused's "grossly disproportionate" response to the deceased's actions (he had stabbed the deceased repeatedly in a frenzied attack).

Errors of fact

10.15 No Scottish case appears to have considered the question of whether a plea of provocation may be founded upon an error of fact (that is, a mistaken belief on the part of the actor that he is under attack or that his partner has been unfaithful). In principle, it seems clear that the plea should be open in such a case.[78] It is submitted, however, that because Scots law requires a justificatory component to the plea (that is, the accused's anger must have been justified),[79] the mistake must be based on reasonable grounds.[80] This is consistent with the general approach of Scots law to mistakes in defence.[81]

The subjective condition: loss of self-control

10.16 The plea will be unavailable unless the accused has killed having lost self-control—or, in more colloquial terms, "in the heat of the moment". Accordingly, in *HM Advocate v Hill*,[82] Lord Patrick directed the jury that if they were "satisfied that the prisoner killed these two people not in the heat of the moment but after an interval when his blood had

---

[76] 1994 J.C. 245.

[77] See, e.g. R.B. Mison, "Homophobia in manslaughter: the homosexual advance as insufficient provocation" (1992) 80 *California Law Review* 133–178; C. Wells, "Provocation: the case for abolition" in *Rethinking English Homicide Law* (A. Ashworth and B. Mitchell (eds), 2000), pp.85–106. For a counter-argument to Mison's position, see J. Dressler, "When 'heterosexual' men kill 'homosexual' men: reflections on provocation law, sexual advances and the 'reasonable man' standard" (1995) 85 *Journal of Criminal Law and Criminology* 726–763.

[78] See the English case of *R. v Brown* (1776) 1 Leach 148; 168 E.R. 177. In *R. v Letenock* (1917) 12 Cr.App.R. 221, the Court of Appeal held that a *drunken* mistake could form the basis for a plea of provocation, but it is less likely that this approach would be followed in Scotland given the general approach taken to intoxication as a defence. Indeed, if, as is said in *Drury v HM Advocate*, 2001 S.L.T. 1013, provocation operates by negating *mens rea*, then provocation following on from a drunken mistake may be regarded as a case where the accused would have had *mens rea* but for his intoxication, meaning that *mens rea* is presumed by applying a legal fiction (see above, para.8.10).

[79] See above, para.10.04.

[80] The position might, however, be different in a jurisdiction which does not adopt such a restrictive approach to the categories of recognised provocation. *Cf.* D. O'Connor and P.A. Fairall, *Criminal Defences* (3rd edn, 1996), para.11.28. Dressler has also argued for unreasonable mistakes of fact to be excluded from the scope of the plea, although he would not adopt a restrictive approach to the question of what may be considered provocation. J. Dressler: "Why keep the provocation defense? Some reflections on a difficult subject" (2002) 86 *Minnesota Law Review* 959–1002 at p.1000.

[81] See above, paras 12.22–12.23.

[82] 1941 J.C. 59.

cooled—killed them from motives of revenge",[83] they should convict him of murder and not culpable homicide. The fact that the killing is deliberate does not bar the plea of provocation, provided that the accused was not "master of his emotions".[84]

The point might be thought to be theoretically awkward, because it can be argued that if a person has genuinely lost self-control, there is no basis for convicting him of any criminal offence and so he should be acquitted on the basis that his conduct is involuntary.[85] While such an argument is superficially attractive, it is based on a misconception, as *total* loss of self-control is not required for a successful plea of provocation.[86]

While there are obvious difficulties in delineating degrees of self-control (and it is doubtful that such a task would be worthwhile), the point does not appear to pose difficulties in practice, and there is no evidence that juries are encouraged to take an overly restrictive approach to the plea because of the reliance on the concept of self-control. More difficulty, perhaps, is caused by the requirement that the loss of self-control must have followed immediately upon the provocation.

Immediacy and loss of self-control

The plea of provocation will be unavailable unless the killing is an immediate response to the provocation.[87] In *Thomson v HM Advocate*,[88] the accused killed his business partner after a minor altercation. The accused drew attention to a history of acrimonious business dealings (essentially claiming that the deceased had been cheating him). The appeal court took the view that: 10.17

> "far from supporting a plea of provocation, the evidence of the breakdown in the business relations, and the appellant's belief that he was being cheated, would provide a clear motive for murder. In all the reported cases, where provocation has been allowed to be considered by the jury, there has been some element of immediate retaliation to provocative acts. In the present case, that element is absent."[89]

The basis for excluding the plea in such cases, according to Hume, is that the interval between the provocation and the killing shows the accused "to have acted deliberately, and to have been master of his emotions".[90] This suggests that the point may, in fact, be evidential rather than

[83] 1941 J.C. 59 at 62.

[84] Hume, i, 252. The subheading in Hume's *Commentaries* at this point ("No excuse if the killing be deliberate") is liable to mislead. The law is correctly stated in the text: the plea is excluded if the accused "appears to have acted deliberately *and* to have been master of his emotions" (emphasis added). See also Gordon, para.25.16.

[85] C. Howard, *Australian Criminal Law* (2nd edn, 1970), p.323, criticised by A.J. Ashworth, "The doctrine of provocation" [1976] C.L.J. 292–320 at pp.314–315.

[86] Ashworth, fn.85 above, p.315.

[87] *David Peter* (1807) Hume, i, 253. *Cf. Walter Redpath* (1810) Hume, i, 252.

[88] 1986 S.L.T. 281.

[89] At 284 *per* the Lord Justice-Clerk (Ross).

[90] Hume, i, 252. It may be significant that Hume considered Scots and English law to be identical on this point. It has been argued that English law historically recognised a temporary loss of self-control as being sufficient without it also being "sudden" (as was later insisted upon in *Duffy* [1949] 1 All E.R. 932). See J. Horder, "Provocation and loss of self-control" (1992) 108 L.Q.R. 191–193.

substantive—in other words, that an interval is proof that the accused did not, in fact, lose self-control. There may, however, be cases where an interval is not factually incompatible with a genuine loss of self-control on the part of the accused,[91] which calls a strict application of the immediacy rule into question.

The point is particularly significant in cases involving cumulative provocation (notably by way of domestic violence), and as such has caused difficulties for the English courts.[92] In Scotland, the courts have not been required to fully confront the issue, as it appears that the Crown have frequently been willing to accept pleas of guilty to culpable homicide in cases where an accused (invariably female) has killed a violent partner.[93]

The objective condition: the "ordinary person"

10.18 *Drury v HM Advocate* establishes that a plea of provocation cannot succeed if the accused's response to the provocation has gone beyond that which might be expected of an ordinary person. It is not clear, however, to what extent characteristics of the accused may be attributed to this "ordinary person". What if the accused (for example) has a mental illness,[94] or is intoxicated?[95] Should the jury measure their reaction against that of a sober ordinary person with no mental illness, or can these characteristics be taken into account?

There is very little authority on this point in Scots law, beyond some *dicta* to the effect that a jury may not take into account the fact that an accused's capacity for self-control may have been affected by drink or drugs.[96] This may be because the "ordinary man" did not properly emerge as the objective limb of the provocation test until *Drury*, and a test of proportionality which requires the jury to consider the relationship between the provocation and the response does not obviously lend itself to subjectivization. In *Drury*, it was observed that:

> "Since in the present case it is not said that the appellant had any special characteristics which would have affected the way in which he acted, I do not need to consider how such a test is to be applied in the

[91] See *Chhay* (1994) 72 A.Crim.R. 1 at 13, *per* Gleeson C.J.: "times are changing, and people are becoming more aware that a loss of self-control can develop even after a lengthy period of abuse, and without the necessity for a specific triggering incident".

[92] See, generally, Law Commission, *Partial Defences to Murder* (Consultation Paper No. 173, 2003), paras 4.18–4.28.

[93] At least since *HM Advocate v Greig*, May 1979, unreported (see the Casebook, para.10.42) where the jury convicted of culpable homicide rather than murder despite strong directions by the trial judge to the effect that there was no basis for a successful plea of provocation. See J. Chalmers, C.H.W. Gane and F. Leverick, "Partial defences to homicide in the law of Scotland: a report to the Law Commission for England and Wales", in Law Commission, *Partial Defences to Murder* (Consultation Paper No. 173 (Appendices), 2003), pp.151–183, 181–183; C. Connelly, "Women who kill violent men", 1996 Jur. Rev. 215–217.

[94] As in *R. v Smith (Morgan)* [2001] 1 A.C. 146.

[95] As in *R. v Morhall* [1996] A.C. 90.

[96] *Berry v HM Advocate* (1976) S.C.C.R. (Supp.) 156 at 157, *per* Lord Keith. See also *HM Advocate v McKean*, 1997 J.C. 32. The jury in the latter case was also directed to take the accused's "general psychological state" into account, but this may have been a reference to her distress at learning of her partner's infidelity rather than to any abnormality of mind. See also *HM Advocate v Robert Smith* (1893) 1 Adam 34, where the accused was found to be suffering from diminished responsibility brought on by cumulative provocation, but because the case could be dealt with as one of diminished responsibility, no question of subjectivization arose.

case of an accused who comes, for instance, from a particular minority ethnic background or who suffers from a particular physical handicap or defect in personality which might have affected his reaction. In other jurisdictions, where matters are regulated by statute, these questions have been hotly debated and they have recently divided the Privy Council, the New Zealand Court of Appeal and the House of Lords. I therefore prefer to express no view on the point, unless and until it arises for discussion."[97]

In the more recent case of *Cochrane v HM Advocate*,[98] it was held that, in considering a plea of coercion, the jury should consider "whether an ordinary sober person of reasonable firmness, sharing the characteristics of the accused, would have responded as the accused did".[99] The jury could not, therefore, take into account evidence from a psychologist that the accused was "on the borderline mentally handicapped range" and a "highly compliant individual".[1] The appeal court upheld the correctness of this decision, but observed (without reaching any conclusive view) that different considerations might apply to the plea of provocation, given that provocation is mitigatory rather than exculpatory in effect.[2]

This is as much as Scots law has had to say on the subject.[2a] As was noted in *Drury*,[3] the question is one which has proved controversial in other jurisdictions, particularly as a result of the controversial decision in *R. v Smith (Morgan)*.[4] It is not appropriate to rehearse the entire debate here, which has a long history prior to *Smith*, but it may be briefly sketched out as follows. In *Smith*, a majority of the Appellate Committee held that *all* the personal characteristics of the defendant—including a lack of self-control—were to be taken into account in deciding whether he was in fact provoked to kill as he did. The decision was strongly criticised,[5] and the point was recently revisited by nine judges sitting as the Judicial Committee of the Privy Council in *Attorney-General for Jersey v Holley*.[6] In that case, a majority of the Committee held that *Smith* was **10.19**

[97] 2001 S.L.T. 1013 at [29], *per* the Lord Justice-General (Rodger), referring to *Luc Thiet Thuan v The Queen* [1997] A.C. 131; *R. v Rongonui* [2000] 2 N.Z.L.R. 385 and *R. v Smith (Morgan)* [2001] 1 A.C. 146.

[98] 2001 S.C.C.R. 655. See above, paras 5.20–5.22.

[99] At [29] *per* the Lord Justice-General (Rodger).

[1] At [7] *per* the Lord Justice-General (Rodger).

[2] See 2001 S.C.C.R. 655 at [25], *per* the Lord Justice-General (Rodger).

[2a] See, however, *Bone v HM Advocate*, 2006 S.L.T. 164, where the appellant was convicted of the culpable homicide of her daughter by witnessing and countenancing an assault upon the child by her co-accused. Expert evidence had been led at trial to the effect that she had severely impaired mental functioning and was affected by three forms of personality disorder. In allowing her appeal against conviction, it was held that the jury should have been directed that, in deciding whether she had failed to take reasonable steps to prevent the assault on the child, they should have had regard to her physical and psychological condition.

[3] See above, para.10.18.

[4] [2001] 1 A.C. 146.

[5] See, in particular, T. Macklem and J. Gardner, "Compassion without respect? Nine fallacies in *R. v Smith*" [2001] Crim. L.R. 623–635. The question was recently considered by the Law Commission: see *Partial Defences to Murder* (Law Com. No. 290, 2004), where, amongst other recommendations, it is suggested (at para.3.110) that the jury should be entitled to take into account the defendant's age, but no other personal characteristic.

[6] [2005] UKPC 23. In *R. v James* [2006] EWCA Crim 14, the Court of Appeal confirmed that *Holley* should be regarded as overriding *Smith* despite being a decision of the Judicial Committee and not the Appellate Committee of the House of Lords.

wrongly decided. The majority referred approvingly to Lord Diplock's remarks, in *R. v Camplin*,[7] on how a judge should direct the jury on this question:

> "He should . . . explain to them that the reasonable man referred to in the question is a person having the power of self-control to be expected of an ordinary person of the sex and age of the accused, but *in other respects* sharing such of the accused's characteristics as they think would affect the gravity of the provocation to him; and that the question is not merely whether such a person would in like circumstances be provoked to lose his self-control but also whether he would react to the provocation as the accused did."[8]

It will be noted that such a direction permits the jury to take into account personal characteristics of the accused, beyond age and sex, which are relevant to the gravity of the provocation, and thus avoids the absurdity of (for example) the case where an impotent man is taunted about his lack of virility, but the jury is asked to consider how such taunts might affect a hypothetical reasonable man, not suffering from impotence.[9] Beyond this, however, personal characteristics of the defendant are to be left out of account. The problem of "characteristics relevant to gravity" is necessarily more acute in a jurisdiction which recognises provocation by words alone. In Scotland, where provocation must be by violence or infidelity, it is less likely to arise as a live issue, which is another explanation for the matter not having yet come before the courts. If it does though, it is submitted that a direction in the terms quoted would be appropriate.

The "reasonable retaliation" rule

10.20 As was noted earlier, the "ordinary person" test did not form part of the Scots law of provocation before the decision in *Drury v HM Advocate*.[10] Prior to *Drury*, the requirement was one of proportionality: the provocation "must bear a reasonable relation to the resentment which it excites".[11] At one point, it was held that this meant that "cruel excess" in retaliation would bar the plea,[12] but the appeal court later disapproved this terminology (as it was already used in the law of self-defence, and thus might lead to confusion in the context of provocation), preferring instead to say that "the retaliation used by the accused must not be

---

[7] [1978] A.C. 705.

[8] At 717, and quoted in *Holley* at [10], *per* Lord Nicholls of Birkenhead (emphasis added by Lord Nicholls).

[9] *Bedder v DPP* [1954] 1 W.L.R. 1119.

[10] 2001 S.L.T. 1013.

[11] *HM Advocate v Smith*, High Court at Glasgow, February 1952, unreported, *per* the Lord Justice-General (Cooper) (reported on another point at 1952 J.C. 66), quoted in *Drury v HM Advocate*, 2001 S.L.T. 1013 at [33], *per* the Lord Justice-General (Rodger). Lord Justice-General Cooper had previously been quoted as using the phrase "reasonable retaliation" (see Gordon, para.25.19 and previous editions), although the appeal court had earlier noted that the word "relation" should probably be substituted for "retaliation": see *Robertson v HM Advocate*, 1994 S.L.T. 1004. It is not clear whether Lord Rodger is correcting an error in the text as quoted in Gordon's *Criminal Law* or emending Lord Cooper's original charge.

[12] *Lennon v HM Advocate*, 1991 S.C.C.R. 611.

grossly disproportionate to the violence which has constituted the provocation".[13]

It might be thought that a proportionality requirement is unnecessary if an "ordinary person" test is to be invoked; ordinary persons presumably do not, after all, react in a grossly disproportionate fashion. However, the *Drury* court declined to overrule the earlier authorities which had laid down a requirement of proportionality:

> "... we did not in the event hear any substantial argument as to the validity of the requirement, as a matter of law, that in the case of provocation by assault the retaliation should not be grossly disproportionate to the assault constituting the provocation. I accordingly express no view on the point, except to note that, even in England and New Zealand, where there is no requirement that, as a matter of law, the response should be proportionate to the provocation, the nature and degree of the accused's response are nonetheless aspects of the evidence to which the jury can have regard when deciding whether the accused reacted in the way in which an ordinary man would have been liable to react."[14]

The logical consequence of this seems to be that the earlier decisions requiring proportionality must remain binding upon trial judges. The point might be important in a case such as *Robertson v HM Advocate*,[15] where the accused had responded to the deceased's (relatively minor) provocation[16] by repeatedly stabbing the accused in a manner which the Crown pathologist considered to indicate "an assailant who had completely lost control of his temper".[17] Because of the requirement of proportionality, the plea could not succeed. But if no such requirement exists, a jury might, at least theoretically, conclude that the ordinary person could have been liable to react in a disproportionate fashion, and thereby accept the plea.[17a]

Misdirected retaliation

What is the rule where A is provoked by B, and retaliates by killing C?[18] **10.21**
The point is not as unlikely as it may seem at first sight. For example, suppose that C intercedes to prevent A attacking B and is killed himself as a result.[19] The point has not been fully considered by the Scottish courts. One case which is briefly noted by Hume suggests that the plea of

---

[13] *Robertson v HM Advocate*, 1994 S.L.T. 1004 at 1006, *per* the Lord Justice-Clerk (Ross). See also *Low v HM Advocate*, 1994 S.L.T. 277.

[14] *Drury* at [35], *per* the Lord Justice-General (Rodger), under reference to *Phillips v The Queen* [1969] 2 A.C. 130 at 138C-D, *per* Lord Diplock; *R. v Campbell* [1997] 1 N.Z.L.R. 26, lines 10–15, *per* Eichelbaum C.J.; *R. v Rongonui* [2002] 2 N.Z.L.R. 425 at [136]–[138], *per* Elias C.J.

[15] 1994 J.C. 245.

[16] The provocation was alleged to have arisen "partly by the act of the deceased in laying his hand on the appellant's upper thigh and requesting a kiss, and partly by the assault both by presenting a knife at the appellant with a similar demand for a kiss." See *Robertson*, at p.249.

[17] At 249.

[17a] The question of whether a proportionality requirement continues to form part of the Scots law of provocation was under consideration by a Full Bench at the time of writing: see *Gillon v HM Advocate*, 2005 G.W.D. 33-627.

[18] This discussion assumes that A is aware that B is responsible for the provoking act. As to the situation where A mistakenly believes that C is responsible, see above para.10.15.

[19] As in *R. v Scriva (No. 2)* [1951] V.L.R 298.

provocation should be open to the accused in such a case, although the facts are not entirely clear.[20] The authorities in other jurisdictions are mixed,[21] although courts have sometimes been compelled to conclude that the plea is unavailable because of the wording of statutory provisions on the defence and have not been free to consider the issue as one of principle.[22]

It is submitted that the Scottish courts should hold that the plea is not excluded in such cases. As was noted earlier, the plea of provocation in Scots law contains elements of both justification and excuse: the accused is justified in his anger, but merely partially excused in having acted on that anger. Provided that there is a sufficient basis for the accused having been provoked,[23] then, if an ordinary person would have been liable to act against a third party in the way in which he did, the plea should not be barred. Because ordinary persons are unlikely to act against third parties in this way, the plea will be more difficult to sustain, but in principle it should remain available.

Self-induced provocation

10.22 Hume was firmly of the view that, if the provocation could be said to have been self-induced (that is, the accused had himself initially provoked the deceased), then the accused could not rely on the deceased's provocation to reduce his crime to culpable homicide:

> "If John strike James a blow with the hand, and James return it with severe blows of a staff; whereupon John draws, but gives James time to do the like, and thus they fight and James is killed; this is murder by the Scottish practice; however such a case might be resolved in the courts of England."[24]

Gordon suggests that this is "probably no longer the law", but the point does not appear to have been addressed in any modern Scottish case. The leading English cases of *R. v Edwards*[25] (actually a decision of the Privy

---

[20] *John Christie* (1733) Hume, i, 245. See also Gordon, para.25.30. *Cf.*, however, Hume, i, 240, who appears to have found it of significance that the victim of a provoked killing was "guilty of a wrong [and] justly deserved to receive, upon the spot, a severe chastisement of his person." In *HM Advocate v McKean*, 1996 S.C.C.R. 402, a case of provocation based on a revelation of infidelity, the revelation was made by a third party (the child of the accused's partner). This is, however, not a proper case of "misdirected retaliation": the wrong has still been committed by the party towards whom the accused acts violently.

[21] Provocation is excluded in most Australian jurisdictions in such cases: see, e.g. *R. v Kenney* [1983] 2 V.R. 470, noted in D. O'Connor and P.A. Fairall, *Criminal Defences* (3rd edn, 1996), para.11.14. In England, provocation would have been unavailable at common law in such circumstances (*R. v Simpson* (1915) 11 Cr.App.R. 218; *R. v Duffy* [1949] 1 All E.R. 932), but is now available as a result of the statutory language found in s.3 of the Homicide Act 1957: see *R. v Twine* [1967] Crim. L.R. 710; *R. v Davies* [1975] Q.B. 691.

[22] See O'Connor and Fairall, fn.21 above, paras 11.14–11.15. In *R. v Kauba-Paruwo* [1963] P & N.G.L.R. 18, the Supreme Court of Papua New Guinea appeared to regret being bound by statutory provisions to this effect.

[23] *cf.* F. McAuley, "Anticipating the past: the defence of provocation in Irish law" (1987) 50 M.L.R. 133–157 at p.143, who argues that the plea should not be available in such cases: as C has not acted unlawfully, his actions "cannot be relied on as a basis for retaliatory action of any kind". However, the plea of provocation does not require that the deceased be at fault, simply that the accused's anger be justified. Fault on the part of the deceased will normally be present, but should not be regarded as essential.

[24] Hume, i, 248.

[25] [1973] A.C. 648.

Council) and *R. v Johnson*[26] provide some guidance as to how the point might be addressed, but the point remains an open one in Scots law.[27]

In *R. v Edwards,*[28] the defendant had been blackmailing the victim. During a meeting between the two, the victim attacked the defendant with a knife and the defendant managed to wrestle the knife from the victim before stabbing and killing him. The trial judge withdrew provocation from the jury on the basis that the provocation was self-induced by the defendant's blackmailing conduct. The Privy Council disagreed and held that where the reaction of the person blackmailed went beyond what might reasonably be predicted as a result of the defendant's conduct, the defendant should not be denied the partial defence of provocation. It was said, however, that the plea should be ruled out where the defendant was responding to the "predictable results" of his own blackmailing conduct.[29]

In *R. v Johnson,*[30] however, it was held that the Privy Council had taken **10.23**
too restrictive a view of the issue. Here, the defendant had behaved "in an unpleasant way" in a nightclub. The victim poured beer over him and pinned him to a wall and in response the defendant produced a flick knife and killed her. Provocation was not left to the jury on the basis that it had been self-induced. On appeal, this was said to be incorrect, no such restriction being found in the statutory formulation of the plea in English law.[31] The court held that it is for the jury to decide whether or not the provocation was enough to make a reasonable man[32] do as the defendant did, taking into account all of the circumstances, including whether or not the provocation was self-induced.[33]

Both of these cases deal with provocation by violence. In the Australian case of *R. v Allwood,*[34] it was said that the allegedly provoking remarks of the deceased could not be relied upon by the defendant, as he had "sought out the deceased", "was determined to speak with her [and] selected the subject matter and controlled the course of the conversation", while "he knew the answers that could be expected from her".[35] The point is of less importance in Scots law, given that the only recognised form of provocation by words is a revelation of infidelity, and that an actor who already knows that his partner has been unfaithful cannot avail himself of the plea when the revelation is repeated a second time.[36] Nevertheless, it may be that the actor who deliberately seeks out a confrontation, suspecting infidelity, is not entitled to the defence if his fears prove to be correct —although that is one possible interpretation of the facts of *HM Advocate v Hill,*[37] where the plea was left to (and accepted by) the jury.

---

[26] [1989] Crim. L.R. 738.

[27] See also A.J. Ashworth, "Self-induced provocation and the Homicide Act" [1973] Crim. L.R. 483–492.

[28] [1973] A.C. 648.

[29] At 658.

[30] [1989] Crim. L.R. 738.

[31] Homicide Act 1957, s.3.

[32] In Scotland, the "ordinary person": see above, para.10.18.

[33] This less restrictive approach was also followed in *R. v Baille* [1995] Crim. L.R. 739.

[34] (1975) 18 A.Crim.R. 120.

[35] At 133 *per* Crockett J.

[36] *McCormack v HM Advocate*, 1993 S.L.T. 1158, noted above, para.10.12.

[37] 1941 J.C. 59.

The Effect of a Successful Plea of Provocation

10.24 A successful plea of provocation will reduce murder to culpable homicide. For a period in the twentieth century, it appears to have been thought that a successful plea might go further and render the accused guilty merely of assault. While directions to this effect were given by trial judge in at least two cases,[38] the correctness of such directions was doubted elsewhere,[39] and the appeal court later ruled that the plea could not have this effect.[40]

Where the charge is one of attempted murder, the position is less clear. It appears that the appropriate verdict is one of guilty of assault.[41] It has been argued that it is unnecessary to reduce the offence in such cases, as attempted murder carries no fixed penalty.[42] Although this is correct, the principle of "fair labelling" remains important, and if it is inappropriate to describe someone who kills under provocation as a murderer, it must be equally inappropriate to describe someone who has attempted to kill under provocation as having attempted to commit murder.

Provocation as a Defence to Crimes Other than Murder

10.25 The discussion of provocation in this chapter has, up until now, been confined to the applicability of provocation as a partial defence in murder cases. It has, however, sometimes been suggested that provocation can operate as a complete defence (rather than just a plea in mitigation) to assault. In *Hillan v HM Advocate*,[43] the accused claimed that he had been induced to enter the cubicle of a public lavatory, whereupon the complainer had made indecent suggestions to him, and that he had then struck the complainer. He pled both self-defence and provocation, and the sheriff-substitute found him guilty of "assault under provocation". On appeal, the conviction was quashed. The Lord Justice-Clerk (Aitchison) observed that:

> "Provocation is frequently a plea in reduction of the quality of the crime, as where it is sufficient to reduce the crime of murder to culpable homicide. But also in certain cases it may amount to a complete defence to the crime libelled, so that, on its being satisfactorily established, the proper verdict is one of acquittal. Again, it may neither reduce the quality of the crime nor afford a complete defence, but only be effectual to establish mitigating circumstances

---

[38] *HM Advocate v Gilmour*, 1938 J.C. 1; *McCluskey v HM Advocate*, 1959 J.C. 39.

[39] *HM Advocate v Sheppard*, 1941 J.C. 67; *HM Advocate v Delaney*, 1945 J.C. 138.

[40] *McDermott v HM Advocate*, 1973 J.C. 8. This is consistent with the rule that any assault which causes death is necessarily at least culpable homicide: see *Bird v HM Advocate*, 1952 J.C. 23.

[41] *Brady v HM Advocate*, 1986 J.C. 68; *Salmond v HM Advocate*, 1992 S.L.T. 156. See also *HM Advocate v Blake*, 1986 S.L.T. 661 (a diminished responsibility case). This is theoretically problematic, as not all attempts to kill need involve an assault, but does not appear to have presented any difficulty in practice. See further, J. Chalmers, "Reforming the pleas of insanity and diminished responsibility: some aspects of the Scottish Law Commission's discussion paper" (2003) 8 S.L.P.Q. 79–94 at pp.86–87.

[42] Jones and Christie (2nd edn), para.9–66, although the authors do not repeat this view in the third edition (see para.9–65).

[43] 1937 J.C. 53.

that go to the sentence to be imposed. This distinction between the plea in justification and the plea in palliation should always be kept in view..."[44]

There can be no question of "reduction" of the crime outside of the law of homicide, but the suggestion that provocation may either justify assault *or* merely operate as a plea in mitigation is an important one. Unfortunately, having identified the distinction, the Lord Justice-Clerk does not clearly indicate how the distinction is to be drawn. His opinion may be read, however, as suggesting that provocation may be a complete defence to assault provided that (a) the provocation is by violence[45] and (b) the accused's retaliation does not amount to "cruel excess". If these criteria are not satisfied, then provocation would be merely a plea in mitigation.

Depending on the interpretation which is given to the term "cruel excess", it is difficult to imagine many instances of a successful provocation plea of this nature which would not also satisfy the criteria for self-defence. Indeed, Lord Mackay in *Hillan* appears to suggest that the case is to be regarded as one of provocation rather than self-defence because the accused might possibly have extricated himself from the situation without using quite as much force as he did.[46] Nevertheless, a minor excess of force in self-defence will not bar that plea, because it is recognised that proportionality between the attack and the response is a matter that should not be "weighed in too fine scales".[47] **10.26**

It may be, therefore, that the proper plea in *Hillan* would have been one of self-defence rather than provocation, and that the case should no longer be taken as authority for the existence of provocation as a complete defence to assault. Despite the fact that there is some historical support for such a defence,[48] the Lord Justice-General (Rodger) took the view in *Drury v HM Advocate* that it "has now fallen into disfavour":

> "The reason for any change is, presumably, that it is nowadays thought that, with an organised police force throughout the land, an individual can never be justified in resorting to violence to deter and punish his assailant."[49]

That view, while *obiter*, should probably be taken as an accurate statement of the modern law. It is, however, arguable that because the *Drury* court treats provocation as negating the "wickedness" required for the *mens rea* of murder, provocation should also be regarded as negating

---

44 1937 J.C. 53 at 58.

45 The question of provocation by infidelity was not raised in *Hillan*. In *HM Advocate v Callander*, 1958 S.L.T. 24 (a case of assault where provocation by infidelity was claimed) it appears to have been assumed that acquittal on the basis of provocation was not an option which was open to the jury, but in that case the accused's response (assault with a bottle to severe injury) would clearly have fallen foul of any "cruel excess" rule.

46 See 1937 J.C. 53 at 62: "To my thinking it is rather monstrous that, if there was any sexual approach of the sort indicated here, a young man with proper morals who endeavours to escape from it should be held properly subjected to a criminal blot on his record because it may possibly be that he could have got rid of the old man's bestiality a little more easily, which at the same time he did him no actual physical hurt other than bleeding his nose."

47 *HM Advocate v Doherty*, 1954 J.C. 1 at 5, *per* Lord Keith. See above, para.3.15.

48 See Hume, i, 334–334; Macdonald, 116; *Isabella Cobb or Fairweather* (1836) 1 Swin. 354 at 391, *per* Lord Moncrieff.

49 *Drury v HM Advocate*, 2001 S.L.T. 1013 at [16], *per* the Lord Justice-General (Rodger).

"evilness" in the *mens rea* of assault (that is, evil intent).[50] It seems clear, however, that this was not a conclusion intended by the *Drury* court.[51] It has also been observed that if provocation were a complete defence to assault, then this would pose difficulties with regard to the current practice of allowing provocation to reduce attempted murder to assault, since it might entail the consequence that a person who attempted to kill under provocation was guilty of no offence at all, which clearly cannot be correct.[52]

[50] *Smart v HM Advocate*, 1975 J.C. 30; *Lord Advocate's Reference (No. 2 of 1992)*, 1993 J.C. 43.

[51] For further discussion, see J. Chalmers, "Collapsing the structure of criminal law", 2001 S.L.T. (News) 241–245 at pp.243–244. Such an approach to the meaning of "evil" in "evil intent" would be difficult to reconcile with *Lord Advocate's Reference (No. 2 of 1992)*, where it was said (at 49 *per* the Lord Justice-Clerk (Ross)) that "[i]t has often been said that evil intention is of the essence of assault... But what that means is that assault cannot be committed accidentally or recklessly or negligently".

[52] M.G.A. Christie, "The coherence of Scots criminal law: some aspects of *Drury v HM Advocate*", 2002 Jur. Rev. 273–290 at pp.289–290.

Chapter 11

DIMINISHED RESPONSIBILITY

Theoretical Basis

The plea of diminished responsibility, on the basis of an abnormality of mind suffered by the accused at the relevant time, permits a conviction for culpable homicide where he would otherwise be convicted of murder. It is regarded as distinctively Scottish and has formed the basis for statutory reform in a number of jurisdictions—most notably in its incorporation into English law in the Homicide Act 1957. Nevertheless, it has not always been enthusiastically accepted by the Scottish courts. In *Kirkwood v HM Advocate*, Lord Normand opined that "there is no doubt that the defence of impaired responsibility is somewhat inconsistent with the basic doctrine of our criminal law that a man, if sane, is responsible for his acts, and, if not sane, is not responsible".[1] Such a position—that there is no intermediate state between responsibility and irresponsibility—may seem initially attractive, and it appears to have formed the basis of a number of arguments against the recognition of "diminished responsibility" defences.[2] **11.01**

Insofar as the argument rests on the concept of "responsibility", however, it is merely linguistic. "Responsibility", here, is a legal concept, not medical, psychological or philosophical.[3] An argument which demonstrates that responsibility cannot be diminished, even if successful, can serve only to show that the doctrine is inappropriately named, not that its existence, scope or effects are in any way objectionable. It must be remembered that the plea has not always been referred to as "diminished responsibility", as demonstrated by Lord Normand's use of slightly different terminology, and in *Dingwall*, Lord Deas spoke of culpable homicide including "murder with extenuating circumstances".[4] As the appeal court recognised in *Lindsay v HM Advocate*,[5] the doctrine is best regarded simply as a plea in mitigation. If that characterisation of the plea is accepted, the objections to its recognition become more difficult to state, unless one is prepared to make the unlikely argument that

---

[1] 1939 J.C. 36 at 41, *per* the Lord Justice-General (Normand). See also *HM Advocate v Higgins* (1913) 7 Adam 229 at 233, *per* Lord Johnston: "I can understand limited liability in the case of civil obligation, but I cannot understand limited responsibility for a criminal act. I can understand irresponsibility, but I cannot understand limited responsibility—responsibility which is yet an inferior grade of responsibility."

[2] See, e.g. S.J. Morse, "Undiminished confusion in diminished capacity" (1984) 75 *Journal of Criminal Law and Criminology* 1–55, particularly at pp.35–36; R.F. Sparks, "Diminished responsibility in theory and practice" (1964) 27 M.L.R. 9–34.

[3] See *Galbraith v HM Advocate*, 2002 J.C. 1 at [22], *per* the Lord Justice-General (Rodger).

[4] (1867) 5 Irv. 466 at 479.

[5] 1997 J.C. 19.

blameworthiness can never be reduced, only negated.[6] The plea may be classified as a "partial excuse",[7] although whether it is regarded as a partial excuse or a plea in mitigation (classifications which are not incompatible) makes no difference to its practical operation.

In summary, the doctrine of diminished responsibility, as recognised in Scots law, is concerned with the blameworthiness of the accused. Its operation rests on twin justifications. First, it is necessary in order to avoid the fixed penalty (imprisonment for life) which currently attaches to a conviction for murder[8] (and, of course, it developed against the background of a mandatory sentence of death).[9] Secondly, it is a practical application of the principle of "fair labelling".[10] It recognises that the labelling of the accused as a criminal is a penalty in itself, particularly where the label attached is "murderer".[11] There are certain killers—even intentional killers—for whom that label is unfairly stigmatic and unrepresentative of the blame which fairly attaches to their actions.[12] For that reason, where the criteria for the diminished responsibility plea are satisfied, they are entitled to be convicted of culpable homicide rather than murder, and the trial judge is not to be bound by the mandatory penalty in sentencing them, although imprisonment for life remains an option.[13]

Diminished responsibility and *mens rea*

11.02 When, in *Drury v HM Advocate*,[14] the appeal court suggested that provocation operated by negating the *mens rea* of murder, in that it demonstrated that the accused's intention to kill, or recklessness, was not "wicked",[15] it might have been assumed that diminished responsibility operated in the same fashion. Despite this, when shortly after *Drury*, diminished responsibility was reshaped by a full bench in *Galbraith v HM Advocate*,[16] no mention was made of this "*mens rea*" approach and the court proceeded on the basis that diminished responsibility simply reduced murder to culpable homicide. This is consistent with the view, noted above, that diminished responsibility is essentially a plea in mitigation. It is possible, however, that an accused might plead in an

---

[6] See D. Husak, "Partial defenses" (1998) 11 *Canadian Journal of Law and Jurisprudence* 167–192 at pp.171–172.

[7] M. Wasik, "Partial excuses in the criminal law" (1982) 45 M.L.R. 520–433.

[8] CPSA 1995, s.205.

[9] See *Royal Commission on Capital Punishment 1949–1953: Report* (Cmd. 8932, 1953), para.413: "like the law relating to provocation ... it is a device to enable the courts to take account of a special category of mitigating circumstances in cases of murder and to avoid passing sentence of death in cases where such circumstances exist."

[10] See Ashworth, *Principles of Criminal Law*, pp.88–90.

[11] *Cf. Report of the Committee on Mentally Abnormal Offenders* (Cmnd. 6244, 1975), para.19.16 (suggesting that if the mandatory life sentence for murder were removed, diminished responsibility could also be abolished and the jury empowered to return a verdict noting "extenuating circumstances", the circumstances of extenuation not being restricted by law).

[12] This means, necessarily, that the verdict is not simply a description of the actions of the accused (that is, not simply a statement that the accused has killed intentionally or with wicked recklessness), but says something more general about the accused's culpability.

[13] *Kirkwood v HM Advocate*, 1939 J.C. 36.

[14] 2001 S.L.T. 1013.

[15] An approach which has been heavily criticised. See paras 3.11 and 10.05.

[16] 2002 J.C. 1.

appropriate case that an abnormality of mind meant that he did not possess the *mens rea* of murder at the relevant time—perhaps because he was unable to foresee the consequences of his actions. If the *mens rea* of murder is in fact negated in this way,[17] he would be entitled to be acquitted of murder without reference to any doctrine of diminished responsibility.[18]

Historical Development

The law prior to *HM Advocate v Dingwall*

Although the foundation of the plea of diminished responsibility in Scots law is generally taken to be Lord Deas's charge to the jury in *HM Advocate v Dingwall*,[19] it can in fact be traced back rather further than that, to a passage in Mackenzie's *Matters Criminal*: 11.03

> "It may be argued, that since the Law grants a total Impunity to such as are absolutely furious, that therefore it should by the Rule of Proportions, lessen and moderat the Punishments of such, as though they are not absolutely mad, yet are Hypocondrick and Melancholly to such a Degree, that it clouds their Reason; *qui sensum aliquem habent sed diminutum*..."[20]

As Walker has shown, this marks a significant difference in approach from Hale, writing in England around the same time, who recognised "partial insanity" but held that it "seems not to excuse ... in the committing of any offence for its matter capital".[21]

Although Walker suggests that "in all probability", Mackenzie's treatment "marks the point at which the Scottish lawyers began to diverge [from the English] on this subject",[22] Hume made some effort to halt any divergence. Rather than following Mackenzie's approach, he adopted that of Hale, arguing that if account were to be taken of "the inferior degrees of derangement", this could only be done by way of an application for mercy to the King.[23]

At the same time, however, Hume notes the 1704 case of *John Somerville*,[24] which may in fact be the first Scottish case to recognise a partial defence of diminished responsibility. Somerville, a town-officer of Edinburgh, "had shot a soldier of the town-guard, one of a party which had 11.04

---

[17] Subject, of course, to the rules excluding any "defence" of voluntary intoxication: see Ch.8.

[18] For discussion, see S.J. Morse, "Diminished capacity" in *Action and Value in Criminal Law* (S. Shute, J. Gardner and J. Horder (eds), 1993), pp.239–278, at pp.240–247.

[19] (1867) 5 Irv. 466.

[20] Mackenzie, 9. The Latin phrase may be translated as "who have a certain amount of awareness, though reduced": Walker, below, fn.21, p.145, fn.6.

[21] M. Hale, *The History of the Pleas of the Crown* (1736), p.30. See N. Walker, *Crime and Insanity in England, Volume 1: The Historical Perspective* (1968), Ch.8.

[22] At 140.

[23] Hume, i, 44 ("the culprit has to seek his relief, in the course of application for mercy to the King"). *Cf.* Hume (1st edn, 1797), i, 36 ("relief... must be sought either in the discretion of the prosecutor, who may restrict his libel to an ordinary pain, or in the course of application to the King for mercy"). The first edition's reference to prosecutorial discretion as a potential solution was subsequently excised by Hume.

[24] Hume, i, 42 and 44.

been sent to seize him, on his becoming outrageous".[25] Following what Hume describes as a "special and an awkward verdict" by the jury, the Court: "sustained the defence of his being mad, relevant to assoilzie him from the ordinary pain".[26]

Although both Hume and Alison describe the case as one where the plea of insanity (or furiosity) was "successful"[27]—and indeed it was, insofar as it spared Somerville's life—it does not appear to have resulted in a full acquittal.[28] Although he was absolved from "all corporal pains", a fine was imposed and assythment awarded.[29] Maclaurin, however, notes that Somerville was ordered to be imprisoned until a certificate of reconvalescence was granted.[30] The nature of the verdict and disposal in *Somerville* is, perhaps unavoidably, unclear: but Hume described it as a "middle course", "hardly to be approved of as a precedent".[31]

Be that as it may, mental disorder short of insanity gradually came to be recognised as a factor operating in mitigation of punishment, and the first use of what would eventually become the accepted terminology can be found in Bell's note of the 1835 case of *William Braid*, where it is said that a doctor was examined after Braid's guilty plea "to shew that the state of the pannel's mind diminished his responsibility, although it did not take it entirely away".[32] Such mitigation could, however, only operate in the case of offences "inferring arbitrary pains" (that is, where sentence of death was not fixed by law),[33] and in capital cases, the aberration of *Somerville* aside, it remained the case that the most the jury could do was to make a recommendation to mercy, in the hope that it would be acted upon.[34]

---

[25] Hume, i, 42.

[26] Hume, i, 43. The verdict is quoted in full in a footnote.

[27] Hume, i, 42; Alison, *Principles*, 649. Alison states that the jury's verdict was "such ... as amounted to sustaining the defence of insanity", but that is difficult to reconcile with the disposal of the case.

[28] Walker, above, fn.21, at p.141, regards it as a case "in which the court recognised ... partial insanity as a legal ground for mitigating punishment".

[29] Hume, i, 44.

[30] Maclaurin, 99.

[31] Hume, i, 44.

[32] Bell's Notes, 5. In *Galbraith v HM Advocate*, 2002 J.C. 1, the Lord Justice-General (Rodger) notes that the exact term "diminished responsibility" can be found as early as 1873, in an American textbook: *Galbraith*, at [24] (citing F. Wharton, *A Treatise on Mental Unsoundness, Embracing a General View of Psychological Law* (3rd edn, 1873), xiv).

[33] Bell's Notes, 5, and see the cases of *Thomas Henderson* (1835) (theft) and *James Ainslie* (1842) (assault) cited there. See also *Robert Bonthorn* (1763) Hume, i, 38 (assault); *Alex. Carr* (1854) 1 Irv. 464 (slandering, insulting and threatening judges); *Thos. Wild* (1854) 1 Irv. 552 (mobbing, rioting and assault); *Dorothea Pearson or Rodgers* (1858) 3 Irv. 105 (plagium).

[34] Hume cites the following examples: *Alexander Campbell* (1809) Hume, i, 38; *Susan Tinny* (1816) Hume, i, 41. See also *Robert Thomson* (1739) Hume, i, 40, Maclaurin, 85; *Agnes Crockat* (1756) Hume, i, 42, although it does not appear that the exercises of mercy in these two cases followed on from any recommendations of the jury, and both Hume and Alison (*Principles*, 648) appear to view the transportation-pardon issued in *Thomson* as correcting an error by the jury. See also *Samuel Rogers* (1831) Alison, *Principles*, 653, where the jury's recommendation was not given effect to. Gordon (para.11.11) notes that the jury "were more or less directed to bring in a recommendation" in *James Denny Scott* (1853) 1 Irv. 132 and *John McFadyen* (1860) 3 Irv. 650.

HM Advocate v Dingwall

11.05 The accused in *HM Advocate v Dingwall*[35] was described as "habitually and irreclaimably" addicted to drinking, and subject to occasional attacks of *delirum tremens*. Although kind to his wife when sober, the reverse was true when he had been drinking and the means of getting more drink were kept from him. While his access to whisky was rationed (being in debt, he had executed a trust deed in favour of a solicitor, who arranged his lodgings and authorised him five bottles of whisky a month), on Hogmanay he had drunk about half-a-dozen additional glasses at different houses and places in the town. After returning home (and drinking a further glass), he had an argument with his wife over a pint bottle of whisky which he thought she had hidden, and later on stabbed her to death as she was dozing. He was tried for murder, and the relevant part of Lord Deas' charge to the jury is reported as follows:

> "There remained the question whether the offence was anything short of murder? And here his Lordship said that it was very difficult for the law to recognise it as anything else. On the other hand, however, he could not say that it was beyond the province of the jury to find a verdict of culpable homicide if they thought that was the nature of the offence ... Culpable homicide in our law and practice, included what, in some countries, was called murder with extenuating circumstances. Sometimes the crime of culpable homicide approached the very verge of murder; and sometimes it was a very minor offence. The state of mind of a prisoner might, his Lordship thought, be an extenuating circumstance ... and he could not therefore exclude it from the consideration of the jury here ... in making up their minds whether, if responsible to the law at all, the prisoner was to be held guilty of murder or culpable homicide."[36]

11.06 The jury took little time to unanimously find Dingwall guilty of culpable homicide.[37] If this was revolutionary, it was not immediately recognised as such,[38] and in 1890 a writer in the *Juridical Review* still felt able to assert that the law "unfortunately does not ... recognise *degrees of criminal responsibility*, or responsibility with a diminished degree of imputability",[39] with *Dingwall* being dismissed as an example of a case of a judge "forced by an impulse of humanity, as he often is, to substantially advise the jury ... to find [the accused] guilty of a minor charge, on the testimony of the experts, in violation of the test asserted by himself".[40] Following *Dingwall*, however, the option of convicting an accused of culpable homicide rather than murder, on the ground of mental infirmity

---

[35] (1867) 5 Irv. 466.

[36] (1867) 5 Irv. 466 at 479–480.

[37] The length of their deliberations is very precisely recorded in the Scottish Law Reporter as having been 27 minutes: 4 S.L.R. 249 at 250–251.

[38] The Scottish Law Reporter report of the case is concerned primarily with questions as to the admissibility of evidence, and notes Lord Deas' directions on culpable homicide very briefly indeed (4 S.L.R. 249), while the case appears not to have been thought worthy of reporting in the Scottish Jurist, although a case heard at the same court the next day is reported: *Alexander Robertson* (1867) 5 Irv. 480; (1867–1868) 40 Sc. Jur. 1.

[39] E.F. Willoughby, "The criminal responsibility of the insane" (1890) 2 Jur. Rev. 220–233 at p.233 (emphasis in original).

[40] Willoughby, above, fn.39, at p.227. The text quoted is Willoughby's; the claim that *Dingwall* is an example of such a case is made by the editor of the *Review* in a footnote.

short of insanity, appears to have been regularly left to juries—mostly, but not always, by Lord Deas himself.[41]

In the case of *John McLean*[42] (a housebreaking case which was certified to the High Court for sentence on account of the peculiarity of the accused's mental condition), Lord Deas took the opportunity, speaking for himself and three other members of the court,[43] to cement the doctrine he had developed. Stating that allowing mental weakness to mitigate sentence "brings up an important general question, upon which ... Judges have not always been agreed",[44] he continued that:

> "I am of opinion that, without being insane in the legal sense, so as not to be amenable to punishment, a prisoner may yet labour under that degree of weakness of intellect or mental infirmity which may make it both right and legal to take that state of mind into account, not only in awarding the punishment, but in some cases, even in considering within what category of offences the crime shall be held to fall."[45]

At this stage, no sign of dissent amongst the judiciary can be discerned. Dissent was not, however, to be long in coming.

The twentieth-century cases prior to *HM Advocate v Savage*

11.07 In *HM Advocate v Aitken*,[46] the accused had killed his wife, who had been unfaithful. A plea of provocation would have been unsustainable, given that he had known of her infidelity for some time, while two medical witnesses testified that he was sane. His counsel, however, sought to argue that the facts of the case "shewed a long series of acts of grave provocation by the wife, tending to produce in the panel a morbid state of mind in which he ceased to have that full control over his actions which the law required" for guilt of murder.[47]

In making this submission, he relied on the earlier case of *HM Advocate v Robert Smith*,[48] where the accused's "mental equipoise" had become disturbed due to incessant persecution by his fellow workers,[49] culminating in Smith shooting the deceased after he was "booed" on one occasion. The jury had returned a verdict of culpable homicide, following evidence that the accused might have been "physiologically unable to resist provocation at the last" due to his mental instability.[50] The case had been roundly criticised as representing a "large and dangerous extension" to the doctrine in *Dingwall*,[51] even though Lord McLaren had stressed the

[41] The cases are as follows: *John Tierney* (1875) 3 Coup. 152; *Andrew Granger* (1878) 4 Coup. 86; *Thomas Ferguson* (1867) 5 Irv. 466; *Helen Thomson or Brown* (1882) 4 Coup. 596; *Francis Gove* (1882) 4 Coup. 598; *HM Advocate v Robert Smith* (1893) 1 Adam 34; *HM Advocate v Abercrombie* (1896) 2 Adam 163.

[42] (1876) 3 Coup. 334.

[43] The Lord Justice-Clerk (Moncrieff), Lords Young and Craighill.

[44] (1876) 3 Coup. 334 at 337.

[45] *ibid.*

[46] (1902) 4 Adam 88.

[47] At 93–94.

[48] (1893) 1 Adam 34

[49] At 50 *per* Lord McLaren.

[50] At 52 *per* Lord McLaren.

[51] See the anonymous note in the *Juridical Review*, (1893) 5 Jur. Rev. 268, arguing that there was "not the faintest trace of any recognised morbid condition" in the accused.

need for a "physiological" disturbance,[52] and it may be that Lord Stormonth Darling had criticisms of this nature in mind when he directed the *Aitken* jury that:

> "The rule of law ... that there might be a degree of insanity, not sufficient to destroy criminal responsibility, and yet sufficient to modify the quality of the crime, was one which had been undoubtedly received and acted on within comparatively recent times. But it was a rule which required to be applied with great caution. It could only be applied if a jury were satisfied that there was something amounting to brain disease."[53]

In the later case of *HM Advocate v Higgins*,[54] Lord Johnston went further, explicitly dissenting from the view put forward by Lord Deas in *Dingwall*.[55] This was, as Gordon observes, a "rearguard action", "possible only because of the absence of any Criminal Appeal Court".[56] Lord Johnston's concerns do not, however, appear to have been shared by other members of the High Court, who continued to leave the plea of "diminished responsibility" (although the terminology had not yet crystallised)[57] to juries in accordance with Lord Deas' views.[58] Similarly, the proposition that mental weakness short of insanity might serve to reduce murder to culpable homicide was uncritically received in the textbooks.[59]

HM Advocate v Savage

In *Savage*,[60] the accused was tried for murder, and lodged a special defence of insanity. The trial judge, the Lord Justice-Clerk (Alness), observed that murder might be reduced to culpable homicide in certain circumstances: **11.08**

> "Formerly there were only two classes of prisoner—those who were completely responsible and those who were completely irresponsible. Our law has now come to recognise in murder cases a third class, the

[52] For a discussion of the significance of this, see Gordon, para.11.17.

[53] (1902) 4 Adam 88 at 94–95. The jury found Aitken guilty as libelled, "with a strong and unanimous recommendation to mercy".

[54] (1913) 7 Adam 229.

[55] At 233: "[Lord Deas'] doctrine appears to have received some countenance from other judges. While I am bound to regard their views with the utmost respect, I desire very humbly to enter my protest against this doctrine being accepted as part of the criminal law and practice of Scotland until the matter is more deliberately dealt with by a larger Court than usually nowadays sits for the trial of criminal cases, and is authoritatively defined and explained. In particular, I cannot help feeling that the combination of the idea of defective or impaired or degenerate mental condition with the whole other circumstances of the case is fallacious, and really leads either to a groping after temporary instantity or to the involving the jury in the assumption of the quality of mercy which resides with the Crown."

[56] Gordon, para.11.18.

[57] The exact phrase "diminished responsibility" appears to have first been used in the reporter's headnote to *HM Advocate v Edmonstone* (1902) 2 S.L.T. 233, where Lord Guthrie (at 224) stated that "his responsibility must be held as diminished by the enfeeblement of his faculties". See also *William Baird* (1835) Bell's Notes 5 ("diminished his responsibility").

[58] See *HM Advocate v Graham* (1906) 5 Adam 212; *HM Advocate v Edmonstone* (1902) 2 S.L.T. 223. See also *HM Advocate v McClinton* (1902) 4 Adam 1 at 25–26, *per* the Lord Justice-General (Kinross).

[59] Anderson, 6; Macdonald (3rd edn, 1894), 16.

[60] 1923 J.C. 49.

class which I have described, namely those who, while they may not merit the description of being insane, are nevertheless in such a condition as to reduce the quality of their act from murder to culpable homicide."[61]

Following on from this, he went on to give what was subsequently taken to be a definition of the plea of diminished responsibility:

> "It is very difficult to put it in a phrase, but it has been put in this way: that there must be aberration or weakness of mind; that there must be some form of mental unsoundness; that there must be a state of mind which is bordering on, though not amounting to, insanity; that there must be a mind so affected that responsibility is diminished from full responsibility to partial responsibility—in other words, the prisoner in question must be only partially accountable for his actions. And I think one can see running through the cases that there is implied—as Lord Stormonth-Darling in terms said in [*Aitken*]—that there must be some form of mental disease ..."[62]

This formulation was subsequently adopted by trial judges in two cases, and in one of those was accepted by a Full Bench on appeal.[63] The term "diminished responsibility" crystallised around this time as well.[64] In the later case of *Connelly v HM Advocate*,[65] the appeal court interpreted Lord Alness' directions as listing a set of criteria,[66] which required to be read as a set of criteria (all of which required to be satisfied) rather than as alternatives. Most importantly, the requirement of "mental disease" was crucial: "it is the presence or absence of that particular characteristic, which has been variously described, which marks the borderline between what is acceptable and what is not".[67] Thereafter, in *Williamson v HM*

[61] At 50.

[62] At 51, citing *HM Advocate v Aitken* (1902) 4 Adam 88 (where Lord Stormonth-Darling had used the term "brain disease": see above, para.11.07).

[63] *HM Advocate v Braithwaite*, 1945 J.C. 55, *per* the Lord-Justice Clerk (Cooper); *Carraher v HM Advocate*, 1946 J.C. 108 at 111–112, *per* Lord Russell (the trial judge), and at 117, *per* the Lord Justice-General (Normand). Lord Alness' directions are also quoted by the Court of Appeal in *R. v Spriggs* [1958] 1 Q.B. 270, a case concerned with the proper interpretation of s.2 of the Homicide Act 1957. They do not appear to have been quoted to the jury in *Muir v HM Advocate*, 1933 J.C. 46, although the trial judge's directions are not clear from the report of that case.

[64] The first use by a judge of the exact phrase "diminished responsibility" is by the Lord Justice-General (Clyde) in *Muir v HM Advocate*, 1933 J.C. 46 at 48. See also *Kirkwood v HM Advocate*, 1939 J.C. 36 at 37, *per* the Lord Justice-General (Normand). Lord Keith later observed that he had not found the term "used by a judge before 1909", but this is probably a reference to the reporter's headnote in *HM Advocate v Edmonstone* (1909) 2 S.L.T. 223 rather than to a direct judicial quotation. See Keith, "Some observations on diminished responsibility", 1959 Jur. Rev. 109–118 at p.112.

[65] 1990 J.C. 349.

[66] Subsequently described as "precise criteria": *Williamson v HM Advocate*, 1994 J.C. 149 at 153, *per* the Lord Justice-General (Hope).

[67] 1990 J.C. 349 at 359, *per* the Lord Justice-General (Hope). See also *Martindale v HM Advocate*, 1994 S.L.T. 1093.

Advocate,[68] a case where the four expert witnesses agreed that the accused did not suffer from a mental illness, but agreed that he did have a personality disorder (or at least "abnormal traits in his personality"), the appeal court held that the trial judge had been correct to withdraw the plea of diminished responsibility from the consideration of the jury.[69]

Galbraith v HM Advocate

The accused in *Galbraith*[70] stood trial for the murder of her husband, whom she alleged had abused her over a period of years. One psychologist gave evidence that she was "suffering from a form of post-traumatic stress disorder", and another that she had been in a state of "learned helplessness" as a result of prolonged abuse.[71] It was noted that neither witness was medically qualified. A third expert witness, who was medically qualified, testified that the accused had been suffering from clinical depression at the relevant time. The trial judge, having quoted Lord Alness' directions in *Savage* to the jury, went on to direct them, unless they were able to accept the third expert's evidence, they "would not, in law, be entitled to sustain a plea of diminished responsibility because the element of some form of mental disease is an essential element in the plea".[72] The jury convicted her of murder, and her appeal was remitted to be heard by a bench of five judges.[73] **11.09**

The court concluded, in a single opinion delivered by the Lord Justice-General (Rodger), that it was wrong to regard Lord Alness' directions in *Savage* as having laid down a series of criteria for the defence. Although the report of *Savage* gives very little clue as to the facts of the case, Lord Rodger demonstrated by reference to newspaper reports of the trial that Savage's own claim to a verdict of culpable homicide appears, in fact, to have been based on having been drunk at the time (a matter which was in dispute), and a tendency to lose control of his actions when intoxicated.[74] Accordingly, the court concluded, Lord Alness, having left the matter to the jury, could not have intended the term "mental disease" to have the narrow meaning which it was given in later cases such as *Williamson*.[75]

If the *Savage* directions were not a definition, of course, this raised the question of what an appropriate definition of the plea was. The court noted that "both counsel found it much easier to tear down the somewhat fragile structure that our predecessors had erected than to suggest what we should raise up in its place".[76]

---

[68] 1994 J.C. 149.

[69] *cf.* R. Darjee and J. Crichton, "Personality disorder and the law in Scotland: a historical perspective" (2003) 14 *Journal of Forensic Psychiatry and Psychology* 394–425, who note at p.398 that, from the reported cases discussed in Gordon's *Criminal Law*, "it is clear that some people who would be described as personality disordered today were being found to be of diminished responsibility in homicide cases in the late nineteenth century".

[70] 2002 J.C. 1.

[71] At [7].

[72] At [11].

[73] As the appeal court notes, the basis for the jury's decision is not *ex facie* obvious and it may have been unrelated to the judge's directions on diminished responsibility. See [5].

[74] Although it is now established that intoxication is no basis for a plea of diminished responsibility (*Brennan v HM Advocate*, 1977 J.C. 38), decisions including *HM Advocate v Campbell*, 1921 J.C. 1 (cited in *Savage*, and overruled in *Brennan*) supported the proposition that voluntary intoxication might operate to reduce what would otherwise be murder to culpable homicide. See *Galbraith*, at [38].

[75] *Galbraith*, at [39].

[76] At [21].

After some discussion, the court concluded that the appropriate test was this: whether "at the relevant time, the accused was suffering from an abnormality of mind which substantially impaired the ability of the accused, as compared with a normal person, to determine or control his acts".[77] This test is remarkably similar to that found in s.2 of the (English) Homicide Act 1957,[78] although that may not be inappropriate given that s.2 was drafted in order to "introduce into English law the Scottish doctrine of diminished responsibility".[79] Alongside this general test, two specific abnormalities are excluded: any abnormality arising from voluntary intoxication,[80] or "psychopathic personality disorder".[81]

It is this test, therefore, which forms the basis of the modern law: the twin requirements of "abnormality of mind" and "substantial impairment", alongside the exclusion of certain specified abnormalities. There is, as yet, little case law addressing the interpretation of this test, but some guidance may legitimately be drawn from English case law given the similarity between the test formulated by the *Galbraith* court and the statutory language found in the 1957 Act.

The Modern Law

11.10 As the law presently stands, in order to find an accused guilty of culpable homicide on the basis of diminished responsibility, the jury must be satisfied that, at the relevant time, (1) the accused was suffering from an abnormality of mind, which was (2) recognised by the appropriate science; and (3) that this abnormality substantially impaired his ability, as compared with a normal person, to determine or control his acts.

It may not be necessary to tell the jury much more than this, in the same way as the English Court of Appeal, shortly after the passing of the Homicide Act 1957, was content to endorse judicial directions which did little more than leave the bare language of s.2 to be construed by the jury.[82] The definition may be glossed by incorporating Lord Rodger's observation in *Galbraith* that "in colloquial terms, there must, unfortunately, have been something far wrong with the accused, which affected the way he acted".[83] Difficult questions may arise, however, where the "abnormality" is argued to be one which is excluded from the scope of the

---

[77] 2002 J.C. 1 at [54], point 2. A colloquial gloss on this test is offered later, at point 4: "In every case, in colloquial terms, there must, unfortunately, have been something far wrong with the accused, which affected the way he acted".

[78] "Where a person kills or is a party to the killing of another, he shall not be convicted of murder if he was suffering from such abnormality of mind (whether arising from a condition of arrested or retarded development of mind or any inherent causes or induced by disease or injury) as substantially impaired his mental responsibility for his acts and omissions in doing or being a party to the killing." For criticism of this statutory wording and provisional proposals for reform, see *A New Homicide Act for England and Wales* (Consultation Paper No. 177, 2005), paras 6.34–6.61.

[79] HC Deb, col.318 (November 27, 1956) (statement of the Attorney-General). See further, J. Chalmers, "Abnormality and Anglicisation: first thoughts on *Galbraith v HM Advocate (No. 2)*" (2002) 6 Edin. L.R. 108–117.

[80] "brought on by the accused himself taking drink or controlled drugs or sniffing glue": 2002 J.C. 1 at [54], point 5.

[81] 2002 J.C. 1 at [54], point 5.

[82] *R. v Spriggs* [1958] 1 Q.B. 270, criticised by J.E. Hall Williams, "The Homicide Act, 1957, and diminished responsibility—an abdication of responsibility?" (1958) 21 M.L.R. 318–320.

[83] 2002 J.C. 1 at [54], point 4.

defence, and more so if such an abnormality is combined with one which is not excluded, for example, where intoxication acts to exacerbate the effects of post-traumatic stress disorder.[84]

"Abnormality of mind"

The *Galbraith* court did not discuss the meaning of the term "abnormality of mind" in great depth, and it may be that the term is not susceptible of much in the way of further definition. In the leading English case of *R. v Byrne*,[85] the Court of Appeal offered the following commentary of the same phrase as found in the Homicide Act 1957: **11.11**

> "... [it] means a state of mind so different from that of ordinary human beings that the reasonable man would term it abnormal. It appears to us to be wide enough to cover the mind's activities in all its aspects, not only the perception of physical acts and matters and the ability to form a rational judgment whether an act is right or wrong, but also the ability to exercise will-power to control physical acts in accordance with that rational judgment."[86]

This definition does two things: first, it emphasises the need for the abnormality to be significant in nature (although trivial abnormalities would fail at the "substantial impairment" hurdle in any case). Secondly, and more importantly, it emphasises the breadth of the concept.[87] It is only limited, it seems, by policy reasons, and the *Galbraith* court identified two types of abnormality of mind which are presently excluded from the scope of the plea: voluntary intoxication[88] and "psychopathic personality disorder".[89] Furthermore, it will not serve "merely to show that an accused person has a very short temper, or is unusually excitable and lacking in self-control".[90] Such a condition is not, however, "excluded"; it simply does not amount to an abnormality of mind for the purposes of the plea.

The policy reasons for the twin exclusions are not entirely clear.[91] Voluntary intoxication was firmly excluded as a basis for a plea of **11.12**

[84] As may have been the case in *HM Advocate v McLeod*, High Court at Forfar, October 24, 2002, unreported: see below, para.11.14.

[85] [1960] 2 Q.B. 396.

[86] At 403 *per* Lord Parker C.J., approved in *Rose v The Queen* [1961] A.C. 496 (PC).

[87] In English law, the scope of "abnormality of mind" is limited by the bracketed phrase which immediately follows it in s.2 of the Homicide Act 1957: "whether arising from a condition of arrested or retarded development of mind or any inherent causes or induced by disease or injury". See further, R.D. Mackay, "The abnormality of mind factor in diminished responsibility" [1999] Crim. L.R. 117–125.

[88] *Galbraith*, at [43]: "no mental abnormality ... which is brought on by the accused himself taking drink or drugs or sniffing glue". *Cf.* the Scottish Law Commission's *Discussion Paper on Insanity and Diminished Responsibility* (Scot. Law Com. D.P. No. 122, 2003), para.3.18, suggesting that intoxication is not within the scope of the plea in any case because "states of acute intoxication by themselves ... are not symptomatic of any underlying condition." There is, however, no basis in Scots law for requiring an "underlying condition" in order for the plea to succeed, and there might be good reasons for allowing a plea to succeed on the basis of *involuntary* intoxication. *Cf.* the position in New South Wales, where an "underlying condition" is expressly required by statute: Crimes Act 1900, s.23A(1).

[89] *Galbraith*, at [43]; *Carraher v HM Advocate*, 1946 J.C. 108.

[90] *HM Advocate v Braithwaite*, 1945 J.C. 55 at 58–59, *per* the Lord Justice-Clerk (Cooper); *Galbraith v HM Advocate*, 2002 J.C. 1 at [51].

[91] For further discussion, see J. Chalmers, "Reforming the pleas of insanity and diminished responsibility: some aspects of the Scottish Law Commission's discussion paper" (2003) 8 S.L.P.Q. 79–94 at pp.88–94.

diminished responsibility by a Full Bench in *Brennan v HM Advocate*,[92] but that decision was based on certain assumptions as to the nature of diminished responsibility which are no longer valid following *Galbraith*.[93] The exclusion is, however, broadly consistent with the general approach of the Scottish courts to any "defence" of intoxication.[94] Although the *Galbraith* court refers to the exclusion as applying to any mental abnormality "brought on by the accused himself", it is assumed that this refers only to transient abnormalities, and a permanent abnormality of mind caused by substance abuse remains a valid basis for the plea.[95] In principle, involuntary intoxication should also be a legitimate basis for the plea.[96]

The exclusion of "psychopathic personality disorder" is more problematic, however. Psychopathy is not, in fact, included in the two major international classifications of mental disorders,[97] and it is not clear to what extent conditions which are included in these classifications would be regarded as sufficiently analogous to psychopathy so as to be themselves excluded from the scope of the plea.[98] Although *Carraher v HM Advocate*[99] is sometimes interpreted—and indeed is so interpreted by *Galbraith*—as firmly excluding psychopathy from the scope of diminished responsibility, it is not quite as clear cut as that. The view has been taken elsewhere that it left the door open for a plea to be based on psychopathy in future cases,[1] and it appears that such pleas were in fact accepted in practice.[2] Furthermore, the decision appears to have been reached against the background of a fear "that psychiatrists might label all habitual criminals as psychopaths",[3] which might be thought to be unwarranted in modern practice.[4] The matter must depend on the evidence led in any particular case—particularly as it is unlikely that expert witnesses will unanimously adopt a diagnosis of "psychopathic personality disorder" in

---

[92] 1977 J.C. 38. See also *HM Advocate v MacLeod*, 1956 J.C. 20 at 22, *per* Lord Hill Watson: "If a man is not shown by the evidence to be within the category of one with a diminished responsibility when sober, he cannot place himself within the category of diminished responsibility by taking drink."

[93] Specifically, that a "mental disease" was required for the plea and that it could properly be understood as "borderline insanity". See further, Chalmers, above, fn.91, at p.90.

[94] See Ch.8.

[95] See *Galbraith*, at [52]; *Alexander Milne* (1863) 4 Irv. 301 at 343–344, *per* the Lord Justice-Clerk (Inglis).

[96] *cf. R. v O'Connell* [1997] Crim. L.R. 683 (effects of sleeping drug not a basis for a plea of diminished responsibility). It is submitted that the result in that case is a consequence of the language of s.2 of the Homicide Act 1957 and need not be followed by the Scottish courts.

[97] World Health Organisation, *International Classification of Diseases (ICD-10)* (1992); American Psychiatric Association, *Diagnostic and Statistical Manual of Mental Disorders (DSM-IV)* (1994).

[98] See J.H.M. Crichton, R. Darjee and D. Chiswick, "Diminished responsibility in Scotland: new case law" (2004) 15 *Journal of Forensic Psychiatry and Psychology* 552–565 at pp.557–558.

[99] 1946 J.C. 108.

[1] Lord Keith, "Some observations on diminished responsibility", 1959 Jur. Rev. 109–118 at p.115; T.B. Smith, *A Short Commentary on the Law of Scotland* (1962), p.160; *Minutes of Evidence Taken Before the Royal Commission on Capital Punishment* (1950), Q 5192 (evidence of the Faculty of Advocates).

[2] Darjee and Crichton, above, fn.69, at pp.406–410; *HM Advocate v Gordon* (1967) 31 J.C.L. 270.

[3] Darjee and Crichton, above, fn.69, at p.160. See also Gordon, para.11.21.

[4] On the incidence of psychopathy among the prison population, see D. Cooke, *Psychological Disturbance in the Scottish Prison System: Prevalence, Precipitants and Policy* (1994), pp.83–84.

isolation from other disorders, if indeed that term is used at all.[5] It is submitted that it would generally be undesirable to exclude particular diagnoses from the scope of the plea, particularly given the difficulties involved in directing a jury where a combination of excluded and non-excluded abnormalities are involved.[6]

The Scottish Law Commission has recently recommended statutory reform to the effect that psychopathy (or any other personality disorder) should not be excluded from the scope of the plea.[7]

Excluded and non-excluded abnormalities combined

Difficult questions arise when an accused who pleads diminished responsibility was voluntarily intoxicated at the relevant time. The issue has arisen in one case post-*Galbraith*, *HM Advocate v McLeod*.[8] In that case, the accused was suffering from post-traumatic stress disorder at the relevant time, and had also voluntarily inhaled butane gas. The trial judge directed the jury that they could not convict of culpable homicide if the gas inhalation was the "sole substantial cause" of his violent acts, but that they could accept the plea of diminished responsibility if they were satisfied that the post-traumatic stress disorder was a substantial cause (even if the intoxication was also a cause). **11.13**

This approach is open to criticism in that it suggests that the basis of the diminished responsibility plea is causal in nature: that is, that the abnormality of mind in some way "caused" the homicide. That is not, however, a question which the jury would normally be asked to consider in relation to a plea of diminished responsibility. In England, a causal approach to the problem of intoxication (as was formerly taken by the courts)[9] was heavily criticised, on the basis that it was inconsistent with the language of the Homicide Act 1957, which requires the jury to consider whether the abnormality of mind "substantially impaired" the "mental responsibility" of the accused.[10]

Because Scots law has not adopted the "mental responsibility" approach, but instead asks whether the accused's ability to "determine or control his acts" was substantially impaired, a causal approach is easier to defend. It may, however, be unnecessarily complex, and there is much to be said for simply asking the jury to consider whether—leaving the effects of intoxication out of account—the underlying condition is, in itself,

---

[5] In *HM Advocate v Menzies*, High Court at Edinburgh, September 29–October 8, 2003, the accused's plea of diminished responsibility appears to have been largely based on anti-social personality disorder (which might be regarded as analogous to psychopathy). A defence witness also gave evidence that the accused was suffering from hallucinations and paranoid schizophrenia. He was convicted of murder. See Crichton, Darjee and Chiswick, above, fn.98, at pp.561–562 ("Case 12").

[6] See below, para.11.13.

[7] *Report on Insanity and Diminished Responsibility* (Scot. Law Com. No. 195, 2004), paras 3.24–3.34. See also Law Commission, *A Criminal Code for England and Wales* (Law Com. No. 177, 1989). Clause 56(2) of the Draft English Code explicitly defines "mental abnormality" for the purposes of diminished responsibility as *including* "psychopathic disorder".

[8] High Court at Forfar, October 24, 2002, unreported. See *Report on Insanity and Diminished Responsibility* (Scot. Law Com. No. 195, 2004), para.3.38; J. Casey, "Intoxication and diminished responsibility", 2003 Jur. Rev. 331–334.

[9] Under English law prior to *R. v Dietschmann* [2003] 1 A.C. 1209, the jury were asked to consider whether, if the defendant had not taken drink, (i) he would have killed as he in fact did and (ii) he would have been under diminished responsibility when he did so. See *R. v Atkinson* [1985] Crim. L.R. 314; *R. v Egan* (1992) 95 Cr.App.R. 278.

[10] G.R. Sullivan, "Intoxicants and diminished responsibility" [1994] Crim. L.R. 156–162.

sufficient to meet the requirements of the plea.[11] This avoids the intoxicated accused being subjected to a causation requirement which is difficult to apply and is not applied to other pleas of diminished responsibility. Although it may seem artificial to ask the jury to disregard the effects of intoxication, the accused may in fact only have been assessed by expert witnesses when sober.

The situation will be even more difficult if the accused is diagnosed with a number of abnormalities of mind, one of which might be excluded on the basis that it amounts to psychopathy. In such a scenario, asking a jury to draw conclusions as to the causative effects of some abnormalities but not others is likely to be wholly unrealistic, and there may be no workable course other than to disregard the psychopathy "exclusion" in such cases.

Alcoholism and addiction to other intoxicating substances

11.14 The foregoing discussion of the effects of intoxication combined with another abnormality of mind assumes that the two are separable in some way. In many cases, however, the two may be linked, in that the abnormality of mind may be causally linked to the intoxication. In *HM Advocate v McLeod*,[12] the jury were directed that, just as evidence of intoxication was to be disregarded, so was any evidence of a causal link between the abnormality of mind and the intoxication:

> "... to the extent that PTSD [post-traumatic stress disorder] may have caused the accused to get into a habit of butane gas intoxication, that is not relevant to the defence of diminished responsibility ... PTSD is only relevant to the extent that it may have had a direct effect on the accused's mind ..."[13]

The position might be different, however, if the evidence were sufficient to suggest that the accused's capacity to avoid developing such a habit had itself been substantially impaired by the abnormality of mind.

In *R. v Tandy*,[14] the Court of Appeal was prepared to accept that intoxication induced by alcoholism was a relevant basis for a plea of diminished responsibility, but only if the "craving for drink" was such as to render the defendant's drinking involuntary.[15] This has been heavily criticised as effectively imposing a requirement of total impairment, rather than the "substantial impairment" of responsibility required by the English statute.[16]

---

[11] See *R. v Dietschmann* [2003] 1 A.C. 1209. Both the Scottish Law Commission and Dr Casey (above fn.8) equate the trial judge's approach in *McLeod* with that of the Appellate Committee in *Dietschmann*. It is submitted that the two are in fact significantly different, given that the approach taken in *Dietschmann* does not require the jury to consider questions of causation.

[12] High Court at Forfar, October 24, 2002, unreported.

[13] The quote is taken from J.H.M. Crichton, R. Darjee and D. Chiswick, "Diminished responsibility in Scotland: new case law" (2004) 15 *Journal of Forensic Psychiatry and Psychology* 552–565 at p.559.

[14] [1989] 1 W.L.R. 350. See also *R. v Inseal* [1992] Crim. L.R. 35.

[15] For criticism, see J. Tolmie, "Alcoholism and criminal liability" (2001) 64 M.L.R. 688–709 at pp.699–700, arguing that the court set "a requirement that even the most chronic alcoholic will find difficult to meet on the facts. Even if the alcoholic in question does not have choice about whether or not they will drink they will often have an apparent choice about when and where they commence drinking". See also G.R. Sullivan, "Intoxicants and diminished responsibility" [1994] Crim. L.R. 156–162 at pp.157–158.

[16] See Tolmie, above, fn.15, at pp.798–701; J. Goodcliffe, "*R v Tandy* and the concept of alcoholism as a disease" (1990) 53 M.L.R. 809–814.

"Recognised by the appropriate science" and the requirement of expert evidence

In *Galbraith*, Lord Rodger is quite clear that the abnormality of mind "must be one that is recognised by the appropriate science".[17] This suggests that the earlier view, expressed in particular by Lord Deas[18] and Lord Keith,[19] that a jury is entitled to find diminished responsibility in the absence of expert evidence is no longer to be regarded as correct. This requirement may be contrasted with Lord Normand's earlier protestation that the court "has a duty to see that trial by judge and jury according to law is not subordinated to medical theories",[20] but in modern practice it is difficult to envisage any scenario where the defence could be successfully pled in the absence of expert evidence.[21] **11.15**

In principle, the question of whether the accused was suffering from diminished responsibility is one for the jury, and not an expert witness.[22] Despite this, it is clear from the reported cases prior to *Galbraith* (and, indeed, *Galbraith* itself) that medical witnesses have in the past been asked without objection whether they considered that the accused was suffering from diminished responsibility.[23] Whether this practice will be affected by *Galbraith* remains to be seen. In a commentary on *Galbraith*, three forensic psychiatrists, acknowledging that expert witnesses have been criticised for "going beyond the boundaries of their expertise" in giving evidence in such cases,[24] suggested that the practice should change as a result:

> "This judgement appears to clarify the role of expert witnesses ... [It is] for the jury to decide to what degree 'abnormality of mind' reduces responsibility for what happened. The expert's role is therefore to comment on the presence of 'abnormality of mind' and how that abnormality affected the individual. It is not to opine, as in the pre-Galbraith era, whether an accused was 'suffering from diminished responsibility'."[25]

Lord Rodger's endeavour to formulate the test "in colloquial terms" as "there must, unfortunately, have been something far wrong with the accused, which affected to the way he acted"[26] may be seen as an attempt **11.16**

[17] 2002 J.C. 1 at [54], point 4.

[18] *HM Advocate v Gove* (1882) 4 Coup. 598 at 599.

[19] *Minutes of Evidence Taken Before the Royal Commission on Capital Punishment* (1950), Q 5192.

[20] *Carraher v HM Advocate*, 1946 J.C. 108 at 117.

[21] See *R. v Dix* (1981) 74 Cr.App.R. 306 at 311, *per* Shaw L.J. (noting that while the statutory formulation of the plea in English law "does not in terms require that medical evidence be adduced in support of a defence of diminished responsibility, it makes it a practical necessity if that defence is to begin to run at all").

[22] See *Walkers on Evidence*, para.16.1.3: "A question is normally inadmissible if its purpose is to elicit an opinion on the actual issue before the court." See also M. Redmayne, *Expert Evidence and Criminal Justice* (2001), pp.168–169.

[23] *Galbraith v HM Advocate*, 2002 J.C. 1 at [53]. See also the questions asked in *Connelly v HM Advocate*, 1991 S.L.T. 397.

[24] See, e.g. E. Griew, "The future of diminished responsibility" [1988] Crim. L.R. 75–87 at pp.82–84. Such criticism has not been confined to writing by lawyers: see D. Chiswick, "Use and abuse of psychiatric testimony" (1985) 290 *British Medical Journal* 975–977.

[25] J.H.M. Crichton, R. Darjee and D. Chiswick, "Diminished responsibility in Scotland: new case law" (2004) 15 *Journal of Forensic Psychiatry and Psychology* 552–565 at p.558.

[26] *Galbraith v HM Advocate*, 2002 J.C. 1 at [51].

to demedicalise the test and emphasise that the question is one for the jury, but the difficulty of achieving the aim of demedicalisation is demonstrated by a subsequent case where (the plea of diminished responsibility having been accepted by the Crown) a psychiatrist adopted exactly the language used by Lord Rodger.[27]

There are authorities in other jurisdictions which might be taken to suggest that a jury may not be entitled to reject a plea of diminished responsibility where there is unchallenged medical evidence that the accused is within the scope of the plea,[28] but that seems difficult to reconcile with the principle that the question is ultimately one for the jury and not the expert witness. The jury is probably only restricted in this way where the evidence is so clear and convincing that a verdict of guilty of murder could be challenged on appeal as one which no reasonable jury could have returned.[29]

"Substantially impaired his ability . . . to determine or control his acts"

11.17 Whether the abnormality of mind "substantially impaired the ability of the accused, as compared with a normal person, to determine or control his acts"[30] is a question of fact for the jury. The requirement that the impairment be "substantial" presumably means no more than that the impairment must be more than something "trivial or minimal",[31] and, conversely, that it is not necessary for the accused to show that he *could not* have done otherwise. In other words, the defence is not one of irresistible impulse.

In *R. v Byrne*,[32] Lord Parker C.J. remarked that:

> ". . . in a case where the abnormality of mind is one which affects the accused's self-control the step between 'he did not resist his impulse' and 'he could not resist his impulse' is, as the evidence in this case shows, one which is incapable of scientific proof. *A fortiori* there is no scientific measurement of the degree of difficulty which an abnormal person finds in controlling his impulses. These problems which in the present state of medical knowledge are scientifically insoluble, the jury can only approach in a broad, common-sense way."[33]

[27] *HM Advocate v Gorrie (Alison)*, High Court at Edinburgh, August 2003, unreported. See the *Herald,* August 15, 2003, which quotes a psychiatrist as having said in evidence led prior to sentencing that "I consider there must unfortunately have been something far wrong with Alison Gorrie which affected the way she acted at the time of the offence."

[28] See *R. v Mathieson* [1958] 1 W.L.R. 474; *R. v Bailey* [1961] Crim. L.R. 828; *R. v Chester* (1981) 5 A.Crim.R. 296. *Cf. Walton v The Queen* [1978] A.C. 788 (PC), where *Mathieson* and *Bailey* were distinguished, on the basis that the medical evidence led by the defence was such that the jury were entitled to regard it "as not entirely convincing", even though no medical evidence had been led by the Crown. See also *R. v Kiszko* (1979) 68 Cr.App.R. 62; *R. v Sanders* (1991) 93 Cr.App.R. 245 (noting that there may be other relevant circumstances beyond the medical evidence for the jury to consider).

[29] On the court's power to allow an appeal on this basis, see *AJE v HM Advocate*, 2002 J.C. 215.

[30] *Galbraith v HM Advocate*, 2002 J.C. 1 at [54], point 1.

[31] See *R. v Lloyd* [1967] 1 Q.B. 175.

[32] [1960] 2 Q.B. 396.

[33] At 404.

Diminished Responsibility as a Defence to Crimes Other Than Murder

Should the doctrine extend to crimes other than murder?

It has occasionally been argued that the doctrine of diminished responsibility should not be restricted to murder. Here, the rationale for the plea is crucial. If the sole basis for the plea is the avoidance of the mandatory penalty, then there is no case for extending it beyond murder. If, however, the rationale also encompasses labelling concerns, then there may be a case for extending the applicability of the plea. Two different questions should be addressed, although the first is frequently ignored or subsumed within the second. **11.18**

First, there is the question of whether the doctrine should apply to inchoate forms of murder (in practice, attempted murder, although incitement and conspiracy to murder under diminished responsibility are not logically inconceivable). In Scotland, it appears that diminished responsibility may reduce attempted murder to assault.[34] In England, by contrast, because the statutory form of the plea applies only to prevent a person being "convicted of murder"[35] it does not apply to a charge of attempted murder.[36]

If the plea exists only to avoid the mandatory life sentence for murder, then the English approach is clearly the correct one, as no mandatory sentence attaches to attempted murder, and the courts should take into account the circumstances of "diminished responsibility" when imposing sentence.[37] It must also be remembered, however, that the label of "murderer" is a strong and stigmatic one, properly reserved for the most serious class of killers. For that reason, it seems inappropriate to designate a person labouring under diminished responsibility as having "attempted" to murder. Indeed, it is illogical to label him as having attempted to place himself within a class to which he could, in the event, never have been assigned. For that reason, the Scottish approach seems preferable in principle, although it might raise practical difficulties if the attempt to kill did not involve an assault. Nevertheless, the label remains inapposite under the Scottish approach, as it does not indicate that the accused has tried to kill, and a better approach might be for diminished

---

34 *HM Advocate v Blake*, 1986 S.L.T. 661, discussed below, para.11.20.

35 Homicide Act 1957, s.2(1).

36 Consequently, for example, a defendant who, suffering from an abnormality of mind such as to amount to diminished responsibility, attacks two individuals simultaneously with an intention to kill or to do serious bodily harm, may be convicted of one count of manslaughter and one of attempted murder if one victim dies and the other does not: see, e.g. *R. v Mohammed* [1996] 1 Cr.App.R. (S) 317. The Criminal Law Revision Committee proposed that the plea (along with provocation) should apply to attempted murder: *Fourteenth Report: Offences Against the Person* (Cmnd. 7844, 1980), para. 98.

37 See, e.g. *R. v Nixon* (1994) 15 Cr.App.R. (S) 492; *R. v Drinkald* (1988) 10 Cr.App.R. (S) 380.

responsibility to reduce attempted murder to "attempted culpable homicide".[38]

11.19 Secondly, there is the question of whether the doctrine should be widened out to apply to all crimes:

> "... in principle, there seems no just reason why a mentally abnormal defendant should be denied the opportunity to show that he was less responsible for, say, a shoplifting offence than his mentally normal counterpart would have been, and no good reason why such a finding should not appear on the trial record."[39]

The opportunity referred to is never "denied" to an accused person, however, who is always entitled to plead what might be referred to as "diminished responsibility" in mitigation. Given this, we may assume that the presence or absence of the plea in cases other than murder will not affect the sentence imposed, but merely the label attached to the offence. Here, it is doubtful that there is any benefit to the accused. For example, compare a verdict of "guilty of theft" with one of "guilty of theft under diminished responsibility". Such a change in the form of verdict, rather than benefiting the accused in the way that a reduction from murder to culpable homicide does, instead doubly stigmatises the accused (by labelling him as being both a criminal *and* mentally ill).[40] One might argue that such stigma is unobjectionable—indeed, even that the label is a fair one[41]—but viewed in these terms, a widened plea would hardly present any "opportunity" to the accused, and might in fact dissuade him from placing the extenuating circumstances before the court. It might also suggest that mental illness or disorder may only be a mitigating factor when the technical requirements of the plea of diminished responsibility are satisfied, which is not the case at present.

---

[38] In *HM Advocate v Blake*, 1986 S.L.T. 661, Lord Brand indicated that the verdict of guilty of assault would be reached by deletion of the words "and did attempt to murder her" from the indictment. An alternative approach might be to substitute the word "kill" for "murder", thus (presumably) making the verdict one of guilty of attempted culpable homicide. It is not clear that "attempted culpable homicide" exists in Scots law (*cf.* Gordon, para.11.03 fn.24), but there seems no good reason why it should not. The only obvious objection might be that it is incoherent because "attempt" implies "intention", but it is settled that this is not the case in Scots law: *Cawthorne v HM Advocate*, 1968 J.C. 32. This assumes that, just as a charge of murder includes an implied alternative charge of culpable homicide (Renton and Brown, para.8–02), so a charge of attempted murder includes an implied alternative charge of attempted culpable homicide.

[39] R.D. Mackay, *Mental Condition Defences in the Criminal Law* (1995), p.206. See also R.D. Mackay "Some thoughts on reforming the law of insanity and diminished responsibility in England", 2003 Jur. Rev. 57–80 at p.79. For a more detailed argument to similar effect (arguing for a generic verdict of "guilty but partially responsible"), see S.J. Morse, "Diminished rationality, diminished responsibility" (2003) 1 *Ohio State Journal of Criminal Law* 289–308. See also R.G. Meakin, "Diminished responsibility: some arguments for a general defence" (1988) 52 J.C.L. 406–413.

[40] This argument is drawn from J. Chalmers, "Reforming the pleas of insanity and diminished responsibility: some aspects of the Scottish Law Commission's Discussion Paper" (2003) 8(2) S.L.P.Q. 79–94 at p.88.

[41] *cf.* J. Gardner and T. Macklem, "No provocation without responsibility: a reply to Mackay and Mitchell" [2004] Crim. L.R. 213–218 at pp.216–218. Alternatively, one might argue that it is wrong for the verdict to carry a stigma: that is a noble but unrealistic position which does not address the difficulty of dissuading accused persons from pleading diminished responsibility in mitigation.

An alternative argument in favour of a general "partial defence" of diminished responsibility might rest on the proposition that such a determination should properly be one for the jury, rather than the trial judge.[42] Such an argument, however, carries less weight in a jurisdiction where less significance is accorded to the role of the jury,[43] and would provide no basis for recognising a general partial defence in summary proceedings (save perhaps, for the sake of consistency).

The current legal position

Although "diminished responsibility", in the broad sense of the term, 11.20
may be pleaded in mitigation of sentence for any crime,[44] it is only in relation to murder that it modifies the offence of which the accused is convicted. It has occasionally been suggested that the doctrine might be applied to other offences, at least if "there is postulated a crime which may be reduced from a higher to a lower category",[45] but it is difficult to envisage many other offences where it might sensibly operate, as culpable homicide operates as a "second-order" form of homicide in a manner which few, if any, other offences do.

Perhaps the most obvious analogy would be the offences of wilful and culpable and reckless fireraising, but it would seem illogical to convict a person of "culpable and reckless" fireraising when their actions were admittedly intentional, albeit that their powers of self-control were impaired by an abnormality of mind.[46] Indeed, given that the doctrine of diminished responsibility is justified by reference to the principle of fair labelling, applying it in this way would be self-contradictory. Because the term "culpable homicide" does not expressly attribute any particular state of mind to the accused, no such problem arises when the doctrine is applied to murder. It has also been suggested that the doctrine could operate to reduce rape to indecent assault,[47] but as each *nomen juris*

---

[42] See, e.g. Morse, above, fn.39, at p.299 ("Partial responsibility is an explicitly normative judgment that should be made, therefore, by the community's representatives at the guilt phase, and not by judges at sentencing.") This is, however, question-begging: why should the jury be afforded this role in relation to "partial responsibility" but not extenuating circumstances more generally?

[43] *cf.* P. Duff, "The defendant's right to trial by jury: a neighbour's view" [2000] Crim. L.R. 85–94.

[44] See, e.g. *Andrews v HM Advocate*, 1994 S.C.C.R. 190; *Arthur v HM Advocate*, 1994 S.C.C.R. 621. In both of these cases, the use of the term "diminished responsibility" is that of the reporter rather than the court.

[45] Keith, above, fn.1, at p.113. Macdonald, 117 (in a passage which does not appear in earlier editions) suggests that on principle, "weakness of mind not amounting to insanity would appear to be available in mitigation of guilt of assault", but this clearly refers only to sentence and not to the category of offence.

[46] Gordon (para.11.04) notes that in *JF Wilson* (1877) 3 Coup. 429, where the accused pleaded guilty to wilful fireraising and his "weakness of mind" was taken into account in sentencing, "it was not suggested that his plea should have been only to culpable and reckless fire raising". However, it seems to have been thought at that time that the difference between wilful and culpable and reckless fire-raising rested, peculiarly, on the nature of the property set alight rather than to the culpability of the accused, and so such an offence modification would have been inappropriate. See J. Chalmers, "Fire-raising: from the ashes?", 2000 S.L.T. (News) 57–62.

[47] J.L. Edwards, "Diminished responsibility—a withering away of the concept of criminal responsibility?" in *Essays in Criminal Science* (G.O.W. Mueller (ed.), 1961), pp.301–341, at p.305. For criticism, see Gordon, para.11.04.

denotes a different *actus reus*, the principle of fair labelling would again be violated.[48]

The point may not matter very much given that murder is now the only offence where it is necessary to reduce the category of the crime in order to avoid a fixed sentence of life imprisonment.[49] It might be considered surprising that the doctrine was not, in its early stages, applied in respect of other offences which were then punishable by death,[50] but it may simply have been that the relevant offences were regarded as only nominally capital at the time at which the doctrine was developed.[51]

It has now been said by the appeal court on two occasions that the doctrine is restricted to murder, and absent statutory intervention, this must be regarded as final.[52] What is not clear, however, is whether the doctrine extends to inchoate forms of murder and, in particular, to attempted murder. In *HM Advocate v Blake*,[53] the trial judge directed the jury that if they were satisfied that the accused was of diminished responsibility at the relevant time, they could return a verdict of "guilty of assault under deletion of attempted murder on the ground of diminished responsibility".[54] This approach is not without its problems, as not all attempted murders will involve an assault—consider, for example, an attempt to murder by poisoning.[55] In almost all cases, however, it will avoid the inappropriate labelling of the accused as someone who has attempted to commit murder, while at the same time avoiding the awkward wording of an "attempted culpable homicide" verdict. Nevertheless, there is probably no reason to exclude the possibility of a conviction for attempted culpable homicide.[56]

Pleading Provocation and Diminished Responsibility Together

11.21 There has been some concern in English law about the potential overlap between the partial defences of provocation and diminished responsibility, and the difficulties that may be caused when they are pled in the

---

[48] On the possibility of distinguishing generally between "first degree" and "second degree" offences, which would answer this difficulty, see J. Horder, *Excusing Crime* (2004), Ch.4.

[49] In this regard, note the statement of the Home Secretary shortly before the government decided to introduce diminished responsibility into English law: "It may be illogical to confine diminished responsibility to murder, but that objection does not seem to me to be conclusive. Murder is *sui generis* because the penalty is death." HC Debs, cols 2553–2554 (February 16, 1956), and see N. Walker, *Crime and Insanity in England, Volume I: The Historical Perspective* (1968), pp.149–150.

[50] T.B. Smith, *A Short Commentary on the Law of Scotland* (1960), p.161, fn.51.

[51] Gordon, para.11.04.

[52] *HM Advocate v Cunningham*, 1963 J.C. 80 at 84, *per* the Lord Justice-General (Clyde); *Brennan v HM Advocate*, 1977 J.C. 38 at 48, *per* the Lord Justice-General (Emslie).

[53] 1986 S.L.T. 661.

[54] At 663 *per* Lord Brand.

[55] See Chalmers, "Reforming the pleas of insanity and diminished responsibility", above, fn.40, at p.87, fn.62.

[56] See Gordon, para.7.83.

same trial.[57] It has been argued that the two pleas should in fact be merged,[58] although such proposals have been criticised[59] and recently rejected by the Law Commission.[60]

The issue does not appear to have arisen in the Scottish cases, and there are good reasons why any difficulties are likely to be far less acute than under English law. First, the restrictive approach adopted by Scots law to the plea of provocation, whereby provocation must be by non-trivial violence or infidelity in order for the defence to run,[61] means that fewer cases will provide an arguable basis for both pleas. *Dingwall*[62] itself involved a "provocation" in the broadest sense—the accused having believed that his wife had hidden a whisky bottle from him—but that clearly does not make his plea in any way one of provocation under Scots law, any more than the harassment and "booing" involved in *Robert Smith*[63] would have amounted to provocation. Secondly, Scots law has not yet gone so far as English law formerly did in permitting abnormalities of mind to be taken into account in applying the objective condition in provocation,[64] one of the factors which is perceived as having (at least temporarily) narrowed the gap between the two pleas in English law.[65]

In deciding whether the abnormality of mind "substantially impaired" the accused's ability to "determine or control" his actions, a jury must necessarily have regard to the surrounding circumstances—self-control does not exist in a vacuum—and if the provoked accused cannot avoid a murder conviction on the basis of this provocation alone, then the jury will be entitled to have regard to the provocation as background material relevant to a plea of diminished responsibility.[66] The plea of diminished responsibility in Scots law is broad enough to allow surrounding circumstances to be taken into account.[67] Indeed, Lord Deas in *Dingwall* went so far as to suggest that the jury might consider the accused's "habitual kindness to his wife" in deciding whether to return a verdict of culpable homicide.[68]

---

[57] See R.D. Mackay, "Pleading provocation and diminished responsibility together" [1988] Crim. L.R. 411–423.

[58] R.D. Mackay and B.J. Mitchell, "Provoking diminished responsibility: two pleas merging into one?" [2003] Crim. L.R. 745–759.

[59] J. Chalmers, "Merging provocation and diminished responsibility: some reasons for scepticism" [2004] Crim. L.R. 198–212; J. Gardner and T. Macklem, "No provocation without responsibility: a reply to Mackay and Mitchell" [2004] Crim. L.R. 213–218. For a response to the latter article, see R.D. Mackay and B.J. Mitchell, "Replacing provocation: more on a combined plea" [2004] Crim. L.R. 219–223.

[60] *Partial Defences to Murder* (Law Com. No. 290), paras 5.98–5.101.

[61] See above, paras 10.08–10.14.

[62] *HM Advocate v Dingwall* (1867) 5 Irv. 466, discussed above, para.11.05.

[63] *HM Advocate v Robert Smith* (1893) 1 Adam 34, discussed above, para.11.07.

[64] See above, paras 10.18–10.19.

[65] See Mackay and Mitchell, "Provoking diminished responsibility", above fn.58.

[66] This assumes that it is preferable to be convicted of culpable homicide by reason of provocation rather than by reason of diminished responsibility. For a defence of this position, see Gardner and Macklem, above fn.59. There is a further question about the extent to which "abnormalities of mind" should be taken into account in applying the objective tests which form part of defences such as self-defence or provocation, and this issue is discussed throughout this book in the context of each relevant defence.

[67] *cf.* Horder, above, fn.48, Ch.4, especially pp.152–160.

[68] *HM Advocate v Dingwall* (1867) 5 Irv. 466 at 479, *per* Lord Deas.

CHAPTER 12

ERROR OF FACT

INTRODUCTION

Error of fact is an example of what was described in Ch.1 as a failure of proof defence. The claim being made is that, due to an error of fact made by the accused, all or part of the *mens rea* element of a particular offence is not satisfied. To this extent it is not really a "defence" at all, but is part of the definitional element of the offence.[1] **12.01**

The main context in which the issue has arisen is in relation to consent in sexual offences, with a line of case law establishing that even an unreasonable mistake that the complainer was consenting provides a defence to a charge of rape or indecent assault.[2] This is not the only context in which relevant error can occur. An error about ownership or consent can be a defence to theft[3] and an error about the death of a former spouse can be a defence to bigamy.[4] The issue can also arise in the context of substantive defences such as self-defence where, for example, the accused mistakenly believes that he is about to be attacked.[5]

RELEVANT ERROR

Error of fact is relevant when it negates *mens rea*. Thus, using Jones and Christie's example,[6] if A shoots and kills B because of his mistaken belief that he is shooting and killing a deer, A does not have the *mens rea* for murder, i.e. an intention to kill[7] or wicked recklessness towards the death of a human being. In this sense, error of fact is not operating as a substantive defence. The accused should not be convicted because he has not satisfied an element of the offence definition. **12.02**

A relevant error should normally result in acquittal on the charge in relation to which the offence definition is not satisfied. The accused might still be convicted of an alternative offence. In the example above, the accused could be convicted of culpable homicide if he was grossly negligent in arriving at the erroneous conclusion that B was a deer. In *HM Advocate v Williamina Sutherland*,[8] the accused killed a child while folding up a bed in which, unknown to her, the child was lying. The error was

[1] For further discussion of failure of proof defences, see paras 1.06 *et seq*.

[2] See *Meek v HM Advocate*, 1983 S.L.T. 280; *Jamieson v HM Advocate*, 1994 J.C. 88; *Marr v HM Advocate*, 1996 J.C. 199 and the discussion in paras 12.13 *et seq*.

[3] See *Dewar v HM Advocate*, 1945 J.C. 5 and the discussion in paras 12.10 *et seq*.

[4] See the English case of *R. v Tolson* (1889) 23 Q.B.D. 168.

[5] For an example, see *Owens v HM Advocate*, 1946 J.C. 119. For discussion, see paras 12.22 *et seq*.

[6] Jones and Christie, para.8–49.

[7] Or, following *Drury v HM Advocate*, 2001 S.L.T. 1013, a "wicked intention" to kill. See paras 3.11 and 10.05 for discussion.

[8] (1856) 2 Irv. 455.

relevant insofar as it negated the *mens rea* for murder,[9] but she was still convicted of culpable homicide on the basis of her gross negligence.[10]

In addition, a relevant error could negate one form of *mens rea* for an offence, but conviction could still result if the accused satisfies another form. An example might be rape, where an error as to the consent of the complainer means that the accused does not possess an intention to have sexual intercourse without consent, but, if his error was made recklessly, he might satisfy the alternative form of *mens rea*, recklessness as to consent.[11] Whether this could ever occur under Scots law as it stands at the moment is open to doubt. Recklessness as to consent to sexual intercourse is judged subjectively and thus to satisfy this form of the *mens rea* of rape the accused must have been aware of a risk that the complainer was not consenting.[12] It is difficult to see how the accused who genuinely believed that the complainer was consenting could be aware of a risk that she was not.[13]

Irrelevant Error

The general principle

12.03 Error of fact operates as a 'defence' only to the extent that it can be demonstrated to have affected *mens rea*. This is seen in *McIver v HM Advocate*.[14] Here, the appellant was convicted of culpable homicide after he had run over the deceased in his car. The appellant and the deceased had argued in the street, following which the appellant drove his car to the end of the road, turned it round and drove back directly towards the deceased at speed. At trial he claimed that he had a defence of error of fact because he had mistakenly believed that the deceased would get out of the way of the car before it hit him. The appeal court rejected his defence on the basis that it had no effect on the *mens rea* for assault[15]:

> "... the error to which we were referred was no more than an explanation for why the appellant acted as he did, and on its own it was no defence at all. To drive a car at someone may itself constitute an assault if there is a hostile intention, even if there is no intention of causing actual injury ... If he was proved to have an evil or hostile

---

[9] At 457.

[10] See also the cases listed by Gordon at para.9.28: *Edmund F. Wheatly* (1853) 1 Irv. 225; *HM Advocate v Wood* (1903) 4 Adam 150; *HM Advocate v AB* (1887) 1 White 532; *David Buchanan* (1817) Hume, i, 192.

[11] *Jamieson v HM Advocate*, 1994 J.C. 88 at 92; *Lord Advocate's Reference (No. 1 of 2001)*, 2002 S.L.T. 466 at [44], *per* the Lord Justice-General (Cullen).

[12] *Lord Advocate's Reference (No. 1 of 2001)*, 2002 S.L.T. 466 at [44], *per* the Lord Justice-General (Cullen).

[13] It would be different if recklessness were judged objectively. This does leave open the question of the accused who is reckless in arriving at his *belief* that the complainer is consenting. For discussion, see V. Tadros, "Recklessness and the duty to take care" in *Criminal Law Theory: Doctrines of the General Part* (S. Shute and A.P. Simester (eds), 2002), pp.227–258.

[14] 1991 S.L.T. 81.

[15] The charge was one of unlawful act culpable homicide (death resulting from an assault). The case was decided before the *Lord Advocate's Reference (No. 2 of 1992)*, 1993 J.C. 43, where it was held that the *mens rea* of assault, evil intention, simply referred to an intention to injure or to make the victim fear injury (hence the references to "hostile" or "evil" intention). The appellant's error would still have been entirely irrelevant, even if the case had been decided subsequent to the *Lord Advocate's Reference*.

intention towards the deceased, then any error or mistaken belief on his part about what the deceased would do at the last moment to avoid the car was of no consequence at all."[16]

Error as to identity

12.04 An error as to identity[17] is generally irrelevant as long as the two objects or people concerned fall into the same legal category. The reason for this is that specific identity is not normally an element requiring *mens rea*.[18] If the accused shoots person A in the mistaken belief that he is person B, this error has no effect on the *mens rea* for murder, which is intention to kill[19] or wicked recklessness towards a human being. Likewise, if the accused rapes a white woman believing her to be a black woman, he will still possess the *mens rea* for rape, which is the intention to have sexual intercourse with a woman without her consent or recklessness as to her consent.[20]

Aberratio ictus

12.05 *Aberratio ictus*[21] refers to the situation where the accused aims an act at B but accidentally the recipient of the act becomes C. An example is the accused who aims to shoot B but accidentally shoots C instead, either as a result of his poor aim or of C interposing himself between the accused and B. *Aberratio ictus* differs from an error as to identity. In the latter, the accused has killed the person he aimed at as a target, whereas in the former, the person aimed at is not the one killed.[22] The error might best be conceptualised as an error in execution compared to an error in perception.[23]

Where a crime can be committed recklessly or negligently, *aberratio ictus* is irrelevant (assuming that the accused's error in execution *was* actually reckless or negligent). Where a crime can only be committed intentionally,[24] the position is more complicated. If some way of holding

[16] *McIver v HM Advocate*, 1991 S.L.T. 81 at 83.

[17] Sometimes termed *error in objecto*. See Gordon, para.9.12; M.E. Badar, "*Mens rea*—mistake of law and mistake of fact in German criminal law: a survey for international criminal tribunals" (2005) 5 *International Criminal Law Review* 203–246 at p.239; J.H. Pain, "*Aberratio ictus*: a comedy of errors – and deflection" (1978) 95 S.A.L.J. 480–504 at p.480.

[18] Where some characteristic of the victim *is* an element requiring *mens rea*, and the offence is not one of strict liability, then the error would be a relevant one. It is difficult to find a modern example of an offence that would satisfy these conditions. Gordon gives the historical example of killing a policeman on duty which, between 1957 and 1965, was a capital offence. If the accused killed a policeman on duty in the belief that he was a private citizen, then this would mean that he was not guilty of capital murder (although he would be guilty of non-capital murder). See Gordon, para.9.11.

[19] Or, if *Drury v HM Advocate*, 2001 S.L.T. 1013 is followed, "wicked intention" to kill. See paras 3.11 and 10.05 for discussion.

[20] *Jamieson v HM Advocate*, 1994 J.C. 88 at 92; *Lord Advocate's Reference (No. 1 of 2001)*, 2002 S.L.T. 466 at [44], *per* the Lord Justice-General (Cullen). The examples are Gordon's (at para.9.11).

[21] Which roughly translates as "act goes amiss" (Badar, above, fn.17, at p.239).

[22] Bader, above, fn.17, at p.239.

[23] In this sense, it might be said that *aberratio ictus* is not an error of fact at all and is not therefore relevant to this discussion. It is dealt with by Gordon, however, under the heading of error of fact and so deserves some consideration here.

[24] The most notable examples of common law crimes that can only be committed intentionally are assault (*Lord Advocate's Reference (No. 2 of 1992)*, 1993 J.C. 43), theft (Hume, i, 73) and wilful fire-raising (*Byrne v HM Advocate*, 2000 J.C. 155).

that the accused intended to cause the harm that actually occurred cannot be found, the error in execution may well negate *mens rea*.[25]

The way that the law has tended to deal with this is through the doctrine of transferred intent,[26] whereby the accused's intention to, say, assault A is "transferred" to B, when B accidentally becomes the victim.

12.06 Although he does not use the term transferred intent, there is support for the doctrine in Hume. Hume makes no distinction between *error in objecto* and *aberratio ictus*. Both are irrelevant errors that should not affect the fact of the accused's conviction:

> "A criminal charge may be good, though there is no evidence of a purpose to injure the very person who has been the sufferer on the occasion. For instance, in a trial for fire-raising, it cannot affect the judgment of the Court, not ought it of the Jury, that the house which has been consumed is not the house of an enemy, which the panel meant to destroy, and to which he applied the fire, but that of another person, to him unknown, and to which, by the shifting of the wind, or some other accident, the flames have been carried. The same is true in a case even of homicide, that crime to which a special malice may seem more natural than to most others. If John make a thrust at James, meaning to kill, and George, throwing himself between them, receive the thrust, and die, who doubts that John shall answer for it, as if his mortal purpose had taken place on James?"[27]

Hume was followed in *Roberts v Hamilton*.[28] Here, the accused was convicted of assault, after aiming a blow at A who was fighting with her son. She intended to hit A but she actually hit B, who was trying to break up the fight. Her conviction for assault was upheld on appeal, with the appeal court stating that:

> "In our opinion the passage in Baron Hume at i, 22 ... is of general application and is not confined to cases of homicide. In particular his statement would apply to a case of assault. No doubt, as observed in Macdonald, if the act of the assailant is not directed against the person of anyone, he will not be guilty of assault because he will lack the necessary *mens rea*. If, however, his act is directed against the person of A, but he causes injury to another, B, in our opinion, he is guilty of assault."[29]

---

[25] Not everyone agrees that *mens rea* is negated by *aberratio ictus*. If it is accepted that the *mens rea* for murder, for example, is an intention to kill a human being, rather than a particular named victim, then *mens rea* is not negated simply because the actual victim was not the originally intended target. See Pain, above, fn.17, at p.117; M. Senevirante, "Prenatal injury and transferred malice: the invented other" (1996) 59 M.L.R. 884–892 at p.890. This would, however, depend on the *mens rea* of the offence in question and this argument does not seem to have been accepted by the Scottish courts, at least in relation to wilful fire-raising (see the discussion of *Byrne v HM Advocate*, 2000 J.C 155 in para.12.07).

[26] For detailed discussion, see A. Ashworth, "Transferred malice and punishment for unforeseen consequences" in *Reshaping the Criminal Law* (P. Glazebrook (ed.), 1978), pp.77–94; A.M. Dillof, "Transferred intent: an inquiry into the nature of criminal culpability" (1998) 1 *Buffalo Criminal Law Review* 501–536; D. Husak, "Transferred intent" (1996) 10 *Notre Dame Journal of Law, Ethics and Public Policy* 65–97; Pain, above, fn.17.

[27] Hume, i, 22.

[28] 1989 J.C. 91.

[29] At 95.

Nonetheless, the doctrine of transferred intent was rejected in relation to wilful fire-raising in *Byrne v HM Advocate*,[30] where the appeal court held that: **12.07**

> "... if the Crown are to secure a conviction of wilful fire-raising in respect of any subjects, they must satisfy the jury that the accused actually intended to set fire to those subjects".[31]

They continued:

> "The jury may infer the necessary intention from all the relevant circumstances, but there is no room for any doctrine of transferred intent."[32]

Roberts v Hamilton was not mentioned at all in *Byrne*. This led Gordon to conclude that *Roberts v Hamilton* "stands virtually alone in modern times"[33] and that, as both assault and intentional fire-raising cannot be committed recklessly, the same approach should apply to both. Gordon's preferred approach is the *Byrne* approach.[34]

Whether *aberratio ictus* is seen as a relevant error that negates *mens rea* (at least where *mens rea* is expressed in the form of intention) or an irrelevant one that is dealt with by the doctrine of transferred intent is perhaps of limited practical relevance. Even if the accused who makes such an error cannot be convicted of assault,[35] then a conviction for reckless injury[36] should still be possible.[37] Likewise, if the offence in question was wilful fire-raising, a conviction for culpable and reckless fire-raising[38] would presumably not be ruled out.

Error as to mode of act

Error as to mode of act refers to the situation where the accused intends a result to come about by one mode but it actually comes about by another. An example would be the accused who intended to shoot A, but whose shot hit a heavy object which fell on A's head and killed him.[39] **12.08**

---

[30] 2000 J.C. 155. For comment on *Byrne*, see J. Chalmers, "Fire-raising: from the ashes?" 2000 S.L.T. (News) 57–62.

[31] At 163.

[32] At 164. See also *Blane v HM Advocate*, 1991 S.C.C.R. 578, where it was held that an intention to set fire to moveable property could not be transferred to the heritable property that was destroyed by the fire. See also *McKelvie v HM Advocate*, 1997 S.L.T. 758, where *Blane* was applied.

[33] Gordon, para.9.10.

[34] Gordon, para.9.12.

[35] And it should be noted in this context that assault does not require actual injury, merely some sort of approach to the victim that led him to fear injury (*Atkinson v HM Advocate*, 1987 S.C.C.R. 534 at 535). Thus, where the accused intended to harm one person, but actually ended up harming another, it may be possible to convict him of an assault in relation to his intended victim, if his act was such that the intended victim would have feared injury.

[36] *HM Advocate v Harris*, 1993 J.C. 150.

[37] Assuming there has been actual injury.

[38] Provided that the Crown has libelled culpable and reckless fireraising as an alternative charge: see *Byrne v HM Advocate*, 2000 J.C. 155 at 164.

[39] The example is Andrew Ashworth's in *Principles of Criminal Law*, p.198. See also Gordon's example, at para.9.14. In a sense, like *aberratio ictus*, this is not an error of fact, but an error in execution and thus arguably does not fall within the scope of this chapter. However, Gordon discusses it in his chapter on error of fact and so it is briefly mentioned here.

There is a lack of Scottish authority as to how this type of error should be treated. Gordon suggests that the position is the same as that of an error as to the identity of the victim: it is an irrelevant error making no difference to whether or not *mens rea* is satisfied. Consequently, in Ashworth's example, it is irrelevant that the heavy object in fact kills A—the accused will still have the *mens rea* for murder.[40] Once again this will depend on the offence definition. Gordon gives the example of the accused who intends to rob a safe and takes with him a non-corrosive substance that he intends to use to melt the safe lock. In fact it is explosive and the safe blows up. The error would be relevant if he was charged with theft by opening lockfast places by means of explosives, but not if he was charged with theft by opening lockfast places.[41]

Relevant Error: Must it be Reasonable?

12.09 Where an error of fact negates *mens rea* an acquittal should result. Thus the accused who genuinely believes that a woman is consenting to sexual intercourse does not possess one form of *mens rea* for rape, an intention to have sexual intercourse without consent.[42]

The question that has divided courts, legislators and commentators alike is whether or not the accused's mistaken belief must be a reasonable one. Early Scots authority (Hume and the case of *Dewar v HM Advocate*[43]) seemed to suggest that only a reasonable error of fact would serve to ground an acquittal. Later authority (*Meek v HM Advocate*[44] and *Jamieson v HM Advocate*[45]) suggests that an unreasonable error will suffice although there is debate over whether this principle is confined to sexual offences or operates more widely. The position is further complicated by a range of statutory sexual offences that permit only reasonable error to ground an error of fact defence. The waters are also muddied by the fact that the infamous English case on which the appeal court based its decisions in *Meek* and *Jamieson*—*R. v Morgan*[46]—has now been overruled by statute,[47] taking English law back to the position whereby only a reasonable belief in consent is a defence to rape.[48]

---

[40] On this, see also Ashworth, *Principles of Criminal Law*, p.198. For a discussion in relation to South African law, see D. O'Connor, "Mistake and ignorance in criminal cases" (1976) 32 M.L.R. 644–662 at pp.655–657.

[41] Gordon, para.9.14.

[42] There is a further issue as to whether or not he might satisfy the alternative form of *mens rea*: recklessness as to consent (*Jamieson v HM Advocate*, 1994 J.C. 88 at 93; *Lord Advocate's Reference (No. 1 of 2001)*, 2002 S.L.T. 466 at [44], *per* the Lord Justice-General (Cullen)). It has already been noted, however, that this is unlikely, given that recklessness is judged subjectively (see para.12.02 above).

[43] 1945 J.C. 5.

[44] 1983 S.L.T. 280.

[45] 1994 J.C. 88.

[46] [1976] A.C. 182.

[47] Sexual Offences Act 2003, s.1(1). For discussion, see para.12.18.

[48] And indeed to the various other sexual offences provided for in ss.1–4 of the Sexual Offences Act 2003 (discussed in para.12.18).

The early authorities on reasonable error

Until *Meek v HM Advocate*,[49] it could be stated with some confidence that only reasonable error of fact was a relevant error that could operate to provide a defence. Hume says nothing about error in relation to sexual offences, but discusses it in relation to theft, specifically in the context of claim of right.[50] A claim of right is an error about a concept of the civil law that negates *mens rea*. An example is the accused who mistakenly believes that he is the owner of an item of property. If he takes possession of that property, his error means that he does not have the *mens rea* of theft, i.e. an intention to appropriate the property of another.[51] **12.10**

For Hume, only reasonable error would serve to ground a claim of right:

> "... it does not amount to theft, though the taker mean to dispose of the thing as his own, if he take it in the belief, no matter how erroneous, if serious, and withal excusable, that the thing is his own ... It has already been remarked, that to make way for this construction, the person must however be excusable for believing, that the thing which he has taken is his own. For as to that sort of belief, if such it may be called, which is directly in the face of law, and is grounded only in the violent passions of the man, or his blind prejudices in his own favour, it is what the Judge can have no regard to, and what none of the lieges can be allowed to entertain."[52]

Further support for this proposition comes from *Dewar v HM Advocate*.[53] The case concerned the manager of a crematorium who was convicted of theft after he removed the lids of coffins passed to him for cremation. The exact nature of his defence was unclear[54] but it seems to have been treated by the appeal court as an error about the ownership of the coffin lids that, if established, would negate the *mens rea* of theft.

What is clear is that the appeal court assumed that any error needed to be reasonable in order to be relevant. At trial, in a direction that was described by the appeal court as one that "could not have been more favourable to the appellant than it was",[55] the trial judge instructed the jury to consider not only whether or not Dewar's belief that he was entitled to appropriate the coffin lids was false but also: **12.11**

> "... whether he ever had any colourable ground for holding such a view, or whether the statements made by him ... were made recklessly without any justification for belief in their accuracy".[56]

---

49 1983 S.L.T. 280.

50 The issue of claim of right is discussed in more detail in paras 13.13 *et seq*.

51 *Black v Carmichael; Carmichael v Black*, 1992 S.L.T. 897.

52 Hume, i, 73–74. See also Burnett, 117; Alison, *Principles*, 271, 273. Macdonald (at 11) is cited by Gordon (at para.9.27) as additional authority for the proposition that error of fact must be reasonable. It seems likely from the context in which Macdonald was writing, however, that he was referring to mistake in relation to a substantive defence such as self-defence. Mistakes in defence are discussed in paras 12.22 *et seq*.

53 1945 J.C. 5.

54 See the discussion of the case in relation to error of law at paras 13.15 *et seq*.

55 *Dewar v HM Advocate*, 1945 J.C. 5 at 13.

56 *ibid*. at 8.

The trial judge re-emphasised this point later, referring to whether Dewar "may have entertained an honest and reasonable belief based on colourable grounds"[57] before proceeding to cite with approval the passage from Hume noted above.[58]

Thus, admittedly on the basis of a single case relating to the *mens rea* of theft, at this point in time it could be concluded that only reasonable error of fact could provide a defence.[59] The process by which this position changed started with the English case of *R. v Morgan*[60] which, given that it was relied upon in the later Scottish cases, is worthy of some discussion.

The English developments—*Morgan* and its influence

12.12 Until *R. v Morgan*,[61] it was relatively safe to assume that English law, like Scottish law, required error of fact to be reasonable.[62] If this was the case, *Morgan* marked a change of direction.[63] In *Morgan*, the appellants had been invited by an army colleague to have sexual intercourse with his wife. They had been told that the complainant would most likely struggle but that this would be a sign that she was enjoying herself. They were convicted of rape and appealed on the basis that the trial judge should have instructed the jury that an honest unreasonable belief in consent would ground an acquittal.[64] The appeal was unsuccessful,[65] but, on a 3/2 majority,[66] the House of Lords held that a mistaken belief in consent to sexual intercourse should acquit a defendant of rape, even if that mistake was unreasonable.

The majority of the House of Lords based their decision on logic. That is, because the *mens rea* of rape requires an intention to have *non-consensual* sexual intercourse, logic dictates that the defendant who honestly believes he is having *consensual* sexual intercourse does not possess *mens rea*, regardless of how unreasonable his belief may be.[67] As Lord Hailsham explained:

---

57 *Dewar v HM Advocate*, 1945 J.C. 5 at 8.

58 At para.12.10.

59 Further support for the proposition was provided by the fact that error about an element of a substantive defence needed to be reasonable. See *Owens v HM Advocate*, 1946 J.C. 119; *Crawford v HM Advocate*, 1950 S.L.T. 279 and the discussion in paras 12.22 *et seq.*

60 [1976] A.C. 182.

61 *ibid.*

62 Based primarily on the case of *R. v Tolson* (1889) 23 Q.B.D. 168 and subsequent bigamy cases.

63 For a detailed discussion of *Morgan*, its history and its influence, see R. Singer, "The resurgence of *mens rea*: II—honest but unreasonable mistake of fact in self defense" (1986–1987) 28 *Boston College Law Review* 459–519.

64 The trial judge had instructed the jury that if they were satisfied that the complainant did not consent, they needed to consider whether or not the defendants "honestly and reasonably" believed that she did (*R. v Morgan* [1976] A.C. 182 at 187).

65 The appellants' case was not helped by the fact that their story was inconsistent. They told the police on initial interview that Mrs Morgan had struggled throughout but repudiated their statements at trial, claiming instead that she eventually came to "co-operate in proceedings with evident relish" (*R. v Morgan* [1976] A.C. 182 at 204, *per* Lord Cross of Chelsea).

66 Lord Simon of Glaisdale and Lord Edmund-Davies dissenting.

67 For criticism of this application of logic, see R.H.S. Tur, "Subjectivism and objectivism: towards synthesis" in *Action and Value in Criminal Law* (S. Shute, J. Gardner and J. Horder (eds), 1996), pp.213–237, at p.222.

> "Once one has accepted, what seems to me abundantly clear, that the prohibited act in rape is non-consensual sexual intercourse, and that the guilty state of mind is an intention to commit it, it seems to me to follow as a matter of inexorable logic that there is no room for a 'defence' of honest belief or mistake, or of a defence of honest and reasonable belief or mistake. Either the prosecution proves that the accused had the requisite intent, or it does not. In the former case it succeeds, and in the latter it fails. Since honest belief clearly negatives intent, the reasonableness or otherwise of that belief can only be evidence for or against the view that the belief and therefore the intent was actually held."[68]

Morgan met with a mixed response from commentators, opinion dividing according to whether a subjectivist or objectivist view of the proper auspices of the criminal law was preferred.[69] In response, the government set up an advisory committee chaired by Mrs Justice Heilbron to examine the law of rape,[70] but the committee endorsed the *Morgan* approach.[71]

For a while following *Morgan*, it did seem that its influence would be restricted to rape.[72] In *R. v Kimber*,[73] however, the *Morgan* approach was extended by the Court of Appeal to indecent assault.[74] In *B v DPP*,[75] it was extended by the House of Lords to an error about age, in the context of the statutory offence of inciting a girl under the age of 14 to commit an act of gross indecency.[76] It was held that an unreasonable belief that a girl was 14 or over should provide a defence.[77]

The Scottish response

The first indication that *Morgan* would be followed in Scotland came in an *obiter* comment in *Meek v HM Advocate*.[78] In *Meek*, the appellants had been convicted of rape, but appealed on the basis that the trial judge 12.13

---

[68] *R. v Morgan* [1976] A.C. 182 at 214. See also Lord Cross of Chelsea at 202; Lord Fraser of Tullybelton at 237.

[69] For positive comment, see R. Cross, "Centenary reflections on Prince's case" (1975) 91 L.Q.R. 540–553; D. Cowley, "The retreat from *Morgan*" [1982] Crim. L.R. 198–208; J.C. Smith, "Comment on *Morgan*" [1975] Crim. L.R. 717. For criticism, see Tur, above, fn.67, and also E.M. Curley, "Excusing rape" (1976) 5 *Philosophy and Public Affairs* 325–360.

[70] *Report of the Advisory Group on the Law of Rape* (Cmnd. 6352, 1975).

[71] Although they expressed strong concern about a number of other issues, such as the use of sexual history evidence in rape trials. Statutory reform also made it clear that rape could be committed recklessly: Sexual Offences Act 1956, s.1 (as amended by the Sexual Offences (Amendment) Act 1976). The statutory definition of rape in English law has since been subject to a number of further amendments. For the latest of these, see para.12.18 below.

[72] E.g. in *R. v Phekoo* [1981] 1 W.L.R. 1117, the Court of Appeal quite clearly restricted *Morgan* to rape and held that only a *reasonable* belief that persons were squatters and not entitled to be in the defendant's premises would be a defence to harassing them intentionally to make them leave. For discussion, see Cowley, above, fn.69.

[73] [1983] 1 W.L.R. 1118.

[74] At 1122–1123, *per* Lawton L.J. In *Kimber*, the Court of Appeal explicitly disapproved the suggestion in *R. v Phekoo* [1981] 1 W.L.R. 1117 that the House of Lords intended to confine the views they expressed in *Morgan* to cases of rape (*Kimber*, at 1124).

[75] [2000] 2 A.C. 428.

[76] Indecency with Children Act 1960, s.1.

[77] *B v DPP* [2000] 2 A.C. 428 at 463, *per* Lord Nicholls of Birkenhead; at 476, *per* Lord Steyn. For criticism, see J. Horder, "How culpability can, and cannot, be denied in under-age sex crimes" [2001] Crim. L.R. 15–30.

[78] 1983 S.L.T. 280. For comment on *Meek*, see C. Gane, *Sexual Offences* (1992), pp.44–46.

should have directed the jury that, if they honestly but mistakenly believed the complainer was consenting, they should be acquitted. The appeal court took the view that there was no reason to consider the defence of error.[79] They did make it clear, however, that, in an appropriate case, they would favour the *Morgan* approach:

> "We have no difficulty in accepting that an essential element in the crime of rape is the absence of an honest belief that the woman is consenting. The criminal intent is, after all, to force intercourse upon a woman against her will[80] and the answer to the certified question given by the majority of their Lordships in *Morgan* is one which readily accords with the law of Scotland. The absence of reasonable grounds for such an alleged belief will however have a considerable bearing upon whether any jury will accept that such an 'honest belief' was held."[81]

Such a case arrived in *Jamieson v HM Advocate*.[82] Once again, this was a case in which the appellant appealed against his conviction for rape on the basis that the trial judge should have given a *Morgan* direction on honest belief in consent.[83] The Lord Justice-General (Hope) started by stating that the *mens rea* of rape "includes the intention to have intercourse with the woman without her consent" and thus:

> "The absence of a belief that she was consenting is an essential element in it. If a man has intercourse with a woman in the belief that she is consenting to this he cannot be guilty of rape. Now, the question whether the man believed that the woman consented is a question of fact. It is a question which the jury must decide, if it is raised, on the evidence. The grounds for his belief will be important, and if he has reasonable grounds for it the jury may find it easier to accept that he did honestly believe that the woman consented. But it will be open to the jury to accept his evidence on this point even if he cannot give grounds for it which they consider to be reasonable, and if they accept his evidence, they must acquit him."[84]

---

[79] Given that there were two conflicting accounts of the facts: the complainer alleged that the sexual intercourse was not consensual on the basis that she had objected and was distressed, whereas the appellants gave evidence of willing compliance in an orgy.

[80] This has since changed. In the *Lord Advocate's Reference (No. 1 of 2001)*, 2002 S.L.T. 466, a seven judge bench of the appeal court held that the *actus reus* of rape consists of sexual intercourse with a female person without her consent, replacing the previously accepted definition of sexual intercourse with a female person by overcoming her will. The change does not affect the approach taken to honest unreasonable error as to consent, which was reaffirmed in the *Reference* (at [28]–[30] *per* the Lord Justice-General (Cullen)).

[81] *Meek v HM Advocate*, 1983 S.L.T. 280 at 281. *Morgan* was also cited with approval (albeit in an *obiter* comment) in *Ross v HM Advocate*, 1991 J.C. 210 at 229, *per* Lord McCluskey.

[82] 1994 J.C. 88. For comment on *Jamieson*, see P.W. Ferguson, "The *mens rea* of rape", 1996 S.L.T. (News) 279–281.

[83] *Jamieson v HM Advocate*, 1994 J.C. 88 at 91.

[84] *ibid.* at 92.

In doing so, both the *obiter* comment in *Meek*[85] and the decision in *Morgan*[86] were cited with approval by the appeal court. The definition of rape has since been considered in detail by a seven judge court in the *Lord Advocate's Reference (No. 1 of 2001)*,[87] but the case concerned the *actus reus* of rape and nothing was said to overrule *Jamieson* in relation to *mens rea*. 12.14

At this stage, two points are worth making. First, as the Lord Justice-General noted in *Jamieson*, intention to have sexual intercourse without consent is one of two forms of *mens rea* for rape, the other being recklessness as to the complainer's consent.[88] Thus, if the accused had intercourse with a complainer who had not consented but he "acted without thinking or was indifferent as to whether or not he had her consent",[89] then the *mens rea* element of rape is satisfied.[90]

Secondly, it was made clear in both *Meek* and *Jamieson* that an absence of reasonable grounds for a belief in consent may be compelling evidence that this belief was not actually held by the accused.[91] As such, the occasions on which a defence of unreasonable belief in consent is successful are likely to be extremely rare.

The impact of *Jamieson*

The question arises of whether the principle expressed in *Jamieson* is confined to the offence of rape. *Marr v HM Advocate*[92] indicates that in relation to indecent assault, at least, an honest but unreasonable error of fact relating to consent will acquit. The case was a slightly odd one, in that the presiding sheriff had given a *Jamieson* direction on the effect of an unreasonable belief in consent, but the appellant (a taxi driver who was convicted of indecent assault) appeared to be arguing that this was a misdirection.[93] The appeal court held that the passage in *Jamieson* relating to honest belief in consent applies to both indecent assault and rape.[94] 12.15

What is less clear is the impact of *Jamieson* in contexts other than consent in sexual offences, given the earlier authority of *Dewar* (and indeed Hume) in relation to theft. If the *Jamieson* principle extends beyond consent in sexual offences, then an error of fact relating to the consent of the owner or the ownership of property need no longer be based on reasonable grounds to succeed as a defence to a charge of theft. Nothing was said in *Jamieson* (or *Meek*) to indicate whether or not *Dewar*

---

85 *Jamieson v HM Advocate*, 1994 J.C. 88 at 92.

86 *ibid.* at 92.

87 2002 S.L.T. 466.

88 *Jamieson v HM Advocate*, 1994 J.C. 88 at 92; *Lord Advocate's Reference (No. 1 of 2001)*, 2002 S.L.T. 466 at [44], *per* the Lord Justice-General (Cullen).

89 *Jamieson v HM Advocate*, 1994 J.C. 88 at 92.

90 It has already been noted, however, that it is unlikely that this form of *mens rea* would ever be satisfied by an accused who honestly believed he had the complainer's consent, given that recklessness is judged subjectively (see para.12.02 above).

91 *Meek v HM Advocate*, 1983 S.L.T. 280 at 281; *Jamieson v HM Advocate*, 1994 J.C. 88 at 92.

92 1996 J.C. 199.

93 And, as the appeal court pointed out (at 210), the trial judge's direction was actually *more* favourable to the appellant than the one for which he was arguing.

94 *Marr v HM Advocate*, 1996 J.C. 199 at 201. *Cf.* the sexual offences contained in Part 1 of the Criminal Law (Consolidation) (Scotland) Act 1995 (discussed in para.12.17).

was still good law and the case was not even referred to in either *Jamieson* or *Meek*.[95]

The preferable view would seem to be that *Jamieson* has application beyond sexual offences. The decision in *Jamieson* was based on logic: the accused who honestly (albeit unreasonably) believes that the complainer is consenting cannot possess the *mens rea* of an intention to have non-consensual sexual intercourse. It would seem to follow that the accused who honestly (albeit unreasonably) believes that he has the owner's consent to take an item of property or that an item of property does not belong to another cannot have the *mens rea* of theft: an intention to appropriate another's property without their consent.[96] Some support for this conclusion can be drawn from *Sandlan v HM Advocate*,[97] a case of theft where Lord Stewart charged the jury on mistaken belief in ownership without indicating that such a belief needed to be reasonable.[98]

The issue of intoxicated error of fact

12.16 *Jamieson* left open the question of unreasonable error of fact made while the accused was intoxicated. It would seem to follow from *Donaldson v Normand*,[99] however, that an unreasonable error of fact made by the accused while in a state of self-induced intoxication would not be a defence.[1]

This would place Scots law in line with English law. Even when *Morgan* was still authoritative,[2] an intoxicated unreasonable mistake did not serve to exculpate.[3] It would also be consistent with Canadian law.[4]

---

[95] Gordon doubts that any distinction between rape and theft is sustainable (at para.9.32). Neither the Casebook (at para.9.19) nor Jones and Christie (at para.8–54) reach any firm conclusion on the matter.

[96] On this, compare J. Chalmers, "Acquaintance rape: a reply", 2000 S.L.T. (News) 163–167 at p.164 ("there is no way whatsoever in which a person who believes that they have the owner's consent to take a piece of property can be said to intend to appropriate another's property without their consent") with S. McCall, "Acquaintance rape: time for reform", 2000 S.L.T. (News) 123–127 at p.124 (*Jamieson* has "set rape apart from other offences in relation to errors of material fact").

[97] 1983 J.C. 22; 1983 S.C.CR. 71 (the relevant aspect of the case, the charge to the jury, is only reported in the S.C.C.R. report).

[98] The appeal in the case concerned evidential matters. Lord Stewart's charge to the jury included the following passage: "If you believed [the evidence of the accused] or it raised in your mind a reasonable doubt to the effect that he genuinely thought the goods that were to be taken were [the co-accused's] own goods, then he couldn't be guilty of theft . . . because he would lack the criminal intention to take the goods without the permission of the owner" (*Sandlan v HM Advocate*, 1983 S.C.C.R. 71 at 83).

[99] 1997 J.C. 200.

[1] "... where the absence or apparent absence of *mens rea* is attributable to the self-induced intoxication, that cannot produce any kind of defence" (at 203). *Cf.* Casebook, at para. 9.19. *Donaldson v Normand* was a case of culpable and reckless conduct, where the accused had failed to tell police officers who were searching him that he had a syringe with an unguarded needle on his person. There is no suggestion, however, that the appeal court intended their statement to be restricted to this context.

[2] It has now been overruled by statute (see para.12.18).

[3] In *R. v Fotheringham* (1989) 88 Cr.App.R. 206, the Court of Appeal, despite accepting the authority of *Morgan* in relation to mistake in consent generally, held that "in rape self-induced intoxication is no defence, whether the issue be intention, consent or, as here, mistake as to the identity of the victim" (at 212 *per* Watkins J.).

[4] While Canadian law allows unreasonable belief in consent to ground an acquittal on a charge of sexual assault, the Supreme Court has made it clear that it is not a defence when it arises from self-induced intoxication (*Pappajohn v The Queen* [1980] 2 S.C.R. 120).

Error as a statutory defence

12.17 The approach taken in *Jamieson* can be contrasted with that taken to error about the *age* of the complainer in statutory sexual offences, where any mistake made must have a reasonable basis. Various sexual offences are provided for by the Criminal Law (Consolidation) (Scotland) Act 1995, the majority of which have a definitional element of sexual intercourse with a complainer of a certain age and all of which require a mistake about age to be reasonable in order to provide a defence.[5]

For example, s.5(3) of the Act creates the offence of unlawful sexual intercourse with any girl of or over the age of 13 and under the age of 16, but provides that it shall be a defence where the accused "had reasonable cause to believe that the girl was his wife; or being a man under the age of 24 years who had not previously been charged with a like offence,[6] had *reasonable* cause to believe that the girl was of or over the age of 16 years".[7] This means that while Scots law followed *Morgan*[8] in permitting an unreasonable error about consent to ground an acquittal on a charge of rape, it did not follow the English case of *B v DPP*[9] in allowing an unreasonable error about the age of the complainer to do so.[10]

Various other statutory offences also provide specifically for a defence of reasonable error of fact. For example, s.8 of the Building (Scotland) Act 2003 creates the offence of undertaking construction work on a building without a building warrant. Section 8(4) of the Act provides a defence where the accused had "reasonable cause to believe that a building warrant had been granted".[11] Some statutes set an even stricter standard and allow a defence of error of fact only where the accused had "no reasonable cause to suspect" the truth. For example, s.18(1) of the Terrorism Act 2000 makes it an offence to enter into an arrangement to conceal terrorist property. Section 18(2) provides a defence where the accused had no reasonable cause to suspect that the arrangement in question concerned terrorist property.[12]

Post-*Jamieson* developments and the possibility of reform

12.18 There is a strong possibility that *Jamieson*[13] will be over-ruled by statute, at least in relation to sexual offences. The Scottish Law Commission, in its Discussion Paper on *Rape and Other Sexual Offences*,[13a] considered

[5] For a discussion of whether or not the distinction between mistake in relation to consent (where an unreasonable belief suffices) and mistake in relation to age (where mistake must be reasonable) is justifiable, see C. Gane, *Sexual Offences* (1992), p.46.

[6] On this, see *McMaster v HM Advocate*, 2001 S.C.C.R. 517: "the clear purpose of this subsection is to allow the defence of mistake as to the girl's age on one occasion but to refuse it on subsequent occasions, the accused having received unequivocal notice of the rules involved in having intercourse with young girls" (at [11]).

[7] s.5(5), emphasis added. Similar provisions are contained in ss.2(b); 3(2)(a); 8(2); 9(2); 13(8); and 15. See also s.311(5) of the Mental Health (Care and Treatment) (Scotland) Act 2003.

[8] See para.12.12 above.

[9] [2000] 2 A.C. 428. See para.12.12 above for discussion.

[10] Both *Morgan* and *B v DPP* have now been overruled in England by the Sexual Offences Act 2003. See para.12.18 below.

[11] For another example, see s.18(2)(b) of the Children (Scotland) Act 1995.

[12] See also the Betting, Gaming and Lotteries Act 1963, s.10(5); Dangerous Dogs Act 1991, s.1(7)(b); Serious Organised Crime and Police Act 2005, s.129(4); Timeshare Act 1992, s.1B(3)(a). Statutory defences are not the primary focus of this book (see para.1.04), so these provisions are not discussed further here.

[13] *Jamieson v HM Advocate*, 1994 J.C. 88.

[13a] (D.P. No. 131, 2006).

the arguments for and against the *Jamieson* rule but did not reach a firm conclusion on the matter, finding "the arguments between the different opinions to be finely balanced".[13b] The matter was put out to consultation, with a report anticipated in 2007.

The likelihood of the review process eventually leading to the demise of the *Jamieson* rule is increased by the fact that *Morgan*,[14] the English case on which the Scottish appeal court relied, has now been overruled by statute.[15] After a lengthy review of the law relating to sexual offences,[16] the Sexual Offences Act 2003 now provides that a person (A) commits the offence of rape if (a) he intentionally penetrates the vagina, anus or mouth of another person (B) with his penis, (b) B does not consent to that penetration, and (c) A does not reasonably believe that B consents.[17] Whether a belief is reasonable is to be determined having regard to all the circumstances, including any steps A has taken to ascertain whether B consents.[18]

If Scotland does replace *Jamieson* with a rule requiring error about consent to be reasonable, then the question remains of the impact this would have on unreasonable error of fact in other contexts, such as theft. Given that it is not even absolutely certain that *Jamieson* over-ruled *Dewar v HM Advocate*[19] in the first place,[20] this is an issue on which it is near impossible to reach a firm conclusion. It is worth mentioning that the Draft Criminal Code leaves the issue in no doubt by requiring all errors of fact to be reasonable, whether in relation to consent, the ownership of property or some other state of affairs.[21]

[13b] At para.4.45.

[14] *R. v Morgan* [1976] A.C. 182.

[15] The effect of *Morgan* has also been reversed by statute in New Zealand (Crimes Act 1961, s.128, as amended by Crimes Amendment Act (No. 3) 1985, s.2).

[16] See the initial consultation paper: *Setting the Boundaries: Reforming the Law on Sexual Offences* (2000). This was followed by a White Paper: *Strengthening Protection against Sex Offenders and Reforming the Law on Sexual Offences* (Cm. 5668, 2002). The eventual legislation does not follow precisely the recommendations set out in either the consultation paper or the White Paper. For discussion of the consultation paper's proposals, see N. Lacey, "Beset by boundaries: the Home Office Review of Sex Offences" [2001] Crim. L.R. 3–14. For discussion of the resulting legislation, see J. Temkin and A. Ashworth, "The Sexual Offences Act 2003: (1) Rape, sexual assaults and the problems of consent" [2004] Crim. L.R. 328–346.

[17] s.1(1). Similar provisions are made in s.2 in relation to assault by penetration; in s.3 in relation to sexual assault; and in s.4 in relation to the offence of causing a person to engage in sexual activity without consent. The offences provided for in ss.2–4 are new offences created by the Sexual Offences Act 2003 to cover sexual assaults that do not fall under the definition of rape. Likewise, ss.9–12 provide that only reasonable mistake in relation to the age of the complainant can provide a defence to various charges including sexual activity with a child (s.9); causing or inciting a child to engage in sexual activity (s.10); engaging in sexual activity in the presence of a child (s.11); and causing a child to watch a sexual act (s.12). This means that *B v DPP* [2000] 2 A.C. 428 (where an unreasonable belief that the complainer was 14 or over provided a defence to a charge of inciting a girl under the age of 14 to commit an act of gross indecency) is no longer good law.

[18] s.1(2).

[19] 1945 J.C. 5. *Dewar* seemed to require an error about the ownership of property to be reasonable to provide a defence to theft (see paras 12.10 *et seq*.).

[20] Although this is the most plausible conclusion. See paras 12.15 *et seq*.

[21] Draft Criminal Code, s.28(1) and (3).

Should error of fact be reasonable in order to provide a defence?

Jamieson, like *Morgan* in the English context, was decided on the basis of logic. There is no discussion in *Jamieson* of wider issues, such as whether the unreasonably mistaken accused is sufficiently morally blameworthy to merit criminal liability.[22] This has not prevented the issue receiving considerable critical attention from commentators.[23] **12.19**

There are two main arguments for requiring error to be reasonable. First, in the specific context of rape (or other sexual offences), it has been suggested that the harm caused to a non-consenting complainer is so great and the cost to the accused in establishing consent so small, that the law is justified in imposing a duty to ascertain the facts before proceeding. As Pickard puts it:

> "There can be no doubt that it is a major harm for a woman to be subjected to non-consensual intercourse notwithstanding that the man believes he has her consent. There can be little doubt that the cost of taking reasonable care is insignificant compared with the harm which can be avoided through its exercise: indeed the only cost I can identify is the general one of creating some pressure towards greater explicitness in sexual contexts. To accept an honest but unreasonable belief in consent as a sufficient answer in these circumstances is to countenance the doing of a major harm that could have been avoided at no appreciable cost."[24]

It has been suggested that this argument applies to errors of fact in other contexts. Shute has argued that there is a far wider range of circumstances in which we have a moral duty to avoid imposing excessive and unreasonable risks of serious harm on our fellow citizens, where we could avoid doing so at little cost to ourselves. He gives the example of a gun owner who points a gun at his friend's head without realising that pulling the trigger would rotate the cylinder and fire a live bullet.[25]

The second (and related) argument is one of deterrence. Once again, this argument has tended to be made in the context of sexual offences, but **12.20**

[22] There is a similar absence of discussion in *Morgan* itself, or at least among the majority judges. In his dissenting opinion, Lord Simon of Glaisdale does deal with wider issues than that of logic (*R. v Morgan* [1976] A.C. 182 at 221). The one exception among the majority judgments is that of Lord Cross of Chelsea who does *briefly* touch on issues of moral blameworthiness before ultimately being persuaded by arguments of logic (*Morgan*, at 202–203).

[23] See E.M. Curley, "Excusing rape" (1976) 5 *Philosophy and Public Affairs* 325–360; F. McAuley, "The grammar of mistake in criminal law" (1996) 31 *Irish Jurist* 56–82; T. Pickard, "Culpable mistakes and rape: relating *mens rea* to the crime" (1980) 30 *University of Toronto Law Journal* 75–98; D.P. Bryden, "Redefining rape" (2000) 3 *Buffalo Criminal Law Review* 317–479; V.J Dettmar, "Culpable mistakes in rape: eliminating the defense of unreasonable mistake of fact as to victim consent" (1984–1985) 89 *Dickinson Law Review* 473–499; H. Power, "Towards a re-definition of the *mens rea* of rape" (2003) 23 O.J.L.S. 379–404; C. Gane, *Sexual Offences* (1992), pp.44–46.

[24] Pickard, above, fn.23, at p.77. Lacey calls this the "decisive argument" (Lacey, above, fn.16, at p.12).

[25] S. Shute "Second Law Commission Consultation Paper on Consent: (1) Something old, something new, something borrowed: three aspects of the project" [1996] Crim. L.R. 684–693 at p.689. See also J. Horder, *Excusing Crime* (2004), p.73.

has wider application. By requiring a reasonableness standard, the criminal law encourages us to take more care in forming our beliefs and, assuming that deterrence is effective in this respect,[26] offers greater protection to the potential victims of rape against sexual violation.[27] In this context, it has been suggested[28] that to fail to have a reasonableness requirement may contravene Art.3 of the ECHR. This is on the basis that the state has a positive obligation to protect citizens from potential violations of their Art.3 rights by private individuals.[29] Permitting an honest but unreasonable belief in consent to ground an acquittal might not provide effective deterrence and thus might not offer adequate protection.[30]

Both of these two arguments for allowing only reasonable error to ground an acquittal have most force in relation to relatively serious offences. Here, the potential for harm to a victim is great and the need for protection is most compelling. This raises the issue of whether reasonable error should be required in relation to some offences but not others. Bryden has suggested that theft and rape should be treated differently on the basis that the harm caused by an unreasonable error of fact is so much more serious in relation to rape than it is in relation to theft. Those who negligently take valuable property usually return it (voluntarily or not) without causing serious harm. This is not the case for rape, where the harm is more serious and cannot be undone in the same way.[31]

The main argument *against* allowing only a reasonable mistake to acquit[32] is that the accused who makes an honest but unreasonable mistake of fact is not sufficiently blameworthy to merit the imposition of criminal liability. As Singer puts it:

> " ... the engine of the criminal law is to be ignited primarily for imposing blame, and an actor who honestly believes the facts allow her to act legally, is not blameworthy, however badly mistaken".[33]

[26] Compare R. Singer, "The resurgence of *mens rea*: II—honest but unreasonable mistake of fact in self defense" (1986–1987) 28 *Boston College Law Review* 459–519 at p.510 with D.P. Bryden, "Redefining rape" (2000) 3 *Buffalo Criminal Law Review* 317–479 at p.337.

[27] Bryden, above, fn.26, at p.335; Curley, above, fn.23, at p.345; Gane, above, fn.23, at p.45; C. Wells, "Swatting the subjectivist bug" [1982] Crim. L.R. 209–220 at pp.212–213.

[28] H. Power, "Towards a re-definition of the *mens rea* of rape" (2003) 23 O.J.L.S. 379–404 at p.339.

[29] *A v United Kingdom* (1999) 25 E.H.R.R. 3.

[30] For further discussion of the positive obligations doctrine, see A. Mowbray, *The Development of Positive Obligations under the European Convention on Human Rights by the European Court of Human Rights* (2004); J. Rogers, "Applying the doctrine of positive obligations in the European Convention on Human Rights to domestic substantive criminal law in domestic proceedings" [2003] Crim. L.R. 690–708; F. Leverick, "Is English self-defence law incompatible with Article 2 of the ECHR?" [2002] Crim. L.R. 347–362; F. Leverick, "What has the ECHR done for victims?" (2004) *International Review of Victimology* 177–200.

[31] Bryden, above, fn.26, at p.336.

[32] Other than arguments related to 'logic'.

[33] Singer, above, fn.26, at p.512. See also M.F. Brinig, "The mistake of fact defense and the reasonableness requirement" (1977–1978) 2 *International School of Law Review* 209–233 at p.217; E. Keedy, "Ignorance and mistake in the criminal law" (1908–09) 22 *Harvard Law Review* 75–96 at p.84. *Cf.* Curley, above, fn.23, at p.347; Pickard, above, fn.23, at p.83.

This argument does have some force in relation to rape, which is an offence that carries a certain stigma and for which a long sentence of imprisonment may potentially result. It has been pointed out that this could be dealt with by convicting the unreasonably mistaken accused not of rape, but of a lesser offence.[34] Whether or not this is appropriate, in terms of labelling the seriousness of the experience from the victim's perspective, is open to question. **12.21**

There is also the concern that the mentally abnormal actor who does not have the capacity to realise that there was no consent could be unfairly convicted under a reasonableness requirement,[35] although this could be catered for by taking personal characteristics into account in applying the test of reasonableness.[36]

Mistakes in Defence

Error of fact can also arise in the context of substantive defences.[37] The approach in Scotland has been to maintain a distinction between error in relation to an offence element and error in relation to an element of a substantive defence, with the latter needing to be reasonable in order to ground an acquittal. Thus, in relation to self-defence, a mistaken belief in the need to use self-defensive force must be based on reasonable grounds in order to acquit.[38] This reasonableness requirement remained intact despite *Jamieson v HM Advocate*,[39] where the appeal court appeared to rule out the extension of the unreasonable belief principle to defences: **12.22**

> "We wish to say that we are not to be taken ... as casting any doubt on the soundness of the dicta in [the self-defence cases of *Owens* and *Crawford*]. Nor are we to be taken as suggesting that in any other case, where a substantive defence is based on a belief which is mistaken, there need not be reasonable grounds for that belief. The reason why, in rape cases, the man's belief need not be shown to be based on reasonable grounds for his belief to be relevant as a ground of acquittal is because of the particular nature of the *mens rea* which is required to commit the crime."[40]

---

[34] Wells has suggested "negligent sexual invasion" (Wells, above, fn.27, at p.213). Power has suggested grading rape as first degree, second degree and third degree rape, with this last least serious category being reserved for the defendant who believes that the victim is consenting but is procedurally and substantially negligent in so believing (Power, above, fn.28, at p.381).

[35] Home Office, *Setting the Boundaries: Reforming the Law on Sexual Offences* (2000), at para.2.13.16.

[36] R.H.S. Tur, "Subjectivism and objectivism: towards synthesis" in *Action and Value in Criminal Law* (S. Shute, J. Gardner and J Horder (eds), 1995), pp.213–237, at p.237; Power, above, fn.28, at p.397.

[37] On this, see also Ch.3 (self-defence) and Ch.10 (provocation).

[38] *Owens v HM Advocate*, 1946 J.C. 119 at 125; *Crawford v HM Advocate*, 1950 S.L.T. 279 at 282. For further discussion, see paras 3.10 *et seq.*

[39] 1994 J.C. 88. See paras 12.13 *et seq.*

[40] At 93. The requirement for a reasonable belief in the need to use self-defensive force has been approved on a number of occasions post-*Meek* and post-*Jamieson*. See, e.g. *Jones v HM Advocate*, 1990 J.C. 160 at 172; *Burns v HM Advocate*, 1995 J.C. 154 at 159.

There is some suggestion that the comments made by the appeal court on the definition of murder in *Drury v HM Advocate*[41] have the potential to change this position. In *Drury*,[42] the *mens rea* for murder was defined not as an intention to kill but a *wicked* intention to do so, where the term "wickedness" referred to the absence of any applicable justification or excuse defence.[43] If murder requires a wicked intention (that is, one which excludes action taken in, for example, self-defence), then it is arguable that the accused who makes an honest mistake of fact, regardless of whether or not his mistake is reasonable, is not acting with wicked intent and will therefore not have the requisite *mens rea* for murder.[44] At worst, this would leave him facing the possibility of a conviction for culpable homicide.

12.23 Since it was decided, *Drury* has not proved influential outside the narrow confines of the law on provocation.[45] Thus, for the time being, it is probably safe to assume that the distinction between error in relation to offence and defence elements still stands, and that an error of fact concerning a substantive defence must be reasonable in order to ground an acquittal.[46]

By contrast, English law *has* extended the *Morgan* principle to error of fact relating to a defence element, at least in cases of self-defence.[47] It was established soon after *Morgan* (and based on similar issues of 'logic') that mistake about the existence of an attack does not need to be reasonable to ground an acquittal on the basis of self-defence; an honest but unreasonable belief will suffice.[48] This leaves English and Scots law occupying diametrically opposed positions. In English law an unreasonable mistake of fact relating to an offence element will *not* serve to acquit (at least where the error relates to belief in consent in sexual offences), whereas an unreasonable error of fact relating to a substantive defence (self-defence) *will* do so. In Scots law, for the time being at least, *Jamieson* still represents the position on error of fact relating to an offence element, whereas an error of fact relating to a substantive defence must be based on reasonable grounds.

Opinion is divided over whether there should be any distinction between offence elements and substantive defences in this respect and

---

[41] 2001 S.L.T. 1013.

[42] A case concerned with the partial defence of provocation. See Ch.10 for detailed discussion.

[43] *Drury v HM Advocate*, 2001 S.L.T. 1013 at [11], *per* the Lord Justice-General (Rodger). See also Lord MacKay at [9]; Lord Johnston at [18]; and Lord Nimmo-Smith at [2].

[44] On this, see F. Leverick, "Mistake in self-defence after *Drury*", 2002 Jur. Rev. 35–48 at pp.40–42 and J. Chalmers, "Collapsing the structure of criminal law: *Drury v HM Advocate*", 2001 S.L.T. (News) 241–245.

[45] On this, see para.3.11.

[46] See para.3.11 for further discussion of the possible impact of *Drury* in this respect.

[47] Despite the fact that *Morgan* has now been overruled in the Sexual Offences Act 2003 (see para.12.18), the position in relation to defences has not changed.

[48] *R. v Williams* [1987] 3 All E.R. 411; *R. v Beckford* [1988] A.C. 130; *R. v Oatridge* [1992] 94 Cr.App.R. 367. See also the Privy Council case of *Shaw v R.* [2001] UKPC 26. See Leverick, above, fn.44, and para.3.11 for detailed discussion of the approach taken by English law.

what the nature of any such distinction should be.[49] The view is taken here that, even if it is accepted that logic requires error of fact about an offence element to acquit, there is no obvious reason why this should automatically be extended to defences.[50] Indeed, there is an argument that where the accused has caused the harm prohibited by an offence, and has done so with a blameworthy state of mind, he should put forward a good reason why we should not blame him for his conduct in order to benefit from a complete defence, and that an unreasonable error of fact does not constitute such a good reason.[51]

[49] For an argument that no distinction should be made, see P.W. Ferguson, "The *mens rea* of rape", 1996 S.L.T. (News) 279–281 at p.280. For an argument that only error in relation to a defence element need be reasonable, see A.P. Simester, "Mistakes in defence" (1992) 12 O.J.L.S. 295–310. For an argument that while error in relation to an offence element (specifically error as to consent in sexual offences) need be reasonable, no such requirement should exist in relation to defences, see C. Wells, "Swatting the subjectivist bug" [1982] Crim. L.R. 209–220 at p.214.

[50] This is based on the assumption that a conceptual distinction can be made between offences and substantive defences. For further discussion, see Ch.1.

[51] For a detailed defence of this position, see Leverick, "Mistake in self-defence after *Drury*", above, fn.44; Simester, above, fn.49.

CHAPTER 13

ERROR OF LAW

INTRODUCTION

The defence of error of law has generally not found favour in the majority of common law jurisdictions. Scotland is no exception. For the most part,[1] the maxim *ignorantia iuris neminem excusat*[2] is a fundamental principle of Scots criminal law.[3] **13.01**

This can be contrasted with the more favourable treatment given to error of fact, where a reasonable (and sometimes *unreasonable*) error as to an element of an offence (or defence) generally exculpates.[4] It can also be contrasted with the treatment given to error of law in many continental jurisdictions, where a reasonable or unavoidable error of law generally does provide a defence.[5]

The blanket term error of law covers a wide range of situations from a simple claim of complete ignorance that, for example, shooting a trespasser is unlawful[6] to the accused who has acted on a mistaken interpretation of the criminal law provided by officials in response to a request as to the legality of specific conduct.[7] It is certainly more difficult to justify withholding the defence in the latter scenario than in the former, especially if the conduct involved was not an obvious moral transgression.

In the early 20th century, academic commentators focused primarily on defending the error of law rule.[8] More recently, the widely held view has been that a blanket rule barring an error of law defence is unfair and that reasonable mistake of law should exculpate,[9] although commentators **13.02**

---

[1] See paras 13.09 *et seq.*

[2] Ignorance of the law excuses no-one.

[3] Hume, i, 25; *Tennant v Gilmour*, 1923 J.C. 19; *Clark v Syme*, 1957 J.C. 1; *Lord Advocate's Reference (No. 1 of 2000)*, 2001 J.C. 143; *HM Advocate v H*, 2002 S.L.T. 1380; *Brown v Frame*, 2005 J.C. 320.

[4] *Jamieson v HM Advocate*, 1994 S.L.T. 537; *Marr v HM Advocate*, 1996 J.C. 199. Error of fact is discussed in Ch.12.

[5] See para.13.23.

[6] *Andrew Ewart* (1828) Syme 315.

[7] *Roberts v Local Authority for Inverness* (1889) 2 White 385.

[8] E. Keedy, "Ignorance and mistake in the criminal law" (1908–09) 22 *Harvard Law Review* 75–96; J. Hall, "Ignorance and mistake in criminal law" (1957) 33 *Indiana Law Journal* 1–44; L. Hall and S. Seligman, "Mistake of law and *mens rea*" (1940–1941) 8 *University of Chicago Law Review* 641–683; R.M. Perkins, "Ignorance and mistake in criminal law" (1939) 88 *University of Pennsylvania Law Review* 35–70.

[9] B.R. Grace, "Ignorance of the law as an excuse" (1986) 86 *Columbia Law Review* 1392–1416; D. Husak, "Ignorance of law and duties of citizenship" (1994) 14 L.S. 105–115; D. Husak and A. von Hirsch, "Culpability and mistake of law" in *Action and Value in Criminal Law* (S. Shute, J. Gardner and J. Horder (eds), 1996), pp.157–174; P. Matthews, "Ignorance of the law is no excuse?" (1983) 3 L.S. 174–192; D. O'Connor, "Mistake and ignorance in criminal cases" (1976) 32 M.L.R. 644–662; A.T.H. Smith, "Error and mistake of law in Anglo-American criminal law" (1985) 14 *Common Law World Review* 3–32.

differ as to what mistakes are considered reasonable.[10] In fact, it is difficult to think of another defence where the balance of academic opinion is so out of step with the law as it stands.

In Scots law, exceptions to the maxim *ignorantia iuris neminem excusat* have on occasion been made,[11] but the law is patchy and under-developed. The authorities, such as they are, certainly do not lead to the conclusion that any reasonable mistake of law would provide a defence. Indeed, abiding by the maxim has led to some rather harsh decisions.[12]

A final issue to be addressed is whether a distinction should be made between error (or mistake) of law and ignorance of law. The two concepts are conceptually different. Ignorance implies a complete lack of knowledge of the existence of a particular law whereas error implies some flawed knowledge of the law. Someone who has consulted the relevant case law or statute but has misunderstood it can be said to be in error, whereas someone completely unaware of the case law or statute's existence can be described as ignorant. The two concepts are not, however, considered sufficiently different to be examined separately.[13] Unless stated otherwise, the chapter will proceed on the basis that the two terms are interchangeable.

Ignorantia Iuris Neminem Excusat: The Traditional Justifications

13.03 The rule that error of law is no defence has traditionally been justified by one of (or a combination of) four arguments.

First, everyone is expected to know the law and thus a failure to do so cannot negate culpability in any way.[14] This argument implies that law and morality are not separate. The inference is that if one did not know that a particular act was contrary to the criminal law, then one certainly ought to have known it.[15]

While this argument may have had some force in the past when the criminal law generally did track community moral values,[16] in modern times the presumption that everyone knows the law is largely fictional.[17] With the rise of purely regulatory offences, much modern legislation is completely devoid of moral content.[18] In this context, a distinction has

[10] E.g. compare Ashworth, *Principles of Criminal Law*, p.234 with R.G. Singer, "The proposed duty to inquire as affected by recent criminal law decisions in the United States Supreme Court" (1999–2000) 3 *Buffalo Criminal Law Review* 701–754 at p.709.

[11] See, e.g. *Roberts v Local Authority for Inverness* (1889) 2 White 385 (discussed in para.13.27); *Paterson v Ritchie*, 1934 J.C. 42 (discussed in para.13.17); *MacLeod v Hamilton*, 1965 S.L.T. 305 (discussed in paras 13.19–13.20).

[12] See, e.g. *Tennant v Gilmour*, 1923 J.C. 19 and *Brown v Frame*, 2005 J.C. 320.

[13] It is not even that easy to distinguish them conceptually. Is the accused who mistakenly believes it is permissible to kill a trespasser mistaken as to the law because he wrongly believes he has a valid defence or is he ignorant of the law because he does not know that what he is doing is prohibited?

[14] Hume, i, 25.

[15] For a more recent version of this argument, see Hall, above, fn.8, at p.23.

[16] Grace, above, fn.9, at p.1392.

[17] T. White, "Reliance on apparent authority as a defence to criminal prosecution" (1977) 77 *Columbia Law Review* 775–809 at p.784.

[18] F.B. Sayre, "Public welfare offenses" (1933) 33 *Columbia Law Review* 55–88; S.P. Green, "Why it's a crime to tear the tag off a mattress: overcriminalization and the moral content of regulatory offences" (1997) 46 *Emory Law Journal* 1533–1615.

been made between conduct that is *malum in se* and conduct that is *malum prohibitum*.[19] While it is relatively easy to defend the error of law rule in relation to the former, it is less easy to do so in relation to the latter.[20]

The second traditional argument supporting the maxim was made by Austin, who argues that the defence, if recognised, would present insurmountable difficulties of proof: **13.04**

> "... if ignorance of the law were admitted as a ground of exemption, the Courts would be involved in questions which it were scarcely possible to solve, and which would render the administration of justice next to impracticable ... Whether the party was *really* ignorant of the law, and was so ignorant of the law that he had no *surmise* of its provisions, could scarcely be determined by any evidence accessible to others."[21]

That the defence is too difficult to prove is not in itself a particularly convincing argument for rejecting it.[22] Rather, Austin's objections to admitting the defence appear to be that (a) requiring the prosecution to prove on every occasion that the accused was not ignorant of the law would waste scarce state resources; and (b) the defence would be open to abuse and would allow culpable individuals to escape conviction.[23]

Whether ignorance of the law is any more difficult to prove than many of the other issues involving mental states that arise in criminal cases is questionable[24] and, as Matthews points out,[25] the argument proves too much. If Austin's argument is accepted, it surely applies to error of fact as much as it does to error of law[26] yet it is never seriously argued that error of fact should not be a defence. What it might suggest at most is that the burden of proof should be placed with the defence.[27]

Likewise any fear that the defence would be open to abuse does not appear to have been borne out in those jurisdictions where reasonable error of law is accepted as a defence. For example, in South Africa, since the defence was recognised in *de Blom*[28] very few cases have been raised and even fewer have been successful.[29] This observation is especially **13.05**

[19] For an explanation of the difference and a detailed account of the history of the distinction, see H. Wechsler, "Note: The distinction between *mala prohibita* and *mala in se* in criminal law" (1930) 30 *Columbia Law Review* 74–86.

[20] M. Travers, "Mistake of law in *mala prohibita* crimes" (1995) 62 *University of Chicago Law Review* 1301–1331 at p.1322.

[21] J. Austin, *Lectures on Jurisprudence* (4th edn, R. Campbell (ed.) 1879), at p.498 (emphasis in original).

[22] O.W. Holmes, *The Common Law* (1882), p.48.

[23] Austin, above, fn.21, at p.499.

[24] Holmes, above, fn.22, at p.48.

[25] P. Matthews, "Ignorance of the law is no excuse?" (1983) 3 L.S. 174–192 at p.187.

[26] *cf.* L. Hall and S. Seligman, "Mistake of law and *mens rea*" (1940–1941) 8 *University of Chicago Law Review* 641–683 at p.651.

[27] Holmes, above, fn.22, at p.48.

[28] *S v de Blom* 1977 (3) S.A. 513 (A).

[29] K. Amirthaligham, "*Mens rea* and mistake of law in criminal cases: a lesson from South Africa" (1995) 18 *University of New South Wales Law Journal* 428–442 at p.440. See also (on Germany) M.E. Badar, "*Mens rea*—mistake of law and mistake of fact in German criminal law: a survey for international criminal tribunals" (2005) 5 *International Criminal Law Review* 203–246 at p.243; and (on Scandinavia) J. Andenaes, "*Ignorantia legis* in Scandinavian criminal law" in *Essays in Criminal Science* (G. Mueller (ed.), 1961), pp.217–231.

noteworthy since in South Africa even an *unreasonable* error serves to exculpate.[30]

Even if one accepts Austin's argument, it certainly does not provide good reason to reject the defence where difficulties of proof do not arise to the same extent—for instance in cases where the accused relied on the erroneous legal advice of an official.[31]

13.06 A third argument is that any defence of error of law should be rejected because it would encourage ignorance of the law. As Holmes states:

> "... to admit the excuse at all would be to encourage ignorance where the law-maker has determined to make man know and obey, and justice to the individual is rightly outweighed by the larger interests on the other side of the scales".[32]

Even if one accepts the utilitarian nature of this argument,[33] it can be questioned on several counts. It is far from obvious that the fact that error of law is no defence is well known, never mind that it would *actually* deter individuals from efforts to know the criminal law.[34] Further, it has been argued that, if the aim is to maximise knowledge of the law, a *reasonable* mistake of law defence would not discourage people from acquiring such knowledge.[35] That standard would surely encourage individuals to make a reasonable attempt to learn the law, as those who did not would be negligent and denied the defence. If the defence is denied *entirely*, the individual will be punished regardless of his attempts to learn the law.

13.07 Finally, even if one accepts Holmes' argument, it does not apply in circumstances where an individual has done everything reasonably possible to learn the law, such as ask the advice of officials charged with its interpretation.[36]

The fourth and final argument that has traditionally been made in support of the maxim is that to recognise ignorance of the law as a defence would contradict the principle of legality:

> "If that plea [ignorance of the law] were valid, the consequence would be: whenever a defendant in a criminal case thought the law was thus and so, he is to be treated as though the law was thus and

---

[30] See para.13.23 below.

[31] See paras 13.25 *et seq.*

[32] Holmes, above, fn.22, at p.48. See also R.M. Perkins, "Ignorance and mistake in criminal law" (1939) 88 *University of Pennsylvania Law Review* 35–70 at p.41.

[33] Implicit in it is that justice to the individual is outweighed by the societal interest in having individuals know and obey the law: see E.C. Walker, "Criminal law—mistake of law defense based on reasonable reliance on apparent authority" (1978) 14 *Wake Forest Law Review* 136–149 at p.139. For an argument that utilitarian arguments are of dubious value in this context, see J. Parry, "Culpability, mistake and official interpretation of law" (1997) 25 *American Journal of Criminal* Law 1–78 at pp.32–35.

[34] P. Brett, "Mistake of law as a criminal defence" (1965–1967) 5 *Melbourne University Law Review* 179–204 at p.196.

[35] D.M. Kahan, "Ignorance of the law *is* an excuse—but only for the virtuous" (1997–1998) 96 *Michigan Law Review* 127–154 at pp.133–134.

[36] Brett, above, fn.34, at p.195; A.T.H. Smith, "Error and mistake of law in Anglo-American criminal law" (1985) 14 *Common Law World Review* 3–32 at p.17. It might also be said that, like Austin's argument, Holmes' argument applies equally to error of fact as it does to error of law.

so, *i.e., the law actually is thus and so*. But such a doctrine would contradict the essential requisites of a legal system, the implications of the principle of legality."[37]

Hall's argument is unconvincing. It might have some merit if error of law operated as a justification defence, but if it is conceptualised as an excuse, then its recognition implies no challenge to the legal order. It is possible to view the conduct concerned as wrongful, yet blameless.[38] This does not result in subjective rules of law; it simply excuses the violation of the law that has taken place.[39]

In the modern context, Ashworth has attempted to construct an alternative argument based on a "duty of citizenship".[40] For Ashworth, individuals have rights and responsibilities within the society in which they live. One such duty of citizenship is to take reasonable steps to become acquainted with the criminal law in so far as it affects one's activities.[41] **13.08**

Ashworth's argument, like those that have gone before it, has been criticised, most prominently by Husak.[42] Husak questions the existence of a duty to know the law on the basis that no-one attempts to inform citizens of such a duty in the same way as, for example, their duty to pay tax or to vote.[43] He also argues that, even if the duty exists, it does not in itself show why an individual who is ignorant of the law is blameworthy to the extent that criminal liability should be imposed.[44]

Ashworth and Husak are not as far apart as Husak's criticism might suggest. Ashworth never suggested that there is an absolute duty upon citizens to know the law per se, only a duty to take reasonable steps to learn the law in so far as it relates to their activities. For Ashworth any reasonable mistake of law should provide an excuse. And, although he comes to it via a slightly different route, this is precisely what Husak also argues.[45] Where they differ is in relation to the circumstances in which ignorance of the law is considered reasonable.[46]

---

[37] J. Hall, "Ignorance and mistake in criminal law" (1957) 33 *Indiana Law Journal* 1–44 at p.19 (emphasis in original).

[38] M. Gur-Arye, "Reliance on a lawyer's mistaken advice: should it be an excuse from criminal liability?" (2001–2002) 29 *American Journal of Criminal Law* 455–480 at p.462.

[39] It is perhaps unfair to criticise Hall on this basis, given that he was writing in 1957, some time before the distinction between justification and excuse defences became well established in the literature (see Ch.1 for a discussion of the development of this distinction).

[40] Ashworth, *Principles of Criminal Law*, p.233.

[41] *ibid.*, p.233.

[42] D. Husak, "Ignorance of law and duties of citizenship" (1994) 14 L.S. 105–115.

[43] Husak, above, fn.42, at p.108.

[44] Husak, above, fn.42, at p.108. The question also arises of how Ashworth would treat the individual who is in error about the duty to take steps to become acquainted of the law.

[45] For Husak, unless the defendant is at least negligent, i.e. if he makes a mistake of law that any reasonable person would have made, it is hard to see why he should be punished (Husak, above, fn.42, at p.114).

[46] On this, see para.13.24.

The General Rule: Error of Law is No Defence

13.09 Authority for the proposition that error of law is no defence can be found in Hume. Hume discusses error of law in the context of the requirement for dole[47] and states that dole is not negated by a belief that the conduct concerned was not criminal:

> "It is not material to the notion of guilt, that the offender have himself been fully conscious of the wickedness of what he did. Though he were persuaded that it was innocent, or even meritorious, (such are the miserable effects of fanaticism in politics, and in religion,) yet still this cannot save him from the judgment of the law; which must be determined by the nature of the act, and its evil consequences to the public, and not by any allowance for those strange delusions, which are as dangerous as the vices of the most thorough malefactor."[48]

Although, as Gordon points out,[49] the concept of dole in the general sense no longer plays any part in modern Scots criminal law, the proposition that error of law is no defence has remained.

Perhaps because of this clear authority in Hume, there are few reported cases in which error of law has been raised as a defence. A case that might be interpreted as a rare exception is *Andrew Ewart*.[50] In *Ewart*, the accused was charged with murder after having shot and killed the deceased in the mistaken belief that he was about to steal dead bodies from a graveyard. In reality, the deceased was a friend of the accused who had been a fellow member of a team of individuals guarding the churchyard after a series of attempts to take away the bodies buried there.

13.10 In the address to the jury, the defence appeared to be trying to rely upon an error of law defence and, in the circumstances, not an entirely unreasonable one[51]:

> "But even if he was to be held legally accountable for what he had done, they would recollect that he acted under mistaken notions, and in the discharge, as he thought, of a sacred and imperative duty. The people of Scotland had been hitherto allowed to believe, that it was lawful to protect the graves of their departed friends in this manner. It was a most erroneous belief; but they were misled into it by the authorities under whose observation placards, giving notice of watchmen being stationed at night with firearms, were exhibited at the gate of almost every churchyard."[52]

---

47 "... that corrupt and evil intention, which is so essential ... to the guilt of any crime" (Hume, i, 21).

48 Hume, i, 25.

49 At para.9.20.

50 (1828) Syme 315.

51 The case involves both an error of fact (the accused mistakenly believed that the deceased was a thief) and an error of law (the accused mistakenly believed that the criminal law permitted him to shoot someone stealing dead bodies). The mistake of fact is irrelevant to the present discussion.

52 *Andrew Ewart* (1828) Syme 315 at 320.

In his charge to the jury, Lord Gillies rejected this defence as irrelevant:

> "Could the defence of the churchyard, even had he had better reason to think it invaded, have proved any justification? It could not."[53]

The issue also arose in *Tennant v Gilmour*.[54] Here, the accused had been charged with a breach of the Explosives in Coal Mines Order 1913. The Order regulated the use of explosives in opening up coal mines. It provided that, in the interests of safety, any person "firing the shot[55] shall not approach . . . the shot-hole until an interval has elapsed of not less than . . . an hour". The accused had placed two explosive devices in position and retired to a safe distance after lighting the fuses. When one of them failed to explode, instead of waiting for the regulation one hour, he returned to light the fuse, believing (wrongly) that it had not been lit. It exploded, injuring him and his companion.

At trial, the accused claimed that he did not believe that he had breached the Order because he did not think that he had "fired the shot". His defence was successful at trial, but the Crown appealed against his acquittal. On appeal, the Lord Justice-General (Clyde) admitted that the Order was "not expressed as clearly as might be desired" but that "[i]f he did misconstrue the Order—as well he might, in my opinion—that does not excuse him".[56] **13.11**

It is sometimes suggested that the issue of error of law arose in *Dewar v HM Advocate*.[57] The case certainly seems to feature prominently in discussions of error of law.[58] The case concerned the manager of a crematorium who was convicted of theft after he removed the lids of coffins passed to him for cremation. Implicit in his defence was a claim that what he did was not criminal, although this was never presented coherently as an error of law defence.[59] Nothing was said by the appeal court, however, about the general principle that error of law is no defence. The case appears to have been treated as a claim of error about a concept of the civil law (the ownership of the coffin lids) that negated *mens rea*.[60] As such, it is discussed in more detail later in this chapter.[61]

There was some reference to the issue of ignorance of the law in *HM Advocate v H*,[62] a case where the accused, who was charged with rape, lodged a devolution minute on the basis that the redefinition of rape in the *Lord Advocate's Reference No. 1 of 2001*[63] was contrary to Art.7 of the

---

[53] *Andrew Ewart* (1828) Syme 315 at 321.

[54] 1923 J.C. 19.

[55] By which was meant lighting a fuse.

[56] *Tennant v Gilmour*, 1923 J.C. 19 at 22.

[57] 1945 J.C. 5.

[58] Jones and Christie, para.8–45; Casebook, para.2.40 (where it is the only case extract included under the heading error of law, a puzzling inclusion as there are more relevant authorities).

[59] Perhaps not surprisingly as given the authority of Hume and subsequent cases it would almost certainly have failed.

[60] And the appeal court made it clear that even if this was the claim being made by Dewar, they did not accept it.

[61] See paras 13.15 *et seq.*

[62] 2002 S.L.T. 1380.

[63] 2002 S.L.T. 466. A seven judge bench of the appeal court held that the *actus reus* of rape consisted of sexual intercourse with a female person without her consent, replacing the previously accepted definition of sexual intercourse with a female person by overcoming her will.

ECHR. The detail of *HM Advocate v H* need not concern us here.[64] It is sufficient to observe that, in the course of his judgment, Lord MacLean stated that:

> "It has often been said that 'ignorance of the law will not excuse unlawful conduct' [Lord MacLean refers to *Millar v Dickson* here[65]]. The conduct alleged ... is certainly unlawful, and the Minuter cannot in my opinion plead ignorance in relation to it."[66]

13.12 Despite these conclusive authorities, an attempt to raise ignorance of the law as a defence was made recently in *Brown v Frame*.[67] Here, the appellant had been convicted of an offence under s.172 of the Road Traffic Act 1988, which requires anyone suspected of a road traffic offence to state the identity of the driver of the vehicle at the time the alleged offence was thought to have been committed. A car registered in the appellant's name had been caught on video camera driving above the speed limit. He was asked to attend at the police station to view the video, where he was asked who was driving the vehicle at the time. He was not told that failure to answer constituted an offence. The appellant answered that he was "unable to say",[68] before launching a verbal attack on the police for wasting resources on matters such as these. On appeal, it was argued that he should not have been convicted, given that he did not realise it was an offence to refuse to answer this question.

His defence of ignorance of the law was ruled out by the appeal court. The opinion of the court was delivered by Lord Osborne, who started by pointing out that there is nothing in the legislation to say that the individual must be warned that failure to comply with s.172 amounts to an offence and, in the absence of a direct provision of this nature, no reason emerges from the legislation itself as to why this must be done.[69] In upholding the conviction, he concluded that to allow a defence in this case:

> "would amount to an unwarranted departure from the maxim *ignorantia iuris neminem excusat*".[70]

---

[64] The accused's argument was rejected out of hand by Lord MacLean.

[65] *Millar v Dickson*, 2002 S.C. (P.C.) 30 was a case where the accused sought suspension of his conviction on the basis that it was heard by a temporary sheriff. In the context of whether or not the accused could be said to have waived his right to protest because he did not make a complaint at the time of the hearing, the issue arose of whether it could be presumed that every accused knew the law. In addressing this issue, Lord Hope approved the following passage in *Evans v Bartlam* [1937] A.C. 473: "For my part I am not prepared to accept the view that there is in law any presumption that anyone, even a judge, knows all the rules and orders of the Supreme Court. The fact is that there is not and never has been a presumption that every one knows the law. *There is the rule that ignorance of the law does not excuse, a maxim of very different scope and application*" (at 479 of *Evans v Bartlam*; *Millar v Dickson*, at [34], emphasis added).

[66] *HM Advocate v H*, 2002 S.L.T. 1380 at [5].

[67] 2005 J.C. 320.

[68] At [2].

[69] At [8].

[70] At [12].

Thus, as a general rule, error of law is no defence.[71] This principle is reflected in the Draft Criminal Code, which distinguishes between an error concerning a "state of affairs" and an error as to the requirements of the criminal law. The former is a defence, if it is reasonable. The latter is not.[72]

Exceptions to the Rule

Error of civil law that negates *mens rea*

An error relating to a concept of the *civil* law does provide a defence to a criminal charge where that error negates *mens rea*.[73] Although traditionally considered under the heading "error of law" by criminal law texts,[74] this type of error is more akin to an error of fact than an error of criminal law, as it relates to a mistake about particular circumstances relevant to a prohibited act.[75] It is sometimes described as a defence of "claim of right": a claim by the accused that he thought he had the legal right to act as he did. **13.13**

Typically errors of this nature are most likely to arise in relation to the ownership of property. An example is the accused who enters into a contract to buy a car.[76] He believes that the agreement has the effect of transferring ownership to him, whereas it is really a hire-purchase agreement where ownership does not pass until the final payment is made. When he sells the car on to a third party, he might seem to have committed theft. It is possible to argue, though, that he is not guilty because he has no intention to appropriate the property of another. He thinks the car is his. The *mens rea* for theft is not therefore established.[77]

Errors of the civil law can arise in contexts other than that of property. In other jurisdictions, the issue has arisen in relation to the defendant's

[71] Although, in the English context, see *Secretary of State for Trade and Industry v Hart* [1982] 1 W.L.R. 638, where the Queen's Bench Division held that an offence under the Companies Act that required the defendant to have acted "knowingly" meant that knowledge of *the law* was required in order for a conviction. The offence in question was then contained in s.13 of the Companies Act 1976 (see now the Companies Act 1989, s.28) which provides that a person who acts as auditor of a company at a time when he knows that he is disqualified is guilty of a criminal offence. Anyone who is a director of the company in question, as the defendant was, is automatically disqualified. The court held that, to be convicted of this offence, the defendant must have known not only that he was a director, but also that directors were disqualified from acting as auditors (at 487–488 *per* Ormrod L.J.; at 485 *per* Woolf J.). Gordon describes this as a "curious case" (at para.9.16, fn.56). *Cf.* the view taken by the House of Lords in *Grant v Borg* [1982] 1 W.L.R. 638 at 647, *per* Lord Bridge. For a case where it was held that the word "wilfully" in the offence definition required the prosecution to prove knowledge of illegality on the part of the defendant, see the United States Supreme Court's decision in *Ratzlaf v United States*, 510 U.S. 135 (1994). For comment, see M. Travers, "Mistake of law in *mala prohibita* crimes" (1995) 62 *University of Chicago Law Review* 1301–1331. *Cf.* the Australian High Court's decision in *Iannella v French* (1968) 119 C.LR. 84.

[72] ss.28(1) and (3).

[73] Errors of the civil law and errors that negate *mens rea* are sometimes discussed separately, but this is misleading—error relating to a concept of the civil law is a defence *because* it negates an element of the offence definition.

[74] See Jones and Christie, para.8–45; R.A.A. McCall Smith and D. Sheldon, *Scots Criminal Law* (2nd edn, 1997), pp.119–120; Casebook, para.2.42.

[75] B.R. Grace, "Ignorance of the law as an excuse" (1986) 86 *Columbia Law Review* 1392–1416 at p.1394.

[76] The example is drawn from the Casebook, para.2.42.

[77] Casebook, para.2.42.

belief that he was entitled to vote in an election[78]; that a third party did not have lawful control over a child[79]; and that he was not lawfully married.[80]

13.14 Although the distinction can sometimes be subtle, these claims are different conceptually to a claim by the accused that, in full awareness of all the facts and circumstances, he did not realise his behaviour was criminal. All of the examples above involve a mistake about a legal concept that belongs to the civil law such as 'property belonging to another', 'lawful control over a child' or the state of being married. They do not involve a claim that, for example, stealing property that *does* belong to another is not a crime.

In relation to theft, the issue is dealt with by Hume, who states that:

> "... it does not amount to theft, though the taker mean to dispose of the thing as his own, if he take it in the belief, no matter how erroneous, if serious, and withal excusable, that the thing is his own; as may happen in many cases of disputed sale, legal diligence, succession, and other modes of conveyance".[81]

Hume makes it clear, though, that the defence is limited to errors that are reasonable:

> "It has already been remarked, that to make way for this construction, the person must however be excusable for believing, that the thing which he has taken is his own. For as to that sort of belief, if such it may be called, which is directly in the face of law, and is grounded only in the violent passions of the man, or his blind prejudices in his own favour, it is what the Judge can have no regard to, and what none of the lieges can be allowed to entertain."[82]

13.15 Modern case authority pertaining to errors of civil law is limited. *Roberts v Local Authority for Inverness*[83] could be categorised as a case in which an error of the civil law occurred, but this was complicated by the fact that the accused had received mistaken advice from officials on the matter and thus the case appears to have been decided on this basis.[84] It is not clear how the case would have been decided if the error was the accused's alone.

A case sometimes discussed in this context is *Dewar v HM Advocate*,[85] although it is debateable as to whether it really has much to contribute to the discussion.[86] The appellant was the manager of a crematorium, who was convicted of the theft of lids from coffins entrusted to him for

---

[78] And therefore not committing the offence of falsely stating himself to be qualified to vote: *R. v Dodsworth* (1837) 173 E.R. 467.

[79] And therefore he would not be committing an offence if he removed that child: *Re: Owens* [2000] 1 Cr.App.R. 195.

[80] And therefore could not be found guilty of the offence of bigamy: *R. v Gould* [1968] 2 Q.B. 65.

[81] Hume, i, 73. See also *Ker and Stables* (1792) Hume, i, 73.

[82] Hume, i, 74. On this, see *Alexander Williamson* (1767) Alison, *Principles*, 272; *John Lockhart* (1800) Alison, *Principles*, 272.

[83] (1889) 2 White 385.

[84] As such it is discussed in para.13.27, where the full facts are outlined.

[85] 1945 J.C. 5.

[86] *Dewar* is also discussed in the context of error of fact, where it is of more relevance (see Ch.12).

cremation along with the bodies they contained. Instead of burning the coffin lids, he removed them, stored them and ultimately disposed of them "in various utilitarian ways".[87]

At trial, Dewar claimed, among other things, that (a) he thought that the coffins were abandoned to him to do as he pleased and (b) he thought that he was entitled to treat the lids as ownerless scrap and to appropriate them.[88] The Lord Justice-Clerk (Cooper), in charging the jury, appears to have treated this claim as an error of civil law (the ownership of the property) that, if established, would serve to negate the *mens rea* of theft. He told the jury that they must consider "whether he may have entertained an honest and reasonable belief based on colourable grounds",[89] before proceeding to read the passage from Hume quoted above.[90] Presumably, the jury were not convinced that his belief was honest and reasonable, as Dewar was convicted.

The appeal court seemed to treat the case as a question of whether the *mens rea* of theft had been established. The court concluded that it had, implying that they too did not believe Dewar's claim that he thought he was entitled to dispose of the lids. The Lord Justice-General (Normand) stated that the presiding judge "took a lenient view when he instructed the jury",[91] and the direction "could not have been more favourable to the appellant than it was".[92] The evidence of the appellant, according to the Lord Justice-General was: **13.16**

> "... a plain assertion of his *unlimited right of property* in a thing which he knew was sent to him under contract for the purpose of destruction, and of destruction only along with the bodies, and this applies both to the coffins and to the lids. Accordingly, in my opinion, there was misappropriation of property which he knew was sent to him merely for destruction by a prescribed method. That being so, there is no doubt that there was evidence upon which the jury were entitled to find the appellant guilty of theft."[93]

While the defence was obviously not established on the facts, *Dewar* suggests that an error relating to the ownership of property *could* succeed in establishing a defence to a charge of theft. It most likely did not succeed in *Dewar* because it was not reasonable.

Another case that might be said to fall into this category (although it is not at all clear) is *Paterson v Ritchie*.[94] Here the accused was charged with fraud, having obtained a widow's pension while she was cohabiting with another man. She was aware of the relevant statutory provision, which prohibited anyone living together "as man and wife" from claiming a **13.17**

---

87 *Dewar v HM Advocate*, 1945 J.C. 5 at 11.

88 A further claim that he believed the removal of the lids was a common practice in other crematoria, he admitted at trial was unfounded in fact. It was unlikely to have provided a defence even if honestly held.

89 *Dewar v HM Advocate*, 1945 J.C 5 at 8.

90 Hume, i, 74, quoted at 10 of *Dewar v HM Advocate*, 1945 J.C. 5 and para.13.14 of this chapter.

91 *Dewar v HM Advocate*, 1945 J.C. 5 at 12.

92 *ibid.* at 13.

93 *ibid.* at 12 (emphasis added). See also *Herron v Diack and Newlands*, 1973 S.L.T. (Sh. Ct) 27, which relied on *Dewar*.

94 1934 J.C. 42. Gordon describes it as "a difficult case" (at para.9 19).

widow's pension,[95] but did not believe it applied to her. Although she was living with her partner, he was actually married to someone else. She thought, as a result, that she could not possibly be "cohabiting together as man and wife" with him. The sheriff-substitute agreed with her interpretation of the statute and acquitted her.

The appeal court upheld the sheriff-substitute's decision, accepting that it was not clear whether one could cohabit with a man "as man and wife" where that man was already married to someone else. The court went on, however, to say that the law had been misinterpreted by the respondent and the sheriff-substitute. In future, anyone in the same position would be convicted since the court had now given notice of the true meaning of the statute.[96]

The significance of this case is unclear. It might suggest that a defence of 'claim of right' can only succeed when the civil law concept in question (here "cohabitation as man and wife") is unclear (or perhaps, as Gordon suggests,[97] where the error made by the accused is shared by the trial judge). If this is the correct interpretation of the case, then it would seem that the defence can only succeed on the first occasion it is raised in relation to a particular concept of the civil law (or at least that it cannot succeed once an appeal court has given a definitive ruling on the concept in question). This is surely incorrect. As Gordon points out,[98] the defence of claim of right is a recognised exception to the irrelevance of error of law and there is no suggestion in Hume or otherwise that it is limited to cases where the civil law concept is ambiguous or unclear. If the case has any significance at all, it is probably to suggest that an error relating to a concept of the civil law can be a defence only where the error is reasonable (and the ambiguity of the concept might be relevant in assessing reasonableness). The error is deemed unreasonable where the appeal court has given a definitive ruling on the meaning of the concept in question.[99]

13.18 An error relating to a concept of civil law provides a defence, so long as it negates an element of the offence. A mere misconception about the availability of a legal remedy does not. In *Clark v Syme*,[1] the accused was charged with malicious mischief after killing a sheep belonging to his neighbour. Sheep had been straying onto his land from a neighbouring property across a derelict boundary wall. At trial, he claimed that he thought he had a legal right to kill the sheep because it was trespassing on his land and he had given due warning to his neighbour about this. The presiding sheriff-substitute accepted this claim and found the accused not guilty. On appeal this was reversed.

---

95 Under s.21(1) of the Widows' Orphans' and Old Age Contributory Pensions Act 1925, any person who was, with another, "cohabiting together as man and wife" was prohibited from claiming such a pension.

96 *Paterson v Ritchie*, 1934 J.C. 42 at 48.

97 At para.9.19.

98 *ibid.*

99 Although as Gordon points out (para.9.23), this is rooted in the rather unrealistic view that it is reasonable to expect widows to read law reports! For another case that *could* have been dealt with on the basis of an error of civil law (but in the event was decided on other grounds), see *Kane v Friel*, 1997 J.C. 69. For examples of the defence of error of civil law in the English context, see Theft Act 1968, s.2(1)(a); Criminal Damage Act 1971, s.2.5(2)(a); *R. v Smith (David)* [1974] Q.B. 354.

1 1957 J.C. 1.

The Lord Justice-General (Clyde) delivered the opinion of the court and held that the respondent's belief, that he had a legal right to engage in this conduct, was irrelevant:

> "If, as in the case of *Ward v Robertson*,[2] it was not clear whether the appellant (*sic*) knew that by doing what he did he was doing or was likely to do damage, the Crown might fail; for the necessary wilfulness might not then be present. But in this case no such doubt could possibly arise. The respondent in this case acted deliberately. He knew what he was doing and he displayed in his actings a complete disregard of the rights of others. The mere fact that his criminal act was performed under a misconception of what legal remedies he might otherwise have had does not make it any less criminal."[3]

Unpublished/inaccessible law

A further exception to the principle that error of law is no defence has **13.19**
been made where the law in question was unpublished or was otherwise inaccessible. This exception to the general rule would seem to be warranted. The principle of legality and, in particular, the notion that individuals should receive fair notice of what conduct is and is not punishable is certainly one basis upon which the defence should be recognised.[4] Alternatively, it might be said that the accused is not blameworthy for her failure to know the law, as she could not have reasonably discovered it even if she tried.

There is, perhaps, an additional question of whether this should apply to *all* criminal offences or solely those which are *mala prohibita*.[5] Husak and von Hirsch argue for the former, stating that "[e]ven ill-willed defendants should receive fair notice of the legal rules they are expected to observe".[6] The view one takes depends to a certain extent on whether the defence is granted on the basis of the principle of legality or on the basis that the accused cannot be blamed for her ignorance of the law. If the latter, then it would seem to make sense to withhold the defence where the accused ought to have known that the conduct was prohibited.

The principle that it would be unfair to convict an accused when the law in question was not made reasonably accessible appears to have been followed in *MacLeod v Hamilton*.[7] Here, the accused had parked her car in an area of Edinburgh in which waiting was not permitted. The statutory chain by which the offence in question was created was a complicated one, but, in essence, she had breached art.7 of the Edinburgh Corporation (Tollcross Area—Various Streets) Traffic Order 1964, which prohibited waiting on certain roads at certain times of day. The primary legislation that permitted the making of such an order was the Road Traffic Act 1960 and s.29 of that Act required that a local authority

---

[2] 1938 J.C. 32, a case of malicious mischief where the accused did not realise that by his actions he was damaging a crop of grass.

[3] *Clark v Syme*, 1957 J.C. 1 at 5. *Clark v Syme* was followed in the *Lord Advocate's Reference (No. 1 of 2000)*, 2001 J.C. 143.

[4] Although see J. Hall, "Ignorance and mistake in criminal law" (1957) 33 *Indiana Law Journal* 1–44, who uses the principle of legality to make the opposite argument.

[5] The distinction between conduct which is *mala in se* and *mala prohibita* was noted in para.13.03.

[6] D. Husak and A. von Hirsch, "Culpability and mistake of law" in *Action and Value in Criminal Law* (S. Shute, J. Gardner and J. Horder (eds), 1996), pp.157–174, at p.173.

[7] 1965 S.L.T. 305.

provide notice of any such order and provided for regulations to be made concerning the manner of publication. Such regulations were, in fact, made but the notice in question did not conform to them. Among other things, the regulations required that "adequate information as to the effect of the order" be given. In the event, a sign was placed in the street stating that it was a "controlled zone" and that waiting was only permitted "if authorised by the Order".

13.20 The accused claimed at her trial that she had not known that parking was prohibited and her defence succeeded. The Crown appealed, but the appeal court upheld the acquittal on the basis that the law in question had not been adequately publicised:

> "Unless these traffic signs were there accordingly and the opportunity was thus afforded to the public to know what they could not legally do, no offence would be committed. It would, indeed, be anomalous and absurd were the position otherwise. Apart altogether from persons familiar with the restrictions, visitors or long-distance travellers could not reasonably be expected to know of the existence of the restrictions in any particular street."[8]

The value of *MacLeod v Hamilton* as an authority on unpublished law generally may be limited, however, given that specific provisions were made governing publication, which were not followed.

Outside Scotland, exceptions to the rule that error of law is no defence have also been made where the law in question was either unpublished or inaccessible to those at whom it was targeted. One example is the Privy Council case of *Lim Chin Aik v R.*[9] The appellant in this case had been convicted of a breach of an Order made under s.9 of the Immigration Ordinance 1952 prohibiting him (and only him) from entering Singapore. No provision had been made to inform the appellant about the Order. It was accepted that he was unaware of the Order, but he was convicted after the Singapore High Court held that this was no defence. The Privy Council disagreed:

> "It was said on the respondent's part that the Order ... once made, became part of the law of Singapore of which ignorance could [not[10]] provide an excuse upon a charge of contravention of the section. Their Lordships are unable to accept this contention. In their Lordships' opinion ... the maxim cannot apply to such a case as the present where it appears that there is in the State of Singapore no provision ... for the publication in any form of an order of the kind made in the present case or any other provision designed to enable a man by appropriate inquiry to find out what 'the law' is".[11]

[8] At 308 *per* the Lord Justice-General (Clyde). *MacLeod v Hamilton* was applied by the English Divisional Court in a similar case, *James v Cavey* [1967] 2 Q.B. 676 (at 681 *per* Winn L.J.).

[9] [1963] A.C. 160.

[10] The word "not" is omitted from both the A.C. ([1963] A.C. 160) and W.L.R. ([1963] 2 W.L.R. 42) versions of the case report, but this is presumably a mistake. In the All E.R. version ([1963] 1 All E.R. 223), the relevant passage reads: "of which ignorance could provide no excuse on a charge of contravention of this section" (at 226).

[11] *Lim Chin Aik v R* [1963] A.C. 160 at 171, *per* Lord Evershed.

Once again, though, the value of the authority might be questioned on the basis that the law in question applied only to a single named individual.[12] 13.21

In the US, a defence of ignorance of the law was allowed by the Supreme Court in *Lambert v California*[13] where an order was made not concerning an individual but a class of persons. Here, the appellant had been convicted under a Los Angeles Order that made it a criminal offence for "convicted persons" to remain in Los Angeles for more than five days without registering with the police. The appellant had a previous conviction for forgery but was unaware of the Order and had no reason to be aware of it.

It was held by the Supreme Court that to disallow the defence would breach the principle of due process and, especially, the requirement of notice:

> "Where a person did not know of the duty to register and where there was no proof of the probability of such knowledge, he may not be convicted consistently with due process. Were it otherwise, the evil would be as great as it is when the law is written in too fine a print to read or in a language foreign to the community."[14]

All of these cases—*MacLeod v Hamilton*, *Lim Chin Aik* and *Lambert*— involved delegated legislation. In this context, it is worth mentioning s.3(2) of the Statutory Instruments Act 1946. The Act applies to both Scotland and England and Wales and s.3(2) provides for a defence of ignorance of the law where the accused is convicted of an offence created by statutory instrument and that statutory instrument has not been issued by the Stationery Office or otherwise publicised.[15] 13.22

It is likely to be much harder for the accused to establish a defence of ignorance of the law on the basis of an offence created by primary legislation or, more likely in Scotland, the common law. Gordon doubts that, for example, a lack of knowledge of the provision would be a defence to s.21 of the Firearms Act 1968 that prevents a discharged prisoner from possessing a firearm within five years of his discharge.[16]

Ignorance of the law might also provide a defence in cases where it would have been impossible for the particular accused to have known of it. Robinson provides the example of a ship that sailed carrying cargo that becomes embargoed, where the legislation is passed before the ship sets sail but is not announced until after the ship has set sail.[17] Cases of this nature are likely to be quite rare, and there is certainly no reported authority in Scotland.

---

[12] Gordon (para.9.24) states that where an ordinance refers only to one person it may or may not properly be called law. However, he argues that a wider defence of ignorance of publication should be recognised.

[13] (1957) 355 U.S. 225. For comment, see A.F. Brooke, "Note: when ignorance of the law became an excuse: *Lambert* and its progeny" (1991–92) 19 *American Journal of Criminal Law* 279–312.

[14] At 229–230 *per* Douglas J.

[15] For comment, see D. Lanham "Delegated legislation and publication" (1974) 37 M.L.R. 510–524. For an English case where the defence was successfully raised, see: *Simmonds v Newell, Macnay v Newell (aka Defiant Cycle Company v Newell)* [1953] 1 W.LR. 826. The defence has not been raised in any reported Scottish case.

[16] Although as there is no Scottish authority on this issue, this conclusion cannot be reached with any certainty.

[17] Robinson, *Criminal Law Defenses*, §181(d). Advances in communications technology mean that it is perhaps no longer accurate to say that it would have been impossible to discover the law in this situation.

In an early English case, the defence of ignorance of the law was denied in exactly such a case, *R. v Bailey*,[18] a decision criticised as unfair.[19] A conviction seems unjustified if the accused could not have known about a particular provision of the criminal law (assuming that the conduct in question is not something that it could be reasonably anticipated would be criminalised).

A wider defence?

13.23 With the exception of reliance on official advice, which is considered sufficiently distinct to be discussed separately,[20] the exceptions to the maxim described so far are the only ones that have been made in Scots law. The somewhat unpersuasive arguments supporting the maxim,[21] however, suggest that a wider error of law defence might be justified.

One possibility is that any error of law (even an unreasonable one) should provide a defence. Few have argued that it should[22] on the basis that this would provide a route to escape conviction for the blameworthy, who *ought* to have known that their conduct was criminal. The South African experience is of relevance here.[23] Since the case of *S v de Blom*,[24] an expansive defence of error of law has existed in South Africa. In *de Blom*, it was held by the Appellate Division that, in relation to any offence with a *mens rea* of intention, an honest mistake of law, even an unreasonable one, should provide a defence.[25] This approach should be seen in the context of the highly subjective approach taken to *mens rea* in South African law. For offences of intention in South Africa, *mens rea* includes a concept of *dolus*[26] and any honest mistake of law operates to negate *mens rea*. The only exception to this is where negligence suffices as *mens rea* and here only a reasonable mistake of law would exculpate.

The approach taken in *de Blom* has been subject to extensive criticism within South Africa.[27] Critics have argued that, where the accused *ought* to have known that his conduct was criminal, he deserves to be blamed and should be convicted. Indeed, Snyman has suggested that that the rule in *de Blom* can lead to such unjust results that the courts have quietly decided not to apply it.[28]

---

[18] (1800) Russ & Ry 1; 168 E.R. 651. See the US case of *The Cotton Planter*, 6 F. Case 620 (1810) where, on a very similar set of facts, a New York Circuit Court reached the opposite decision.

[19] See, e.g. D. Ormerod, *Smith and Hogan Criminal Law* (11th edn, 2005), p.120.

[20] See paras 13.25–13.36.

[21] See paras 13.03–13.08.

[22] For an example of a commentator who comes close to doing so, see R.G. Singer, "The proposed duty to inquire as affected by recent criminal law decisions in the United States Supreme Court" (1999–2000) 3 *Buffalo Criminal Law Review* 701–754.

[23] For discussion of South African law, see K.A. Mirthaligham, "*Mens rea* and mistake of law in criminal cases: a lesson from South Africa" (1995) 18 *University of New South Wales Law Journal* 428–442; C.R. Snyman, "Confusion concerning the defence of ignorance of law" (1994) 111 S.A.L.J. 1–5; C. Turpin, "Defence of mistake of law" [1978] C.L.J. 8–11.

[24] 1977 (3) S.A. 513 (A). The case is reported in Afrikaans, but a translation is provided in J. Burchell and J. Milton, *Cases and Materials on Criminal Law* (2nd edn, 1997), p.364.

[25] *Per* Rumpff C.J., delivering the judgment of the court, with which the other four judges concurred.

[26] See J. Burchell, *Principles of Criminal Law* (3rd edn, 2005), p.152.

[27] R.C. Whiting, "Changing the face of *mens rea*" (1978) 95 S.A.L.J. 1–8; Snyman, above, fn.23, at pp.4–5.

[28] Snyman, above, fn.23, at p.4. One example that he provides is *S v Coetzee en 'n ander* 1993 (2) S.A.C.R. 191 (T).

There is less reason to object to a rule that permits a defence of *reasonable* error of law. The most convincing argument *for* recognising error of law as a defence in these circumstances is that the accused who has made a reasonable error of law is simply not morally blameworthy.[29] 13.24

Permitting a reasonable error of law defence would bring Scotland into line with continental jurisdictions. For example, the German Penal Code permits the defence whenever an error of law is unavoidable.[30] The French Penal Code permits the defence in relation to errors of law the accused was not in a position to avoid.[31]

Determining whether or not an error of law is reasonable may cause some difficulties. Much would centre on the nature of the conduct in question and whether or not there was any reason to suspect or to anticipate that it might be criminalised.[32] Certainly the defence would be difficult to plead in relation to any activity that would cause or risk causing injury.[33] It would also be difficult to plead by an accused engaged in a business or specialised activity, as it seems reasonable to expect such a person to be informed about the rules of criminal liability relating to that business or specialised activity.[34]

None of these difficulties is in itself a bar to recognising the defence. The courts regularly deal with questions of reasonableness in other areas of the law, so there seems no reason to think that it would cause undue difficulty in relation to error of law.

Reliance on Official Advice

A final category of cases in which error of law has been held to be a defence is where the accused has relied on a mistaken interpretation of the law provided by officials ("reliance on official advice").[35] 13.25

While there are some conceptual similarities between reliance on official advice and renunciation of the right to prosecute,[36] and there may be

[29] B.R. Grace, "Ignorance of the law as an excuse" (1986) 86 *Columbia Law Review* 1392–1416 at p.1413; D. Husak, "Ignorance of law and duties of citizenship" (1994) 14 L.S. 105–115 at p.114; A.T.H. Smith, "Error and mistake of law in Anglo-American criminal law" (1985) 14 *Common Law World Review* 3–32 at p.22.

[30] German Penal Code, art.17. For discussion in English, see G. Arzt, "Ignorance or mistake of law" (1976) 24 *American Journal of Comparative Law* 646–679; R. Youngs, "Mistake of law in Germany—opening up Pandora's Box" (2000) 64 J.C.L. 339–344; M.E. Badar, "*Mens rea*—mistake of law and mistake of fact in German criminal law: a survey for international criminal tribunals" (2005) 5 *International Criminal Law Review* 203–246.

[31] Article 122–3. See also the Austrian Criminal Code, art.9 and the widespread recognition of the defence in Scandinavian countries: J. Andenaes, "*Ignorantia legis* in Scandinavian criminal law" in *Essays in Criminal Science* (G. Mueller (ed.), 1961), pp.217–231.

[32] J. Parry, "Culpability, mistake and official interpretation of law" (1997) 25 *American Journal of Criminal Law* 1–78 at p.72.

[33] D. Husak and A. von Hirsch, "Culpability and mistake of law" in *Action and Value in Criminal Law* (S. Shute, J. Gardner and J. Horder (eds), 1996), pp.157–174, at p.168.

[34] Ashworth, *Principles of Criminal Law*, p.234; Husak and von Hirsch, above, fn.33, at pp.169–170. *Cf.* R.G. Singer, "The proposed duty to inquire as affected by recent criminal law decisions in the United States Supreme Court" (1999–2000) 3 *Buffalo Criminal Law Review* 701–754 at p.709. If the accused has been *misinformed* about the rules relating to his business or specialised activity, he may have a defence of reliance on official advice (see paras 13.25 *et seq.*).

[35] See Gordon, para.9.22; A. Ashworth, "Official advice and mistakes of law" [1998] Crim. L.R. 435–436.

[36] Discussed in Ch.17.

some overlap, the two concepts are for the most part distinguishable. Reliance on official advice covers the situation where the accused, *in advance of embarking on a course of conduct*, has sought the advice of officials as to whether or not his intended conduct would be illegal and has been told that it is not. Renunciation of the right to prosecute is generally concerned with cases where the accused, already having engaged in the conduct in question, has been told by the Crown that he will not be prosecuted for it.

It is, however, possible for renunciations to be general in their terms and have prospective effect, and here the two concepts may overlap. Here, the distinction is this: a renunciation must be a statement by the public prosecutor and is clearly recognised as a defence, whereas reliance on official advice might concern statements by another public official, but is only much more tentatively recognised in law, if at all.[37]

Of all the possible exceptions to the maxim *ignorantia iuris neminem excusat*, reliance on official advice has attracted the most attention in the academic literature, which overwhelmingly supports the defence.[38] Even the strongest supporters of the maxim[39] usually relent in relation to reliance on official advice, since the defence does not contradict the principles on which the maxim rests.[40] There are no real difficulties of proof,[41] as the defence does not require proof that the accused was ignorant of the law; only that he sought advice and was misled. Likewise, allowing the defence cannot be said to encourage ignorance of the law.[42] On the contrary, if it has any influence on behaviour at all,[43] it ought to encourage individuals to seek official advice, secure in the knowledge that if this proves wrong, they will escape criminal liability.

The arguments for its recognition

13.26 Three main arguments have been made in favour of the defence.[44] The first is what has been termed the 'estoppel' argument, whereby the state should be barred from prosecuting in cases where it has misled the accused into thinking that the conduct in question is not criminal.[45]

---

[37] See paras 13.27 *et seq.*

[38] A. Ashworth, "Testing fidelity to legal values" in *Criminal Law Theory: Doctrines of the General Part* (S. Shute and A.P. Simester (eds), 2002), pp.299–330; S.D. Billimack, "Reliance on an official interpretation of the law: the defense's appropriate dimensions" 1993 *University of Illinois Law Review* 565–588; J. Parry, "Culpability, mistake and official interpretation of law" (1997) 25 *American Journal of Criminal Law* 1–78; T. White, "Reliance on apparent authority as a defence to criminal prosecution" (1977) 77 *Columbia Law Review* 775–809.

[39] See J. Hall, "Ignorance and mistake in criminal law" (1957) 33 *Indiana Law Journal* 1–44 at p.27; R.M. Perkins, "Ignorance and mistake in criminal law" (1939) 88 *University of Pennsylvania Law Review* 35–70 at p.42.

[40] Although this did not prevent the English Law Commission from recommending that the strict principle that error of law is no defence be retained, even in reliance on official advice cases, despite admitting that it raised issues of fairness (*Codification of the Criminal Law: A Report to the Law Commission* (Law Com. No. 143, 1985), at paras 9.5–9.6). For criticism see G. Williams, "The Draft Code and reliance on official statements" (1989) 9 L.S. 177–188 at p.177.

[41] Austin's objection to allowing a general error of law defence (see para.13.04 above).

[42] Holmes' objection to allowing a general error of law defence (see para.13.06 above).

[43] On this, see Parry's scepticism about utilitarian justifications of the defence (Parry, above, fn.38, at p.32).

[44] These are comprehensively set out by Ashworth in "Testing fidelity", above, fn.38, at pp.304–309; Billimack, above, fn.38, at pp.577–580; and Parry, above, fn.38, whose whole paper is concerned with the arguments for recognising the defence.

[45] Billimack, above, fn.38, at p.578; Robinson, *Criminal Law Defenses*, §183(c).

Ashworth describes this as an argument based on maintaining the integrity of the criminal justice process.[46] The moral authority and legitimacy of the system would be compromised, he states, if it engaged in what is effectively self-contradiction. This argument is only convincing, of course, if the official providing the advice and the criminal court system are held to be part of the same system.

A second, and to some extent related, argument is that to disallow the defence would contradict essential notions of due process, in particular that the accused be given due notice of conduct deemed criminal.[47] In many instances, the requirement of due notice is something of a fiction, given that individuals do not generally examine case law or legislation before they commit criminal offences. It is simply that by virtue of the publication of statutes and the reporting of cases, individuals are deemed to have been given notice of what constitutes criminal conduct. As Parry points out,[48] however, in the situation where the accused has relied on official advice, it could be argued that the accused has been given *actual but incorrect* notice and thus the imposition of punishment would seem to contravene fundamental principles of fairness. After all, the accused did not know and, if one accepts this argument, could not reasonably have been expected to know, that his conduct was criminal.[49] This does depend on an assumption: that a state official's advice as to the law is treated as akin to a declaration of the law itself.

A third argument in favour of allowing the defence is that not to do so would contradict basic principles of criminal responsibility because, assuming certain conditions are satisfied, the accused who acts on the basis of mistaken official advice is simply not morally blameworthy.[50] On the contrary, the accused who, uncertain about whether or not his planned conduct conforms to the criminal law, has done all we can reasonably expect of him when he seeks the advice of a competent official.

The authorities

There is only one reported case in Scotland where the issue has been discussed and no general principles were set down. In *Roberts v Local Authority for Inverness*,[51] the accused was convicted of an offence under a regulation that prohibited moving cattle from one local authority area to another without a licence and without lawful authority or excuse. His defence was that, when he applied for a licence, the responsible inspector appointed by the local authority told him that no licence was needed for the journey. **13.27**

His conviction was quashed by the High Court. The Lord Justice-Clerk (Macdonald) delivered the opinion of the court and accepted that "the appellant acted in perfect *bona fides* upon ... the inspector's statement

---

[46] Ashworth "Testing fidelity", above, fn.38, at p.308. See the similar argument he makes in the same article about entrapment, discussed in Ch.20.

[47] Billimack, above, fn.38, at p.578.

[48] Parry, above, fn.38, at p.52.

[49] A. Ashworth, "Testing fidelity to legal values" in *Criminal Law Theory: Doctrines of the General Part* (S. Shute and A.P. Simester (eds), 2002), pp.299–330, at p.307.

[50] Ashworth "Testing fidelity", above, fn.49, at p.305; S.D. Billimack, "Reliance on an official interpretation of the law: the defense's appropriate dimensions" 1993 *University of Illinois Law Review* 565–588 at p.577; J. Parry, "Culpability, mistake and official interpretation of law" (1997) 25 *American Journal of Criminal* Law 1–78 at p.21.

[51] (1889) 2 White 385.

that no licence was necessary".[52] He went on to state that the only remaining question was whether or not this constituted "lawful authority or excuse" under the statute and he concluded that it did:

> "... in my opinion it would be a case of gross oppression if the sentence pronounced convicting the appellant was allowed to stand. I have no hesitation in saying that there is in the facts proved sufficient to warrant us finding that there was a lawful excuse for what the appellant did."[53]

He continued:

> "It is monstrous to suppose that a man who acts on the advice of the authorised servant of the Local Authority, who declines to give him a certificate because it is unnecessary, is to be found guilty of an offence."[54]

What is not clear is whether *Roberts* establishes some sort of general defence of reliance on official advice in Scots law or whether its application, if indeed it has any, is confined to offences where an exception of "lawful authority or excuse" exists.[55]

13.28 The Draft Criminal Code allows reliance on official advice as its sole exception to the principle that error of the criminal law is no defence,[56] but the commentary expresses no conclusive opinion on the value of *Roberts* as an authority, stating only that *Roberts* "may" have been an example of this principle.[57]

If Scots law did not accept reliance on official advice as a defence, it would be out of line with the majority of common law jurisdictions. English law recently recognised the defence,[58] ignoring a long line of authorities in which the defence had (at times very unfairly) been ruled out.[59] Given that Scots law has followed the English approach to entrapment,[60] a conceptually similar defence, it would not be unreasonable to conclude that a similar approach to reliance on official advice would be taken, especially given the absence of any contrary Scottish authority.[61]

The English case in which the defence first succeeded was

---

[52] At 391.

[53] At 391–392.

[54] At 392.

[55] *Roberts* has not been relied upon in any subsequently reported case. It is also unclear what would have happened if the error, which was an error relating to a concept of the civil law, was the accused's alone. It may be that this in itself would have provided a defence (see paras 13.13–13.18).

[56] s.28(2).

[57] Commentary to Draft Criminal Code, at 71.

[58] In *Postermobile v Brent LBC* [1998] Crim. L.R. 435. It was dealt with not as a substantive defence, but as an abuse of process (see below).

[59] See *Surrey County Council v Battersby* [1965] 2 Q.B. 194 (and the comment on the case by P. Brett, "Mistake of law as a criminal defence" (1965–1967) 5 *Melbourne University Law Review* 179–204); *Cambridgeshire and Isle of Ely County Council v Rust* [1972] 1 Q.B. 426; *R. v Bowsher* [1973] Crim. L.R. 373; *R. v Arrowsmith* (1975) 1 Q.B. 678.

[60] In *Brown v HM Advocate*, 2002 S.L.T. 809, the appeal court adopted into Scots law the principles set out by the House of Lords on entrapment in *R. v Loosely, Attorney General's Reference (No.3 of 2000)* [2001] UKHL 53. See Ch.20.

[61] Although, as Scots law has not followed English law on abuse of process generally, this conclusion cannot be drawn with any certainty. See Ch.19.

Postermobile v Brent LBC.[62] Here, a company was advised by two members of the local council's planning department that erection of advertising boards would not require planning consent and was therefore not illegal. The company was subsequently prosecuted for displaying advertisements without the appropriate planning consent. The Divisional Court held that the prosecution should have been stayed as an abuse of process.[63] Schiemann L.J. stated that it is important "that the citizen should be able to rely on what a public official tells him"[64] and that he saw:

> "... no substantial public purpose being served in continuing to prosecute an individual who has come to the Council for advice as to whether something which he proposes to do is lawful, is advised that it is and then in reliance on that representation does that very thing".[65]

The council had argued that the individuals whose advice had been sought were only junior officials, but the court did not find this to be a bar to the defence, stating that it was not as though the defendants had requested planning advice from one of the council's gardeners.[66]

What is not clear is the extent to which the decision in *Postermobile* turned on the fact that the advising and prosecuting body were one and the same (the local council). *Postermobile* has not been considered in any subsequently reported case. It may be that where the official body from which the advice has been obtained is not also the prosecuting body, the previous English authorities in which the defence was ruled out[67] are still authoritative. 13.29

The defence of reliance on official advice has long been recognised in the United States, with the first reported successful case, *Long v State*,[68] being decided in 1949 by the Supreme Court of Delaware. The US Supreme Court first allowed the defence in 1959 in *Raley v Ohio*,[69] basing it on the constitutional requirement for due process and fairness to the individual.[70] In Canada, the defence, termed "officially induced error of law", was first recognised by the Supreme Court in *R. v Jorgensen*[71] and its existence has since been confirmed in *Lévis (City) v Tétreault*.[72a] Here

---

[62] [1998] Crim. L.R. 435. For comment, see A. Ashworth, "Official advice and mistakes of law" [1998] Crim. L.R. 435–436.

[63] The procedural basis of the defence is discussed in para.13.34 below.

[64] *Postermobile v Brent LBC* [1998] Crim. L.R. 435 at p.435.

[65] This passage is not reported in the Crim. L.R. case report, but see the Lexis transcript of *Postermobile*, at 3.

[66] *Postermobile v Brent LBC* [1998] Crim. L.R. 435 at 435.

[67] *Surrey County Council v Battersby* [1965] 2 Q.B. 194; *Cambridgeshire and Isle of Ely County Council v Rust* [1972] 1 Q.B. 426; *R. v Bowsher* [1973] Crim. L.R. 373; *R. v Arrowsmith* (1975) 1 Q.B. 678.

[68] 65 A.2d 489 (1949). The advice in question in this case actually came from an attorney (on which, see paras 13.35 *et seq.*).

[69] 360 U.S. 423 (1959), confirmed in *Cox v Louisiana*, 379 U.S. 559 (1965). For a history of the defence in the US, see P.S. Cremer, "The ironies of law reform: a history of reliance on officials as a defense in American criminal law" (1978–1979) 14 *California Western Law Review* 48–91.

[70] *Raley v Ohio*, 360 U.S. 423 (1959) at 437–440; *Cox v Louisiana*, 379 U.S. 559 (1965) at 568–575.

[71] [1995] 4 S.C.R. 55. Prior to this, it had been accepted by the lower courts (e.g. by the Nova Scotia County Court in *R. v Maclean* (1974) 17 C.C.C. (2d) 84 and by the Ontario Court of Appeal in *R. v Cancoil Thermal Corporation* (1986) 27 C.C.C. (3d) 295). *Jorgensen* itself contains a comprehensive history of the defence in Canadian law (at [12]–[24]).

[72a] 2006 S.C.C. 12.

the appellant had been charged with knowingly selling obscene material without lawful justification or excuse. He claimed in his defence that he had relied on the Ontario Film Review Board's approval of the material in concluding that it was not obscene. The case was actually decided on another ground,[72] but Lamer C.J. wrote at some length about officially induced error of law and held that it would have been a defence if the other ground of appeal had not succeeded. Lamer C.J. based the defence in notions of fairness[73] and individual culpability.[74]

The requirements of the defence

13.30 The only Scottish authority, *Robertson*, does not set out the dimensions of a defence of reliance on official advice. Accordingly, it is necessary to look to other jurisdictions.

The requirement for advice

13.31 The first requirement that might form part of the defence is that the accused acted on the basis of official *advice*.[75] In *Robertson*, this was not in issue—the accused had clearly sought the advice of a local authority official about his planned conduct. A question that arises, however, is whether *actual* advice is necessary or whether *implied* advice might suffice. Glanville Williams has argued that the defence should be allowed wherever:

> "... contraventions have for a substantial time been known to the relevant officers and have not been made subject to a prosecution or warning, thus leading to a reasonable belief that conduct is non-criminal or that the law will not be enforced".[76]

Reliance on implied advice seemed to have been ruled out as a defence in the English case of *London Borough of Redbridge v Jaques*[77] but this was decided before *Postermobile*. Subsequent to *Postermobile*, the defence appears to have been accepted in *R. v Liverpool Magistrates' Court ex*

---

[72] That the *mens rea* of the offence was not satisfied. Lamer C.J. issued a separate opinion in which he considered the defence of officially induced error of law. The majority concurred in the result, but chose not to address the issue of officially induced error, given that it was not the central issue in the case (at [123] *per* Sopinka J., for the majority). The Supreme Court has now approved Lamer C.J.'s opinion and formally recognised the defence in *Lévis (City) v Tétreault*, 2006 S.C.C. 12.

[73] *R. v Jorgensen* [1995] 4 S.C.R. 55 at [6]. See also *Lévis (City) v Tétreault*, 2006 S.C.C. 12 at [22].

[74] *R. v Jorgensen* [1995] 4 S.C.R. 55 at [9].

[75] And that the advice was given in good faith in the full knowledge of the circumstances. In the US, the defence has been disallowed where the defendant withheld details of his planned conduct. See, e.g. *United States v Stirling*, 439 U.S. 824 (1978).

[76] G. Williams, "The Draft Code and reliance on official statements" (1989) 9 L.S. 177–188 at p.185.

[77] [1970] 1 W.L.R. 1604. The facts of *Jaques* provide an example of the sort of case Williams is referring to. The respondent had been acquitted of the offence of wilfully obstructing free passage along the highway under s.121(1) of the Highways Act 1957. For many years previously, in the full knowledge of the police and the local authority, he had been operating a fruit and vegetable stall every Thursday on a public road in front of a row of shops that were closed for early closing on Thursday. On appeal, Lord Parker C.J., delivering the judgment of the Court of Appeal, stated that he felt sorry for the respondent, but that in originally acquitting him, the justices had acted out of sympathy and the act was unlawful. He remitted the case back to the justices with a direction to convict, although he suggested that the penalty be minimal.

parte Slade.[78] The case arose out of an earlier occasion on which Slade was prosecuted under the Dangerous Dogs Act 1991 for having a pit bull terrier in a public place without being muzzled and kept on a lead. His defence was that his dog was not a pit bull terrier. On the day of the trial, the expert witness for the prosecution failed to attend and the case collapsed. On returning to the police station the following day, the police let the defendant take the dog, but did not tell him that the prosecution had decided that they would prosecute him again for having a dog in a public place without a muzzle when he left the station. When the prosecution did exactly that and brought a fresh prosecution against him, this was stayed by the Queen's Bench Division on the basis that it was an abuse of process. The court noted that the defendant:

> "... could reasonably assume that he would not be prosecuted for doing what he did and the police could have but did not disabuse him of that belief ... Given the consequences of a conviction [at the time there was mandatory destruction of the dog], it was unfair to try the defendant for the offence and offensive to the court's sense of justice and propriety, so as to be an abuse of process."[79]

Actual reliance

The second requirement that can be gleaned from the operation of the defence in other jurisdictions is that the accused must have actually *relied* on the advice he was given. For example, in *Jorgensen*, the Canadian Supreme Court held that the accused must have actually relied on specific advice, by showing that advice was given prior to the act and in response to a question "specifically tailored to the accused's situation".[80] **13.32**

Reasonable reliance

A third requirement that can be gleaned from authorities in other jurisdictions is that the accused's reliance on the advice must have been reasonable in the circumstances.[81] This raises the question of when is it reasonable to rely on advice. Various considerations have been suggested by case law[82] and commentators.[83] The status of the official is likely to be one factor.[84] In *Jorgensen*, the Canadian Supreme Court held that, in general, "government officials who are involved in the administration of the law in question will be considered appropriate officials"[85] but otherwise provided no specific guidance.[86] Ashworth has suggested that an official who was too junior or who was not in the right department might be ruled out.[87] **13.33**

---

78 [1998] 1 W.L.R. 531.

79 At 536 *per* Pill L.J.

80 *R. v Jorgensen* [1995] 4 S.C.R. 55 at [35], approved in *Lévis (City) v Tétreault*, 2006 S.C.C. 12 at [27].

81 *R. v Cancoil Thermal Corporation* (1986) 27 C.C.C. (3d) 295 at 303; *R. v Jorgensen* [1995] 4 S.C.R. 55 at [33]; *Lévis (City) v Tétreault*, 2006 S.C.C. 12 at [26].

82 *R. v Cancoil Thermal Corporation* (1986) 27 C.C.C. (3d) 295 at 303.

83 A. Ashworth, "Excusable mistake of law" [1974] Crim. L.R. 652–662 at p.660.

84 This raises the question of whether it might ever be reasonable to rely on the advice of a lawyer other than one acting on behalf of the state (see paras 13.35 *et seq.*).

85 *R. v Jorgensen* [1995] 4 S.C.R. 55 at [30], *per* Lamer C.J.

86 Lamer C.J. did think that the Ontario Film Review Board (the body that approves films for playing in Ontario) would count as an official body for the purposes of the defence which, here, centred on whether or not a film was obscene.

87 A. Ashworth, "Testing fidelity to legal values" in *Criminal Law Theory: Doctrines of the General Part* (S. Shute and A.P. Simester (eds), 2002), pp.299–330, at p.305.

Another factor is the nature of the conduct in question. It would seem less reasonable to rely on advice where the course of conduct advised is obviously morally blameworthy; for instance, where personal injury or damage to property would result.[88]

It has also been suggested that the ambiguity of the law might be a relevant factor to consider in determining whether it was reasonable to follow the advice given.[89] It would, on this view, be less reasonable to follow advice where the language of the provision is clear and the advice differs from its clear meaning.

Finally, Ashworth[90] has suggested that it may not be reasonable for a defendant to rely on official advice where she is herself an expert and knows the advice is probably wrong.

The procedural mechanism

13.34 A further question arises of the procedural mechanism for dealing with the accused who has relied on official advice. The stance one takes on this issue depends to an extent on the rationale favoured for the defence. If one takes the view that reliance on official advice reduces culpability, then a substantive defence would seem a logical remedy. If one accepts that reliance on official advice is not about culpability, but the integrity of the criminal justice system, then the appropriate remedy is a stay of proceedings.

In *Roberts*, reliance on official advice was regarded as a substantive defence. This was, though, on the basis that it constituted a "lawful excuse" for conduct under a statute that provided for a defence of "lawful authority or excuse". It was not regarded as a free-standing defence under common law. The approach that has been favoured in other common law jurisdictions is that, if proved, it operates not as a substantive defence, but as a matter that should lead to a stay of proceedings.

In England, in *Postermobile*, the prosecution brought against the defendants was stayed as an abuse of process, mirroring the approach taken to the issue of entrapment by the English courts.[91] In Canada, the Canadian Supreme Court in *Jorgensen* held that officially induced error of law should not operate as a defence leading to an acquittal but it should lead to a judicial stay of proceedings. Lamer C.J. found this kind of official inducement "procedurally similar to entrapment."[92]

The Scottish appeal court has already followed the English approach to entrapment,[93] although seemingly via the Scottish procedural mechanism of a plea in bar of trial based on oppression,[94] rather than the English procedural mechanism of abuse of process.[95] Assuming the court was prepared to recognise the defence at all, it seems relatively safe to conclude that a Scottish court would take the same approach if a suitable case arose.

---

[88] J. Horder, *Excusing Crime* (2004), p.271.

[89] *R. v Cancoil Thermal Corporation* (1986) 27 C.C.C. (3d) 295 at 303.

[90] Ashworth, "Testing fidelity to legal values" above, fn.87, at p.305.

[91] See *R. v Loosely, Attorney General's Reference (No.3 of 2000)* [2001] UKHL 53 (discussed in Ch.20).

[92] *R. v Jorgensen* [1995] 4 S.C.R. 55 at [37]. See also *Lévis (City) v Tétreault*, 2006 S.C.C. 12 at [25].

[93] In *Brown v HM Advocate*, 2002 S.L.T. 809.

[94] Some support for this can be found in *Roberts v Local Authority for Inverness* (1889) 2 White 385, where the Lord Justice-Clerk (Macdonald) did state that if a conviction was allowed, this "would be a case of gross oppression" (at 392).

[95] See Ch.19.

The advice of a private lawyer

A further question is whether or not reliance on official advice should operate as a defence where the incorrect advice was obtained from a private lawyer.[96] The balance of academic opinion is that it should, although there have been notable dissenters on this point.[97] **13.35**

The question has never arisen in Scots law, although the Draft Criminal Code appears to exclude a private lawyer's advice from the defence, defining official advice as "advice from a national or local government official charged with some responsibility for the area of activity in question".[98]

In English law, a case where the official advice was provided by a lawyer has not arisen since *Postermobile*,[99] but the procedural approach taken would seem to suggest that reliance on a private lawyer's advice would not be sufficient to stay proceedings, as the advice would not have stemmed from a state agent.[1]

Those arguing for the recognition of a defence of reliance on the advice of a private lawyer have tended to focus on the fact that in some circumstances[2] relying on the advice of a lawyer may well be more reasonable than relying on the advice of, say, a junior official.[3] One's conclusion on this matter might well depend on the rationale (and the procedural basis) one accepts for the defence of reliance on official advice in the first place. If it is seen as a defence based on abuse of process then the defence should probably be restricted to advice provided by state officials; it is only if the defence is based on notions of culpability that a lawyer's advice might be allowed.[4]

The most common argument that has been made *against* allowing a lawyer's advice in this context is the potential for abuse.[5] This was found to be persuasive in the US case of *Hunter v State*,[6] where the defence was rejected by the Supreme Court of Tennessee on the basis that it: **13.36**

> "... would be productive of disastrous results, opening a way of escape from prosecution for the criminally inclined through a door held ajar by ignorant, biased or purchasable advisors".[7]

---

96 As opposed to a lawyer acting in an official capacity for the state.

97 See, e.g. M. Guy-Arye, "Reliance on a lawyer's mistaken advice: should it be an excuse from criminal liability?" (2001–2002) 29 *American Journal of Criminal Law* 455–480.

98 s.28(3)(b).

99 For a case that ruled out the defence prior to *Postermobile*, see *Cooper v Simmons* (1862) 7 H & N 707; 158 E.R. 654.

1 Although the issue was left open in *R. v Jorgensen* [1995] 4 S.C.R. 55 (and was not clarified in *Lévis (City) v Tétreault*, 2006 S.C.C. 12), the same can be said of Canada. In the US, although the very first case in which the defence was recognised was one where the advice was provided by a private lawyer (*Long v State*, 65 A.2d 489 (1949)), since then, the defence has generally been ruled out. The majority of US states follow the Model Penal Code which allows the defence only where advice has been provided by "the public officer or body charged by law with responsibility for the interpretation, administration or enforcement of the law defining the offense" (s.2.04(3)(b)). See Gur-Arye, above, fn.97, at fn.35.

2 For example, where the lawyer is a highly experienced specialist in the area of law in question.

3 Ashworth, *Principles of Criminal Law*, p.237; J. Parry, "Culpability, mistake and official interpretation of law" (1997) 25 *American Journal of Criminal* Law 1–78 at p.72.

4 Unless one takes the view that even private lawyers are part of the state's justice system.

5 Gur-Arye, above, fn.97, at p.466, although she does not think this is the strongest argument for rejecting the defence, accepting as she does some of the counter- arguments set out below.

6 (1928) 12 S.W. 2d 361.

7 At 363. See also *State v Downs*, 21 S.E. 689 (1895). *Cf. Long v State*, 65 A.2d 489 (1949).

The main fear is that lawyers might be tempted by financial or other incentives to provide incorrect advice, and thus immunity from prosecution for their clients.[8] A number of counter-arguments can be made in this context. By making it a requirement of the defence that the accused must *actually* have relied on the advice in guiding his conduct, this would seem to rule out instances where the accused and his lawyer concocted a scheme to escape conviction.[9] It has also been pointed out that lawyers who have been bribed to give erroneous advice are likely to be subject to disciplinary action.[10] In addition, it might be said that this argument could equally apply to public officials, as there seems to be no reason for thinking that as a class they would be less subject to the temptations of bribery than lawyers.[11]

Gur-Ayre sets out a number of additional arguments against recognising reliance on a private lawyer's advice as a defence, although none of them are particularly convincing. Her main concern is what she terms the social cost of recognising the excuse.[12] Allowing the defence will open up the possibility of courts having to make judgments about a lawyer's reputation, given that an element of the defence will be how reasonable it was to rely on the advice, a factor that relates to the reputation and quality of the lawyer in question.[13] This, she suggests, harms the interests of justice in a number of ways. First, it is likely to raise questions of the appearance of bias if a judge rules that a particular lawyer's advice is of poor quality and is then faced with deciding a subsequent case in which that lawyer is involved.[14] Secondly, she states, because those lawyers judged to have a good reputation will be able to command high fees, those on lower incomes are less likely to be able to use the reliance on official advice defence and "immunity from prosecution will become a question of economics".[15] While these arguments possibly have some merit, they are highly speculative and must be weighed against the cost of denying the defence in terms of convicting those who did not act in a blameworthy manner.[16] Having said that, the circumstances in which the conditions of the defence will be made out are likely to be rare in practice.

---

[8] L. Hall and S. Seligman, "Mistake of law and *mens rea*" (1940–1941) 8 *University of Chicago Law Review* 641–683 at p.652.

[9] S.D. Billimack, "Reliance on an official interpretation of the law: the defense's appropriate dimensions" 1993 *University of Illinois Law Review* 565–588 at p.579.

[10] A.T.H. Smith, "Error and mistake of law in Anglo-American criminal law" (1985) 14 *Common Law World Review* 3–32 at p.8.

[11] Billimack, above, fn.9, at p.580.

[12] M. Guy-Arye, "Reliance on a lawyer's mistaken advice: should it be an excuse from criminal liability?" (2001–2002) 29 *American Journal of Criminal Law* 455–480 at p.467.

[13] Gur-Arye, above, fn.12, at p.467.

[14] *ibid.* at p.467.

[15] *ibid.* at p.468.

[16] Although Gur-Arye does point out that the accused still had a choice about whether or not to engage in the conduct in question. In consulting a lawyer in the first place, that person must have been in a state of some uncertainty about the legality of the conduct and therefore it is the individual who should bear the risk of conviction (Gur-Ayre, above, fn.12, at p.474).

Chapter 14

INSANITY IN BAR OF TRIAL

Introduction

The plea of insanity in bar of trial operates to prevent a person from being tried when he is unable to properly participate in the process, in that he cannot instruct the defence or understand the proceedings. The use of the term "insanity" in this context is unfortunate. Not only is that term stigmatic and no longer used medically,[1] it fails to reflect the breadth of the plea, which can apply in circumstances far removed from any popular understanding of the term. As far back as 1975, the Thomson Committee recommended that it be replaced with "unfitness to plead on account of mental disorder",[2] while the Scottish Law Commission has more recently recommended that the plea be renamed "unfitness for trial".[3] These recommendations have yet to be acted on. **14.01**

The plea serves a number of purposes. First, the law recognises that where an accused person is unable to participate in his trial, the risk of wrongful conviction is consequently increased. That is not, however, the only (or probably even the principal) justification for the plea. There may be cases where guilt can be conclusively established even though the accused is unfit to plead (just as guilt might be conclusively established where a competent accused refuses to participate in the trial process): indeed, the modern process of an "examination of facts" assumes that at least some form of accurate ascertainment of the relevant facts is possible.[4] More convincingly, the plea protects the "moral dignity"[5] of the process: as the Criminal Law Revision Committee has observed, "[t]o go through the motions of trying a person unable to understand what was taking place would be absurd and might be cruel".[6] Duff has argued that the rationale of the plea can be understood by reference to the idea of participation in the criminal trial: "a criminal trial is a process of argument and judgment which is meant to be conducted *with* the defendant".[7] That rationale is consistent with the right to a fair trial under Art.6 of the

[1] See the *Report of the Committee on Mentally Abnormal Offenders* (Cmnd. 6244, 1975), para.18.18: "the continued use of the words 'insanity' and 'insane' in the criminal law long after their disappearance from psychiatry and mental health law has been a substantial source of difficulty, and we attach importance to the discontinuance of the use of these words in the criminal law".

[2] *Criminal Procedure in Scotland (Second Report)* (Cmnd. 6218, 1975), para.52.13.

[3] *Report on Insanity and Diminished Responsibility* (Scot. Law Com. No. 195, 2004), para.4.10.

[4] See below, paras 14.10–14.13.

[5] R.J. Bonnie, "The competence of criminal defendants: beyond *Dusky* and *Drope*" (1993) 47 *University of Miami Law Review* 539–601 at p.543.

[6] Criminal Law Revision Committee, *Third Report: Criminal Procedure (Insanity)* (Cmnd. 2149, 1963), para.21.

[7] R.A. Duff, *Trials and Punishments* (1985), p.35.

ECHR,[8] and is reflected in the test applied by the courts in modern practice, which is essentially an assessment of the accused's ability to participate in the process.

Insanity as a plea in bar of trial differs from insanity as a substantive defence[9] in two ways. First, it is concerned with the accused's state of mind at the time of the trial, rather than at the time the offence was committed. Secondly, the test which is applied differs between the two pleas. This is because insanity as a substantive defence is concerned with the accused's responsibility for acts committed, while insanity as a plea in bar of trial is concerned with the accused's capacity to participate in the criminal process. A successful plea in bar of trial says nothing about whether the accused was in fact responsible for his alleged actions at the relevant time.

The Test to be Applied

14.02 The test to be applied where insanity is pleaded in bar of trial has not developed in a particularly coherent fashion, and the modern law rests on a number of passages from trial judges' charges to juries and some appellate decisions which are not easily reconcilable.

Although there are a number of reported cases on the plea in bar in the Justiciary Reports, they are generally reports of proceedings at first instance where the matter was dealt with by the trial judge, and so no exposition of the relevant principles was called for,[10] particularly as the court rarely rejected the views of medical witnesses that the accused was unfit to plead.[11] Consequently, although the medical evidence given is sometimes narrated, it is difficult to establish what test was being applied, and in some cases the medical witnesses were simply asked directly whether they considered the accused a "proper object for trial" or similar.[12] In some cases, the note of the medical evidence indicates that court and counsel were concerned primarily about the accused's capacity to instruct counsel,[13] and, on one occasion, knowledge of right from wrong.[14]

Although the importance of the accused knowing right from wrong was given some weight by the remarks of the Lord Justice-Clerk (Macdonald) in *HM Advocate v Robertson*,[15] it has not featured in subsequent case law,

[8] See *Report on Insanity and Diminished Responsibility* (Scot. Law Com. No. 195, 2004), paras 4.24–4.30. The Commission concludes (at para.4.29) that the Convention case law requires that the accused be able to "effectively participate" in the trial.

[9] On which, see Ch.7.

[10] See *John Warrand* (1825) Shaw 130; *William Douglas* (1827) Shaw 192, Syme 184; *Mary Paterson* (1842) 1 Broun 200; *James Daly* (1846) Ark 213; *Thomas or Alexander Smith* (1858) 3 Irv. 167; *Thomas Arnot* (1864) 4 Irv. 529; *Joannis Manolatos* (1864) 4 Irv. 485.

[11] There are exceptions: see *John Caldwell* (1866) 5 Irv. 241, where the reasons for the plea being repelled are not stated, although it is clear that the evidence in its favour was weak. See also *HM Advocate v Cameron*, 1946 S.N. 74.

[12] See *Euphemia Lees* (1845) 2 Broun 484, where the medical witnesses were questioned in these terms by the trial judge, Lord Mackenzie. See also *Archibald Robertson* (1836) 1 Swin. 15.

[13] See, e.g. *Adam Sliman* (1844) 2 Broun 138. Lord Moncrieff also states in that case (at 140) that "[t]he real question is, does he understand the meaning of pleading 'guilty' or 'not guilty'?" See also *Euphemia Lees* (1845) 2 Broun 484; *Peter Peanver* (1850) J. Shaw 462.

[14] *John Caldwell* (1866) 5 Irv. 241.

[15] (1891) 3 White 6 at 16–17.

which has concentrated instead on the capacity of the accused to instruct counsel and (more recently) to comprehend the proceedings.

The first substantive discussion of the plea is found in *HM Advocate v Brown*.[16] In that case, the accused was charged with murder, the allegation being that he had iced a shortbread cake with a strychnine icing and then sent it through the post, whereupon the recipient's housekeeper died after eating a portion. The Solicitor-General suggested that he might be unfit to plead to the charge, but this was strongly resisted by Brown's counsel. The court consequently decided that it was inexpedient to deal with the matter by way of a preliminary inquiry, and that the matter should be left to the jury after trial (as was then possible).[17] At the trial, evidence was led that Brown was prone to epileptic fits and that epileptic patients might partially or totally forget what they had done when in an epileptic state. The Lord Justice-General's charge to the jury constitutes the first detailed judicial pronouncement on the plea: **14.03**

> "On this question for your determination of whether the prisoner is or is not insane, I must consider with you what that class of insanity means. It means insanity which prevents a man from doing what a truly sane man would do and is entitled to do—maintain in sober sanity his plea of innocence, and instruct those who defend him as a truly sane man would do.
>
> You have heard about instructions being given for the defence. That is a good enough test to a certain extent, but not a complete one. There is one matter which has been left out of view. The learned counsel has said to you that he has received such instructions as a sane man would give. But that is not enough. There is something which is not generally asked about, and that is that the person who is giving these instructions should not only intelligently, but without obliteration of memory as to what has happened in his life, give a true history of the circumstances of his life at the time the supposed crime was committed. It is just there that the question you have to determine lies...
>
> It is a duty imposed on you ... to say whether in your judgment he is in the condition of a truly sane man, who can not only tell his counsel how to defend him, but can tell his counsel, with the certainty of not being deceived, what he was really doing at the time during which the act is said to have been committed."[18]

Essentially, this repeats the test of capacity to instruct counsel found in the earlier cases,[19] but seems to add in an additional prong to the test, suggesting that an individual may also be unfit to plead if he is unable to give an account of the relevant circumstances to those defending him. Although *Brown* has continued to be referred to as authoritative,[20] it is **14.04**

---

[16] (1907) 5 Adam 312.

[17] On the modern position, see below, para.14.12.

[18] (1907) 5 Adam 312 at 343–345.

[19] See above, para.14.02.

[20] See, e.g. *Stewart v HM Advocate (No. 1)*, 1997 J.C. 183.

difficult to understand why this is so, given that the appeal court has now twice ruled that amnesia is not a basis for the plea in bar, despite the fact that Lord Dunedin's charge in *Brown* seems to suggest that it should be.[21]

There is no detailed treatment of the plea in bar in the case reports after *Brown* until the decision in *HM Advocate v Wilson* in 1942.[22] Wilson, charged with robbery and murder, was "to all intents and purposes" deaf and dumb, and certain medical witnesses who gave evidence at a preliminary inquiry considered that he was not of "normal intellect".[23] As in *Brown*, the question was left to the jury, given defence counsel's wish to proceed to trial on the instructions of the accused. Lord Wark charged the jury in the following terms:

> "Now, what exactly is meant by saying that a man is unfit to plead? The ordinary and common case, of course, is the case of a man who suffers from insanity, that is to say, from mental alienation of some kind which prevents him giving the instructions which a sane man would give for his defence, or from following the evidence as a sane man would follow it, and instructing his counsel as the case goes along upon any point that arises. Now, no medical man says, and no medical man has ever said, that this accused is insane in that sense. His reason is not alienated, but he may be insane for the purposes of the section of the Lunacy Act to which counsel referred, although his reason is not alienated, if his condition be such that he is unable either from mental defect or physical defect, or a combination of these, to tell his counsel what his defence is and instruct him so that he can appear and defend him; or if, again, his condition of mind and body is such that he does not understand the proceedings which are going on when he is brought into Court upon his trial, and cannot intelligibly follow what it is all about. Now, the question which you have to consider in this case is whether it is proved that the accused is unfit to plead in either of these senses, that is to say, is there any evidence that he was not, and is not, able to instruct his solicitor and counsel as to his defence?"[24]

---

[21] *Russell v HM Advocate*, 1946 J.C. 47; *Hughes v HM Advocate*, 2002 J.C. 23. See below, para.14.06.

[22] 1942 J.C. 75. Lord Constable's opinion in *HM Advocate v Sharp*, 1927 J.C. 66, a case heard between the decisions in *Brown* and *Wilson*, proceeds on the basis that—given that Sharp's condition had not changed since the time of the alleged murder—it was appropriate to apply the test for insanity as a substantive defence. It is now clear that the tests for insanity as a defence and insanity as a plea in bar are clearly distinct: see the opinion of the trial judge in *Stewart v HM Advocate (No. 1)*, 1997 J.C. 183.

[23] See 1942 J.C. 75 at 78, *per* the Lord Justice-General (Normand).

[24] At 80. The statutory reference is to s.87 of the Lunacy Act 1857, under which the jury was competent to determine whether the accused was insane so that he was unfit to plead. The jury found Wilson not guilty.

This direction has since been approved by the appeal court on at least two occasions,[25] and may be taken as representing the modern law.[26] It appears to recognise a plea in bar of trial in two different situations: first, where the accused is incapable of instructing his defence (either before or during the trial) or, secondly, where he is incapable of understanding the proceedings.[27] It may be, of course, that both situations are made out at the same time. The fact that an accused person may not act in his own best interests during the course of the trial is not in itself sufficient to ground the plea in bar.[28] **14.05**

Whether the test is satisfied is a question of fact, and English research suggests that the most common instances of successful pleas in bar have involved schizophrenia, mental impairment, and psychosis.[29] The following issues have caused particular difficulty for the courts, however: amnesia, deaf-mutism, and mental deficiency.

Amnesia

If Lord Dunedin's directions in *Brown* (quoted above)[30] are correct (and they have never been disapproved) then it would seem that an amnesiac should have a good plea in bar of trial, in that they would be unable to give their counsel an account of their actions at the relevant time. However, this view has not found favour with the courts. In *Russell v HM Advocate*,[31] where the accused was said to be suffering from "hysterical amnesia" and unable to remember anything during a period of seven years, including the three-year period relating to the charges of **14.06**

---

[25] See *McLachlan v Brown*, 1997 J.C. 222 at 225, *per* the Lord Justice-General (Rodger); *Stewart v HM Advocate (No. 1)*, 1997 J.C. 183. In *Stewart v HM Advocate (No. 1)*, the Crown unsuccessfully argued before the trial judge that "insane" in terms of s.54(1) of the CPSA 1995 fell to be interpreted according to the law regarding insanity as a defence.

[26] The Scottish Law Commission has recently proposed that the test be reformulated in statute to provide that a person "is unfit for trial if it is established on the balance of probabilities that the person is incapable, by reason of a mental or physical condition, of participating effectively in a trial". In deciding this question, a court would be required to have regard to "(a) the ability of the person to (i) understand the nature of the charge; (ii) understand the requirement to tender a plea to the charge and the effect of such a plea; (iii) understand the purpose of, and follow the course of, the trial; (iv) understand the evidence that may be given against the person; (v) instruct and otherwise communicate with the person's legal representative; and (b) any other factor which the court considers relevant." (*Report on Insanity and Diminished Responsibility* (Scot. Law Com. No. 195, 2004), p.82).

[27] This is remarkably similar to the test formulated by the United States Supreme Court in *Dusky v United States*, 362 U.S. 402, 402 (1960) ("[the] test must be whether he has sufficient present ability to consult with his lawyer with a reasonable degree of rational understanding—and whether he has a rational as well as factual understanding of the proceedings against him"). In England, see the leading of *R. v Pritchard* (1836) 7 C & P 303; 173 E.R. 135. For more detailed discussion of how the competence of the accused should be assessed, see R.J. Bonnie, "The competence of criminal defendants: beyond *Dusky* and *Drope*" (1993) 47 *University of Miami Law Review* 539–601, which appears to have been influential on the Commission's approach to the subject.

[28] See the English cases of *R. v Robertson* [1968] 1 W.L.R. 1767; *R. v M (John)* [2003] EWCA Crim 3452.

[29] See R.D. Mackay, *Mental Condition Defences in the Criminal Law* (1995), p.223, where it is noted that of 302 findings of unfitness to plead between 1976 and 1989, 56% were based on schizophrenia, 21.2% on mental impairment and 10.6% on psychosis. The other "diagnostic groups" noted were brain damage, dementia, personality disorder, deafness and amnesia, with a small number of cases (10) recorded as either "other" or "none".

[30] Para.14.03.

[31] 1946 J.C. 37.

fraud and embezzlement against her, the Lord Justice-Clerk (Cooper) argued that Lord Dunedin's directions in *Brown* did not apply to the case in hand:

> "I do not consider that they were intended to be understood, or are capable of being understood, literally as applying to the case of a sane prisoner—in this case one whom all the medical witnesses adduced have pronounced to be completely sane and normal—for so to read them would come near to paralysing the administration of criminal justice. On any such reading the plea in bar would require to be sustained in most cases in which the accused had been under the influence of drink, or had sustained a head injury, at the time of the crime, or even if he was naturally a person of unreliable memory."[32]

This was followed by the English Court of Appeal in the notorious case of *R. v Podola*,[33] and more recently by the appeal court in *Hughes v HM Advocate*.[34] The principle may not always have been rigorously applied in practice, and empirical research in England has noted that three of 302 unfitness to plead findings between 1976 and 1989 were been based on amnesia.[35]

14.07 Although the Butler Committee concluded that amnesia should not raise an issue of fitness to stand trial,[36] that view was not unanimous and it has been argued that amnesia should operate as a bar to trial in some circumstances.[37] Two points should be made. First, although the cases make it clear that an inability to recall the relevant events is not a basis for a plea of insanity in bar of trial, that does not mean that such a plea could not be based on, for example, anterograde amnesia, which affects the patient's ability to recall new (rather than past) events and might affect the accused's ability to follow and participate in the trial.

Secondly, while *Russell* and *Hughes* may preclude a plea of insanity in bar of trial based on an inability to recall events, they do not preclude a claim that the accused cannot receive a fair trial as a result of this

---

[32] At 48. One other difficulty with recognising a plea of insanity in bar of trial based on amnesia would, historically, have been that the court would have had no option but to make a hospital order, which would frequently have been inappropriate in such cases. Such a disposal is, however, no longer mandatory. See CPSA 1995, s.57, as amended by the Criminal Justice (Scotland) Act 2003, s.2(b).

[33] [1960] 1 Q.B. 325. For the background to the case, see R. Furneaux, *Guenther Podola* (1960). See also *R. v M (John)* [2003] EWCA Crim 3452.

[34] 2002 J.C. 23.

[35] See R.D. Mackay, fn.29 above, p.223, who notes that in view of *Podola* "this might seem an unexpected result".

[36] *Report of the Committee on Mentally Abnormal Offenders* (Cmnd. 6244, 1975), paras 10.1–10.11.

[37] Professors Hill and Walker did not agree with the majority of the committee on this point: para.10.8 of the Report. They suggested that amnesia should operate as a plea in bar only where "the circumstances were such that it was likely to prevent the defendant from giving adequate instructions for his defence" (para.10.9). See also N. Walker, "Butler v the CLRC and others" [1981] Crim. L.R. 596–601 at pp.599–600. See also R.A. Duff, *Trials and Punishments* (1985), pp.120–121.

inability, which might provide a basis for a plea of oppression (or a claim that the accused's Art.6 rights would be breached by proceeding to trial).[38] Such a claim would be a difficult one to make, however, as a lack of awareness of the relevant events does not in itself amount to unfairness: indeed, it has been argued that "[i]n his plight the amnesiac differs very little from an accused who was home alone, asleep in bed, at the time of the crime".[39] Although a number of US courts have accepted, in principle, that amnesia may preclude a fair trial in certain circumstances,[40] such claims appear to have invariably failed on their merits.[41] Similarly, Canadian courts have consistently rejected claims that proceeding to trial where the defendant is an amnesiac is a violation of the Charter right to a fair trial.[42]

Deaf-mutism and other physical conditions

The accused in the leading Scottish case of *Wilson* was a deaf-mute, **14.08** although he appears to also have been mentally impaired (and in any event the jury, in acquitting him, appear to have concluded that the plea in bar was not made out).[43] Hume also notes an early case where it was held that the accused, who had been deaf and dumb from birth, was competent to stand trial with the aid of a skilled interpreter.[44] Physical conditions are, taken alone, unlikely to found a basis for the plea in bar of trial provided that adaptations can be made to allow the accused to appropriately participate in the trial, but in principle the plea should remain available where such adaptations cannot be made.[45] Objections to the use of the term "insanity" are, of course, more acute in such cases, but it is widely recognised that the term is inappropriate regardless of whether physical conditions are included within the scope of the plea.[46] Problems might have arisen where a hospital order was the inevitable consequence of a successful plea in bar, but this is no longer the case.[47]

---

[38] In *Russell*, the trial judge, Lord Sorn, stated that his views might have been different had he been persuaded that the accused's amnesia "must result in an unfair trial and in prejudice" (1946 J.C. 37 at 41). On appeal, Lord Cooper noted that only a "single point of alleged prejudice" had been argued—the possibility that the accused might have forgotten a valid explanation for her actions—concluding that it would "hardly bear inspection, for the appellant had ample opportunity after the charges were made against her and before she partially lost her memory to offer such a complete explanation, if it had any foundation in fact." (1946 J.C. 37 at 46–47).

[39] "Amnesia: a case study in the limits of particular justice" (1961) 71 Yale L.J. 109–136 at p.128.

[40] See, e.g. *Wilson v United States*, 391 F.2d 460 (D.C. Cir. 1968); *State v McIntosh*, 404 N.W.2d 557 (Wis App 1987). See further, Robinson, *Criminal Law Defenses*, §207(b).

[41] See, e.g. *State v Gilbert*, 640 A.2d 822 (Conn. App. 1993); *US v Villegas*, 899 F.2d (2nd Cir. 1990); *US ex rel Parson v Anderson*, 481 F.2d 94 (3rd Cir. 1973); *State v Severns*, 336 P.2d 447 (Kan. 1959); *People v Soto*, 327 N.Y.S.2d 669.

[42] *R. v H (L.J.)* (1997) 120 C.C.C. (3d) 88; *R. v Majid* (1997) 119 C.C.C. (3d) 161; *R. v Boylen* (1972) 18 C.R. N.S. 273. See also *R. v Murphy* (1998) 224 A.R. 30; *R. v Deveraux* (1988) 72 Nfld. & P.E.I.R. 175.

[43] *HM Advocate v Wilson*, 1942 J.C. 75. See also *Jackson v Indiana*, 406 U.S. 715 (1972), where the defendant was both mentally impaired and a deaf-mute.

[44] *Jean Campbell* (1817) Hume, i, 45.

[45] *Report on Insanity and Diminished Responsibility* (Scot. Law Com. No. 195, 2004), paras 4.17–4.19.

[46] *Report on Insanity and Diminished Responsbility*, above, fn.45, at paras 2.19–2.24.

[47] See below, para.14.13.

Mental deficiency

14.09 In *Russell v HM Advocate*, the Lord Justice-Clerk (Cooper) stated that "mental deficiency cannot be pleaded as a plea in bar".[48] That statement, however, was based on the decision in *HM Advocate v Breen*,[49] where it was said only that a claim that an accused was "mentally deficient" within the meaning of the Mental Deficiency (Scotland) Act 1913 was not in itself a plea in bar of trial. In *Stewart v HM Advocate (No. 1)*,[50] Lord Hamilton took the view that the remarks in *Russell* and *Breen* meant no more than that mental deficiency was not per se a plea in bar, and that they were "consistent with the proposition that mental deficiency which results in a person not being a fit object for trial may found such a plea".[51] A plea based on mental impairment has succeeded in at least one case.[52]

Procedural Aspects and the Examination of Facts

14.10 Although the plea in bar exists in order to protect the interests of the accused, a successful plea may not always have been to his benefit. Because, historically, the result of a successful plea was indefinite detention, it ran the risk of two distinct forms of injustice. First, it meant that the accused could be detained without any proof that he had in fact committed any crime—and, because insanity could be alleged by the Crown, this could happen where he neither admitted the crime itself nor pleaded that he was unfit to stand trial. As the panel's counsel in *HM Advocate v Alexander Robertson*[53] strongly, but unsuccessfully, argued when disputing the Crown's right to allege insanity:

> "This is the first case in the history of the Criminal Law where the Crown has indicted a man for trial before this Court, and at the calling of the diet has called witnesses to prove that he is incapable of being tried; and in face of the opposition of the panel, who is anxious to be tried and offers himself for trial, has moved the Court to refuse him trial and order him to be confined in prison during Her Majesty's pleasure. If such procedure were to be sanctioned, the Crown might procure the confinement of any person in prison for life without trial by a jury, by charging him with an offence which he might or might not have committed, and then, instead of proceeding to trial, calling witnesses to prove him insane."[54]

---

48 1946 J.C. 37 at 48.

49 1921 J.C. 30.

50 1997 J.C. 183.

51 At 186.

52 *HM Advocate v S*, High Court at Glasgow, July 1999, unreported. The accused in that case was 13 years of age and suffered from learning difficulties. See C. Connelly and C. McDiarmid, "Children, mental impairment and the plea in bar of trial" (2000) 5 S.L.P.Q. 157–168. This case is noted in the context of nonage at para.9.03 above.

53 *HM Advocate v Alexander Robertson* (1891) 3 White 6.

54 At 15.

Just as the plea might wreak injustice by resulting in the incarceration of an innocent man, so it might result in the true criminal not being apprehended due to a mistaken belief that the offender had been identified.[55]

Secondly, the nature of the condition which rendered the accused unfit to stand trial might not be such as to justify restricting his liberty. In *Barr v Herron*,[56] the accused, an 18-year-old boy who had Down's syndrome, was found to be completely incapable of understanding the proceedings brought against him for an alleged minor breach of the peace. The statutory provisions extant at the time left the sheriff-substitute with no option but to make a hospital order, despite it being a matter of agreement that the best course of action would be to allow him to be returned to the care of his mother.[57] On appeal, the High Court avoided the obvious difficulty by concluding that the statutory requirements had not been complied with (the reasons for the sheriff's finding not being set out in the record of proceedings), meaning that the order was null and void and could not receive effect. This difficulty is now avoided by the fact that detention is no longer an inevitable result of a successful plea in bar, but is now at the discretion of the court.[58] **14.11**

Over time, various solutions have been offered to the first of these difficulties. One is that adopted by the Scottish courts in cases such as *Brown*[59] and *Wilson*,[60] which is to postpone the issue until the end of the trial. It is difficult to understand how this could be considered an acceptable solution: in each case, the accused was given his day in court, but the jury was still invited to decide on his sanity *before* considering whether he had done the act complained of. But postponing the issue until after deciding on guilt or innocence would run contrary to the rationale for the plea, and should rightly be condemned as "bizarre".[61] Even more difficult, for that reason, are proposals to abolish the plea in bar altogether.[62]

A partial solution was adopted in English law in the form of s.4 of the Criminal Procedure (Insanity) Act 1964, which allowed the issue of fitness to plead to be postponed until any time up to the opening of the case for the defence,[63] thus at least allowing the prosecution case to be tested.[64] Such a procedure did not commend itself to the Thomson Committee, which recommended that the plea should be made at the first diet and, if

---

[55] *R. v Roberts* [1954] 2 Q.B. 329 at 329, *per* Devlin J.

[56] 1968 J.C. 20, and see (1968) 32 J.C.L. 113.

[57] Mental Health (Scotland) Act 1960, s.55.

[58] CPSA 1995, s.57. Detention was mandatory where the charge had been one of murder up until s.2(b) of the Criminal Justice (Scotland) Act 2003 came into force. Mandatory detention in all cases would have been likely to contravene Art.5 of the ECHR. Although Art.5 (guaranteeing the right to liberty and security) permits the detention of persons of "unsound mind", not all persons who were unfit to plead in a criminal trial would be regarded as of "unsound mind" for the purposes of the Convention. On the meaning of this phrase, see *Winterwerp v The Netherlands* (1979) 2 E.H.R.R. 387 at [37]–[39].

[59] *HM Advocate v Brown* (1907) 5 Adam 312.

[60] *HM Advocate v Wilson*, 1942 J.C. 75.

[61] R.A. Duff, *Trials and Punishments* (1985), pp 32–33.

[62] See R.A. Burt and N. Morris, "A proposal for the abolition of the incompetency plea" (1972) 40 *University of Chicago Law Review* 66–95.

[63] Criminal Procedure (Insanity) Act 1964, s.4(2).

[64] For the background to the provision, see Criminal Law Revision Committee, *Third Report: Criminal Procedure (Insanity)* (Cmnd. 2149, 1963), paras 13–29; *R. v Burles* [1970] 2 Q.B. 191 at 195, *per* Lord Parker C.J.

successful, followed by a factual inquiry presided over by a judge sitting alone.[65]

14.12 The position was subsequently reformed by what are now ss.54–57 of the Criminal Procedure (Scotland) Act 1995.[66] These provisions are triggered where "the court is satisfied, on the written or oral evidence of two medical practitioners, that a person charged with the commission of an offence is insane so that his trial cannot proceed or, if it has commenced, cannot continue".[67] These provisions apply to all pleas of insanity in bar of trial: there is no room for any common law plea of "mental impairment".[68] It is clear from the statutory provisions that the determination is now one for the judge and cannot be left to the jury as was done in some of the earlier cases.[69]

If a finding of insanity in bar of trial is made, the court shall discharge the trial diet and order that an "examination of facts"[70] be held.[71] Alternatively, the court may desert the diet *pro loco et tempore* on the motion of the prosecutor.[72] At the examination of facts, the court is required to determine whether it is satisfied:

> "(a) beyond reasonable doubt, as respects any charge on the indictment or, as the case may be, the complaint in respect of which the accused was being or was to be tried, that he did the act or made the omission constituting the offence; and
> (b) on the balance of probabilities, that there are no grounds for acquitting him."[73]

If the court is not so satisfied, it must acquit the accused.[74] If the acquittal is on the ground of insanity at the time, this should be stated.[75]

The wording of these provisions may give rise to some confusion. It is

---

[65] *Criminal Procedure in Scotland (Second Report)* (Cmnd. 6218, 1975), para.52.18. The Butler Committee made similar recommendations for English law around the same time (both committees reporting in October 1975): *Report of the Committee on Mentally Abnormal Offenders* (Cmnd. 6244, 1975), paras 10.24 *et seq.*

[66] Originally ss.47–50 of the Criminal Justice (Scotland) Act 1995. The reforms made by these provisions are similar, but not identical, to those made in English law by the Criminal Procedure (Insanity and Unfitness to Plead) Act 1991.

[67] CPSA 1995, s.54(1). In *McLachlan v Brown*, 1997 J.C. 222, it was noted that the terms of this section meant that the court could not directly rely on the evidence of psychologists to satisfy the statutory requirement. The Lord Justice-General (Rodger) observed (at 226) that "If need be, the evidence of a psychologist may be led before the court and the psychiatrists may be asked to give their opinion in the light of that evidence. This will not always be necessary. We note, for instance, that in *Stewart* [*v HM Advocate (No. 1)*, 1997 J.C. 183] there was a joint minute agreeing the terms of a report on the appellant by a clinical psychologist who had examined him. There is therefore no reason to believe that medical practitioners should not be able to furnish the courts with the necessary opinions in cases of mental impairment." See also the further requirements imposed by s.61.

[68] *McLachlan v Brown*, 1997 J.C. 222.

[69] See *Stewart v HM Advocate (No. 1)*, 1997 J.C. 183 at 190, *per* the Lord Justice-Clerk (Cullen).

[70] For a comparative analysis of this procedure, see R.D. Mackay and W.J. Brookbanks, "Protecting the unfit to plead: a comparative analysis of the 'trial of the facts'", 2005 Jur. Rev. 173–195.

[71] Subject to the requirements of s.54(1)(c), the accused may be committed to hospital under a temporary hospital order until the conclusion of the examination of facts.

[72] CPSA 1995, s.54(2).

[73] *ibid.*, s.55(1).

[74] *ibid.*, s.55(3).

[75] *ibid.*, s.55(4).

likely that subsection (a) encompasses only the *actus reus* of the offence,[76] and so the Crown are not required to prove *mens rea* beyond a reasonable doubt in an examination of facts, but need only prove it on a balance of probabilities, the absence of *mens rea* being a possible ground for acquitting the accused. Similarly, defences such as self-defence, where raised, need only be disproved on the balance of probabilities.[77]

The distinction appears to be drawn on the basis that it would be "unrealistic and contradictory" to consider the accused's mental state when he is unfit to be tried in the normal way,[78] or at least to attempt to determine this beyond a reasonable doubt. It is not without difficulty, given that it may be impossible to determine some issues of *actus reus* without consideration of the accused's mental state at the relevant time.[79] It might also be thought unsatisfactory to engage in a procedure which—to all intents and purposes—publicly declared that the accused was guilty of a criminal offence, despite the fact that he was unable to properly participate in the proceedings.[80] The procedure strikes an uneasy, but necessary, balance in attempting to protect the unfit accused from unfounded allegations without negating the purpose served by the plea in bar. **14.13**

The position of partial defences, where the charge is one of murder, is less clear. It has been held in England that the partial defence of diminished responsibility cannot be raised in the analogous English procedure, but this is based on statutory provisions which have no counterpart in Scots law.[81] The Scottish Law Commission has suggested that diminished responsibility is irrelevant in an examination of facts, because it does not lead to an acquittal,[82] but it may be responded that an accused who succeeds in a plea of diminished responsibility, and is convicted of culpable homicide, is thereby acquitted *of murder*.[83] There is, however, a difficulty here, because the statutory provisions do not, at least explicitly, encompass the possibility of alternative verdicts. Consequently, if a partial defence was made out at the examination of facts, the court would

---

[76] See *R. v Antoine* [2001] 1 A.C. 340, which is concerned with the interpretation of "did the act or made the omission charged against him as the offence" in s.4A(2) of the Criminal Procedure (Insanity) Act 1964, which extends to England and Wales only. This is the only question to be considered by an English court where a defendant is unfit to plead, as the 1964 Act has no equivalent of subsection (b) of s.55(1) of the CPSA 1995, and the analogous inquiry in England is therefore significantly more restricted than is the case in Scotland.

[77] In *R. v Grant* [2001] EWCA Crim 2611 the Court of Appeal held that provocation was a matter of *mens rea* (and therefore should not be considered under the equivalent English procedure). In Scots law, that view would appear to be consistent with the decision in *Drury v HM Advocate*, 2001 S.L.T 1013; see para.10.05.

[78] See *R. v Antoine* [2001] 1 A.C. 340 at 375, *per* Lord Hutton.

[79] See *R. (Young) v Central Criminal Court* [2002] 2 Cr.App.R. 12 (*actus reus* involved consideration of the accused's intentions as to his future conduct in order to determine whether his conduct was "dishonest"); *R. v M* [2003] 2 Cr.App.R. 21 (defendant's knowledge of what was planned was relevant to whether he had participated in a joint enterprise, satisfying the *actus reus* of murder).

[80] But *cf.* the *Report of the Committee on Mentally Abnormal Offenders* (Cmnd. 6244, 1975), paras 10.24–10.25.

[81] Homicide Act 1957, s.2, which introduced diminished responsibility into English law, applies only to a person who is liable to be "convicted of murder". As an individual who is unfit to plead is not liable to be convicted of murder, the plea is irrelevant in such cases: *R. v Antoine* [2001] 1 A.C. 340.

[82] *Report on Insanity and Diminished Responsibility* (Scot. Law Com. No. 195, 2004), para.4.3, fn.5. The logic of this point would appear to apply equally to provocation, although the Commission's report refers only to diminished responsibility.

[83] See *HM Advocate v Boyle*, 1993 J.C. 5 at 13, *per* the Lord Justice-General (Hope).

have to acquit the accused of murder,[84] but it is not clear that the court would have any power to make a finding that he had committed the *actus reus* of culpable homicide and that there were no grounds for acquitting him of that charge.[85]

With that in mind, the better view is probably that partial defences are irrelevant in an examination of facts. Prior to 2003, they might have been crucial because, where the charge was one of murder and the findings at the examination of facts were adverse to the accused, the judge would have no option but to make orders detaining the accused without limit of time.[86] The judge is no longer restricted in this way, although such orders may be required if the accused presents a high risk to the safety of the public at large.[87] Given the nature of the findings made by the court in an examination of facts, there would seem to be no need for the court to distinguish between murder and culpable homicide for the purposes of these proceedings.

The procedural issues involved in an examination of facts, including disposal of the case thereafter, and any appeals consequent upon the findings made and/or disposal are not considered further here.[88] It should be noted that, unless the examination of facts results in an acquittal, the accused may be tried at a later date if he is then fit to plead.[89] There are no specific time-limits regarding such prosecutions, although the general rules on time-bar and delay continue to apply.[90]

---

[84] CPSA 1995, s.55(3).

[85] Unless, perhaps, s.55(6) of the 1995 Act (providing that "the rules of evidence and procedure and the powers of the court shall, in respect of an examination of facts, be as nearly as possible those applicable in respect of a trial") is read so as to incorporate the possibility of such findings into the proceedings.

[86] CPSA 1995, s.55(3), prior to the substitution of those provisions by s.2(b) of the Criminal Justice (Scotland) Act 2003. It was because of the equivalent provisions in England that the defendant wished to raise the issue of diminished responsibility in *Antoine*: see *R. v Antoine* [2001] 1 A.C. 340 at 364–365, *per* Lord Hutton. It is not, however, clear that mandatory detention could have been avoided in Scotland prior to 2003 by raising a partial defence at the examination of facts, as s.55(3) made detention mandatory where the offence with which the person "was charged" with murder.

[87] CPSA 1995, s.55(3), as substituted.

[88] See CPSA 1995, ss.55–63; Renton and Brown, paras 26–09 to 29–15.

[89] As to the uncertain status of the original order disposing of the case in such circumstances, see D. Chiswick et al, "Reprosecution of patients found unfit to plead: a report of anomalies in procedure in Scotland" (1990) 14 *Psychiatric Bulletin* 208–210. That article was referred to by Mr Menzies Campbell MP in moving an amendment to the Law Reform (Miscellaneous Provisions) (Scotland) Bill which was intended to make it clear that a subsequent prosecution, if disposed of by a court, would have the effect of terminating an earlier order made by the court (such as a hospital order) when the accused was found unfit to plead. The amendment was withdrawn after the government agreed to consider the matter. See HC Debs, cols 1250–1251 (October 17, 1990).

[90] On which, see Ch.16. For a reported example of such a prosecution, see *HM Advocate v Bickerstaff*, 1926 J.C. 65.

Chapter 15

RES JUDICATA

Introduction

The plea of *res judicata* operates to bar successive prosecutions for the same offence. Although Alison describes the plea as one which "is not unfrequently advanced",[1] there is relatively little case law on the topic in Scotland, compared to other jurisdictions where a voluminous jurisprudence and accompanying literature has been produced.[2] This is probably only to be expected in a small jurisdiction with a longstanding system of (relatively centralised) public prosecution.[3] Nevertheless, the principle is fundamental to criminal procedure, as evidenced by Hume's affront at the suggestion that Scots law might allow a man to stand trial twice for the same offence: **15.01**

> "... a reproach has sometimes been rashly thrown out against our law, (and if true it would indeed be a foul stain,) as if it allowed a prisoner to be brought to repeated trials for the same offence. Now, the truth is, that our practice inviolably maintains the opposite maxim, that no man *shall thole an assize twice* (so we express it); for the same fact; and that this humane rule is by no means understood in so favourable a sense for the prisoner, in the law of England, as in ours."[4]

Two principal justifications are normally offered for the rule.[5] First, it is said to protect against wrongful conviction. The prosecution (which, it is assumed, is generally better resourced than the defence) may receive an unfair advantage by the defence having "shown its hand" at an earlier trial.[6] Similarly, the prosecution should not be allowed a "trial run" at convicting the accused.[7] Secondly, the rule protects the "moral integrity

[1] Alison, *Practice*, 615.

[2] The seminal work is M. Friedland, *Double Jeopardy* (1969), which considers the subject throughout the common-law world, with some reference to the Scottish cases. A more recent treatment of the US position can be found in G.C. Thomas III, *Double Jeopardy: The History, The Law* (1998).

[3] Thus avoiding the difficulties that may arise where separate prosecutorial agencies reach potentially conflicting decisions: see, e.g. *R. v Beedie* [1998] Q.B. 356 (successive prosecutions by the Health and Safety Executive and the Crown Prosecution Service).

[4] Hume, i, 7.

[5] See A. L.-T. Choo, *Abuse of Process and Judicial Stays of Criminal Proceedings* (1993), pp.16–18; *Green v US*, 355 U.S. 184, 187–189 (1957) (Black, J). For a slightly different formulation, see A.J. Ashworth, "Concepts of criminal justice" [1979] Crim. L.R. 412–427 at p.425.

[6] *Double Jeopardy* (Law Com. C.P. No. 156), para.4.5, where it is also noted that the risk of a perverse verdict of conviction is necessarily increased by multiple trials.

[7] *Connelly v DPP* [1964] A.C. 1254 at 1353, *per* Lord Devlin.

of the criminal justice system",[8] by protecting accused persons from the stress and harassment of successive prosecutions.[9]

15.02 Both of these justifications are, in practice, regarded as qualified by countervailing considerations, and successive prosecutions may be permitted in limited circumstances. As regards the first justification (wrongful conviction), the appeal court now has the power to permit a retrial after quashing a conviction, notwithstanding any "advantage" obtaining to the prosecution by reason of having conducted a first trial.[10] There have, furthermore, been moves in some jurisdictions to permit retrials in certain circumstances, such as where the accused had been acquitted but new and compelling evidence comes to light so that it is in the interests of justice to permit a retrial,[11] or where the accused appears to have been acquitted as a result of his own perjury or another offence against the administration of justice.[12] Such proposals have not yet, however, found favour in Scotland, although the courts have allowed persons to be prosecuted for perjury in their own defence.[13]

The second justification (protection from harassment) is qualified by the prosecution's right to ensure that the charges against the accused are properly tried.[14] A second prosecution following on from an abortive trial, or proceedings which were fundamentally null, might be equally stressful and harassing from the perspective of the accused, but will not form a basis for the plea.[15]

Two other justifications are occasionally offered for the principle: first, that it conserves judicial resources[16] and, secondly, that it secures "finality of verdict".[17] The first, however, is of limited importance in a legal system such as Scotland where prosecutorial resources are almost wholly within the control of the state, and there is no significant risk of judicial resources being abused by way of criminal prosecutions brought by private parties.[18] The second is more properly seen as descriptive of the principle rather than as a justification for it.

---

[8] Choo, fn.5 above, at p.17.

[9] Hume, ii, 465; *Hamilton v Byrne*, 1997 S.L.T. 1210 at 1212, *per* the Lord Justice-General (Rodger).

[10] CPSA 1995, s.118(1)(c).

[11] In England, see Part 10 of the Criminal Justice Act 2003.

[12] *Acquittal Following Perversion of the Course of Justice* (New Zealand Law Commission Report 70, 2001). See also ss.54–57 of the Criminal Procedure and Investigations Act 1996, which do not extend to Scotland.

[13] See below, para.15.11.

[14] Subject, of course, to other pleas in bar of trial, as discussed in Chs 9 and 14–20.

[15] See below, para.15.07.

[16] M. Friedland, *Double Jeopardy* (1969), p.6.

[17] *Acquittal Following Perversion of the Course of Justice* (New Zealand Law Commission Report 70, 2001), para.14.

[18] *cf. US v Dixon* (1993) 509 U.S. 688, at 21 n.15 (Scalia J.), where it is suggested that scarcity of resources acts as a safeguard against double jeopardy: "the Government must be deterred from abusive, repeated prosecutions of a single offender for similar offences by the sheer press of other demands upon prosecutorial and judicial resources".

THE SCOPE OF THE RULE

15.03 According to Hume, the pannel was protected against having to thole an assize twice by means of sentence of absolvitor (sentence being of two sorts, "absolvitor or condemnatory").[19] Hume seems, perhaps surprisingly, to have regarded the plea of *res judicata* or tholed assize as one which followed only from sentence of absolvitor, but it is clear from his discussion of sentence condemnatory, where he observes that a sentence regularly delivered may not be retracted, varied or amended,[20] that similar consequences followed from a sentence condemnatory. Alison, by contrast, recognises a unified plea of *res judicata* following on from a former trial which resulted in either a conviction or acquittal.[21]

The plea of *res judicata* is not, however, restricted to cases where the accused has "tholed his assize" (that is, been tried for the offence, with the trial being brought to a valid conclusion). It may also operate where the complaint or indictment on which it is sought to try the accused has previously been held to be irrelevant.[22] It is normal, therefore, to regard the plea as having two forms: first, based on a previous decision as to relevancy, and secondly, based on the accused having previously "tholed an assize".[23]

Previous decision on relevancy

15.04 In *Longmuir v Baxter*,[24] the sheriff-substitute found the libel against the accused to be irrelevant. Instead of bringing an appeal against this decision, the procurator fiscal instead charged the accused with the same offence, this time before the sheriff, who found the indictment relevant. On appeal, it was noted that the point was of some novelty. Longmuir did not have the benefit of a sentence of absolvitor (the sheriff-substitute had purported to assoilzie him from the libel, but it was doubtful whether this was competent). Nevertheless, it was held that the matter should have been treated as *res judicata*, the sheriff-substitute and the sheriff being regarded as the same judge.

The principle does not extend so far as to prevent an accused being tried in the High Court on a libel held irrelevant by the sheriff,[25] as the High Court cannot "be held bound by the decision of an inferior judge".[26] It seems, however, that where a High Court judge has held a libel to be

[19] Hume, ii, 464–465. It would seem appropriate to equate "sentence of absolvitor" with acquittal and "sentence condemnatory" with conviction.

[20] To the extent that the accused in *Margaret Dickson* (1724) Hume, ii, 476, who was hanged for child murder but "revived after being carried from the gallows", could not be hanged a second time and continued to live in Edinburgh "for a good many years".

[21] Alison, ii, 615. Similarly, Macdonald and Anderson appear not to have regarded the previously convicted accused as being in any different a position from the previously acquitted: Macdonald, 272; Anderson, 285. There are, of course, different justifications for recognising a plea of *res judicata* following on from a conviction as opposed to an acquittal, which is evident in the English practice of recognising separately pleas of *autrefois acquit* and *autrefois convict*. For an argument that the two pleas "rest on different principles and serve different functions", see C. Howard, "Res judicata in the criminal law" (1961–1962) 3 *Melbourne University Law Review* 101–136.

[22] See below, para.15.04.

[23] Anderson, 285; Renton and Brown, para.9–08.

[24] (1858) 3 Irv. 287.

[25] *George Fleming* (1866) 5 Irv. 287.

[26] *George Fleming* (1866) 5 Irv. 287 at 292, *per* Lord Cowan. The proceedings before the sheriff had been deserted *pro loco et tempore* after the decision on relevancy.

irrelevant, it would not be permissible to bring the same libel before a different judge in the hope that a different decision would be reached.[27]

It was held in *HM Advocate v M*[28] that the plea could not succeed where "there is a material difference between the two indictments",[29] and so the fact that the sheriff had held a libel irrelevant due to an excessive latitude of time specified in the charges did not preclude the Crown from proceeding upon a fresh, more narrowly drawn, libel.

Previous tholing of an assize

15.05 Here, there are two requirements: the former proceedings must have been for the same offence, and they must have been validly brought to a conclusion.[30]

Proceedings for the same offence

15.06 "Same offence" does not require identity of *nomen juris,* and the prosecutor cannot evade the plea of *res judicata* by charging the same set of facts but describing them as a different offence. According to Hume:

> "As little shall it vary the rule, that the new prosecutor chooses to alter the shape of the former charge, and lay his libel for the same facts, under a new denomination of crime; stating them as fraud perhaps instead of theft, falsehood instead of forgery, assault or riot instead of deforcement or hamesucken, or the like. The Judge will not suffer the law to be evaded on such easy pretences; but will look to the substance of the case, and the situation of the pannel, who still is prosecuted twice for the pains of the same act."[31]

The courts have not, however, articulated a test for determining whether the "same offence" has been charged: the case law has simply not warranted any such development.[32] Nonetheless, it is clear that mere identity of time and place between the two charges will not suffice[33]: the focus is on the identity of the acts alleged. In *Galloway v Somerville*,[34] the plea of *res judicata* was repelled on the basis that there was "nothing ... inconsistent in the respondent being acquitted of the first charge and convicted of the second",[35] which suggests that the question to be asked by the court is whether the two prosecutions might produce inconsistent verdicts: could a particular verdict on one charge dictate the result on another? There is, however, no protection against inconsistent verdicts where the

[27] See *Longmuir v Baxter* (1858) 3 Irv. 287 at 291–292, *per* Lord Deas. This must follow from the principle that "[a] decision of a judge of the High Court of Justiciary is a decision of the High Court of Justiciary" (*Jessop v Stevenson*, 1988 J.C. 17 at 21, *per* the Lord Justice-General (Emslie)) and must therefore be treated as final unless and until it is recalled on appeal.

[28] 1987 J.C. 1. See also *Simpson v McLeod*, 1986 S.C.C.R. 237.

[29] 1987 J.C. 1 at 8, *per* the Lord Justice-Clerk (Ross).

[30] See Alison, *Practice*, 615.

[31] Hume, i, 466. See also Alison, *Practice,* 615–616.

[32] Compare the much more detailed approach formulated in English law: see *Connelly v DPP* [1964] A.C. 1254 at 1305–1306, *per* Lord Morris of Borth-y-Gest, setting out nine governing principles which form the basis of the English plea of *autrefois acquit*.

[33] See *Glen v Colquhoun* (1865) 5 Irv. 203.

[34] (1863) 4 Irv. 444.

[35] (1863) 4 Irv. 444, *per* the Lord Justice-Clerk (Inglis).

second charge is one which could not have been charged at the first trial, the alleged offence not yet having been complete, a point discussed further below.[36]

Proceedings validly brought to a conclusion

Although the former proceedings must have been concluded for *res judicata* to operate, it is not necessary that sentence should have been passed. In *HM Advocate v Sarah Fraser and James Fraser*,[37] the pannels were convicted of murder, and the case certified to the High Court. It was held, however, that as no date had been fixed for the case to call before the High Court, the instance had fallen, and the pannels were discharged.[38] The Crown then sought to reindict them for murder, where it was held that the proceedings were incompetent: it was the *verdict*, rather than the passing of sentence, which amounted to the tholing of an assize.[39] **15.07**

It has been held that solemn proceedings are concluded by the jury returning a competent verdict,[40] and that summary proceedings are concluded by a plea of guilty being accepted.[41] In *Dunlop v HM Advocate*,[42] the Lord Justice-General (Emslie) stated, in general terms, that:

> "It is clear that a plea of tholed assize will fall to be sustained, in solemn procedure, where the trial has been concluded with a determination by the jury of guilt or innocence. In my opinion, a plea of tholed assize will also fall to be sustained in summary procedure where an accused has been convicted or acquitted, or where the proceedings have reached the stage where a plea of guilty has been accepted by the prosecutor and has been recorded. Despite apparent statements to the contrary in Alison, it is not necessary that a sentence or penalty should have been imposed before a plea of tholed assize can be upheld."[43]

If the former proceedings were incompetent in some way, then the plea of *res judicata* will fail.[44] So, for example, subsequent prosecutions have been allowed where the former proceedings were void because a minor had sat on the jury[45]; where proceedings were incompetently held before a single

[36] See below, paras 15.09–15.11.
[37] (1852) 1 Irv. 1; (1852) 1 Irv. 66.
[38] (1852) 1 Irv. 1.
[39] (1852) 1 Irv. 66. See also *McDonald v HM Advocate*, 2003 J.C. 60 at [14], *per* the Lord Justice-General (Cullen). In *Herron v McCrimmon*, 1969 S L.T. (Sh. Ct) 37, however, Sheriff J. Irvine Smith distinguished *Fraser*, taking the view that the plea of *res judicata* required either that the accused had been sentenced, or that the proceedings against him had terminated and no further procedure was competent (including, in particular that it was not competent to impose sentence). *Cf. Pirie v Rivaud*, 1975 S.L.T. (Sh. Ct) 59; *McPhail v McCabe*, 1984 S.C.C.R. 146 (Sh. Ct).
[40] *Dunlop v HM Advocate*, 1974 J.C. 59. The position where the accused pleads guilty before a jury is empanelled is unclear: Renton and Brown, para.9–09.
[41] *Milne v Guild*, 1986 S.L.T. 431.
[42] 1974 J.C. 59.
[43] *Milne v Guild*, 1986 S.L.T. 431 at 434, *per* the Lord Justice-Clerk (Ross).
[44] Alison, *Practice*, 618: "the former proceedings must be one subject to no inherent vice, or fatal irregularity"; *McGlynn v HM Advocate*, 1995 J.C. 196.
[45] *Menzies* (1790) Hume, ii, 469; *John Sharpe* (1800) Hume, ii, 469.

justice rather than two or more[46]; where the former prosecution was time-barred[47]; and where the former "verdict" of the jury was incompetent as having been returned by an incompletely reconvened jury.[48]

Desertion simpliciter and tholed assize

15.08 It is suggested in Renton and Brown that desertion *simpliciter* (whether by the prosecutor or by the court *ex proprio motu*) amounts to the tholing of an assize.[49] It is submitted, however, that the position is not quite this clear. Desertion *simpliciter*, on the motion of the prosecutor, is described by Hume as a "thorough relinquishment or discharge of his right of prosecution".[50] By statute, desertion *simpliciter* by the court in solemn procedure bars the prosecutor from raising a fresh libel in the case unless the court's decision is reversed on appeal.[51] In both cases, this appears to be more in the nature of personal bar, or a renunciation of the right to prosecute[52] than a tholed assize, and so would not bar a private prosecution in the limited circumstances where that remains possible.[53]

In summary proceedings, s.152 of the 1995 Act provides that if the court refuses a motion by the prosecutor to desert *pro loco et tempore* and the prosecutor is unwilling or unable to proceed with the trial, the court must desert the diet *simpliciter*.[54] In that case, there is a similar statutory provision providing that it shall not be competent for the prosecutor to raise a fresh libel unless the court's decision is reversed on appeal.[55] However, it has been held that in summary proceedings, desertion *simpliciter* by the court *at common law* (as opposed to under s.152(2)) does not bar a new prosecution in the absence of prejudice to the accused,[56] although the extent, if any, of a judge's power to desert *simpliciter ex proprio motu* otherwise than under s.152(2) is unclear.[57]

Offences which could not have been charged at the first trial

15.09 It may be that a charge is brought against the accused which could not have been brought at his first trial, because it depends on proof of an event which had not yet occurred. In such a case, the plea of *res judicata* does not apply, as the newly charged offence is one which could not have been charged at the first trial.

The most obvious case is homicide, where a person may stand trial for

---

46 *William McLellan* (1824) Alison, *Practice*, 619.

47 *Whitelaw v Dickinson*, 1993 J.C. 68. The second prosecution was brought under summary procedure rather than solemn procedure, and so the court held that the timebar did not itself bar the second prosecution (but see *Gardner v Lees*, 1996 J.C. 83, noted below, para.16.23). The first prosecution had been deserted *pro loco et tempore* after the timebar issue had been raised, but the court's decision suggests that a second prosecution would have been competent even if the first had purported to reach a conclusion.

48 *Dunlop v HM Advocate*, 1974 J.C. 59.

49 Renton and Brown, para.9–08.

50 Hume, ii, 277.

51 CPSA 1995, ss.72C(1), 81(1) (as amended by the Criminal Procedure (Amendment) (Scotland) Act 2004).

52 See Ch.17.

53 These are noted in the context of renunciation of the right to prosecute (see below, para.17.09).

54 CPSA 1995, s.152(2).

55 *ibid.*, s.152(3).

56 *Mackenzie v Maclean*, 1980 J.C. 89.

57 See *McLeod v Williamson*, 1993 J.C. 25.

assault (or some other relevant crime) before the victim dies, and subsequently be tried for murder or culpable homicide. That may seem unproblematic where the first trial has resulted in a conviction, given that homicide could not have been charged at the earlier trial, and that a fresh trial for homicide does not run the risk of inconsistent verdicts. However, the leading case on the point, *Isabella Cobb or Fairweather*,[58] actually involved an acquittal. The court split evenly on whether the plea of *res judicata* was open to the pannel, with the consequence that the Lord Justice-Clerk (Boyle) (who considered that it *should* be open to her) had no vote, and so the plea was repelled.[59]

An examination of the opinions of the majority suggests that the reasons for the decision may no longer hold. Two of the majority judges appear to have rested their conclusions, at least in part, on the fact that the assault prosecution had been in the Police Court: Lord Meadowbank was concerned that the Superintendent, who had power to act as prosecutor in the police court, should not be effectively granted the power "of discharging prosecutions for crimes not cognizable by that act [the Dundee Police Act]".[60] Similarly, Lord Moncrieff said only that he was "not prepared to hold that a *police* conviction, or a *police* acquittal for assault, can found a defence against the serious charge of murder."[61] These arguments no longer carry as much weight given that summary prosecution other than at the instance of the procurator fiscal has now been all but abolished.[62] Lord Mackenzie's opinion is not restricted in this way, but he appears to have taken the view that it was sufficient to elide the plea of *res judicata* that fresh evidence had been discovered by the prosecutor,[63] a view which appears to find no support elsewhere. 15.10

Nevertheless, subsequent courts (concerned with previous convictions, rather than acquittals) treated *Cobb* as binding upon them,[64] and in *Tees v HM Advocate*[65] the appeal court chose to rely on remarks made by Lord Ardmillan in *James Stewart*[66] to reformulate the rule's rationale:

> "it matters not whether the accused was convicted or acquitted of assault at the initial trial. These cases also show that it is not necessary at the subsequent prosecution for murder or culpable homicide to show that there is any new mode of assault. The

---

[58] (1836) 1 Swin. 354.

[59] Strictly speaking, the rule was that the presiding judge at a sitting of the High Court had no vote unless the other judges were equally divided. The Criminal Appeal (Scotland) Act 1926 provided (in s.12(1)) that this rule should not apply to criminal appeals, as recommended in the *Report of the Committee on Criminal Appeal in Scotland* (Cmd. 2546, 1925), p.10.

[60] (1836) 1 Swin. 354 at 388. See also the earlier case of *John McNeil* (1826) Shaw 162.

[61] (1836) 1 Swin. 354 at 391 (emphasis added).

[62] CPSA 1995, ss.6(3) and 133(5).

[63] (1836) 1 Swin. 354 at 390: "Suppose a party tried for entering a house at night by a window, and acquitted on that charge; and suppose that it was afterwards found that the house-breaker had, while in the house, committed a murder, the party would not be entitled to take advantage of the acquittal on the charge of house-breaking, as a defence against an indictment for murder. There is no principle in our law, which would stretch the plea of *res judicata* to such an extent." The conclusion is, of course, correct, but the subsequent prosecution would be permissible as it is clearly for a different offence, and so *res judicata* simply cannot apply.

[64] *John McNeil* (1826) Shaw 162; *John Stevens* (1850) J. Shaw 287; *James Stewart* (1866) 5 Irv. 310; *Patrick O'Connor* (1882) 5 Coup. 206.

[65] 1994 J.C. 12.

[66] (1866) 5 Irv. 310.

subsequent prosecution for murder or culpable homicide is justified because death has occurred. As Lord Ardmillan stated, death is a new element and creates a new crime."[67]

15.11 A similar logic was applied in the perjury case of *HM Advocate v Cairns*.[68] There, Cairns was acquitted of murder,[69] but allegedly confessed to a newspaper reporter thereafter. As Cairns had given evidence in his own defence, the Lord Advocate chose to prosecute him for perjury. His plea of *res judicata* was repelled, the Lord Justice-Clerk (Grant) remarking that not only could perjury "not have been the subject of a charge at [the first] trial, but it is a crime wholly different in nature from that of which the panel was acquitted and is libelled as having taken place at a different place and on a different date".[70] While evidence would, necessarily, be led to show that he had in fact assaulted and stabbed the deceased, it was "identity of the charges and not of the evidence that is the crucial factor".[71]

If prosecutions for perjury in one's own defence are to be permitted, it is not clear what limits, if any, are placed on the discretion of the prosecutor in bringing them. In the English case of *DPP v Humphrys*,[72] it was suggested that a prosecution for perjury which was, in substance, brought simply to overturn the earlier verdict of acquittal might be halted as an abuse of the process of the court, but it is not clear to what extent (if any) the Scottish courts have the power to halt prosecutions as an abuse of process.[73] If, however, a distinction can be drawn between "legitimate" and "illegitimate" prosecutions for perjury, where should that line be? It has been held in the Supreme Court of Canada that a perjury prosecution following acquittal should only be possible where the Crown "is tendering, in addition to or in lieu of the evidence previously adduced, evidence that was not at the time of the first trial available by the exercise of reasonable diligence",[74] a view which finds some support in Lord Hailsham's speech in *Humphrys*[75] and is readily reconcilable with *Cairns*[76] itself. It might be thought that a "fresh evidence" exception should go

[67] 1994 J.C. 12 at 16, *per* the Lord Justice-Clerk (Ross). See also *McNab v HM Advocate*, 2000 J.C. 80, where a prosecution for attempted murder (disposed of by way of a guilty plea) was followed by a prosecution for murder after the death of the victim.

[68] 1967 J.C. 37. Such a case would not have been possible prior to the Criminal Evidence Act 1898, s.1 of which permitted an accused to give evidence in his own defence.

[69] The verdict was one of not proven rather than not guilty. This is of no significance given that the effect of the two verdicts is identical but may occasionally have caused confusion as to the ratio of the decision: see M. Friedland, *Double Jeopardy* (1969), p.158.

[70] 1967 J.C. 37 at 41.

[71] At 42.

[72] [1977] A.C. 1. See generally P.A. McDermott, *Res Judicata and Double Jeopardy* (1999), Ch.31.

[73] See Ch.19.

[74] *R. v Grdic* [1985] 1 S.C.R. 810 at [31], *per* Lamer J. See also *Double Jeopardy, Pleas and Verdicts* (Law Reform Commission of Canada Working Paper No. 63, 1991), 59–60; *R. v Smith* (1997) 119 C.C.C. (3d) 547. The High Court of Australia, however, in holding that a perjury prosecution following the defendant's acquittal for murder should be stayed as an abuse of process, was not prepared to recognise any such "fresh evidence" exception: *The Queen v Carroll* (2002) 213 C.L.R. 635. See also *R. v El-Zarw* [1994] 2 Qd. R. 67.

[75] *DPP v Humphrys* [1977] A.C. 1 at 40, *per* Lord Hailsham.

[76] 1967 J.C. 37.

further and permit a retrial of the substantive offence regardless of whether the accused had given evidence at the first trial.[77] However, although such a reform might validly be contended for, limiting it to perjury is not illogical. There are good reasons to regard interference with the course of justice as more serious than a failure to admit guilt.[78]

Perhaps paradoxically, there are fewer arguments against a subsequent prosecution for perjury where the accused has been *convicted* at the first trial, because a conviction for perjury would not call the earlier verdict into doubt. There has been at least one such prosecution in Scotland.[79] It has, in fact, been suggested that to allow prosecutions for perjury after conviction but not acquittal is correct in principle,[80] but Lord Hailsham described this proposition as "repugnant to my conscience" in *Humphrys*.[81]

Can the assize be tholed abroad?

As to whether a conviction or acquittal abroad bars a prosecution in Scotland, there is very little authority. It is said in Renton and Brown that "[t]he assize need not be tholed in Scotland",[82] but only one authority—*Macgregor and Inglis*[83]—is cited for this proposition, and it is doubtful whether it supports such a broad statement. That case was not, in fact, directly concerned with the plea of *res judicata*, but instead with whether the Scottish courts could exercise jurisdiction over a person accused of committing fraud by sending a letter from Scotland to a tradesman in England, inducing him to deliver goods to Scotland. Counsel for the pannel argued that the Scottish courts had no jurisdiction: "... the effect of the letters was produced in England, and it is that which constitutes the crime. There cannot be two *loci delicti*. If the pannel be put upon his trial for this offence in England, it will not avail him to plead that he has already been tried and punished for it in Scotland."[84] The court rejected this argument, with the Lord Justice-Clerk (Hope) stating that: 15.12

[77] *cf.* Part 10 of the Criminal Justice Act 2003, which does not apply in Scotland. For discussion, see I. Dennis, "Prosecution appeals and retrials for serious offences" [2004] Crim. L.R. 619–638.

[78] *cf. Acquittal Following Perversion of the Course of Justice* (New Zealand Law Commission Report 70, 2001), viii ("No case has been established in New Zealand for a 'new evidence' exception to the rule against double jeopardy. Our first condition for a retrial is that the accused has committed an 'administration of justice' offence.") The Commission's proposals would, subject to certain restrictions, allow a full retrial where it is more likely than not that the acquitted person would not have been acquitted of the primary offence but for an administration of justice offence, of which he has subsequently been convicted.

[79] *Milne v HM Advocate*, 1996 S.L.T. 775, but see the sheriff's remarks on sentencing noted in the S.C.C.R. report: 1995 S.C.CR. 751.

[80] M. Friedland, *Double Jeopardy* (1969), p.160.

[81] [1977] A.C. 1 at 31.

[82] Renton and Brown, para.9–09.

[83] (1846) Ark 49. See also *Hilson v Easson* (1914) 7 Adam 390, where it was held that a plea of tholed assize could not be based upon the fact that the commission of the offence had been "taken into consideration" in sentencing the accused when he had been convicted by an English court of a similar offence. This would not in fact even form the basis for an equivalent plea in English law: *R. v Nicholson* [1947] 2 All E.R. 535.

[84] (1846) Ark 49 at 60 (Moncrieff). The statement about English law was probably incorrect at the time: see *R. v Roche* (1775) 168 E.R. 169 at 169; 1 Leach 134 at 135, *per* Burland B. ("a final determination in a Court having competent jurisdiction is conclusive in all Courts of concurrent jurisdiction"). It is certainly incorrect now: see *R. v Thomas (Keith)* [1985] 1 Q.B. 604.

> "We must hold that the Courts of England would do justice. If a man has been tried for theft in England, we would not try him again here. There may be two countries where he may be tried."[85]

Not only is this statement strictly *obiter*, in its own terms it relates only to offences over which two jurisdictions, both part of the United Kingdom, have jurisdiction.[86] There are legitimate reasons for distinguishing such cases from ones where there have been prosecutions in a foreign country,[87] and it is significant that the protection against double jeopardy offered by the Seventh Protocol (which the UK has yet to ratify)[88] to the ECHR clearly recognises such a distinction:

> "No one shall be liable to be tried or punished again in criminal proceedings under the jurisdiction of the same State for an offence for which he has already been finally acquitted or convicted in accordance with the law and penal procedure of that State."[89]

15.13 Although the UK is a signatory to the Convention Between the Member States of the European Communities on Double Jeopardy,[90] which would provide for some protection (subject to exceptions) against successive trials in two contracting states, the United Kingdom has yet to ratify this Convention, which has never entered into force.[91]

In the absence of clear authority, therefore, the point remains to be properly resolved by the Scottish courts as one of principle. It may be noted that the English courts, while accepting as a general rule that the principle of double jeopardy may be guaranteed internationally, have

---

[85] (1846) Ark 49 at 60.

[86] To similar effect, see *Clements v HM Advocate*, 1991 J.C. 62 at 71, *per* the Lord Justice-General (Hope), a case concerned with drugs offences purportedly committed in part on a train travelling between London and Edinburgh. In *HM Advocate v M*, 1987 J.C. 1, the Lord Justice-Clerk (Ross) suggested (at 8) that the plea of *res judicata* required both libels to be at the instance of the same prosecutor—in which case the principle clearly could not apply internationally—but this was *obiter* and appears to be a misreading of the authority cited (*Longmuir v Baxter* (1858) 3 Irv. 287 at 291–292, *per* Lord Deas).

[87] Both the European Convention on the International Validity of Criminal Judgments (1970), arts 53(1) and 35(1) and the European Convention on the Transfer of Proceedings in Criminal Matters (1972), arts 35 to 37—neither of which the UK has yet signed—provide for some protection against successive prosecutions in separate states, but provide for exceptions where the act concerned "was directed against either a person or an institution or any thing having public status in that State [where the second prosecution is brought], or if the subject of the [earlier] judgment had himself a public status in that State", or where the state concerned claims territorial jurisdiction over the act. Similar exceptions—although slightly narrower as regards the territorial exception—are found in the Convention Between the Member States of the European Communities on Double Jeopardy (Cm. 438, 1987).

[88] The reasons for this appear to relate to aspects of the Protocol unrelated to double jeopardy: see *Rights Brought Home: The Human Rights Bill* (Cm. 3782, 1997), para.4.15.

[89] Protocol No. 7 to the Convention for the Protection of Human Rights and Fundamental Freedoms (1984), art.4(1). See also art.14(7) of the International Covenant on Civil and Political Rights (1966) (which the UK has ratified), which is in slightly more ambiguous language: "No one shall be liable to be tried or punished again for an offence for which he has already been finally convicted or acquitted in accordance with the law and penal procedure of each country."

[90] Cm. 438, 1987.

[91] It will not do so until it is ratified by all those states which were members of the European Communities at the time it opened for signature: art.6(2). At the time of writing, this would require ratification by the UK, Greece and Spain.

refused to apply it where the defendant was never really in jeopardy at his first trial.[92] If a plea based on a foreign conviction is rejected, it will be appropriate to have regard, in passing sentence, to any sentence imposed by the foreign court.[93]

International practice is not uniform, although the tendency in common law jurisdictions has been to recognise that prosecutions can be barred by proceedings abroad[94]—with the notable exception of the United States.[95] Future moves towards the creation of an international double jeopardy (*ne bis in idem*) principle within the European Union are likely.[96]

Res Judicata and Pleas in Bar of Trial

The principle of *res judicata* applies to pleas in bar of trial, and so, if a plea in bar on the ground of (for example) undue delay is upheld, the Crown may not relitigate the issue by raising a fresh libel.[97] It does not, however, appear to apply against the accused, and so in *Stewart v HM Advocate*,[98] where the accused's plea of insanity in bar of trial had failed, there was held to be no bar to him raising the issue a second time after the indictment had fallen and the Crown had been given leave to indict him again. **15.14**

[92] *R. v Thomas (Keith)* [1985] 1 Q.B. 604, where the defendant had been convicted *in absentia* in Italy of a crime essentially identical to the one with which he was charged in England, but could not be extradited to Italy to serve his sentence.

[93] See *Hilson v Easson* (1914) 7 Adam 390 at 397–398, *per* the Lord Justice-General (Strathclyde), and at 402, *per* Lord Anderson.

[94] See *R. v Aughet* (1919) 13 Cr.App.R. 101; *R. v Thomas (Keith)* [1985] 1 Q.B. 604; *S v Pokela*, 1968 (4) S.A. 702; D. Lanham, *Cross-Border Criminal Law* (1997), pp.48–49; *Double Jeopardy, Pleas and Verdicts* (Law Reform Commission of Canada Working Paper No. 63, 1991), 17–18. As regards Continental jurisdictions, see European Parliament Legal Affairs Committee, *Report on the application of the "non bis in idem" principle in criminal law in the European Community* (1984). Cross border criminal activities may, of course, involve separate and distinct violations of the laws of two jurisdictions: see, e.g. *R. v Lavercombe and Murray* [1981] Crim. L.R. 435.

[95] The double jeopardy clause of the US constitution does not prohibit successive prosecutions by different "sovereigns" and for this purpose even the Federal and different State governments in the US are regarded as different sovereigns. See *Bartkus v Illinois* 359 U.S. 121 (1959); D. Braun, "Praying to false sovereigns: the rule permitting successive prosecutions in the age of cooperative federalism" (1992) 20 *American Journal of Criminal Law* 1–78; S. Guerra, "The myth of dual sovereignty: multijurisdictional drug law enforcement and double jeopardy" (1995) 73 *North Carolina Law Review* 1159–1210.

[96] See M. Fletcher, "Some developments to the *ne bis in idem* principle in the European Union" (2003) 66 M.L.R. 769–780; G. Stessens and C. van den Wyngaert, "The international *non bis in idem* principle: resolving some of the unanswered questions" (1999) 48 I.C.LQ. 779–804.

[97] *McNab v HM Advocate*, 1994 S.C.C.R. 632 (Sh Ct).

[98] 1997 J.C. 217.

CHAPTER 16

TIME BAR AND DELAY

CUSTODY TIME LIMITS

Overview

Scots law has applied statutory time limits to custody before trial since 1701.[1] The detail of these provisions has evolved over time and is currently contained in two separate provisions of the Criminal Procedure (Scotland) Act 1995: s.65 (solemn proceedings) and s.147 (summary proceedings). Although the side notes to the statutory provisions read "Prevention of delay in trials", it has been observed that custody time limits are in fact intended to prevent the indefinite detention of untried persons[2]: a person serving a sentence of imprisonment for another offence is no more entitled to insist that his trial be held within the custody time limit than one who has been admitted to bail.[3] Such persons are, of course, both entitled to the benefit of general common law, statutory and ECHR protections against delay, all of which are discussed later in this chapter. **16.01**

Until very recently, the principal rule—that regarding detention in solemn proceedings—was referred to as the "110 day rule",[4] that being the longest period of time an accused could be held in custody before trial in solemn proceedings,[5] subject to the power of the court to extend the period.[6] The Bonomy Review of High Court procedure, however, concluded that, notwithstanding the common perception of the 110-day rule as the "jewel in the crown" of the Scottish criminal justice system, it should in fact be relaxed. The real "jewel in the crown", it was argued, was the 80-day rule, under which the Crown was required to serve an indictment upon the accused with 80 days of committal for trial. While that obligation was "one which the Crown consistently meet",[7] the 110-

[1] APS X, 272, c.6 (1701). See Hume, ii, Ch.4.

[2] *Wallace v HM Advocate*, 1959 J.C. 81 at 77, *per* Lord Sorn.

[3] See below, para.16.06.

[4] Dating from 1887: see the Criminal Procedure (Scotland) Act 1887, s.43.

[5] Prior to 1980, the trial required to be completed within the 110-day period. In 1975, the Thomson Committee recommended that in order to "provide a definite instead of an indefinite terminal date and obviate difficulties that have arisen due to unforseen delays in completing trials", the period should only run to the commencement of the trial: *Criminal Procedure in Scotland (Second Report)* (Cmnd. 6218, 1975), para.15.07. This recommendation was given effect by the Criminal Justice (Scotland) Act 1980, s.14.

[6] See below, para.16.07.

[7] *Improving Practice: 2002 Review of the Practices and Procedure of the High Court of Justiciary*, para.9.2.

day time limit was, in practice, "regularly extended".[8] Accordingly, it was suggested that a preliminary hearing[9] should be required to commence within the 110 day period, but that the trial itself should not be required to commence until, at latest, 140 days after committal.[10]

16.02 The 80-day rule remains, but the period within which the accused must be brought to trial has now been extended to 140 days by the Criminal Procedure (Amendment) (Scotland) Act 2004.[11] Because the 2004 reforms, however, related only to High Court procedure, there are now three sets of custody time limits: those applying in summary procedure, those applying in solemn procedure in the sheriff court, and those applying in the High Court. These dates are as follows (running from full committal or the bringing of the complaint):

In High Court procedure:

(a) the indictment must be served within 80 days;
(b) a preliminary hearing must be commenced within 110 days;
(c) the trial must be commenced within 140 days.[12]

In solemn procedure in the sheriff court:

(a) the indictment must be served within 80 days;
(b) the trial must be commenced within 110 days.[13]

In summary procedure:

- the trial must be commenced within 40 days of the bringing of the complaint.[14]

Calculation of the periods

16.03 It was held in *Hazlett v McGlennan*[15] that, in calculating the 40-day period, the day from which the period runs is itself excluded and the period ends at the end of the 24 hours of the final day. That is consistent with, and was based upon, general principles relating to the calculation of

---

[8] *Improving Practice: 2002 Review of the Practices and Procedure of the High Court of Justiciary*, para.9.2 (noting that extensions were granted in 23% of custody cases in 2001, "a high figure, bearing in mind that roughly 55% of cases result in pleas of guilty").

[9] Referred to as a "preliminary diet" in the *Improving Practice* report. The terminology of "preliminary hearing" is that used in the implementing legislation (the Criminal Procedure (Amendment) (Scotland) Act 2004).

[10] *Improving Practice: 2002 Review of the Practices and Procedure of the High Court of Justiciary*, para.9.8.

[11] 2004 Act, s.6.

[12] CPSA 1995, s.65(4).

[13] *ibid.*, s.65(4).

[14] *ibid.*, s.147. There was, in fact, no statutory regulation of pre-trial detention in summary proceedings prior to 1980: the 40-day rule was recommended by the Thomson Committee and given statutory effect by the Criminal Justice (Scotland) Act 1980. See *Criminal Procedure in Scotland (Second Report)* (Cmnd. 6218, 1975), para.15.19 and s.14(2) of the 1980 Act.

[15] 1993 S.L.T. 74.

time periods,[16] and it is thought that it applies equally to the time-limits governing solemn procedure.[17]

In solemn procedure, the periods run while an accused who has been "committed for any offence until liberated in due course of law" is "detained by virtue of that committal".[18] Accordingly, it was held in *K v HM Advocate*[19] that two children who had been committed to prison, but later granted bail on the condition that they reside at (separate) named List D schools with secure units, continued to be "detained by virtue of that committal" even after bail had been granted, and so the custody time limits continued to run. The court stressed that the matter was a factual one: the children "although granted bail, were not set at liberty ... the bail orders did not result in their release from custody".[20]

Two points should be emphasised. First, detention requires "the intervention of some outside agency to ensure that the person remains where he has been put",[21] and so a bail condition that the person remain within his own home (save for court appearances) was held not to amount to "detention".[22] Secondly, the detention must be *by virtue* of the committal order,[23] and so it was held that where a child had been detained beyond the expiry of the 110-day period as a result of the decisions of the school's deputy principal and a social worker, "who were influenced by considerations which were unconnected with the committal warrant", the custody time limit had not been exceeded.[24]

Multiple committals for the same offence

Section 65(4) of the 1995 Act provides that "an accused who is committed for any offence until liberated in due course of law shall not be detained by virtue of that committal" for longer than the relevant maximum periods. In *HM Advocate v Muir*,[25] the following sequence of events took place: the accused (a) was committed by virtue of a warrant granted **16.04**

[16] *Frew v Morris* (1897) 24 R. (J.) 50 at 51, *per* the Lord Justice-Clerk (Macdonald): "I think that in the ordinary sense of our criminal law the word "time" means the day on which the fact or offence occurred, and the rule of law applies, that in computing a period from the time or day of the occurrence of any event, the day of that occurrence is not to be counted." See also *Lees v Lovell*, 1992 S.L.T. 967, which was relied upon in *Hazlett*.

[17] Renton and Brown, para.9–30.

[18] CPSA 1995, s.65(4). In summary procedure, the 40-day period runs while "a person charged with an offence in summary proceedings" is "detained in that respect": CPSA 1995, s.147(1).

[19] 1993 S.L.T. 77.

[20] At 80 *per* the Lord Justice-General (Hope). The situation had arisen because the court had originally not committed the children to the local authority—the default course of action where a child is committed for trial and not released on bail or ordained to appear—because certificates were produced to the effect that they were so unruly that they could not safely be detained in this way (Criminal Procedure (Scotland) Act 1975, s.24(1): see now CPSA 1995, s.51). They were, as a result, committed to prison and the arrangements for detention in List D schools were made at a later stage.

[21] *Brawls v Walkingshaw*, 1995 S.L.T. 139 at 141, *per* the Lord Justice-General (Hope).

[22] *Brawls v Walkingshaw*, 1995 S.L.T. 139 (a case concerned with the 40-day limit in summary procedure). The court remarked that such conditions should not be imposed save in exceptional circumstances. On the compatibility of such bail conditions with Art.5 of the ECHR, see *McDonald v Dickson*, 2003 S.L.T. 467.

[23] In summary procedure, the period only runs while a person charged with an offence is "detained in that respect" (CPSA 1995, s.147(1)), but the practical effect of this provision would appear to be identical for these purposes.

[24] *X, Petr*, 1996 S.C.C.R. 436 at 446, *per* the Lord Justice-Clerk (Ross).

[25] 1998 J.C. 20.

by the sheriff; (b) thereafter granted bail, and (c) committed to prison again after the trial judge granted a warrant following his failure to appear at court. The Crown then applied for an extension of the relevant time limit, which the single judge held was unnecessary as "that committal" in the statute referred to the committal by virtue of the warrant granted by the trial judge, in which case there was no question of the time limit expiring. On appeal, it was held that this interpretation was incorrect: the key words were "committed for any offence", and even if the accused was committed to prison by virtue of separate warrants over distinct periods, these required to be aggregated for the purposes of the custody time-limits.[26]

Multiple committals for different offences

16.05 Where the accused is subject to two different committals at the same time, the second being granted where he is imprisoned as a result of the first, the second committal does not interrupt the first and the relevant time limits must be considered separately in respect of each committal.[27] Where, however, the accused has been liberated in respect of one committal and is subsequently committed in respect of other charges, time spent imprisoned as a result of the second committal warrant does not count towards the custody time limit applicable to the first.[28]

Interruptions of the period, and detention for other reasons

16.06 The relevant period is necessarily interrupted by release from custody (or even escape).[29] Where an accused is committed to prison pending trial, and is thereafter sentenced to a term of imprisonment on a different charge, any time spent serving that sentence is left out of account in calculating the custody time limit.[30] Similarly, where a person who is already serving a sentence of imprisonment is committed,[31] the custody

[26] The Crown's request for an extension was granted. See also *HM Advocate v Bickerstaff*, 1926 J.C 65, where the court assumed (but did not decide) that the periods covered by successive committals (the accused having been detained in an asylum in the interim) fell to be aggregated.

[27] *Ross v HM Advocate*, 1990 S.C.C.R. 182. The desirability of bringing the accused to trial on a series of charges at the same time may justify an extension of the time limit applicable in respect of the earlier committal: see *HM Advocate v Dickson*, 1949 S.L.T. (Notes) 58. On extensions generally, see below, paras 16.07–16.08.

[28] *HM Advocate v Boyle*, 1972 S.L.T. (Notes) 16.

[29] *HM Advocate v McCann*, 1977 J.C. 1 at 8, *per* the Lord Justice-Clerk (Wheatley).

[30] *Wallace v HM Advocate*, 1959 J.C. 71. In *Lockhart v Robb*, 1988 S.C.C.R. 381 (Sh. Ct), however, it was held that where the accused pled guilty to a summary complaint and was detained in custody until the diet to which the court had deferred sentence, this did not—not being a "sentence"—interrupt the period of detention in respect of another summary complaint on which he had yet to be tried. While that serves to distinguish *Robb* from *Wallace*, it is not clear that the distinction is justified in principle.

[31] *cf. HM Advocate v Lewis*, 1993 S.L.T. 435, where the accused absconded from prison in England, having been sentenced in Scotland but transferred to an English prison in terms of s.26(1) of the Criminal Justice Act 1961. He was later arrested in Scotland, charged with various offences committed after he had absconded, and fully committed in custody. He was detained for more than 110 days, and it was held that the custody time limit had therefore been breached, because the original sentence had to be treated as if it had been passed by an English court (s.26(4) of the 1961 Act) and therefore did not provide a basis for his detention in Scotland.

time-limit will not commence running until the date on which he is due to be released.[32] The same principle applies where an accused who has been released on licence in respect of a previous sentence has that licence revoked and is recalled to prison.[33]

Extending the periods

Solemn procedure: the 80, 110 and 140-day periods

Prior to 2004, the 80-day period could be extended by a single judge of the High Court on "cause shown",[34] but the 110-day period could only be extended in the following circumstances[35]: **16.07**

> "(a) the illness of the accused or of a judge;
> (b) the absence or illness of any necessary witness; or
> (c) any other sufficient cause which is not attributable to any fault on the part of the prosecutor."[36]

As a result of the Criminal Procedure (Amendment) (Scotland) Act 2004, however, either the 80-day, 110-day or 140-day periods may simply be extended on "cause shown".[37] This change means that prior case law (of which there is, in fact, surprisingly little) on the court's power to extend the 110-day period must be read with this change in mind.[38] Given that the statutory language—"cause shown"—is now identical to the provisions on extending the 12-month period, resort may be had to the case law on extensions of that period.[39] In substance, the principal consequence of the statutory reform is that fault on the part of the Crown will no longer act as an absolute bar to an extension being granted.[40]

It must be remembered, however, that the appeal court has acknowledged that "the consequences of an extension of the 110 day period are more serious for the accused than an extension of the 12-month period",[41] a factor which—notwithstanding the change wrought by the 2004 Act—it

---

[32] *HM Advocate v Park*, 1967 J.C. 70, and see the note of the case at (1967) 31 J.C.L. 269 (sub nom *HM Advocate v Meechan*); *Hartley v HM Advocate*, 1970 J.C. 17. What matters is the date on which the accused was *due* to be released, and not the date on which he might *factually* have been released, and so in *Brown v HM Advocate*, 1988 S.C.C.R. 577, it was held that a practice of releasing prisoners on a Friday where they were due for release on the following Sunday fell to be disregarded for this purpose

[33] *Follen v HM Advocate*, 2001 S.C.C.R. 255.

[34] CPSA 1995, s.65(5) (as originally enacted).

[35] *ibid.*, s.65(7) (as originally enacted).

[36] *ibid.*, s.65(7) (as originally enacted). On the interpretation of this statutory language, see *HM Advocate v Macaulay* (1892) 3 White 131 at 135, *per* the Lord Justice-Clerk (Macdonald).

[37] CPSA 1995, s.65(5) (as amended), which also provides that the extension may now be granted by a sheriff where the accused has been served with a copy of the indictment accompanied by a notice calling upon him to appear and answer to the indictment in the sheriff court.

[38] See, generally, Renton and Brown (5th edn), para.7–40.

[39] On which see below, paras 16.12–16.22.

[40] It had already been held, however, that taking a "calculated risk" regarding the commencement of trials did not act as a bar to an extension: *Gildea v HM Advocate*, 1983 S.L.T. 458.

[41] *Beattie v HM Advocate*, 1995 S.L.T. 946 at 949, *per* the Lord Justice-General (Hope), who observes also that the statutory language applicable at the time did not "permit the court to extend the 110-day period in order to suit the convenience of the court or its administrators". As to the circumstances in which that might now amount to "cause shown", see the case law on extensions of the 12-month period due to "pressure of business", discussed below, para.16.21.

is submitted should continue to be taken into account in deciding whether or not to grant an extension.

It had been held that the statutory language prior to 2004 did not preclude retrospective extension of the 110-period.[42] Retrospective extensions should be competent under the new statutory language (in the same way as they have been held competent in respect of the 12-month period),[43] but the point is now of less importance given that exceeding the period merely entitles the accused to be admitted to bail and does not operate to bar a trial.[44]

Summary procedure: the 40-day period

16.08 The sheriff is entitled to extend the 40-day period by virtue of s.147(2) of the 1995 Act, which provides as follows:

> "The sheriff may, on application made to him for the purpose, extend the [40-day period] and order the accused to be detained awaiting trial for such period as he thinks fit where he is satisfied that delay in the commencement of the trial is due to—
>
> (a) the illness of the accused or of a judge;
> (b) the absence or illness of any necessary witness; or
> (c) any other sufficient cause which is not attributable to any fault on the part of the prosecutor."

This language is identical to that which applied to the 110-day period prior to 2004. It has been suggested (with regard to the 110-day period) that the words "any other sufficient cause" must be interpreted as meaning a cause of a "similar nature" to that specified in sub-section (a) or (b).[45] In that context, it has also been held that the fact that the Crown wishes to conduct further investigation with a view to bringing more serious charges against the accused will not be a ground for an extension.[46]

The consequences of exceeding the periods

Custody limits in solemn proceedings

16.09 Prior to the Criminal Procedure (Amendment) (Scotland) Act 2004, where an accused was detained for more than 110 days, he was to be "liberated forthwith and thereafter he shall be for ever free from all question or process for that offence".[47] Following suggestions, noted in the Bonomy Review, that "[s]uch a final determination, within four

---

42 *HM Advocate v Bickerstaff*, 1926 J.C. 65. A retrospective extension also appears to have been sought in *HM Advocate v Dickson*, 1949 S.L.T. (Notes) 58.

43 See below, para.16.12.

44 See below, para.16.09.

45 *HM Advocate v Macaulay* (1892) 3 White 131 at 135, *per* the Lord Justice-Clerk (Macdonald).

46 *HM Advocate v MacTavish*, 1974 J.C. 19.

47 CPSA 1995, s.65(4), as initially enacted. Where only the 80-day period (within which the accused must be served with an indictment) had been exceeded, the accused was required to be liberated but was not rendered free from prosecution thereby: *HM Advocate v McCann*, 1977 J.C. 1.

months of the commencement of an investigation, is regarded by many as an absurd and unjust outcome for the human error of miscalculating the period of time in custody", which "could result in substantial injustice",[48] the position was modified by statute. Now, an accused is merely "entitled to be admitted to bail" at the expiry of the 80, 110 or 140 day (as the case may be) limits, and is not rendered immune from prosecution thereby.[49]

Custody limits in summary proceedings

Where a person charged with an offence in summary proceedings is detained for more than 40 days by virtue of a complaint, he must "be liberated forthwith and thereafter he shall be for ever free from all question or process for that offence".[50] This rule, which is subject to the power of the sheriff to extend the 40-day period,[51] was not altered by the 2004 Act.[52] **16.10**

The 11- and 12-Month Periods in Solemn Procedure

In solemn procedure, the 11- and 12-month periods run from the first appearance of the accused on petition in respect of an offence. The first period applies only in High Court cases, where a preliminary hearing must be commenced within 11 months. In all solemn cases, the trial must be commenced within 12 months. **16.11**

Prior to 1980, there was no statutory provision regulating the length of time taken to bring solemn proceedings to trial. In 1975, the Thomson Committee noted that there were "complicated cases where years elapse between first court appearance and ultimate disposal", and described this as "socially unacceptable" and a position which "cannot in our view be allowed to continue."[53] Accordingly, the committee recommended a statutory maximum period of 12 months from first appearance on petition to the commencement of the trial,[54] a recommendation which was given statutory effect in 1980.[55] The 11-month period is a result of the

48 *Improving Practice: 2002 Review of the Practices and Procedure of the High Court of Justiciary*, para.9.21. No reference was made to the possibility of a retrospective application to extend the period, on which see above, para.16.07.

49 CPSA 1995, s.65(4), as amended by the Criminal Procedure (Amendment) (Scotland) Act 2004, s.6.

50 CPSA 1995, s.147(1).

51 *ibid.*, s.147(2). The question of whether a retrospective application under s.147(2) is permissible appears not to have been decided, but by analogy with the position in solemn proceedings (see above, para.16.07) it seems likely that it would be regarded as competent.

52 It was, of course, wholly outwith the remit of the Bonomy Review and appears not to have been considered by the McInnes Committee: see *The Summary Justice Review Committee: Report to Ministers* (2004).

53 *Criminal Procedure in Scotland (Second Report)* (Cmnd. 6218, 1975), paras 15.08–15.09.

54 *Criminal Procedure in Scotland (Second Report)* (Cmnd. 6218, 1975), para.15.09.

55 Criminal Justice (Scotland) Act 1980, s.14.

introduction of preliminary hearings by the Criminal Procedure (Amendment) (Scotland) Act 2004, as recommended by the Bonomy Review.[56]

The 11- and 12-month periods run regardless of whether or not the accused is in custody.[57]

Extending the 11- and 12-month periods[58]

Procedural aspects

16.12 Where an indictment has been served on the accused in respect of the High Court, the 11- or 12-month period may be extended by a single judge of the High Court on cause shown. In any other case, the 12-month period may be extended by a sheriff on cause shown.[59]

The periods run from the date of the first appearance of the accused on petition in respect of the offence and are independent of the indictment.[60] Accordingly, there is no need for an indictment to be in existence when an extension is sought,[61] while, when an extension is granted, it remains in effect even where an indictment falls.[62]

In terms of the statutory provisions, there is no requirement for an application for an extension to be in writing or for notice to be given to the accused, and so there can be no objection to notice not being given where the accused cannot be traced and has no known solicitor.[63] However, it has been said that, where it is possible to do so, it is only fair and just that notice should be given so that an opportunity is given to the accused (or his agent) to put forward reasons why the application should not be granted,[64] and extensions have been quashed where such notice was not given.[65] Where an application for an extension is refused, a renewed application for an extension based on materially different facts

---

[56] *Improving Practice: 2002 Review of the Practices and Procedure of the High Court of Justiciary*, Chs 8–9.

[57] In *McGuire v HM Advocate*, 2000 S.C.CR. 896, it was argued before the trial judge that the 12-month period did not run while the accused was in custody. That submission was rejected by the trial judge as unsound, a decision which was not challenged on appeal. See also *HM Advocate v McGill*, 1997 S.C.C.R. 230; *Lyle v HM Advocate*, 1992 S.L.T. 467, both of which proceed on the basis that the 12-month period runs regardless of whether the accused is in custody.

[58] Identical considerations apply to applications to extend either period: *HM Advocate v Freeman*, 2006 S.L.T. 35.

[59] CPSA 1995, s.65(3). The question of the 11-month period being extended by the sheriff does not arise as the 11-month period relates only to preliminary hearings, which are a feature of High Court procedure. Where the 11- or 12-month period is extended, the clerk of court shall send a copy of the order of the court to the governor of any institution in which the accused is detained: Criminal Procedure Rules 1996, r.12.5(3).

[60] CPSA 1995, s.65(1).

[61] *HM Advocate v Caulfield*, 1999 S.L.T. 103.

[62] *McDonald v HM Advocate*, 1988 J.C. 74.

[63] *Ferguson v HM Advocate*, 1992 J.C. 133.

[64] *ibid.* at 137, *per* the Lord Justice-Clerk (Ross).

[65] *Sandford v HM Advocate*, 1987 S.L.T. 399 (accused could not be traced but intimation should have been made to his known solicitor). In *Voudouri v HM Advocate*, 2003 S.C.C.R. 448, it is noted that, at an earlier stage of the proceedings, the Crown had consented to the quashing of an extension on the ground that no notice had been given and the hearing was outwith the presence of the accused and his solicitor. A fresh extension was, however, granted.

and circumstances may competently be brought before a sheriff or single High Court judge.[66] An extension may be sought retrospectively.[67]

Where a motion for extension is made, or an extension granted, it is implicit that the extension will begin to run when the original period expires.[68] While the court may specify that the extension is to commence on an earlier date, if that is done it should be made clear at the time that the motion is moved and granted.[69]

The general test to be applied

Extensions should be for no longer than is reasonably necessary.[70] **16.13**
While the decision as to whether or not to grant an extension will always depend on the individual facts and circumstances of the particular case,[71] the court must apply the general two-stage test laid down in *HM Advocate v Swift*,[72] where the court held that "the first question for the judge concerned is...: 'Has a sufficient reason been shown which might justify the grant of an extension?'; and the second question is: 'Ought I in the exercise of my discretion in all the relevant circumstances of the case, to grant the extension for that reason?'"[73] This approach follows logically from the wording of the statute, which requires "cause shown" in order that the court *may* grant an extension. Accordingly, it does not follow that an extension will be granted merely because cause has been shown; that is a matter for the court's discretion.[74] The appeal court will be reluctant to interfere with the discretion of the sheriff or trial judge where the correct test has been applied,[75] although the appeal court will more closely review the question of whether the first stage of the test (that is, has cause been shown?) has been satisfied, as this does not involve the exercise of a discretion. Where the sheriff or trial judge has wrongly concluded that cause has not been shown (or has taken irrelevant factors into account), the court may consider the matter *de novo*.[76]

---

66 *Goldie v HM Advocate*, 2003 S.L.T. 1078, where it is noted that, if the facts and circumstances are unchanged, a fresh application is inappropriate and the Crown should instead take an appeal under the CPSA 1995, s.65(8).

67 *HM Advocate v M*, 1987 J.C. 1. See also *HM Advocate v McGinlay*, 1999 S.L.T. 1297.

68 *Millar v HM Advocate*, 1994 S.L.T. 461.

69 *ibid.* at 463, *per* the Lord Justice-General (Hope). In that case, the sheriff had ordered that the extension was to run from "this date", being eight days before the expiry of the 12-month period. It was held that the sheriff was entitled, in view of the "genuine misunderstanding" this had caused, to grant the Crown's request for an extension of a further eight days.

70 *Garrow v HM Advocate*, 1999 J.C. 209; *Squires v HM Advocate*, 1996 S.C.C.R. 916 (the fact that information had been received saying that a vital witness was ill and unable to travel until the next day did not justify a 30-day extension).

71 *Garrow v HM Advocate*, 1999 J.C. 209 at 215, *per* the Lord Justice-General (Rodger); *McGuire v HM Advocate*, 2000 S.C.C.R. 896 at 907, *per* Lord Cameron of Lochbroom.

72 1984 J.C. 83.

73 1984 J.C. 83 at 89, *per* the Lord Justice-General (Emslie). See, however, *Ellis v HM Advocate*, 2001 J.C. 115, where the court expressed reservations about the appropriateness of this test but declined to express a view on the matter in the absence of fuller argument. Despite these comments, *Swift* has been repeatedly applied by the courts both before and after *Ellis*.

74 *Ferguson v HM Advocate*, 1992 J.C. 133.

75 See, e.g. *Skead v HM Advocate*, 1999 S.L.T. 1357.

76 See, e.g. *HM Advocate v McGill*, 1997 S.C.C.R. 230.

Factors relevant to the exercise of discretion

16.14 **Fault on the part of the Crown.** In *Stenton v HM Advocate*,[77] the court said that "where all that can be said by way of explanation of the need for the extension is that a mistake has been made by the Crown, then that is not a reason of the kind which may be capable of providing a justification for an extension"[78]: in other words, there would be no "cause shown" in such cases and the first stage of the *Swift* test would not be satisfied. That *dictum* is not, however, readily reconcilable with the general body of case law on the subject, and in the subsequent case of *Ellis v HM Advocate*,[79] it was said that *Stenton* should not be read as laying down any wider rule "to the effect that an extension can never be granted where the underlying cause for seeking the extension is a mistake on the part of the Crown, however minor".[80]

Following *Ellis*, it seems that a distinction can be drawn between "minor" and "major" errors. Where the error which has resulted in the Crown being unable to meet the time limit is a major one, there is no cause shown for an extension and the court is precluded from exercising its discretion to extend the limit.[81] Examples of major errors include a failure by the Crown to serve the indictment on the accused,[82] serving an indictment which is fundamentally null for want of specification of a locus,[83] and a decision by the procurator fiscal to put case papers into the Crown's collection system at the sheriff court rather than taking them back to the office personally when he knew that a fresh indictment had to be served within five days in order to comply with the 12-month period (in the event they did not reach his desk for nine days).[84]

A failure to appreciate when the 12-month period expires has normally been held not to be a ground for an extension,[84a] although the cases are not entirely consistent.[85] It has been suggested that a mistake in calculation—such as might be due to a leap year—might be excusable and a

[77] 1998 J.C. 278.

[78] *ibid.* at 283, *per* Lord Coulsfield.

[79] 2001 J.C. 115.

[80] *ibid.* at [14], *per* the Lord Justice-General (Rodger).

[81] *Palmer v HM Advocate*, 2002 S.C.C.R. 980 at [6]–[7], *per* Lord MacLean. See, however, *HM Advocate v Crawford*, 2006 S.L.T. 456 at [15], *per* Lord Johnston: "However fundamental an error may be, the question whether it can be excused depends on the reasons for it being made rather than the intrinsic nature of it or its result."

[82] *HM Advocate v Swift*, 1984 J.C. 83, as interpreted in *HM Advocate v Fitzpatrick*, 2002 S.C.C.R. 758 at [11], *per* the Lord Justice-Clerk (Gill). As to the position where the indictment is not served due to a failure on the part of the police, see below, para.16.16.

[83] *Stenton v HM Advocate*, 1998 J.C. 278. See, however, *Rennie v HM Advocate*, 1998 S.C.C.R. 191, where the fact that the extension was required due to the Crown having served an irrelevant indictment did not act as a bar to granting an extension.

[84] *Palmer v HM Advocate*, 2002 S.C.C.R. 980.

[84a] *Lyle v HM Advocate*, 1992 S.L.T. 467 (mistaken belief that the period did not start to run until the accused, who was already serving a sentence was released from custody); *Bennett v HM Advocate*, 1998 S.L.T. 1258.

[85] See *McGuire v HM Advocate*, 2000 S.C.C.R. 896, where the case did not proceed because of the absence of witnesses, and the Crown wrongly failed to apply for an extension of the 12-month period on the belief that it was not running due to the accused being in custody. An extension was granted in this case, but it is distinguishable on the basis that the Crown's error was simply the cause of the failure to apply for an extension, and not the cause of the *need* for an extension itself.

ground for an extension.[86] It has also been held that a failure to realise that the date on which the 11-month period expired was a Sunday could be treated as a minor error and a ground for an extension,[86a] although one of the judges who heard the case suggested that if the same mistake were to recur in the future it would "be difficult to argue" that it should not be treated as a major error.[86b]

Minor errors, by contrast, will not bar an extension provided that the Crown acts properly and promptly thereafter. Accordingly, *bona fide* errors in the conduct of a trial which have resulted in desertion *pro loco et tempore* being required have resulted in extensions being granted where the accused cannot be brought to a second trial within the time limit.[87] Where, however, the Crown compounds a minor error by subsequent actings, this will be regarded as a major error and will not provide a basis for an extension.[88] It seems that the fact that the Crown have chosen to indict the case towards the end of the time-limit, leaving little or no room for manoeuvre if problems arise, is not in itself to be regarded as fault or risk-taking and will not weigh against granting an extension.[89]

An extension was refused in one case where the Crown had intimated readiness to proceed to trial at an intermediate diet but did not cite witnesses until a later date, and essential witnesses were, in the event, unavailable at the trial diet, leading to further delays.[90]

[86] *Lyle v HM Advocate*, 1992 S.L.T. 467 at 450, *per* the Lord Justice-General (Hope).

[86a] *HM Advocate v Freeman*, 2006 S.L.T. 35. The 11-month period in that case expired on Sunday June 5, 2005. The Crown served an indictment on the accused on the May 5, 2005. A preliminary hearing must be held not less than 29 clear days after service of an indictment (CPSA 1995, s.66(6)(b)), and the first clear day in this case was Saturday June 4, 2005. Accordingly, the earliest date on which the preliminary hearing could be held was Monday June 6, 2005, one day after the expiry of the 11-month period.

[86b] *Freeman*, at [19], *per* Lord Abernethy.

[87] *McCulloch v HM Advocate*, 2001 J.C. 100; *Ellis v HM Advocate*, 2001 J.C. 115, where the court noted that to hold otherwise would have the effect of converting a desertion *pro loco et tempore* into a desertion *simpliciter*.

[88] *HM Advocate v Fitzpatrick*, 2002 S.C.C.R. 758 at [11], *per* the Lord Justice-Clerk (Gill). So, e.g. in *HM Advocate v Willoughby*, 2000 S.C.C.R. 73, the trial was adjourned to a non-existent sitting of the High Court, with the effect that the indictment was deemed to have fallen. The Crown could have served a fresh indictment but instead obtained a warrant for a sitting on the relevant date. The trial judge held that this had "simply compounded the original error", the Crown "must have known" this was incompetent and should have been aware that the original indictment had fallen; accordingly the motion for extension was refused. An extension would in fact have been unnecessary had the Crown served a fresh indictment promptly, but it is implicit in the case that the initial mistake, taken alone, might have been cause for an extension. See also *Brown v HM Advocate*, 1999 S.L.T. 1369, where an "accumulation of errors" led to the motion for an extension being refused.

[89] *HM Advocate v Fitzpatrick*, 2002 S.C.C.R. 758 at [16], *per* the Lord Justice-Clerk (Gill); *Singh v HM Advocate*, 2004 S.C.C.R. 651 at 656, *per* Lord Penrose. But see *HM Advocate v McNally*, 1999 S.L.T. 1377, where a different view was taken by the trial judge (at 1379 *per* Lord Coulsfield). The decision was reversed on appeal, but without specifically contradicting the trial judge's views on this point.

[90] *Langan v Normand*, 1997 S.C.C.R. 306.

16.15 **Absence of fault on the part of the Crown.** It has been said that absence of fault on the part of the Crown is not conclusive in deciding whether or not to grant an extension[91] (and it could obviously not amount in itself to "cause shown"), but it is "plainly a material consideration".[92]

16.16 **Fault on the part of persons other than the Crown.** Where it is impossible to comply with the time-limit because of fault on the part of persons other than the Crown, an extension is likely to be granted. The reported cases concern fault on the part of court staff in giving incorrect information to the procurator fiscal's office,[93] or fault on the part of the police in failing to serve indictments timeously.[94] The cases make it clear that it is the Crown's responsibility to have given appropriate instructions and have appropriate systems in place[95]: if an indictment was not served by the police because of negligence on the part of the Crown it appears that the case for an extension would not be made out.[96]

16.17 **Offence seriousness.** The courts have said that the seriousness of the crime is a relevant factor in deciding whether or not to grant an extension,[97] but it must be borne in mind that the 11- and 12-month periods apply only in solemn procedure and so necessarily concerned with serious cases. Accordingly, offence seriousness does not appear to have been given particular weight outside of crimes such as murder,[98] rape,[99] and attempting to pervert the course of justice.[1]

---

[91] *Mejka v HM Advocate*, 1993 S.L.T. 1321 at 1323, *per* the Lord Justice-Clerk (Ross).

[92] *Ashcroft v HM Advocate*, 1997 S.L.T. 60 at 61, *per* the Lord Justice-Clerk (Ross).

[93] *Anderson v HM Advocate*, 1996 J.C. 138; *Siddiqi v HM Advocate*, 1998 J.C. 190 (where there was held to be degree of fault on the part of the Crown, but not such as to warrant refusing an extension).

[94] *McGinty v HM Advocate*, 1985 S.L.T. 25; *HM Advocate v Davies*, 1994 S.L.T. 296; *Garrow v HM Advocate*, 1999 J.C. 209; *Singh v HM Advocate*, 2004 S.C.C.R. 651.

[95] See, e.g. *Coutts v HM Advocate*, 1992 S.C.C.R. 87.

[96] See *HM Advocate v Finlay*, 1998 S.C.C.R. 103 at 106–107, *per* the Lord Justice-Clerk (Cullen): "In a situation in which the reason for the application is that there was a failure on the part of the police, when acting on behalf of the Crown, to serve the copy indictment in accordance with the Act of Adjournal, it is in my view for the Crown to demonstrate that this occurred without fault on their part." But it may be that a minor degree of contributory fault on the part of the Crown is excusable: see *Siddiqi v HM Advocate*, 1998 J.C. 190.

[97] *Forrester v HM Advocate*, 1997 S.C.C.R. 9; *Main v HM Advocate*, 1999 S.L.T. 881 (where the point was conceded by counsel for the accused). Earlier cases suggest that the relevant question is whether the charges are of "unusual or exceptional gravity": *HM Advocate v Swift*, 1984 J.C. 83 at 90, *per* the Lord Justice-General (Emslie); *Lyle v HM Advocate*, 1992 S.L.T. 467 at 470, *per* the Lord Justice-General (Hope).

[98] *HM Advocate v Fitzpatrick*, 2002 S.C.C.R. 758 (attempted murder).

[99] *Ellis v HM Advocate*, 2001 J.C. 115. Similarly, *Rennie v HM Advocate*, 1998 S.C.C.R. 191 (accused had appeared on petition on a charge of rape; indictment was to libel shameless indecency where the complainer was a young child to whom the accused was *in loco parentis*).

[1] *HM Advocate v Davies*, 1994 S.L.T. 296. The court did not consider the other crimes charged as being of an exceptional nature, but its decision nevertheless extended the 12-month period in respect of all the offences charged. Although it is not absolutely clear whether the court, in terms of the relevant statutory provisions, has the power to grant a "partial" extension only, the periods are expressed as relating to the offence (rather than to the petition) and so an extension in respect of one offence but not another would seem to be competent.

Witness unavailability. Where a crucial witness is unable to give evidence, then an extension will often be appropriate,[2] but this is not the case where the situation is unlikely to change.[3] It has been held to be appropriate to grant an extension to allow an essential witness (who was ill at the relevant time) to give oral evidence at a later date,[4] even though hearsay evidence of a statement he had made earlier could have been admitted instead.[5] In one case, it was said that the fact that the relevant witness had been excused attendance *prior* to the request for an extension meant that it was "extremely difficult, if not impossible" for the motion to be made.[6] **16.18**

Other factors which have been described as relevant to the decision to grant an extension are the absence of prejudice to the accused,[7] and the length of the extension sought.[8]

Unavailability of the accused. Although this should not normally arise, given that expiry of the 11- or 12-month periods cannot bar "the trial of an accused for whose arrest a warrant has been granted for failure to appear at a diet in the case",[9] it has been held sufficient to justify granting an extension when it does.[10] In *HM Advocate v Rowan,*[11] where the accused was on remand in custody in England, an extension was granted. Noting that the English authorities had no power to competently transfer the accused to Scotland while he was held on remand, the court observed that legislation to permit the transfer of prisoners on remand in such circumstances was "urgently needed in order to avoid the risk of injustice due to delay".[12] The government's response was to legislate to the effect that, in calculating the 12-month period, detention "other than while serving a sentence of imprisonment or detention" elsewhere in the UK (or any of the Channel Islands or the Isle of Man) was to be left out of account.[13] **16.19**

---

[2] *Aslam v HM Advocate*, 2000 J.C. 325; *Main v HM Advocate*, 1999 S.L.T. 881 (where the complainer was hiding in order to avoid giving evidence). See also *Squires v HM Advocate*, 1996 S.C.C.R. 916, although in that case the decision to grant an extension was reversed on appeal on the basis that insufficient information had been put forward to warrant an extension, at least of the length granted.

[3] *HM Advocate v Caulfield*, 1999 S.L.T. 1003.

[4] *Forrester v HM Advocate*, 1997 S.C.C.R. 9.

[5] In terms of CPSA 1995, s.259.

[6] *Ferguson v HM Advocate*, 1992 J.C. 133 at 138–139, *per* the Lord Justice-Clerk (Ross). In that case, it was also noted that another witness was abroad on holiday and the Crown position was that if his evidence had to be led the Crown would have to pay for his holiday to have him brought to the trial. The court observed that it was "not persuaded that that would have been a proper basis for seeking to show cause to this court as to why an extension should be granted" (*per* Lord Ross at 139).

[7] *HM Advocate v Swift*, 1984 J.C. 83 at 90, *per* the Lord Justice-General (Emslie); *HM Advocate v Fitzpatrick*, 2002 S.C.C.R. 758 at [14], *per* the Lord Justice-Clerk (Gill); *HM Advocate v Freeman*, 2006 S.L.T. 35 (where even if the time limit had been observed, the defence would not have been ready to go to trial).

[8] *HM Advocate v Swift*, 1984 J.C. 83 at 90, *per* the Lord Justice-General (Emslie).

[9] CPSA 1995, s.65(2).

[10] *HM Advocate v Brodie*, 1996 S.C.C.R. 862, where the accused had disappeared, possibly abroad, and there was the possibility that extradition proceedings might have to be taken. The commentary by Sheriff Gordon to the S.C.C.R. report (at 865) noted that the case "falls among almost all possible stools. The accused did appear on petition but he was not fully committed and not bailed, so that there was no domicile of citation at which he could be cited. As a result the Crown were not able to avoid the operation of [the time limit] by taking a warrant."

[11] 1995 S.L.T. 434. See also *Duffy v HM Advocate*, 1991 S.C.C.R. 685.

[12] 1995 S.L.T. 434 at 440, *per* the Lord Justice-General (Hope).

[13] CPSA 1995, s.65(10), as amended (which now applies equally to the 11-month period).

16.20 **Conduct of the defence.** The fact that proceedings have been delayed at the request of the defence may be a factor weighing in favour of an extension being granted.[14] In a case where an extension was necessary only because of a plea in bar being successfully taken by the defence before the sheriff, a decision which was overturned on appeal by the Crown, this was held to be a reason justifying an extension.[15]

16.21 **Pressure of business.**[16] In a frequently cited passage, the Lord Justice-General (Emslie) said in *McGinty v HM Advocate*[17] that "[o]f course it will not do for the Crown to say that there has not been time to serve an indictment to permit a trial to commence within 12 months as the result of mere pressure of business ..."[18] That statement (which was strictly *obiter*) has, however, been distinguished in subsequent cases, with the appeal court in *Rudge v HM Advocate*[19] observing that Lord Emslie was referring to pressure of business on the Crown.[20] In that case, pressure of business on the *court* (specifically, regarding accommodation for trials at Ayr Sheriff Court) was held to be sufficient warrant for an extension.[21] An extension was granted in one case where the Crown were unable to proceed to trial within the 12-month period due to choosing to start another trial first which, unforeseeably, took longer than expected.[22]

As noted by Sheriff Gordon in his commentary to *Rudge v HM Advocate*,[23] this approach is objectionable on the basis that the accused's right to be brought to trial within 12 months in solemn procedure is a right against the state as a whole, not just against the prosecutor. More recently, in *Warnes v HM Advocate*,[24] the appeal court seems to have demonstrated an unwillingness to distinguish between pressure of business on the part of the Crown and the court, noting that the right to be brought to trial within 12 months in solemn procedure "is a very important right [which] can be given effect ... only if all the constituent parts of the criminal justice system—including the courts, the Crown and,

---

[14] *Ellis v HM Advocate*, 2001 J.C. 115, where the need for the extension only arose because of an earlier adjournment at the request of the defence. In refusing the accused's appeal against the grant of an extension, the court observed that, had the trial gone ahead at the earlier date and the same problem which led to the trial being deserted *pro loco et tempore* had arisen, the Crown could have started a new trial within the 12-month period.

[15] *HM Advocate v McGill*, 1997 S.C.C.R. 230. See also *Rimmer v HM Advocate*, 2002 S.C.C.R. 22, where it was held to be relevant that the application for extension had been delayed while appellant's advisers were actively considering whether to lodge a petition to the *nobile officium*, the need for an extension being dependent on the outcome of that petition.

[16] See also Sheriff Gordon's commentary to *Tudhope v Mathieson*, 1981 S.C.C.R. 231 (Sh. Ct) at 239, where it is noted that the High Court adopted a practice of granting extensions to the 110-day period during a strike by court staff.

[17] 1985 S.L.T. 25.

[18] 1985 S.L.T. 25 at 26, and see *Riaviz v HM Advocate*, 2003 S.L.T. 1110. The situation is different where the Crown are ready to proceed to trial, but the defence move for an adjournment and pressure of business makes it difficult for the Crown to find a new trial date within the 12-month period: *HM Advocate v Sinclair*, 1984 S.C.C.R. 347.

[19] 1989 S.L.T. 591.

[20] As noted by Sheriff Gordon in his commentary to *Rudge* (in the report of the case 1989 S.C.C.R. 105).

[21] To similar effect, see *Dobbie v HM Advocate*, 1986 S.L.T. 648; *Fleming v HM Advocate*, 1992 S.C.C.R. 575. A stricter view was taken in *Beattie v HM Advocate*, 1995 S.L.T. 946, but that case was concerned with the 110-day period and as such an extension not only delayed the trial but resulted in the accused being kept in custody for a longer period.

[22] *Skead v HM Advocate*, 1999 S.L.T. 1357.

[23] See the report of the case at 1989 S.C.C.R. 105.

[24] 2001 J.C. 110.

so far as publicly funded, the defence—have adequate resources to ensure that, as a rule, trials can be begun within twelve months".[25] It may be, therefore, that the distinction drawn in earlier cases is no longer sustainable.

Miscellaneous factors. Because, as noted earlier, applications for an extension must necessarily be decided on their own particular facts, there are a number of reported cases which do not involve the application of general principles or fall into any obvious category, but may nevertheless be relied upon by way of analogy in future cases. They are noted here as follows: **16.22**

- In a case where three co-accused had been placed on petition, but the Crown had decided that there was insufficient evidence to proceed to trial against the third until the trial of the other two had concluded and they could be precognosed, it was held that this was a ground for an extension given that the Crown had acted legitimately and promptly.[26]
- Where it was not possible to take a prosecution for fraudulent evasion of VAT to trial within the 12-month period because of ongoing negotiations regarding a financial settlement with Customs and Excise, an extension was granted.[27]
- Although the convenience of trying two accused at the same time is not in itself a basis for depriving one of them of the protection of the time limits,[28] an extension may be justified in such cases in order to prevent a vulnerable witness from having to give evidence on two separate occasions.[29] An extension may also be justified in order to try all the outstanding charges against an accused on a single indictment.[29a]
- In a case where it was held that the sheriff had acted wrongly by deserting the trial *pro loco et tempore*, the 12-month limit was extended, seemingly without discussion by the court, in order to allow a fresh trial to take place.[30]
- The fact that the accused is currently serving a sentence of imprisonment is not a relevant consideration.[31]
- The fact that previous extensions to the time limits have been necessary, while part of the case history, will not in itself justify a further extension.[32]
- Where fresh evidence came to light after the extension of the 12-month period, but it was conceded that the Crown could have discovered this earlier, having failed to initiate enquires until too

[25] At [9] *per* Lord Philip.

[26] *Hogg v HM Advocate*, 2002 S.L.T. 639. This decision appears to assume that it is necessarily legitimate in such cases for the Crown to only proceed to trial against the first two accused towards the end of the 12-month period, and does not consider whether it would in fact have been possible for both trials to have taken place within the period, or for the first trial to have been expedited.

[27] *Voudouri v HM Advocate*, 2003 S.C.C.R. 448.

[28] *Mejka v HM Advocate*, 1993 S.L.T. 1321.

[29] *Ashcroft v HM Advocate*, 1997 S.L.T. 60.

[29a] *Allan v HM Advocate*, 2005 S.C.C.R. 613.

[30] *HM Advocate v Sinclair*, 1986 J.C. 113.

[31] *HM Advocate v McGill*, 1997 S.C.C.R. 230.

[32] *Riaviz v HM Advocate*, 2003 S.L.T. 1110.

late a point, there was held not to be a basis for a retrospective extension.[33]

The consequences of exceeding the 11- or 12-month periods

16.23 Prior to 1996, the statutory provisions relating to the 12-month rule provided that, unless the trial was commenced within a period of 12 months from the first appearance of the accused on petition in respect of that offence, he should "be discharged forthwith and thereafter he shall be for ever free from all question or process for that offence".[34] It was initially held that this had no relevance to summary proceedings, and so it was open to the Crown to "reduce" solemn proceedings to summary ones by prosecuting the accused on complaint after the expiry of the 12-month period.[35] However, in *Gardner v Lees*,[36] a Full Bench held that the statutory language was plain and unambiguous, and so rendered a summary prosecution after the expiry of the 12-month period incompetent.[37] Legislation was, shortly thereafter, passed to overturn the effect of this decision, and so expiry of the 12-month period now only renders subsequent prosecutions *on indictment* incompetent.[38] The same consequence follows where the preliminary hearing is not commenced within 11 months.[39]

Prescription

16.24 It was authoritatively decided in *Sugden v HM Advocate*[40] that there is no common-law rule of prescription in Scots law. In that case, a majority of the court (a Whole Court but for the absence of the Lord Justice-General) rejected the existence of a rule of "vicennial prescription" which the accused argued had been established by the earlier case of *HM Advocate v Macgregor*.[41] The court acknowledged, however, that a lapse of time might result in the court sustaining a plea in bar of trial on the basis that "grave prejudice to the accused might result if the trial were allowed to proceed".[42] Such a plea would not, of course, be one of prescription, but of oppression on the basis of delay or (in modern practice) a plea that

[33] *Stewart v HM Advocate*, 1994 S.L.T. 518.

[34] CPSA 1995, s.65(1) (as originally enacted); Criminal Procedure (Scotland) Act 1975, s.101(1) (which reads "he shall be forthwith set at liberty and declared for ever free from all question or process for the crime with which he was charged").

[35] *MacDougall v Russell*, 1986 S.L.T. 403. See also *Whitelaw v Dickinson*, 1993 S.L.T. 599.

[36] 1996 J.C. 83.

[37] This did not *necessarily* render such "reduced" prosecutions incompetent as it was open to the Crown to seek retrospective extensions of the 12-month period: see *McDowall v Lees*, 1996 J.C. 214; *Normand v Walker*, 1996 J.C. 100 and subsequent cases such as *Keddie v Crowe*, 1997 S.L.T. 738; *Langan v Normand*, 1997 S.C.C.R 306; *McDonald v Gordon*, 1997 S.L.T. 1069.

[38] Criminal Procedure and Investigations Act 1996, s.73, amending CPSA 1995, s.65(1). These provisions were held to have retrospective effect in *Cairns v Miller*, 1997 S.L.T. 1233. Because s.65(1) now only bars trial on indictment outwith the 12-month period, it would seem not to bar a private prosecution by way of criminal letters after the period has expired. *Cf.*, however, Renton and Brown, para.3–09, where the contrary seems to be assumed. On the effects of the original wording of s.65(1) on a private prosecution, see *Gardner v Lees*, 1996 J.C. 83, where earlier dicta in *C. v Forsyth*, 1995 S.L.T. 905 are disapproved.

[39] CPSA 1995, s.65(1), as amended.

[40] 1934 J.C. 103.

[41] (1773) Mor. 11146.

[42] *Sugden v HM Advocate*, 1934 J.C. 103 at 113, *per* the Lord Justice-Clerk (Aitchison).

proceeding to trial would be incompatible with the right to trial within a reasonable time under Art.6(1) of the ECHR. This plea is discussed later in the chapter.[43]

Prescription in summary procedure

Although there is no common-law rule of prescription in Scots law, there is a statutory rule relating to offences triable only summarily. Section 136 of the Criminal Procedure (Scotland) Act 1995 provides as follows: **16.25**

> "(1) Proceedings under this Part of this Act in respect of any offence to which this section applies shall be commenced—
> (a) within six months after the contravention occurred;
> (b) in the case of a continuous contravention, within six months after the last date of such contravention,
> and it shall be competent in a prosecution of a contravention mentioned in paragraph (b) above to include the entire period during which the contravention occurred.
> (2) This section applies to any offence triable only summarily and consisting of the contravention of any enactment, unless the enactment fixes a different time limit.
> (3) For the purposes of this section proceedings shall be deemed to be commenced on the date on which a warrant to apprehend or to cite the accused is granted, if the warrant is executed without undue delay."[44]

A variety of statutes make specific provision for particular time-limits to apply to particular offences.[45] Such provisions are not discussed further here.[46]

Calculating the six-month period

The start of the period. The six-month period starts to run from the date of the contravention or, in the case of a "continuous" contravention, from the last date of such contravention.[47] Whether an offence is a "continuing" one or not will depend on the drafting of the particular statutory provision.[48] In *A & C McLennan (Blairgowrie), Limited v* **16.26**

---

[43] See below, paras 16.33 *et seq*.

[44] Prior to the 1995 Act, the six-month prescriptive period applied to all summary prosecutions for statutory offences (except where the relevant statute applied a different rule), whether or not these were also triable on indictment. See s.331 of the Criminal Procedure (Scotland) Act 1975. It is noted in Renton and Brown (at para.9–39) that "[t]he reason for the restriction in the 1995 legislation is unclear". Offences which are normally triable only summarily may be libelled as an additional or alternative charge in an indictment (CPSA 1995, s.292(6)), in which case the prescriptive period will not apply (Renton and Brown, para.9–41).

[45] See, e.g. Road Traffic Offenders Act 1988, s.6; Misuse of Drugs Act 1971, s.25(5).

[46] Some aspects of certain provisions are noted in Renton and Brown, paras 9–46 to 9–47.

[47] CPSA 1995, s.136(1).

[48] *British Telecommunications Plc v Nottinghamshire CC* [1999] Crim. L.R. 217. In that case, an offence of failing to properly reinstate a street after works (New Roads and Street Works Act 1991, s.71) was held to be a continuing one, meaning that the prosecution did not fall foul of the six-month time limit applicable under English law (Magistrates' Courts Act 1980, s.127) even though the prosecution was commenced over three years after the defendant had excavated the footpath in question. See, to similar effect, *Thames Water Utilities Ltd v Bromley LBC*, March 4, 2000, DC.

MacMillan,[49] it was held that an offence of failing to notify the change of ownership of a vehicle "forthwith" after sale was complete once notification had not been made "as soon as is reasonably possible", and was therefore not a continuing offence. Accordingly, a prosecution commenced 6 months and 11 days after the sale was incompetent.

16.27 **Duration.** The six-month period—"month" meaning calendar month[50]—is calculated with the date of the contravention left out of account.[51]

16.28 **Commencing the proceedings.** Proceedings may be commenced either by "actual commencement" or by "deemed commencement".[52] Actual commencement will be effected by service and receipt of the complaint.[53] If that cannot be established, resort may be had to s.136(3) of the 1995 Act, according to which (as noted earlier) proceedings shall be "deemed to be commenced on the date on which a warrant to apprehend or to cite the accused is granted, if the warrant is executed without undue delay".[54]

The reference to a "warrant to cite" is confusing,[55] as the 1995 Act itself operates as sufficient warrant to cite the accused.[56] In *Keily v Tudhope*,[57] the reference in s.136(3) to a "warrant to cite" was held to refer to an order of the court assigning a diet for the disposal of the case under s.139(1)(a), and accordingly proceedings will be deemed to commence on the date the diet is assigned.[58]

In *Shaw v Dyer*,[59] a citation was sent to the accused's father in error. A solicitor did, however, appear for the accused at the assigned diet, and argued that the proceedings were barred by prescription as the execution of the citation could not establish commencement within six months. It

---

49 1964 J.C. 1.

50 Interpretation Act 1978, s.5 and Sch.1; *Farquharson v Whyte* (1886) 1 White 26.

51 *Lees v Lovell*, 1992 J.C. 169, where it was held that proceedings commenced on December 29 in respect of an offence committed on June 29 were competent. See also *Hazlett v McGlennan*, 1992 S.L.T. 74; *Tudhope v Lawson*, 1983 S.C.C.R. 435 (the latter case applying the same principle in respect of a different statutory timebar).

52 *Keily v Tudhope*, 1986 J.C. 103 at 107, *per* the Lord Justice-Clerk (Ross). *Cf. Tudhope v Bruckner*, 1985 S.C.C.R. 352.

53 *Keily v Tudhope*, 1986 J.C. 103 at 107, *per* the Lord Justice-Clerk (Ross), and see also *Orr v Lowdon*, 1987 S.C.C.R. 515. See, however, *Robertson v Page*, 1943 J.C. 32, where it was said, *obiter*, that (at 38 *per* Lord Carmont) "commencement of proceedings ... takes place when the complaint is placed before the Clerk of Court and a diet is fixed by him".

54 As to the formalities required for a valid warrant, see the general discussion in C.N. Stoddart, *Criminal Warrants*, (2nd edn, 1999), paras 1.15–1.22. There are two reported decisions specifically concerned with the validity of warrants in this context: *Welsh v Normand*, 1995 S.C.C.R. 81 (warrant for apprehension did not contain the accused's name or serial number of the case; held that it was "plainly referable" to the accused and the complaint against him, being stapled to the complaint, and was therefore valid); *Tudhope v Senatti Holdings Ltd*, 1984 S.C.C.R. 251 (Sh. Ct) (undated 'warrant' held to be *ex facie* invalid as not bearing a date before the expiry of the prescriptive period).

55 See *Tudhope v Buckner*, 1985 S.C.C.R. 352 (Sh. Ct) at 353, *per* Sheriff Gordon, observing that the statutory provision (then s.331(3) of the Criminal Procedure (Scotland) Act 1975) is "somewhat ineptly framed in the context of the Act as a whole as no warrant to cite is granted from the date of which any period of delay can be calculated. What happens is that the order assigning a diet is treated as if it were a warrant to cite, and delay is reckoned as from its date".

56 CPSA 1995, s.140.

57 1986 J.C. 103 (the decision being taken under reference to identical provisions in the Criminal Procedure (Scotland) Act 1975).

58 In accordance with s.140, the 1995 Act itself is sufficient warrant to cite the accused to that diet, and so a warrant to cite is not specifically granted when the diet is assigned.

59 2002 S.L.T. 826.

was held that, given the solicitor's appearance, the accused must have actually received the complaint at some date, and that proceedings would have commenced on that date. There was, therefore, "at least an initial onus on the accused to set up his preliminary defence based on time bar", but as no attempt had been made to discharge that onus and "no reference [had been] made to when the accused actually received or became aware of the complaint in question",[60] the plea had to fail.

Deemed commencement and undue delay

The prosecutor can only take advantage of the "deemed commencement" rule in s.136(3) where the warrant to apprehend or cite has been executed without "undue delay". In *Smith v Peter Walker and Son (Edinburgh) Ltd*,[61] the following definition of "undue delay" (taken from Renton and Brown) was approved: **16.29**

> "What constitutes undue delay must be a question of fact in each case. It must not be due to any act for which the prosecutor is responsible. The expression 'without undue delay' implies that there has been no slackness on his part and that any delay in execution is due to some circumstance for which he is not responsible, e.g. the conduct of the accused."[62]

The absence of prejudice to the accused is not the same as the absence of undue delay.[63] Where a warrant has been executed after the expiry of the six-month period, it is for the prosecutor to show that there has been no undue delay in order to "avail himself of the very limited latitude allowed to him"[64] by s.136(3). This may, in some cases, require evidence to be led,[65] and in one case where a plea to the competency on the basis of prescription was taken without prior notice to the fiscal, it was held oppressive for the sheriff to demand an immediate explanation and refuse an adjournment.[66]

The relevant question is whether there has been undue delay from the date that the warrant was granted, and the period between the warrant being granted and the expiry of the six-month period is not to be left out of account in answering this question.[67] By contrast, delays in progressing matters prior to the expiry of the six-month period are less likely to be regarded as undue.[68] By contrast, where the warrant is received in the prosecutor's office after the expiry of the six-month period, it is of "supreme importance" that the matter proceeds without delay.[69] Pressure

---

[60] At [5] *per* Lord Marnoch.

[61] 1978 J.C. 44.

[62] At 48 *per* the Lord Justice-General (Emslie), quoting from Renton and Brown (4th edn, 1972), para.13–08. See now Renton and Brown, para.9–48.

[63] *Harvey v Lockhart*, 1991 J.C. 9.

[64] *Smith v Peter Walker and Son (Edinburgh) Ltd*, 1978 J.C. 44 at 48, *per* the Lord Justice-General (Emslie).

[65] *McCartney v Tudhope*, 1986 J.C. 7. But not always: *Kennedy v Carmichael*, 1991 S.C.C.R. 458.

[66] *McGlennan v Johnston*, 1991 S.C.C.R. 895.

[67] *MacNeill v Cowie*, 1985 J.C. 23; *McNeillie v Walkingshaw*, 1991 S.L.T. 892.

[68] See *Alexander v Normand*, 1997 S.L.T. 370; *McKay v Normand*, 1996 S.L.T. 624.

[69] *Galloway v Clark*, 2001 S.C.C.R. 734 (warrant for apprehension received in the prosecutor's office the day after the six-month period expired; a delay of five days while a covering letter to be sent with the warrant to the police was typed was held to be "undue").

of business is not an excuse which prevents delay from being regarded as "undue".[70] Where no explanation is given for a delay in the prosecutor's office, that may be regarded as undue even if it is only for a matter of days.[71]

16.30 **Police procedures.** The passage of time involved in normal police procedures which result in warrants being executed a number of days after receipt has consistently been held not to amount to undue delay,[72] to the extent that, even where the warrant has only been received by the prosecutor the day before the expiry of the six-month period, there has been held to be no obligation on the prosecutor to seek to expedite the normal procedure.[73] Similarly, it was held legitimate in one case for the prosecutor to attempt postal service where a warrant was received one day before the expiry of the period, there being no reason to believe that service via the police would be any more effective. Consequently, the delay occasioned due to the postal service failing, necessitating subsequent personal service, did not amount to undue delay.[74]

It has been said that the prosecutor is not responsible for police procedures,[75] but has a duty to enquire if there appears to be a long delay in the execution of a warrant.[76] It is, however, the responsibility of the prosecutor to ensure that an appropriate system is in place for transmission of warrants to the police and their execution thereafter: provided that such a system normally operates efficiently, a slightly extended delay due to abnormal circumstances will not be regarded as undue.[77] Similarly, the prosecutor is not responsible for a delay in the sheriff clerk's office.[78] The police cannot be expected to make repeated futile attempts to execute a warrant, and so in one case a lengthy period of inaction following three failed attempts was held not to amount to undue delay.[79]

A police policy of not executing warrants on persons involved in High Court proceedings until after proceedings had concluded has been held to be sound policy, compliance with which did not constitute undue delay.[80]

---

[70] *McCartney v Tudhope*, 1986 J.C. 7 (the fact that the police officer responsible was required to serve or attempt to serve 300 complaints and citations in a two week period was not a relevant factor). See also *Tudhope v Mathieson*, 1981 S.C.C.R. 231 (the prosecutor could have executed the warrant but chose not to do so given limited court facilities due to a strike by court staff; held that this was undue delay).

[71] *Robertson v Carmichael*, 1993 S.C.C.R. 841 (four days); *Carmichael v Sardar & Sons*, 1983 S.C.C.R. 433 (Sh. Ct) (six days). But see *McNeillie v Walkingshaw*, 1991 S.L.T. 892 (three days unexplained delay in the prosecutor's office prior to the expiry of the six-month period; sheriff was entitled to conclude there had not been undue delay).

[72] *Tudhope v Brown*, 1984 S.C.C.R. 163; *Kennedy v Carmichael*, 1991 S.C.C.R. 458.

[73] *Beattie v Tudhope*, 1984 S.L.T. 423; *Stagecoach Ltd v MacPhail*, 1986 S.C.C.R. 184.

[74] *Ross Inns Ltd v Smith*, 1987 S.L.T. 121.

[75] *Singh v Vannet*, 1999 S.L.T. 985.

[76] *Wilson v Vannet*, 2000 J.C. 152; see also *Singh v Vannet*, 1999 S.L.T. 985.

[77] *MacLeod v Hingston*, 1999 S.C.CR. 717.

[78] *Anderson v Lowe*, 1991 S.C.C.R. 712.

[79] *Alexander v Normand*, 1997 S.L.T. 370.

[80] *Melville v Normand*, 1996 S.L.T. 826.

Fault or absence on the part of the accused. Where a delay in executing a warrant is due to the non-cooperation or deliberate absence of the accused, this will not be "undue".[81] In two cases where the accused was unavailable for personal service due to being at sea, the resultant delays in serving the complaint were held not to be undue.[82] 16.31

Where the accused was held in prison in England, and it would have taken around 28 days for his transfer to Scotland to allow the warrant to be executed, delaying the execution of the warrant by a further 10 days to await his release was held not to be undue.[83]

Warrant never executed. In *Chow v Lees*,[84] the Crown obtained a warrant for the accused's apprehension, but rather than execute it, wrote to the accused informing him of the warrant and stating that he would refrain from executing it on condition that he appeared personally at the sheriff court on the relevant date. The appeal court held that it was "wholly satisfied that Parliament could never have intended that a person who appears in court in response to a letter of this kind should be entitled to argue that the proceedings are time-barred simply because by appearing the accused has made it unnecessary for the warrant to be executed",[85] and that proceedings would not be time-barred provided that the prosecutor had acted without undue delay in inviting the appellant to appear. While the result reached is desirable and clearly in accordance with the spirit of the legislation, it is difficult to reconcile with the statutory language, according to which s.136(3) can only be relied upon where the warrant has been "executed without undue delay"—yet the warrant in *Chow* was never executed at all.[86] 16.32

Trial Within A Reasonable Time

The common law guarantee: oppression

Prior to Art.6(1) of the ECHR being given effect in Scots law, the accused was protected from the consequences of delay by way of the common law plea of oppression. As originally formulated in *HM Advocate v Leslie*[87] (and approved by the appeal court in *Tudhope v McCarthy*[88]), the test was a bipartite one: (1) was there undue delay? and (2) did it result in gross or grave prejudice?[89] In *McFadyen v Annan*,[90] a Full Bench held that this test was unsound, the real question being "if the delay, whether caused by the Crown or not, has been such as to prejudice the prospects of fair trial".[91] Accordingly, the court formulated the test as follows: 16.33

---

[81] *Nicolson v Skeen* (1974) S.C.C.R. Supp. 74; *Young v MacLeod*, 1993 S.C.C.R. 479.
[82] *Aird v MacNab* (1972) 36 J.C.L. 114; *Buchan v McNaughtan*, 1991 S.L.T. 410.
[83] *Young v MacPhail*, 1992 S.L.T. 98.
[84] 1997 J.C. 137. See also *Young v Smith*, 1981 S.L.T. (Notes) 101.
[85] At 140 *per* the Lord Justice-General (Rodger).
[86] *Aird v McNab* (1972) 36 J.C.L. 114 is similarly problematic.
[87] January 31, 1984, unreported (reported on another point at 1985 J.C. 1).
[88] 1985 J.C. 48.
[89] At 52 *per* the Lord Justice-Clerk (Wheatley), quoting the test adumbrated by Lord Hunter in *Leslie*.
[90] 1992 J.C. 53.
[91] At 61 *per* the Lord Justice-Clerk (Ross).

> "the real question which the court has to consider in all cases where delay is alleged is whether the delay has prejudiced the prospects of a fair trial. This involves the court asking itself whether the risk of prejudice from the delay is so grave that no direction by the trial judge could be expected to remove it. In the case of summary procedure the question must be whether the risk of prejudice from the delay is so grave that the sheriff or justice could not be expected to put that prejudice out of his mind and reach a fair verdict".[92]

The court stressed that the plea would only be exceptionally upheld, which is unsurprising given the requirement for the accused to demonstrate prejudice. In *HM Advocate v H*,[93] Lord Bonomy observed that a plea of oppression, prior to Art.6(1) of the ECHR being given effect in Scots law, seldom succeeded, due to the need to demonstrate that the accused could not receive a fair trial on account of the delay:

> "It has perhaps been a surprising feature of Scottish criminal procedure that in the past the strict timetable for bringing those in custody to trial, including the renowned 110 day rule, should not be complemented by rules designed to ensure that those not in custody, who are subject to serious criminal charges but not active proceedings, and who are presumed innocent, should have their fate determined within a reasonable time. The introduction of such a right under the Convention must be welcomed by those interested in the rights of persons who face serious criminal charges in a society which prides itself in the presumption of innocence as a fundamental element of criminal procedure. That right now exists for the protection of all of us who may at any time be rightly or wrongly the subject of such charges."[94]

Accordingly, although the common law plea of oppression remains open to the accused,[95] it appears to have been largely supplanted by Art.6(1) of the ECHR.

Article 6(1) of the European Convention on Human Rights

16.34 Article 6(1) of the ECHR provides that "[i]n the determination of his civil rights and obligations or of any criminal charge against him, everyone is entitled to a fair and public hearing within a reasonable time". Because s.57(2) of the Scotland Act 1998 provides that the Lord Advocate (as a member of the Scottish Executive) has no power to do any act which is incompatible with Convention rights, the court has no discretion to allow a prosecution brought by the public prosecutor to proceed where it has not been brought within a reasonable time.[96] It is not necessary for

---

[92] At 61 *per* the Lord Justice-Clerk (Ross).

[93] 2000 J.C. 552.

[94] At 553–554.

[95] See, e.g. *HM Advocate v Little*, 1999 S.L.T. 1145, where counsel for the accused (in arguing that the trial was barred by Art.6(1)) expressly reserved the right to take a plea based on oppression at a later stage. The plea is treated in more detail in Renton and Brown, paras 9–23 to 9–23.1.

[96] *HM Advocate v R* [2002] UKPC D3. The position is different in England: *Attorney-General's Reference (No. 2 of 2001)* [2003] UKHL 68. By contrast, an unreasonable delay in hearing an appeal against conviction does not mean that the conviction must be quashed as a result: *Mills v HM Advocate (No. 2)* [2002] UKPC D2, although it may result in a reduction of sentence: *Mills; Gillespie v HM Advocate (No. 2)*, 2003 S.L.T. 210.

the accused to show that he has been prejudiced by the delay in order to establish a breach of Art.6(1),[97] as the protection is not directly concerned with prejudice but aims to "avoid that a person charged should remain too long in a state of uncertainty about his fate".[98] The right to trial within a reasonable time has been treated in some detail elsewhere[99] and, accordingly, only an overview of the (considerable) case law is provided here.

It has been held that "[t]he threshold of proving a breach of the reasonable time requirement is a high one, not easily crossed".[1] The decision is, however, one for the trial judge and his decision will not be open to challenge on appeal where he has ascertained the facts and applied the proper test.[2]

The "reasonable time" period guaranteed by Art.6(1) runs from the date at which the person is "charged",[3] and applies to "the whole of the proceedings in issue, including appeal proceedings".[4] "Charged", for these purposes, may be defined as "the official notification given to an individual by the competent authority of an allegation that he has committed a criminal offence".[5] While this will normally be the date on which the person concerned is charged by the police,[6] it may in fact be an earlier date in appropriate cases.[7] It has been suggested in a number of cases that the reasonable time period will commence when the allegation is put to the individual concerned by the police in interviewing him.[7a] In all these cases, however, the point appears to have been conceded by the Crown rather than being argued. In *Attorney-General's Reference (No. 2 of 2001)*,[7b] it was held that "the relevant time period commences at the earliest time at which a defendant is officially alerted to the likelihood of criminal proceedings against him, which in England and Wales will

---

[97] *Mills v HM Advocate (No. 2)* [2002] UKPC D2; *Dyer v Watson* [2002] UKPC D1 at [50], *per* Lord Bingham; *Crummock (Scotland) Ltd v HM Advocate*, 2000 J.C. 408 at [6], *per* Lord Weir. See also A. Webster, "Delay and article 6(1): an end to the requirement of prejudice?" [2001] Crim. L.R. 786–794 (written prior to *Mills*).

[98] *Stögmüller v Austria* (1969) 1 E.H.R.R. 155 at 191; see also *McLean v HM Advocate*, 2000 J.C. 140.

[99] See Renton and Brown, paras 9–26.9 to 9–26.9.3; A. Ashworth and B. Emmerson, *Human Rights and Criminal Justice* (2001), paras 14–38 to 14–44; R. Clayton and H. Tomlinson, *The Law of Human Rights* (2000), paras 11.219–11.221; K. Starmer, *European Human Rights Law* (1999), paras 7.33–7.40.

[1] *Dyer v Watson* [2002] UKPC D1 at [52], *per* Lord Bingham of Cornhill. See also (quoting this statement): *HM Advocate v R* [2002] UKPC D3 at [109], *per* Lord Rodger of Earlsferry; *Attorney-General's Reference (No. 2 of 2001)* [2003] UKHL 68 at [22], *per* Lord Bingham of Cornhill.

[2] *Dyer v Watson* [2002] UKPC D1 at [161], *per* Lord Rodger of Earlsferry; *HM Advocate v Morton*, 2003 S.C.C.R. 305 at [14], *per* the Lord Justice-General (Cullen).

[3] *Eckle v Federal Republic of Germany* (1983) 5 E.H.R.R. 1 at [73].

[4] *Eckle*, at [76].

[5] *Eckle*, at [73]; *IJL v United Kingdom* (2001) 33 E.H.R.R. 11 at [131].

[6] As, e.g. in *HM Advocate v Little*, 1999 S.L.T. 1145.

[7] *Eckle*, at [73], gives potential examples of the date at which the person is "charged" as "the date of arrest, the date when the person concerned was officially notified that he would be prosecuted or the date when preliminary investigations were opened". See also *X v UK* (1978) 14 D.R. 26, where the DPP gave immediate consideration to the possibility of further charges against X after the end of a Crown Court trial where he was sentenced to imprisonment; it was held that the "reasonable time" period ran from that date and not from the issue of an indictment over a year later.

[7a] *Robb v HM Advocate*, 2000 J.C. 368; *Reilly v HM Advocate*, 2000 J.C. 632; *Dyer v Watson* [2002] UKPC D1 at [96], *per* Lord Hope of Craighead.

[7b] [2003] UKHL 68.

ordinarily be when he is charged or served with a summons",[7c] which casts some doubt on the concession made in the Scottish cases.[7d]

In *Unterschutz v HM Advocate*,[8] however, it was held that an interview under caution conducted by the Inland Revenue could not amount to a "charge": at most, it was an investigation undertaken with a view to ascertaining whether a criminal offence had been committed, and in any event the Inland Revenue was not a "competent authority",[9] having no power to prosecute (and not potentially acting under the direction of the public prosecutor, as might the police).

Establishing whether there has been unreasonable delay

16.35 Whether or not there has been an unreasonable delay will depend on the circumstances of each individual case. The relevant question is whether there has been unreasonable delay looking at the case as a whole, not simply at one particular aspect of it.[10] In *Gibson v HM Advocate*,[11] the appeal court said that "unless it is clear that a previous case was closely analogous in its circumstances to the case in hand, it seems to us that the stage has been reached where reference to prior authority will seldom be of real assistance. In each individual case, what will determine the issue—and whether there really is an issue—will be specific circumstances which appear to be in point".[12]

Guiding principles were, however, laid down by the Judicial Committee in *Dyer v Watson*.[13] In that case, it was held that the court should initially "consider the period of time which has elapsed. Unless that period is one which, on its face and without more, gives grounds for real concern it is almost certainly unnecessary to go further..."[14] If, however, real cause for concern is shown:

> "... two consequences follow. First, it is necessary for the court to look into the detailed facts and circumstances of the particular case. The Strasbourg case law shows very clearly that the outcome is closely dependent on the facts of each case. Secondly, it is necessary for the contracting state to explain and justify any lapse of time which appears to be excessive."[15]

The Judicial Committee observed that the European Court had identified three areas as "calling for particular inquiry": the complexity of the case, the conduct of the accused, and the manner in which the case has been

---

[7c] At [29], *per* Lord Bingham of Cornhill.

[7d] There is some support for the concession in *Howarth v United Kingdom* (2000) 31 E.H.R.R. 861. However, it was observed in *Attorney-General's Reference (No. 2 of 2001)* [2003] UKHL 68 at [28], *per* Lord Bingham of Cornhill, that the question of whether the time period commenced at H's first police interview or his charge 4½ months later was not crucial to the case, which was concerned with delay at a much later stage.

[8] 2003 J.C. 70. See also *IJL v United Kingdom* (2001) 33 E.H.R.R. 11 at [131] (interviews by DTI inspectors did not constitute a "charge" for the purposes of Art.6(1)).

[9] See also *HM Advocate v Shell UK*, 2003 S.L.T. 1296 (doubting whether the Health and Safety Executive could be considered a "competent authority" for these purposes).

[10] See, e.g. *Hendry v HM Advocate*, 2001 J.C. 122 (long police delay in executing warrant did not in itself amount to unreasonable delay overall).

[11] 2001 J.C. 125.

[12] At [10] *per* Lord Prosser.

[13] [2002] UKPC D1.

[14] At [52] *per* Lord Bingham of Cornhill. Consequently, the Crown will not be required to explain the delay: see, e.g. *McNab v HM Advocate*, 2000 J.C. 80.

[15] At [52] *per* Lord Bingham of Cornhill.

dealt with by the administrative and judicial authorities.[16] These are noted below, along with a number of other factors which have been identified as relevant. Where no reason has been offered for the delay (or a significant part thereof), it will be more difficult for the court to conclude that the reasonable time requirement has been complied with.[17]

Relevant circumstances

Complexity. The complexity of the case may justify proceedings taking longer than would otherwise be expected.[18] It may be legitimate to postpone proceedings against one accused while proceedings against another person involved in the same alleged offence are concluded.[19] In *Boddaert v Belgium*,[20] it was held that there was no violation of Art.6(1) where the authorities postponed the murder case against the accused to await the outcome of the trial for another murder with which his co-accused had been charged. **16.36**

Conduct of the accused. While a decision by the accused to, for example, raise preliminary matters such as pleas in bar of trial—and even appeal against decisions of a trial judge on such points—will inevitably involve some delay in proceedings, delay caused by such actions is not to be disregarded but should result in the courts and prosecuting authorities acting promptly to ensure that the case progresses promptly thereafter.[21] In *Henworth v United Kingdom*,[22] it was noted that the collapse of a retrial was due to the defendant's attempt to defend himself, but that did not prevent the overall delay being considered unreasonable.[23] **16.37**

Manner in which the case has been dealt with. The fact that there is a satisfactory explanation for part of the time elapsed does not mean that this time is to be left out of account in considering whether there has been an unreasonable delay overall.[24] There is an obligation on the state to ensure that the legal system is "organised ... so as to allow the courts to comply" with the requirement of trial within a reasonable time,[25] **16.38**

[16] At [53]–[55] *per* Lord Bingham of Cornhill.

[17] See, e.g. *HM Advocate v H*, 2000 J.C. 552.

[18] *Wemhoff v Germany* (1968) 1 E.H.R.R. 55; *Ringeisen v Austria (No. 1)* (1973) 1 E.H.R.R. 455. For examples of cases where the courts have taken complexity into account, see *Crummock (Scotland) Ltd v HM Advocate*, 2000 J.C. 408; *Morrison v HM Advocate*, 2002 S.L.T. 795. Although complexity may excuse a degree of delay, it will be necessary to show that the complexity is the *reason* for that delay: see *HM Advocate v McGlinchey*, 2000 J.C. 546 at 571, *per* the Lord Justice-General (Rodger).

[19] *HM Advocate v Workman*, 2000 J.C. 383. As regards extending the 12-month rule in such circumstances, see *Hogg v HM Advocate*, 2002 S.L.T. 639, noted above para.16.22.

[20] (1993) 16 E.H.R.R. 242.

[21] *Cunningham v Ralph*, 2004 S.C.C.R. 549. The courts will, however, be reluctant to assume that a particular case should have been "fast-tracked", not being in the same position as the prosecutor and being able to compare one case with others: *HM Advocate v Wright*, 2001 S.C.C.R. 509 at [9], *per* Lord Prosser.

[22] (2005) 40 E.H.R.R. 33.

[23] See also *Smirnova v Russia* (2004) 39 E.H.R.R. 22, where the fact that the accused was not always willing to submit to the court's jurisdiction did not prevent a finding that Art.6(1) had been breached overall.

[24] See *HM Advocate v Morton*, 2003 S.C.C.R. 305 at [11], *per* the Lord Justice-General (Cullen).

[25] *Buchholz v Federal Republic of Germany* (1981) 3 E.H.R.R. 597 at [51].

although the need to prioritise some cases over others is relevant to determining whether the requirement has been complied with.[26] A temporary backlog of business will not result in a breach of Art.6(1) provided that reasonably prompt remedial action is taken.[27]

16.39 **Age of the accused.** The courts have recognised a particular need to expedite cases where the accused is a child.[28] In *Smith v Angiolini,*[29] the court—in sustaining the plea in bar based on Art.6(1)—placed some stress on the fact that the case should have been given priority as involving a young *complainer*, but did not explain how the accused's Art.6(1) right was affected by this consideration.

16.40 **Detention.** The fact that the accused has been held in custody pending trial is a relevant factor—persons detained pending trial being entitled to "special diligence" on the part of the authorities[30]—but given the protection afforded by custody time limits in Scots law,[31] this should not normally be a significant factor in practice. Conversely, the fact that the appellant has been at liberty throughout may weigh against finding a breach of Art.6(1).[32]

16.41 **The consequences of the delay.** Although it is not necessary for the accused to show prejudice in order to establish a breach of Art.6(1), the existence of prejudice might assist in establishing a breach.[33]

16.42 **What is "at stake".** The court should also consider what is "at stake" for the accused.[34] In the unusual case of *McNab v HM Advocate*[35]—where the accused was already serving a sentence for attempted murder and was charged with murder after the victim died—the appeal court seems to have considered that her previous plea of guilty meant that there was not "much scope for uncertainty as to the outcome of a trial for murder", something which had "the effect of significantly narrowing what was at stake"[36] and seemingly therefore making the need to take the case to trial promptly less compelling.

---

[26] See *O'Brien v HM Advocate*, 2001 S.L.T. 1101 at [10], *per* Lord Prosser (referring to a "bona fide prioritisation of work"); *Gibson v HM Advocate*, 2001 J.C. 125 at [14], *per* Lord Prosser.

[27] *Buchholz v Federal Republic of Germany* (1981) 3 E.H.R.R. 597 at [51]; *Valentine v HM Advocate*, 2002 J.C. 58.

[28] *K v HM Advocate*, 2001 S.L.T. 1261; *HM Advocate v P*, 2001 S.L.T. 924. But not, perhaps, when the child is almost an adult: *HM Advocate v Cook*, 2001 S.L.T. (Sh Ct) 53. At the least, the consideration will be of less weight the closer the child is to adulthood: see *Haston v HM Advocate*, 2003 S.C.C.R. 740.

[29] 2002 S.L.T. 934.

[30] *Kreps v Poland*, European Court of Human Rights, unreported, July 26, 2001 at [52]. See also *Abdoella v Netherlands* (1995) 20 E.H.R.R. 585 at [24].

[31] See above, paras 16.01–16.23. See also *Dyer v Watson* [2002] UKPC D1 at [24], *per* Lord Bingham, where it is said that the custody time limits "effectively preclude a breach of the reasonable time requirement".

[32] *McLarnon v Griffiths*, 2004 S.C.C.R. 397.

[33] *Clark v HM Advocate*, 2004 S.L.T. 9; *Hansen v HM Advocate*, 2005 S.C.C.R. 293 (financial prejudice).

[34] *Henworth v United Kingdom* (2005) 40 E.H.R.R. 33.

[35] 2000 J.C. 80.

[36] At 86 *per* the Lord Justice-Clerk (Cullen).

Chapter 17

RENUNCIATION OF THE RIGHT TO PROSECUTE

Introduction

In Scots law, it is established that a statement by the public prosecutor that a prosecution will not be brought for a particular offence is binding and will operate as a bar to a subsequent prosecution at the instance of the Crown.[1] By contrast, English law has tended to deal with the question as one of "abuse of process",[2] meaning that a decision not to prosecute does not have the near-absolute finality which is accorded to it by Scots law. For example, the (English) *Code for Crown Prosecutors* states as follows: **17.01**

> "People should be able to rely on decisions taken by the Crown Prosecution Service. Normally, if the Crown Prosecution Service tells a suspect or defendant that there will not be a prosecution, or that the prosecution has been stopped, that is the end of the matter and the case will not start again. But occasionally there are special reasons why the Crown Prosecution Service will re-start the prosecution, particularly if the case is serious."[3]

Scots law, by contrast, appears to leave no room for such "special reasons". Perhaps paradoxically, the Scottish position is linked to the constitutional independence of the Lord Advocate, as it avoids any need for the courts to engage in a review of the merits or propriety of a decision taken by the public prosecutor. On one view, in upholding the accused's plea that the right to prosecute has been renounced, the court is not interfering with the prosecutor's exercise of discretion. Instead, it does no more than to confirm the validity of the prosecutor's earlier decision to fetter his own discretion.[4]

Indeed, the ability of the prosecutor to fetter his own discretion in this way is considerable, and may extend as far as allowing the prosecutor to,

---

[1] *Thom v HM Advocate*, 1976 J.C. 48. As regards subsequent private prosecutions, see below, para.17.09. The position of a *socius criminis* (accomplice immunity) is discussed below, para.17.14.

[2] In England, see *R. v Croydon Justices, ex parte Dean* [1993] Q.B. 796; *R. v Bloomfield* [1997] 1 Cr.App.R. 135.

[3] Crown Prosecution Service, *Code for Crown Prosecutors* (2004), s.12(1). Section 12(2) gives examples of "special reasons" (including a "clearly wrong" original decision and "cases which are stopped because of a lack of evidence but where more significant evidence is discovered later").

[4] It is also consistent with the reluctance of the Scottish courts to recognise any general doctrine of "abuse of process" in criminal procedure: see Ch.19. Because the doctrine of renunciation is founded upon the role of the prosecutor as "master of the instance" (see, e.g. *Boyle v HM Advocate*, 1976 J.C. 32 at 37, *per* Lord Cameron), there is no parallel principle at the appellate level, where the prosecutor no longer has this role. Consequently, a concession by the Crown that it does not resist an appeal against conviction does not bind the court to give effect to that concession: *Howitt v HM Advocate; Duffy v HM Advocate*, 2000 S.C.C.R. 195 at 200, *per* the Lord Justice-Clerk (Cullen).

in advance, issue a binding statement that prosecution will not take place in certain circumstances.[5] Such "general" renunciations (as opposed to what may be described as "personal" renunciations) raise distinct issues, which are dealt with below.[6]

Justifying the Doctrine

17.02 The doctrine of renunciation might be sought to be justified on the basis that "there is a clear public interest to be observed in holding officials of the state to promises made by them in full understanding of what is entailed by the bargain".[7] However, such a rationale leaves a number of questions unanswered. First, it is unclear why a promise by the prosecutor should be privileged over a promise by other agencies such as the police.

Secondly, it is one thing to argue that the prosecutor should be held to a *bargain*—and so, for example, a promise not to prosecute on one charge in return for a guilty plea on another,[8] or an agreement that the individual concerned will give evidence in another prosecution might be held binding. Scots law, however, requires nothing by way of "bargain" in order for the doctrine to operate—and so if the prosecutor advises the accused that no proceedings are to be taken simply because there is insufficient evidence available, a subsequent prosecution will be barred even where new evidence unexpectedly (and even unforeseeably) comes to light.[9] Indeed, if it is the case that the state may sometimes be bound to bring a criminal prosecution in order to protect certain Convention rights,[10] then it is arguable that allowing renunciation to bar a prosecution might in certain circumstances be itself a violation of the ECHR.[11]

17.03 Thirdly, general renunciations present special difficulties. Here, three different types of renunciation may be distinguished on the basis of practice to date:

(1) A statement that certain types of evidence will be regarded as an insufficient basis for a prosecution;

---

[5] *Lockhart v Deighan*, 1985 S.LT. 549 (where the point was conceded by the Crown).

[6] See below, paras 17.11–17.13.

[7] *Chu Piu-Wing v Attorney-General* [1984] H.K.L.R. 411 at 417, *per* McMullin V-P; *R. v Croydon Justices, ex parte Dean* [1993] Q.B. 769 at 778, *per* Staughton L.J.

[8] See *DPP v Edgar* (2000) 164 J.P. 471 at [20], *per* Schiemann L.J.: "compromises of this kind between prosecution and defence, where the defence agrees to plead to some charges in return for the prosecution dropping others, are a commonplace of our criminal proceedings and they occur in magistrates courts and crown courts. It is important in principle that such compromises should generally be stuck to and the integrity of the criminal process requires that they should be."

[9] *cf. X v Sweeney*, 1982 J.C. 70, where the complainer was initially unfit to give evidence but later recovered and sought to bring a private prosecution.

[10] A possible interpretation of cases such as *X & Y v Netherlands* (1986) 8 E.H.R.R. 235 and *A v United Kingdom* (1999) 27 E.H.R.R. 611. See F. Leverick, "What has the ECHR done for victims? A United Kingdom perspective" (2004) 11 *International Review of Victimology* 177–200 at pp.189–192.

[11] See further, S.C. Styles, "The renunciation by the Crown of the right to prosecute and the European Convention on Human Rights" (2000) 4 Edin. L.R. 283–307.

(2) A statement that the Lord Advocate does not consider that a certain course of conduct falls within the scope of the criminal law[12];

(3) A statement that prosecutions will not be brought for certain types of conduct even though such conduct *does* fall within the scope of the criminal law.[13]

There is, it is submitted, nothing objectionable in principle about the first or second type of renunciation, as these merely represent a formally stated view that prosecutions in such circumstances would not lead to a conviction, in which case proceedings would necessarily be inappropriate.[14] Such renunciations do not (as has been suggested elsewhere) in effect "change the limits of the criminal law".[15]

The third type, however, presents more difficulty, as it might be regarded as inappropriate that the Lord Advocate should have the power to restrict the scope of the criminal law by means of a general renunciation. In the Privy Council case of *Attorney-General of Trinidad and Tobago v Phillip*,[16] Lord Woolf remarked that:

> "... while a pardon can expunge past offences, a power to pardon cannot be used to dispense with criminal responsibility for an offence which has not yet been committed. This is a principle of general application which is of the greatest importance. The state cannot be allowed to use a power to pardon to enable the law to be set aside by permitting it to be contravened with impunity."[17]

A general renunciation by the Lord Advocate, however, might have exactly this effect. The closest the Lord Advocate has come to making such a statement would appear to be in respect of homosexual **17.04**

---

[12] *cf.* the English case of *Postermobile Plc v Brent LBC* [1998] Crim L.R. 435, where it was held to be an abuse of process for a borough council to prosecute a company for the unlawful display of posters after the company had sought advice from the council as to necessary planning consents and had been advised by council officials that no planning consent was required. As to the extent to which statements such as this might give rise to a defence of error of law by way of reliance on official advice, see the discussion of *Postermobile* and other cases in paras 13.28–13.29.

[13] The first type is exemplified by *Lockhart v Deighan*, 1985 S.L.T. 549 and subsequent cases (see below, para.17.11). The statement following on from *Law Hospital NHS Trust v Lord Advocate*, 1996 S.L.T. 848 is ambiguous in this respect and might be regarded as being either of the second or third type.

[14] *R. (Pretty) v DPP* [2001] UKHL 61 at [122], *per* Lord Hobhouse of Woodborough. This assumes, of course, that the statement of renunciation is properly drafted. *Cf. Hain v Ruxton*, 1999 J.C. 166, discussed below, para.17.11.

[15] C.T. Reid, "Renouncing the right to prosecute" (1998) 43 J.L.S.S. 117–118 at p.118.

[16] [1995] 1 A.C. 396.

[17] At 411. See also *R. (Pretty) v DPP* [2001] UKHL 61.

conduct,[18] where (while the age of consent to male homosexual acts was 21),[19] a Crown Office circular (subsequently made public) was issued in the following terms:

> "1. Where both of the participants are over 18 years but one or both are under 21 years and the act has taken place in private and where there are circumstances pointing to exploitation, corruption, or breach of trust, prosecution would be appropriate. Where the Procurator Fiscal receives a report involving individuals in this age group and none of these circumstances is present, but the Procurator Fiscal considers there are other circumstances which would justify proceedings, a report should be made to the Crown Office for consideration by Crown Counsel.
>
> 2. When both of the participants are over 16 years but one or both are under 18 years and the act appears to have been consensual and in private, the Procurator Fiscal should report the case to Crown Office for consideration by Crown Counsel."[20]

Although this has been regarded as a general renunciation by one writer,[21] it is clear that it is not sufficiently unequivocal to have any such effect.[22] The terms of the circular did not bar prosecutions, but instead imposed a requirement of consideration by Crown Counsel before a prosecution could take place.[23]

A statement by the Lord Advocate that a certain act, although criminal, was never to be prosecuted, might well be objectionable in principle

---

[18] The Lord Advocate has also stated that "he will not authorise the prosecution of a qualified medical practitioner (or any person acting upon the instructions of such a practitioner) who, acting in good faith and with the authority of the Court of Session, withdraws or otherwise causes to be discontinued life-sustaining treatment or other medical treatment from a patient in a persistent, or permanent, vegetative state, with the result that the patient dies." See *Law Hospital NHS Trust v Lord Advocate*, 1996 S.C. 301; 1996 S.L.T. 848 (the statement being printed as an appendix to the *Scots Law Times* report, at 867). The *Law Hospital* court did not decide whether such actions would be a criminal offence, taking the view that the Court of Session, although able to rule that such withdrawal was lawful as a matter of civil law, had no jurisdiction over criminal matters. It is not clear whether the Lord Advocate's statement is made on the basis that such actions do not amount to a criminal offence, or on the basis that they are criminal but do not warrant prosecution (or, indeed, whether the Lord Advocate reached a final view on the question of criminality before issuing the statement). See, however, *R. (Pretty) v DPP* [2001] UKHL 61 at [82], *per* Lord Hope of Craighead (after referring to the Lord Advocate's statement): "What Mrs Pretty seeks is an undertaking, before the event occurs, that if her husband helps her to commit suicide he will not be prosecuted. I am not aware of any case where the Lord Advocate has given an undertaking of that kind. It is not his function to permit individuals to commit acts which the law treats as criminal."

[19] It is now 16: Sexual Offences (Amendment) Act 2000, s.1(3).

[20] Crown Office Circular 2025/1 (issued December 20, 1991). See *McDonald v HM Advocate*, 1997 S.L.T. 1237, where it is noted that the terms of the circular were set out in the *Report on an Inquiry into Allegations of a Conspiracy to Pervert the Course of Justice in Scotland* (HC 377, published on January 26, 1993, paras 3.4 *et seq.*), and that the responsible minister had referred to these directions in the House of Commons on February 8, 1994 (HC Debs, col.179w (February 8, 1994)).

[21] S.C. Styles, "The renunciation by the Crown of the right to prosecute and the European Convention on Human Rights" (2000) 4 Edin. L.R. 283–307 at pp.288–289.

[22] On the requirement that the renunciation be unequivocal, see below para.17.06.

[23] In any event, the policy may be regarded as exceptional given that differential ages of consent for homosexual and heterosexual intercourse might have been regarded at the time as of doubtful compatibility with the European Convention of Human Rights, a position which was in fact later held to be incompatible: *Sutherland v United Kingdom* [1998] E.H.R.L.R. 117.

and open to challenge[24]—although how such a policy might be challenged is another matter, given that it is not clear to what extent decisions of the Lord Advocate are amenable to judicial review.[25]

The Development of the Doctrine

Personal renunciation

The modern doctrine appears to have developed as an extension of the rule that desertion *simpliciter*, on the motion of the Crown, bars a future prosecution for the same offence (in contrast to desertion *simpliciter* by the court *ex proprio motu*, which may not always have this effect).[26] Hume states the rule as follows: **17.05**

> "... if the prosecutor, being present, shall himself move the Court to desert the diet *simpliciter*, and thus neither allude to any dilatory cause for dropping his present libel, nor intimate any purpose to raise a new one; such a measure cannot well be construed any otherwise, than as a thorough relinquishment or discharge of his right of prosecution."[27]

In its terms, however, this passage only applies where proceedings have been initiated and then abandoned—and even then, only to cases abandoned in a particular form. The principle was extended beyond such instances by a Full Bench in the leading case of *Thom v HM Advocate*,[28] which concerned a letter from the procurator fiscal to the accused's solicitor containing the following passage:

> "Although I am left in the end of the day with a strong suspicion that Mr Thom is responsible for the defalcations in question, I have come to the conclusion, having considered the whole matter, that the case is not good enough to put before a jury, nor for that matter do I think that I could persuade my sheriff to convict on a summary prosecution—because of the number of loose ends that appear to exist in the evidence relating to what occurred in Mr Thom's former office. As a result, therefore, I am taking no further steps in this matter and your client, accordingly, may uplift his bail."[29]

---

[24] *cf. R. v Commissioner of Police of the Metropolis, ex parte Blackburn* [1968] 2 Q.B. 118 at 136, *per* Lord Denning M.R., stating that the Commissioner can "make policy decisions and give effect to them, as, for instance, was often done when prosecutions were not brought for attempted suicide. But there are some policy decisions with which, I think, the courts in a case can, if necessary, interfere. Suppose a chief constable were to issue a directive to his men that no person should be prosecuted for stealing any goods less than £100 in value. I should have thought that the court could countermand it. He would be failing in his duty to enforce the law." See also *per* Salmon L.J. at 138–139 and Edmund Davies L.J. at 148–149.

[25] See Styles, above, fn.21, at pp.304–307.

[26] *HM Advocate v Hall* (1881) 4 Coup. 500; *Mackenzie v Maclean*, 1980 J.C. 89. See further above, para.15.08.

[27] Hume, ii, 277 (quoted with approval by the Lord Justice-General (Inglis) in *HM Advocate v Hall* (1881) 4 Coup. 500 at 508). The argument for the accused in *Thom v HM Advocate*, 1976 J.C. 48 was made under reference to this passage. See also Alison, *Practice*, 356–357, which is to the same effect.

[28] 1976 J.C. 48.

[29] At 48.

17.06 This was followed by an announcement to the press that no proceedings were to be taken in respect of the charge on which Mr Thom had appeared on petition. An indictment was, however, served on the accused some four months later, in identical terms to that charge. On appeal, the Crown conceded that it would be incompetent to prosecute on a charge where the Lord Advocate had "made a public announcement which falls to be construed as ... a relinquishment or discharge"[30] of his right of prosecution, but argued, first, that the relinquishment had to be in open court, and secondly, that the procurator fiscal had made "no more than a statement of present intention".[31]

The court rejected the Crown's construction of the procurator fiscal's statements, concluding that they were an "unequivocal and unqualified announcement on behalf of the Lord Advocate"[32] that no further steps were to be taken in the prosecution. The court then went on to consider the Crown's contention that the statement should be in open court to be effective. While considering that the renunciation should be a "public act", the court concluded that there was no "justification in principle or good sense" for such a restriction, and that Thom's prosecution had therefore been incompetent.[33] The weight placed by the *Thom* court on a careful interpretation of the statements alleged to amount to a renunciation suggests that there is no room for a plea founded on a mistaken belief that the right to prosecute has been renounced.[34]

The court has confirmed elsewhere that a statement of present intention does not operate as a renunciation, and so, in *Murphy v HM Advocate*,[35] a letter from the procurator fiscal stating that "It is ... my intention to proceed against Mr Murphy on a summary complaint ..." was held not to bar the Crown from subsequently deciding to prosecute the accused on indictment. Where, however, the Crown has agreed to accept a plea of guilty from the accused in particular terms, it seems that this may operate to bar the prosecutor from resiling from that agreement.[36] This may be the only situation in which a renunciation can be implied (and even then only from an express statement from the Crown that it is prepared to accept a certain plea): it would certainly not be possible to imply

[30] At 51.

[31] At 51.

[32] At 52. *Cf.* Styles, fn.21 above, at p.286, where it is stated that the *Thom* court held "that a Crown statement of non-prosecution could be binding on the Crown, even although there was no explicit renunciation of the right to prosecution, merely a declaration that there was no present intention to prosecute". This is, however, irreconcilable with the interpretation of the procurator fiscal's letter adopted by the court: "we have no doubt that the letter by itself cannot be read as a mere statement of the intention of the Crown for the time being" (1976 J.C. 48 at 52).

[33] 1976 J.C. 48 at 52.

[34] A conclusion which seems to be confirmed by *McDonald v HM Advocate*, 1997 S.L.T. 1237: see below paras 17.12–17.13. See also *Carter v Robertson*, 2005 S.C.C.R. 181.

[35] 2002 S.L.T. 1416. See also *HM Advocate v M*, 1986 S.C.C.R. 624 at 628, *per* Sheriff MacLeod.

[36] See *HM Advocate v Nairn*, 2000 S.L.T. (Sh Ct) 176, although Sheriff Stewart appears to have considered the issue to be more of a balancing exercise, stating (at 178) that "In reaching this conclusion I am influenced by the fact that a relatively long period has elapsed since the accused first appeared on petition and that the Crown has had ample opportunity to reflect on the terms of any charge brought against him." See also *DPP v Edgar* (2000) 164 J.P. 471. If there has been merely an *offer* to accept a plea in certain terms, which has not been accepted by the accused, then this will not operate as a renunciation: *Latto v Vannet*, 1998 S.L.T. 711.

renunciation from, for example, a mere delay in bringing a prosecution[37] (although delay may of itself give rise to a plea in bar of trial in certain cases).[38]

Despite stating in *Thom* that renunciation should be a "public act", the court paid particular attention to the terms of the letter written to Thom's solicitor. It was subsequently held by Lord Kincraig in *HM Advocate v Stewart* that such a letter was sufficient to bar future prosecution without being announced to the press: "So long as the Lord Advocate's decision is communicated to the accused, to his agent or to one who could be reasonably expected to communicate it to the accused, it does not seem to me to be material that it is not published."[39] Nor, according to Lord Kincraig, was it necessary that the accused should at any time have been charged with the offence in question, as Mr Thom had been.[40] Such a conclusion is only logical—it might be regarded as odd indeed if a decision to abandon proceedings against an individual at an earlier stage were to leave that person in a less secure position than where proceedings reach the stage of court proceedings—but it does mean that the modern principle is very far removed from the doctrine of desertion *simpliciter* on the prosecutor's motion, where its origins lie. **17.07**

Because renunciation must be a public act, it follows that a decision to prosecute would not be challengeable on the basis that it runs contrary to unpublished Crown Office guidance which happens to be within the knowledge of the accused or his agent (perhaps, for example, through previous employment as a procurator fiscal).[41]

Who can renounce the right to prosecute?

It is clear from *Thom* that a statement by a procurator fiscal can amount to a renunciation of the right to prosecute, such a statement being treated as one made on behalf of the Lord Advocate.[42] Statements by other public authorities will not, however, have such an effect. In *Huston v Buchanan*, it was held that any statements by the police (the content of which was a matter of dispute) "could not bind the Crown and could not constitute any bar to proceedings being taken by the Crown".[43] **17.08**

[37] *cf. R. v Bradford Stipendiary Magistrates, ex p Daniel*, June 6, 1997, Divisional Court, *per* Owen J.: "No doubt the Applicants thought the prosecution's delay had removed their worries over prosecution for good. It is possible that they may feel that it is unfair that now they should be faced with that which seemed to have gone away. However, it is sometimes in the nature of preliminary proceedings to produce such feelings."

[38] See Ch.16.

[39] 1980 J.C. 84 at 88, *per* Lord Kincraig.

[40] See, however, *HM Advocate v Waddell*, 1976 S.L.T. (Notes) 61, where Lord Robertson took the view that a renunciation could not be effective where the accused had not been charged and committed on the relevant charges at the time the statement was made. That position would appear to be no longer tenable now that it is accepted that renunciations can have a *general* prospective effect: see *Lockhart v Deighan*, 1985 S.L.T. 549 and subsequent cases, discussed below, para.17.11.

[41] See also *R. v Inland Revenue Commissioners, ex parte Allen* [1997] S.T.C. 1141, where it was held that A would not have been entitled to rely on knowledge of internal Inland Revenue procedures which his adviser had obtained during a period of employment with the Revenue.

[42] *Thom v HM Advocate*, 1976 J.C. 48 at 52. This is consistent with the present understanding that an act of a procurator fiscal is an act of the Lord Advocate for the purposes of s.57 of the Scotland Act 1998: see *Starrs v Ruxton*, 2000 J.C. 208 at 213, *per* the Lord Justice-Clerk (Cullen); *Montgomery v HM Advocate* [2003] 1 A.C. 641 at 676, *per* Lord Clyde.

[43] 1995 S.L.T. 86 at 88, *per* the Lord Justice-Clerk (Ross). See also *McGhee v Maguire*, 1996 S.L.T. 1012.

It would appear not to matter that the person to whom the statement is made might genuinely believe that the police are entitled to grant such assurances.[44] The assurance might, however, have some effect if the accused had prejudiced himself as a result of it. In *Huston*, the appellants had been interviewed by the police after the alleged statement that no action was to be taken against them. The court accepted that this might provide a basis for an objection to the admissibility of any evidence of the interviews which the Crown sought to lead at trial.[45] The court also suggested that "any question of oppression" which might arise could be raised at the trial.[46]

In *HM Advocate v Weir*,[46a] a clerk confused two cases and wrote a letter to the wrong individual (in the name of the principal procurator fiscal depute, but signed by the clerk) advising that no further proceedings were to be taken. The sheriff upheld a plea in bar of trial, holding that the letter could not be construed otherwise than as an unequivocal and unqualified renunciation of the right to prosecute. In allowing an appeal by the Crown, the High Court held that the sheriff had misdirected herself because "she failed to deal with the logically prior question whether, at the date of the letter, there was a decision to be intimated".[46b] Because the Crown had not actually decided not to prosecute Weir, the clerk had no authority to write the letter and it could not bind the Crown.

If the court is correct in its characterisation of the "logically prior question", it would have made no difference if the clerk had prepared the letter and it had been signed by the procurator fiscal (in error) personally, because there would still have been no decision to intimate. Taken one step further, that would mean that a person who receives a letter renouncing the right to prosecute is not entitled to rely on it even if it is signed by the procurator fiscal (or even the Lord Advocate), which threatens to strip renunciation of much of its meaning. It may be that the error was not such as to make it an abuse of process to continue with the prosecution, but given that Scots law has so far largely avoided recognising the concept of abuse of process in criminal proceedings[46c] and has preferred to deal with breaches of promises not to prosecute by way of the renunciation doctrine, the decision in *Weir* is difficult to justify.

The effect of renunciation on non-Crown prosecutions

17.09 Although a renunciation by the Crown will bar the Lord Advocate from concurring in a private prosecution, it does not preclude the High Court from permitting an individual to proceed with such an action.[47] The point is likely to be of limited importance given that private summary

---

[44] This is implicit in *Huston v Buchanan*: see also *Dacorum Borough Council v El-Kalyoubi* [2001] EWHC Admin 1052.

[45] See 1995 S.L.T. 86 at 87–88, *per* the Lord Justice-Clerk (Ross). On the admissibility of statements "unfairly obtained", see *Walkers on Evidence*, paras 9.11 *et seq*.

[46] This raises the question of what is meant by "oppression" in such a context, and specifically whether the plea of oppression can operate to bar a prosecution as an "abuse of process". This is discussed further in Ch.19.

[46a] 2005 S.C.C.R. 821.

[46b] At [12], *per* the Lord Justice-Clerk (Gill).

[46c] See Ch.19.

[47] *X v Sweeney*, 1982 J.C. 70. In English law, where a general right of private prosecution has been expressly preserved by statute (s.6(1) of the Prosecution of Offenders Act 1985), the courts have had some difficulty with the question of whether it is an abuse of process for a private prosecution to be brought after a person has accepted a caution. See *Hayter v L* [1998] 1 W.L.R. 854 and *Jones v Whalley* [2006] UKHL 41.

prosecution is now largely precluded by statute[48] and that private prosecutions under solemn procedure are exceptionally rare.[49]

Can a personal renunciation have prospective effect?

The case law on personal renunciations is exclusively concerned with decisions not to prosecute (or not to continue a prosecution) in respect of an alleged offence which has already occurred. As such, it leaves open the question of whether the Lord Advocate would be entitled to assure an individual that he could embark on a particular course of action without facing the risk of prosecution. **17.10**

In the English case of *R. (Pretty) v DPP*, the claimant suffered from motor neurone disease and wished "to be able to take steps to bring her life to a peaceful end at a time of her choosing".[50] That would, however, have required the assistance of another person because of her physical incapacity. Accordingly, the Director of Public Prosecutions was requested to give an undertaking that he would not consent to the prosecution of her husband under s.2 of the Suicide Act 1961 (complicity in another's suicide) if he were to assist her to end her life.[51] That request was refused,[52] and Mrs Pretty sought judicial review of the Director's decision.

In holding that Mrs Pretty was not entitled to such an undertaking, the Appellate Committee took the view that the Director had no power to give an undertaking "that a crime yet to be committed would not lead to prosecution".[53] Some reference was made to the Scottish prosecutorial statements which have been regarded as general renunciations, but the members of the Appellate Committee seemed inclined to view these as statements of policy rather than binding undertakings.[54] In fact, the Scottish courts have regarded these statements as being binding on the prosecution, as is discussed below.

General renunciation

Just as the Crown can renounce the right to prosecute in a particular case, it appears that the right to prosecute an entire class of cases may be *prospectively* renounced. The issue first arose as a result of a statement made in order to cater for possible inaccuracies in breath tests carried out to determine whether a motorist had been driving with excess alcohol. **17.11**

[48] CPSA 1995, ss.6(3) and 133(5).

[49] Only two such prosecutions were brought in the 20th century: *J & P Coats Ltd v Brown*, 1909 J.C. 29 and *X v Sweeney*, 1982 J.C. 70. There were, however, a number of unsuccessful attempts to bring such prosecutions: see *McBain v Crichton*, 1961 J.C. 25; *Trapp v M*, 1971 S.L.T. (Notes) 30; *Meehan v Inglis*, 1975 J.C. 9.

[50] [2001] UKHL 61 at [1], *per* Lord Bingham of Cornhill.

[51] No prosecution may be brought for this offence except by or with the consent of the Director of Public Prosecutions: Suicide Act 1961, s.2(4).

[52] For the terms of the refusal (which states that immunities will not be granted by the Director or the Attorney-General "no matter how exceptional the circumstances"), see [2001] UKHL 61 at [115], *per* Lord Hobhouse of Woodborough.

[53] [2001] UKHL 61 at [39], *per* Lord Bingham of Cornhill. See also Lord Hobhouse of Woodborough at [117]. In part, this conclusion appears to have been reached on the basis that such an undertaking would have run contrary to the declaration in the Bill of Rights 1689 that "the pretended power of suspending the laws or the execution of laws by regal authority without consent of Parliament is illegal".

[54] [2001] UKHL 61 at [39], *per* Lord Bingham of Cornhill, at [81]–[82], *per* Lord Hope of Craighead, and at [122], *per* Lord Hobhouse of Woodborough. *Cf.* the comments of Lord Steyn at [66].

Following the passing of the Transport Act 1981, the Home Office issued guidance to the effect that the police would not proceed against offenders with a breath-test result of less than 40 microgrammes of alcohol in 100 millilitres of breath (the prescribed limit being 35 microgrammes), in order to cater for the possibility of the breath-testing machine "reading high".[55]

This guidance applied to England and Wales only, and the Crown Agent was asked to clarify the Scottish position. His response, published in the *Journal of the Law Society of Scotland*, was as follows:

> "The position in Scotland is that no proceedings will be instituted for contraventions of section 6 of the Road Traffic Act 1972, as amended by Schedule 8 to the Transport Act 1981, on the basis of a breath/alcohol reading of less than 40 microgrammes. It will, however, be a matter for individual procurators fiscal to decide whether proceedings are appropriate in such cases for a contravention of section 5 of the Road Traffic Act 1972 (driving, etc, when under the influence of drinks [sic] or drugs)."[56]

In *Lockhart v Deighan*,[57] it was conceded by the Crown that no prosecution could be brought in breach of the undertaking contained in the Crown Agent's letter. It was held, however, that the letter could not bar Deighan's prosecution as—although he had given two breath samples, both of which were below the 40 microgramme level, he had thereafter exercised his statutory right to provide a blood sample, which had been assessed as over the statutory limit.[58] Furthermore, although the *prosecution* had been brought after the Crown Agent's letter was written and published, the option of a blood sample had been given to him before both of those events.

It was, however, held in later cases that it was unfair and oppressive for the police to give a suspect the option of providing a blood sample when he had provided a breath sample below the 40 microgramme level,[59] and that a prosecution should not be allowed to proceed in such a case despite the fact that it was brought on the basis of a blood/alcohol reading rather than a reading of the type specified in the Crown Agent's letter.[60] These decisions cannot be explained on the basis of renunciation, and instead appear to indicate the operation of an abuse of process doctrine.[61]

In *Hain v Ruxton*,[62] the accused had provided a breath sample of 39 microgrammes some four hours after driving, on the basis of which a prosecution was brought alleging a level of 67 microgrammes (a figure arrived at by "back counting") at the time of the alleged offence. It was held that this prosecution was in fact barred by the terms of the Crown

---

55 Home Office Circular No. 46/1983, (1983) 133 N.L.J. 323–324.

56 "Drinking and driving" (1983) 28 J.L.S.S. 405–406.

57 1985 S.L.T. 549.

58 100 milligrammes of alcohol in 100 millilitres of blood (the prescribed limit being 80 milligrammes).

59 Under s.8(2) of the Road Traffic Act 1998, a person who has provided two breath samples, the lower of which contains no more than 50 microgrammes of alcohol per 100 millilitres of breath, is entitled to claim that it should be replaced by a blood or urine sample. The police must inform the person of this right: *Woodburn v McLeod*, 1986 S.L.T. 325.

60 *Benton v Cardle*, 1998 S.L.T. 310; *McConnachie v Scott*, 1998 S.L.T. 480.

61 See below, para.19.09.

62 1999 J.C. 166.

Agent's letter, which led to a revised letter being issued to specifically exclude such cases (and certain others) from the terms of the general renunciation.[63]

Making and revoking a general renunciation

Because the cases on general renunciation have proceeded on the basis of concessions by the Crown that such statements are binding in their terms, there has been no discussion of the form which a general renunciation should take, or who is entitled to make it. Those statements which have been regarded as general renunciations appear to have all been made by either the Lord Advocate or the Crown Agent. Because an individual procurator fiscal cannot normally be regarded as having responsibility for prosecution policy across Scotland as a whole, it presumably follows that he cannot make an effective general renunciation—although it may be that a procurator fiscal could validly make such a declaration in respect of prosecutions to be brought in the particular sheriff court or courts for which he is responsible. **17.12**

A general renunciation obviously cannot be made by an individual without responsibility for the prosecution of crime, and an accused person is not entitled to rely on a mistaken belief that such a renunciation has been made. In *McDonald v HM Advocate*,[64] the accused (who was indicted on various charges of shameless indecency and sodomy, four of which referred to complainers of 16 years of age) argued that he could rely, in bar of trial, on a newspaper report to the effect that the Lord Advocate was about to issue guidelines to procurators fiscal stating that men should not normally be prosecuted for consensual homosexual sex in private where both of the parties were aged 16 or over.

The appeal court rejected this claim, noting that the declared prosecution policy of the Lord Advocate referred only to parties over the age of 18 years,[65] adding "that the proposition that the Crown could be bound by the publication of an untrue report of its prosecution policy unless steps were taken to refute that report with a similar degree of publicity is totally lacking in authority and is fundamentally unsound".[66] Even if the report were accurate, it seems unlikely that it could have been **17.13**

[63] See "New breath test device" (1999) 44(8) J.L.S.S. 15, which states that "proceedings may, in future, be taken, even where two samples of a suspect's breath have been analysed and a lower reading of 39µg or less obtained, if" (a) "in terms of section 7(3)(b) of the Road Traffic Act 1988, as amended, the officer requests blood/urine because the machine is considered to be unreliable"; (b) "in terms of section 7(3)(bb) of the same Act, the police officer in question requires the accused to provide a specimen of blood/urine on the basis that he has 'reasonable cause to believe that the (breath analyser) device has not produced a reliable indication of the proportion of alcohol in the breath of the person concerned'"; or (c) "the readings are obtained in circumstances where a back calculation indicates that the suspect had a breath alcohol level in excess of the prescribed limit at the time the driving is alleged to have occurred." The first of these three exceptions is odd and suggests that the letter may be erroneously drafted, as s.7(3)(b) is not concerned with reliability, but with the unavailability of a breath-testing device or the impracticability of using it. S.C. Styles, "The renunciation by the Crown of the right to prosecute and the European Convention on Human Rights" (2000) 4 Edin. L.R. 283–307 at p.289, states that this letter effectively overturns the decisions in *Benton v Cardle* and *McConnachie v Scott* (above, fn.60). This must, however, be regarded as incorrect as the police did not rely upon s.7(3)(bb) of the 1988 Act in either case, but instead informed the persons concerned of their right to replace the specimen of breath under s.8(2) of the Act.

[64] 1997 S.L.T. 1237.

[65] For the terms of this policy, see above, para.17.04.

[66] 1997 S.L.T. 1237 at 1239, *per* the Lord Justice-Clerk (Cullen).

regarded as having the effect of a renunciation, given that it only stated that guidelines were to be drafted and issued, and that these would only state that prosecutions should normally not take place (not "never take place") where the parties were both aged 16 or over.

It appears that general renunciations can be revoked by a subsequent statement,[67] and the Crown Agent's revised letter regarding prosecutions for driving with excess alcohol necessarily proceeds on that assumption. It is not clear, however, whether such statements can have retrospective effect. The revised letter states that no proceedings may be brought "in future" in certain cases which would have been barred by the terms of the first letter, but does not make it clear whether such prosecutions might be based on conduct prior to the letter being issued.

This may depend on the type of general renunciation which is to be revoked. If it is, like the Crown Agent's letters, a renunciation of type (1) identified above[68]—a statement that certain evidence will be regarded as an insufficient basis for a prosecution—then it may be legitimate for revocation to be given retrospective effect. This is because a statement of this nature cannot give rise to any legitimate expectation on the part of a member of the public that he is entitled to conduct himself in a particular fashion: no motorist, for example, could have concluded that he was entitled to drive with a certain level of alcohol in his breath on the basis of the Crown Agent's letter. If, by contrast, it is a revocation of type (2) or (3),[69] then it is submitted that it must fall to be regarded differently. A medical practitioner who has withdrawn treatment in good faith and on the authority of the Court of Session, in reliance on the Lord Advocate's statement that he will not be prosecuted for such actions, has a legitimate expectation that he will not be prosecuted for his conduct.[70]

Accomplice Immunity and the Police, Public Order and Criminal Justice (Scotland) Act 2006

17.14 A witness who is called to testify as a *socius criminis* acquires immunity from prosecution and may plead this in bar of a subsequent trial.[71] For these purposes a *socius criminis* is a witness who "is called by the Crown for the express purpose of testifying that he was an accomplice in the crime charged".[72] A witness who is (or may be) an accomplice but is called

---

[67] *McDonald v HM Advocate*, 1997 S.L.T. 1237 at 1239, *per* the Lord Justice-Clerk (Cullen).

[68] See above, para.17.03.

[69] See above, para.17.03.

[70] *cf. Attorney-General's Reference (No. 44 of 2000)* [2001] 1 Cr.App.R. (S) 460 at [37], *per* Rose V-P: "if the Crown, by whatever means the Crown is prosecuting, make representations to a defendant on which he is entitled to rely and on which he acts to his detriment by, as in the present case, pleading guilty in circumstances in which he would not otherwise have pleaded guilty, that can properly be regarded as giving rise to a legitimate expectation on his part that the Crown will not subsequently seek to resile from those representations ..." This is concerned with representations made after a prosecution has commenced, but the principle would seem to be the same.

[71] The subject is comprehensively reviewed by P.W. Ferguson, "A note on accomplice immunity", 2002 S.L.T. (News) 79–85. See also C.N. Stoddart, "The immunity rule" (1983) 28 J.L.S.S. 453–457.

[72] *O'Neill v Wilson*, 1983 J.C. 42 at 49, *per* the Lord Justice-General (Emslie).

for a different purpose and not invited to incriminate himself is not entitled to immunity from future prosecution.[73] The same applies to a person who is otherwise involved in the criminal activity with which the first trial is concerned—so, for example, if A is charged with assaulting B in a brawl, and B gives evidence against A at the first trial, B will not be able to plead immunity if he is subsequently prosecuted for assaulting A.[74]

The reason for the immunity is that, if it were not granted, the *socius* would be immune from answering any questions which might tend to incriminate him.[75] Hume and Alison characterised the immunity as a form of renunciation of the right to prosecute—"by the very act of calling him as a witness, the prosecutor discharges all title to molest him for the future, with relation to the matter libelled",[76] although the general law on renunciation of the right to prosecute appears to have developed independently of the position of the *socius*. Despite Hume and Alison's characterisation of the rule, the courts have suggested that the immunity arises "by operation of law"[77] rather than by way of a personal bar on the part of the prosecutor, and it has been held—in contrast to the position regarding renunciation generally[78]—to bar a subsequent private prosecution of the *socius*.[79]

At common law, the immunity was absolute and was not conditional on the testimony offered by the *socius* in court. Alison strongly defended this rule:

> "This privilege is absolute, and altogether independent of the prevarication or unwillingness with which the witness may give his testimony. Justice indeed may often be defeated by a witness retracting his previous disclosures, or refusing to make any confession after he is put into the box; but it would be much more put in hazard if the witness was sensible that his future safety depended on the extent to which he spoke out against his associate at the bar. The only remedy, therefore, in such a case, is committal of the witness for contempt or prevarication, or indicting him for perjury, if there are sufficient grounds for any of these proceedings."[80]

However, shortly before this book went to press, the Scottish Parliament passed the Police, Public Order and Criminal Justice (Scotland) Bill. Once the Act is brought into force, s.97 will create a power on the part of a prosecutor, "if of the opinion that for the purposes of the investigation or prosecution of any offence it is appropriate to give any person immunity from prosecution", to give that person a "conditional immunity notice". Where such a notice is given, no proceedings for an offence specified in **17.15**

---

[73] *Cochrane v HM Advocate*, 2002 S.L.T. 1424, where it is also said (although probably *obiter*) that the immunity cannot apply where the second charge is in different terms to the first. For criticism, see Ferguson, fn.71 above.

[74] *McGinley and Dowds v MacLeod*, 1963 J.C. 11; *O'Neill v Wilson*, 1983 J.C. 42.

[75] *O'Neill v Wilson*, 1983 J.C. 42 at 49–50, *per* the Lord Justice-General (Emslie). On the privilege against self-incrimination generally, see *Walkers on Evidence*, para.12.13.

[76] Hume, ii, 367.

[77] *HM Advocate v Weatherly* (1904) 4 Adam 353 at 355, *per* Lord McLaren: "I do not think that this discharge is the act of the Lord Advocate any more than it is the act of the judge who accepts the evidence. It is really a discharge by operation of law arising from the fact that the witness by the proper legal authority has been cited to give evidence." See also *Macmillan v Murray*, 1920 J.C. 13.

[78] See above, para.17.09.

[79] *Hare v Wilson* (1829) Syme 373.

[80] Alison, *Practice*, 453.

the notice may be brought against the person concerned, and any ongoing proceedings must be discontinued.[81]

The notice "must specify the conditions to which its application is subject [and] may specify the circumstances to which it applies or the circumstances to which it does not apply", and will have effect and cease to have effect accordingly. When it has ceased to have effect, a prosecutor must give a written "cessation notice" to the person concerned. This notice does not cause the immunity notice to cease to have effect, as this will already have happened. Instead, it operates as a formal notification of this fact and the date of the cessation notice will be relevant for the purposes of calculating certain time bars which are modified in these circumstances.[82] It should still be open to an accused to plead in bar of trial that there is no proper basis for the cessation notice and that the original immunity notice remains in effect.

The Executive, in response to concerns raised by the Law Society of Scotland when the Bill was passing through Parliament, explained that s.97 was intended to alter the law regarding to the immunity of a *socius*.[83] According to the Crown Agent, the provisions were necessary because Crown Office was "seriously hamstrung in dealing with the middle rankers in serious criminal organisations":

> "At present, we have either to take a very high risk and give people who might have committed serious offences immunity from prosecution or wait until they have been right through the system and convicted and then hope that they will co-operate with us, by which time, the major offenders might already have disappeared; indeed, they may be committing more serious offences."[84]

It should be noted, however, that s.97 is not limited in its terms to granting immunity to a *socius*: the only restriction is that the immunity must be granted for the purposes of the investigation or prosecution of any offence. The statute, on its face, would appear to give the prosecutor the power to license a person to commit a crime for these purposes. The statute modifies the position at common law by providing that where the conditional immunity notice has ceased to have effect, communications between the prosecutor or anyone else and the person to whom the notice was given cannot provide a basis for a plea in bar of trial.[85] That seems to leave room for an argument that the common law rule has not been altered because the immunity arises by operation of law and is not simply a question of personal bar,[86] but the purpose of the legislation is clear.

---

[81] s.97(2).

[82] ss.97(5) (time limit for commencement of trial on indictment) and 97(6) (time limits for commencement of proceedings).

[83] "... where a person who has been granted immunity under section 88(1) [as it was numbered in the Bill as introduced] gives evidence as an accomplice against another accused person as a condition of his/her immunity, but in some way fails to fully adhere to the conditions attached to the immunity whereby it is revoked by the prosecutor, the effect of section 88(8) will be that the prosecutor can still proceed against the individual. However if an individual gave evidence against an accused person as an accomplice out with the scope of the terms of section 88, then the normal common law rules about a *socius criminis* would apply." See Justice 2 Committee, *Stage 1 Report on the Police, Public Order and Criminal Justice Bill* (S.P. Paper 491, 2006), Vol.2 (Evidence).

[84] Justice 2 Committee Official Report, November 1, 2005, col.1743.

[85] s.67(8)(b).

[86] See above, para.17.14.

CHAPTER 18

OPPRESSION: PREJUDICIAL PUBLICITY

INTRODUCTION

Although concerns about the effect of prejudicial publicity on the accused's right to a fair trial are long-standing,[1] it is only relatively recently that such prejudice has been recognised as a relevant plea in bar of trial. Historically, while the High Court of Justiciary might have acted to prohibit or punish prejudicial publicity as a contempt of court, there appears to have been no suggestion that such publicity might deprive the Crown of their right to put the accused on trial. While the court recognised a duty "to ensure that persons charged on indictment in Scotland shall receive a fair and impartial trial",[2] that was a duty discharged by acting against prejudicial publicity, and not by preventing a trial from proceeding.[3] **18.01**

By contrast, concern about proceeding to trial or verdict, notwithstanding such publicity, is a creature of modern jurisprudence. The issue appears first to have been raised, indirectly, in the contempt case of *Atkins v London Weekend Television*.[4] There, the day before Ms Atkins—a nursing sister—was to go on trial charged with assault to the danger of life by attempting to block the air supply of a severely brain-damaged girl, London Weekend Television chose to broadcast a programme called "The Living Dead". That programme, in juxtaposing Ms Atkins' prosecution with two other cases, created a contrast which the High Court considered resulted in "the clear insinuation that the real if not the only question which would arise out of the petitioner's trial would be whether she was medically and morally justified in committing the acts charged".[5]

In granting the prayer of Ms Atkins' contempt petition, the court observed that the result of the broadcast was to create "a real question whether fair and impartial investigation by a criminal court of the charges against the petitioner is now possible".[6] It appears that the Crown subsequently decided not to proceed with the prosecution.[7]

The question did not squarely arise until the case of *Stuurman v HM Advocate*.[8] In that case, contempt proceedings had been successfully taken against the publishers and the editors of a newspaper, as well as those **18.02**

---

[1] For some early examples, see the contempt cases of *Robert Emond* (1829) Shaw 229; *Smith v John Ritchie & Co* (1892) 3 White 408; *Cowie v Outram & Co Ltd* (1912) 6 Adam 556. Judicial concern about the effects of prejudicial publicity in civil cases may be traced back slightly further: see *Henderson v Laing* (1824) 3 S. 384; *McLauchlan v Carson* (1826) 5 S. 147.

[2] *Atkins v London Weekend Television*, 1978 J.C. 48 at 52, *per* the Lord Justice-General (Emslie).

[3] For a general discussion of legal responses to prejudicial publicity, see B. Naylor, "Fair trial or free press: legal responses to media reports of criminal trials" [1994] C.L.J. 492–501.

[4] 1978 J.C. 48.

[5] At 55 *per* the Lord Justice-General (Emslie). See further below, para.18.14.

[6] At 56 *per* the Lord Justice-General (Emslie).

[7] See *HM Advocate v Fraser*, 2000 S.C.C.R. 412 at 418, *per* Lord Osborne.

[8] 1980 J.C. 111.

responsible for a series of radio broadcasts, in respect of publicity immediately following the arrest of a number of persons charged with drugs offences.[9] The accused persons tabled pleas in bar of trial, arguing that they could not expect to receive a fair trial in the light of the prejudicial publicity. While these pleas ultimately failed, a Full Bench accepted that the court did have "power to intervene to prevent the Lord Advocate from proceeding upon a particular indictment".[10] The following test was formulated:

> "this power will be exercised only in special circumstances which are likely to be rare. The special circumstances must indeed be such as to satisfy the Court that, having regard to the principles of substantial justice and of fair trial, to require an accused to face trial would be oppressive. Each case will depend on its own merits, and where the alleged oppression is said to arise from events alleged to be prejudicial to the prospects of fair trial the question for the Court is whether the risk of prejudice is so grave that no direction of the trial Judge, however careful, could reasonably be expected to remove it."[11]

Although the plea in *Stuurman* was in the form of a plea in bar of trial, the point may arise mid-trial as well, and trial diets have on occasion been deserted *pro loco et tempore* because of publicity during the trial itself.[12] Indeed, publicity occurring at this stage may be regarded as considerably more damaging, because there is little or no time for the jury's recollection of it to fade before beginning their deliberations.[13] The test as formulated in *Stuurman* is in fact drawn from an earlier case where the court had to consider whether a trial diet should have been deserted after one juror claimed to have been approached by a man who wished to bribe her to persuade the jury to acquit one of the accused,[14] and although it will normally be applied to a plea in bar of trial, it may equally be applied to a motion to desert the trial diet.

The *Stuurman* test has been regularly applied by the courts and remains valid today. It was reconsidered by the Judicial Committee of the Privy Council in *Montgomery v HM Advocate*,[15] where the point was raised as a devolution issue, the appellants' argument being that the pretrial publicity meant that the Lord Advocate would be acting in breach of their right to a fair trial under Art.6(1) of the ECHR if he were to bring them to trial. The Judicial Committee considered that the *Stuurman* test remained valid in the Art.6(1) context, subject to the caveat that it was not permissible to balance the right to a fair trial against the public interest in the detection

---

[9] For the proceedings against the newspaper, see *HM Advocate v George Outram & Co Ltd*, 1980 J.C. 51.

[10] 1980 J.C. 111 at 123, *per* the Lord Justice-General (Emslie).

[11] 1980 J.C. 111 at 123, *per* the Lord Justice-General (Emslie). This means that the court should uphold the plea in bar where a fair trial "cannot reasonably be expected", rather than requiring the accused to prove that a fair trial is impossible: see *Beggs v HM Advocate*, 2001 S.C.C.R. 836 at [6], *per* Lord Coulsfield. *Cf. McLeod v HM Advocate*, 1997 J.C. 212 at 215, *per* the Lord Justice-Clerk (Cullen).

[12] The first such case appears to have been *HM Advocate v Trainer*, August 28, 1987, High Court at Paisley, unreported (see A.J. Bonnington, "Contempt of court: a practitioner's viewpoint", 1988 S.L.T. (News) 33–38; *Adams, Petr*, 1987 S.C.C.R. 650). See also *Kilbane v HM Advocate*, 1990 S.L.T. 108.

[13] See below, para.18.10.

[14] *Stewart v HM Advocate*, 1980 J.C. 103.

[15] 2001 S.C. (P.C.) 1.

and prosecution of crime, as had previously been suggested.[16] In ECHR terms, the question is technically one of objective impartiality—whether "the fear of the accused that any future jury will lack impartiality can be objectively justified"—but the application of the *Stuurman* test is sufficient to answer that question.[17]

Although the European Commission on Human Rights has accepted that prejudicial publicity might be such as to breach an accused's right under Art.6(1), such claims have not in practice met with success.[18] The position is similar in the Scottish jurisprudence, where the *Stuurman* test has never been held to be satisfied.[19] The Scottish courts have, however, been prepared to hold that a trial diet must be deserted *pro loco et tempore* because of prejudicial publicity during the trial itself,[20] or that a trial cannot take place in a particular location because of prejudicial publicity in that locality.[21] It appears that a lower threshold may require to be satisfied where the accused is pleading merely that the trial should take place in a different venue rather than that it should be halted altogether, an issue which is discussed later in this chapter.[22] In principle, it should also be open to the accused to argue that the trial, rather than being halted altogether, should be delayed in order to ameliorate the effects of prejudicial publicity.[23] **18.03**

The decision as to whether the *Stuurman* test is satisfied is a question of fact for the trial judge,[24] which requires a risk assessment of the residual impact of the publicity on a notional juror.[25] To that end, the judge must weigh a number of factors in the balance. The decision will usually be based principally on an examination of copies of the relevant material placed before the court. In one exceptional English case (the Maxwell fraud trial), the court was also presented with evidence derived from opinion polls designed to gauge the effects of the publicity, but the trial judge commented that "I do not believe I would have reached a significantly different conclusion as to the effects of publicity without the assistance of these and I hope that their use in this case will not be taken as precedent in the future."[26]

---

[16] In *X v Sweeney*, 1982 J.C. 70, discussed below, para.18.18. See *Montgomery v HM Advocate*, 2001 S.C. (P.C.) 1 at 29, *per* Lord Hope of Craighead.

[17] See *HM Advocate v Fraser*, 2000 S.C.C.R. 412 at 419, *per* Lord Osborne.

[18] See *X v Austria* (1963) 11 C.D. 31; *X v Norway* (1970) 35 C.D. 37; *X v United Kingdom* (1978) 2 Digest 558; *Berns and Ewart v Luxembourg* (1991) 67 D.R. 137; *Baragiola v Switzerland* (1993) 75 D.R. 120. See also *HM Advocate v Fraser*, 2000 S.C.C.R. 412 at 416 and 418, *per* Lord Osborne (noting submissions by counsel regarding the absence of any successful claims of a breach of Art.6(1) based on prejudicial publicity).

[19] *HM Advocate v Fraser*, 2000 S.C.C.R. 412 at 416, *per* Lord Osborne. By contrast, prejudicial publicity has resulted in a number of English prosecutions being barred by the courts there. See A.J. Bonnington, "Cross borders: cross purposes" (1996) 146 N.L.J. 1312; D. Corker and D. Young, *Abuse of Process in Criminal Proceedings* (2nd edn, 2003), Ch.9.

[20] See *Adams, Petr*, 1987 S.C.C.R. 650; *Kilbane v HM Advocate*, 1990 S.L.T. 108.

[21] See *HM Advocate v Mitchell*, 1994 S.L.T. 144; *McLeod v HM Advocate*, 1997 J.C. 212.

[22] See below, paras 18.24–18.25.

[23] Such a plea appears to have been unsuccessfully made in *Kilbane v HM Advocate*, 1990 S.L.T. 108.

[24] See *Lambert v HM Advocate*, 1993 S.L.T. 339 at 341, *per* Lord Allanbridge (stressing the importance of the sheriff's local knowledge).

[25] See *Montgomery v HM Advocate*, 2001 S.C. (P.C.) 1 at 24, *per* Lord Hope of Craighead, citing *Attorney-General v MGN Ltd* [1997] 1 All E.R. 456 at 461, *per* Schiemann L.J.

[26] D. Corker and M. Levi, "Pre-trial publicity and its treatment in the English courts" [1996] Crim. L.R. 622–632 at pp.630–631. On the use of such surveys, see also A.J. Posey and L.M. Dahl, "Beyond pretrial publicity: legal and ethical issues associated with change of venue surveys" (2002) 26 *Law and Human Behavior* 107–125.

While the decision will always depend on the facts of the particular case, some guidance can be drawn from decisions which have considered the weight to be given to certain factors (and which factors are not to be taken into account).

Factors to be Taken into Account

The capacity of the jury to disregard prejudicial publicity

18.04 The courts have evaluated the deleterious effects of prejudicial publicity against a background of healthy confidence in the abilities of juries: "the entire system of trial by jury is based upon the assumption that the jury will follow the instructions which they receive from the trial judge and that they will return a true verdict in accordance with the evidence."[27] Accordingly, juries are assumed to be capable of disregarding most prejudicial publicity.

Juries, it has been said, are comprised of "ordinary folk ... good, sensible people",[28] whom the law of evidence assumes are capable of disregarding irrelevant material where appropriate: "[i]f they can do that, which is far from easy, they can disregard what has been said in a newspaper".[29] The nineteenth-century warning of Lord Ellenborough that, "[b]y their own public declarations we know that the minds of jurymen", when faced with pretrial reports of the evidence against the accused, "are often pre-occupied by such statements, and that they proceed with terror to the discharge of their duty, from the apprehension that an antecedent bias may influence their verdict",[30] is now a long-forgotten historical curiosity.[31]

This assumption as to the abilities of the jury is as much pragmatic as anything else. In the words of the former Chief Justice of the Supreme Court of Canada, while the theory of trial by jury may be disputed, "until the paradigm is altered by Parliament, the Court should not be heard to call into question the capacity of juries to do the job assigned to them. The ramifications of any such statement could be enormous..."[32] Similarly, the jurisdiction to halt a trial on the basis of prejudicial publicity necessarily assumes that judges are capable of evaluating the effects of prejudicial publicity on juries: it may be that judges are well placed to do that by virtue of having observed juries over a long period of time, but a

---

[27] *Montgomery v HM Advocate*, 2001 S.C. (P.C.) 1 at 30, *per* Lord Hope of Craighead. For similar expressions of confidence in the abilities of juries, see the Canadian, Australian and Irish authorities cited by Lord Hope in *Montgomery*, at 30–31. See also *R. v Kray* (1969) 53 Cr.App.R. 412 at 414, *per* Lawton J.; *Attorney-General v News Group Newspapers* [1987] Q.B. 1 at 19, *per* Sir George Waller ("In my opinion the risk of prejudicing juries is very often exaggerated.").

[28] *R. v Horsham Justices, ex parte Farquharson* [1982] Q.B. 762 at 794, *per* Lord Denning M.R.

[29] *R. v Coughlan; R. v Young* (1976) 64 Cr.App.R. 33 at 37, *per* Lawton L.J. (noting that juries "are expected to disregard what one accused says about another in his absence").

[30] *R. v Fisher* (1811) 2 Camp. 563 at 570; 170 E.R. 1253 at 1255 (a prosecution for criminal libel based on reports of preliminary examinations taken *ex parte* before a magistrate).

[31] Another curiosity (noted by Corker and Levi, fn.26 above, at p.623) is that it is taken for granted in modern practice that a jury should ideally come to court with no prior knowledge of the facts of the case or of the persons involved, which is at odds with the jury's role historically.

[32] *Corbett v R.* [1988] 1 S.C.R. 670 at [40], *per* Dickson C.J.

more convincing justification is simply that there is no better alternative, and that judges must simply do "the best they can in what are undoubtedly difficult circumstances".[33]

Jury research

Although there is a considerable body of research into the effects of publicity on jury decision-making, that research has rarely been considered by the courts.[34] Indeed, none of the Scottish cases prior to *Montgomery v HM Advocate*[35] even acknowledged the existence of such research. **18.05**

In *Montgomery*,[36] Lord Hope of Craighead referred to research conducted for the New Zealand Law Commission, stating that it "suggests that the impact of pre-trial publicity and of prejudicial media coverage during the trial, even in high profile cases, is minimal".[37] This New Zealand research is particularly significant, because it involved actual jury trials (48 over a period of nine months, including as many "high profile" cases as practicable), as opposed to laboratory-based jury research, the applicability of which to actual trials may be disputed. Data—in addition to that generated by the trial process itself—was collected by means of questionnaires and conducting interviews with the judge and jurors (where they consented) after the conclusion of the trial.[38]

The researchers found that, "despite the emphasis in [the] sample upon high-profile cases, very few of the jurors who were aware of pre-trial publicity knew anything of the case beyond a hazy recollection of the bare essentials of the incident".[39] The effects of knowledge beyond this appeared to be countered by conscious efforts to put preconceptions to one side, and by the effect of jury deliberations (other jurors making it clear in one case that they did not want to know about one juror having seen the case on television).[40] Publicity during the trial was also considered to have limited impact, as jurors who followed press and television coverage often regarded themselves as better informed than the media, and were in any event "told bluntly" by other jurors that details of media coverage were irrelevant to deliberations.[41] **18.06**

Given that the New Zealand study is the only jury research which has been referred to in the Scottish cases, it must be stressed that it runs counter to the orthodox view in the psychological literature, which is that

[33] *Attorney-General v MGN Ltd* [1997] 1 All E.R. 456 at 462, *per* Schiemann L.J.

[34] In the Supreme Court of Canada in 1994, Lamer C.J., in considering whether jurors are adversely affected by publicity, went so far as to say that "[t]here is no data available on this issue" and that the matter had to be dealt with as one of "common sense": *Dagenais v Canadian Broadcasting Corporation* [1994] 3 S.C.R. 835 at [87], *per* Lamer C.J. In *Gisborne Herald Co Ltd v Solicitor General* [1995] 3 N.Z.L.R. 563, the New Zealand Court of Appeal acknowledged the existence of a body of research on the issue, but did not consider it in depth, simply noting that there was "a body of empirically based research evidence which gives grounds for scepticism" as to whether jurors were unaffected by publicity.

[35] 2001 S.C. (P.C.) 1.

[36] *ibid.*

[37] 2001 S.C. (P.C.) 1 at 30, citing W. Young, N. Cameron and Y. Tinsley, *Juries in Criminal Trials: Part Two* (New Zealand Law Commission Preliminary Paper 37, 1999). See also M. Chesterman, J. Chan and S. Hampton, *Managing Prejudicial Publicity: An Empirical Study of Criminal Jury Trials in New South Wales* (2001).

[38] See *Juries in Criminal Trials: Part Two*, para.1.6.

[39] *ibid.*, para.7.51.

[40] *ibid.*, paras 7.52–7.53.

[41] *ibid.*, paras 7.54–7.56.

pretrial publicity "has damaging effects on potential jurors; jurors exposed to pretrial publicity render guilty verdicts more often than those not so exposed. This has been found both with simulated jurors, and in real cases."[42]

This is not the place for a full review of the psychological literature.[43] However, it may be observed that, from a legal perspective, there are four particular factors which may lead to the findings of such research studies being treated with caution by the courts.[44]

18.07 First, the courts have placed considerable weight on the transient effects of publicity, stating that "public memory of newspaper articles and news broadcasts and of their detailed contents" is "notoriously short".[45] Given this working assumption, studies of the effects of pretrial publicity which expose mock jurors to both "pretrial publicity" and a "trial" in a single session, or in two sessions in short succession, are of limited value in evaluating the approach of the courts.[46] Such research may be more readily applied to evaluating the effect of prejudicial publicity on the eve of, or during, trial—a situation in which the courts have been far more ready to discontinue proceedings, at least temporarily.[47]

Secondly, research will often involve specifically drawing the attention of mock jurors to simulated "pretrial publicity"—perhaps specifically requesting that they read it.[48] This is unlikely to be regarded by the courts as an accurate simulation of the effect of pretrial publicity which forms part of a much broader set of stories reported by the media, each unlikely to receive the potential juror's full attention, and the courts have stressed

---

[42] S.M. Fulero, "Afterword: the past, present and future of applied pretrial publicity research" (2002) 26 *Law and Human Behavior* 127–133 at p.127 (citing 20 research studies and other publications). See also N.M. Steblay, J. Besirevic, S.M. Fulero and B. Jimenez-Lorente, "The effects of pretrial publicity on juror verdicts: a meta-analytic review" (1999) 23 *Law and Human Behavior* 219–235.

[43] The literature is very extensive. Useful starting points include the following: T.M. Honess, "Empirical and legal perspectives on the impact of pre-trial publicity" [2002] Crim. L.R. 719–727 and a special issue of *Law and Human Behavior* on pretrial publicity (issue 26(1), 2002).

[44] In *Lockhart v McCree*, 476 U.S. 162 (1986), a majority of the US Supreme Court referred to three jury research studies relied upon by the defendant, noting that the studies "were based on the responses of individuals randomly selected from some segment of the population, but who were not actual jurors sworn under oath to apply the law to the facts of an actual case involving the fate of an actual capital defendant. We have serious doubts about the value of these studies in predicting the behaviour of actual jurors" (Rehnquist J., at 171). See further, B.H. Bornstein, "The ecological validity of jury simulations: is the jury still out?" (1999) 23 *Law and Human Behavior* 75–91; C.A. Studebaker *et al*, "Studying pretrial publicity effects: new methods for improving ecological validity and testing external validity" (2002) 26 *Law and Human Behavior* 19–41.

[45] *Stuurman v HM Advocate*, 1980 J.C. 111 at 123, *per* the Lord Justice-General (Emslie). See below, para.18.10.

[46] See, e.g. L. Hope, A. Memon and P. McGeorge, "Understanding pretrial publicity: predecisional distortion of evidence by mock jurors" (2004) 10 *Journal of Experimental Psychology: Applied* 111–119; S. Fein, S.J. Morgan, M.I. Norton and S.R. Sommers, "Hype and suspicion: the effects of pretrial publicity, race, and suspicion on jurors' verdicts" (1997) 53 *Journal of Social Issues* 487–502 (mock jurors read pretrial publicity articles "a few days" in advance of the trial transcript).

[47] See below, para.18.10.

[48] See, e.g. Fein *et al*, above, fn.46, at p.493 ("Participants in the four pretrial publicity (PTP) conditions received a packet of articles in their campus mailboxes with a cover letter that asked them to read the articles over the next few days, after which they would receive further instructions.")

the artificiality of considering the effects of particular items of media coverage in isolation.[49]

Thirdly, research may involve participants reading a summary of a "trial", or perhaps a transcript, before reaching a "verdict". The courts have, however, held to the view that the trial process itself has a curative effect: "the drama, if I may use that term, of a trial almost always has the effect of excluding from recollection that which went before."[50]

Fourthly, the courts have placed considerable weight on the effect of jury deliberations in negating the effects of any prejudices held by individual jurors.[51] Research with mock jurors returning an individual verdict leaves any such effects out of account.

Not all studies are, however, subject to these limitations, at least to their full extent.[52] The difficulty is that the courts have assumed that the effects of publicity are weakened or ameliorated by a number of factors not replicated in most research studies, and so the available research normally does not provide a basis on which to evaluate the working assumptions employed by the courts.

The capacity of judges to disregard prejudicial publicity

The courts' faith in the system of trial by jury has been paralleled by a near-absolutist faith in the immunity of judges from prejudice caused by publicity. It appears that a plea based on prejudicial publicity is almost certain to fail in summary proceedings, because it is accepted that a judge is capable of disregarding the extraneous influence of prejudicial publicity.[53] In principle, it *might* be possible for a plea to succeed if the court were satisfied that the publicity was such as to irredeemably taint the evidence of potential witnesses, as opposed to tainting the deliberations of the judge.[54] This could, however, be regarded as simply being a matter which the judge could consider in evaluating the evidence (although, perhaps paradoxically, it might then require evidence to be led as to the nature and content of the prejudicial publicity) **18.08**

The effect of the trial process

Alongside this reliance on the abilities of fact-finders to disregard prejudicial publicity, the courts have expressed faith that the trial process itself will work to correct the effects of prejudicial publicity in two ways: **18.09**

---

[49] See below, para.18.16.

[50] *R. v Kray* (1969) 53 Cr.App.R. 412 at 415, *per* Lawton J. See below, para.18.09.

[51] *Pullar v HM Advocate*, 1993 J.C. 126.

[52] See, in particular, T.M. Honess, E.A. Charman and M. Levi, "Factual and affective/evaluative recall of pretrial publicity: their relative influence on juror reasoning and verdict in a simulated fraud trial" (2003) 33 *Journal of Applied Social Psychology* 1404–1416, examining recall of real-life pretrial publicity in the context of a trial simulation, during or soon after the actual trial. See also T.M. Honess, M. Levi and E.A. Charman, "Juror competence in processing complex information: implications from a simulation of the Maxwell trial" [1998] Crim. L.R. 763–773.

[53] *Tudhope v Glass*, 1981 S.C.C.R. 336 (Sh. Ct). The same principle applies to lay justices: see *Aitchison v Bernardi*, 1984 S.L.T. 343. See also *R. v Croydon Magistrates' Court, ex parte Simmons* [1996] C.L.Y. 1662. In *Tudhope v Glass*, reference was made to the decision in *Stirling v Herron*, 1976 S.L.T. (Notes) 2, where it was held not to be improper for the same sheriff to preside over two consecutive trials concerning different charges against the same accused. Similarly, a sheriff is capable of disregarding inadvertently disclosed previous convictions: see, e.g. *Clampett v Stott*, 2002 J.C. 89.

[54] An argument unsuccessfully attempted in *Tudhope v Glass*, 1981 S.C.C.R. 336 (Sh. Ct).

first, because the evidence of the witnesses will be open to the test of cross-examination (thereby minimising any effect which publicity might have on the evidence given),[55] and secondly, that the trial process will act to focus the jurors' attention on the issues[56] and to exclude recollection of the pretrial publicity.[57] One consequence of this, it has been suggested, is that a plea in bar based on prejudicial publicity will have less chance of success where the trial is to be lengthy and complex.[58]

The timing of prejudicial publicity and its transient effects

18.10 In *Stuurman v HM Advocate*,[59] the Lord Justice-General (Emslie) remarked that "public memory of newspaper articles and news broadcasts and of their detailed contents" was "notoriously short",[60] a phrase repeated by the courts on numerous occasions since.[61]

Consequently, the courts have been prepared to accept that the effect of even the most prejudicial publicity can be ameliorated over time.[62] For example, although the appeal court in *Beggs v HM Advocate*[63] entertained "grave doubts" as to whether a fair trial could legitimately have been commenced within the 110-day period because of publicity drawing attention to a previous conviction (which had been quashed on appeal),[64] the extended delay caused by the accused's flight to the Netherlands and subsequent extradition meant that the plea in bar of trial failed, as the bulk of the publicity was now over 18 months old. Similarly, in *X v Sweeney*,[65] although the case had received "massive coverage" in the press, including details of an alleged "confession" by one of the accused, the court was prepared to hold that the "notoriously short" public

---

[55] See *Stuurman v HM Advocate*, 1980 J.C. 111 at 123, *per* the Lord Justice-General (Emslie).

[56] *Ex parte The Telegraph Plc* [1993] 1 W.L.R. 980 at 988, *per* Lord Taylor C.J.

[57] *R. v Kray* (1969) 53 Cr.App.R. 412 at 415, *per* Lawton J.

[58] D. Corker and M. Levi, "Pre-trial publicity and its treatment in the English courts" [1996] Crim. L.R. 622–632 at p.629, and see *Attorney-General v BBC* [1997] E.M.L.R. 76 at 79–80, *per* Auld L.J.

[59] 1980 J.C. 111.

[60] At 123.

[61] *X v Sweeney*, 1982 J.C. 70 at 86, *per* the Lord Justice-General (Emslie); *Spink v HM Advocate*, 1989 S.C.C.R. 414 at 415, *per* the Lord Justice-General (Emslie); *Lambert v HM Advocate*, 1993 S.L.T. 339 at 341, *per* Lord Allanbridge; *McLeod v HM Advocate*, 1997 J.C. 212 at 215, *per* the Lord Justice-Clerk (Cullen). In *R. v Derby Stipendiary Magistrate, ex parte Brooks*, February 17, 1994, D.C., Scott Baker J. observed that "In most cases, one day's headline news is the next day's firelighter. Most members of the public do not remember in any detail what they have seen on television, heard on the radio or read in the newspapers except for a very short period of time."

[62] See also *R. v Stone* [2001] EWCA Crim 297 at [62], *per* Kennedy L.J. ("... people do forget. Even if they do not forget entirely, the passage of time makes it easier for them to set aside that which they are told to disregard").

[63] 2001 S.C.C.R. 836.

[64] *R. v Beggs* (1990) 90 Cr.App.R. 430.

[65] 1982 J.C. 70. The decision is, however, affected by the court's reliance on the public interest in the prosecution of crime, which would probably now be regarded as an illegitimate consideration: see below, para.18.18.

memory of newspaper reports meant that the case could fairly proceed to trial barely four months after the "confession" had appeared in print.[66]

There is, of course, little or no room for relying on the transient effects of publicity where the publicity occurs during the trial itself[67]: and so in *R. v Magee*,[68] the trial judge, having refused to stay proceedings on the basis of pretrial reports revealing the criminal backgrounds of the defendants, felt constrained to grant a stay once similar reports were published during the trial. Similarly, while Scottish prosecutions have occasionally been deserted *pro loco et tempore* due to prejudicial publicity during the course of the trial, pleas in bar have not been successful in preventing subsequent prosecutions.[69]

The likelihood of memory of the publicity fading may depend on its nature. It has been suggested, for example, that allegations made against a prominent individual will be likely to recede more slowly from the minds of potential jurors,[70] and that reports of "spectacular and dramatic" events will be similarly memorable.[71]

The content and style of the publicity

The fact that a particular case has attracted widespread publicity, or indeed that the accused has come to widespread public attention for other reasons, does not in itself amount to prejudicial publicity.[72] The nature of the publicity, that is, the information it conveys and the manner in which it does so, will be crucial in assessing its effect. **18.11**

For example, where an accused faces a second trial, for whatever reason, it is highly unlikely that fair and accurate contemporaneous reports of the evidence given at his first trial will form a basis for a successful plea in bar.[73] The position may be different where the reports

---

[66] The "confession" had appeared in the *Daily Record* on January 19, 1982, shortly before the Lord Advocate (who had previously renounced the right to prosecute, believing that the complainer would be unable to give evidence) indicated the possibility of a private prosecution. The appeal court, in its decision of the 1st April, granted permission for a private prosecution and rejected the accused persons' claims that it would be oppressive to put them on trial because of the prejudicial publicity. The case proceeded to trial on the 24th May after further pleas in bar were repelled by the trial judge: see *Sweeney v X*, 1982 S.C.C.R. 509.

[67] Or on the eve of trial: see *X v Sweeney*, 1982 J.C. 70 at 89, *per* Lord Cameron.

[68] Woolwich Crown Court, January 1997, unreported: see *Attorney-General v Associated Newspapers Ltd* [1998] E.M.L.R. 711 and D. Corker and D. Young, *Abuse of Process in Criminal Proceedings* (2nd edn, 2003), para.9.39. The proceedings were permanently stayed, thus preventing a further prosecution from being brought, although this may have been partially due to the fact that this was the second occasion on which the defendants had stood trial, rather than on prejudice alone.

[69] *Kilbane v HM Advocate*, 1990 S.L.T. 108. See also *Adams, Petr*, 1987 S.C.C.R. 650, although it is not clear whether a plea in bar was taken in respect of the second trial in that case.

[70] *HM Advocate v The Scotsman Publications Ltd*, 1999 S.L.T. 466.

[71] *HM Advocate v News Group Newspapers Ltd*, 1989 S.C.C.R. 156.

[72] See *HM Advocate v Fraser*, 2000 S.C.C.R. 412 at 420, *per* Lord Osborne (noting that much of the publicity was concerned with the disappearance of the complainer—which was later to become the basis of a murder charge against the accused—and not with the charge of attempting to murder the complainer which the accused then faced). See also J. Cooper "Media coverage—from the Taylor twins to Leah Betts" (1997) 147 N.L.J. 963–964.

[73] See *Spink v HM Advocate*, 1989 S.C.C.R. 414.

are not contemporaneous, but are published on the eve of or during the retrial.[74]

Furthermore, the content of the publicity will affect the extent to which its effects can be remedied by direction from the judge. Where the publicity is simply erroneous (for example by confusing the identities of two different persons) it may be possible for the inaccuracy to be made clear in open court.[75] Where, by contrast, the publicity reveals material which, accurate or not, should not be known to the jury—such as a previous conviction of the accused—or amounts to comment which is not necessarily inaccurate but which trespasses on the issues which the jury have to determine,[76] it will be less easy to remedy by way of direction.

It has been said that a jury must be credited with sufficient common sense to recognise innuendo or ludicrous speculation for what it is,[77] although in one contempt case the High Court gave short shrift to the argument which counsel, appearing for a tabloid newspaper, appeared to advance: "that readers do not really believe what they read in such newspapers and that the style in which such articles ... were written showed that they were really designed more to entertain than inform", describing this as a "wholly unpersuasive argument".[78] There is, no doubt, a distinction between basic factual information (such as a claim that the accused did a particular act or has a criminal record) and "ludicrous speculation", which will be readily disregarded.

In assessing prejudice, the courts have considered the following types of publicity to be particularly prejudicial. This is by no means a closed list, and simply reflects the reported cases which have come before the courts to date.

Previous convictions

18.12 The importance attached to juries not normally knowing of any previous convictions of the accused, or indeed, other misconduct which is unrelated to the case before the court, is clear from the relevant rules of evidence.[79] With this in mind, the courts have considered references to the accused's criminal background to be particularly prejudicial,[80] an

[74] *cf.* the position regarding disclosure of previous convictions to a jury during the course of a trial, which may require the trial diet to be deserted: see, e.g. *Binks v HM Advocate*, 1984 J.C. 108.

[75] *HM Advocate v McDougall and Bell*, June 11, 1986, Glasgow Sheriff Court, unreported. See A.J. Bonnington, "Contempt of court: a practitioner's viewpoint" 1988 S.L.T. (News) 33–38 at p.35.

[76] See, e.g. *R. v Taylor and Taylor* (1994) 98 Cr.App.R. 361, discussed below, para.18.15.

[77] *HM Advocate v Fraser*, 2000 S.C.C.R. 412 at 420, *per* Lord Osborne. The same applies to information which is patently incorrect: *HM Advocate v McGill and Strain*, March 3, 1987, High Court at Glasgow, unreported: see A.J. Bonnington, above, fn.75, at p.36.

[78] *Cox and Griffiths, Petrs*, 1998 J.C. 267 at 271, *per* the Lord Justice-General (Rodger).

[79] See CPSA 1995, s.101; *Walkers on Evidence*, para.7.8.1.

[80] *Beggs v HM Advocate*, 2001 S.C.C.R. 836. In England, see *Attorney-General v Morgan* [1998] E.M.L.R. 294 at 305, *per* Pill L.J.; *Attorney-General v Associated Newspapers* [1998] E.M.L.R. 711 (a contempt case following on from the stay of proceedings granted in *R. v Magee*, Woolwich Crown Court, January 1997, unreported); *R. v Hassan and Caldon*, Isleworth Crown Court, July 1995, unreported (noted in D. Corker and D. Young, *Abuse of Process in Criminal Proceedings* (2nd edn, 2003), para.9.37). See also *Hinch v Attorney-General* (1987) 164 C.L.R. 15 at 28, *per* Mason C.J., at 71, *per* Toohey J., and at 88, *per* Gaudron J.; *Gisborne Herald Co Ltd v Solicitor General* [1995] 3 N.Z.L.R. 563. *Cf.*, however, *R. v Stone* [2001] EWCA Crim 297 at [60], *per* Kennedy L.J., noting that "there are a variety of ways in which that knowledge [of previous convictions] may come to the attention of a jury in a particular case without the trial being rendered unfair".

approach which is vindicated by the available research evidence.[81] Such prejudice is unlikely to be alleviated even where the reports make it clear that the conviction was quashed on appeal, particularly where the implication is that the accused had nonetheless committed the crime concerned.[82]

Direct statements of the accused's guilt

In *HM Advocate v Mitchell*,[83] the sheriff noted that no-one reading the newspaper reports in question "could doubt that the *Evening Times* is utterly convinced that [the accused] are guilty of defrauding many innocent customers".[84] The sheriff's decision to uphold a plea in bar of trial was upheld, but on the basis that the accused could be indicted to stand trial in a different sheriff court district.[85] Reports of an alleged confession by the accused (or perhaps statements by others implicating the accused) might equally be regarded as prejudicial.[86] **18.13**

It is not strictly necessary that the accused be named so long as he or she is identifiable, and so, in *R. v Reade*,[87] it was held that police officers accused of extracting confessions from members of the Birmingham Six would be unable to obtain a fair trial because the publicity surrounding the quashing of the Six's convictions meant that the jury would be liable to conclude that there had already been a judicial declaration that those police officers involved in the investigation were guilty of offences against the course of justice. It is probably essential that the accused is in some way identified by the publicity: in *Atkins v London Weekend Television*,[88] a television programme on euthanasia might well have barred the accused's trial (had the Crown not chosen to voluntarily drop the prosecution) because it specifically included a discussion of the accused's impending prosecution. By contrast, a general broadcast or report concerned with the subject of euthanasia would be unlikely to be sufficiently prejudicial, even if it alleged that the practice was common.[89]

[81] See S. Lloyd-Bostock, "The effects on juries of hearing about the defendant's previous criminal record: a simulation study" [2000] Crim. L.R. 734–755.

[82] *Beggs v HM Advocate*, 2001 S.C.C.R. 836.

[83] 1994 S.L.T. 144.

[84] At 146 *per* Sheriff Russell.

[85] On such "transfer of venue" cases, see below, paras 18.24–18.25.

[86] *cf. X v Sweeney*, 1982 J.C. 70. See also *Rideau v Louisiana* 373 U.S. 723 (1963). The same might apply to, e.g. a report that the accused had offered to plead guilty to a lesser charge: *HM Advocate v Trainer*, August 28, 1987, High Court at Paisley, unreported, but see *HM Advocate v McMurray*, November 6, 1985, High Court at Airdrie, unreported. Both cases are discussed in A.J. Bonnington, "Contempt of court: a practitioner's viewpoint" 1988 S.L.T. (News) 33–38, and see also *Adams, Petr*, 1987 S.C.C.R. 650.

[87] Central Criminal Court, October 15, 1993, unreported. See the *Independent*, October 19, 1993; Corker and Young, above, fn.80, para.9.28. *Cf R. v Alcindor*, June 11, 1990, unreported: see Corker and Young, para.9.29. *Reade* may be contrasted with *R. v Bow Street Metropolitan Stipendiary Magistrate, ex parte DPP* (1992) 95 Cr.App.R. 9 (pre-trial publicity no bar to a charge of conspiracy to pervert the course of justice brought against three police officers involved in the investigation which led to the conviction of the Guildford Four).

[88] 1978 J.C. 48.

[89] Compare *Atkins* with *Attorney-General v English* [1983] 1 A.C. 116. *Cf. Dagenais v Canadian Broadcasting Corporation* [1994] 3 S.C.R. 835.

Statements restricting the scope of the accused's defence

18.14 In *Atkins v London Weekend Television*,[90] the High Court considered that media reports juxtaposing Ms Atkins' imminent trial with what might be described as two "euthanasia" cases resulted in "the clear insinuation that the real if not the only question which would arise out of the petitioner's trial would be whether she was medically and morally justified in committing the acts charged".[91] In fact, as the court noted, her plea of not guilty necessarily raised the question of whether she was the person who had attempted to block the complainer's air supply, and indeed whether any attempt to block the air supply had taken place at all. While the insinuation was such as to suggest that the accused might have no legally valid defence (beyond the hope for a merciful jury verdict) whatsoever, the same principle should apply where the scope of the accused's defence is restricted in other ways, for example, where a newspaper report implies that the accused did in fact inflict injuries on the complainer but leaves open the plea of self-defence. Although not conclusive of the accused's guilt, such statements would tend to exclude the "defence" of a simple denial of the offence charged, and as such might well be regarded as prejudicial.

Inaccurate reporting of trial proceedings

18.15 In the English case of *R. v Taylor and Taylor*,[92] the Court of Appeal quashed the appellants' murder convictions because of (in addition to non-disclosure of crucial information to the defence) press coverage of the trial which was described as "unremitting, extensive, sensational, inaccurate and misleading".[93] McCowan L.J. commented that:

> "What, in fact, they [the press] did was not reporting at all; it was comment, and comment which assumed guilt on the part of the girls in the dock. But the Press is no more entitled to assume guilt in what it writes during the course of a trial, than a police officer is entitled to convince himself that a defendant is guilty and suppress evidence, the emergence of which he fears might lead to the defendant's acquittal."[94]

The court declined to order a retrial, concluding that the publicity had been such as to make a fair trial impossible.[95]

The likely exposure of jurors to the prejudicial material

18.16 The court will consider the likelihood of the prejudicial material coming to the attention of potential jurors. This involves a consideration of whether, and to what extent, the publication circulates in the area from

---

[90] 1978 J.C. 48.

[91] At 55 *per* the Lord Justice-General (Emslie).

[92] (1994) 98 Cr.App.R. 361.

[93] At 368 *per* McCowan L.J. (quoting the trial judge, Blofeld J.).

[94] At 369.

[95] The court noted that the defence might have asked for the jury to be discharged at the first trial, but accepted that there were valid reasons for no such request having been made: see *per* McCowan L.J. at 369.

which jurors are likely to be drawn.[96] In *HM Advocate v Fraser*,[97] Lord Osborne considered it of significance that most of the newspaper reports before him had their widest circulation in Aberdeen and Glasgow, while the trial was expected to take place in Edinburgh.[98] Similarly, it is unlikely that jurors will specifically seek out material about the accused which may have been published in the past and is now available in archival form, via the internet or otherwise.[99]

The court will bear in mind that a consideration of the full body of material placed before it is likely to be a "somewhat artificial exercise", as no juror will be likely to have seen the material in its full extent or have concentrated on it in such detail.[1] Although the exercise is normally a speculative one, in one Scottish case where a prejudicial radio broadcast was made during the course of the trial, the jury were polled by the clerk of court to establish how many of them had heard the programme in question.[2]

The possibility of prejudice tainting the evidence

It has been accepted that publicity may have a prejudicial effect by tainting the evidence of witnesses: **18.17**

> "... publicity may be important not only by affecting the minds of potential jurors, but also by affecting the minds and the recollections of witnesses or their readiness to draw inferences from what they have seen or remembered. That is a risk which has to be borne in mind generally. There may be cases in which the risk becomes more specific as, for example, where identification by eyewitnesses is likely to be an issue in the trial."[3]

Factors Which Should Not Normally be Taken into Account

The public interest in the detection and suppression of crime

Prior to the decision of the Judicial Committee in *Montgomery*,[4] it appeared to be accepted that the public interest in the detection and suppression of crime was a valid factor to be taken into consideration. This was one of the reasons why the appeal court in *X v Sweeney*[5] was prepared to hold that the accused persons could stand trial for rape regardless of the extensive media coverage of their case, including a high-profile report of an alleged confession: **18.18**

---

[96] See *Montgomery v HM Advocate*, 2001 S.C. (P.C.) 1 at 24, *per* Lord Hope of Craighead, citing *Attorney-General v MGN Ltd* [1997] 1 All E.R. 456 at 461. See also *Attorney-General v Independent Television News Ltd* [1995] 2 All E.R. 370.

[97] 2000 S.C.C.R. 412.

[98] See also *Gisborne Herald Co Ltd v Solicitor General* [1995] 3 N.Z.L.R. 563.

[99] See *HM Advocate v Beggs (No. 2)*, 2002 S.L.T. 139.

[1] See *Montgomery v HM Advocate*, 2001 S.C. (P.C.) 1 at 24, *per* Lord Hope of Craighead.

[2] *HM Advocate v Trainer*, August 28, 1987, High Court at Paisley, unreported. See A.J. Bonnington, "Contempt of court: a practitioner's viewpoint" 1988 S.L.T. (News) 33–38 at pp.36–37. As to the possibility of questioning *potential* jurors, see below, para.18.20.

[3] *Beggs v HM Advocate*, 2001 S.C.C.R. 836 at [28], *per* Lord Coulsfield. See also *Tudhope v Glass*, 1981 S.C.C.R. 336 (Sh. Ct).

[4] 2001 S.C. (P.C.) 1.

[5] 1982 J.C. 70.

"In considering what the answer should be [to the question of whether the plea in bar should be upheld] I have not forgotten that while the public interest in securing fair trial of accused persons is of the highest importance, so too is the public interest in the fair administration of justice and the detection and trial of alleged perpetrators of crime. Great weight must be given to this latter aspect of the public interest in this case, for the crimes alleged are of a particularly serious and horrible nature. In light of this consideration, and my assessment of the probable course which presentation of available evidence at a trial would follow, can I confidently affirm now that fair and impartial trial of the three respondents cannot reasonably be secured? I have come to be of opinion that I cannot so affirm. Trials in cases which have become notorious are not uncommon ..."[6]

As Lord Hope of Craighead observed in *Montgomery v HM Advocate*,[7] however, this raises the possibility of a conflict with the Convention right to a fair trial.[8] Consequently:

"in order to preserve its [the *Stuurman* test's] integrity for this purpose ... it should be recognised that in the application of art 6(1) to the facts of the case there is no such balancing exercise. The right of the accused to a fair trial by an independent and impartial tribunal is unqualified. It is not to be subordinated to the public interest in the detection and suppression of crime."[9]

18.19 Removing the public interest in the detection and suppression of crime from the equation might give some cause for concern and, at the very least, there are pragmatic reasons why the courts are likely to be unwilling to uphold pleas in bar of trial in "notorious" cases. Before *Montgomery,* in *R. v West (Rosemary)*,[10] where particularly horrifying allegations had given rise to widespread publicity, Lord Taylor C.J. remarked that: "[the] question raised on behalf of the defence is whether a fair trial could be held after such intensive publicity adverse to the accused. In our view it could. To hold otherwise would mean that if allegations of murder are sufficiently horrendous so as inevitably to shock the nation, the accused cannot be tried. That would be absurd."[11]

Such a consequence would certainly be undesirable, but it is unclear why it should be regarded as absurd. More importantly, it is submitted that Lord Taylor's observations are incorrect. It should be remembered that widespread publicity is not in itself prejudicial—it depends on the

---

6 At 85 *per* the Lord Justice-General (Emslie).

7 2001 S.C. (P.C.) 1.

8 See also *Hinch v Attorney-General* (1987) 164 C.L.R. 15 at 54–55, *per* Deane J.: "The right to a fair and unprejudiced trial ... is a touchstone of the existence of the rule of law. It is difficult, if not impossible, to envisage any situation in which countervailing public interest considerations could outweigh the detriment to the due administration of justice involved in public prejudgment by the mass media of the guilt of a person awaiting trial."

9 2001 S.C. (P.C.) 1 at 29. While this could be interpreted as meaning that a "balancing exercise" is not permissible where the point is raised as a devolution issue, but is where it is raised at common law, this would be an unsatisfactory distinction and the better view is probably that *Montgomery* has effectively modified the common law test. This appears to be the view taken in Renton and Brown, para.9–25.

10 [1996] 2 Cr.App.R. 374.

11 At 386.

nature of that publicity and the aspersions which it casts upon the accused.[12] Notoriety and shock are not synonymous with prejudice: allegations may be memorable but if they are reported as allegations rather than as statements of fact and fairly represent the allegations which will be made at trial, they will not be regarded as sufficiently prejudicial to justify preventing a trial from taking place.

The possibility of challenging jurors

In *HM Advocate v Hunter*,[13] in responding to a motion that the trial be moved from Dundee to Edinburgh because of pretrial publicity in the local press, the Solicitor-General submitted that counsel for the accused, when the jurors were empanelled, could exercise his right to challenge a particular juror.[14] It is not clear, however, how the defence would acquire knowledge of any juror's awareness of prejudicial publicity, and in *Spink v HM Advocate*, the appeal court expressly disapproved a suggestion by the sheriff that jurors "might be asked if they have any particular knowledge gleaned from earlier newspaper reports which might preclude them from carrying out their duty as jurors in the trial of the appellant".[15] **18.20**

In one English case, counsel was granted permission to examine potential jurors as they came into the box to be sworn,[16] and questionnaires were administered in the Maxwell fraud trial to "sift out" potential jurors.[17] However, the Court of Appeal has stressed that such measures must be confined to exceptional cases.[18]

In any event, the Scottish courts have taken a much more restrictive approach to any suggestion of "jury vetting" than have the English.[19] It seems that the most that can legitimately be done is to "ask jurors at the appropriate time if there are any reasons known to them which would make it desirable that they should not take part in the particular trial."[20] The capacity of this method to reveal prejudice is limited, as it "seems unlikely that a prejudiced juror would recognize his own personal prejudice, or, knowing it, would admit it"[21] and so the ability to challenge a juror for cause should not, in most cases, be regarded as ameliorating the effects of prejudicial publicity.

---

[12] See above, paras 18.11–18.15.

[13] 1988 J.C. 153.

[14] See 1988 J.C. 153 at 154, *per* Lord Brand.

[15] 1989 S.C.C.R. 413 at 416, *per* the Lord Justice-General (Emslie).

[16] *R. v Kray* (1969) 53 Cr.App.R. 412 at 416, *per* Lawton J.: "No one must leave this court thinking that my judgment on this point amounts to a license for counsel to examine and cross-examine prospective jurors as to what they believe or do not believe. Indeed, I want to stress—and I cannot stress too strongly—that the combination of facts which have brought about the situation with which I have had to deal in this case is, in my view, wholly exceptional." *Kray* was distinguished in the Australian cases of *R. v Stuart and Finch* [1974] Qd. R. 297 and *Murphy v The Queen* (1989) 167 C.L.R. 94.

[17] See D. Corker and M. Levi, "Pre-trial publicity and its treatment in the English courts" [1996] Crim. L.R. 622–632 at pp.628–629.

[18] *R. v Andrews (Tracey)* [1999] Crim. L.R. 156. See also *R. v Kray*, above, fn.16. *Cf. R. v Stone* [2001] EWCA Crim 297 at [62], *per* Kennedy L.J.

[19] See P.W. Ferguson, "Jury vetting", 1997 S.L.T. (News) 287–291.

[20] *Spink v HM Advocate*, 1989 S.C.C.R. 413 at 416, *per* the Lord Justice-General (Emslie).

[21] *Murphy v R.* (1989) 167 C.L.R. 94 at 103, *per* Mason C.J. and Toohey J. (quoting A. Friendly and R.L. Goldfarb, *Crime and Publicity* (1967), pp.103–104).

The conduct of the police or Crown

18.21 A plea in bar on the ground of prejudice will not be aided by reference to any fault, delay or otherwise improper conduct on the part of the authorities.[22] The court's power to prevent a trial where there has been prejudicial publicity exists to protect the accused's right to a fair trial and not to punish the police or the Crown. If "there has been publicity which is sufficiently prejudicial to meet the *Stuurman* test, then the accused is entitled to protection on that ground without reference to any question of fault or delay on the part of the authorities".[23]

Fault on the part of the accused

18.22 In *R. v Savundranayagan and Walker*,[24] the Court of Appeal dismissed Savundranayagan's appeal against conviction based, in part, on the televising of an interview prior to his trial, observing that "[it] hardly lies in his mouth to complain" given that he "voluntarily went to the television interview when he must have strongly suspected that he was about to be arrested and eventually tried".[25] In *R. v Andrews*,[26] where an appeal against conviction based on prejudicial publicity failed, it was noted that the adverse publicity was in part due to the defendant's request that reporting restrictions be lifted at the committal proceedings, but the decision to dismiss the appeal did not rest on this ground.[27]

Although it has been argued that the factor of "defendant deserts" is "an important one in conditioning judicial reactions",[28] it is submitted that—now that Art.6(1) is recognised as the foundation of this area of the law[29]—fault on the part of the accused is not a relevant consideration except in the unlikely event that the criteria for waiver of the Convention right are satisfied.[30]

Deterring potential witnesses from coming forward

18.23 In *Tudhope v Glass*,[31] the accused's agent argued that pretrial publicity might have the effect of deterring potential witnesses from coming forward. Sheriff Kearley rejected this argument, indicating that he was "far from satisfied that this is truly a likely consequence of pre-trial publicity—indeed I think the opposite may be argued",[32] and that even if a bare possibility of such a consequence remained, it did not amount to sufficient reason for upholding the plea in bar. It might be that

---

[22] As to the circumstances, if any, in which misconduct might amount to an abuse of process, see Ch.19.

[23] *Beggs v HM Advocate*, 2001 S.C.C.R. 836 at [26], *per* Lord Coulsfield, rejecting an argument that the Crown could have applied for a petition warrant earlier, therefore making the proceedings "active" within the terms of s.2 of the Contempt of Court Act 1981.

[24] [1968] 1 W.L.R. 1761.

[25] [1968] 1 W.L.R. 1761 at 1766, *per* Salmon L.J.

[26] [1999] Crim. L.R. 156.

[27] In *Beggs v HM Advocate*, 2001 S.C.C.R. 836, it appears that no argument was made that adverse publicity created by the accused's decision to leave the country and resist extradition should be left out of account, although it is not clear from the report whether such publicity constituted a significant part of the material before the court. See also *Terris v HM Advocate*, 1992 G.W.D. 13–711.

[28] Corker and Levi, above, fn.17, at p.624, fn.12.

[29] *Montgomery v HM Advocate*, 2001 S.C. (P.C.) 1.

[30] See *Millar v Dickson* [2001] UKPC D4.

[31] 1981 S.C.C.R. 336 (Sh. Ct).

[32] At 339.

exceptional types of publicity (for example, reports of death threats to defence witnesses), could be regarded as having a deterrent effect, but pretrial publicity in itself cannot normally be expected to operate in this fashion.

Transfer of Venue

An accused may take a plea in bar of trial on the basis that the prosecution should not be deserted *simpliciter*, but instead deserted *pro loco et tempore* on the basis that the case can be brought to trial in a different court.[33] In one High Court case, the motion made by the accused was described as a "motion for transfer".[34] **18.24**

It is not clear whether the test to be applied in such cases is identical to that which is to be applied where the accused's contention is that no trial should take place at all. In *McLeod v HM Advocate*,[35] the Lord Justice-Clerk (Cullen) stated that:

> "All the earlier decisions, from *X v Sweeney* onwards, to which we were referred, with the exception of *HM Advocate v Mitchell*, were cases in which the effect of upholding a submission that material prejudice had been caused to the accused, to the extent of making a fair trial impossible, would have been that no trial could take place at all. It is in that context that Lord Avonside, in *Stuurman*, discussed at length the relationship between the court and the Lord Advocate as public prosecutor and arrived at the conclusion that nothing short of oppression would entitle the court to prevent an indictment proceeding to trial. Where, however, a trial can proceed in a different court, the question must assume a somewhat different aspect. The decision in *Mitchell* established that the fact that a trial can take place in another court is a relevant consideration. In that context, there must be greater room for taking account of the perception of the proceedings by the public and, indeed, by the accused himself. We would add that, in our experience, the Crown have, from time to time, readily agreed to a transfer to a different court in circumstances of this kind."[36]

However, it is now established that, in applying the *Stuurman* test, the court is not to have regard to the public interest in the prosecution of crime.[37] This would suggest that the fact that a trial can take place in a different court is no longer a relevant consideration. Either a fair trial can reasonably be expected, or it cannot. The current legal position is unresolved, and there are two possible positions, as follows: **18.25**

1. That the question is simply whether a fair trial can reasonably be expected or not. If it cannot, the trial cannot proceed. The

[33] *Kilbane v HM Advocate*, 1990 S.L.T. 108; *HM Advocate v Mitchell*, 1994 S.L.T 144; *McLeod v HM Advocate*, 1997 J.C. 212. In Renton and Brown, however, it is noted that "[t]his course is not available in the Sheriffdom of Glasgow and Strathkelvin, which is not divided into districts": para.9–26.

[34] *HM Advocate v Hunter*, 1988 J.C. 153 at 156.

[35] 1997 J.C. 212.

[36] At 215–216.

[37] See above, paras 18.18–18.19.

question of whether it can proceed in a different court (or at a different time) is irrelevant to the question of whether the plea in bar should succeed, but may be relevant to how the prosecution choose to proceed thereafter. If a fair trial can reasonably be expected, the choice of which court to proceed in is one for the prosecutor's discretion.

2. That even where a fair trial can reasonably be expected (and so a plea in bar would fail), the accused is entitled to have the case heard elsewhere where this is in the interests of justice. It is not clear from *McLeod* what test would be applied to such a motion by the accused. In any event, it will require a balancing of the interests of the accused in having the trial moved against the "well established principle that a trial should *prima facie* take place in the locality, so far as practicable, of the alleged crime".[38]

---

[38] *HM Advocate v Hunter*, 1998 J.C. 153 at 156, *per* Lord Brand.

CHAPTER 19

OPPRESSION AND ABUSE OF PROCESS

INTRODUCTION

It is clearly established in Scots law that, where an accused's right to a fair trial has been prejudiced because of delay or pretrial publicity, this will provide a basis for a plea of oppression in bar of trial.[1] What is less clear is whether the plea of oppression extends to circumstances where the accused's prospects of a fair trial will not be prejudiced, but it in some way offends against the legitimacy of the judicial process to put him on trial: in other words, his prosecution is an abuse of process.[2] **19.01**

In the English case of *R. v Martin*,[3] Lord Hope of Craighead explained that:

> "an abuse of process is something so unfair and wrong that the court should not allow a prosecutor to proceed with what is in all other respects a regular proceeding. Thus it is no answer to a claim that there was an abuse of process to show that the proceedings at the trial itself were entirely fair."[4]

Influenced by the constitutional position of the Lord Advocate, however, the Scottish courts have been reluctant to accept that the actions of the Scottish public prosecutor in bringing a prosecution could be halted as an abuse of the process of the court.[5] In the civil context, the discretion of the Lord Advocate has been stated in near-absolute terms:

> "In our system the Lord Advocate alone possesses the function, in indictable offences, of deciding whether he will prosecute or whether he will withdraw a prosecution, and there is no appeal to any Court against his decision on these matters. No Court or magistrate can compel or direct or recommend to him what he should do. These are matters exclusively for him and exclusively within his province."[6]

---

1 See above, para.16.33 and Ch.18.

2 Attempts have been made to link the concepts of oppression and abuse of process in at least two recent appeals, but the appeal court did not enter into any discussion of the point in either case. See *Sinclair v HM Advocate*, 2004 S.C.C.R. 499 at [9] (where the grounds of appeal alleged that the conduct of the prosecution "was oppressive and represented an abuse of process"); *Tant v HM Advocate*, 2003 S.C.C.R. 506 at 509 (where the grounds of appeal argued that the conduct of the advocate-depute at trial "was oppressive and an abuse of process").

3 [1998] A.C. 917.

4 At 930.

5 It might be that a private prosecutor could be regarded as abusing the process of the court, but such an individual normally has no automatic right of prosecution but must instead seek the concurrence of the Lord Advocate or the permission of the High Court, a procedure which in itself acts as a safeguard against abuse of process. See, e.g. *J. & P. Coats Ltd v Brown*, 1909 J.C. 29 and *X v Sweeney*, 1982 J.C. 70.

6 *Hester v MacDonald*, 1961 S.C. 370 at 378, *per* the Lord President (Clyde) (citing Alison, *Practice*, 87).

19.02 The very existence of the plea of oppression demonstrates, however, that the position is not quite so absolute. According to Burnett, the prosecutor's discretion may be restrained "by the interference of the Court of Law upon any case of hardship or oppression towards the party accused, by undue delay or otherwise, in conducting the trial".[7] "Oppression", however, is not a term with any clear or obvious meaning,[8] and this ambiguity has dogged the Scottish case law on the point. It may be that Burnett's statement should be taken as indicating no more than that the court may prevent a prosecution from proceeding to trial where the accused's right to a fair trial has been prejudiced; alternatively, it may indicate that the court has broader powers to prevent any prosecution which would be an abuse of process.

At first sight, one of the leading authorities on the plea of oppression, *HM Advocate v Stuurman*,[9] appears to have decided that oppression is restricted to cases of prejudice, as the headnote to the *Justiciary Cases* report of the case asserts that the court held that "oppression occurs only when the risk of prejudice to the accused is so grave that no direction of the trial Judge could reasonably be expected to remove it".[10] That is, however, a misreading of what was in fact said by the Full Bench in that case, which is as follows:

> "As the authorities show, the High Court of Justiciary has power to intervene to prevent the Lord Advocate from proceeding upon a particular indictment but this power will be exercised only in special circumstances which are likely to be rare. The special circumstances must indeed be such as to satisfy the Court that, having regard to the principles of substantial justice and of fair trial, to require an accused to face trial would be oppressive. Each case will depend on its own merits, and *where the alleged oppression is said to arise from events alleged to be prejudicial to the prospects of fair trial* the question for the Court is whether the risk of prejudice is so grave that no direction of the trial Judge, however careful, could reasonably be expected to remove it."[11]

Two points arise. First, it is clear that the court did not hold that oppression was restricted to cases of alleged prejudice, but in fact left that question open: if anything, these remarks suggest that oppression could be made out in the absence of prejudice. Secondly, oppression is not confined to cases where the accused's right to a fair trial is prejudiced, but applies also in cases where the "principles of substantial justice" might be violated by proceeding to trial, although the meaning of "substantial justice" is not elaborated on.

19.03 Despite this, the High Court has more recently asserted, in the case of

---

[7] Burnett, 309 (a passage quoted with approval by the Lord Justice-Clerk (Aitchinson) in *Sugden v HM Advocate*, 1934 J.C. 103 at 113).

[8] See, e.g. the use of the term in s.76 of the Police and Criminal Evidence Act 1984 and the Court of Appeal's interpretation of the term in *R. v Fulling* [1987] Q.B 426, discussed in R. Munday, "The court, the dictionary and the true meaning of 'oppression': a neo-Socratic dialogue on English legal method" (2005) 26 Stat. L.R. 103–124. The interpretation of the 1984 Act is of little, if any, assistance here, but serves to demonstrate the malleability of the term.

[9] 1980 J.C. 111.

[10] At 112.

[11] 1980 J.C. 111 at 123, *per* the Lord Justice-General (Emslie) (Opinion of the Court) (emphasis added).

Mitchell v HM Advocate,[12] that "an examination of the authorities cited in the course of argument" (which included *Stuurman*) "demonstrates, in our view, that a plea of oppression can only be upheld if the alternative is that the accused person will be subject to such prejudice that he will not obtain a fair trial".[13] *Mitchell* was, in fact, not the most suitable case for such a point to be addressed. The court was clear that there was in any event "no appearance of injustice" in allowing the prosecution to proceed, meaning that counsel's argument based on the existence of an abuse of process doctrine would have failed in any event.

There are, in fact, a number of decisions of the appeal court which suggest that prosecutions may be halted on the ground of an abuse of process by the prosecution.[14] No coherent body of principles can yet be discerned from these cases, and it is convenient to deal with each of them in turn.

Cases Recognising Abuse of Process as a Basis for a Plea of Oppression

Mowbray v Crowe

Mowbray v Crowe[15] is the most important of the "abuse of process" cases. In this case, the accused (who was 17 years old) was cautioned and charged by the police. About four months later, the procurator fiscal wrote to her to advise her that a report had been received from the police. The fiscal's letter went on to say that "I am currently considering this matter but before I decide whether to institute Court proceedings against you I would be obliged if you would attend at this office in order that I may discuss the matter with you." The accused attended for interview as requested—without having been advised that she was not required to attend, might wish to take legal advice, and could be accompanied by a solicitor. Subsequently, a decision was taken to prosecute her: the appeal court held that the prosecution should be halted as oppressive. 19.04

The court approved a statement in Renton and Brown's *Criminal Procedure* that "Oppression arises when something is done in a cause which amounts to unfairness to the accused from which he is entitled to get relief",[16] and went on to state that:

> "We readily accept that the respondent has no intention of seeking to lead evidence of what the appellant may have said at the interview, but knowing what her defence is must give the Crown an advantage which they would not have had if the interview had not taken place. Not only that but it is well established that justice must not only be

---

12 2003 J.C. 89.

13 At [10] *per* Lord Macfadyen. For criticism of the case, see J. Chalmers, "Oppression and abuse of process" (2003) 8 S.L.P.Q. 232–236. There is, however, some support for the conclusion reached by the court in *Hamilton v Byrne*, 1997 S.L.T. 1210 at 1211, *per* the Lord Justice-General (Rodger).

14 See also the decision of Sheriff Boyle in *Normand v McQuillan*, 1987 S.C.C.R. 440 (Sh. Ct); the decision of Sheriff Stewart in *HM Advocate v Nairn*, 2000 S.L.T. (Sh Ct) 176 (discussed above, para.17.06), and *Beggs v HM Advocate*, 2001 S.C.C.R. 836 at [26], *per* Lord Coulsfield.

15 1993 J.C. 212.

16 At 218 *per* the Lord Justice-Clerk (Ross), citing Renton and Brown (5th edn), para.16–35. See now Renton and Brown, para.29–54.

done but must be seen to be done, and in our judgment justice is not seen to be done if the prosecutor has behaved in the way in which the respondent behaved in the present case by interviewing the appellant without warning her that she did not require to attend for interview nor advising her that she might wish to take legal advice and could be accompanied by a solicitor at the interview. By doing so he secured for the Crown an unfair advantage in any subsequent trial of the appellant on this complaint."[17]

19.05 The concept of an "unfair advantage" is not developed further by the court, and it might be interpreted as one possible formulation of a prejudice-based test. Two subsequent cases, however, make it clear that *Mowbray* can only be understood as having been decided on the basis of a disapproval of the prosecutor's conduct. In *Macdonald v Munro*[18] and *Sloan v Crowe*,[19] the Crown had instructed a psychiatric examination of the accused in order to comply with their statutory obligations under s.376(5) of the Criminal Procedure (Scotland) Act 1975.[20] In both cases, this had the incidental consequence that the Crown obtained details of the nature of the accused's defence. The appeal court held, however, that in neither case did this amount to an "unfair advantage" such as to ground a plea of oppression, the *Sloan* court stating that the case was not "in any respect analogous to the cases to which reference was made [including *Mowbray*], where there was no doubt that investigations had been carried out on behalf of the prosecutor for the sole purpose of informing the prosecutor about the circumstances of the offence".[21]

But if this distinction is to be drawn, the decision in *Mowbray* cannot be explained on the basis of prejudice alone, because the consequences of the prosecution obtaining advance notice of the accused's line of defence are unaffected by whether or not such notice has been legitimately or illegitimately obtained. If such notice is liable to place the accused at undue risk of a miscarriage of justice (and it is not clear why it should),[22] then it will do so regardless of the means by which it has been obtained. Accordingly, it is submitted that *Mowbray* should be regarded as recognising that the plea of oppression may extend to prevent a prosecution which is an abuse of process. In *Mitchell v HM Advocate*,[23] however, the appeal court appears to have accepted a submission by the advocate-depute that *Mowbray* "could not be regarded as setting up an alternative

---

[17] At 219 *per* the Lord Justice-Clerk (Ross).

[18] 1997 S.L.T. 446.

[19] 1996 S.L.T. 1094.

[20] "Where it appears to the prosecutor in any court before which a person is charged with an offence that the person may be suffering from mental disorder, it shall be the duty of such prosecutor to bring before the court such evidence as may be available of the mental condition of such person." See now CPSA 1995, s.52(1), which replaces "such prosecutor" and "such person" with "the prosecutor" and "that person" but is otherwise identically worded.

[21] 1996 S.L.T. 1094 at 1095–1096, *per* the Lord Justice-General (Hope).

[22] In *HM Advocate v O'Neill*, 1992 J.C. 22, the Lord Justice-General (Hope) appears to suggest that the prejudice test may be defined in this way. See 1992 J.C. 22 at 28 (referring to the court's "power to disallow procedure which, in its opinion, might lead to a miscarriage of justice").

[23] 2003 J.C. 89.

test" to that of prejudice, but the basis for this submission (or its acceptance) is not explained by the court and it is difficult to see how *Mowbray* can be interpreted otherwise.[24]

MacLeod v Tiffney

In *MacLeod v Tiffney*,[25] it was held to be a basis for a plea of oppression that the procurator fiscal had obtained information relevant to the accused's defence by, prior to his trial, extensively questioning him about a complaint he had made about the conduct of the police on the occasion in question.[26] Reference is made to the accused being prejudiced by this procedure, but it is not clear what the court means by "prejudice" in this context. The procedure employed might hamper the conduct of his defence in tactical terms, but it is difficult to see how it might place the accused at risk of wrongful conviction in the way that delay or adverse pretrial publicity might. **19.06**

In the subsequent case of *Normand v Ramage*,[27] the prosecution of two persons who had made statements regarding complaints about the police prior to their trial was held to be barred on the basis of oppression, but the prosecution of their two co-accused was not held to be barred in this way as "there was no basis for concluding that justice had not been seen to be done".[28] Significantly, the court was prepared to consider at some length whether there was a basis for the plea of oppression despite an express concession by counsel for the co-accused that they had not been prejudiced.

Bennett, Petr

In *Bennett, Petr*,[29] the accused had faced prosecution in England shortly beforehand. Before the English courts, he had successfully argued that his prosecution in England for various offences of dishonesty should be stayed as an abuse of process, because he had been brought from South Africa into the jurisdiction of the courts illegally and in disregard of extradition procedures.[30] This involved departing from a number of earlier decisions, including the Scottish case of *Sinclair v HM Advocate*,[31] according to which "the Scottish court cannot enquire into the actions of a foreign government and its officers which have resulted in the arrest **19.07**

---

[24] See also *Ucak v HM Advocate*, 1998 J.C. 283 at 289, *per* the Lord Justice-Clerk (Cullen), suggesting that the basis of *Mowbray* is that the principle that justice must be seen to be done had been breached by "the conduct of the prosecutor securing an unfair advantage over the accused".

[25] 1994 J.C. 77.

[26] Guidelines issued by the Lord Advocate around the time of the interview in this case make it clear that, where a complaint has been made against the police, "information obtained from that person at interview [should be] kept entirely separate from all persons involved in the prosecution of the charges which have been brought against him" (*MacLeod v Tiffney*, 1994 J.C. 77 at 87, *per* the Lord Justice-General (Hope)). Provided such procedures are followed, the fact that an accused person is interviewed about a complaint against the police prior to his trial will not in itself found a plea of oppression: see *Bott v Anderson*, 1995 S.L.T. 1308.

[27] 1995 S.L.T. 130.

[28] 1995 S.L.T. 130 at 133, *per* the Lord Justice-Clerk (Ross).

[29] 1995 S.L.T. 510.

[30] See *R. v Horseferry Road Magistrates' Court, ex parte Bennett* [1994] 1 A.C. 42. Following the decision of the Appellate Committee, the Divisional Court quashed Bennett's committal for trial after hearing evidence: see *Bennett, Petr*, 1995 S.L.T. 510 at 513, *per* the Lord Justice-General (Hope).

[31] (1890) 17 R. (J.) 38.

there and delivery into the hands of an authorised officer here of a person who has been charged with crimes in this country".[32]

Bennett was subsequently prosecuted in Scotland for other offences. The Lord Advocate made independent inquiries into the alleged disregard of extradition procedures and took the view, contrary to the assumption on which the English proceedings had taken place, that no impropriety had occurred. The appeal court held that this was a view which the Lord Advocate was entitled to reach, and that this was the end of the matter. The court indicated, however, that had the facts of the case been different, "we would have wished the decision in *Sinclair v HM Advocate* to be reviewed by a larger court", as there "may well be room . . . for regarding at least some of the dicta in *Sinclair*, if not the decision itself, as out of line with modern thinking on this subject not only in England but in other legal systems".[33] While these comments are necessarily tentative, they do appear to suggest that the Scottish courts should have some power to halt proceedings on the basis of abuse of process,[34] there being no suggestion that Bennett could not have received a fair trial.[35]

Grugen v Jessop

19.08 *Grugen v Jessop*[36] concerned the statutory rule that a person charged with a summary offence shall not be detained for more than 40 days (subject to the sheriff's power to extend the period), unless his trial is commenced within that period.[37] Here, the procurator fiscal had commenced a trial shortly before the end of that period, in the knowledge it could not be finished that day due to the unavailability of certain witnesses. After leading the available witnesses, she moved for an adjournment and opposed the granting of bail to the accused. The accused appealed against the sheriff's decision to grant the adjournment and refuse bail, arguing that the procurator fiscal's actions amounted to an abuse of process. The court was prepared to entertain this argument in its own terms: "[t]he question for us really is whether what happened on that day can properly be described as an abuse of process",[38] but concluded that it was not, noting that the procurator fiscal would almost certainly have been granted an extension of the 40-day period had she requested one instead of commencing the trial,[39] and that the delay in holding the trial was in part due to the accused's failure to attend for trial at an earlier date. Although this case proceeds on the explicit assumption that the

---

[32] *Bennett, Petr*, 1995 S.L.T. 510 at 515, *per* the Lord Justice-General (Hope) (describing *Sinclair* as "clear authority" for this view).

[33] *Bennett, Petr*, 1995 S.L.T. 510 at 517, *per* the Lord Justice-General (Hope). See also *Torres v HM Advocate*, 1998 S.L.T. 811 at 816, *per* the Lord Justice-Clerk (Cullen).

[34] See C. Gane and S. Nash, "Illegal extradition: the irregular return of fugitive offenders" (1996) 1 S.L.P.Q. 277–304. This is the basis on which Bennett's prosecution in England had been halted: *R. v Horseferry Road Magistrates' Court, ex parte Bennett* [1994] 1 A.C. 42.

[35] See also *HM Advocate v Vervuren*, 2002 S.L.T. 555, where the trial judge considered herself bound by *Bennett* but in any event was not satisfied that the accused's allegations that his human rights had been breached in the process of extradition had been made out.

[36] 1988 S.C.C.R. 182.

[37] See now CPSA 1995, s.147, which is discussed in Ch.16.

[38] 1988 S.C.C.R. 182 at 185, *per* the Lord Justice-General (Emslie).

[39] If it had not been possible to extend the time limit in this way, it might have been argued that the prosecutor's actions were an exploitation of a legislative loophole such as to amount to an abuse of process. *Cf. R. (Wardle) v Leeds Crown Court* [2001] UKHL 12; *R. v J* [2004] UKHL 42; *M v HM Advocate*, 2006 J.C. 71.

Scottish courts have jurisdiction to intervene in respect of an abuse of process by the prosecution—and is a rare example of the Scottish courts directly using the terminology "abuse of process"—it has not been influential. It appears to be referred to in only one other reported case, and for a completely different point.[40]

Benton v Cardle

In *Benton v Cardle*,[41] the accused had been stopped while driving. He gave two breath samples to the police, both of which were analysed as showing a level of 37 microgrammes of alcohol per 100 millilitres of breath. These readings could not have formed the basis for a prosecution for driving with excess alcohol, as the Crown Agent had previously stated that prosecutions would not be brought on the basis of breath/alcohol readings of less than 40 microgrammes.[42] The accused did not know this, however, and was informed by the police of his right to substitute a sample of blood.[43] He availed himself of that right, and was prosecuted for driving with excess alcohol on the basis of the reading obtained from his blood sample. The appeal court held that the sheriff should have sustained a plea to the competency of the complaint: "the conduct of the police in this case, by drawing the attention of the appellant to his right [to give a sample of blood] at a time when the Crown had disabled itself from prosecuting him, amounted to unfairness and oppression of such a nature that the prosecution should not be allowed to proceed".[44] This may be regarded as a decision based on abuse of process: it may alternatively be regarded as a decision based on the blood sample having been unfairly obtained (although why it would be appropriate to deal with such an issue as one of competency rather than admissibility of evidence is unclear). It was followed in the later case of *McConnachie v Scott*[45] where the accused had pled guilty to driving with excess alcohol on the basis of similar facts, but the appeal court was nevertheless prepared to quash his conviction. **19.09**

Brown v HM Advocate

In *Brown v HM Advocate*,[46] the appeal court held that the court has the power to halt a prosecution on the basis of entrapment (an issue which is discussed elsewhere in this book).[47] The court was heavily influenced by the decision of the Appellate Committee in *R. v Loosely*,[48] which had held that a prosecution of a crime committed as a result of entrapment might be stayed as an abuse of process. Given that *Loosely* is predicated on the basis of an inherent jurisdiction to stay proceedings as an abuse of process, it would seem to follow that the *Brown* court proceeded on the assumption that the Scottish courts also possess such a power (and Lord Clarke specifically approved Lord Nicholls' statement in *Loosely* that **19.10**

[40] *Hazlett v McGlennan*, 1993 S.L.T. 74, which is concerned with the calculation of time as concerns the 40-day period. See para.16.03.
[41] 1988 S.L.T. 310.
[42] See above, para.17.11.
[43] Road Traffic Act 1972, s.8; *Woodburn v McLeod*, 1986 S.L.T. 325.
[44] At 313 *per* the Lord Justice-Clerk (Ross).
[45] 1988 S.L.T. 480.
[46] 2002 S.L.T. 809.
[47] See Ch.20.
[48] [2001] UKHL 53.

"[e]very court has an inherent power and duty to prevent abuse of its process").[49] In *Mitchell v HM Advocate*, however, the appeal court appeared to accept a submission by the advocate-depute that the *ratio* of *Brown* should be confined to the "discrete subject" of entrapment,[50] although it is doubtful whether the approach taken in *Brown* can, as a matter of principle, be restricted in this way.[51]

M v HM Advocate

19.10A In *M v HM Advocate*,[51a] the Crown brought a prosecution for rape but invited the jury to convict instead of the statutory offence of unlawful sexual intercourse with a girl aged between 13 and 16.[51b] At the time, prosecutions for the latter offence could only be commenced within a year of the offence,[51c] a period which had elapsed before the prosecution for rape had begun. M appealed against conviction, arguing that the Crown's actions were improper as a circumvention of the statutory time bar.[51d] In refusing the appeal, Lord Hamilton remarked that:

> "Where in Scotland the Crown prosecute on a charge of rape . . . it is right to assume, in the absence of compelling reasons to the contrary, that they do so on the basis, first, that they have before them information which, in the considered judgment of Crown counsel, supports such a charge and, second, that it is in the public interest to prosecute on that charge."[51e]

Although the point is not developed further by the court, this might be taken to imply that, if there *were* reason to contest these assumptions, the prosecution could be challenged as oppressive and an abuse of process: otherwise, these observations are meaningless and irrelevant.[51f]

What Should Amount to an Abuse of Process?

19.11 Although, as noted above, there are various decisions of the appeal court which support the proposition that abuse of process should be recognised in Scots law, it is far from clear exactly what might be held to be an abuse of process. The only two situations that are clearly recognised are those where the prosecution has improperly obtained information about the

---

[49] 2002 S.L.T. 809 at [5], *per* Lord Clarke (citing *R. v Loosely* [2001] UKHL 53 at [1], *per* Lord Nicholls of Birkenhead). See also *per* Lord Philip at [14]–[15]. Lord Marnoch, by contrast, held (at [12]) that "the nature of unfairness in entrapment, namely conviction of a crime artificially created by the agents of the State, can, I think, readily be seen as a form of prejudice to the accused". This approach, however, necessarily involves a wider interpretation of the term "prejudice" than has hitherto been found in the Scottish cases, and so is probably no different in substance from the other members of the court.

[50] See 2003 J.C. 89 at [9], *per* Lord Macfadyen.

[51] J. Chalmers, "Oppression and abuse of process" (2003) 8 S.L.P.Q. 232–236 at p.235.

[51a] 2006 J.C. 71.

[51b] Criminal Law (Consolidation) (Scotland) Act 1995, s.5(3).

[51c] Criminal Law (Consolidation) (Scotland) Act 1995, s.5(4), which was repealed by the Protection of Children and Prevention of Sexual Offences (Scotland) Act 2005, s.15.

[51d] Relying, inter alia, on *R. v J* [2004] UKHL 42.

[51e] At [13].

[51f] *Cf. Webster v Dominick*, 2005 J.C. 65 at [60], *per* the Lord Justice-Clerk (Gill), where concern is expressed about the possible use of charges of "shameless indecency" (an offence effectively abolished by the *Dominick* court) to circumvent the time-bar under s.5(4) of the Criminal Law (Consolidation) (Scotland) Act 2005.

nature of the accused's defence,[52] and (perhaps) those situations where the accused has been brought into the jurisdiction of the court in disregard of extradition procedures.[53]

Unsurprisingly, no general test has been formulated by the courts given their reluctance to acknowledge any such general jurisdiction. The closest is the *Mowbray v Crowe*[54] court's comments that "justice must not only be done but must be seen to be done",[55] but that is not a concrete test which may be readily applied to particular scenarios. Nor, however, are alternative tests based on such considerations as whether "the affront to fair play and decency [in compelling an accused to stand trial] is disproportionate to the societal interest in the effective prosecution of criminal cases"[56] or whether the prosecution is an "affront to the public conscience".[57]

It is doubtful that any particularly precise test can be formulated. Inevitably, any abuse of process jurisdiction will be required to address a "panoply of diverse and sometimes unforeseeable circumstances",[58] and it will be necessary for any claims of abuse of process to be decided both by reference to a general test and by analogy with previous decisions. Should the Scottish courts develop the doctrine of abuse of process beyond the embryonic form in which it has been recognised to date, it may be that useful lessons can be drawn from decided cases elsewhere.[59] It is unlikely that any abuse of process doctrine will operate to bar a prosecution where the alleged abuse is the result of the conduct of private individuals acting independently of the state.[60]

The Justification for Recognising an Abuse of Process Jurisdiction

Because Scots law already recognises the plea of oppression where the **19.12** accused's right to a fair trial has been prejudiced (and recognises an at least analogous plea in cases of entrapment), any abuse of process jurisdiction would necessarily be residual and would not operate to protect the accused's right to a fair trial or any associated procedural right. As such, it operates not to protect the accused but to prevent the court from becoming complicit in unacceptable behaviour on the part of the state:

> "The court is, in effect, saying it cannot condone or be seen to lend a stamp of approval to behaviour which transcends what our society perceives to be acceptable on the part of the state. The stay of the prosecution of the accused is the manifestation of the court's disapproval of the state's conduct. In this way, the benefit to the accused is really a derivative one."[61]

[52] *Mowbray v Crowe*, 1993 J.C. 212; *MacLeod v Tiffney*, 1994 J.C. 77.
[53] *Bennett, Petr*, 1995 S.L.T. 510.
[54] 1993 J.C. 212.
[55] At 219 *per* the Lord Justice-Clerk (Ross).
[56] *R. v Conway* [1989] 1 S.C.R. 1659 at [22], *per* L'Heureux-Dubé J.
[57] *R. v Latif* [1996] 1 W.L.R. 104 at 113, *per* Lord Steyn.
[58] *R. v O'Connor* [1995] 4 S.C.R. 411 at [73], *per* L'Heureux-Dubé J.
[59] For English law, see, generally, D. Corker and D. Young, *Abuse of Process and Fairness in Criminal Proceedings* (2nd edn, 2003).
[60] See also the discussion of "private entrapment" below, paras 20.27–20.29.
[61] *R. v Mack* [1988] 2 S.C.R. 903 at [77], *per* Lamer J.

In the English case of *DPP v Humphrys*,[62] Viscount Dilhorne argued that there were "considerable dangers" in recognising a power inherent in the court to halt a prosecution as an abuse of process:

> "A judge must keep out of the arena. He should not have or appear to have any responsibility for the institution of a prosecution. The functions of prosecutors and of judges must not be blurred. If a judge has power to decline to hear a case because he does not think it should be brought, then it soon may be thought that the cases he allows to proceed are cases brought with his consent or approval."[63]

19.13 It may be that the fears of Viscount Dilhorne are too strongly stated: provided that the abuse of process jurisdiction is restricted to exceptional and flagrant abuses, it does not involve affording the court any general power to review the exercise of prosecutorial discretion.[64] Nevertheless, the English courts of appeal have, in recent years, regularly found it necessary to remind lower courts that the power to halt a prosecution as an abuse of process is only to be exercised in the most exceptional circumstances:

> "The question whether or not to prosecute is for the prosecutor. Most of the points relied on in support of an argument of abuse [of process] are more properly to be relied on as mitigation. If a prosecutor obtains a conviction in a case which the court feels on reasonable grounds should never have been brought, the court can reflect that conclusion in the penalty it imposes. The circumstances in which it can intervene to stop the prosecution, however, are very limited indeed. At present many applications to stay are made in quite inappropriate circumstances. Sometimes courts are wrongly persuaded to accede ... It should be generally appreciated that a successful application to stay which leads to a successful appeal by the prosecutor renders the client no service."[65]

19.14 Despite the concerns expressed by Viscount Dilhorne, however, the power of the English courts to stay a prosecution as an abuse of process has now been clearly recognised,[66] notwithstanding a significant rearguard action by some of the most senior members of the judiciary.[67] A

---

62 [1977] A.C. 1.

63 At 26.

64 See *DPP v Humphrys* [1977] A.C. 1 at 46, *per* Lord Salmon.

65 *Environment Agency v Stanford*, June 30, 1998, DC, unreported, *per* Lord Bingham of Cornhill C.J. See also *R. (on the application of Tunbridge Wells Borough Council) v Sevenoaks Magistrates' Court* [2001] EWHC Admin 897 at [52], *per* Rose L.J.; *Dacorum Borough Council v El-Kalyoubi* [2001] EWHC Admin 1052 at [34], *per* Kennedy L.J.

66 See, in particular, *Connelly v DPP* [1964] A.C. 1254 at 1296, *per* Lord Reid, at 1354, *per* Lord Devlin, and at 1365, *per* Lord Pearce; *DPP v Humphrys* [1977] A.C. 1 at 45–46, *per* Lord Salmon, and at 55, *per* Lord Edmund-Davies; *R. v Horseferry Road Magistrates' Court, ex parte Bennett* [1994] 1 A.C. 42; *R. v Loosely* [2001] UKHL 53. See also *Mills v Cooper* [1967] 2 Q.B. 459 at 467, *per* Lord Parker C.J.; *R. v Thomson Holidays Ltd* [1974] Q.B. 592; *Hunter v Chief Constable of the West Midlands Police* [1982] A.C. 529 at 536, *per* Lord Diplock.

67 In addition to Viscount Dilhorne's comments, see *Connelly v DPP* [1964] A.C. 1254 at 1300, *per* Lord Morris, and at 1337–1338, *per* Lord Hodson; *R. v Horseferry Road Magistrates' Court, ex parte Bennett* [1994] 1 A.C. 42 at 70–71, *per* Lord Oliver of Aylmerton. See also *R. v Chairman, County of London Quarter Sessions, ex parte Downes* [1954] 1 Q.B. 1 at 6, *per* Lord Goddard C.J.

similar jurisdiction has been recognised by the courts of other Commonwealth jurisdictions,[68] although the Supreme Court of Canada has more recently demonstrated a reluctance to grant a stay of proceedings where a fair trial remains possible and further proceedings will not perpetuate the abuse of process.[69] Such doubts disclose an inevitable discomfort with the purpose of any abuse of process jurisdiction: although it "protect[s] the communal interest in judicial integrity by not condoning oppressive state conduct", it means that the accused receives "an undeserved windfall from the perspective of corrective justice".[70]

It has been necessary for the courts and the legislature to develop safeguards against abuse of the processes of the civil courts because the right of access to a civil court is not normally in the hands of a public prosecutor who may be presumed to act responsibly.[71] The fact that abusive prosecutions are hardly ever brought in the criminal courts should not, however, detract from the constitutional importance of the residual power of the courts to halt such prosecutions if necessary.[72] It should instead serve to emphasise that any abuse of process jurisdiction is one which should be exercised sparingly, and only in the most exceptional cases. In English law, abuse of process plays a necessarily residual role but encompasses, perhaps most significantly, breach of promises not to prosecute and cases of entrapment,[73] both of which are recognised in their own right as bars to proceedings in Scotland.[74] Accordingly, any residual role for abuse of process in the Scottish courts is likely to be very small indeed.

[68] In Australia, see *Barton v The Queen* (1980) 147 C.L.R. 75. In New Zealand, see *Moevao v Department of Labour* [1980] N.Z.L.R. 464; *Fox v Attorney-General* [2002] 3 N.Z.L.R. 62.

[69] See K. Roach, "The Attorney General and the Charter revisited" (2000) 50 *University of Toronto Law Journal* 1–40 at pp.9–12, citing *Canada v Tobiass* [1997] 3 S.C.R. 391; *R. v Curragh* [1997] 1 S.C.R. 537; *R. v Latimer* [1997] 1 S.C.R. 217. See also *R. v Regan* [2002] 1 S.C.R. 297.

[70] Roach, fn.69 above, at p.11.

[71] *cf. Connelly v DPP* [1964] A.C. 1254 at 1357, *per* Lord Devlin (noting the civil courts' attempts to extend the doctrine of *res judicata*): "I think it is likely that there would have been a similar development in criminal procedure, had it not been that prosecutions fell largely into the hands of public authorities, who in practice impose restrictions on themselves."

[72] See *DPP v Humphrys* [1977] A.C. 1 at 46, *per* Lord Salmon.

[73] See, generally, D. Corker and D. Young, *Abuse of Process and Fairness in Criminal Proceedings* (2nd edn, 2003); A. L.-T. Choo, *Abuse of Process and Judicial Stays of Criminal Proceedings* (1993).

[74] See above, Ch.17 (renunciation) and below, Ch.20 (entrapment). The English doctrine of abuse of process may, however, extend in some cases to a breach of a promise by the police (rather than the prosecutor) not to prosecute: see, in particular *R. v Croydon Justices, ex parte Dean* [1993] Q.B. 769. This would not be within the scope of the Scottish plea that the prosecutor has renounced the right to prosecute: see above, para.17.08.

Chapter 20

ENTRAPMENT

Introduction

Entrapment is a claim by the accused that he was induced by deception into committing a criminal offence. Most commonly, the deception is on the part of a police officer or other state official,[1] but in some jurisdictions entrapment has been claimed where the entrapper was a private citizen, such as a journalist.[2] **20.01**

Claims of entrapment tend to arise where the authorities are more likely to resort to covert policing methods for the detection of criminal activity, such as in the detection of victimless crimes or crimes that victims are reluctant to report.[3] As such, the vast majority of reported cases have involved either the supply of prohibited drugs[4] or the breach of alcohol licensing regulations.[5]

The treatment of entrapment has divided the common law legal world. In the federal jurisdiction of the United States, it is regarded as a substantive defence.[6] In England and Wales and Canada it is treated as a matter that should lead to a stay of proceedings.[7] In Australia and New Zealand it is regarded as a matter relating to the exclusion of evidence.[8] The approach taken by Scots law changed recently, in *Brown v HM Advocate*.[9] Prior to *Brown*, Scots law had taken the exclusion of evidence approach. In *Brown*, however, the appeal court held that entrapment, if proven, should lead to a stay of proceedings, bringing Scotland into line with England and Canada.

To date, there has been little discussion of entrapment in the Scottish context.[10] Even in the most recent edition of Gordon, coverage is limited **20.02**

---

[1] For some this would be a definitional requirement. See G. Dworkin, "The serpent beguiled me and I did eat: entrapment and the creation of crime" (1985) 4 *Law and Philosophy* 17–33 at p.17.

[2] See paras 20.27 *et seq*.

[3] Either because the offence is consensual or because the victim is reluctant to bring his affairs to the attention of the authorities. See A. L.-T.Choo, *Abuse of Process and Judicial Stays of Criminal Proceedings* (1993), pp.148–149; J.D. Heydon, "The problems of entrapment" [1973] C.L.J. 268–286 at pp.269–270.

[4] *HM Advocate v Harper*, 1989 S.C.C.R. 472 (Sh. Ct); *Weir v Jessop*, 1991 J.C. 146; *R. v Loosely, Attorney General's Reference (No.3 of 2000)* [2001] UKHL 53 (the leading case in England and Wales, a decision of the House of Lords).

[5] *Marsh v Johnston*, 1959 S.L.T. (Notes) 28; *Cook v Skinner*, *MacDonald v Skinner*, 1977 J.C. 9.

[6] See para.20.07.

[7] See para.20.09.

[8] That is, evidence obtained by entrapment will be excluded, but, assuming that other evidence is available, the trial will continue. See para.20.08. For discussion of the merits of each of these approaches, see paras 20.07–20.09.

[9] 2002 S.L.T. 809.

[10] Prior to *Brown*, see C. Fraser, "Undercover law enforcement in Scots law", 1994 S.L.T. (News) 113–118, discussing the decision in *Weir v Jessop*, 1991 J.C. 146. For limited comment on *Brown*, see S. Christie, "Conspiracy and entrapment" (2002) 70 S.L.G. 109–110. Entrapment is not mentioned in the Draft Criminal Code.

to a single paragraph,[11] although this is understandable, given that the text was written before *Brown*, when entrapment was still treated as a matter relating to the exclusion of evidence. The absence of discussion in Scotland is compensated for to some extent by academic comment in other jurisdictions. The decision of the House of Lords in *R. v Loosely, Attorney General's Reference (No.3 of 2000)*[12] and the European Court of Human Rights in *Teixeira de Castro v Portugal*[13] both attracted a flurry of academic comment.[14] The plea has also been extensively discussed in the US, where, until recently, there was a divergence of opinion between a majority and minority of the Supreme Court.[15]

Theoretical Basis

20.03 There are a number of possible justifications for the acquittal of someone who has been entrapped into engaging in what would otherwise have been criminal conduct.[16] One possibility is that the entrapped accused is insufficiently morally blameworthy to merit a criminal conviction, entrapment operating as an excuse defence on the basis that the accused has been tricked into performing an act he would not otherwise have performed.

Although critics have been quick to demolish this idea,[17] it is difficult to find any published work in which the authors argue seriously that this is the reason why entrapment should acquit.[18] Whereas there may be cases in which the deceptive practices of police officers are so coercive that the accused cannot be blamed for giving in, these cases can be subsumed under the substantive defence of coercion.[19] Where the conduct of police officers does not go so far as to constitute coercion, then, as Altman and

[11] See para.9.21, where Gordon simply notes that Scots law "may recognise a limited form of a defence of entrapment" or at least may accept that evidence is inadmissible when obtained by entrapment.

[12] [2001] UKHL 53.

[13] (1998) 28 E.H.R.R. 101.

[14] On *Loosely*, see A. Ashworth, "Testing fidelity to legal values" in *Criminal Law Theory: Doctrines of the General Part* (S. Shute and A.P. Simester (eds), 2002), pp.299–330; A. Ashworth, "Re-drawing the boundaries of entrapment" [2002] Crim. L.R. 161–179; S. Bronitt, "The law in undercover policing: a comparative study of entrapment and covert interviewing in Australia, Canada and Europe" (2004) 33 *Common Law World Review* 35–80; S. McKay, "Entrapment: competing views on the effect of the Human Rights Act on English criminal law" (2002) 6 E.H.R.L.R. 764–774. On *Teixeira*, see A. Ashworth and M. Strange, "Criminal law and human rights in 2002" (2003) 2 E.H.R.L.R. 139–156; C. Barsby and D.C. Ormerod, "Entrapment: police officers posing as drug users" [2002] Crim. L.R. 301–304; D. Ormerod and A. Roberts, "The trouble with *Teixeira*: developing a principled approach to entrapment" (2002) 6 *International Journal of Evidence and Proof* 38–61.

[15] See para.20.07.

[16] For a discussion far more detailed than we provide here, see the special issue of the *Journal of Social Issues* devoted to entrapment: (1987) 43(3).

[17] See, e.g. C.D. Moore, "The elusive foundation of the entrapment defense" (1995) 89 *Northwestern University Law Review* 1151–1188 (devoting a whole paper to criticism of the notion that entrapment is an excuse defence); A. Altman and S. Lee, "Legal entrapment" (1983) 12 *Philosophy and Public Affairs* 51–69 at p.59; Ashworth, "Testing fidelity to legal values", fn.14 above, at p.322; L. Katz, *Bad Acts and Guilty Minds* (1987), p.158.

[18] One exception is R.J. Allen, M. Luttrell and A. Kreeger, "Clarifying entrapment" (1999) 89 *Journal of Criminal Law and Criminology* 407–431 at p.420.

[19] For an example, see the Ontario Court of Appeal case of *R. v Woods* [1969] 3 C.C.C. 222. For discussion of coercion, see Ch.5.

Lee state, "[t]he fact that someone is tempted into some reprehensible action by another does not in general relieve the first person of responsibility for the action".[20]

A second possibility is that entrapment should acquit because this will deter wrongful conduct on the part of state officials.[21] This was the only rationale contemplated by the English Law Commission when they last considered the issue.[22]

There are at least two difficulties with this argument. The first is that it **20.04** is not at all clear that ordering an acquittal is the best way of achieving this result.[23] A more effective deterrent would surely be the threat of disciplinary procedures for the individual officers concerned. The second is that it simply does not explain what is so wrong with conduct constituting entrapment that it is important to deter it in the first place.[24]

A third possible rationale for recognising the entrapment defence relates to preserving the integrity of the criminal justice process. The argument is that the moral authority and legitimacy of the court is compromised if it acts on the basis of the wrongful practices of law enforcement officers.[25] The difficulty with this argument is that, like the argument based on deterrence, it fails to explain what is so wrong about entrapment that it would compromise the integrity of the courts to prosecute a case in which it had occurred.

The answer to this question can be found in a number of inter-linked reasons. The first is that it is inconsistent and hypocritical for the state to prohibit crime on one hand while encouraging it on the other. As well as being a waste of state resources (which are, after all, obtained from taxpayers),[26] it destroys the coherence of the criminal justice system if one part of the system creates crime simply for another part of the system to punish it.[27]

The second is that it seems to offend the rule of law to allow law **20.05** enforcement officers to themselves engage in unlawful activity solely for the purpose of inducing others to commit criminal offences.[28]

---

[20] Altman and Lee, above, fn.17, at p.59. That is not to say that culpability is *never* reduced by entrapment, just that it is insufficiently reduced to merit a complete defence. See *Jacobson v United States*, 503 U.S. 540 (1992), where the defendant's culpability was surely reduced by the persistent attempts of the authorities to persuade him to purchase pornographic images of young boys.

[21] P. Mullock, "The logic of entrapment" (1985) 46 *University of Pittsburgh Law Review* 739–752.

[22] In *Report on Defences of General Application* (Law Com. No. 83, 1977), at paras 5.1–5.54. Scepticism about this rationale led the Law Commission to reject the defence entirely. For criticism, see A. Ashworth, "Entrapment" [1978] Crim. L.R. 137–140; D. Birch, "Excluding evidence from entrapment: what is a fair cop?" (1994) 47 *Current Legal Problems* 73–99 at p.82.

[23] See Ashworth, "Testing fidelity to legal values", fn.14 above, at p.317; J.C. Carlson, "The act requirement and the foundations of the entrapment defense" (1987) 72 *Virginia Law Review* 1011–1108 at p.1919; R.A. Duff, "I might be guilty, but you can't try me: estoppel and other bars to trial" (2003) 1 *Ohio State Journal of Criminal Law* 245–259 at p.252.

[24] See Duff, fn.23 above, at p.252.

[25] See A. Ashworth, "Re-drawing the boundaries of entrapment" [2002] Crim. L.R. 161–179 at p.162.

[26] M.F.J. Whelan, "Lead us not into (unwarranted) temptation: a proposal to replace the entrapment defense with a reasonable suspicion requirement" (1985) 133 *University of Pennsylvania Law Review* 1193–1230 at p.1213.

[27] Duff, fn.23 above, at p.252; G. Dworkin, "The serpent beguiled me and I did eat: entrapment and the creation of crime" (1985) 4 *Law and Philosophy* 17–33 at p.24.

[28] A. Ashworth, "Testing fidelity to legal values" in *Criminal Law Theory: Doctrines of the General Part* (S. Shute and A.P. Simester (eds), 2002), pp.299–330, at p.319.

The third is the possibility that entrapment techniques could be used as a tool of political oppression. Permitting entrapment carries with it the danger of abuse of state power, allowing, for example, the harassment of those whose lifestyles or political beliefs have offended a state official.[29]

The fourth is that entrapment threatens privacy and physical and mental integrity. It has been argued that citizens are surely entitled to get on with their lives free of state interference unless they forfeit this right by giving rise to a reasonable suspicion that they have committed a crime. If traps are set for people who have done nothing to arouse the reasonable suspicions of the authorities, this infringes their right to security of the person for no good reason.[30]

20.06 All of these four justifications together explain why the integrity of the criminal justice system would be compromised if the courts permitted a prosecution to take place where entrapment had occurred.[31]

The integrity argument has found favour with the House of Lords. In *Loosely*,[32] Lord Nicholls stated that:

> "Every court has an inherent power and duty to prevent abuse of its process. This is a fundamental principle of the rule of law. By recourse to this principle courts ensure that executive agents of the state do not misuse the coercive, law enforcement functions of the courts and thereby oppress citizens of the state. Entrapment . . . is an instance where such misuse may occur. It is simply not acceptable that the state through its agents should lure its citizens into committing acts forbidden by the law and then seek to prosecute them for doing so. That would be entrapment. That would be a misuse of state power, and an abuse of the process of the courts."[33]

No doubt influenced by *Loosely*, this was also the rationale adopted by the appeal court in *Brown*. Lord Clarke made the argument most explicitly:

> "It does seem to me that it is for the court, in any civilised system of criminal jurisprudence, to seek to ensure that the police, or prosecuting authority, in that system, in exercising their powers and in performing their duties, do not descend to methods which cross the line from detecting crime and pursuing criminals, to instigating criminal conduct by provoking or inciting persons to commit crimes. To countenance such conduct, once it is identified, may be to countenance the pollution of the moral integrity of the machinery of justice."[34]

---

[29] J. Braithwaite, B. Fisse and G. Geis, "Covert facilitation and crime: restoring balance to the entrapment debate" (1987) 43 *Journal of Social Issues* 5–41 at p.9; A. Altman and S. Lee "Legal entrapment" (1983) 12 *Philosophy and Public Affairs* 51–69 at p.52.

[30] Braithwaite *et al*, fn.29 above, at p.9; Whelan, fn.26 above, at p.1213. Although *cf.* K. Hofmeyr, "The problem of private entrapment" [2006] Crim. L.R. 319–336 at p.334 and D. Squires, "The problem with entrapment" (2006) 26 O.J.L.S. 351–376 at p.370.

[31] This does, of course, assume that the criminal justice system has such a unity that the later stages of the process—and especially the trial—are compromised if there has been wrongdoing by the police at an earlier stage. See Ashworth, "Testing fidelity to legal values", fn.28 above, at p.319.

[32] *R. v Loosely, Attorney General's Reference (No.3 of 2000)* [2001] UKHL 53.

[33] At [1], a passage adopted by Lord Philip in *Brown v HM Advocate*, 2002 S.L.T. 809 at [10].

[34] *Brown v HM Advocate*, 2002 S.L.T. 809 at [2].

PROCEDURAL BASIS

A substantive defence?

20.07 One possibility is that entrapment can operate as a substantive defence to a criminal charge in the same way as, for example, coercion or necessity. If one takes the view that entrapment operates to reduce culpability, then a substantive defence would be the logical remedy.

This is the approach taken in the federal jurisdiction of the US, although the basis claimed for the defence is unconvincing, relating not to a lack of culpability as such, but to a principle of statutory interpretation.[35] In a line of cases stemming from *Sorrells v United States*,[36] a majority of the US Supreme Court has consistently held that entrapment entitles the accused to a complete acquittal on the basis that all criminal statutes should be read as excluding the entrapped individual from their scope.[37]

What the Supreme Court does not do is explain exactly why the entrapped individual should be regarded as lying outside the scope of criminal statutory provisions. The justifications advanced in *Sorrells*, such as they are, seem to relate more to the abuse of government power than to any lack of culpability on the part of the accused.[38] As such, the approach of the majority has been criticised as a fiction by academic commentators[39] and by a line of minority judgments of the Supreme Court, which favour an approach to entrapment based on abuse of process.[40]

A ground upon which evidence can be excluded?

20.08 A second approach is to exclude evidence obtained by entrapment on the basis that it would be unfair to the accused to admit this evidence. This was the approach of the Scottish and English courts until relatively

---

35 A rationale that would sit uneasily in Scotland, given that the vast majority of the criminal law is not statutory.

36 287 U.S. 435 (1932).

37 For a detailed account of the history and development of the defence of entrapment by the US Supreme Court, see: F.W. Bennett, "From *Sorrells* to *Jacobson*: reflections on six decades of entrapment law and related defenses in federal court" (1992) 27 *Wake Forest Law Review* 829–870; D.D. Camp, "Out of the quagmire after *Jacobson v United States*: towards a more balanced entrapment standard" (1993) 83 *Journal of Criminal Law and Criminology* 1055–1097; J.D. Lombardo, "Causation and objective entrapment: towards a culpability-centred approach" (1995) 43 *UCLA Law Review* 209–261; P. Mullock, "The logic of entrapment" (1985) 46 *University of Pittsburgh Law Review* 739–752; R. Roiphe, "The serpent beguiled me: a history of the entrapment defense" (2003) 33 *Seton Hall Law Review* 257–302.

38 See Hughes J. at 448 and 452 of *Sorrells v United States*, 287 U.S. 435 (1932).

39 J.C. Carlson, "The act requirement and the foundations of the entrapment defense" (1987) 72 *Virginia Law Review* 1011–1108 at p.1038; L. Katz, *Bad Acts and Guilty Minds* (1987), p.158.

40 See, e.g. the dissenting opinions of Roberts J. in *Sorrells v United States*, 287 U.S. 435 (1932) at 456; Frankfurter J. in *Sherman v United States*, 356 U.S. 369 (1958) at 379; Stewart J. in *United States v Russell*, 411 U.S. 423 (1973) at 441–442; Brennan J. in *Hampton v United States*, 425 U.S. 484 (1976) at 496.

recently[41] and is still the approach taken by the High Court in Australia[42] and in New Zealand.[43]

The exclusion of evidence approach has found some support among academic commentators, albeit primarily those who were writing before *Loosely* was decided.[44] The approach has been criticised on two fronts. The first is that it potentially produces arbitrary and, therefore, unfair results.[45] The second is that it misses the point that it is the *offence* that is manufactured by the State, not solely the evidence of the State official. The exclusion of the evidence does not address the issue that, without State intervention, there would have been no crime in the first place.[46]

A ground for ordering a stay of proceedings?

20.09 A third procedural option for dealing with cases in which entrapment has been established is to stay the proceedings. This is not the same as regarding entrapment as a substantive defence. A stay of proceedings indicates not that the accused is innocent, but that it is an accusation he should not have to answer in court due to some factor that makes the trial as a whole illegitimate.[47]

This was the minority view of the US Supreme Court for a long time[48] and it is the well-established approach taken to entrapment by the Canadian Supreme Court.[49] Indeed, if one accepts that entrapment is not about culpability, but rather that it is about compromising the integrity of

---

[41] Until *R. v Loosely, Attorney General's Reference (No.3 of 2000)* [2001] UKHL 53 in England and *Brown v HM Advocate*, 2002 S.L.T. 809 in Scotland. See paras 20.12–20.13 (England) and paras 20.10–20.11 (Scotland).

[42] *Ridgeway v The Queen* (1995) 184 C.L.R. 19 (although see the dissenting opinions of Toohey J., Gaudron J. and McHugh J.). *Ridgeway* was approved relatively recently (albeit before *Loosely* was decided in the House of Lords) in *Nicholas v The Queen* [1998] H.C.A. 9. For comment on *Ridgeway*, see K. Grevling, "Illegality, entrapment and a new discretion" (1996) 112 L.Q.R. 41–46.

[43] *Police v Lavalle* [1979] 1 N.Z.L.R. 45; *R. v Loughlin* [1982] 1 N.Z.L.R. 236. The approach was recently confirmed in *Burns v Ministry of Fisheries* [2003] D.C.R. 311.

[44] J.D. Heydon, "The problems of entrapment" [1973] C.L.J. 268–286 at p.285; D.K. Allen, "Entrapment and exclusion of evidence" (1980) 42 M.L.R. 450–456 at p.453; D. Birch, "Excluding evidence from entrapment: what is a fair cop?" (1994) 47 *Current Legal Problems* 73–99 at p.85.

[45] Take two accused who have engaged in identical conduct as a result of entrapment by the police: assuming that the evidence of the officer who entrapped them is excluded, whether or not each accused is convicted will depend solely on the availability of additional evidence sufficient to prove the offence and not on any objective difference in the conduct of either the accused or the police officer concerned. See A. Choo, "A defence of entrapment" (1990) 53 M.L.R. 453–471 at p.463; C. Fraser, "Undercover law enforcement in Scots law", 1994 S.L.T. (News) 113–118 at p.114.

[46] Choo, above, fn.45, at p.463; Fraser, above, fn.45, at p.114; G. Robertson, "Entrapment evidence: manna from heaven or fruit of the poisoned tree?" [1994] Crim. L.R. 805–816 at p.812.

[47] R.A. Duff, "I might be guilty, but you can't try me: estoppel and other bars to trial" (2003) 1 *Ohio State Journal of Criminal Law* 245–259 at pp.246–247.

[48] From *Sorrells v United States*, 287 U.S. 435 (1932) until *Mathews v United States*, 485 U.S. 58 (1988), where one of the justices who had previously been a supporter of the minority view abandoned his dissent and sided with the majority.

[49] Since *R. v Mack* [1988] 2 S.C.R. 903, where the Canadian Supreme Court adopted the minority opinion of Estey J. in *Amato v The Queen* [1982] 2 S.C.R. 418.

the criminal justice system, then it seems to follow that the appropriate procedural mechanism is to stay proceedings on this basis.[50]

One possible difficulty with this approach, as noted by Ashworth,[51] is that staying proceedings is such a drastic measure that the courts might use it too sparingly, leading to injustice in particular cases. However, as Ashworth points out, this is not in itself a convincing principled reason to reject the approach.[52]

So which of these three possible approaches has found favour in Scots law? Initially, at least, entrapment was treated as a matter relating to the exclusion of evidence[53] and this remained the case until 2002 when, in *Brown v HM Advocate*,[54] the appeal court shifted their position and held that it was more properly a plea that, if established,[55] should result in a trial being barred.[56] The developments leading up to *Brown* and the change in approach are considered in more detail below.

Historical Development

Scots law prior to *Brown*

Prior to *Brown*, entrapment was dealt with as an issue of admissibility of evidence. This can be seen in a series of cases starting with *Marsh v Johnston*,[57] where the evidence of two undercover police officers who had purchased drinks outside of licensing hours was held to be admissible to prove a breach of licensing regulations. The licence holder appealed against his conviction on the basis that this evidence should not have been admitted. The appeal court held that it had not been unfair to admit the evidence, because the police officers had not "pressed the appellant to commit an offence" or "tricked him into committing an offence which he would not otherwise have committed".[58] **20.10**

In *Cook v Skinner*; *MacDonald v Skinner*,[59] it was confirmed that *Marsh v Johnston* established that the correct way to deal with cases such as these was to consider whether or not it would have been fair to the accused to admit the evidence. Like *Marsh v Johnston*, this was a case where the appellants had been convicted of licensing offences on the basis of the evidence of undercover police officers who had purchased drinks outside of licensing hours. The appeals were unsuccessful.[60] The appeal

[50] A. Ashworth, "Re-drawing the boundaries of entrapment" [2002] Crim. L.R. 161–179 at p.164. *Cf.* D. Ormerod and A. Roberts, "The trouble with *Teixeira*: developing a principled approach to entrapment" (2002) 6 *International Journal of Evidence and Proof* 38–61, who argue for a rather puzzling hybrid approach (at pp.58–60).

[51] A. Ashworth, "Testing fidelity to legal values" in *Criminal Law Theory: Doctrines of the General Part* (S. Shute and A.P. Simester (eds), 2002), pp.299–330, at p.330.

[52] And it might be said that excluding evidence obtained by entrapment can be an equally drastic measure if the evidence obtained by entrapment is the main source of evidence in the case.

[53] See the cases referred to in paras 20.10–20.11.

[54] 2002 S.L.T. 809.

[55] In *Brown* it was not. See para.20.14.

[56] The precise procedural mechanism by which this should take place was a subject of disagreement between the three judges who delivered options. See paras 20.14–20.15.

[57] 1959 S.L.T. (Notes) 28. Prior to *Marsh v Johnston*, see the civil case of *Southern Bowling Club v Ross* (1902) 4 F. 405.

[58] At 28.

[59] 1977 J.C. 9.

[60] There were two conjoined appeals, both stemming from essentially the same set of facts.

court stated that the test for whether evidence should be excluded was whether the police officer engaged in conduct amounting to "inducement to commit an offence which, but for the pressure, encouragement or inducement, would never have been committed at all".[61]

The admissibility of evidence approach continued in *HM Advocate v Harper*,[62] the first reported case to consider entrapment in relation to the purchase of drugs by undercover police officers. Here, a police officer approached an ice cream van driven by the accused and asked him if he had "a couple of trips".[63] The accused asked who had sent him and the police officer answered "Wee Prunie".[64] The accused then produced a pack of brown tablets and the transaction was completed. The accused objected to the admissibility of this evidence at his trial, but the objection was repelled by the presiding sheriff.

20.11 The sheriff stated that there was no 'defence' of entrapment known to Scots law[65] and proceeded on the basis of whether or not it would be fair to admit the evidence. He concluded that it would, given that there had been "no trick or inducement, nor [had] the accused been duped into committing a crime which he would not otherwise have committed".[66] It might have been different, Sheriff Spy noted, if "the accused had said something initially disclaiming all knowledge of what was being asked for and had then been pressed, enticed or otherwise cajoled into committing a crime".[67]

Finally, the leading case prior to *Brown* was *Weir v Jessop*.[68] Here, the appellant had been convicted of possession of cannabis with intent to supply after the evidence of a police officer who had knocked on his door and asked him to supply the drug was ruled to be admissible. His appeal against conviction failed, the appeal court holding that it had not been unfair to admit the evidence, given that the police officer concerned had not induced the appellant to commit an offence he would otherwise not have committed.[69]

The approach taken by the Scottish courts changed with the decision of the appeal court in *Brown v HM Advocate*.[70] The impetus for the change undoubtedly came from the English House of Lords case *R. v Loosely, Attorney General's Reference (No.3 of 2000)*,[71] a decision that all three

[61] At 13.

[62] 1989 S.C.C.R. 472 (Sh. Ct).

[63] At 473.

[64] At 473.

[65] At 474.

[66] At 474 (drawing on the language used in *Cook v Skinner*, 1977 J.C. 9).

[67] At 474.

[68] 1991 J.C. 146. For comment, see C. Fraser, "Undercover law enforcement in Scots law", 1994 S.L.T. (News) 113–118. For another case in which the admissibility of evidence was challenged on the basis that it had been obtained by entrapment, see *Seyton v McNaughtan*, 1993 S.C.C.R. 125. The challenge was unsuccessful and the issue was not raised on appeal.

[69] At 155 *per* the Lord Justice-Clerk (Ross); at 156 *per* Lord Morison; at 160 *per* Lord Caplan. See also *Porter v HM Advocate*, 2005 J.C. 141, where entrapment was dealt with at the original trial (which took place in 1997, prior to *Brown v HM Advocate*, 2002 S.L.T. 809) in terms of exclusion of evidence. The trial judge directed the jury that the undercover officer must not have "caused the suspects to commit a crime that but for his intervention they would not otherwise have committed" (at [34]), a direction that was held not to constitute a misdirection by the appeal court (at [42]). (The trial took place prior to *Thompson v Crowe*, 2000 J.C. 173, where it was held that issues of admissibility of evidence were for the trial judge, not the jury, to decide).

[70] 2002 S.L.T. 809.

[71] [2001] UKHL 53.

judges in *Brown* drew on extensively.[72] For this reason it is worth examining briefly the nature of the change in the law in England, before returning to *Brown*.

A brief history of entrapment in English law

Until 1980, the English courts, like the Scottish courts, dealt with entrapment by taking the exclusion of evidence approach. Thus, in *Brannan v Peek*,[73] the evidence of a police officer who had deliberately misled the defendant as to his identity to induce him to accept an unlicensed bet was excluded on the basis that it would have been grossly unfair to admit it. This changed in *R. v Sang*,[74] where the House of Lords held that entrapment was not a sufficient basis for the exclusion of evidence and could operate as nothing more than a plea in mitigation. This reflected a climate of general hostility towards the entrapment 'defence' in England and Wales,[75] with the Law Commission recommending in 1977 not only that it should not operate as a complete defence or to exclude evidence, but that it should not even be relevant in mitigation of sentence.[76] **20.12**

The power of the courts to exclude evidence on the basis that it was obtained by entrapment was restored indirectly in the Police and Criminal Evidence Act 1984. Under s.78 of the Act, courts were given the general power to exclude evidence if to admit it would cause unfairness to the defendant. There was nothing in the Act to prevent courts from reaching the conclusion that evidence obtained by entrapment fell into this category, a fact that was explicitly acknowledged by the Court of Appeal in *R. v Smurthwaite and Gill*.[77]

This was the position in English law when the conjoined cases[78] of *R. v Loosely, Attorney General's Reference (No. 3 of 2000)*[79] came to be decided by the House of Lords. Three of their Lordships issued

[72] To the extent that they did not issue their own detailed guidance on the issue of entrapment but instead were content to state that Scots law should follow English law (*Brown v HM Advocate*, 2002 S.L.T. 809 at [13], *per* Lord Marnoch; at [15] *per* Lord Philip).

[73] [1948] 1 K.B. 68.

[74] [1980] A.C. 402.

[75] A hostility that does not appear to have been shared in Scotland.

[76] *Report on Defences of General Application* (Law Com. No. 83, 1977), paras 5.33, 5.37. This recommendation was never implemented. For criticism, see A. Ashworth, "Entrapment" [1978] Crim. L.R. 137–140.

[77] (1993) 98 Cr.App.R. 437. For a detailed account of the history of entrapment in English law up until this point, see G. Robertson, "Entrapment evidence: manna from heaven or fruit of the poisoned tree?" [1994] Crim. L.R. 805–816.

[78] Loosely was convicted of the supply of a controlled substance and was appealing against his conviction. The other case was an Attorney General's Reference arising after the acquittal of a defendant on the basis of entrapment. The defence had applied both for the exclusion of the evidence allegedly obtained by entrapment and a stay of proceedings as an abuse of process. The trial judge granted the stay of proceedings, but lifted it the next day. In the event, the prosecution offered no evidence and the defendant was acquitted.

[79] [2001] UKHL 53. For comment, see S. McKay, "Entrapment: competing views on the effect of the Human Rights Act on English criminal law" (2002) 6 E.H.R.L.R. 764–774; D. Ormerod and D. Birch, "The evolution of the discretionary exclusion of evidence" [2004] Crim. L.R. 767–788.

substantive opinions,[80] but all five were in agreement that the most appropriate remedy in a case of entrapment was a stay of proceedings on the basis that an abuse of process had occurred.

20.13 Their Lordships relied heavily on the earlier case of *R. v Horseferry Magistrates Court ex parte Bennett*,[81] in which the House of Lords had held that the abuse of process doctrine could be invoked where an improperly executed extradition had taken place. The House of Lords had, as early as 1964,[82] held that criminal proceedings could be stayed in England where an abuse of process had occurred, but *Bennett* was the first case in which it was acknowledged explicitly that pretrial police or prosecution improprieties may lead to a stay not only if the accused's right to a fair trial is compromised, but also where the continuation of criminal proceedings would "offend the court's sense of justice and propriety".[83]

In *Loosely*, their Lordships regarded entrapment as an abuse of process similar to the one that had occurred in *Bennett*, and thus concluded that it should, likewise, lead to a stay of proceedings.[84] In so doing, the House of Lords adopted the approach that had been taken to entrapment by the Canadian Supreme Court since 1988, in *R. v Mack*.[85]

The procedural basis of the plea of entrapment following *Brown*

20.14 The appellants in *Brown* were convicted of conspiracy to steal motor vehicles after evidence was led from undercover police officers who posed as prospective buyers. They appealed against the conviction on the basis that this evidence should not have been admitted as it was obtained by entrapment. The appeals were refused, as there was no real question of entrapment on the facts, but nonetheless, given the absence of Scottish authority, the appeal court felt it necessary to issue some observations.

All three judges agreed on the broad procedural basis for the plea. Contrary to previous Scottish authorities, the most appropriate way to deal with entrapment is not now by excluding the evidence obtained but by a procedural device whereby the trial is prevented from going ahead at all.[86] There was minor disagreement, however, over exactly what this procedural device should be.

The minority view was taken by Lord Marnoch, who regarded entrapment as a plea in bar of trial based on oppression.[87] The plea in bar

---

[80] Lords Nicholls, Hoffman and Hutton. Lords MacKay and Scott issued brief concurring opinions.

[81] [1994] 1 A.C. 42.

[82] In *Connelly v DPP* [1964] A.C. 1254. See above, paras 19.12–19.14.

[83] *R. v Horseferry Magistrates Court ex parte Bennett* [1994] 1 A.C. 42 at 74, *per* Lord Lowry. For a detailed history and discussion of the abuse of process doctrine, see A. Choo, *Abuse of Process and Judicial Stays of Criminal Proceedings* (1993) (written prior to *Bennett*); A. L.-T. Choo, "Halting criminal prosecutions: the abuse of process doctrine re-visited" [1995] Crim. L.R. 864–874 (written post-*Bennett*).

[84] *R. v Loosely, Attorney General's Reference (No. 3 of 2000)* [2001] UKHL 53 at [16], *per* Lord Nicholls; at [104] *per* Lord Hutton; at [121] *per* Lord Scott. See also *Jenkins v Government of the USA* [2005] EWHC Admin 1051 at [16]. The courts in England can still consider entrapment as an issue of exclusion of evidence if it arises only after proceedings have commenced; however if this does happen, the issue should be considered under the same principles as would govern a stay of proceedings (at [43] *per* Lord Hoffman; at [104] *per* Lord Hutton).

[85] [1988] 2 S.C.R. 903.

[86] *Brown v HM Advocate*, 2002 S.L.T. 809 at [11]–[12], *per* Lord Marnoch; at [14]–[15] *per* Lord Philip; at [2]–[3] *per* Lord Clarke.

[87] *Brown v HM Advocate*, 2002 S.L.T. 809 at [11]–[12].

of trial is a procedural mechanism already well established in Scots law whereby, if sustained, it effectively stops procedure on the libel in question.[88] A plea in bar of trial based on oppression[89] will succeed where the court feels that it would be "oppressive and unfair"[90] for the accused to be put on trial. Oppression has traditionally taken the form of either delay in bringing the accused to trial or prejudicial publicity, with the test being whether or not the oppression complained of has led to prejudice so grave that no direction of the trial judge, however careful, could reasonably be expected to remove it.[91]

The majority view, taken by Lords Philip and Clarke, was that entrapment, if established, should be dealt with in the same way as it is by the English courts, that is, by a stay of proceedings based on an abuse of process.[92] In their view, a plea in bar of trial based on oppression was not an appropriate procedural mechanism because the traditional test of prejudice or unfairness so severe that the accused can no longer have a fair trial is not appropriate to a case involving entrapment. As Lord Philip stated: **20.15**

> "... [i]n entrapment cases, the abuse of state power is so fundamentally unacceptable that it is not necessary to investigate whether the accused has been prejudiced or has been the victim of any form of unfairness. Indeed one can envisage cases of entrapment where it might be difficult to conclude that an accused had been truly (as opposed to theoretically) prejudiced or the victim of unfairness."[93]

The abuse of process doctrine, on the other hand, does not involve assessing the prejudice that would be suffered by the accused if the trial went ahead. Rather, it involves a balancing process between the public interest in prosecuting serious crime and the importance of discouraging the abuse of state power.[94] The difficulty with this approach is that it is not clear whether or not the abuse of process doctrine *does* form part of Scots law at present.[95]

Finally, this is not to say that evidence of entrapment (or at least conduct bordering on entrapment) cannot be relevant in mitigation of

[88] See Renton and Brown, para.9–05 and the discussion of pleas in bar of trial in Chs 14–20.

[89] A plea in bar of trial may be based on factors other than oppression, such as nonage, insanity, *res judicata, socii criminis* or personal bar (renunciation). For discussion, see Renton and Brown, paras 9–05 to 9–20 and Chs 9, 14, 15 and 17.

[90] Renton and Brown, para.9–21.

[91] *Stuurman v HM Advocate*, 1980 J.C. 111; *Montgomery v HM Advocate*, 2001 S.C. (P.C.) 1. For discussion, see Chs 16 and 18.

[92] *Brown v HM Advocate*, 2002 S.L.T. 809 at [13]–[15], *per* Lord Philip; at [2]–[3] *per* Lord Clarke. Indeed, Lord Clarke specifically approved Lord Nicholls' statement in *Loosely* that "[e]very court has an inherent power and duty to prevent abuse of its process" (*Brown*, at [5], *per* Lord Clarke, citing *R. v Loosely, Attorney General's Reference (No. 3 of 2000)* [2001] UKHL 53 at [1], *per* Lord Nicholls of Birkenhead). Entrapment can still be considered as an issue of exclusion of evidence if it arises only after proceedings have commenced, in which case the same principles as those governing a stay of proceedings should apply (*Brown*, at [14] *per* Lord Marnoch).

[93] *Brown v HM Advocate*, 2002 S.L.T. 809 at [14]. *Cf.* Lord Marnoch at [12].

[94] *Brown v HM Advocate*, 2002 S.L.T. 809 at [2], *per* Lord Clarke.

[95] For discussion, see Ch.19. Some indication that entrapment will continue to be considered as a plea in bar of trial based on oppression comes in *HM Advocate v Bowie*, 2004 S.C.C.R. 105, where the appeal court appeared to accept the minority view of Lord Marnoch (at [27]).

sentence. In *MacDonald v HM Advocate*,[96] for example, the appeal court substituted a sentence of nine months' imprisonment with one of 200 hours community service at least in part because the offence was committed in response to requests made by test purchasers.

Requirements of the Plea

Generally in Scots law

20.16 While *Brown* must now be regarded as the leading case on entrapment in Scots law, it says very little about the substantive requirements of the plea. Only Lord Philip attempts to define entrapment, stating that:

> "Entrapment occurs when the state (in the form of the police or other agency) becomes involved in the instigation of crimes which would not otherwise be committed, whether by deception, pressure, encouragement or inducement."[97]

It is clear that the appeal court intend future Scottish courts to follow the approach taken by the House of Lords in *Loosely*[98] and thus it is to this case that we must turn in order to establish the requirements of the plea. In addition to *Loosely*, regard should be paid to the decision of the European Court of Human Rights in *Teixeira de Castro v Portugal*.[99]

The overall test in *Loosely*

20.17 In *Loosely*, it was held that the ultimate question was always "whether the conduct of the police or other law enforcement agency was so seriously improper as to bring the administration of justice into disrepute".[1] This is a balancing process between the "competing requirements that those who commit crimes should be convicted and punished and that there should not be an abuse of process which would constitute an affront to the public conscience".[2] Two factors relevant to the balancing process were highlighted: the conduct of the police and the reason for the operation. Two further factors were identified as *irrelevant* to the balancing process: the seriousness of the offence and the predisposition of the defendant (and his or her criminal record in particular).

It is also worth noting that the two factors relevant to establishing whether or not entrapment has taken place—the conduct of the police and the reason for the operation—mirror those identified by the Canadian Supreme Court. Indeed, the similarity of the guidance given by the House of Lords to that given by the Canadian Supreme Court in *R. v Mack*[3] shows that Canadian law has been influential in the development of English law and (given the approval of *Loosely* in *Brown*) Scots law.

---

96 2003 G.W.D. 19–580.

97 *Brown v HM Advocate*, 2002 S.L.T. 809 at [10].

98 Lord Marnoch at [13]; Lord Philip at [15] of *Brown v HM Advocate*, 2002 S.L.T 809.

99 (1998) 28 E.H.R.R. 101.

1 *R. v Loosely, Attorney General's Reference (No. 3 of 2000)* [2001] UKHL 53 at [25], *per* Lord Nicholls.

2 *R. v Loosely, Attorney General's Reference (No. 3 of 2000)* [2001] UKHL 53 at [104], *per* Lord Hutton.

3 [1988] 2 S.C.R. 903.

Factors considered relevant

The conduct of the police

The first part of the test involves establishing that the conduct of the police[4] went beyond providing an opportunity to commit an offence and instead caused or induced that offence.[5] How is this to be judged? 20.18

In *Loosely* such further guidance as was given centred on whether the conduct of the police went no further than might be expected from others in the same circumstances.[6] Lord Hoffman phrased the test as whether the law enforcement officer "behaved like an ordinary member of the public".[7] He admitted, however, that while this test works well in relation to regulatory offences, such as unlicensed sale of alcohol, it could be problematic in cases involving drug dealing, as "ordinary members of the public" are less likely to become involved in such transactions.[8] In this context, Lord Hutton suggested that any inducement, including a persistent request to supply drugs, would be unproblematic if "consistent with the ordinary temptations and stratagems that are likely to be encountered in the course of criminal activity".[9]

It is also apparent from *Loosely* that, in considering whether or not the conduct of the police constituted entrapment, regard might be had to the characteristics of the accused. Lord Nicholls stated that:

> "In assessing the weight to be attached to the police inducement, regard is to be had to the defendant's circumstances, including his vulnerability. This is not because the standards of acceptable behaviour are variable. Rather, this is a recognition that what may be a significant inducement to one person may not be so to another."[10]

The test in *Loosely* is not inconsistent with the pre-*Brown* Scottish case law on entrapment. In *Weir v Jessop*,[11] the leading case prior to *Brown*, the Lord Justice-Clerk (Ross) held that evidence had not been unfairly obtained because "apart from representing that he would like to obtain cannabis, [the police officer] applied no pressure, encouragement or inducement to incite the appellant to commit an offence which he would otherwise not have committed".[12] In the same case, Lord Morison stressed that a police officer would not be held to have induced an offence 20.19

---

[4] Or, perhaps more accurately, the state authorities, as entrapment could involve state agencies other than the police, such as customs or health and safety officers.

[5] *R. v Loosely, Attorney General's Reference (No. 3 of 2000)* [2001] UKHL 53 at [23], *per* Lord Nicholls, and at [50], *per* Lord Hoffman. See also *R. v Mack* [1988] 2 S.C.R. 903 at [121], [122], [134]–[135].

[6] *R. v Loosely, Attorney General's Reference (No. 3 of 2000)* [2001] UKHL 53 at [23], *per* Lord Nicholls.

[7] *R. v Loosely, Attorney General's Reference (No. 3 of 2000)* [2001] UKHL. 53 at [55], *per* Lord Hoffman.

[8] *R. v Loosely, Attorney General's Reference (No. 3 of 2000)* [2001] UKHL 53 at [55].

[9] *R. v Loosely, Attorney General's Reference (No. 3 of 2000)* [2001] UKHL 53 at [102], quoting with approval from the dissenting judgment of McHugh J. in *Ridgeway v The Queen* (1995) 184 C.L.R. 19, the leading Australian case on entrapment. For further guidance on the sorts of factors that might be taken into account in deciding whether or not an officer went beyond providing an opportunity to commit crime, see the extensive list in *R. v Mack* [1988] 2 S.C.R. 903 at [138]–[148].

[10] *R. v Loosely, Attorney General's Reference (No. 3 of 2000)* [2001] UKHL 53 at [28]. This is consistent with the way in which Scots law deals with confessions obtained by inducement. See *Walkers on Evidence*, para.9.13.1.

[11] 1991 J.C. 146.

[12] At 154.

if "the supply was one which would in any event have taken place as a result of a request by a genuine customer".[13]

Loosely is open to criticism on the basis that it does little to clarify exactly how far a police officer can go before his behaviour constitutes entrapment. The test of whether the conduct went beyond what would be ordinary behaviour in the circumstances is certainly vague. If the ordinary behaviour test is to be the standard, however, it is difficult to see how much more specific it could be without being counter-productive. As Ashworth points out,[14] it would be unwise to specify the number of times a police officer can ask a suspect to supply drugs before this constitutes entrapment, as drug dealers and their clients could simply adjust their behaviour accordingly.[14a]

The reason for the operation

20.20 The second factor for the courts to consider is the reason for the police operation. It is not entrapment if the police have acted "in good faith".[15] There are two main ways in which this can be established: by reasonable suspicion or by the existence of a *bona fide* operation.

The reasonable suspicion route to establishing good faith requires consideration of whether the police had reasonable grounds for suspecting that the accused was likely to commit the offence in question or one of a similar nature.[16]

The *bona fide* operation route to establishing good faith involves consideration of whether the police were "acting in the course of a *bona fide* investigation of offences of a kind similar to that with which the accused has been charged".[17] As long as an officially authorised investigation was taking place into offences of a similar nature, then good faith will be established even if the accused was someone to whom no personal suspicion had previously attached.[18]

An illustration of a case that fell into the *bona fide* operation category is the Canadian Supreme Court case of *R. v Barnes*.[19] Here, Vancouver Police conducted an operation targeting a particular area of Vancouver where they had evidence that drug selling was occurring. One undercover police officer had a hunch that a scruffy looking man was a dealer and approached him asking to buy "weed". After some persistence on the part

[13] At 156. See also *Weir v Jessop*, 1991 J.C. 146 at 159, *per* Lord Caplan; *Marsh v Johnston*, 1959 S.L.T. (Notes) 28 at 28; *Cook v Skinner*, 1977 J.C. 9 at 13; *HM Advocate v Harper*, 1989 S.C.C.R. 472 (Sh. Ct) at 474.

[14] A. Ashworth, "Re-drawing the boundaries of entrapment" [2002] Crim. L.R. 161–179 at p.172.

[14a] For a rare example of a case where the conduct of the police was held to have constituted entrapment, see *R. v Moon* [2004] EWCA Crim 2872. Here, the appellant, a heroin addict, successfully appealed against a decision not to stay her prosecution as an abuse of process. The English Court of Appeal concluded that she had only agreed to supply heroin after persistent pressure from an undercover policewoman (the nature of the pressure is detailed at [5]) and entrapment had therefore been established.

[15] *R. v Loosely, Attorney General's Reference (No. 3 of 2000)* [2001] UKHL 53 at [27], *per* Lord Nicholls.

[16] *R. v Loosely, Attorney General's Reference (No. 3 of 2000)* [2001] UKHL 53 at [27], *per* Lord Nicholls; at [56], *per* Lord Hoffman; at [100], *per* Lord Hutton.

[17] *R. v Loosely, Attorney General's Reference (No. 3 of 2000)* [2001] UKHL 53 at [100], *per* Lord Hutton, quoting with approval from the dissenting judgment of McHugh J. in *Ridgeway v The Queen* (1995) 184 C.L.R 19.

[18] *R. v Loosely, Attorney General's Reference (No. 3 of 2000)* [2001] UKHL 53 at [65], *per* Lord Hoffman.

[19] [1991] 1 S.C.R. 449.

of the police officer, he agreed and was arrested. A majority of the Supreme Court held that entrapment had not taken place. Reasonable suspicion had not been established, nor could it be established by factors such as length of hair or manner of dress. The operation *was* held to be a *bona fide* enquiry, however, given that it had been approved by the authorities and the operation took place in a well-defined location (six city blocks) in which it was suspected that criminal activity was occurring.[20]

Another example of a case that would not meet the reasonable suspicion requirement but would meet the *bona fide* operation requirement is *DPP v Williams and O'Hare*,[21] a decision of the English Court of Appeal that was approved by the House of Lords in *Loosely*. Here, police officers left a van containing cigarettes unguarded in public view with its rear door open to see if passers-by would be tempted to steal them. Two men did so and the Court of Appeal held that the police conduct did not amount to entrapment. In *Loosely*, Lord Hoffman stated that: **20.21**

> "If the trick had been the individual enterprise of a policeman in an area where such crime was not suspected to be prevalent, it would have been an abuse of state power. It was justified because it was an authorised investigation into actual crime, and the fact that the defendants may not have previously been suspected or even thought of offending was their hard luck."[22]

On the other hand, as a hypothetical example of a case where neither the reasonable suspicion nor the *bona fide* operation requirement would be met, Lord Hoffman in *Loosely* mentions the police officer who decides unilaterally that he wants to increase his performance and leaves an unattended wallet in a park.[23] If a passer-by takes the wallet, this would constitute entrapment on the basis that no suspicion had previously attached to that individual and no *bona fide* operation was involved.[24]

It is this second aspect of the plea of entrapment—the good faith test—that has attracted most critical comment. The reason for requiring the police to have acted in good faith is consistent with the underlying rationale for the defence: it is an abuse of power (and a waste of resources) for the State to interfere with the private lives of citizens by offering them an opportunity to commit an offence where there is no

---

[20] At [23] *per* Lamer C.J. McLachlin J. delivered a strong dissenting opinion (see para.20.22).

[21] (1994) 98 Cr.App.R. 209. For comment, see D. Birch, "Excluding evidence from entrapment: what is a fair cop?" (1994) 47 *Current Legal Problems* 73–99. For criticism of the decision, see A. Ashworth, "Re-drawing the boundaries", above, fn.14, at p.175; G. Robertson, "Entrapment evidence: manna from heaven or fruit of the poisoned tree?" [1994] Crim. L.R. 805–816 at p.811.

[22] *R. v Loosely, Attorney General's Reference (No. 3 of 2000)* [2001] UKHL 53 at [65], *per* Lord Hoffman.

[23] The example is drawn by Lord Hoffman from the Canadian Supreme Court case of *R. v Mack* [1988] 2 S.C.R. 903.

[24] *R. v Loosely, Attorney General's Reference (No. 3 of 2000)* [2001] UKHL 53 at [58], *per* Lord Hoffman.

suggestion that they have previously engaged in criminal activity or considered doing so.

20.22 As such, the reasonable suspicion route to establishing good faith is relatively uncontroversial.[25] The *bona fide* operation route to establishing good faith is less so. Allowing good faith to be established simply by information that an operation has been authorised means that the mere fact that a local area is a crime "hot-spot" justifies interference with the private life of any person who happens to be in the relevant place at the relevant time, regardless of whether or not there is any suspicion that they are engaged in criminal activity. It is questionable whether such interference into the lives of randomly selected individuals is justified.[26] Perhaps more importantly, the *bona fide* operation requirement is potentially discriminatory because it promotes the over-policing of minorities who tend to be more highly represented in high crime areas and who are therefore more likely to be targeted with opportunities to commit crime. It is these concerns that led McLachlin J. to issue a dissenting opinion in the Canadian Supreme Court case of *Barnes*:

> " . . . the notion is that individuals should be free to go about their daily business—to go shopping, to visit the theatre, to travel to and from work, to name but three examples—without courting the risk that they will be subjected to the clandestine investigatory techniques of agents of the state. A further risk inherent in overbroad undercover operations is that of discriminatory police work, where people are interfered with not because of reasonable suspicion but because of the colour of their skin or, as in this case, the quality of their clothing and their age."[27]

One way to deal with these concerns might be to adopt the solution proposed by Ormerod and Roberts: to identify suspicious individuals through surveillance and only then to engage in targeting.[28]

Factors considered irrelevant

The seriousness of the offence

20.23 In *Loosely*, it was made clear that the nature of the offence is relevant only to the extent that some offences, drugs offences in particular, are more difficult to detect without using pro-active techniques and, therefore, the courts are more likely to find the use of such techniques

---

[25] Although it has been pointed out that the robustness of the reasonable suspicion test will depend on how closely the grounds for suspicion are scrutinised: "In principle there ought to be demonstrable support from surveillance reports or other documented sources" (A. Ashworth, "Re-drawing the boundaries of entrapment" [2002] Crim. L.R. 161–179 at p.168).

[26] A. Ashworth, "Re-drawing the boundaries", above, fn.25, at p.168; S. Bronitt, "The law in undercover policing: a comparative study of entrapment and covert interviewing in Australia, Canada and Europe" (2004) 33 *Common Law World Review* 35–80 at p.72; D. Ormerod and A. Roberts, "The trouble with *Teixeira*: developing a principled approach to entrapment" (2002) 6 *International Journal of Evidence and Proof* 38–61 at p.169.

[27] *R. v Barnes* [1991] 1 S.C.R. 449 at [76].

[28] Ormerod and Roberts, above, fn.26, at p.169.

acceptable.[29] What is not relevant in considering whether or not entrapment is established is the *seriousness* of the offence.[30]

This represents a departure from the approach in some other jurisdictions, especially those where entrapment is still considered as a matter of exclusion of evidence. The Australian High Court, in considering whether or not to exclude evidence on the basis that it was obtained by entrapment, balances the public interest in the conviction and punishment of the guilty against the public interest in maintaining the integrity of the courts. The weight to be given to the public interest in the conviction and punishment of the guilty will "vary according to the degree of criminality involved".[31]

This raises the question as to whether there are any offences in English or Scots law to which entrapment could not operate as a bar to prosecution. There is no suggestion in either *Brown* or *Loosely* that this is the case and the other grounds upon which a plea in bar of trial can be based (insanity, nonage, and so on) operate regardless of the nature of the offence. Indeed, it might be argued that it is *more* important to ensure that entrapment operates as a bar to trial in relation to serious charges, given the greater adverse consequences for the accused of being convicted of a relatively serious offence.

The pre-disposition of the accused

At the federal level in the United States, where entrapment is regarded as a substantive defence, a plea of entrapment requires two factors to be established: government inducement and an absence of pre-disposition to engage in criminal conduct.[32] Thus the entrapment defence is effectively ruled out for anyone who is held to be pre-disposed to commit criminal offences of the type charged. **20.24**

The focus on pre-disposition has been criticised because it removes *entirely* the protection of the entrapment defence from anyone who has relevant previous convictions, regardless of how extreme the conduct of the police officers.[33]

---

[29] *R. v Loosely, Attorney General's Reference (No. 3 of 2000)* [2001] UKHL 53 at [26], *per* Lord Nicholls; at [66], *per* Lord Hoffman.

[30] *R. v Loosely, Attorney General's Reference (No. 3 of 2000)* [2001] UKHL 53 at [66], *per* Lord Hoffman.

[31] *Ridgeway v The Queen* (1995) 184 C.L.R. 19 at 38. The seriousness of the offence would most likely be considered relevant by the Scottish courts if entrapment was still regarded as a matter of exclusion of evidence: see *Lawrie v Muir*, 1950 J.C. 19 at 27.

[32] Known as the Sorrells-Sherman test, as it is drawn from the two leading federal cases, *Sorrells v United States*, 287 U.S. 435 (1932) and *Sherman v United States*, 356 U.S. 369 (1958).

[33] R.J. Allen, M. Luttrell and A. Kreeger, "Clarifying entrapment" (1999) 89 *Journal of Criminal Law and Criminology* 407–431 at pp.413–414; C. Fraser, "Undercover law enforcement in Scots law", 1994 S.L.T. (News) 113–118 at p.117; G. Robertson, "Entrapment evidence: manna from heaven or fruit of the poisoned tree?" [1994] Crim. L.R. 805–816 at p.813. For a defence of the pre-disposition requirement, see F.W. Bennett, "From *Sorrells* to *Jacobson*: reflections on six decades of entrapment law and related defenses in federal court" (1992) 27 *Wake Forest Law Review* 829–870 at p.865; J.D. Lombardo, "Causation and objective entrapment: towards a culpability-centred approach" (1995) 43 *UCLA Law Review* 209–261 at p.214; R. Roiphe, "The serpent beguiled me: a history of the entrapment defense" (2003) 33 *Seton Hall Law Review* 257–302 at p.293.

Fortunately, the debate need not detain us unduly here as the position in English (and by implication Scots) law is clear: the pre-disposition of the accused to commit criminal offences is irrelevant to whether or not entrapment has taken place.[34] As Lord Nicholls states in *Loosely*:

> "... the existence or absence of predisposition in the individual is not the criterion by which the acceptability of police conduct is to be decided. Predisposition does not make acceptable what would otherwise be unacceptable conduct on the part of the police or other law enforcement agencies. Predisposition does not negative misuse of state power."[35]

The impact of the ECHR

20.25 Entrapment was considered by the European Court of Human Rights in *Teixeira de Castro v Portugal*,[36] and thus the question arises of whether the approach taken by the House of Lords (and by the Scottish courts if, as suggested in *Brown*, they will follow *Loosely*) differs in any respect from that taken by the European Court.

The events that were the basis of the applicant's case in *Teixeira* stemmed from an approach made by two police officers to a third party, VS. The police officers indicated that they wished to buy heroin. VS put them in touch with the applicant, whom the police then approached with an offer to buy 20 grams of heroin for 200,000 escudos. The applicant agreed to obtain the drugs and did so by going to another man's house, before returning to his own house, where the police officers were waiting. When the applicant produced the heroin, they revealed their identity. He was convicted of dealing in heroin and sentenced to six years' imprisonment.

It was argued by the applicant that his Art.6 right to a fair trial had been breached because he had been incited to commit the offence by police officers. The applicant had no previous convictions and claimed that he would never have committed the offence if it had not been for the police involvement.

The European Court agreed that Art.6 had been violated. Three main factors appear to have led the Court to arrive at this conclusion. First, the operation did not take place as part of an official anti-drug trafficking

---

[34] Although as Ashworth (in *Principles of Criminal Law*) points out, there remains a danger that the reasonable suspicion requirement might effectively bring in predisposition by the back door, if reasonable suspicion can be established by previous convictions alone (at 238).

[35] *R. v Loosely, Attorney General's Reference (No. 3 of 2000)* [2001] UKHL 53 at [22]. See also Lord Hoffman at [68].

[36] (1998) 28 E.H.R.R. 101. For comment, see D. Ormerod and A. Roberts, "The trouble with *Teixeira*: developing a principled approach to entrapment" (2002) 6 *International Journal of Evidence and Proof* 38–61. See also *Edwards and Lewis v United Kingdom* (2005) 40 E.H.R.R. 24, where the European Court re-stated the principles it set down in *Teixeira*. The central issue in *Edwards and Lewis*, however, was not whether or not entrapment had occurred, but whether the Crown should have disclosed evidence that might have assisted the applicants in establishing entrapment.

operation ordered and supervised by a judge.[37] Secondly, the authorities had no basis upon which to suspect that the applicant was involved in criminal activity.[38] Thirdly, the conduct of the police officers caused a crime that would otherwise not have been committed.[39] In this context, the European Court distinguished between "passive" and "active" conduct on the part of the officers:

> "... the two police officers did not confine themselves to investigating [the applicant's] criminal activity in an essentially passive manner, but exercised an influence such as to incite the commission of the offence".[40]

The decision in *Teixeira* has been criticised. It has been pointed out that, contrary to the Court's view that there was no good reason to suspect that the applicant was involved in the supply of drugs, this requirement was actually met, on the basis of the information provided by VS.[41] The distinction between active and passive conduct has also been criticised as effectively meaningless. Although the Court described the conduct of the police as "active", the officers did nothing other than offer the market rate for drugs, with no pressure or repeated requests to supply, and the applicant complied as promptly as he could. If this constitutes actively creating a crime, then there is very little by way of deceptive policing techniques that would *not* do so.[42] **20.26**

Nonetheless, the House of Lords in *Loosely* held that *Teixeira* was consistent with English law.[43] The factors emphasised (a supervised/authorised operation, the need for a reasonable suspicion) are not inconsistent with those emphasised in *Loosely* (reasonable suspicion, a *bona fide* operation). The one exception to this is the active/passive conduct distinction. This was described by Lord Hoffman in *Loosely* as "unhelpful",[44] but he did not consider that the decision in *Teixeira* meant that no police officer could ever take an active step such as offering to buy an illegal substance:

> "I do not believe that the court intended to lay down such a rigid and prescriptive rule. The description of the policeman's conduct [by the European Court of Human Rights] must be seen as one of the

[37] At [38]. This is not something that would happen in the Scottish context as it is a practice specific to inquisitorial systems of criminal justice. The equivalent would perhaps be the *bona fide* operation requirement (see paras 20.20–20.22).

[38] At [38]. Elsewhere in the judgment, the Court uses the term pre-disposition ("[t]here is no evidence to support the government's argument that the applicant was predisposed to commit offences", at [38]), which is unfortunate given the manner in which it has been used in the US cases—see para.20.24.

[39] At [39].

[40] At [38]. The distinction between active and passive conduct was also made in *Cook v Skinner*, 1977 J.C. 9 (at 13), although, given that the House of Lords in *Loosely* was critical of this terminology and Scots law is likely to follow *Loosely*, this is perhaps of little significance.

[41] Ormerod and Roberts, above, fn.36, p.44.

[42] Ormerod and Roberts, above, fn.36, at p.44. An exception is perhaps the type of conduct that took place in *DPP v Williams and O'Hare* (1994) 98 Cr.App.R. 209, where police officers simply left a van containing cigarettes unguarded in public view with its rear door open (see para.20.21 above).

[43] *R. v Loosely, Attorney General's Reference (No. 3 of 2000)* [2001] UKHL 53 at [31], *per* Lord Nicholls; at [74] *per* Lord Hoffman; at [112] *per* Lord Hutton.

[44] *R. v Loosely, Attorney General's Reference (No. 3 of 2000)* [2001] UKHL 53 at [69], *per* Lord Hoffman.

various factors which led to the court's conclusion that there had been an abuse of police power which denied the defendant a fair trial."[45]

Private Entrapment

20.27 Thus far, it has been assumed that entrapment relates only to what might be termed public entrapment: offences induced by the police or other state officials. The question arises of how the courts should approach the issue of *private* entrapment: where the accused is induced to commit a crime by someone who is not a police officer or state official.[45a] A good example, and one that has been the subject of English case law,[46] is where the entrapper is an investigative journalist who induces the accused into, for example, supplying drugs, and then publicises that fact in the press.

Whether or not private entrapment is recognised depends to some extent on the underlying rationale for the 'defence'. It would, for example, be entirely consistent to allow a defence of private entrapment if the underlying rationale for the defence was one of culpability. If the underlying rationale behind the defence relates to preserving the integrity of the criminal justice system, however, then it is less clear that private entrapment should operate as a defence.[46a] It does not reflect badly on the criminal justice system to prosecute the accused where the entrapper was a private individual.[47]

Scottish case law sheds no light on the situation as no reported case has involved private entrapment. English case law seems to suggest that the plea would be ruled out, although there has only been limited case law since *R. v Loosely, Attorney General's Reference (No. 3 of 2000)*[48] was decided by the House of Lords and the approach taken to entrapment changed from a matter of exclusion of evidence to a matter of abuse of process.

20.28 Prior to *Loosely* in *R. v Hardwicke and Thwaites*,[49] the Court of Appeal held that the trial judge had erred in equating private entrapment with public entrapment. Kennedy L.J., delivering the judgment of the court, stated that accepting evidence obtained by entrapment would involve the

[45] *R. v Loosely, Attorney General's Reference (No. 3 of 2000)* [2001] UKHL 53 at [75].

[45a] For a detailed discussion of private entrapment, see K. Hofmeyr, "The problem of private entrapment" [2006] Crim. L.R. 319–336.

[46] See the cases referred to in paras 20.28–20.29.

[46a] This is the conclusion reached by Kate Hofmeyr in her detailed examination of the principle of private entrapment. See K. Hofmeyr, "The problem of private entrapment" [2006] Crim. L.R. 319–336 at p.336.

[47] There is perhaps an argument that if the state allows prosecution to take place in a case of private entrapment, it is condoning the deception that took place. This is a weaker argument for recognising the defence, however, than where the entrapper is a state official. Ashworth does consider whether or not citizens have a general right not to be subjected to temptation designed to test their willingness to commit crime or whether this right is only state related (in "Re-drawing the boundaries of entrapment" [2002] Crim. L.R. 161–179 at p.176). He concludes (surely correctly) that the difficulty with founding any such right is that criminal law is founded on an assumption of individual autonomy. Absent other considerations, the mere fact that someone is persuaded to engage in criminal activity by another does not normally serve to absolve them of criminal responsibility.

[48] [2001] UKHL 53.

[49] [2001] Crim. L.R. 220. The case involved the supply of cocaine by the Earl of Hardwicke to an undercover journalist.

court in condoning malpractice among law enforcement agencies. This, he stated, could undermine public confidence and bring the criminal justice system into disrepute. He continued:

> "Obviously that is not a consideration that applies with anything like the same force when the investigator allegedly guilty of malpractice is outside the criminal justice system altogether."[50]

Likewise, in *R. v Tonnessen*,[51] albeit in a sentencing appeal, the Court of Appeal stated that:

> "If these men had been police officers that would provide mitigation of sentence. Different considerations however must apply when the tempters are investigative journalists. They are not officers of the law whose prime purpose is to detect crime, apprehend criminals and bring them to justice."[52]

In *R. v Shannon*,[53] however, the issue of entrapment was dealt with by the Court of Appeal without a single reference to the fact that this was a case of private entrapment involving an undercover journalist and did not involve state officials at all. It is difficult to draw any firm conclusions from this, though, as entrapment was still operating at this time as a ground upon which evidence could be excluded and not as a factor that could result in a stay of proceedings.[54] **20.29**

In *Loosely* no explicit mention is made of the issue of private entrapment. It is clear, however, that the rationale for recognising the defence set out in *Loosely* is the undesirability of the courts' involvement in state created crime.[55] On this basis, it seems reasonable to conclude that private entrapment would not be treated in the same way as public entrapment.[56] Since *Loosely* was decided, there have been two reported English cases where the issue has arisen, but neither of them discusses private entrapment in any depth and, indeed, they take contradictory approaches. In *R. v Marriner*,[57] the appellants appealed against their conviction for offences relating to football violence on the ground, among others, that the trial judge should have stayed proceedings on the basis of entrapment. The main source of evidence against them stemmed from two undercover journalists, who befriended the appellants and exposed their violent activities in a BBC television programme. Somewhat surprisingly, the Court of Appeal did not rule out the possibility that private entrapment could ground a stay of proceedings, although in this particular case, the court endorsed the decision of the trial judge. No mention was made of

[50] At [22].

[51] [1998] 2 Cr.App.R. (S) 238.

[52] At 329. Although this did not prevent the court from recognising the fact of the entrapment in sentencing. The original sentence of 12 months' imprisonment was replaced with one of six months on the basis, among others, that there was an element of entrapment by an investigative journalist.

[53] [2001] 1 Cr.App.R. 168. See also *R. v Morley and Hutton* [1994] Crim. L.R. 919.

[54] See paras 20.12–20.13.

[55] *R. v Loosely, Attorney General's Reference (No. 3 of 2000)* [2001] UKHL 53 at [2], *per* Lord Nicholls; at [35] *per* Lord MacKay of Clashfern.

[56] It might be argued that the court should not endorse the impropriety of a private individual as this in itself could be seen as an abuse of process (see D. Ormerod, *Smith and Hogan Criminal Law* (11th edn, 2005), p.345). This is a weaker argument, however, than where the impropriety was on the part of the state.

[57] [2002] EWCA Crim 2855.

Loosely. In *R. v Paulssen*,[58] the alleged entrapment was undertaken by a police informer, but he was acting on his own initiative without the knowledge of the authorities. Here, the Court of Appeal did rely on *Loosely* to hold that, because of the lack of state involvement, the trial judge was correct in refusing to stay proceedings. Given that the rationale for recognising entrapment as an abuse of process in *Loosely* related specifically to the behaviour of the state, the approach taken in *Paulssen* seems more convincing than that taken in *Marriner*. Thus, as the appeal court relied so heavily on *Loosely* in *Brown*, it does seem unlikely that a Scottish court would stay proceedings on the basis of private entrapment. This tentative conclusion is bolstered by the fact that all three of the appeal court judges in *Brown* referred to entrapment specifically as state induced crime.[59]

[58] [2003] EWCA Crim 3109.

[59] *HM Advocate v Brown*, 2002 S.L.T. 809 at [11], *per* Lord Marnoch; at [10], *per* Lord Philip; at [2], *per* Lord Clarke. Although see *Shannon v United Kingdom* [2005] Crim. L.R. 133, a decision on admissibility where the European Court of Human Rights did not rule out the possibility that a prosecution based on evidence obtained by private entrapment could infringe Art.6 (in this particular case the application was declared inadmissible).

INDEX

(all references are to paragraph number)